Franz Liszt

THE VIRTUOSO YEARS

1811–1847

ALSO BY ALAN WALKER

A Study in Musical Analysis

An Anatomy of Musical Criticism

EDITOR OF

Frédéric Chopin:
Profiles of the Man and the Musician

Franz Liszt:
The Man and His Music

Robert Schumann:
The Man and His Music .

Alan Walker

Franz Liszt

VOLUME ONE

The Virtuoso Years

1811 · 1847

REVISED EDITION

Cornell University Press

ITHACA, NEW YORK

Revised Edition first published 1988 by Cornell University Press.
Published by arrangement with Alfred A. Knopf, Inc.

Music examples drawn by Paul Courtenay.

LIBRARY OF CONGRESS CATALOGING IN PUBLICATION DATA
Walker, Alan, 1930–
Franz Liszt.
Includes bibliographical references.
Contents: v. I. The virtuoso years, 1811–1847.
1. Liszt, Franz, 1811–1886. 2. Composers—Biography.
ML410.L7W27   780'.92'4[B]   87-24459
ISBN 0-8014-9421-4

Printed in the United States of America

Cornell University Press strives to utilize environmentally responsible
suppliers and materials to the fullest extent possible in the publishing of
its books. Such materials include vegetable-based, low-VOC inks and
acid-free papers that are also either recycled, totally chlorine-free, or
partly composed of nonwood fibers.

Paperback printing   10   9   8   7   6   5   4   3

*To Lisztians across the world,
wherever they may be, these volumes
are affectionately dedicated.*

Contents

PROLOGUE

BOOK ONE: THE YOUNG PRODIGY, 1811–1829

The Great Comet of 1811 ∼ birth in Raiding ∼ family hardships ∼ childhood sickness ∼ mistaken for dead ∼ his musical awakening ∼ first piano lessons from Adam Liszt ∼ growing up in Hungary ∼ influence of church and Gypsies ∼ Adam appeals to Prince Esterházy ∼ a first encounter with Czerny: "Nature herself had formed a pianist" ∼ début in Oedenburg ∼ triumph in Pressburg and departure for Vienna.

Settling down in Vienna ∼ piano lessons with Czerny ∼ theoretical studies with Salieri ∼ Salieri's letter ∼ "Franzi's" first published composition ∼ début in Vienna's town hall ∼ the press dub him "Little Hercules" ∼ plays in the Vienna Redoutensaal ∼ the myth of Beethoven's public embrace ∼ a visit to Beethoven ∼ a farewell journey to Hungary, May 1823: "I am Hungarian" ∼ plays to the Franciscan fathers in the monastery at Pest.

The tours begin ∼ Prince Metternich intercedes ∼ Liszt plays in Munich, Augsburg, Stuttgart, and Strassburg ∼ arrival in France ∼ friendship with the family Erard ∼ Cherubini refuses to admit Liszt to the Paris Conservatoire ∼ studies with Reicha and Paer instead ∼ Liszt is taken up by the Paris press: "Le petit Litz" ∼ two visits to England, 1824–25 ∼ a letter from Adam Liszt ∼ *Don Sanche* produced in Paris, October 1825 ∼ maturing piano style: Twelve Studies ∼ a third visit to England, 1827.

BOOK TWO: THE GROWING VIRTUOSO, 1830–1834

Book Three: The Years of Pilgrimage, 1835–1839

men: his speech of acceptance ∼ the ceremony is misunderstood beyond Hungary's borders ∼Liszt takes up the pen against his critics ∼ he raises money for a Hungarian National Conservatory of Music ∼ he revisits the Franciscan monks in Pest ∼ he receives the freedom of the city of Oedenburg ∼ Liszt sees again his birthplace in Raiding ∼ a visit to the Gypsies; he describes their encampment ∼ the Hungarian Rhapsodies are born ∼ the case of "Josi" Sárai, the Gypsy violinist.

Illustrations

xi

Preface to the Revised Edition

Important developments have taken place in the world of Liszt scholarship since this volume first went to press, in 1983. Most noteworthy is the belated publication of Lina Ramann's *Lisztiana*.[1] This book contains many of the basic documents Ramann used to construct her "official" three-volume biography of Liszt, which appeared during the fourteen-year period 1880–94. It had always been known that Liszt granted Ramann some personal interviews, but their extent had never before been properly chronicled. Moreover, she struck up a long correspondence with Liszt and various members of his circle, and she gradually acquired a mass of detailed information about him of a type never before assembled. Nonetheless, her biography was dismissed as mere hagiography because parts of it were thought (not without justification) to have been written by Princess Carolyne von Sayn-Wittgenstein, Liszt's mistress and companion. We now know differently. Ramann herself was partly to blame for the problem. Because of the "sensitive" nature of much of the material, she placed an embargo on its use by others and left instructions that her archives could not be opened until fifty years after her death. Meanwhile, all her papers were transferred to the Goethe- und Schiller-Archiv in Weimar, where they were known to only a small handful of scholars. With the publication of *Lisztiana* in 1983, all that has changed. Ramann's place in the hierarchy of Liszt scholars will have to be reassessed.

Then there was the reappearance of Beethoven's Conversation Books for the period February–July 1823, in a new and thoroughly reliable edition,[2] which raised afresh the vexed question of Schindler's forged entries and how they

---

1. RL (1983).
2. BK (1983).

might affect the only recorded meeting between the master and the eleven-
year-old Liszt in Vienna, in April 1823. The simple answer is that they do not.
Some new perspectives must nonetheless be considered, for Schindler's
spurious additions have been wrongly assumed to discredit the entire Liszt-
Beethoven connection.

Finally, the year 1986 saw the centenary of Liszt's death, with commemorative festivals all over the world. Some of these events were significant, particularly the ones mounted in Budapest, Paris, and Washington, for they brought
together an international cast of scholars, some of whom toil on the leading
edge of the discipline. Liszt's piano playing, his composing methods, and his
religious convictions all came under fresh scrutiny, to say nothing of such esoteric issues as his health, the size of his bank balance, and the watermarks on
his stationery. All things are grist to the biographer's mill. One of the unexpected pleasures of the Liszt jubilee year, in fact, was the discovery that the art
of iconography has made such rapid strides of late that it has been raised to the
level of a research tool. What a man wears as he comports himself before the
camera, it seems, can occasionally yield as much biographical information as a
letter or a diary entry. The best collection of Liszt photographs to appear in recent times is Ernst Burger's *Franz Liszt: Eine Lebenschronik in Bildern und
Dokumenten*, which has changed the existing chronology of a number of
well-known paintings and lithographs.

In view of these and other developments, it seemed to me that nothing short
of a revised text would do if the present volume were to continue to meet the
requirements of modern scholarship. Two people in particular encouraged me
in this task. Mária Eckhardt, the director of the Liszt Memorial Museum and
Research Centre in Budapest, made many helpful suggestions, and the time
we spent together in the City of the Magyars, working on the text of the Hungarian edition of this book in the summer of 1985, remains a pleasant memory
for me. But it was Geraldine Keeling who persuaded me to look afresh at
Liszt's concerts, and in particular at the great tours of Europe he undertook
from 1838 to 1847, with a view to providing the reader with more detail than I
had originally considered to be either desirable or necessary. My inertia was
overcome by her winning combination of charm, tact, and practical advice.
The sort of help I received from both scholars is beyond praise, and it is a pleasure to acknowledge it here.

It has been well said that it takes a life to study a life. As the modern Liszt biographer proceeds along his journey, he does well to carry with him both a
mirror and a lamp—the one to reflect more accurately the changing landscape
that now surrounds him, the other to illuminate the dark paths that still lie
ahead. Only then may he be sure that his work remains worthy of its topic.

Rome, June 1987   Alan Walker

Acknowledgements

During the ten years which have elapsed since I embarked on the present volume, my travels have taken me to many different parts of the world—Germany, Hungary, Italy, Austria, Czechoslovakia, England, and America—in pursuit of authentic material connected with Liszt. I have made many friends in the course of my long tours abroad, and without their assistance this volume would not have achieved its final form. In particular I owe a debt of gratitude to my colleagues in Hungary, and especially to Veronika Vavrinecz of the National Széchényi Library, Budapest, who acted as my assistant and guide on all my visits to that city. Her devotion to my work has been a source of encouragement to me, and it is a pleasure to acknowledge that fact here. Among the Hungarian musicologists with whom I enjoyed personal contact over the years, and who generously placed the fruits of their scholarship at my disposal, were Mária Párkai-Eckhardt, Dr. Dezső Legány, Miklós Forrai (secretary-general of the Budapest Liszt Society), Imre Achátz, Dr. László Eösze, and Dr. István Kecskeméti (head of the Music Division of the Széchényi Library). They showered me with hospitality and information in almost equal profusion, and I enjoyed many happy hours in their company; few were the occasions, in fact, when they failed to illuminate some obscure corner or other of Liszt's life and personality, and many of the remote details of Liszt's career which I have woven into the narrative of this work were first brought to my attention in that country. In the case of Dezső Legány a simple expression of thanks is hardly adequate. In countless ways he proved himself to be a staunch ally, and his unrivalled grasp of the minutiae of Liszt's life always ensured that my encounters with him were both stimulating and rewarding.

Weimar remains by far the largest centre for Liszt research today. The Goethe- und Schiller-Archiv not only holds most of Liszt's papers and manuscripts relating to his years of permanent residence there (1848–61), but also many personal items of interest to the biographer (e.g., passports, civic honours, citations, newspaper files, and photographs); it contains as well the holographs of thousands of letters to and from Liszt which span his career. Weimar also has on permanent display an important museum collection of Lisztiana in the Hofgärtnerei, Liszt's occasional home for the last seventeen years of his life, and the site of his world-famous masterclasses. On all my trips to Weimar I was received with courtesy and kindness, and I wish to extend to the officials there, but particularly to Dr. Gerhard Schmid and the staff of the Goethe- und Schiller-Archiv, my grateful thanks for making my visits so productive. My sojourns were further enlivened by Dr. Horst Förster, who arranged forays into Eisenach, Jena, and other nearby towns in the old kingdom of Thuringia which still echo with Liszt's presence, and to him too I owe thanks.

Vienna, Eisenstadt, Unterfrauenhaid, and Raiding all contain documents which must be consulted before the biographer of Liszt can claim that his work is complete; dispersed throughout the tiny villages of the Burgenland and western Hungary are the parish registers which record the movement of the Liszt family from one community to another throughout the seventeenth and eighteenth centuries. My tours of these villages, which took place mainly during the years 1977 and 1978, were made in the company of Dr. Karl Emmerich Horvath, to whom I am indebted for some details about Liszt's childhood in Raiding and its environs.

Bayreuth contains many of Liszt's unpublished family letters, between Liszt and his mother on the one hand, and Liszt and his three children on the other. Much of this legacy was passed down through Cosima Liszt-Wagner and is now in the paradoxical position of being part of the city of Bayreuth's Wagner archives, kept in the former home of Houston Stewart Chamberlain. I want to thank the director of the Archive, Dr. Manfred Eger, and the Wagner Stiftung for permission to work there and for giving me unrestricted access to these documents.

Most of my research in Italy was carried out in the Vatican Library. Monsignor Charles Burns helped me to smooth over many a difficulty, and I am particularly grateful to him for his assistance in procuring microfilms of rare material. Nor should I forget to extend my thanks to the administrators of the Canadian Academic Centre in Rome for making my stay there so comfortable.

For the staffs of the British Library in London and the Library of Congress in Washington, D.C., I have nothing but praise. Across the years they helped me to locate a great variety of material with efficiency and despatch, and my sojourns in these halls of learning were among the highlights of my transatlantic travels. As for the many libraries, archives, and museums in other parts of the world which so readily answered my calls for assistance, it is impossible for me to thank them all individually, although I have a duty to mention the following: the Bibliothèque Nationale, Paris; the Royal Library, Windsor; the National Library of Wales; McMaster University Library, Ontario; the Burgenland Museum, Eisenstadt; the City of Bratislava Museum, Czechoslovakia; and the Liszt Museum in Sopron, Hungary. I am especially grateful to Frau Hedwig Jusits of this last institution for drawing my attention during a visit there to some of Liszt's hitherto unpublished concert programmes, which give details of his recitals in Sopron (Oedenburg) in 1840. Other institutions that provided materials or answered specific requests for information include the Turkish Embassy in Ottawa, the Paris Conservatoire of Music, the Geneva Conservatoire of Music, the City of Geneva Archive, and the City of Boulogne-sur-Mer Archive. It is a special pleasure for me to acknowledge the assistance of Pierre-André Wimet, president of the Department for Historical Monuments in Pas-de-Calais, whose knowledge of the history of Boulogne is unrivalled and who traced for me a number of rare documents relating to Liszt's stays in that city and to Adam Liszt's death there in 1827. Various other scholars were good enough to deal with sporadic inquiries of a specialized nature, including Edward Waters, former chief of the Music Division of the Library of Congress, Dr. Charles Suttoni, Professor Jacques Vier, Professor Gabriele Erasmi, and Dr. Bálint Sárosi, Hungary's leading expert on Gypsy music, and I am happy to record my appreciation here. It was a stroke of good fortune that brought in Eva Resnikova as my copy editor at the house of Knopf. From the start, she treated my text with the same respect as if it had been her own. Many of her helpful suggestions were incorporated into the narrative and helped to produce a better book.

Last but first, I want to mention two people who helped me with much of the research, who sifted through hundreds of microfilms, photocopies, and magazine articles, prepared synopses, paraphrases, and translations, and generally did all that they could to lighten my burden. To Pauline Pocknell, my loyal assistant, who holds with Blake the "holiness of the minute particular" and has saved me from many an inconsistency, I extend my warmest personal regards. As for László Jambor, music librarian at McMaster University, Ontario, his unflagging energy in the face of an unremitting hail of questions, challenges, and rebuttals over half a decade has won my lasting admiration. In both cases, the work of these individuals went far beyond the call of duty, and I shall long remember our years of toil together.

Weimar, May 1982   ALAN WALKER

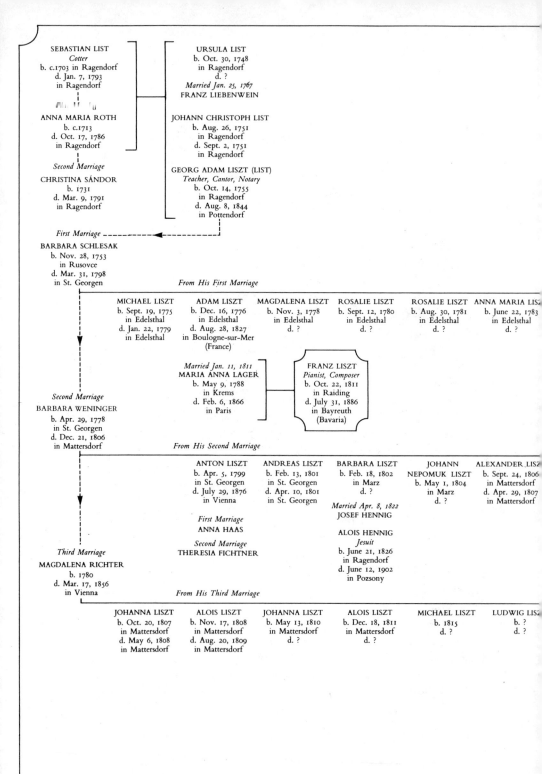

The Liszt Family Tree I

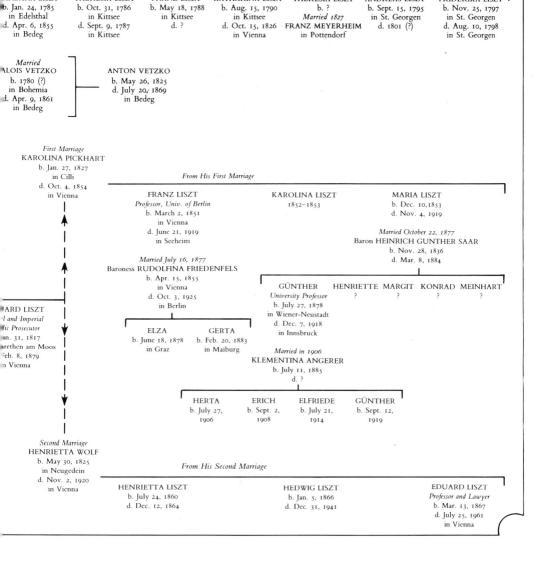

ARBARA LISZT	THERESIA LISZT	FRANZ LISZT	KATHARINA LISZT	THERESIA LISZT	ANDREAS LISZT	FRIDERIKA LISZT
b. Jan. 24, 1785	b. Oct. 31, 1786	b. May 18, 1788	b. Aug. 15, 1790	b. ?	b. Sept. 15, 1795	b. Nov. 25, 1797
in Edelsthal	in Kittsee	in Kittsee	in Kittsee	*Married 1827*	in St. Georgen	in St. Georgen
d. Apr. 6, 1855	d. Sept. 9, 1787	d. ?	d. Oct. 15, 1826	FRANZ MEYERHEIM	d. 1801 (?)	d. Aug. 10, 1798
in Bedeg	in Kittsee		in Vienna	in Pottendorf		in St. Georgen

Married
ALOIS VETZKO
b. 1780 (?)
in Bohemia
d. Apr. 9, 1861
in Bedeg

ANTON VETZKO
b. May 26, 1825
d. July 20, 1869
in Bedeg

First Marriage
KAROLINA PICKHART
b. Jan. 27, 1827
in Cilli
d. Oct. 4, 1854
in Vienna

From His First Marriage

FRANZ LISZT
Professor, Univ. of Berlin
b. March 2, 1851
in Vienna
d. June 21, 1919
in Seeheim

KAROLINA LISZT
1852–1853

MARIA LISZT
b. Dec. 10, 1853
d. Nov. 4, 1919

Married October 22, 1877
Baron HEINRICH GUNTHER SAAR
b. Nov. 28, 1836
d. Mar. 8, 1884

Married July 16, 1877
Baroness RUDOLFINA FRIEDENFELS
b. Apr. 15, 1855
in Vienna
d. Oct. 3, 1925
in Berlin

GÜNTHER	HENRIETTE	MARGIT	KONRAD	MEINHART
University Professor	?	?	?	?
b. July 27, 1878				
in Wiener-Neustadt				
d. Dec. 7, 1918				
in Innsbruck				

ELZA
b. June 18, 1878
in Graz

GERTA
b. Feb. 20, 1883
in Maiburg

Married in 1906
KLEMENTINA ANGERER
b. July 11, 1885
d. ?

HERTA	ERICH	ELFRIEDE	GÜNTHER
b. July 27, 1906	b. Sept. 2, 1908	b. July 21, 1914	b. Sept. 12, 1919

ARD LISZT
l and Imperial
ic Prosecutor
an. 31, 1817
arethen am Moos
Feb. 8, 1879
n Vienna

Second Marriage
HENRIETTA WOLF
b. May 30, 1825
in Neugedein
d. Nov. 2, 1920
in Vienna

From His Second Marriage

HENRIETTA LISZT	HEDWIG LISZT	EDUARD LISZT
b. July 24, 1860	b. Jan. 5, 1866	*Professor and Lawyer*
d. Dec. 12, 1864	d. Dec. 31, 1941	b. Mar. 13, 1867
		d. July 25, 1961
		in Vienna

The Liszt Family Tree II

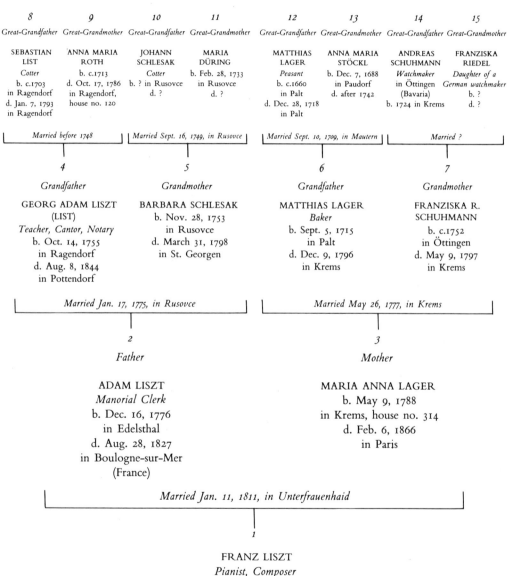

8	9	10	11	12	13	14	15
Great-Grandfather	*Great-Grandmother*	*Great-Grandfather*	*Great-Grandmother*	*Great-Grandfather*	*Great-Grandmother*	*Great-Grandfather*	*Great-Grandmother*
SEBASTIAN LIST	ANNA MARIA ROTH	JOHANN SCHLESAK	MARIA DÜRING	MATTHIAS LAGER	ANNA MARIA STÖCKL	ANDREAS SCHUHMANN	FRANZISKA RIEDEL
Cotter	*Cotter*	*Cotter*	b. Feb. 28, 1733 in Rusovce d. ?	*Peasant*	b. Dec. 7, 1688 in Paudorf d. after 1742	*Watchmaker* in Öttingen (Bavaria) b. 1724 in Krems	*Daughter of a German watchmaker* b. ? d. ?
b. c.1703 in Ragendorf d. Jan. 7, 1793 in Ragendorf	b. c.1713 d. Oct. 17, 1786 in Ragendorf, house no. 120	b. ? in Rusovce d. ?		b. c.1660 in Palt d. Dec. 28, 1718 in Palt			

Married before 1748	Married Sept. 16, 1749, in Rusovce	Married Sept. 10, 1709, in Mautern	Married ?

4	5	6	7
Grandfather	*Grandmother*	*Grandfather*	*Grandmother*
GEORG ADAM LISZT (LIST)	BARBARA SCHLESAK	MATTHIAS LAGER	FRANZISKA R. SCHUHMANN
Teacher, Cantor, Notary	b. Nov. 28, 1753 in Rusovce d. March 31, 1798 in St. Georgen	*Baker*	b. c.1752 in Öttingen d. May 9, 1797 in Krems
b. Oct. 14, 1755 in Ragendorf d. Aug. 8, 1844 in Pottendorf		b. Sept. 5, 1715 in Palt d. Dec. 9, 1796 in Krems	

Married Jan. 17, 1775, in Rusovce	Married May 26, 1777, in Krems

2	3
Father	*Mother*
ADAM LISZT	MARIA ANNA LAGER
Manorial Clerk	b. May 9, 1788 in Krems, house no. 314 d. Feb. 6, 1866 in Paris
b. Dec. 16, 1776 in Edelsthal d. Aug. 28, 1827 in Boulogne-sur-Mer (France)	

Married Jan. 11, 1811, in Unterfrauenhaid

1

FRANZ LISZT
Pianist, Composer
b. Oct. 22, 1811
in Raiding
Registered in Unterfrauenhaid
d. July 31, 1886
in Bayreuth
(Bavaria)

Concordance Table of
Cities, Towns, and Villages

The map of Europe has been redrawn several times during the past hundred and fifty years. Two world wars, a number of smaller European ones, various uprisings, insurrections, and revolutions have all conspired to change the face of the globe beyond recognition. The treaties of Versailles, St. Germain, and Trianon (1919) and, during World War II, the Yalta Conference (1945) settled the fate of millions of Europeans at the stroke of a pen. People went to bed as Austrians and Germans; they woke up next morning as Poles, Czechs, or Yugoslavs. Some of their children would one day wake up again as Russians.

What this means for the biographer of any important European figure of the nineteenth century can easily be imagined. At the very outset, he is faced with a dilemma: how to identify the very towns, cities, and countries which form the backdrop to his story. To take a simple example: the ancient city of Breslau was once part of Germany; today it belongs to Poland and is called Wrocław. A more notorious case is that of Pressburg, one of the musical capitals of the world. This Austrian name goes back nearly a thousand years. Yet the city always belonged to Hungary, and Hungarians always called it Pozsony. In 1919 Pozsony passed to Czechoslovakia and is today called Bratislava. How is the biographer to proceed? Does he use the names of places as they once were? Or does he adopt their modern equivalents? If he chooses the former, he will probably confuse the general reader, who will be quite unable to find such places on a map. If he chooses the latter, however, he will raise the ire of the serious scholar, who is committed to historical context, to the continuity of the discipline, and to comparing and contrasting each new contribution to his subject with all the others in the field.

In this book cities, towns, and villages will be known as Liszt himself called them, which happened to be as common nineteenth-century usage dictated. The reason is self-evident. Liszt was one of the greatest travellers of his time. His correspondence is studded with place names. To transpose them all, in the light of everything that has since befallen the modern world, would quickly lead to chaos; to say that Liszt played in Chemnitz in 1840 is one thing; to say that he played in Karl Marx Stadt in 1840 is quite another. The following concordance table reveals at a glance many of those places associated with Liszt, with his family, and with his friends and colleagues, which have meanwhile changed

Place Name	Alternative Name	Originally in	Now in (* = *no change*)
AACHEN	Aix-la-Chapelle	Germany	*
BRESLAU	Wrocław	Germany	Poland
BRÜNN	Brno	Moravia	Czechoslovakia
CHEMNITZ	Karl Marx Stadt	Germany	*
CONSTANTINOPLE	Istanbul	Turkey	*
CZERNOVTSY	Czernowitz	Austria	USSR
DANZIG	Gdansk	Germany	Poland
DEUTSCHKREUTZ	Németkeresztúr	Hungary	Austria
EDELSTHAL	Nemesvölgy	Hungary	Austria
EISENSTADT	Kismarton	Hungary	Austria
ELISABETGRAD	Kirovograd	Ukraine	USSR
ESTERHÁZA	Fertőd	Hungary	*
ESZÉK	Osijek	Hungary	Yugoslavia
FORCHTENAU	Fraknó	Hungary	Austria
FÜNFKIRCHEN	Pécs	Hungary	*
GLOGAU	Głogów	Germany	Poland
GRAN	Esztergom	Hungary	*
HERMANNSTADT	Nagyszeben later Sibiu	Hungary	Rumania
KITTSEE	Köpcsény	Hungary	Austria
KLAUSENBURG	Kolozsvár, later Cluj	Hungary	Rumania
KÖNIGSBERG	Kaliningrad	Germany	USSR
LACKENBACH	Lakompak	Hungary	Austria
LEMBERG	Lvov	Austria	USSR
LIEGNITZ	Legnica	Germany	Poland

names. The Burgenland, for example, is particularly rich in associations with Liszt's childhood. This narrow strip of land used to be in western Hungary; it has since been transferred to Austria. Many of its towns and villages had mixed populations. Quite logically, then, they often had two names—one Hungarian, the other German. There are still Hungarian Liszt scholars who never refer to Eisenstadt; they talk only of Kismarton. There are still Austrian Liszt scholars who never refer to Sopron; they talk only of Oedenburg. Such a practice is deeply rooted in national pride. I record it here merely to alert the English-speaking reader to a possible source of error and confusion.

Place Name	Alternative Name	Originally in	Now in (* = *no change*)
LIVORNO	Leghorn	Italy	*
MAFFERSDORF	Vratislavice	Bohemia	Czechoslovakia
MARZ	Márcfalva	Hungary	Austria
MATTERSDORF	Nagymarton	Hungary	Austria
MITAU	Jelgava	Latvia	USSR
NAGYENYED	Aiud	Hungary	Rumania
NEISSE	Nysa	Germany	Poland
OEDENBURG	Sopron	Hungary	*
OROSZVÁR	Karlburg, later Rusovce	Hungary	Czechoslovakia
PRESSBURG	Pozsony, later Bratislava	Hungary	Czechoslovakia
RAAB	Györ	Hungary	*
RAGENDORF	Rajka	Hungary	*
RAIDING	Doborján	Hungary	Austria
ST. GEORGEN-AM- LEITHAGEBIRGE	Lajtaszentgyörgy	Hungary	Austria
ST. PETERSBURG	Petrograd, later Leningrad	Russia	USSR
STANISLAV	Ivano-Frankovsk	Ukraine	USSR
STETTIN	Szczecin	Germany	Poland
TILSIT	Sovetsk	Germany	USSR
TYRNAVIA	Nagyszombat, later Trnava	Hungary	Czechoslovakia
UNTERFRAUENHAID	Lók	Hungary	Austria
ZIMONY	Zemun	Hungary	Yugoslavia

Franz Liszt

THE VIRTUOSO YEARS

1811–1847

Prologue

Liszt and the Literature

Do not entangle yourself in too many details.
LISZT TO LINA RAMANN, C.1881[1]

I fear that [Ramann] will be unable to see
the wood for the trees.
LISZT TO PRINCESS VON SAYN-
WITTGENSTEIN, 1877.[2]

I

The normal way biography is written is to allow the basic materials—letters, diaries, manuscripts—to disclose the life. And if those materials are missing, one goes out and finds them. That did not happen with Liszt. Because of the unparalleled fame, even notoriety, enjoyed by Liszt during his lifetime (eclipsing by far that of all his musical contemporaries), a complete reversal of the "normal" process took place. Everywhere he went Liszt lived out his life in a blaze of publicity. People clamoured for literature about him. And so the biographies came first; the hard evidence turned up later. Most of the energy expended by the modern Liszt researcher has to do with correcting the former in the light of the latter. Liszt himself entertained no illusions about his biographers. They often irritated him, and for good reason; some of them, as we shall discover, had a genuine talent for invention. Occasionally Liszt corrected their work. By the time he had reached old age, however, he was resigned to his fate: the groundwork for that generous supply of misinformation, half-truth, and legend which taints the Liszt literature to this day had already been prepared.

The earliest biography was that of Joseph d'Ortigue (1802–66), whose "Etude biographique" was published in the *Gazette Musicale de Paris* in 1835,

---

1. WA, Kasten 351, no. 1; unpublished.
2. LLB, vol. 7, p. 181.

when Liszt, already a European figure, was only twenty-three years old. It was based on materials supplied by Anna Liszt, his mother, and Countess Marie d'Agoult, his first mistress—a combination of sources not likely to inspire confidence.[3] Liszt himself was dissatisfied with it, little realizing, when he suggested one or two changes, that it was the harbinger of much worse to come. Six years later, in 1841, Johann Wilhelm Christern (1809–77) came forward with his panegyric *Franz Liszts Leben und Wirken.* A valuable copy of this rare book, now in the possession of the Library of Congress, Washington, D.C., was corrected and annotated by Liszt himself. His corrections reveal the extent of Christern's shortcomings, and the remarkable objectivity with which Liszt viewed himself as a biographical topic, a rarely acknowledged aspect of his character. Liszt's editorial changes, made on interleaved blank pages in pen and ink,[4] cover the details of his early childhood, his amours, his religious leanings. These changes are sometimes detrimental even to Liszt himself, and spoil Christern's idealized image of him. In fact, they are a model of common sense and good taste, and set a standard of decency for his later biographers which, unfortunately, these ladies and gentlemen were disinclined to follow. The very next year, 1842, saw the publication of *Franz Liszt* by the Berlin critic Ludwig Rellstab (1799–1860). This hastily assembled collection of reviews and newspaper articles was timed to coincide with Liszt's long-awaited concerts in Berlin, which he gave during the winter of 1841–42. Two years later, in 1844, Gustav Schilling (1803–81) wrote his *Franz Liszt: Sein Leben und sein Wirken aus nächster Beschauung.* This book, too, was evidently intended to capitalize on Liszt's successful tours of Europe. Liszt must have read both books, but his reactions are unknown.

Already these early publications establish the model for the later ones. Neither F. J. Fétis, in his Liszt entry in the *Biographie universelle des musiciens* (1844, 2d ed. 1875), nor Ludwig Nohl, in his *Franz Liszt* (1882), shows much advance on d'Ortigue's pioneering effort—not, at any rate, as far as the early part of Liszt's career is concerned. By 1850, in fact, the hard information about his childhood and early youth had become stubbornly fixed in the literature, and even though much of it is palpably false (for instance, the supposed public embrace by Beethoven during the boy's 1823 "farewell" recital in Vienna), it is dutifully repeated to this day. These, then, are custom-built biographies, instantly recognizable as such. They take in one another's paragraphs as friendly

---

3. This study was spotted almost at once by Robert Schumann, who commissioned a complete German translation for his magazine, the *Neue Zeitschrift für Musik.* D'Ortigue's piece was therefore transmitted across the whole of Germany. The work of translation was carried out by Emil Flechsig (1808–78), and it was published in six instalments (NZfM, vol. 4, nos. 4, 5, 6, 7, 8, and 10, 1836).
4. Carl Engel published a list of these annotations in his useful review of the Washington copy called "Views and Reviews," MQLN, July 1936.

neighbours take in one another's washing: they neither give nor receive any public acknowledgement for such a basic, mutual activity.[5]

I I

The reader already familiar with the broad outlines of Liszt's life will recall that the early 1840s were years of crisis in his relationship with Countess Marie d'Agoult. This liaison terminated, in fact, in 1844. The full story of that ill-starred romance and its tragic consequences for the lovers themselves, and above all for their three children, will be told in its proper place. What has to be observed here is that Marie was humiliated, and her humiliation quickly turned to hatred. In 1846, after she had adopted her well-known pseudonym "Daniel Stern," she dipped her pen in vitriol and published her first novel, *Nélida* (the title of which is an anagram of the name Daniel). This work is a thinly disguised account of Liszt and Madame d'Agoult herself, in which Liszt is depicted as Guermann, a painter who is artistically impotent, and Marie as Nélida, a woman of noble breeding who, despite her selfless devotion to Guermann, is callously abandoned. This autobiographical novel was first published in serial form in 1846 in the *Revue Indépendante;* it then reappeared almost at once in hardcover.[6] Its publication caused Liszt some embarrassment. Not content to insert the blade, Marie twisted the hilt. A second edition of her book appeared in 1866 and did him professional harm in France. But still worse was to follow. In 1869, when Liszt was fifty-eight years old and an abbé of the Roman Catholic Church, a young pupil, Olga Janina, the so-called Cossack Countess, crossed his path. Olga was pathological. She became briefly enamoured of Liszt, who, after trying to shake her off, was a witness to her attempted suicide in his Budapest apartment. Olga was finally deported from the Hungarian capital by the Budapest police.[7] These experiences seemed suffi-

---

5. These, of course, represent by no means all the writings about Liszt during the first thirty years of his life. He was the topic of constant comment in the European press; the professional journals, especially the ones published in France and Germany, often carry long reports about his activities. Among the more interesting are the *Musikalische Berichte aus Paris* (1841), written by Heine, articles by Berlioz in the *Journal des Débats,* and Robert Schumann's classic pieces on Liszt's Leipzig concerts in the *Neue Zeitschrift für Musik* (1840).

As for the many newspaper reports from other lands, they are to be found in practically every country through which Liszt toured. They are often set pieces which merely unroll the same tired biographical information, not unlike the press handouts artists still carry around with them today, whose function is largely cosmetic. Two stimulating exceptions are *Bohemia* and *Buda-Pesti Rajzolatok,* newspapers which served the Czech and Hungarian-speaking populations of Central Europe, respectively. Their accounts of the pianist's visits to Prague (1840) and Pest (1839–40) are highly rewarding to the serious Liszt researcher.

6. In two volumes (Brussels, 1846). The following year it also appeared in a Spanish translation (Burgos, 1847).

cient to justify this twenty-six-year-old's going into retirement to write her "memoirs," the first batch of which appeared as an autobiographical novel, *Souvenirs d'une cosaque* (1874), under the pseudonym "Robert Franz." Then, lest her readership fail to grasp the facts behind her fiction, she wrote two further novels, "replies" to the first, called *Les Amours d'une cosaque par un ami de l'Abbé "X,"* and *Le Roman du pianiste et de la cosaque* (1874–75). For these two literary efforts Olga felt constrained to adopt another pseudonym, "Sylvia Zorelli." In his brilliant exposé of this troublesome parasite, the Hungarian scholar Dezső Legány shows that Olga's real name was not Janina but Zielinska.[8] She took the name Janina from her husband, Karel Janina Piasecki, whom she married in her eighteenth year and then abandoned, because it had a better "ring" to it among the aristocratic circles of Central Europe in which she wanted to mix. She was not a Cossack; least of all was she a countess. Whatever pretensions she had to a moneyed background she owed to her father, Ludwik Zielinski, who manufactured boot polish in Lemberg. Everything that Olga tells us about herself in her books is pure fiction, created to obscure her mundane origins. It is truly astonishing that the slander she spread about Liszt, which caused him pain in his old age, is still believed today. The scandal no longer lies in Olga's books; it lies in the books of those who continue to cite what she said in order to add a dash of colour to what might otherwise be a drab account of Liszt's final years. We shall have occasion to meet Olga Zielinska-Piasecka again in Volume III of the present biography.

Liszt had now become a dubious figure to the world at large. His close friends, pupils, and acquaintances grieved to see this great artist depicted as a buffoon. They lamented the absence of any serious biographer, someone who would view Liszt's life with scholarly concern rather than merely help to bury it under a growing mound of literary debris. Liszt's two great contemporaries Schumann and Chopin, co-founders with him of the Romantic movement in music, had already found outstanding biographers. Joseph Wasielewski's *Robert Schumann* had appeared as early as 1858, and Moritz Karasowski's *Life of Chopin* followed in 1877. Both are foundation works on their respective composers. And both books, not unnaturally, cast Liszt in a minor supporting role. Liszt was now sixty-six, and approaching the twilight of his life. Where was *his* biographer? It was at this point that Princess Carolyne von Sayn-Wittgenstein, his second mistress and companion for thirty years, decided to intervene.

I I I

Whatever Liszt's later biographers have said against Carolyne, and they have said a great deal, it was never possible for them to charge her with harbouring

---

7. HL, p. 259.
8. LLM, pp. 207–8.

spite and animosity towards Liszt, a man she loved with fierce and proud possessiveness down to the day of her death. Unlike Marie d'Agoult, Carolyne never turned on Liszt, never publicly maligned and defamed his character. In fact, it was her dearest wish to see that her idol had a lasting monument, a multivolume "authorized" biography written by an independent scholar. The story of how an obscure music teacher named Lina Ramann (1833–1912) took on the awesome task of writing Liszt's biography makes fascinating reading.[9] Until recently it was thought that Ramann was an accomplice of the princess, appointed to carry out her directives. Thanks to the belated publication of Ramann's *Lisztiana* (1983), we can see that her original research was far more extensive than anyone had supposed. Through her diary entries, her personal reminiscences of Liszt and Carolyne, and, above all, the biographical questionnaires that she sent to Liszt, we are afforded a rare glimpse into the biographer's workshop.

Ramann would doubtless have been capable of writing a dispassionate biography if she had been left to get on with it. The German press had warmly praised two of her earlier books;[10] and an article on Liszt's music published before she knew him shows that she was not antipathetic to her subject. But the princess had some old scores to settle. She set out to influence Ramann's text and attempted to alter it to her advantage. After 1878, the conflict between the two became acute, and Ramann had to fight to retain her integrity. "Do you really think that I am an instrument whose mechanism can be controlled according to the will of the player?" she asked Carolyne. "Can I see only with your eyes, think only your thoughts, feel only your feelings?"[11] On one issue, however, Ramann failed to resist the princess: Marie d'Agoult (whom the princess never met but with whom she knew posterity would compare her) was cast in the poorest light. Since Marie died in 1876, shortly before the chapter on her was written, she had no opportunity to defend herself. There is little question that Cosima Wagner was right when she charged that this mendacious attack on her mother was inspired by the princess. Ramann's *Franz Liszt als Künstler und Mensch* occupied her for twenty years. Although her style is fulsome, even fawning, it was not unusual for the nineteenth century to idealize its heroes, and it was widely believed that her book had, at last, done justice to its subject.

But in 1933–34 a literary event of capital importance occured. Daniel Ollivier, Liszt's grandson, published the *Correspondance de Liszt et de la Comtesse*

---

9. For an account of Ramann herself, consult the useful biographical sketch by Marie Ille-Beeg in IRL.

10. *Die Musik als Gegenstand der Erziehung* (1868), and *Allgemeine Erzieh- und Unterrichtslehre der Jugend* (1869).

11. RL, p. 131.

d'Agoult in two volumes.[12] Now, for the first time, we were given the other side of the picture. This publication represented nothing less than the moral rehabilitation of Marie d'Agoult. Throughout Liszt's long years abroad, especially the period 1838–47, when he was away on concert tours, he had maintained a regular correspondence with Marie. She preserved some five hundred of his letters to her; most of hers to him were destroyed. These letters quickly became an essential tool for all subsequent Liszt research. They are full of lively observations, of great practical interest to the biographer. Liszt's tours took him all over Europe. With the practised eye of a seasoned traveller, he packed his letters with minute detail. People, places, events—all were brought to life for Marie, who could only share his spectacular successes at a distance. Included in this correspondence were great and moving love letters, in the grand Romantic tradition, and they proved conclusively that far from being the passing diversion Ramann had made her out to be, Marie was at the heart of Liszt's emotional life for ten years.

Neither the princess nor Ramann could be sure that this remarkable collection of letters still existed when they embarked on their posthumous campaign of denigration against Marie d'Agoult. But they felt reasonably safe. Marie, after all, had silently hugged these letters to herself for thirty-five years or more. Why had she not used them in her bitter quarrels with Liszt? She was surely deterred by a simple reservation: she, in turn, could not be certain that her letters to Liszt had been destroyed, that they might not some day be used against her. The *Correspondance* posed a mutual threat. The result was a stalemate. Since 1934 the question has often been asked: How far was Liszt implicated in Ramann's biography? The answer is clearly important to some scholars, since Liszt's honour appears, to them, to be at stake. This was the chief talking-point of *The Man Liszt* (1934) by Ernest Newman, the most vocal of Liszt's critics.

---

12. The dramatic story of how Ollivier came into possession of these priceless letters is worth telling, since it shows how shifting are the foundations on which biography rests. Marie d'Agoult bequeathed all her papers to Louis de Ronchaud, her literary executor, who was at her bedside when she died in 1876. Ronchaud, the director of the Louvre, lived in bachelor apartments in the Louvre itself. When he died in 1887 one of his female relatives gained admittance to his rooms and systematically began to burn bundles of papers in the fireplace. Portions of the d'Agoult legacy had already been consigned to the flames when a young assistant director, Georges Lafenestre, walked in and stopped her from completing this senseless act of vandalism. The bundles which were saved, including the Liszt-d'Agoult *Correspondance,* were entrusted to Marie's heirs and eventually passed to her grandson Daniel Ollivier. Today these holographs are in the Bibliothèque Nationale (NAF Archives Daniel Ollivier no. 25179). In 1927 Ollivier published Madame d'Agoult's *Mémoires,* constructed from a loose assemblage of her papers. Such was the interest aroused by this book that he followed it some six years later with the two volumes of *Correspondance.* For many years the world assumed that Ollivier had published all the letters in his possession, and, more important, had published them complete. It is now apparent that this was not the case. What the world requires, in fact, is a completely new edition of the Liszt-d'Agoult *Correspondance* which will restore the material omitted by Ollivier.

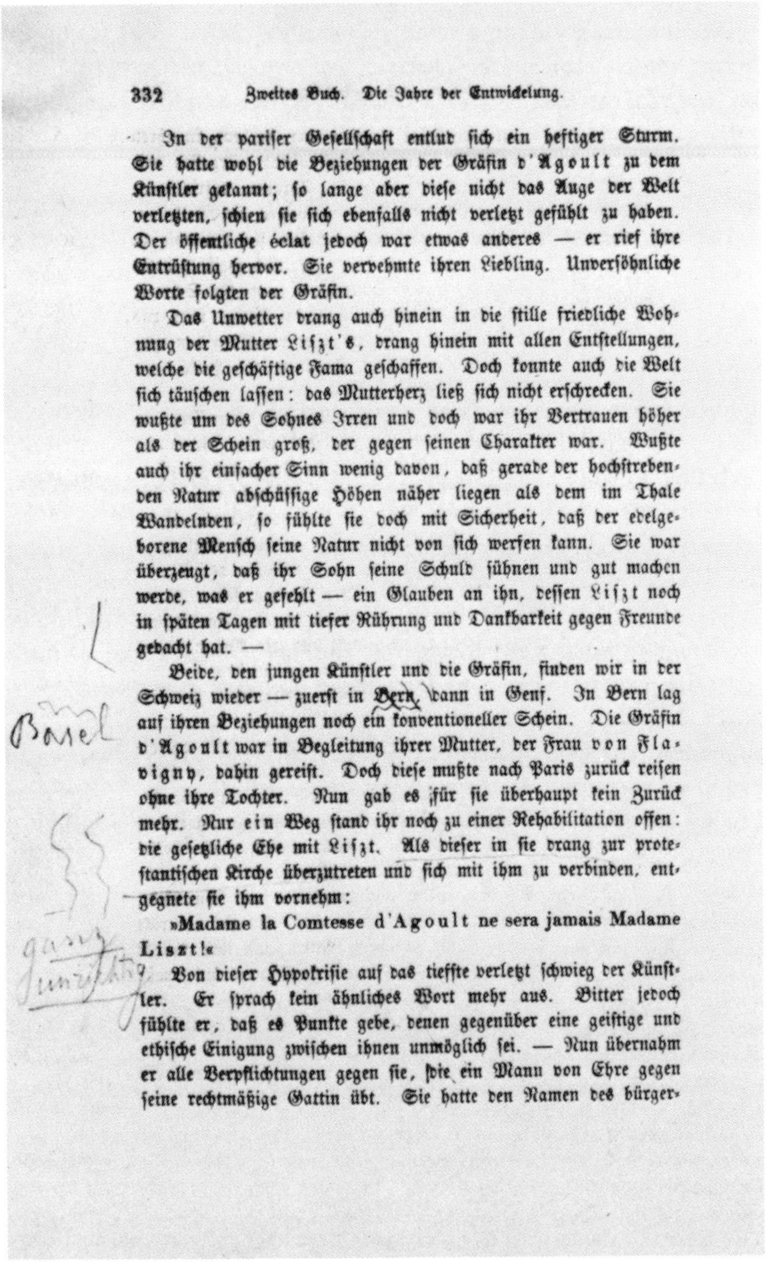

332   Zweites Buch. Die Jahre der Entwickelung.

In der pariser Gesellschaft entlud sich ein heftiger Sturm. Sie hatte wohl die Beziehungen der Gräfin d'Agoult zu dem Künstler gekannt; so lange aber diese nicht das Auge der Welt verletzten, schien sie sich ebenfalls nicht verletzt gefühlt zu haben. Der öffentliche éclat jedoch war etwas anderes — er rief ihre Entrüstung hervor. Sie verfehmte ihren Liebling. Unversöhnliche Worte folgten der Gräfin.

Das Unwetter drang auch hinein in die stille friedliche Wohnung der Mutter Liszt's, drang hinein mit allen Entstellungen, welche die geschäftige Fama geschaffen. Doch konnte auch die Welt sich täuschen lassen: das Mutterherz ließ sich nicht erschrecken. Sie wußte um des Sohnes Irren und doch war ihr Vertrauen höher als der Schein groß, der gegen seinen Charakter war. Wußte auch ihr einfacher Sinn wenig davon, daß gerade der hochstrebenden Natur abschüssige Höhen näher liegen als dem im Thale Wandelnden, so fühlte sie doch mit Sicherheit, daß der edelgeborene Mensch seine Natur nicht von sich werfen kann. Sie war überzeugt, daß ihr Sohn seine Schuld sühnen und gut machen werde, was er gefehlt — ein Glauben an ihn, dessen Liszt noch in späten Tagen mit tiefer Rührung und Dankbarkeit gegen Freunde gedacht hat. —

Beide, den jungen Künstler und die Gräfin, finden wir in der Schweiz wieder — zuerst in Bern, dann in Genf. In Bern lag auf ihren Beziehungen noch ein konventioneller Schein. Die Gräfin d'Agoult war in Begleitung ihrer Mutter, der Frau von Flavigny, dahin gereist. Doch diese mußte nach Paris zurück reisen ohne ihre Tochter. Nun gab es für sie überhaupt kein Zurück mehr. Nur ein Weg stand ihr noch zu einer Rehabilitation offen: die gesetzliche Ehe mit Liszt. Als dieser in sie drang zur protestantischen Kirche überzutreten und sich mit ihm zu verbinden, entgegnete sie ihm vornehm:

»Madame la Comtesse d'Agoult ne sera jamais Madame Liszt!«

Von dieser Hypokrisie auf das tiefste verletzt schwieg der Künstler. Er sprach kein ähnliches Wort mehr aus. Bitter jedoch fühlte er, daß es Punkte gebe, denen gegenüber eine geistige und ethische Einigung zwischen ihnen unmöglich sei. — Nun übernahm er alle Verpflichtungen gegen sie, wie ein Mann von Ehre gegen seine rechtmäßige Gattin übt. Sie hatte den Namen des bürger-

[Marginal handwritten corrections: "Basel"; "ganz unrichtig"]

A page from Lina Ramann's biography,
with Liszt's handwritten corrections.

Certainly Liszt gave Ramann a number of interviews in the late 1870s; much of
the information about his early years, in fact, could have come only from
him.[13] But there was no suggestion that he was asked even to approve the
manuscript before publication. That fact ceases to be astonishing once we remember the context within which the enterprise unfolded. Ramann lived in
Nuremberg, Carolyne lived in Rome (she and Liszt had not lived together
since 1860, twenty years earlier, and saw little of one another). He was an el
derly man. He had been publicly praised and pilloried all his life. He had made
at least two attempts conscientiously to correct the work of previous biographers. Enough was enough. Polite lack of interest seems to have been Liszt's
attitude towards his "official" biography. For the rest, a glance at the dates set-
tles two-thirds of the question: the last two volumes were published after
Liszt's death.

The most incriminating piece of evidence against Liszt is his personal copy
of volume I, now in the Weimar archives, which contains a number of marginal
notes in his own handwriting, made sometime after 1880. The chapter on Marie
was left untouched. That, say his critics, points to his complicity. Not one of
them perceived an alternative, and very human, explanation. Since Liszt knew
that this chapter was the work of Carolyne, he faced an almost impossible
choice: he could either pick up his pen and expose her, or he could do nothing
and risk being exposed himself. He was damned if he did and damned if he
didn't. As his eye roved across those pages it must have paused at one of
Carolyne's sentences: "He was too noble and too proud to abandon a woman
at a moment when she had a right to appeal to his heart." Liszt, we may be
sure, savoured the irony of these words to the full.

There are fashions in all things; biography is no exception. Marie d'Agoult

---

13. Between the years 1874 and 1881, while Ramann was preparing her biography, it became her
habit to send Liszt handwritten questionnaires with spaces beneath each question for his reply.
These holographs are all preserved in the Weimar archives (WA, Kasten 351, no. 1). Ramann put
more than one hundred questions to Liszt about his life and work, and his replies are often detailed. In sifting through these documents, which seem to be unknown to Liszt's biographers, the
modern observer is struck with great force by two things. First: however painful the question,
Liszt does not shirk the answer; we know this with certainty because his replies can today be objectively verified, and they reveal Liszt to be a truth-teller of an unusual order. Second: the relationship between Ramann and Liszt was as detached as that between a lawyer and his client. The
charge of collusion must be discounted. On one occasion Liszt balks at one of Ramann's questions.
She asks him to provide details about the death of his son, Daniel. The subject is apparently too
sensitive for him to deal with in writing, and he replies that the matter ought to be handled orally
the next time that they meet. Closely related to these questionnaires is the extant correspondence
between Ramann and Liszt, the main body of which consists of a series of twenty-nine letters
which are in reality amplifications of, or supplements to, his autobiographical responses to
Ramann's questions (WA, Kasten 326). It is from the correspondence, in fact, that we receive
proof that Liszt granted Ramann personal interviews. On August 30, 1874, shortly after she began
work on her biography, he wrote, "Before the first volume appears I am available for a few hours'
conference—next May or June in Weimar or Nuremberg" (where Ramann lived). These questionnaires are included in *Lisztiana* (1983). See RL, pp. 387–408.

is generally perceived today as a "wronged woman." Is this a definitive picture? Her *cri de coeur,* uttered only three years after their sensational elopement to Geneva, and enshrined forever in her *Mémoires* ("Franz had abandoned me for such small motives!"), has haunted Liszt's biographers for half a century; they have been hard pressed to handle the accusation dispassionately. Ever since the publication of Jacques Vier's masterly *La Comtesse d'Agoult et son temps* in six volumes (1955–63), however, it has been clear that the "long-suffering" image of Marie is not entirely truthful and would itself have to be revised. Vier had access to many unpublished archives in France. He toiled for more than fifteen years on his magnum opus and consulted, among other esoteric documents, the hitherto unknown diaries of Charles d'Agoult, the husband whom Marie had in turn abandoned. By the time the first volume of Vier's biography of Marie appeared, he had already made two extremely useful contributions to the Liszt literature,[14] and was therefore well equipped to do his subject justice. The picture that emerges is refreshingly candid. Vier had a great respect for evidence, and he went where it led him; he had no interest in writing a book that would merely please Marie's admirers. He demonstrated that the frustrations with which Marie was undoubtedly beset after her ten-year liaison with Liszt was finally ended sprang as much from the divisions in her complex make-up as from her association with the famous pianist. She would, in all likelihood, have been a "wronged woman" whoever crossed her path. It is clearly in Liszt's posthumous interests to incorporate Vier's scholarly findings into any subsequent biography of the man, since few aspects of his life have been more severely criticized in modern times than his "abandonment" of Madame d'Agoult. If, therefore, the present life of Liszt treats Marie with somewhat less deference than is customary nowadays, that is because the balance of evidence has started to shift away from her, and that fact must inevitably affect the narrative.

I V

Meanwhile, what of Liszt's other letters? The really important collections had been available to scholars for many years, although it has to be said that this was rarely reflected in the literature. They were mostly published during the period 1893–1918 under the editorship of La Mara (Marie Lipsius, 1837–1927). The chief volumes are

> *Franz Liszts Briefe* (8 vols.), Leipzig, 1893–1905:
> vol. 1, *Von Paris bis Rom*

---

14. See VAMA and VFL.

vol. 2, *Von Rom bis ans Ende*
vol. 3, *Briefe an eine Freundin*
vols. 4–7, *Briefe an die Fürstin Sayn-Wittgenstein*
vol. 8, *Neue Folge zu Band I und II*

Briefe hervorragender Zeitgenossen an Franz Liszt (3 vols.),
Leipzig, 1895–1904

*Briefwechsel zwischen Franz Liszt und Carl Alexander,
Grossherzog von Sachsen,* Leipzig, 1909

Franz Liszts Briefe an seine Mutter, Leipzig, 1918.

La Mara was fifty-six years old when she published the first volume of Liszt's letters in 1893. By the time she had finished her great task, with the appearance of her last volume in 1918, she was an old lady of eighty-one. Such tireless devotion to Liszt's cause commands respect. La Mara edited other important collections, too, including Liszt's correspondence with Wagner and with Hans von Bülow. Altogether she had made at least four thousand letters (either to or from Liszt) available to his biographers by the year 1918. Why were they so rarely consulted? They are source documents of some significance; they illuminate a great personality possessed of a warm generosity of spirit and an enormous range of interests. Liszt's worldwide connections alone are of perennial fascination.

It must be stressed that, valuable though they are, these are not "critical" editions. La Mara did not scruple to omit a number of letters from the series. She also subjected some of the correspondence to censorship. Perhaps the material to suffer most was the *Briefe an eine Freundin,* which is known to the world only in its mutilated form. The anonymous *Freundin* was Agnès Street-Klindworth, who, according to La Mara, became a pupil of Liszt in the 1850s during his tenure at Weimar. La Mara first gained access to these letters through the good offices of Agnès Street's elder son, George, in 1892, and she appears to have been taken aback by their content. There was evidence that Liszt and Agnès had not only forged a strong emotional bond during the years 1853–55, but had also become lovers, one of their secret trysts being her apartment on the Carlsplatz, less than a mile from the Altenburg, where Liszt now lived with his "official" mistress, Princess von Sayn-Wittgenstein. Liszt confided to Agnès his frustrations over the tug-of-war he was then enduring with Marie d'Agoult over the future of their three children, whom he was about to remove from Paris to Germany, and he allowed himself to make some ambivalent references to his family in unguarded moments. La Mara doubtless thought that she was serving many interests by expurgating all the "sensitive" material these letters contained. After all, Cosima

Liszt-Wagner was still alive and would have been sure to protest at this treatment of herself and her father. Marie von Sayn-Wittgenstein, the daughter of the princess, could also have construed these uncensored letters to be a slur on her mother's memory. Then there was Liszt himself, who had asked Agnès to destroy all his letters (he had consigned hers to the flames) and who would have been deeply perturbed to think that his request had been ignored. By publishing a mutilated version of the letters, however, La Mara cast a shadow over her editorial work in general and created a climate of unease among modern Liszt scholars. Nothing short of a revised edition of her eleven volumes will satisfy the requirements of modern scholarship, a daunting enterprise which has not yet even begun and which is unlikely to be carried out in this century. Until then, the luckless Liszt biographer is well advised to consult the holographs or the *Abschriften,* which are held in Weimar, and to compare them carefully with La Mara's published texts.

The reverential attitude which La Mara adopted towards her work is symbolized by her prefaces to these volumes, most of which are signed "La Mara, October 22," irrespective of the actual year in which they were published. This particular day, of course, was Liszt's birthday, and La Mara's editorial work does indeed form a remarkable gift to his memory. La Mara had known Liszt personally. She had met him for the first time in Weimar, in 1856, as an impressionable girl of nineteen, and had been at once ensnared by his powerful personality. In her autobiography,[15] written some sixty years later, she still held Liszt in awe, and found a perfect title for her chapter on him, which even her severest critics could not improve upon: "Liszt, My Destiny." There was, in fact, a touch of absurdity about her particular brand of hero worship, which reached its peak in her volume *Liszt und die Frauen* (1911). This book contains twenty-six biographies of women whom Liszt is supposed to have esteemed. It bears the dedication "zum 100. Geburtstag Liszts," surrounded by a decorative border of hearts. Those women who tainted Liszt's life with scandal (Lola Montez and Olga Janina, for example) have been excluded.

La Mara's editions of Liszt's correspondence are misleading in one other respect, albeit a minor one. While the titles are in German, the contents are mainly in French, the language in which Liszt always preferred to communicate. Liszt, in fact, was never at home in the German language. It is true that he was brought up in a German-speaking part of western Hungary, by German-speaking parents, and that German was therefore his mother tongue. But from the age of eleven, after he had moved to Paris, he was educated in French. (The ease with which the young boy made the linguistic transition is borne out by a juvenile letter to Sébastien Erard, which he wrote while on a visit to London when he was twelve years old, and which already shows an idiomatic grasp of

---

15. LDML.

the language.[16]) Thereafter he lost his German; it was only in later life and with difficulty that he recovered its partial use. This is rather surprising when we recall that the mature Liszt spent thirteen years (1848–61) in Weimar. But the facts speak for themselves. Here are a few passages culled from his correspondence covering a period of twenty-two years or more. The italics are Liszt's.

> Excuse the *spelling* and *writing* of these lines! You know that I never write *German.* [17]

> Allow me . . . to thank you . . . in *French,* as this language becomes more and more familiar and easy to me, whereas I am obliged to make an effort to patch up more or less unskillfully my very halting German syntax.[18]

> What do you say to my German scribbling? I would give a lot if I could get it to the point where, little by little, I could prepare my essays for the press in German. It feels to me all the time, however, like finger exercises in syntax.[19]

> Forgive me, that I write to you today in German.[20]

Examples of his "very halting German syntax" abound. As early as 1833 Liszt had sometimes written letters to Marie d'Agoult in which he temporarily lapsed into faulty German. But it is his letters to his Austrian-born mother that provide the most telling evidence. Here, if anywhere, we would expect Liszt to revert to his mother tongue. Mostly, however, he writes to her in French. These letters to Anna Liszt have never been published in their original language. When La Mara eventually brought out her selection, in 1918, it was in her own German translation, under the aforementioned title *Franz Liszts Briefe an seine Mutter.*

Liszt's letters continue to be published in modern times. Two substantial volumes can be mentioned here: *Franz Liszt : Briefe aus ungarischen Sammlungen, 1835–86* [21] (1966) and *The Letters of Franz Liszt to Olga von Meyendorff, 1871–86* [22] (1979). At the time of writing there are six thousand published letters between Liszt and eight hundred correspondents across the world. These are the staggering figures given in Charles Suttoni's authoritative bibliography[23] (1979) of Liszt's published correspondence. Since many unpublished holographs

---

16. The holograph, dated June 1824, is now in the British Library, M.S. Add. 33965.
17. Letter to Franz von Schober, December 5, 1840, LLB, vol. 1, p. 41.
18. Letter to Theodor Uhlig, June 25, 1851, LLB, vol. 1, p. 99.
19. Letter to Joachim, March 28, 1854, MBJ, vol. 1, p. 179.
20. Letter to Hans von Bülow, March 27, 1855, LBLB, p. 128.
21. PBUS.
22. WLLM.
23. SLAB.

still lurk in the archives of Paris, Bayreuth, and Weimar, these numbers are bound to be revised upwards with the passing years.[24]

Another basic source for the modern biographer is Liszt's *Gesammelte Schriften.* These six volumes of "collected writings"—books, essays, pamphlets—were gathered together and published during the period 1880–83, that is, within Liszt's lifetime at the instigation of Princess Carolyne. The earliest essay to appear over Liszt's signature, "On Future Church Music," dated from 1834; the latest, "John Field and His Nocturnes," from 1859. Since these writings were scattered, and since most of them were originally written in French, the task of assembling them and translating them into German was given to Lina Ramann. She failed to find them all, and the *Gesammelte Schriften* is therefore incomplete.

vol. 1: *F. Chopin* (1852)

vol. 2 (i): *Essays from the "Revue et Gazette Musicale"*
On Future Church Music (1834–35)
On the Position of Artists and Their Place in Society (1835)
On Popular Editions of Important Works (1836)
On Meyerbeer's *Les Huguenots* (1837)
Thalberg's *Grande Fantaisie,* op. 22, and *Caprices,* opp. 15
and 19 (1837)
To M. Fétis (1837)
R. Schumann's Piano Compositions, opp. 5, 11, and 14 (1837)
Paganini: A Necrology (1840)

vol. 2 (ii): *Letters of a Bachelor of Music* (1835–40)
1–3. To George Sand
4. To Adolphe Pictet
5. To Louis de Ronchaud
6. By Lake Como (to Louis de Ronchaud)
7. La Scala (to M. Schlesinger)
8. To Heinrich Heine
9. To Lambert Massart
10. On the Position of Music in Italy (to M. Schlesinger)
11. St. Cecilia (to M. d'Ortigue)
12. To Hector Berlioz

---

24. For example, there are several hundred unpublished letters between Liszt and his three children and Liszt and his mother in the Nationalarchiv der Richard-Wagner-Stiftung in Bayreuth, while the Goethe- und Schiller-Archiv in Weimar holds thousands of unpublished letters to or from Liszt, or letters written by third parties about him. One need only mention the nearly two thousand unpublished letters to Liszt from Princess Carolyne von Sayn-Wittgenstein (to which vols. 4–7 of *Liszts Briefe* form the published counterpart) to appreciate the size of the legacy.

The essays which constitute both parts of volume 2 were later republished in their original French versions by Jean Chantavoine in his important book *Pages romantiques* (1912). This source is preferable to the *Gesammelte Schriften,* since Chantavoine went directly to the issues of the *Gazette Musicale* in which these texts were originally published, and he did not subject them to the editorial changes that mar the German translation. For the most part, the *Bachelor of Music* letters take the form of a travelogue in which Liszt (and Marie d'Agoult) recorded their impressions of music and musical life in Italy during their "honeymoon" years. Modelled on George Sand's *Lettres d'un voyageur,* their primary purpose was to inform Liszt's friends in France of his activities abroad. Writing in the 1860s, Sainte-Beuve found it incredible that thirty years earlier one carried on one's life through the columns of a newspaper. "A sheet with five thousand subscribers," he remarked, "was practically a family of intimates."

vol. 3 (i): *Pages about Dramatic and Stage Works*
    Gluck's *Orpheus* (1854)
    Beethoven's *Fidelio* (1854)
    Weber's *Euryanthe* (1854)
    On Beethoven's Music to *Egmont* (1854)
    On Mendelssohn's Music to *A Midsummer Night's Dream* (1854)
    Scribe and Meyerbeer's *Robert le diable* (1854)
    Schubert's *Alfonso und Estrella* (1854)
    Auber's *La Muette de Portici* (1854)
    Bellini's *Montecchi e Capuletti* (1854)
    Boieldieu's *La Dame blanche* (1854)
    Donizetti's *La favorita* (1854)
    Pauline Viardot-Garcia (1859)
    No Entr'acte Music! (1855)
    Mozart: On the Occasion of his Centenary Festival in Vienna
      (1856)

vol. 3 (ii): *Richard Wagner*
    Tannhäuser and the Song Contest on the Wartburg (1849)
    Lohengrin and Its First Performance at Weimar (1850)
    Der fliegende Holländer (1854)
    Das Rheingold (1855)

vol. 4: *From the Annals of Progress*
    Berlioz and his *Harold* Symphony (1855)
    Robert Schumann (1855)
    Clara Schumann (1855)
    Robert Franz (1855)

Sobolewski's *Vinvela* (1855)
John Field and His Nocturnes (1859)

vol. 5: *Incursions: Critical, Polemical, and Topical Essays*
On the Goethe Foundation at Weimar (1850)
Weimar's September Festival in Honour of the Centenary of
    Carl August's Birth (1857)
Dornröschen: Genast's Poem and Raff's Music (1855)
Marx and His Book *The Music of the Nineteenth Century* (1855)
Criticism of Criticism: Ulibishev and Serov (1858)
A Letter on Conducting: A Defence (1853)

vol. 6: *On the Gypsies and Their Music in Hungary* (1859)

Doubt has been cast on the true authorship of these writings.[25] Liszt relied on a number of people to get his ideas down on paper, but the ideas are still his. In the 1850s, especially, he had secretaries, transcribers, translators, and researchers virtually at his beck and call. Even if it could be proved that much of his work was "ghosted" (and it cannot), Liszt quite clearly held himself responsible for the results, and the conscientious biographer must become acquainted with their contents. Liszt's credentials as an author are explained in detail elsewhere in this book.[26] The main figure behind the controversy will emerge as this survey unfolds.

v

Clearly, less than half a century after Liszt's death his biographers had a formidable task on their hands. Simply to master and evaluate the available material was a daunting enterprise. Add to this the interminable flow of "recollections," "memories," and "diaries" of his pupils and disciples that came off the printing presses in a flood after 1900 and you have a tangled mass of contradictions through which the modern Liszt scholar picks his way with trepidation. Liszt's Weimar masterclasses attracted some of the most brilliant young pianists of the day. Rosenthal, Tausig, Bülow, Siloti, Friedheim—the illustrious roll-call reads like a Burke's Peerage of the realm of pianists—were all pupils of Liszt. There were also many worthless hangers-on, whom Liszt was too soft-hearted to turn away. (Liszt never charged a penny for these classes.) But whoever they were, the quick or the dead, it seemed as if personal contact

25. HFLA and HPL, p. 130.
26. See pp. 20–23.

with Liszt, however slight, was sufficient to stimulate the most recalcitrant pen
into activity. Thus, one of the earliest "memoirs" to appear was Anton Strelezki's*** *Personal Recollections of Chats with Liszt* (1893), and one of the latest
was Arthur Friedheim's *Life and Liszt* (1961). In between, there were dozens
of other "reminiscences" by Liszt's pupils, including Siloti's *My Memories of
Liszt* (1913) and Lamond's *Memoirs* (1949), which earnestly disclose such matters as the warmth of Liszt's handshake or the penetration of his gaze. To be
sure, Liszt's handshake may have been the most memorable event in their lives.
That is sufficient commentary on their work. Liszt, we know, was deeply
perturbed by the biographical activities of his "disciples" and camp followers.
He went through Janka Wohl's copy of Trifonoff's "François Liszt"[28] (1884)
with great care and made scrupulous marginal corrections, puncturing some of
Trifonoff's puffed-up prose with his sharp pen, demolishing one legend after
another. Trifonoff at one point has Liszt (by then an abbé in the Roman
Catholic Church) suggesting to Marie d'Agoult that they turn Protestant in
order to simplify their marriage prospects. Liszt takes up his pen and writes,
"No! That is not true."[29] It is easy to understand why Liszt, wearied beyond
measure by such falsehoods, was often asked why he never wrote his autobiography. His ironic comment cannot be bettered: "It is enough to have lived such
a life as mine."[30]

In 1931 Peter Raabe (1872–1945) made the first scholarly attempt to produce
order out of chaos and published his two-volume work *Franz Liszt: Leben und
Schaffen.* Many Liszt scholars regard this book as definitive. They admire its
calm detachment; Liszt's biography had never before been unfolded so objectively. Its manner was impeccable; but what of its matter? In fact, it contained
a number of flaws, the full extent of which can best be gauged by looking at
the fifteen pages of corrigenda prepared by the author's son, Felix Raabe, who
brought out a second edition in 1968. Without in any way wishing to denigrate
Peter Raabe's work, one must say that his biography gave very little evidence
that for thirty-four years (1910–44) he was the director of the Liszt Museum
in Weimar, and had unrestricted access to its treasures; its thousands of original

---

27. "Strelezki" was an Englishman. His real name was Burnand (1859–1907), and he was born in
Croydon.
28. TL.
29. WFLR, p. 61. See also LLB, vol. 8, p. 377.
30. WFLR, p. 88. Another publication can be mentioned here. In 1853, Liszt had been sent a copy
of the biographical article about him that had appeared in the *Konversations-Lexikon,* published by
Brockhaus. Again the errors were stupid, but Liszt handled them with exemplary detachment. He
pointed out that he had never worn the *bleu-barbot* coat of the St. Simonists, that he had never been
to America, and that while he did not object to being called the "Paganini of the piano," it would
be nice to think that his more recent work might make its way because of his *own* name and gain
for him a worthier mention in any future edition of the *Lexikon.* This reply was extremely dignified,
if one bears in mind that the article had referred to the "poverty of invention" of his music. (LLB,
vol. 1, pp. 162–64.)

documents were his to do with as he willed. Yet he used them only in a passive way, to correct the errors of others. The definitive work the world had a right to expect of him, considering his key position, was not forthcoming. Unfortunately, the sources relating to Liszt's childhood in Hungary and his youth in Paris were unknown to Raabe, and these early periods constitute the weakest sections of his book. Its most valuable feature is the great Catalogue of Works which takes up most of volume 2, and which is still a reliable guide to Liszt's compositions.[31]

VI

The year 1936 was a double anniversary: it was both the fiftieth year of Liszt's death and the one-hundred-and-twenty-fifth year of his birth. A flurry of interest marked the event. Celebrations were mounted across the world, including in Budapest, London, and New York. Papers were read, tributes were made, music was played, lip-service was paid. A remarkable piece of information was disclosed: the complete Liszt bibliography now stood at five thousand titles.[32] And yet, as the Hungarian scholar István Csekey wryly observed, despite all the activity nothing happened. All that the scholars really did during that memorial year, with one notable exception, was to rake over the old, by now familiar information in a desperate attempt to find something new to say.[33] Csekey himself delivered his pioneering study *The Descent and National Identity of Franz Liszt* before the Hungarian Academy of Sciences in 1937, and it was published by them that same year. His valuable updated genealogical tables, an indispensable guide, threw new light on Liszt's family origins.

I mentioned an exception. In the spring and summer of 1936, Emile Haraszti (1885–1958) published his two-part essay "Liszt à Paris" in *La Revue Musicale*. He followed this up with his "Deux Franciscains: Adam et Franz Liszt" in 1937. A few months later came his "Le Problème Liszt" (*Acta Musicologica,* December

---

31. Liszt composed more than thirteen hundred individual pieces of music. They were gathered up by Raabe under 674 catalogue entries. His catalogue formed the basis of the one prepared by Humphrey Searle for *Grove V* (1954), revised and updated by him for *The New Grove* (1980). The original sources for Raabe's catalogue are: (1) two thematic catalogues prepared and published by Liszt himself in 1855 and 1877, respectively; (2) a manuscript catalogue prepared by Princess von Sayn-Wittgenstein; (3) a manuscript list of the repertory played by Liszt on his concert tours, 1838–48. Neither Raabe nor Searle is free from error, and when they refer to the locations of manuscripts (and particularly to the ones in private hands, many of which have long since found their way into other collections) we do well to proceed with caution.

32. KLV.

33. One achievement rightly belongs to 1936, although it passed almost unnoticed. More by accident than by design, the vast thirty-four-volume *Collected Edition* of Liszt's music, begun in 1901, was finally brought to completion. This great enterprise, thirty-five years in the making, was handled by Breitkopf and Härtel under the distinguished editorship of Busoni, Bartók, Vianna da Motta, Raabe, and others.

1937). Within two years, Haraszti had established himself as one of the foremost Liszt scholars of his generation. "Le Problème Liszt" is an important essay, even today. This penetrating study took a hard, critical look at the musicological mess called "Liszt scholarship," and set about the herculean task of putting the field in order. The cunning mendacity of Ramann is censured, the simple carelessness of Raabe is exposed, and the newspapers and magazines of the day are culled for every scrap of information. Haraszti is quite splendid on matters chronological. Dates, names, and places all come up for review and correction. Hungarian by birth, Haraszti lived much of his life in France. He was by nature a "field worker" and spent his life toiling in the archives of Europe, sparing no effort to search out whatever original documentation on Liszt, however esoteric, he could find. His one-man crusade has put everyone else in his debt. He was lucky; he found cache after cache of documents, some of them (Adam Liszt's letters to the administrators of the Paris Opéra, for example, located in that building's archives) of importance to our understanding of Liszt's early years. One has to deserve one's luck, and Haraszti deserved his. And yet he has the vice of his virtues. He was rightly proud of his "sceptical" approach to Liszt. Having so drastically modified the received picture of the composer, Haraszti was occasionally carried away by his success, attempting to rob Liszt of creative achievements which were rightfully his. A good example was Liszt's youthful opera *Don Sanche,* which Haraszti flatly declared to be by Liszt's teacher Paer. The evidence is far from conclusive. A more famous example was the doubt Haraszti cast on the authenticity of Liszt's literary output. "Liszt never wrote anything but his private letters," Haraszti declared.[34] He was convinced that all Liszt's books and articles (contained in the *Gesammelte Schriften*) were a fraud. The works of the 1830s, he said, particularly the *Lettres d'un bachelier-ès-musique,* came from the pen of Marie d'Agoult, while those of the 1850s, including *Chopin* and *Des Bohémiens et leur musique en Hongrie,* were written by Princess von Sayn-Wittgenstein. Liszt, in short, merely allowed these ladies to use his name. A careful reading of Haraszti compels us to say that he was forced to extend the evidence in order to reach so extreme a conclusion. It had been known, almost from the beginning, that Liszt sought literary *collaboration* from his two mistresses. Liszt himself furnished us with circumstantial evidence of that fact. (Incidentally, none of the holographs for the *Lettres* can be found.) Thus, after the initial success of the first group of *Bachelor of Music* essays, we find him writing to Marie d'Agoult in Nohant: "When I arrive at Nohant I shall ask you for one or two articles."[35] The essay to George Sand ("Lettre à un poète voyageur") he even referred to as "ours." Shortly afterwards

---

34. HPL, p. 130. Haraszti's views were summed up in his article "Franz Liszt: Author Despite Himself." (HFLA.)
35. ACLA, vol. 1, p. 189.

he sent Marie the outline of an article about some chamber-music recitals he had recently given with Batta and Urhan. "Here is an outline of the article, which does not have to be too long. . . . The article ought to be written in my personal name. This is an important matter for me. I am asking you for a real service. Try to let me have it within five or six days so that I can have it printed in the *Gazette* on Sunday, February 26, and also in *Le Monde.*"[36] By 1839 Liszt was having second thoughts about the wisdom of leaving so much literary responsibility to others. He wrote to Marie from Vienna: "Do not publish anything in the future on my behalf, either in the *Gazette* or elsewhere."[37] Nonetheless, in 1847 we find Liszt asking Marie to provide a preface for his forthcoming volume of Hungarian Rhapsodies.[38] The idea came to nothing for the simple reason that their relationship was now almost ended. In 1848 Liszt moved to Weimar and installed himself in the Altenburg with his second mistress, Princess von Sayn-Wittgenstein. Peter Cornelius, his secretary and translator during the early 1850s, has left us a harrowing picture in his diary of the way in which the princess meddled in Liszt's literary activities. One famous example was the essay on Wagner's *Das Rheingold.* Cornelius had translated the princess's French manuscript into German. Liszt then revised the text. "Then everything was turned upside down, which pained me no end." After this procedure had been repeated no fewer than four times, poor Cornelius was almost beside himself. "I thought this thing would drive me crazy," he wrote.[39]

All this is compelling testimony in favour of those who would have us believe that Liszt's literary output is a gigantic deception. Yet there is another side to this complex story. In the British Library there exists a detailed twelve-page holograph, a draft of one part of Liszt's early article "On the Position of Artists" (1835) signed by Liszt.[40] Preserved at Weimar is the holograph of Liszt's closely argued preface to his Symphonic Poems;[41] and in the same archive we also find a holograph sketch of his essay "De la fondation Goethe à Weimar" (1850). The existence of these important documents goes some way towards restoring Liszt's credentials as an author. Certainly it demolishes Haraszti's statement that "Liszt never wrote anything." An important question is now raised. Is there any evidence that Liszt's other published articles were originally printed from holographs? The *Pariser Zeitung* of October 2, 1838, observing the emergence of Liszt as a writer in the columns of Schlesinger's *Revue et Gazette Musicale,* voiced the suspicion that Madame d'Agoult was the true

---

36. ACLA, vol. 1, p. 195.
37. ACLA, vol. 1, p. 329.
38. ACLA, vol. 2, p. 389.
39. CAB, vol. 1, pp. 187–88.
40. M.S. Add. 33965, fol. 237–42.
41. WA, Kasten 5, no. 1.

author—whereupon Schlesinger at once published an invitation to anyone who cared to do so to call at the offices of the *Gazette* and scrutinize the originals for himself. Schlesinger would hardly have done this unless he had something to show to his callers.[42] Sometime after 1838 these manuscripts vanished. Liszt himself was puzzled by their disappearance. Years afterwards, when the question of producing a collected edition of his writings arose, their whereabouts became a topical issue.

> What has become of the original French manuscripts of my complete articles I don't in the least know. . . . The only person who could give some particulars would be Mlle L. Ramann, my biographer, who has been for many years past on the lookout for everything related to my prose and music.[43]

Liszt does not say here that the manuscripts were in his handwriting, but he does refer explicitly to "my articles." Elsewhere he directly claims authorship for certain essays: the first four pieces he undertook for the *Gazette* he described unequivocally as "by me."[44] Even if the original manuscripts were one day to come to light, however, and some of them bore the telltale calligraphy of Marie d'Agoult or Carolyne von Sayn-Wittgenstein, what would that prove? In this day and age, when great men "write" their memoirs by the simple expedient of dictating their thoughts into a microphone, the recording later to be transcribed and edited by other hands, we have a far broader conception of "authorship" than the one which would confine it to the mere act of pushing a pen across a sheet of paper. What seems to have happened in Liszt's case is that he provided all the ideas, especially the musical ones (neither Marie nor Carolyne was professionally competent to talk about music[45]), and then his thoughts were put into a polished literary form. Not the least remarkable aspect of the situation is that both of Liszt's mistress-writers seemed content to work in obscurity. Indeed, when asked about the authorship of the Chopin book,

---

42. Liszt's unpublished letters to Maurice Schlesinger refer to the *Bachelor* essays and imply that they are his own. In a letter dated "Frankfurt, September 8, 1841," Liszt writes: "Have the *Bachelier* carefully corrected by Mormais and let the varied fragments from Hamburg, Copenhagen, Luxhaven, and Nonnenwerth be separated by dotted lines, or any type of line of separation as I've indicated." (WA, Kasten 73, no. 6.) Although the particular *Bachelor* essay to which Liszt here refers was never published (what became of it?), he clearly took a close interest in the layout of the printed page—an indication of his personal involvement in these travelogues.

43. LLB, vol. 2, p. 330.

44. LLBM, p. 24.

45. To this statement, however, should be added the little-known fact that Marie d'Agoult was a fairly accomplished amateur pianist, and Liszt praised her playing in the early days of their liaison. In 1833, for example, we find him telling Henri Herz that Marie had "taken up the piano again," that she was working on his (Herz's) Variations on *Euryanthe,* and that she had made "immense

Carolyne replied unhelpfully: "When two beings become completely merged, can it ever be said where the work of one begins or of the other ends?"[46]

Where does this leave the problem? Today, as Serge Gut has pointed out, there are four positions that can logically be taken with regards to Liszt's literary output: (a) *none* of it is by him; (b) *some* of it is by him; (c) *most* of it is by him; (d) *all* of it is by him.[47] No Liszt scholar would now accept the two extremes of either (a) or (d). The evidence obliges him to occupy the middle ground; but just which part of that middle ground he chooses to take, (b) or (c), will depend largely on how he interprets the facts. From this vexed topic only one conclusion can safely be drawn: each article poses a separate problem and demands a separate conclusion. For the rest, whenever the hand of Marie d'Agoult or Carolyne von Sayn-Wittgenstein reveals itself (as, for example, in the notorious *Bachelor* essay on La Scala, which caused Liszt embarrassment and is beyond question the work of d'Agoult; see p. 264) we shall draw attention to it. Adolphe Boschot was witty but not entirely wise when he remarked, "Le style, c'est la femme!"[48]

V I I

No survey of the Liszt literature would be entirely complete without passing reference to the scandal-mongers and myth-makers. Liszt's charisma is such that he has attracted more speculation over his amours, both real and imagined, than any other composer in history. A whole mythology has sprung up concerning the illegitimate progeny he is supposed to have scattered across Europe. The desire to saddle great men with illicit offspring is not new. What is new is the persistence with which such efforts have been directed towards Liszt for the past one hundred years. If only half these tales were true, Liszt would have had no time for composition, no time for piano playing, no time for anything other than the fulfillment of this mundane destiny the myth-makers have carved out for him, and there would consequently be no reason to write a biography of him at all. It is necessary to review this literature not because it is important or true, for it is neither, but because it represents a psychological phenomenon without parallel in the annals of musical biography.

Typical of the field is the case of Ilona Höhnel, who lived in Weimar until 1963 and was known locally as "the last daughter of Liszt." Her mother was

---

progress." (ACLA, vol. 1, p. 35.) But this would hardly qualify Marie to have written the *Bachelor* essays unaided.
46. MAL, p. 168.
47. GLEL, p. 38.
48. BMP, p. 152.

the beautiful Ilona von Kovacsics, the daughter of a Hungarian couple whom Liszt knew well and often visited in their home in Weimar during the 1880s. This young girl, so the story goes, fell deeply in love with the great pianist, who was by then an abbé. Since the relationship soon produced a consequence, the influential parents arranged a marriage for their daughter with a certain Herr Falz. After the birth of the child on August 6, 1882, in Bad Reichenhall, the marriage was dissolved. This child, a daughter, was christened Ilona after her mother. Ilona Falz was highly musical and became a respected piano teacher in Weimar. In 1907 she married a Weimar hairdresser called Höhnel. Her last years were clouded by misfortune. During the closing days of the Second World War, in the spring of 1945, she was run over in a Weimar street by a Russian military vehicle and crippled. For the rest of her life she hobbled on crutches, and she became destitute. A report appeared in the *Hamburger Abend-blatt* in January 1961 calling attention to her plight. "Almost helpless, she depends on the support of her neighbours and on her Social Security allowance of 85 Ostmark. But even today, in old age, her resemblance to her father is so great that this alone would be enough proof of her identity." Where is the documentary evidence for such a tale? It does not exist. There is not a shred of proof to demonstrate Liszt's connection with this unfortunate woman. Yet there are still people in Weimar who believe it, as witness the death mask taken by Professor Günther Kraft and introduced by him as "evidence" of Frau Höhnel's lineage when he pursued this thesis in a lecture delivered in Bayreuth in 1964. We would do better to look up the dates. Ilona von Kovacsics gave birth to her daughter in early August 1882; she therefore conceived in November 1881. Liszt at that time was a thousand miles away; from September to December 1881 he lived in the Villa d'Este outside Rome, and although we have a mass of information about the people he met during these four months, the name of Fräulein von Kovacsics is nowhere to be found. So seductive was the pull of the legend, however, that when Ilona Höhnel died in Weimar on January 24, 1963, those responsible for her burial (she had no living relatives) engraved on her tombstone the epigraph: "*Franz Liszts Tochter.*"[49]

Then there is the strange case of Dr. Carlos Davila. He was the founder of the faculty of medicine in Bucharest, became an army doctor, rose to the rank of general, and held several distinguished positions in Rumania. Davila was born sometime during the 1840s. His childhood was cloaked in mystery, and the circumstances surrounding the place and date of his birth remain obscure. It therefore became a matter of urgency for the Rumanians to provide this impressive figure with a suitable pedigree. For no other reasons, apparently,

---

49. The grave lies in the Stadtfriedhof, Weimar. Had Günther Kraft prepared his lecture with greater care, he would have examined the tombstone before making his pronouncements. This would have enabled him to get Frau Höhnel's birthdate right, to say nothing of her mother's maiden name. She is buried with her grandmother Marie Kovacsics (1837–1919).

than his strong facial resemblance to Liszt and the keen interest shown in Dr. Davila's career by a number of people in Liszt's circle, together with a rough proximity of dates (Liszt passed through Bucharest in 1846 and 1847), the rumour began to circulate in Rumania that Davila was the natural son of Liszt. It soon reached the capitals of Vienna and Paris via the diplomatic network (Davila maintained contacts with aristocrats and politicians in France and the Austro-Hungarian empire) and became established as fact. No authentic documents were ever produced to substantiate this absurd assertion, but it has haunted the Liszt literature until modern times. In 1956 there appeared a book, *Davila: Fils de Liszt?* by Doretta Berthoud, which devoted nearly three hundred pages to the pursuit of the barren hypothesis that Davila was a hitherto unrecognized offspring of Marie d'Agoult and Liszt. This story was "substantiated" by such witnesses as Madame Claire de Charnacée (Marie's legitimate daughter by Charles d'Agoult) and King Carol I of Rumania. When the inquiring reader turns the page he discovers that these "witnesses" are merely cited by other people twice and thrice removed, rendering it impossible to nail down a single verifiable fact. The day after Davila died in 1884, *L'Indépendance roumaine* published an obituary notice which archly referred to him as the offspring of two superior creatures "whose names we all know." That is considerably more than the rest of the world has ever been able to discover, and although a century has meanwhile passed, we are no nearer to establishing Davila's true identity than we ever were.

Equally bogus was the assertion that the pianist and composer Franz Servais had a claim on Liszt's paternity. This case was sensationalized by Ernest Newman in his foolish character assassination of Liszt.[50] Newman set out to show that Servais was the natural son of Liszt and Princess Carolyne von Sayn-Wittgenstein, and he gleefully reminded his readers that it was "common talk" in Weimar that Servais was one of Liszt's sons; that this young man bore a close resemblance both to Liszt and to his deceased son, Daniel; that he possessed an outstanding musical talent; that he was christened Franz; that after the death of his adoptive father, Adrien Servais, he was taken under Liszt's wing (at the request of Madame Servais), who promoted his career; and, finally, that he was born in St. Petersburg in 1847, the very year that Liszt got to know Carolyne. Newman's case collapses the moment we examine the dates. Liszt first met Carolyne in Kiev in February 1847; she did indeed journey to St. Petersburg in 1847—for two months during March and April. Whatever the reason for her trip, then, it was clearly not to produce Liszt's child. This did not stop *Grove V*[51] from referring to the rumour, and it was actually reported as bald fact in *Baker V* ("He was an illegitimate son of Liszt and Princess Carolyne

---

50. NML, p. 182ff.
51. Vol. 7, p. 719.

Sayn-Wittgenstein"), a neat example of biographical work run wild.[52] Liszt, of course, heard the wagging tongues in Weimar during the 'sixties and 'seventies. According to Richard Burmeister, Liszt was once asked during a game of whist if he was indeed the father of Servais. His amusing reply cannot be bettered: "Ich kenne seine Mutter nur durch Correspondenz, und so was kann nicht durch Correspondenz abmachen" ("I know his mother only through correspondence, and one can't arrange that sort of thing by correspondence"). The truly fascinating thing about all these cases—Davila, Ilona Höhnel, and Franz Servais—is that their claims were invariably made for them, never by them. The whole topic is pathological: the creators of such tales have themselves become an object worthy of study.

Even Liszt's most respected colleagues were not above spreading gossip about his personal affairs in general, and about the consequences of his union with Princess Carolyne von Sayn-Wittgenstein in particular. For twelve years (1848–60) Liszt and Carolyne lived under the same roof in Weimar. Their liaison caused much controversy in the small town. Since they produced no children, it became necessary for the upright citizens of Weimar to invent them. According to Carl Maria Cornelius, Carolyne bore Liszt three children and removed herself from Weimar on each occasion for the confinement.[53] We are to conclude that Cornelius received this information directly from his father, Peter Cornelius, who lived in Weimar during the 1850s, was Liszt's secretary and trusted colleague, and was in a position to observe events at first hand. The source appears to be unassailable, and the story has gained credence among Liszt scholars. Unfortunately, Carl Maria was only six years old when his father died in 1874. It cannot be stressed sufficiently that he provided no evidence for his assertion. He simply assumed that his readers would believe him by virtue of his father's close professional association with Liszt during the years in question. *Argumentum ad verecundiam.* Moreover, his book was not published until 1925, so Liszt and Carolyne could not deny the statement. One central fact tells against Cornelius: the passionate attachment of Carolyne to Liszt, which would never have allowed her to give up her children by him, let alone hide them away in a foreign city. Likewise, it would be uncharacteristic of Liszt to aid and abet her in such a covert act. He had openly acknowledged paternity of his three children by Countess Marie d'Agoult (Blandine, Cosima, and Daniel, the only children of Liszt we know of), was proud to give them his name, and fought to have them legitimized in 1845 after his rupture with the countess was complete. He would have behaved no less honourably towards any children of

---

52. *The New Grove* (1980) has also fallen victim to this falsehood, thereby perpetuating its life for at least one more generation. (Vol. 17, p. 188.)

53. CPC, vol. 1, p. 158.

his by Carolyne, the more so since it was his declared wish at this time to marry her.[54] Unless more evidence is forthcoming, Carl Maria Cornelius, too, must be consigned to the scrap heap of innuendo and gossip.

VIII

And what of Liszt today? Books and articles about him abound. The latest bibliographic count puts the total number of Liszt titles at over ten thousand. It would be arrogant of anyone to claim familiarity with them all. But the conscientious Liszt biographer surely has a duty to try. The task confronting him is formidable. For not only must he come to terms with the literature itself; he must understand its history, understand why some of it came to be written at all. He must also familiarize himself with the large quantities of unpublished material still awaiting scrutiny in the archives of Europe and North America. The main centres of original Liszt research today are Weimar, Budapest, and Washington, D.C., with important archives in Rome and Paris. Still other archives will doubtless one day come to light in Russia, a country which Liszt visited three times and with which he maintained lifelong links. One of the more important original sources, practically unknown to Liszt scholars, is the great Esterházy Archive in Budapest. The incalculable treasures in this massive collection have not even been properly catalogued. Hundreds of documents pertaining to Liszt's family were transferred to the National Széchényi Library after World War II, as part of the series now known as Acta Musicalia. These documents were examined afresh by the Hungarian scholar Arisztid Valkó, whose studies have altered our conception of Liszt's early childhood and his family background.[55] The archive contains a vast correspondence between Prince Nicholas Esterházy on the one hand and Liszt's grandfather Georg and his father, Adam, on the other. No one who sifts through this material will be in much doubt about the hardship and privation endured by this family, and about the self-sacrifices Adam made in order to smooth the path for his prodigy son. No musical genius could have been born into more difficult circumstances. The archive is embarrassingly rich in the minutiae of the Liszts' daily life, ranging from the revelation that grandfather Liszt got into trouble with Prince Esterházy for his unauthorized use of the manorial horse and cart in order to drive his young wife to the Vienna Prater, to the touching documents which disclose that Liszt made a nostalgic bid to purchase the humble cottage in Raiding where he was born. Of such stuff as this are biographies made. I have

---

54. LLB, vol. 5, p. 53.
55. VLC.

drawn heavily on this material for my discussion of Liszt's family background in the second half of this prologue.

A final, cautionary word. Only those scholars who have attempted to traverse the whole of this enormous field will appreciate the gaps still waiting to be filled. To identify a few at random: The correspondence between Adam and Anna Liszt during their years of separation (1824–27) has still not come to light. Presumably it perished in flames, along with other valuable family documents belonging to Anna, when the home of Emile Ollivier, her politician grandson-in-law, was burned down during the Paris Commune uprising of 1871. Liszt's second will, made shortly before his death, is still missing. So too is Adam Liszt's diary, which contained much information about Liszt's childhood. And the Vatican Library remains innocent of all knowledge about any documents in its possession which might throw light on the joint machinations of the church and the Wittgenstein family in Russia, an unholy alliance which was powerful enough to stop Liszt's marriage to Princess Carolyne twelve hours before the ceremony was due to take place in Rome, on October 22, 1861. As for all the unpublished peripheral material which has recently become available, but still awaits investigation by the intrepid scholar with limitless time and boundless energy, we may cite in passing the vast Ramann-Wittgenstein correspondence in the Goethe- und Schiller-Archiv, which was placed under a fifty-year embargo after Ramann's death in 1912 because of its "sensitive" material. Into a similar category fall the more than fifteen hundred handwritten missives with which Princess von Sayn-Wittgenstein bombarded the Russian ambassador to Weimar during the 1850s in connection with her divorce case, some of which are two hundred pages long, and which are now held in the Grand Ducal Archives, Weimar. Such material represents but one small corner of the quagmire through which the Liszt biographer wanders at his peril. Just how much information from such sources, once excavated, can usefully be incorporated into a biographical narrative before that narrative sinks beneath the weight of its own learning remains forever a matter of personal judgement. For the biographer has a responsibility towards his reader: namely, to address him. He should heed Voltaire's aphorism: "If you would be dull, tell all."

I X

While my life of Liszt may not "tell all," it has nonetheless been impossible to compress it into fewer than three volumes.

    I *The Virtuoso Years, 1811–1847*
    II *The Weimar Years, 1848–1861*
    III *The Final Years: "Une Vie Trifurquée," 1861–1886*

It arose from a conviction, based on many years of study of the man and his music, together with a close investigation of the literature, that Liszt was the central figure in the Romantic century (Berlioz and Wagner notwithstanding) and that a book was needed to proclaim that fact. The present state of Liszt biography, particularly in the English-speaking world, reflects a sort of Gresham's Law whereby the constant recapitulation of the same events leads only to the most sensational details being recalled. It was high time to redress the balance. Every biographer of Liszt so far has attempted the impossible: he has tried to understand the man without knowing anything about the child. This is an elementary blunder, quite impossible to justify. A man's life does not begin when he is twenty; there is a deep and profound sense in which that life is by then already ended. Volume I, therefore, covers Liszt's family background, his early childhood, and his adolescence in Paris in much greater detail than hitherto. It was a peculiarly difficult book to handle because the sources are so widely scattered, and it took a decade to write. Although the process is long and laborious, the wisdom of taking nothing on trust as far as Liszt is concerned, of consulting original documents whenever possible, particularly when they have a direct bearing on his life, is vindicated in a hundred different ways. The last thing that Liszt needs at this stage of his posthumous career is yet another biography which merely consists of two or three old ones joined together. A great deal of fresh information has been incorporated into the present study, and I make no apology for the rather large number of citations, both primary and secondary, which bolsters the narrative along the way. Given the confused history of Liszt biography hitherto, no other aims seemed worthy.

Liszt's Family Background

To become noble is much more
than to be born noble.

FRANZ LISZT[1]

I

One of the oldest stories to attach itself to Liszt concerns his "aristocratic" descent. Since so many of his biographers repeat it, we should recognize from the outset where the myth began, and why.

When Liszt arrived in Hungary in December 1839, after an absence of sixteen years, he was greeted as a national hero. No other living Hungarian was so widely known. He was, as István Csekey puts it, a "shining star" to the entire Hungarian nation.[2] The Magyar leaders of the opposition party to the ruling government, patriots like Counts Leo Festetics and Lajos Batthyány (executed in the Revolution of 1848–49), who were both identified with the national struggle against Austria, petitioned the interior minister, Count Franz Kollowrat,[3] for a patent of nobility for Liszt.[4] This request, full of political overtones, was flatly rejected, one of the grounds being that Liszt had recently played the

1. KLB, p. 92.
2. CLSH, p. 6.
3. Count Franz Anton Kollowrat-Liebsteinsky (1778–1861) was born in Prague. He is chiefly remembered today for founding, in 1818, the Prague National Museum. This astute politician was summoned to Vienna in 1826 to take charge of the internal affairs of the Austro-Hungarian empire. His reactionary views made him unpopular with the Hungarians, and after the 1848 bloodbath he retired from public life. At his death, he left his entire library of forty thousand volumes to the Prague National Museum.
4. The original petition was destroyed by fire during the 1848 Revolution. A copy owned by the historian Sándor Takáts (1860–1932) survives in the Hungarian State Archive (Secret Police Documents, folder no. 59).

Rákóczy March in Pressburg, a melody with which all patriotic Hungarians identified (it was for that reason considered dangerous by the secret police), and that he had thus helped to fan the flames of national unrest. The Hungarian newspapers took up the story, two of them even publishing diplomas as evidence that Liszt was of noble descent anyway, without, however, offering any proof that Liszt was connected with the "Liszthius" family disclosed in these documents.[5] Other petitions were made in his behalf. On January 13, 1840, for example, the Municipality of Pest, at the instigation of his Hungarian friends, approached the imperial office in Vienna for a patent of nobility. They, too, were turned down, the argument this time being that according to Hungarian law and precedent the rank of nobility was bestowed only for distinction on the field of battle or for a life of service to the Hungarian nation, and Liszt did not qualify on either count. Clearly, Liszt was quite unable to sustain his claim, and he and his political friends let the matter drop. So confident was Liszt that his aristocratic descent was about to be established, however, that in December 1839 he wrote to Countess Marie d'Agoult, his mistress, for advice on the design of a coat of arms.[6]

The issue of Liszt's nobility was raised again in 1851 by his distinguished relative Eduard Liszt, Imperial Public Prosecutor in Vienna, who placed an interesting advertisement in the Hungarian newspaper *Magyar Hirlap*.

> Attention! On the occasion of his sojourn in Pest in the year 1839–40 the piano virtuoso Franz Liszt was offered original documents for sale which proved his family's nobility. We appeal to the holder of these, or similar papers, to contact Professor Eduard Liszt, Vienna, Rossau 123, *as soon as possible* in order to sell these papers to *Ferenc Liszt*.[7]

No one came forward, and no such sale took place. This newspaper advertisement does tell us one thing, however: Liszt had had grounds for believing, ever since 1839, that he might be descended from the nobility, irrespective of whether the Hungarians elevated him to the aristocracy. Thereafter, the search was on for *proof* of that fact. It was not forthcoming, but the rumour of Liszt's "titled" background had taken root in the literature and now started to flower. Some of Liszt's nineteenth-century biographers even quoted the historian Sán-

5. *Buda-Pesti Rajzolatok,* December 17, 1839, and *Pesther Tageblatt,* December 21 and 28, 1839. The first newspaper tried to show a connection with the sixteenth-century family of Count Listhi (see pp. 32–33). The second newspaper, however, wanted to promote a link with a certain Wolfgang Liszt (1397–1492), governor of Styria. Csekey was convinced that both newspapers forged these documents (CLSH, pp. 22–23) to support Liszt's case. The originals were never produced.
6. ACLA, vol. 1, p. 331.
7. Issues of December 7 and 27, 1851, and January 7, 1852.

dor Takáts as their authority, although all he did was to mention the Pest newspaper reports of 1839. Takáts may have felt about such matters as did Bismarck, who used to say, "Was in der Zeitung steht, kann auch wahr sein."[8] The final outcome of these dismal proceedings occurred in 1859, when the Emperor Franz Joseph awarded Liszt the Order of the Iron Crown (third class), which made him eligible, upon petitioning for it, to become an Austrian knight. Liszt duly pursued this opening, and the subsequent correspondence between the Austrian Ministry of the Interior and the Hungarian Registry Office proved conclusively that Liszt's claim to a title, whatever other merits it possessed, could not possibly rest upon a hereditary foundation. The correspondence also made it clear that Liszt himself had at last abandoned such a claim, that is, one based on a "blood tie." Liszt was finally given a knighthood, with his own coat of arms, in 1859, thanks largely to the unremitting efforts of Eduard Liszt, on whom most of the administrative burden fell. The important point to observe is that this title, one of the humblest within the gift of the Emperor Franz Joseph, was an Austrian and not a Hungarian one. The official proclamation, which bears the inscription "Franz Ritter von Liszt," is dated October 30, 1859, and is now in the Weimar archives.[9] Since the knighthood was a hereditary one, it would normally have passed to Liszt's son, Daniel. This gifted youth died in tragic circumstances less than two months later, and so Liszt arranged for his cousin Eduard to assume the title, which was duly transferred in March 1867. The title eventually lapsed in 1961 with the death in Vienna at age ninety-four of Eduard's son, Eduard Ritter von Liszt.

Given this background, it was incomprehensible of Lina Ramann, in her "official" biography of Liszt written twenty years after these events, to revive once more the hoary legend of Liszt's noble descent by asserting, "The name and traditions of the Liszt family belong to the Hungarian nobility."[10] Ramann attempted to show that Liszt was descended from Count Johann Listhi, who flourished in the sixteenth century and who rose to be Regal Chancellor and Bishop of Raab. This claim was bogus. Count József Kemény, in his treatise *The Origin, Rise and Fall of the Family Listhi,* showed conclusively that this noble family had become extinct by 1676. Ramann's case rested on a remarkable coincidence. The last surviving member of the Listhi family, Johann IV, seeing that he was about to end his days childless, obtained a royal permission to sell his estates. In 1670 his lands at Kittsee became the property of Prince Paul Esterházy. It was here, in Kittsee, that Liszt's grandfather Georg Adam Liszt was to become the village schoolmaster between 1786 and 1790. The coinci-

---

8. "What one reads in the newspaper can also be true."
9. WA, Überformate no. 82. Reproduced in BVL, p. 161.
10. RLKM, vol. 1, p. 4.

dence that he lived there, and that three of his children were born there,[11] was the only connection between Franz Liszt and Count Johann Listhi.

Liszt, as we know, was far from happy with Ramann's book, which painted him in false colours. In his personal copy of volume I, now in the Weimar archives, on the page dealing with his "noble" ancestry, he underlined the word "bestimmten" in the phrase "Keine *bestimmten* Urkunden" ("no *decisive* documents"), his last comment on the topic. This did not prevent his descendant Eduard Ritter von Liszt, criminal lawyer and professor at the University of Graz, from reopening the issue in relatively modern times. In his book *Franz Liszt: Abstammung, Familie, Begebenheiten* (1937), Eduard insisted on his family's connection with Count Listhi. Even if he could have proved the link, and he could not, Kemény's study had already shown us that the Listhi family were actually of Saxon origin. This connection, therefore, would not have demonstrated Liszt's Hungarian nobility at all.

This, then, is the origin of Liszt's "noble" ancestry. The political events in Hungary in 1839–40 started it all. The Magyars needed a national hero, and they found one in Liszt. Later the myth was canonized, and incorporated into Liszt's biography by Ramann and embroidered by her followers. Liszt's modern biographer, however, really has no excuse for repeating this groundless tale. Yet it continues to appear. The best known and most influential of Liszt's English biographers so far calmly states, "His own family, like all Magyars not of peasant class, was originally of noble origin. . . . There is no reason to doubt its truth."[12]

II

What kind of family, then, did Liszt come from? The earliest known male ancestor of Liszt was his great-grandfather Sebastian List. He died in 1793 at Ragendorf, in Moson County, when he was ninety years old. He is described in the parish register merely as a "cotter," or tenant farmer. Lina Ramann, in her attempts to give Liszt an aristocratic background, elevated Sebastian to the rank of officer in the First Imperial Regiment of Hussars.[13] This would have been impossible, however, since the First Imperial Regiment was not formed until 1756, by which time Sebastian was fifty-three years old.[14] He was, in fact, the poorest type of cotter, and could not at first even afford to rent, let alone

---

11. Including, confusingly, one who was called Franz Liszt, an uncle of the pianist, born in 1788 (see The Liszt Family Tree I).

12. SL (1967), p. 5.

13. RLKM, vol. 1, p. 5.

14. CLSH, p. 11.

own, a house.[15] He was one of those thousands of German-speaking migrant serfs who entered Hungary from Lower Austria during the first half of the eighteenth century in search of work on the land.

Sebastian married twice. His first wife was Anna Roth (1713–86). The last of their three children, Georg Adam, became Liszt's grandfather. In common with several other members of Liszt's family, Sebastian remarried in extreme old age, and took as his second wife a widow of Ragendorf, Christina Sándor, when he was eighty-three years old.

I I I

Liszt's venerable grandfather Georg Adam was born at Ragendorf in 1755. This remarkable man married three times and fathered twenty-five children. He became in turn a schoolteacher, choirmaster, parish notary, and overseer on several Esterházy estates, including Marz and Mattersdorf. Highly musical, he played the piano, violin, and organ; he also had some knowledge of composition. In later life, he even conducted the choir in the Esterházy chapel at Pottendorf. Three of his children inherited his musical talent—Adam, Barbara, and Eduard—which was in turn transmitted to three of his grandsons: Anton Vetzko, Alois Hennig, and Franz Liszt. By a remarkable coincidence all three grandsons also became priests.[16]

Georg was only nineteen when he married Barbara Schlesak (1753–98), who bore him thirteen children. The young couple set up house in Edelsthal, and Georg immediately embarked on a schoolteaching career which lasted for twenty-five years. He was a village schoolmaster in a number of hamlets now in the Austrian Burgenland, including Edelsthal, Kittsee, Pottersdorf, and St. Georgen. Adam, Franz's father, was the second son of this marriage. Six weeks after the death of his first wife, Georg was married again, this time to Barbara Weniger (1778–1806), who produced five further offspring. Barely seven weeks had elapsed after his second wife's death before Georg took a third, Magdalena Richter (1780–1856), twenty-five years his junior, who bore him seven more children. The youngest son of this last marriage, Eduard Liszt (1817–79), rose to become a brilliant criminal lawyer who finally occupied the position of Royal Imperial Public Prosecutor in Vienna. This precocious boy, apart from being intellectually gifted, was also very musical. At the age of ten he was already playing the organ at the Franciscan church in Wiener-Neustadt. He also

---

15. Later on he lived in "house no. 120," Ragendorf, which belonged to a nobleman called Waldberg. This house became the property of the Modrovich family in 1814, when Franciska Waldberg married Georgius Modrovich (the dwelling was included in her dowry). The building was demolished in 1944. (BLSC, pp. 14, 18–19.)

16. See The Liszt Family Tree I. Also CLSH, p. 13ff.

showed talent as a pianist; in his youth, his piano was his most treasured possession. On September 8, 1834, when Eduard was seventeen years old, there was a terrible fire at Wiener-Neustadt, and the building in which he lived was engulfed. Eduard never forgot the sound made by his piano as it fell through the charred floorboards and crashed to the ground below.[17] After the fire Eduard removed to Vienna, where he enrolled as a law student at the university and was called to the bar in November 1842. There now began an outstanding legal career, which carried him to the top of his profession. Eduard and Franz Liszt were on close terms after 1839,[18] and for more than thirty years Eduard handled Liszt's private business affairs. Although Eduard was six years younger than Liszt, he was, of course, Liszt's uncle. In later life, they removed this anomaly by addressing one another as cousins.

The twenty-five children of Georg and his three young wives arrived in monotonous succession, and although some of them died in infancy, Georg was able to do little more for those who survived than feed and clothe them and send them out into the world as soon as possible. The Liszt clan, in fact, quickly dispersed throughout Hungary and Austria and gradually lost touch with one another.[19] Most of them were destined to remain peasants and work the land. Certainly there was no question of a brilliant education for any of them, although it happened that Adam and Eduard, by dint of their own efforts, rose above their poor background and made their mark upon the world.

I V

An important collection of archival documents in the National Széchényi Library, Budapest, throws light on Georg's long and tragic life.[20] In August 1801, after teaching in the village school of St. Georgen for seven years, he was dismissed from his post. Charges were laid against him by the school principal and an inquiry was begun into his character. Georg was, as we shall see, not entirely blameless, but he fought back. He had taught the children of the Esterházy estates for the past twenty-five years, and there had never been any suggestion that he was unfit for his job. Georg petitioned Prince Esterházy and

---

17. LAFB, p. 46.
18. See Ritter von Liszt's pamphlet *Bemerkungen zur Stammtafel der Familie von Liszt* (Vienna, 1940).
19. Liszt himself remembered hardly any of his relatives, and what he thought of them may be gleaned from a letter to his mother, written in 1850 (LLBM, p. 94): "My ringing phrases in favour of my thirty or forty uncles and aunts, nephews and nieces, would soon be changed into ringing money." In a letter to Eduard Liszt (LLB, vol. 1, pp. 95–96) he complains that the family name has been "compromised by the bulk of our relations, who have been wanting either in noble sentiments, or in intelligence and talent." Liszt, normally the most tolerant of men, had no time for indolence, a vice he detected in his relatives, some of whom he dismissed as little better than "spongers."
20. Acta Mus.

enclosed a certificate, signed by a priest and a judge, confirming that he was an upright man.[21] On September 4, 1801, Superintendent Siess came down from Eisenstadt, called a meeting of the villagers of St. Georgen, and attempted to rehabilitate their ex-schoolteacher. The meeting was a stormy one. The superintendent completely failed to reconcile the parties, the villagers claiming that Georg Liszt's "rough conduct," which had caused them concern in the past, was no longer acceptable.[22] Prince Esterházy now stepped in and offered Georg alternative employment. And so, on October 1, 1801, Liszt's grandfather left St. Georgen, with his wife and nine young children, to work in the lumberyards on the Esterházy estates at Marz. He was forty-six years old. He never returned to schoolteaching again.

Life in Marz was difficult. It was completely different from anything Georg was used to. And he had been there only a short time when suspicion fell on him once again. It seems that he was a careless bookkeeper. Certain supplies of lumber could not be accounted for, and Georg Liszt was suspected of selling the wood for private gain. He was finally cleared, but only after the most thorough investigation, which took more than a year to unfold. The experience left him humiliated and embittered.[23] Once again he changed jobs, this time moving to Mattersdorf. In February 1806 the unfortunate man suffered an accident. The horse and cart which he was driving overturned and he suffered serious bruises; the horse was killed. The medical expenses came to twenty forints. Since Georg was working for Prince Esterházy at the time, he asked for, and received, half the medical expenses and a fresh horse.[24]

Georg's tragic existence is brought home to us by a report dated May 9, 1807, which tells us that he married for a third time without informing his superiors. Forced to explain his action, he reported (in a memo dated June 12, 1807) that his second wife had died the previous December. Twelve small children were left behind. They needed a mother more than he needed a wife, he observed. His position was daily becoming more desperate. Returning home after a long day's work, he often found his children running wild and damaging his modest property. Marriage, he concluded, was the only solution. And so, in February 1807, the fifty-two-year-old widower had taken Magdalena Richter, aged twenty-seven, as his wife.[25]

Henceforth, the old man's character became increasingly unpredictable. He diverted himself and his young wife at the Vienna Prater, Austria's great amusement park, disguising these jaunts as "business trips," borrowing the Esterházys' horse and trap to get there. That landed him in trouble. The horse

21. Acta Mus. no. 4170.
22. Acta Mus. no. 4168.
23. Acta Mus. no. 4181.
24. Acta Mus. no. 4183.
25. Acta Mus. no. 4185.

showed symptoms of exhaustion; the return journey, often completed after nightfall, was at least sixty miles. Georg became the object of at least two more investigations, the outcome of which was that he lost his job in 1812, "for breach of loyalty."[26] A steady stream of appeals now rained down on the prince's head. Georg, who had through long practice become an arch-petitioner, explains that he has made many enemies; perhaps it is they who have turned the prince against him. He is ashamed to live like a beggar, and requests a job. He reminds the prince that during the fire at Mattersdorf in 1808 he saved a great deal of personal property of the prince's subjects from destruction. The prince remained immovable. Soon afterwards his council at Eisenstadt informed Georg that "one who caused his own dismissal should not ask the prince for favours." He was "unworthy" to serve the Esterházys.[27] The next few years were lean ones for Georg Liszt and his family. In 1819, for example, we find the sixty-four-year-old itinerant forced to seek work in a clothing factory at Pottendorf. He might have ended his days disastrously, but there was a touching post-script to his story which brightened his final years and restored his self-respect. In 1820 his phenomenal grandson Franz, then a child of nine, created a sensation in Pressburg with his piano playing. Many of Hungary's leading magnates were present. The old man basked in the small boy's glory. The prince, well aware of the family connection, now looked on Georg in a more favourable light. In 1821 Georg, who was then sixty-six years old, was granted an honorary appointment as organist and choirmaster at Pottendorf.[28] That act, which saved the grandfather from certain ruin, was done out of respect for the child, not for the old man. The following year, 1822, Prince Nicholas presented Georg with one of his pianos from the palace at Eisenstadt, so that he could coach the children of Pottendorf for the church choir.[29] Later on, the prince offered Georg free accommodation. One of the very last descriptions of Georg comes from the chief clerk at Pottendorf (January 19, 1838), who depicted him as an aged man of eighty-three years lacking all possessions; he asked the prince to allow Georg to retain his church appointment, for the only alternative would be for him to beg in the streets. Prince Paul Esterházy, to whom the succession had meanwhile passed, responded that Georg's salary and appointment would be guaranteed for life.[30] The reason for all this benevolence is obvious. The grandfather of the most famous living Hungarian, who at the time of this exchange of correspondence was raising large sums of money for the victims of the Danube floods, was not to be allowed to end his days in poverty. Georg died in his eighty-ninth year, on August 8, 1844, in Pottendorf. News of his

---

26. Acta Mus. no. 3044.
27. Acta Mus. no. 3221.
28. Acta Mus. no. 3302.
29. Acta Mus. no. 3221.
30. Acta Mus. no. 3771.

death was brought to Franz Liszt, who was at that moment in the middle of a concert tour of the French provinces, and his childhood memories of his grandfather came flooding back to him. He wrote from Toulouse to his mother in Paris: "My grandfather is dead. Have a mass said for him on the anniversary of my father's death, August 28. . . . The children should attend the service."[31]

The standard accounts of Liszt's life usually claim that it was Georg, the grandfather, who first Magyarized the family name from List to Liszt. List betrayed the family's Germanic origins; it was, and still is, a fairly common German name. Moreover, it is pronounced "Lischt" by the Magyars. By inserting the "z," Georg is usually credited with avoiding the German pronunciation, adopting a rare family name (few other families in Hungary in the eighteenth century were called Liszt), and, at the same time, linking the word to one of the basic nouns in the Magyar tongue: the word "liszt" in Magyar means "flour." There are strong grounds, however, for supposing that it was not Georg at all who first adopted the new orthography, but his educated son, Adam. As late as 1826 Georg was still signing his name as List.[32] Adam, on the other hand, had consistently signed all letters and documents, even at the turn of the century, as Liszt. Even his school reports from the Royal Gymnasium in Pressburg, dating from the 1790s, refer to the eighteen-year-old Adam as Liszt.[33] The grandfather, then, appears to have copied this spelling from the son, not vice versa. Georg was in his eighties before he used it consistently. In the twilight of his life, he enjoyed being grandfather to the great pianist, and when, in 1843, he signed himself Georg Adam Liszt, he was drawing attention to the family connection.

v

Adam Liszt was born on December 16, 1776, in Edelsthal, a small village in the district of Moson, near Pressburg. He was, as we have seen, the second son of Georg Liszt, and his mother was Barbara Schlesak, the first of Georg's three wives.

As a boy, Adam's chief love was music, for which he possessed a genuine talent. From his prodigiously active father he picked up some knowledge of the various instruments, including the piano and the cello, and he dreamed of becoming a virtuoso. We find him in Eisenstadt, sometime before 1790, playing

---

31. LLBM, p. 58. Liszt is referring to his own children, Blandine, Cosima, and the five-year-old Daniel.
32. LAFB, p. 14.
33. CLSH, p. 16.

the cello in the Esterházys' summer orchestra under the direction of Haydn. In later life he was fond of telling how he had regularly played cards with the great composer on these visits to the summer palace.[34] Until he was thirteen Adam went to school in the village of Kittsee, where his father was the schoolmaster. The following year Georg Liszt lost his job, and was forced to move his large brood to Pottendorf. Adam was now fourteen. Innately shrewd and intelligent, he decided to fend for himself. He left home, never to return, in order to study at the Royal Catholic Gymnasium in Pressburg. The record shows that he remained there for five years, graduating in 1795. Throughout this period he also studied music under the theorist Franz Paul Riegler.[35] Adam, then, enjoyed the benefits of a solid education, thanks largely to his diligence and a determination to better himself. Such was the grasp of his general knowledge that after he married he was able to supplement his meagre income by teaching occasional pupils Latin, geography, history, and music.[36]

The next phase of Adam's life was virtually unknown until 1936, when some unusual documents were discovered.[37] They reveal that in September 1795 Adam Liszt, aged eighteen, entered the Franciscan order as a novice in the monastery at Malacka, near Pressburg. The order holds in its archives a register containing the following entry:

> At Malacka (in the year 1795) on the 21st of September, by order of the Most Reverend Father Provincial, the following men were invested with the clerical habit of our holy order:
>
> 1. Josephus Kmentovics
> 2. A local-born youth, Adam Liszt, from the district of Edelsthal, in the area of Mosoniensi; he speaks the German tongue, trained in rhetoric. Liszt was born 1776 [*sic*], December 16, to honest[38] and Catholic parents; his father's name was Adam, his mother's Barbara; he has already been confirmed. He took his religious name from St. Matthew the Apostle.
> 3. Franciscus Spaidl

---

34. OFL, p. 2. Ninety years later, Liszt wrote, "My father often told me of his dealings with Haydn, and the daily card parties he made up with him." (June 5, 1885, LLB, vol. 2, p. 380.)

35. CLSH and HDF. Since the reforms of Joseph II, the *Gymnasium* had introduced the Hungarian language into its curriculum. According to the records, Adam studied Hungarian with beginners (CLSH, p. 15), but he never mastered the language and later on was quite unable to teach it to his son. See n. 17 on p. 57.

36. VFL, p. 111.

37. They were dealt with almost simultaneously by Vševlad Gajdoš (GFLF), István Csekey (CLSH), and Emile Haraszti (HDF).

38. An ecclesiastical code-word for "born in wedlock."

We know of no reason why Adam should have been drawn to the priesthood. But the fact that his famous son should in turn embrace the church, and become a Franciscan like his father, suggests a profound psychological connection between them of which Liszt's biographers are not always aware. It is remarkable that in both music and the church, Franz Liszt should have fulfilled all of Adam's own frustrated ambitions.[39]

The same register for 1794 contains a further disclosure.

> At Malacka, on October 1, 1794:
>
> A native-born youth, Joseph Wagner, from the district of Comaromiensis, German and Hungarian in language, trained in logic. Born of honest and Catholic parents, father Francis Xavier, mother Elizabeth, already confirmed, was received on April 10; he took his religious name from St. John Capestrano.

Adam and Joseph overlapped by a month at Malacka: Adam was just beginning his year as Joseph ended it. They struck up a lifelong friendship which was terminated only by Adam's death thirty-three years later. (It is strange, as Haraszti says,[40] that a "Liszt-Wagner" friendship should already have existed in Liszt's family background half a century before Liszt and Wagner themselves appeared on the scene.) After completing his novitiate at Malacka, Adam was transferred to the monastery at Tyrnavia. Here, less than two years after entering the priesthood, he began to chafe beneath its restrictions. He petitioned repeatedly to be allowed to leave the order. He was, in fact, dismissed, on July 29, 1797, "by reason of his inconstant and changeable nature."[41] He was twenty years old.

Adam never forgot the Franciscans. His lifelong friendship with Father Capistran Wagner preserved a link with the order and with his fellow novitiates. He returned to the monastery a number of times. In later life, after his marriage, he would baptize his prodigy son Franciscus[42] and would often take the small boy to the monastery and show him the spot where his father had spent his formative years. Such visits were to make deep inroads into the mind of the young Liszt. In 1840, in the midst of his triumphal return to Pest, and long after the death of his father, he withdrew from the celebrations and sought

---

39. Thanks to the researches of Father V. J. Gajdoš (GWLF, p. 299), we now know that there was a Franciscan tradition in the Liszt family reaching back to the first half of the eighteenth century. In the year 1739 a certain Ignatius List entered the Franciscan order at Raab and received the name of Father Antonius. He came from Oedenburg, and the parish registers reveal that he was a cousin of grandfather Georg Liszt. Within the Liszt family circle, as Gajdoš points out, Father Antonius would often have been spoken about.
40. HDF, p. 271.
41. CLSH, p. 15.
42. See p. 56.

out Capistran Wagner (who had meanwhile risen to become the Franciscan monastery's father superior) in order to relive his childhood memories.[43] No one who is even slightly acquainted with Liszt's early life can doubt that when Liszt himself took holy orders in 1865, he was fulfilling all the antecedents of his youth.[44]

Dismissed by the Franciscans, despondent and lacking in purpose, and having little money, Adam enrolled as a student at the University of Pressburg. He studied philosophy during the first semester of 1797–98. Since he lacked the funds to pay his fees, he was forced to withdraw before completing the academic year. The twenty-one-year-old Adam was now obliged to take a job, and he became a clerk at Prince Esterházy's estate at Forchtenau, starting work on January 1, 1798.[45] That was a fateful year for him. Within a few weeks his mother, Barbara, was dead. Shortly afterwards, his father entered into bitter litigation with the school authorities at St. Georgen. (This was the period of the older man's disgrace and eventual dismissal from the teaching profession.) Adam could not look on with unconcern. He gave his eleven motherless young brothers and sisters all his filial help and support. With an authority beyond his years, he used his newfound connections at Forchtenau to secure for his father the job at the Esterházy lumberyards at Marz.[46] After two years at Forchtenau, he was transferred to Kapuvár; but barely two months had elapsed before he asked for a different posting, on the grounds that he could speak no Hungarian.[47] Adam longed to be transferred to Eisenstadt, now the main residence of Prince Nicholas, where the Esterházy orchestra was based. In 1801, attempting to draw attention to his plight, Adam offered the Prince a *Te Deum* for chorus and sixteen instruments, and in a letter he pointed out that he had

---

43. *Társalkodó* (Pest), January 1840, p. 22.

44. In 1856, nine years before he received the tonsure in Rome, Liszt was made an honorary member of the Franciscan order at Pressburg. The meaning of this episode is generally missed. We can understand the gesture at once, however, by recalling that the monasteries of Malacka and Tyrnavia, where Adam served his novitiate, fell under the aegis of Pressburg, the provincial capital. Adam's monastic records were kept there; he was an erstwhile "son" of this particular monastery. Likewise, Adam's birthplace, Edelsthal, was less than ten miles from the monastery and lay within its parish. When, more than sixty years after his father had entered the order, Franz Liszt himself was admitted to those same cloisters, albeit in an honorary capacity, it symbolized a family connection kept alive by Liszt through repeated visits and gifts of money to the monastery. The scrolled diploma marking the honour is now in the Weimar archives. It is signed by Father Provincial Eugenius Koppán and is dated June 23, 1857. (WA, Überformate no. 117.) See GWLF.

45. CLSH, p. 15.

46. It was Adam, we should note, who gave his father entrée into the Esterházy bureaucracy, and not vice versa, as many of Liszt's biographers casually claim. The first job Georg applied for, in fact, was Adam's own at Forchtenau in 1801 (Acta Mus. no. 4172). For the rest of his long life Georg was increasingly dependent on Adam, who gave him much material and financial help.

47. "Nachdem ich der ungarischen Sprache unkundig, welche doch zu diesem Amt höchst nötig ist" ("Since I am unacquainted with the Hungarian tongue, which is very necessary for this position"). CLSH, p. 15. Acta Mus. no. 4204.

studied counterpoint both at the Royal Gymnasium and, later, at the University of Pressburg.[48] Adam had to wait for four years before his wish was granted. In 1805 he was at last transferred to Eisenstadt and embarked on one of the happiest periods of his life. For four years all his spare time was devoted to music. He played second cello in the orchestra, made friends with many of the players, and dreamed incessantly of devoting his life to music. He got to know Hummel, Haydn's successor, who was now in charge of music at the Esterházy palaces; he also met Cherubini, who, in 1805–6, was living in nearby Vienna and who visited Eisenstadt. Hearing Hummel play revived Adam's interest in the piano, and he became proficient enough to tackle the Hummel concertos and, later, to teach them to his son. The high point of this period occurred when Beethoven visited Eisenstadt and, on December 13, 1808, conducted the musicians in a performance of his C-major Mass.[49] There were also marvellous summer outings on the Neusiedler See, that impressive inland lake within the Austrian Burgenland. Once, in July 1805, Adam was a member of Prince Nicholas's yachting party. The prince had bought a new vessel, and Adam took part in the sea trials which occurred on the Neusiedler lake. His clothing was soiled, which is why we know about the incident. Adam sent the cleaning bill to the Esterházys, who paid.[50] These were halcyon days for Adam, but they were soon to end. His situation became tragic when, in 1809, he was abruptly appointed intendant of the sheep flocks at Raiding, in the district of Sopron. Starved of culture, cut off from music and the company of sophisticated friends, Adam looked back with nostalgia to his days in Eisenstadt, now gone forever. Raiding broke Adam's heart. He sank into a chronic depression, characterized by a total inability to come to terms with his mediocre existence, a condition from which he was finally rescued when his son's early genius manifested itself and he began to see his own frustrated ambitions realized through the wonderful career of his child.

VI

No account of Adam's early years would be complete without some reference to his long-time employers the Esterházys, one of the most illustrious aristocratic families in Hungary. The Esterházys had been made princes in 1687 by the Habsburgs for helping to deliver Vienna from the Turks, and they had been allotted gigantic estates in western Hungary. The most brilliant member of the dynasty was Prince Nicholas Joseph (1714–90), an outstanding soldier and

---

48. Acta Mus. no. 3367.
49. Acta Mus. nos. 3396 and 2425.
50. Acta Mus. no. 2114.

patron of the arts. Eisenstadt was the first great palace of the Esterházy family. Built in 1673, it stands to this day. After his travels through France and Italy, however, Nicholas returned to Eisenstadt dissatisfied, and resolved to build his second palace, Esterháza, which lies a few miles away, near the southern edge of the Neusiedler See.[51] Here, amidst a glitter and splendour unmatched since the Renaissance, the prince indulged his love of art. Not for nothing was he called Nicholas the Magnificent. He formed a private orchestra and engaged the services of Joseph Haydn, who remained his Kapellmeister for thirty years. Operas, plays, concerts, intellectual discourse, all were part and parcel of everyday life at Esterháza, a cultural paradise which stood in complete isolation on the rim of the great Hungarian plains. After his death in 1790 the title eventually passed to his grandson, Prince Nicholas II (1765–1833).[52]

Prince Nicholas II was not very musical. He closed down the orchestra at Esterháza, dispensed with Haydn's services, and moved his retinue back to Eisenstadt. From Eisenstadt castle Nicholas II indulged his love of collecting. He collected snail shells, medals, and minerals, all of which were put on display. In 1795 he bought Count Neuperg's impressive library, adding it to the Esterházy family library. But his greatest achievement was his magnificent collection of paintings and engravings. When Nicholas moved back to Eisenstadt he found the Esterházy picture gallery neglected, in much the same state as it was when his grandfather had first acquired it. Nicholas scoured the countryside for paintings, bringing in from his outlying châteaux any worthwhile canvas he could lay hands on. This great collection eventually formed the basis of the Museum of Fine Arts in Budapest. But there was another side to Prince Nicholas. His mania for collecting spread to women. He kept numerous mistresses, dotted about western Hungary, each in her own house, and visited them all in turn. He had a marked appetite for young girls, which his entourage did its best to hush up. We know something of the way he set about deflowering the local maidens, however. At the trials of the infamous Prince zu Kaunitz-Rietburg, who systematically seduced large numbers of young girls, first buying off their parents, it was a part of his defence that others were as guilty as he. Prince Esterházy, he claimed, did exactly the same thing. Kaunitz was eventually expelled from Hungary. Everyone knew that Esterházy's sexual tastes were just as exotic (they were, for example, common knowledge among the musicians of Eisenstadt, one of whom, Tomasini, had a daughter who had been bought by Kaunitz), but no one was prepared to bring him to public account.[53] Between times, Nicholas would often arrange hunting parties and

---

51. Since 1919 Eisenstadt has been in Austria and Esterháza in Hungary. The Austro-Hungarian border was redrawn at Versailles, and the dividing line still separates the two castles (Treaty of Trianon, 1919).
52. His son Prince Anton died in 1794, after only four years as head of the dynasty.
53. The Kaunitz trials are documented in GEFR.

indulge his love of the chase, the other kind. He cut a dashing figure on his dappled stallion, and on Sundays it was his custom to ride the horse straight down the central aisle of the church and dismount at his private pew near the altar.[54] This dissolute man, for all his fabulous wealth, was basically unhappy. At seventeen he had married Princess Marie Hermenegild Liechtenstein, herself only fifteen, after seeing her but once before the wedding ceremony. This was a disastrous match, with scarcely anything to commend it. The princess, in turn, sought a series of lovers, the most notable of whom was Baron Salomon Mayer von Rothschild (1774–1855), who advised the Esterházys on finance. He helped protect the Esterházy fortune, so carefully built up by Nicholas I, against the profligate spending of his grandson, who was now doing his best to place the family's wealth in jeopardy. Nicholas II's children flaunted the Esterházy money with almost equal abandon. His son Paul Anton (1786–1866), as ambassador to London, created a sensation by turning up at George IV's coronation in 1821 wearing a suit of diamonds. Nicholas's saving grace was his strong sense of loyalty. In 1809 Napoleon had tried to persuade the Magyars to elect Nicholas as their king and rid themselves of the Habsburgs. Nicholas, ever mindful of his family's origins, not only refused to betray the Austrian monarchy but raised a regiment of volunteers in defence of its interests.

It was entirely in keeping with Nicholas's autocratic character that he placed an iron grip on the administrative structure that had controlled his family's estates for generations. The Esterházy archives reveal that no detail escaped his eagle eye, be it the shipment of lumber from one village to another or the hiring of simple farmhands. He could be a hard taskmaster, especially if he suspected inefficiency. His strictness in such matters had already been the undoing of Georg Liszt. This duality in his nature is constantly revealed by the archive material. Side by side with memos concerning the sale of a house or the storage of feed grain we find revealing letters, such as the following to his son Paul, dated May 26, 1810:

> In haste! When Frau von Kemmitzer has her child, have it baptized in my name! Nicholas Paulus, if it's a boy; Leopoldine Henriette, if it's a girl! I will write Frau v. Kemmitzer with the next courier. The expenses are to be handsomely paid! N.E.[55]

The profits generated by the labours of his serfs went to subsidize the labours of his mistresses.

This, then, was Adam's employer—rigorous, strict, lecherous, dissolute—a

---

54. See the diary of Lady Frances Shelley (SD, vol. 1, pp. 290–95), who visited Eisenstadt castle in September 1816 and observed the Esterházys at first hand.
55. Original document preserved in the Esterházy archives, Széchényi National Library, Budapest.

bundle of contradictions. When Adam entered his service at Forchtenau, Nicholas was still only thirty-two years old. He held dominion over tens of thousands of his subjects. He owned their land, he owned their villages, he rewarded and punished his people—all according to his own lights. His word was their law. Adam was to remain in the service of this despot for twenty years.

V I I

In the summer of 1810, Adam went on a short visit to Mattersdorf in order to see his father. Georg Liszt, it will be recalled, was working in the Esterházy lumberyards there, and he was again under suspicion of fraud. Adam, a skilled bookkeeper and by now a trusted employee of the Esterházys, might have thought that he could help. It was during this fateful visit that Adam met a young woman who had recently moved to Mattersdorf from Vienna to be with her brother. Her name was Anna Lager and she was twenty-two years old. Anna was destined to become the mother of Franz Liszt, her only child.[56]

---

56. A baffling problem surrounds Liszt's earliest childhood. Every one of his biographers claims that Liszt was Adam's only child. Adam and Anna were married on January 11, 1811. Liszt was born the following October, just over ten months later. There is no record of any other child. After his genius had asserted itself, and the concert tours began, the family was constantly on the move. This generated a great deal of correspondence. Not once in his long letters to friends, colleagues, and employers does Adam mention any other child than his prodigy son Franz Liszt. Yet Liszt himself does. Many years later Liszt, who was unwell at the time, wrote to Marie d'Agoult: "Let my illness be like an absence, like a day or two away from you. . . . If only I hadn't lost a brother from consumption. There was a time when I should have been delighted for a cold to rid me of life. Now I should be broken-hearted to die." (ACLA, vol. 1, p. 59.) This suggests that at some point Liszt had witnessed a family death scene. Close scrutiny of the holograph (Bibliothèque Nationale, NAF Archives Daniel Ollivier no. 25175, doc. no. 7045) proves that these lines are authentic and have not fallen victim to editorial caprice. See p. 202.

It is an indication of the scepticism with which Liszt scholars have approached their task that they have assumed Liszt to have had a memory lapse. (See, for example, CLSH, p. 6.) As if he would invent a brother! It so happens that there is a crucial document in the National Széchényi Library which corroborates Liszt's observation. In July 1812 Georg, the grandfather, having lost his job, arrived at his son's house in Raiding with a wife and eight young children. He was destitute. Liszt, it will be remembered, was then an infant of nine months. On July 10 Georg sent a desperate appeal for help to Prince Esterházy. His letter contains this revealing phrase: "My son also has four young children. He hardly manages to make ends meet, and now I come along and place an additional burden on his family." (Acta Mus. no. 4195.) According to Georg's testimony, then, Adam already had four children by 1812, and Liszt must have been the youngest. A glance at the family tree (p. xvi) shows that Georg could not have been referring to any other son than Adam, for the dates match only his case. Since Adam and Anna had been married a mere eighteen months, the three older children must have resulted from a previous union. Adam was twelve years older than Anna; he was thirty-five when he married her. If this was his second marriage, nothing whatsoever is known of his first. There is a considerable gap in our knowledge of Adam's life from 1800 to 1810, that is, between his twenty-fifth and his thirty-fourth years.

Taken separately, the two documents—Liszt's letter and grandfather Georg's petition—prove nothing. But taken together, they point to an intriguing topic which might yield some interesting results if subjected to further research.

Anna's family can be traced back far into the seventeenth century. Most of her forbears were German-speaking peasants who lived in Lower Austria. Her paternal grandfather, Matthias Lager (1660–1718), was born in Palt, where he spent all his life working as a farmer. He was fifty-five years old when his young wife, Anna Maria Stöckl (1688–c.1742), gave birth to a son, Matthias (1715–96), who eventually moved to Krems, a small village about 40 miles from Vienna, and established himself there as a baker. When Matthias the baker was sixty-two he took a twenty-seven-year-old bride, Franziska Romana Schuhmann (1752–97), a daughter of a Bavarian watchmaker. They established themselves in Krems, house no. 314, and produced a large family. In 1788, when the still-vigorous Matthias was seventy-three years old, his wife presented him with a daughter, Maria Anna.[57]

Anna had a difficult childhood. Her aged father died in 1796, and her mother followed him to the grave six months later, on May 9, 1797, Anna's ninth birthday. Although she had several brothers and sisters in Krems, Anna appears to have moved out of necessity to Vienna and worked there as a chambermaid, moving from one job to another—mainly in the Kärntnerstrasse and Tiefer Graben areas of the city. This experience, far from harming her, seems to have instilled into her the virtues of thrift, honesty, directness, and sheer goodness of heart—qualities for which she was later respected by her son and loved by her three grandchildren, Blandine, Cosima, and Daniel, on whom she lavished much kindness and affection and whom she brought up as her own flesh and blood. Anna lived in Vienna throughout the Napoleonic bombardment and occupation of the city. Later on, she moved to the village of Mattersdorf to be with her brother Franz Lager, who was a soap-maker there. The overseer of the Esterházy estate at Mattersdorf was Liszt's grandfather, Georg, and it was here in 1810, as we have seen, that Anna met his son Adam, who was then thirty-four years old. Within a few weeks Adam had proposed to her, and the marriage took place in the Catholic church at Unterfrauenhaid, a tiny village 2 miles from Adam's home in Raiding, on January 11, 1811.[58] According to the marriage certificate, one of the witnesses was Johann Rohrer, the village schoolmaster, who later became Franz Liszt's childhood mentor.[59]

---

57. The Lager house is now called Theaterplatz 5, and it bears a modest commemorative plaque.
58. Already by September 10, 1810, Adam had petitioned for permission to marry, as any Esterházy employee was bound to do, and he also requested a leave of absence on that account. (Acta Mus. no. 4207.)
59. See n. 14 on p. 57.

Krems

LOWER

AUSTRIA

Vienna

Malacka

Tyrnavia

Pressburg

Danube

Edelsthal

Kittsee

Ragendorf

LEITHAGEBIRGE

Pottendorf

Austria

Wiener-Neustadt

Eisenstadt

St. Georgen

Neusiedlersee

Neunkirchen

Mattersdorf

Marz

Forchtenau

Oedenburg

Deutschkreuz

Esterháza

Lackenbach

Unterfrauenhaid

Raiding

Nikitsch

Hungary

STYRIA

Szombathely

Graz

Güssing

Austrian Burgenland
(formerly western Hungary,
where Liszt's forbears lived)

This, then, was Liszt's family background. For three generations his male forbears had worked on Hungarian soil. They loved the country, they identified with its people, they were absorbed in its culture. They lived, they reproduced, and they died in exactly the same way as thousands of other peasant families of Magyar stock. And in the unlikely event of any one of them being questioned about his "nationality," he would have replied, "Hungarian."

Given the mass of evidence we now have at our disposal concerning Liszt's family background, it is truly remarkable that so seemingly simple and fundamental a matter as his national identity was ever disputed by modern scholars. Emile Haraszti, for example, claimed that Liszt was French in outlook and feeling, and that the Gallic temperament, acquired in his youth, remained with him for life.[60] James Huneker, on the other hand, asserted that Liszt was German, at any rate in the second half of his life.[61] Norbert Dunkel said that Liszt was ashamed of his origins and never spoke of them.[62] As if to complete this round of logical alternatives, Peter Raabe stressed Liszt's "cosmopolitanism."[63] Hungary, he asserted, was to Liszt merely a birthplace, not his homeland. Liszt, it is true, could not even speak Hungarian. He spent his most formative years in France, and spoke French in preference to any other language. Then, at the height of his fame and maturity, he moved to Germany, a country he admired but whose language he never properly mastered,[64] and became the leader of the "Neo-German" school. His last twenty years, his *"vie trifurquée,"* as Liszt called them, were years of endless wandering back and forth across Italy, Hungary, and Germany, with frequent visits to Austria and some to France. This final period seems conclusively to prove Raabe's assertion. Liszt did indeed live an international life.

And yet Raabe and the other scholars are wrong. Liszt was Hungarian in thought and word and deed. He often said throughout his life that he was Magyar; he never once claimed that he was either French or German. He constantly referred to Hungary as "my homeland,"[65] and it gave him immense pleasure to write, "I am part of the national pride."[66] Liszt was always declaring himself for Hungarian causes. He gave many charity concerts for the people of his country, at which he sometimes appeared wearing national dress. He

60. HPL, p. 135.
61. HJL, p. 12.
62. DML, p. 10.
63. RLS, vol. 2, p. 211.
64. See pp. 13–14 for a fuller discussion of Liszt's difficulties with German.
65. RGS, vol. 2, p. 223.
66. LLB, vol. 3, p. 77.

helped to found the great music academy in Budapest which still bears his name. Always he carried his nationality proudly. In 1848 he attempted to buy the humble farm cottage in Raiding where he was born.[67] This does not sound like a man who has no homeland, least of all like a man ashamed of his origins. The fact that Liszt spoke no Hungarian is not important, although Liszt himself always regretted it. Large numbers of nineteenth-century Hungarians never learned their own language. They were part of the Austrian empire and the German tongue dominated their nation, especially the western part of it, where Liszt was born. Even the Princes Esterházy, the leaders of the Magyar nation, could not speak Hungarian. On November 12, 1847, a historic session of the Hungarian parliament was opened in Pressburg by Ferdinand V with eight Hungarian words, the first time the Hungarians had ever heard their own language used in their legislature. The greatest Hungarian politician of the day, István Széchenyi, was there, and he recorded this memorable event in his diary, in German: "Alles war ergriffen, viele weinten" ("Everyone was deeply moved; many were weeping"). Széchenyi himself, the tireless promoter of that symbol of Hungarian unity, the Buda-Pest suspension bridge, learned to speak Hungarian only in later life. In the twilight of Liszt's life he wrote, "I may surely be allowed, in spite of my lamentable ignorance of the Hungarian language, to remain from my birth to the grave Magyar in heart and mind...."[68]

---

67. Acta Mus. no. 3877.
68. Letter to Baron Antal Augusz, dated May 7, 1873. (PBUS, p. 160.)

BOOK ONE

The Young Prodigy
1811 · 1829

Childhood in Hungary

*My son, you are predestined! You will realize
that artistic goal whose spell bewitched my youth
in vain.*

ADAM LISZT[1]

I

The year 1811 was momentous. All Europe was in turmoil. The Napoleonic
Wars had been raging for nearly a decade and had left a trail of devastation
behind them. Napoleon himself was still at the height of his powers, his most
terrible battles yet to be fought. He raised a *grande armée* of half-a-million men
and marched on Russia. The Russians turned and fought at Borodino on September 6, and there was a bloodbath: eighty thousand casualties littered the
field. Napoleon finally took Moscow on September 14, 1812. The Russians
then set fire to the city, making it impossible for him to establish winter quarters there. Now began the arduous, thousand-mile trek back to France. The
first snows fell in October; by early November the hard frost had set in. On
November 6 Napoleon marched with his army through a blinding snowstorm
at minus 20 degrees centigrade. His columns were constantly harassed by the
Cossacks. Under the command of General Kutusov, the Russian army resorted
to guerrilla tactics, striking swiftly and disappearing, often with prisoners. An
English observer with General Kutusov saw sixty dying men, stripped naked,
their necks laid upon a felled tree, while Russian men and women with large
sticks hopped around them, singing in chorus, striking out their brains with
repeated blows.[2] The stragglers from Napoleon's columns were lured into
Russian huts with promises of warmth and food, only to have their throats cut.

---

1. OFL.
2. BNR, p. 222.

The lucky ones were those who simply fell asleep in the snow and froze to death. Entombed in thick ice, they lay there until the following spring. Then the Russian thaw set in. Thousands of corpses, locked in macabre positions, were now revealed along the routes from Smolensk to Warsaw, silent sentinels to this epic tragedy. Eastern Europe had become one vast graveyard. Of the *grande armée*'s half-a-million men, only fifty thousand succeeded in getting back to France.

To the south things were easier. In 1810 Napoleon had married the Arch-duchess Marie Louise, eighteen-year-old daughter of the Emperor of Austria. Within a year she had borne him a son, who was proclaimed King of Rome. This alliance between the Habsburgs and France protected Napoleon's southern flank and brought a temporary stability to the area. But even here, in the cities of Vienna and Munich, Prague and Pressburg, a social phenomenon had emerged on a scale unparalleled in Europe's history. The maimed survivors of the great battles of Austerlitz, Jena, and Eylau had started to trickle back home. They would soon be joined by the wounded soldiers of Borodino, Leipzig, and Waterloo. Wherever one turned, the battle-scarred veterans of the Napoleonic wars could be observed with their missing limbs, eyeless sockets, severed ears, and jagged sabre wounds across the face and hands. These old campaigners were a constant reminder of Europe's agony, and many of them lived into the 1850s and beyond.

Presiding over these grisly scenes, like a ghostly galleon in the skies, was the Great Comet of 1811, one of the astronomical wonders of the age. This astonishing phenomenon illuminated the night skies of Central Europe. Men gazed heavenwards, awestruck by the wondrous sight. They took it to be an omen. Napoleon had actually consulted astrologers and planned his disastrous military campaign against Russia convinced that the comet foretold a great victory for him. The spectacle gradually waxed in intensity, until night was turned to day. By the middle of October the comet's tail was estimated to be at least 100 million miles in length. During the previous August, the tail had divided into two streams, almost at right angles to one another, and it now left a brilliant carpet of light spread across the entire northern hemisphere.[3] Eighteen eleven was a year of ghastly horrors, but brilliant portents. Its greatest son was Franz Liszt.

---

3. The Great Comet, one of the most celebrated of modern times, was discovered by Flaugergues at Viviers on March 26, 1811, and last seen by Wisniewski at Neu-Tscherkask, in south Russia, on August 17, 1812—an unprecedented period of visibility. Sir William Herschel studied the comet in detail and made some precise observations about it *(Philosophical Transactions of the Royal Society of 1812)*. The comet left its mark on many different fields of human activity. One of its more unscientific consequences was the wine crop of that year, which happened to be particularly fine. "Comet wine" was much sought after, and featured in merchants' price lists and auction sales until the 1880s.

11

Immediately after their wedding Adam Liszt and his young bride, Anna, set up house at Raiding, where, as we have seen, Adam had been intendant of the Esterházy sheepfolds since 1809. In those days Raiding was a major sheep-breeding station for the Esterházys, and its combined flocks numbered more than fifty thousand.[4] Adam, with his clerical training and his flair for organization, quickly became one of the Esterházys' trusted employees. Since the sheepfolds were widely dispersed, Adam used to conduct his inspections on horseback. He became a familiar figure during these visits to the surrounding villages, and he built up a wide circle of friends and acquaintances. The family home was a low-lying, whitewashed brick dwelling with tall chimneys, on one level, possessing a courtyard at the front and a small orchard at the back. It stands in Raiding to this day and is indistinguishable from thousands of similar dwellings spread throughout Austria and Hungary. Adam and Anna were to live there for twelve years.

In February 1811, three or four weeks after her marriage, Anna became pregnant. Shortly afterwards occurred the first sighting of the Great Comet. The heavens became more spectacular with every passing week of Anna's term. From time immemorial such marvels have been interpreted as the harbingers of men of destiny; and so it was here. The Tziganes encamped outside Raiding foretold the birth of a great man. The point is not the truth or the falsity of the prophecy; the point is that Anna heard it and later related it to her young son, and this gave him a sense of destiny which he carried with him to the grave. Anna herself was never in doubt that her child was a "chosen one." Four months before Liszt's birth, she fell down a disused well on the Esterházy estate.[5] It was the height of the summer, and that fact probably saved her from drowning, since the water-level was low. She was brought up soaked and bruised, but none the worse for her experience, which she herself characteristically interpreted as a lucky sign. Right up to her confinement, however, there was anxiety that her pregnancy might have been affected; but the child was born without complications in Raiding on Tuesday, October 22, 1811. Anna never conceived again; Franz Liszt was to remain her only child.[6]

Liszt was baptized the next day at the neighbouring village of Unterfrauen-haid, since there was no priest in Raiding,[7] and the details of his birth were entered in the church registry there. The baptismal certificate tells us that Adam

4. GL, p. 159.
5. GL, p. 135. See also APL, August 19, 1886.
6. See n. 56 on p. 45.
7. CLV. Father Johannes Stefanits, who baptized Liszt, looked after both parishes from 1796 to 1838.

Liszt named his son Franciscus,[8] christening him after the Franciscans and also after his godfather, Franciscus Zambothy. The certificate reads

OKTOBER 1811					
23.	Franciscus L.	List Adamus ovium Rationista, Principis Esterházy et Lager Maria Anna	Reiding	Patrini: Zambothy Franciscus et Szalay Julianna	Mersits Georgius capellanus Lookiensis

Adam himself is described on the document as an "ovium Rationista," that is, a sheep accountant. During the baptism service, the infant Liszt was carried to the font by Frau Frankenburg, the mother of the Hungarian writer Adolf Frankenburg, who became a childhood playmate of Liszt's.[9]

As an infant Liszt was weak and sickly. According to his father, the child was attacked by "nervous pains and fever, which more than once imperilled his life."[10] The low-lying marshlands of the Neusiedlersee were a continual source of infection, and the infant mortality rate in this area was high, as a glance at the Liszt family tree shows. Adam had the boy vaccinated, an advanced and radical treatment in those days.[11] On one occasion, just before his third birthday, the sickness reached a crisis: the symptoms resembled those of catalepsy. The parents took him for dead and ordered his coffin made by the village carpenter. He rallied shortly afterwards, but for much of his life he was subject to feverish attacks and fainting spells.[12] Liszt was nursed through this grave illness by his aunt Therese, a younger sister of Anna's, who, in Liszt's own

---

8. Liszt's name was neither the Hungarian Ferenc nor the French François. Least of all was it the German Franz, the name by which he is universally known today. He usually signed himself F. Liszt, thereby doing nothing to resolve the confusion. As a child he was known at home by the diminutives Zischy and Franzi (see the correspondence between Adam and Carl Czerny, LCRT).

9. FM, pp. 24–26.

10. OFL, from the diary of Adam Liszt.

11. Ibid. Edward Jenner's technique of vaccination by grafting had been introduced in 1798.

12. As the child walked onto the platform to make his début at Oedenburg, a fever swept over him (p. 68). Again, during a public concert in Paris in 1835, he collapsed at the keyboard and was carried off the platform "in a fit of hysterics." (RML, vol. 1, pp. 48–49.) In November 1839 Liszt cancelled a concert in Vienna because of a fever which made his hand "tremble fearfully." (LLB, vol. 1, p. 32.) It was a fever which prevented him from fulfilling his engagements in Leipzig in 1840, and which Liszt described as "violent shuddering." (ACLA, vol. 1, p. 414.) Shortly afterwards we find Liszt taking harmful quantities of quinine, while on tour of England, to help fight a chronic feverishness. (ACLA, vol. 2, pp. 29–30.) All his life, those nearest and dearest to him were concerned lest he catch a chill, which always seemed to have more serious consequences for him than for others. ACLA, vols. 1 and 2, is full of such references. Liszt died after contracting a cold, which he neglected, and which culminated in fever and pneumonia.

words, rescued him from death.[13] The boy was taught to read and write by the village schoolmaster, Johann Rohrer. Rohrer was not the village priest, an error still perpetrated in the Liszt literature. The year that the young German-speaking teacher of twenty-two was appointed as Raiding's schoolmaster, there were sixty-seven children registered in the little school: fifty-two boys and fifteen girls. Liszt attended classes with all the other children. Rohrer taught them in a schoolroom measuring approximately 20 feet in length and 14 feet in width.[14] Liszt's general education was neglected, therefore, and he always regretted it. He once told Lina Ramann that in his childhood he had no idea of history, of geography, or of the natural sciences.[15] And in a letter to Princess von Sayn-Wittgenstein he confessed that his poor primary education had always been a handicap to him, and that he had never been able to remedy this capital defect.[16] We have already observed that Liszt's parents, like thousands of other western Hungarians, were German-speaking, and that Raiding itself was a German-speaking village. Liszt therefore grew up unable to speak Magyar.[17]

III

The first few years, then, were difficult ones for Adam and Anna. Until recently, we knew virtually nothing of their married life in Raiding. Much new information has meanwhile come out of the Esterházy archives, and today we have a clearer idea of the hardships they endured. Adam's greatest concern at first was his maverick father, Georg, who had moved with his entire family into their small dwelling at Raiding in July 1812 and stayed there for almost an

---

13. LLBM, p. 110. Liszt was deeply attached to this particular aunt, who used to visit Raiding during his childhood. Her full name was Maria Therese Lager (1790–1856), and in later life she lived in Graz. When she died, Liszt wrote a letter of consolation to his mother: "Dearest Mother, Your dear, good, and excellent sister Therese has passed away! As prepared for this news as one could be, it nevertheless brings a deep mourning to my heart—for you know that I always remember everything good that she rendered me in my childhood, when she rescued me from death, and I remained loyal and deeply devoted to her. If you possess, perhaps, some small object of hers—a book, a cup, or something else of no value, send it to me here, where it will remain dear and precious to me." (Weimar, January 2, 1857.)

14. LHFL. Johann Rohrer (1783–1868) remained the schoolmaster of Raiding for sixty-one years, from 1805 to 1866, retiring when he was eighty-three years old. This is confirmed by the parish records, *Annales Parochiae Lok cum filialibus Lakfalva et Doborján, scriptaeber parachum Joannem Prikoso-vich, A.D. MCMXVIII.* Rohrer's income was recorded as 66 fl., 97 kr. When Liszt revisited his natal village in 1840 he remembered Rohrer and made over a large gift of money to his old teacher. (*Társalkodó* [Pest], vol. 3, no. 25, 1840.)

15. RLKM, vol. 1, p. 152.

16. LLB, vol. 6, p. 184.

17. In later life he tried to correct this drawback by taking lessons in Hungarian from a Budapest monk called Zsigmond Vadász, but soon abandoned the effort. (LLM, p. 131.)

entire year. We learn that Adam was rebuked by the intendant at Eisenstadt for expropriating large quantities of brushwood, manorial property, to use as firewood during the severe winter of 1812.[18] Adam explained that his father's large family was living with him, and they would all otherwise have frozen. The orchard and garden also presented difficulties. The French troops garrisoned near Raiding broke in and caused damage to the fence and the trees. Adam subsequently tried to get the prince to agree to a reduction on his lease.[19] Not the least of Adam's problems concerned the house itself, which was damp, and which eventually ruined his piano. He was forced to sell some of his personal possessions in order to buy a new one, which cost him 550 forints.[20]

There was a brighter side to the picture, however. Adam held frequent chamber-music evenings in his house at which he and his friends from neighbouring communities took part. Adam was not only an amateur cellist and pianist, but he also played the violin and had a good bass voice.[21] Occasionally a distinguished visitor would come down from Eisenstadt and raise the proceedings to a more professional level. Adam knew all the orchestral players at Eisenstadt, about 30 miles away, and Kapellmeister Fuchs, Hummel's successor there, often turned up at Raiding.[22] The young Liszt was surrounded by music from his earliest years.

I V

The boy's musical genius first asserted itself in his sixth year. One day he heard his father playing Ries's Concerto in C-sharp minor and was captivated by it. That same evening, the child spontaneously sang one of the themes of the concerto from memory. His father considered the feat so exceptional that he made him sing it again. Here is an account of that occasion, recorded by Adam in his diary, together with some observations on his son's sickness:

> After his vaccination, a period commenced in which the boy had to struggle alternately with nervous pains and fever, which more than once imperilled his life. On one occasion, during his second or third year, we thought him dead and ordered his coffin made. This agitated

18. Acta Mus. nos. 4205, 4209, 3477.

19. Acta Mus. no. 3471.

20. Acta Mus. no. 3500.

21. Acta Mus. no. 3383.

22. In a revealing letter to an unknown correspondent in Eisenstadt, written from Paris some years later (March 20, 1824), Adam asks to be remembered to all his old colleagues and singles out some of them by name. He writes: "Now, dear friend, some news of Eisenstadt. How are Herren Schubernigg, Steffl, Walch, Fajt, Verex, and Kapellmeister Fuchs? What is my good friend Breuster doing, that fine musician Tomasini, the fat Schuster, and all those thousands of artists?" (DM.)

condition lasted until his sixth year. In that same year he heard me play Ries's Concerto in C-sharp minor. Franz, bending over the piano, was completely absorbed. In the evening, coming in from a short walk in the garden, he sang the theme of the concerto. We made him sing it again. He did not know what he was singing. That was the first indication of his genius.[23]

According to Adam, the boy now incessantly begged to be taught the piano. Adam's reluctance stemmed from his concern over his son's delicate health. Having nearly lost him once, Liszt's parents were resolved to spare the boy any physical strain; throughout his childhood they were watchful and protective. Eventually, Adam took on the task of giving the boy regular lessons. However, after three months' instruction, he tells us, the fever returned, obliging them to discontinue. When they resumed, it was evident that the boy was uniquely endowed, and he started making astonishing progress.

We have hardly any documentary evidence about the lessons themselves. Adam Liszt was well qualified to instruct his son in the rudiments of piano playing, however. And he did more than merely teach him the names of the notes and how to read musical notation. He encouraged the boy to play from memory, to sight-read, and above all to improvise, skills at which he soon became phenomenal. Adam, who had a broad musical background, was familiar with a wide range of repertoire, including much of the keyboard music of Bach, Mozart, Hummel, and early Beethoven. We know that he introduced Liszt to

---

23. OFL, from the diary of Adam Liszt. Since much of our information about Liszt's earlier years comes from Adam Liszt, and since there is so little of it, we have to proceed cautiously over a difficult stretch of ground. Adam seems to have written his diary at a later date, after his son's early triumphs in Pressburg and Vienna, by which time he clearly perceived his boy to be a genius. Without going so far as to suggest that his diary was merely written for posterity, we may infer that Adam realized that a "journal" such as this, carefully tracking his son's progress, would one day prove to be an invaluable basis for biographical articles about his famous child.

Fragments of the diary, which has since disappeared, were first published by Joseph d'Ortigue. In his "Etude biographique" of Liszt (OFL) d'Ortigue publicly thanked Anna Liszt for allowing him access to it. Haraszti, one of the more sceptical of Liszt researchers, insisted that the diary never existed. He claimed that it was nothing more than a random collection of newspaper cuttings pasted into a scrapbook, begun by Liszt's father and later continued by Marie d'Agoult. (HPL, fn. 24.) This miscellany is now in the Versailles library among Madame d'Agoult's papers, under the title "Second Scrapbook." (ASSV.) But the quotations from Adam Liszt used by d'Ortigue and others are not to be found in this "Scrapbook," thus rendering it a quite different source from the diary. Moreover, Adam Liszt himself mentions his diary as early as 1824. In a revealing letter to Carl Czerny, in which Adam described his son's sensational successes on his English tour, he wrote, "Ich könnte Ihnen noch Vieles schreiben, allein mein Tagebuch soll Ihnen einstens alles haarklein sagen" ("I could write still more to you, but my diary will one day tell you everything to the last detail"). (LCRT, p. 241.) Lina Ramann made a number of efforts to find Adam's diary. In the 1870s she sent Liszt a letter asking where it might be located. Liszt replied: "My mother used to possess a few parts of this diary. Since her passing, I don't know what became of them." (WA, Kasten 351, no. 1.) Liszt's answer is further proof that Adam's diary at one time existed.

their works, for he was prepared publicly to exhibit his son playing them. There was a special affinity with Beethoven. Whenever Liszt was asked as a boy what he wanted to be when he grew up, he pointed to the wall where a portrait of Beethoven was hanging. "Ein solcher," he used to reply. "Like him." It is to Adam's credit that once he had recognized his son's genius, he allowed it to blossom without hindrance. He himself tells us that the boy's practice sessions were quite irregular until his ninth year,[24] an indication that Adam was not the harsh disciplinarian some observers have claimed.[25] Adam Liszt was also intelligent enough to know his own limitations; a teacher would one day have to be found who was worthy of his son's gifts.

There is a touching anecdote dating from this period, little known to Liszt's biographers. Adam regularly had his son accompany him on his travels round the Esterházy estates. He used to like to introduce his boy to his musical friends on these trips, and the precocity of "der junge Künstler" was soon widely recognized. As a special treat for his seventh birthday, on October 22, 1818, the small boy was allowed to travel with his father to Lackenbach, where Adam had some business with a wealthy merchant called Ruben Hirschler. The daughter of this merchant, Fanni, had just been given a piano, recently arrived from Vienna. Adam requested the girl to play something for his young son, who, he explained, also loved music. When the lad heard the playing he could say nothing, his eyes filled with tears, and he threw himself weeping into the arms of his father. This scene so moved the elderly merchant that he gave the piano to the boy. It was a wonderful birthday gift. Hirschler's gesture created a warm friendship between the two families. The Liszts often used to drive over from Raiding to Lackenbach (about half an hour's journey) and spend their Sunday afternoons in the Hirschler household.[26]

Another family with whom the Liszts were friendly was the Frankenburgs. Antal Frankenburg, like Adam, was an administrator on the Esterházy estates. The Frankenburgs lived in Deutschkreuz, about 7 miles from Raiding. Adam and Antal visited one another frequently. Antal, like his "cousin Adam," as he affectionately called him, was a passionate Hungarian. He often cursed the Austrian government in Vienna and refused to attend the German-speaking theatre, saying that although his name was German, his heart was Hungarian. Adolf, his gifted writer-son, was an exact contemporary of Franz Liszt, and the two small boys became friends. Many years later, long after he had become a well-known

---

24. OFL, the diary.
25. HLP, part 1, fn. 15. HPL, p. 130.
26. *Budapesti Bazár,* Pesti Hölgy-Divatlap, no. 22, Nov. 15, 1873. Koch (KLV, p. 18), who also reports this anecdote, wrongly calls the Hirschler family "Rehmann." The Hirschlers, in fact, were rich Jews who later fell upon hard times. By 1865 they had been reduced to selling shoes from an old stall in the Vienna market. Fanni herself married into poverty, but she followed Liszt's subsequent career with interest.

author, Adolf wrote a reminiscence of these early years.[27] Frau Frankenburg, enthralled by the phenomenal progress of "Franzi," wanted to put Adolf to the piano as well. But he tells us that his childish mind was frightened by the huge keyboard, because he thought that innumerable tiny demons lived in it and would shoot up from the ebony keys to bite into his fingers. Instead of the piano, he eventually settled for the guitar, which appeared less threatening.

About this time, Franz narrowly escaped serious injury. Adam used to store gunpowder in the house for use on the estate—for tree felling, for hunting, and for defending the sheepfolds against natural predators. The boy used to watch, fascinated, as his father filled his leather gunpowder pouch with this magical substance, primed his gun, and went out on hunting trips. He quickly noticed that only a tiny amount of powder was required to produce an enormous bang, an event which invariably caused him great pleasure. He could not help wondering what might happen if the entire contents of his father's gunpowder pouch were emptied on the old kitchen stove, in which Anna always kept a fire brightly burning. He waited until Adam and Anna were outside, took the pouch, and threw it into the stove. A tremendous explosion shook the house, and half the iron stove was blown out. Franz was knocked to the floor by the blast, a fact that probably saved him from the flying debris. When Adam rushed back into the house and surveyed the destruction, a suitable chastisement was at once carried out. Liszt never forgot the incident, and when he revisited his birthplace in 1881 it was the old stove, which still bore its telltale scars, that brought this memory vividly to life.[28]

v

Among the influences which were already working on the child's character during these early years, two call for special mention. The first was the church. Liszt never lost the faith that he won for himself as a boy through his prayers in the tiny churches of Raiding and Frauendorf.[29] From the outset, he was a deeply religious, mystical child. Nothing seemed to him "so self-evident as heaven, nothing so true as the compassion of God."[30] He dreamed himself incessantly into the world of the saints and the martyrs. Under Adam's guidance, he became familiar with the forms of worship and the symbolic ritual of the Catholic faith. He knew, of course, that his father had once dedicated himself to the priesthood. More than once Adam was to take the small boy on

27. FM, vol. 1, pp. 24–25.
28. ZLEF, vol. 2, p. 102ff. Also SB, p. 58.
29. LLBM, p. 145. Liszt made this comment in 1862. He means Unterfrauenhaid, where he was baptized.
30. Ibid.

a nostalgic trip to the Franciscans and their monastery and point out the place where he had experienced his first religious crisis. These powerful memories never left Liszt; they were to surface many times in later life. In his adolescence he would beg to be allowed to enter a seminary in Paris and die the death of the martyrs. Later still, aged fifty-three, he would finally take holy orders. To interpret such a solemn act, as so many of Liszt's "romantic" biographers have done, as an escape into the refuge of a monastic cell in order to avoid capture by his Egeria, the Princess von Sayn-Wittgenstein, is to reveal scant acquaintance with his earliest years. Liszt's life must be seen whole. The church, as he himself acknowledged, was his vocation almost from the start.[31]

The other influence was equally hypnotic. Among Liszt's most colourful childhood memories was the image of the wandering tribes of dark-skinned Gypsies who trekked back and forth across the plains of Hungary, remarkable people whose customs, language, and music he later described in such vivid detail in *Des Bohémiens et leur musique en Hongrie*. The very best passages in that book are autobiographical; they are first-hand, eye-witness accounts of this proud, nomadic race, and they could have been written by no one but Liszt.[32] The Gypsies entered Hungary from the Balkan Peninsula as early as the fifteenth century. They flourished there simply because they were not subjected to the terrible persecutions which decimated their numbers in Russia, Poland, Turkey, and other less tolerant countries. By the nineteenth century, tens of thousands of them were living in Hungary side by side with the Magyars, although culturally quite separate from them. The Gypsies often camped outside Raiding. Liszt describes how they would form their caravans into a large circle and unfurl their tents. The women would start small fires for the cooking pots while the men would feed and water the horses. Small groups would then enter the village to barter their handmade goods, beg for necessities, and tell fortunes to the suspicious villagers. At nightfall they would build a huge fire in the middle of their encampments, around which singers and dancers would perform. Theirs was a purely improvisatory art. Responding entirely to feeling and emotion, they would sway back and forth to the music, as if under a hypnotic spell.

What Liszt admired in Tzigane music was its improvisatory, impulsive nature. It coincided with his own view of the art as something fundamental to mankind. Here was a living proof, for him, that music was truly innate, for it had been preserved within an ancient people who had received no formal instruction whatever in the art, who could not read music notation, who were illiterate by the civilized standards of the day, and yet whose music had somehow managed to survive across the generations.

The Tziganes, in fact, produced some outstanding musicians. One of the very

---

31. Liszt's will, dated September 14, 1860 (LLB, vol. 5, p. 52).
32. On the complex question of the authenticity of Liszt's books and articles, see pp. 20–23.

best, and one who made a powerful impression on the young Liszt, was the Romany violinist János Bihari.

> I was just beginning to grow up [wrote Liszt] when I heard this great man in 1822. . . . He used to play for hours on end, without giving the slightest thought to the passing of time. . . . His musical cascades fell in rainbow profusion, or glided along in a soft murmur. . . . His performances must have distilled into my soul the essence of some generous and exhilarating wine; for when I think of his playing, the emotions I then experienced were like one of those mysterious elixirs concocted in the secret laboratories of those alchemists of the Middle Ages.[33]

Bihari formed one of the finest Tzigane bands of the day, in which every player was a virtuoso, and between 1802 and 1824 they toured Hungary, Transylvania, and Austria in their colourful national costumes. They internationalized the *friska* and the *csárdás*. One of their favourite renderings was Bihari's fiery arrangement of the Hungarian *Rákóczy* March, a melody he was once reputed to have composed. (This was impossible, since Bihari, true Gypsy musician that he was, could not read, let alone write music notation. We now know that this old Hungarian melody was not written down until 1820, by Michael Scholl, the military bandmaster of the Esterházy regiment in Pest.)[34] Bihari's band once played in Vienna before the emperor, who was so moved by their exotic music that he asked Bihari what he would like as a mark of the Imperial favour. Bihari asked for patents of nobility for his entire Gypsy band! In 1824 the coach in which he was travelling overturned and he broke his left arm. This effectively ended his career, and his band dispersed. Bihari was only fifty-eight when he died in 1827, leaving a widow and an only child in impoverished circumstances, having lavished all his wealth on others during his lifetime. Liszt writes with affection about Bihari's musical personality and has some penetrating things to say about this Romany's life and art. When, in the 1840s, Liszt composed that national epic, the series of fifteen Hungarian Rhapsodies, he must have had constantly before him these childhood scenes and attempted to enshrine them in those unique creations.

---

33. RGS, vol. 6, pp. 345–46. It can surely be no accident that Liszt's own art placed such a high premium on improvisation. A regular feature of his recitals during the 1840s were his fantasies on given themes, publicly announced in advance. He was constantly elaborating variations on standard repertory works, even during performance, a practice which appalled Joachim, among others, and which got Liszt a bad name until he abandoned it and took a more rigorous view of the printed text. Liszt could never bear merely to reproduce music. Something new, fresh, and creative had to take place during each act of music making in order to justify that act at all. His love of arranging, paraphrasing, and transcribing springs from the same source.

34. SC, p. 108.

These twin influences helped to shape Liszt's character for life. The child was father to the man. After his death, Liszt's biographers became fond of diagnosing his character with the damaging phrase "half Gypsy, half Franciscan"—as if to say that neither half was genuine because of the presence of the other. They could never understand how it was possible for one man to embrace both worlds and concluded that Liszt was therefore "a personality at war with himself." Whatever else he was, Liszt was loyal to his background, to the country that bred him, and to the culture that nourished him. For the rest, that simple catch-phrase "half Gypsy, half Franciscan" does not have the merit of originating with Liszt's biographers themselves; that is, it is not based on a study of his early background at all. They merely appropriated it, without acknowledgement, from Liszt. Half in jest he had once written: "I can be described rather well in German: Zu einer Hälfte Zigeuner zur andern Franziskaner."[35] He was visiting Hungary at the time, and rehearsals for his *Graner* Mass were in full swing at the great cathedral of Esztergom. During a brief respite Liszt had returned to his apartments to deal with some correspondence. Unexpectedly the father of Reményi (the violinist) had walked into his room and interrupted the narrative. His presence there later reminded Liszt to write that after a visit to the theatre that evening, he was rushing off to hear the Tziganes—"you know what particular fascination this music exercises over me." Liszt, then, was merely describing his *itinerary* for August 1856, not analysing his character, which was simultaneously bringing him into contact with the sacred and the secular, clerics and Tziganes. If Liszt had not bothered to write that letter, the "Zigeuner-Franziskaner" phrase would never have been uttered. One wonders what some of his twentieth-century biographers would then have fallen back on in its absence.

VI

By 1819 Adam's thoughts had begun to turn towards Vienna, the city of Beethoven, Schubert, Haydn, and Mozart. In those days Vienna was the capital of the musical world. It lay only 50 miles from Raiding, or about three or four hours away by road. Living there was the great piano pedagogue Carl Czerny. Then there was Adam's old friend Hummel, who had also made his reputation in Vienna. But Hummel was on the point of moving to Weimar, to take up the position of court pianist and Kapellmeister,[36] and the prospect of journeying so far seemed unrealistic. Moreover, his fees were high; he charged 1 louis d'or

---

35. LLB, vol. 4, p. 316, August 13, 1856.
36. He held the post from 1819 until his death in 1837. By a curious coincidence, this was the same post that Liszt took up twenty-three years later, in 1842.

a lesson, an exorbitant sum in those days. Old friendships, apparently, counted for nought.

Several key documents help us to determine Adam's intentions at this time. The Esterházy archives contain a number of petitions from Adam to his employer, Prince Nicholas Esterházy, asking to be transferred from Raiding to Vienna (where the Esterházys kept a large staff) for the purpose of improving his son's prospects. These requests were all turned down. Adam was far too valuable an employee to be spared from Raiding. A Vienna posting was a common enough ambition among the provincial stewards scattered across the Esterházy domains, and the prince's Vienna offices were already overcrowded. Adam then played his trump card. Why should not the prince journey to Raiding and hear the boy for himself? If "Franzi" was indeed talented, the prince might well decide to help by finding Adam an opening in Vienna, thus enabling him to support his family while his son was studying there. The go-between was one Szentgály, a steward; Kapellmeister Fuchs also helped to bring these arrangements to fruition.[37] On September 21, 1819, during a hunting party, Prince Esterházy arrived at Raiding and heard the young Liszt play in the presence of Fuchs and others.[38] The event was decisive. While the prince could not be prevailed upon to give Adam his cherished Vienna posting, he did promise to contribute financially towards the boy's education and to grant Adam a year's leave of absence.[39]

Adam was disappointed; he had expected more. It appears that Szentgály had even found an opening for Adam as a wine-controller to the Esterházys in Vienna, but Prince Nicholas refused to sanction the transfer.[40] Politely, but firmly, Adam in turn rejected the paltry sum of 200 florins Nicholas now sent him in fulfillment of his promise. This action was unprecedented. Since the money had already been drawn from the treasury, Adam's refusal caused some administrative headaches for the petty bureaucrats in Eisenstadt.[41] Thereafter, we detect a note of hurt pride in Adam's dealings with Nicholas. Family hardships in Vienna would, in the months to come, oblige Adam to beg for more charitable donations from the prince; but it galled him to do so. It was a source of enormous satisfaction to him, in March 1824, to be able to repay Nicholas all this money with interest—a parting shot he would not have dared fire at his boy's other aristocratic benefactors.[42]

---

37. Johann Nepomuk Fuchs (1766–1839), a former pupil of Haydn, had been appointed Kapellmeister at Eisenstadt in 1809. The composer of many masses and twenty operas, Fuchs was one of Adam's most valued musical colleagues and took an active interest in Franzi's early development.
38. Acta Mus. nos. 170, 4213. See also CLV, p. 633.
39. Acta Mus. no. 3279.
40. Acta Mus. no. 170.
41. Acta Mus. no. 3506.
42. DM, p. 19. Something of Adam's bitterness towards Prince Nicholas rubbed off onto Liszt himself. In his marginal corrections to Johann Christern's biography of him (CFLW), he struck out Prince

On April 13, 1820, Adam petitioned the prince yet again, drawing attention to his son's growing musical powers.

> The fact that within twenty-two months he has easily overcome any difficulty in the works of Bach, Mozart, Beethoven, Clementi, Hummel, Cramer, etc., and can play the hardest piano pieces at sight, in strict tempo, correctly and without any mistakes, represents in my opinion giant progress.[43]

This petition, like the others, was turned down. Starting with this date, Adam became obsessional. The Esterházy documents disclose a father prepared to sacrifice everything for the sake of his talented son. He pointed out that even Eisenstadt, one of the cultural centres of Hungary, was far too limited a place in which to develop his son's artistry, and he now put forward a bold plan. It took the form of an educational curriculum for his son consisting of three broad aims:

1. to send the child to Vienna, where he would receive a proper moral [sic] upbringing;
2. to provide an excellent music teacher who would work with him at least three times a week; the boy would also learn French and Italian;
3. in order to secure rapid progress the boy would attend as often as possible concerts, operas, and sung masses.[44]

The total bill, Adam declared, would come to 1,500 florins. The prince's share would consist only of the educational expenses; living expenses would be taken care of by Adam. This was a desperate compromise borne of Adam's fear that if a bargain could not be struck with his intransigent employer, he and his family might remain forever prisoners of the mud and sheep of Raiding.

The reason for Adam's concern is not hard to find. A few months earlier, in the summer of 1819, he had paid a brief visit to Vienna, taking the seven-year-old boy with him, and had called on Carl Czerny. This visit was carefully documented by Czerny himself. It happens to be one of the best descriptions of the young Liszt to come down to us, all the more valuable because of its objectivity. Czerny was one of the shrewdest pedagogues of the day, a keen observer of music and musicians, and a man well qualified to evaluate musical talent.

Nicholas's name, whom Christern had identified as one of his benefactors, and added the terse comment: "Old Prince E. never did anything for me. . . ." (p. 9) The statement sounds ungrateful, and it is not entirely true. All his father's frustrations as a humble intendant of the Esterházy sheepfolds come out by proxy, so to speak, on such occasions.

43. April 13, 1820. Acta Mus. no. 3500.

44. Acta Mus. no. 170.

One morning in the year 1819, a short time after La Belleville[45] had left us, a man with a small boy of about eight years approached me with a request to let the youngster play something on the fortepiano. He was a pale, sickly-looking child who, while playing, swayed about on the stool as if drunk, so that I often thought he would fall to the floor. His playing was also quite irregular, untidy, confused, and he had so little idea of fingering that he threw his fingers quite arbitrarily all over the keyboard. But that notwithstanding, I was astonished at the talent which Nature had bestowed on him. He played something which I gave him to sight-read, to be sure, like a pure "natural"; but for that very reason, one saw that Nature herself had formed a pianist. It was just the same when, at his father's request, I gave him a theme on which to improvise. Without the slightest knowledge of harmony, he still brought a touch of genius to his rendering. The father (his name was Liszt, and he was a minor official in the service of Prince Esterházy) told me that he himself had taught his son up to now; but he asked me whether, if he came back to Vienna a year later, I myself would accept his little "Franzi." I told him I would be glad to, of course, and gave him at the same time instructions as to the manner in which he should meanwhile continue the boy's education, in that I showed him scale exercises, etc. About a year later Liszt came back to Vienna with his son and occupied a house in the same street where we lived, and I devoted almost every evening to the boy, since I had little time during the day.[46]

This document is important for several reasons. Liszt's first meeting with Czerny is not supposed to have occurred until 1821, after Adam had settled his family in Vienna. But Czerny's statement indicates that they met two years earlier, long before the "official" lessons began. The romantic story of Adam Liszt arriving in Vienna, beseeching the unyielding Czerny to hear his son play, and having Franz, close to tears, break down Czerny's resolve with a dazzling display of pyrotechnics is simply—a legend.[47] Far from being arranged on

---

45. Anne de Belleville (1808–80), another infant prodigy who made Czerny's name known throughout Europe.

46. CEL, pp. 27–28. A document in the Esterházy archives helps us to pinpoint this visit quite accurately. Acta Mus. no. 170 discloses that Adam was given eight to ten days off on August 12, 1819. The primary purpose was to search out employment in Vienna. Since Adam and the boy were back in Raiding by September 21, we may assume that the first encounter between Liszt and Czerny took place in mid-August 1819. This same document, written by Szentgály the steward, also reveals that Adam wanted "to attend his son's concert in Baden" during this trip to Vienna. There is no mention of this Baden concert in the local press, nor is there any corroborating document in the Baden archives. (See CLV, p. 632.)

47. See RLKM, vol. 1, p. 35, where the story originated.

impulse, these lessons were planned in advance, and became the raison d'être for the Liszt family's leaving Hungary. The impending move to Vienna helps to explain why Adam now chose to bring his son to public attention. He needed money, and he was resolved to raise it through concerts and private subscription.

VII

Adam presented his son to the public for the first time at a concert held in the Old Casino,[48] in nearby Oedenburg, in October 1820. The concert was arranged by a blind flautist, one Baron von Braun,[49] who had himself been an infant prodigy but was now out of favour with the public. Liszt was an "additional attraction," the baron doubtless hoping that the presence of a wunderkind on his programme would attract a larger audience and revive his sagging fortunes. Liszt played the Concerto in E-flat major by Ries, and he extemporized a fantasy on popular melodies. His success was overwhelming. Adam touchingly related in his diary that just before the boy seated himself at the piano, the fever attacked him once more, "yet he was strengthened by the playing. He had long manifested a desire to play in public and exhibited much ease and courage."[50]

Emboldened by this success, Adam announced that the boy would appear in a concert of his own at Pressburg, the ancient capital of Hungary. He shrewdly arranged the concert for Sunday, November 26, so that it coincided with a meeting of the Diet, when the city was full of Hungarian magnates. The concert, which was held at noon, was a glittering occasion, for the audience consisted largely of members of the nobility. Franz appeared in a braided Hungarian costume,[51] and was given a tumultuous reception. We still have a press report of the event which appeared in the *Pressburger Zeitung*.

> Last Sunday, on the 26th, at noon, the nine-year-old virtuoso pianist Franz Liszt had the honour of playing the piano before a glittering assembly of local nobility and connoisseurs of music in the home of Count Michael Esterházy. His extraordinary skill and his ability to decipher the most difficult scores and to play at sight everything placed before him was beyond admiration and justifies the highest hopes.[52]

48. This building, which dominated the Casino Platz in Oedenburg, was burned down in 1834.
49. RLKM, vol. 1, p. 25. He died before he was twenty. Some sources refer to the baron as a violinist.
50. OFL, the diary.
51. See the picture opposite.
52. November 28, 1820. This press notice makes it clear that the concert took place not in the palace of Prince Nicholas, but in the home of a lesser relative.

Liszt aged eleven, in Hungarian costume,
a lithograph by Ferdinand Lütgendorff (1823).

A group of Hungarian noblemen now came forward and offered to establish a fund to enable Liszt to pursue his studies abroad. They were led by Counts Amadé, Szapáry, and Michael Esterházy, and for the next six years they guaranteed Liszt an annual stipend of 600 florins.[53]

And so the Liszt family prepared to move to Vienna. There were still difficulties ahead. Adam's finances were in a parlous state, and he had no job. Looking back on those early years, Liszt was astonished that he should ever have survived them. No great composer had ever started from humbler beginnings. Cut off from the civilized world, condemned to lifelong servitude in the tightly run Esterházy domains—it seemed to him in retrospect a miracle that his family succeeded in breaking out of these narrow confines and that he himself leapt to world prominence before he was fifteen years old. For this he thanked his father, to whom he affectionately ascribed an *"intuitive obstinacy—a quality found only in exceptional characters."*[54] As for Anna, a highly practical house-wife, she had looked on anxiously while her husband sacrificed his secure position for the sake of the boy's career. She is said to have given up her dowry of 1,200 gulden, carefully set aside across the years of their marriage, to help towards her "Franzi's" education in Vienna, since she believed unshakeably in the calling of her son.[55]

---

53. CFLW. Liszt confirms this figure in a marginal note on p. 11 of Christern's book. He also inserted the name of Michael Esterházy as one of his principal benefactors. On p. 9, as we have seen, he struck out the name of Prince Nicholas Esterházy, and went on, "I should under no condition want this thoroughly wrong information to gain credence." Even at the end of his life Prince Nicholas was Liszt's bête noire. He was angered by Trifonoff's biographical sketch of him (TL), which had repeated the story that Nicholas had given him "loads of presents" as a child. Liszt scratched out the offending sentence and added, "Prince Nicholas never gave me a single present." (WFLR, p. 216.) The wealth of these Hungarian magnates, incidentally, was beyond calculation. In 1809 the gross returns from the Amadé estates for that year alone were 800,000 florins. (KHC, p. 143.)
54. VFL, p. 111.
55. Acta Mus. no. 3279; GL, p. 135.

Vienna, 1821–1823

Never before had I had so eager, talented, or
industrious a student. . . . After only a year I could
let him perform publicly, and he aroused a degree
of enthusiasm in Vienna that few artists have
equalled.

CARL CZERNY[1]

I

The Liszt family arrived in Vienna in the early spring of 1822. Adam lost no time in contacting Czerny, and the young Liszt was at once placed under his charge. The question of musical theory was more difficult. Adam's choice finally fell upon Antonio Salieri, one of the most distinguished operatic composers of the day. Let us consider these two musicians in greater depth.

Carl Czerny was born in Vienna in 1791. From infancy his piano teacher had been his father, himself a professional musician. By the age of three, Czerny was already playing simple pieces on the piano. His progress thereafter was rapid; by the age of ten, Czerny could play by heart most of the principal piano compositions of the leading masters. One of his father's closest friends was the violinist Wenzel Krumpholz, an enthusiastic admirer of Beethoven. It was thanks to Krumpholz that Beethoven was prevailed upon to hear the ten-year-old Czerny, and was so impressed with the boy's performance of his newly published *Pathétique* Sonata that he agreed to take him as a pupil. That set the seal on Czerny's career. The few years he spent with Beethoven so enhanced his reputation that he was quickly besieged on all sides with requests to take pupils. Teaching soon became his chief preoccupation, and from his fifteenth year that is how he earned his livelihood.

Czerny, a lifelong bachelor, lived in the home of his parents, to whom he was devoted. His industry was staggering. He tells us in his autobiography that

---

1. CEL, p. 28.

he taught from 8 a.m. to 8 p.m., giving twelve lessons a day in the homes of the Viennese nobility.[2] He describes this experience as "lucrative but taxing." Nonetheless, he kept it up for twenty years, finally abandoning teaching entirely in 1836. Although his compositions have never been properly catalogued, they number more than a thousand opuses and consist of symphonies, overtures, concertos, quartets, trios, three hundred religious works, and, best known of all, several hundred studies and exercises for the piano.[3] Added to this was his interest in scientific literature, languages (he could speak Czech, Italian, French, and German), and classical antiquity. Among his unpublished manuscripts are essays, plays, and translations from classical authors. Czerny's pen was indefatigable.

The best account we have of Liszt's lessons with Czerny comes from Czerny himself. Liszt was a "natural," he claimed, who played according to feeling. At first he found his playing wild and exaggerated and saw that he must regulate and strengthen the boy's technique, hitherto badly neglected. An adherent of the "finger-equalization" school, Czerny knew that nothing worthwhile could be achieved in piano playing until the technical foundations were secure. He began by giving the boy massive doses of endurance exercises. For the first few months master and pupil concentrated on scales in all the keys (which Liszt soon played with "masterful fluency"), on correct fingering, on strict rhythm, and on tone production. All these things were instilled into his young pupil, according to Czerny, for the first time. Liszt was made to drop his entire repertory for a barren regime of mechanical exercises. Not surprisingly, a crisis developed between the two which was not resolved until Czerny relented and at last moved his pupil on to an intensive study of Clementi's sonatas, followed by works of Hummel, Ries, Moscheles, Beethoven, and Bach.[4] Especially interesting is Czerny's disclosure that he forced Liszt to learn everything quickly, thus compelling him to become an expert sight-reader. The boy soon acquired a reputation among the Viennese music sellers for being able to sight-read whatever was placed before him. In those days, all the larger music shops in the city displayed pianos in the middle of the sale room, on which the customer might try out new pieces before making his purchase. On one occasion, we are told, Liszt walked into a trap. The shopkeeper, tired of being asked by him for "something very difficult," put Hummel's new Concerto in B minor on the music desk, a work which makes heavy demands. Liszt read it through at sight, much to the shopkeeper's chagrin.[5] Czerny may have been a hard taskmaster, but it was exactly what the boy needed. Liszt was taught to think, and to think independently, about piano playing. Later, in the mid-

2. CEL, p. 25.
3. The most complete catalogue yet to appear may be found in CEL, p. 55.
4. CEL, p. 28.
5. RLKM, vol. 1, p. 40.

1830s, when he was on the brink of that historic breakthrough in his playing which Liszt scholars to this day call "transcendental," he was able to look back in gratitude to these months of toil and know that Czerny had been absolutely right. Indeed, he was to symbolize that fact by dedicating his Transcendental Studies to his old master.

Since the Liszt family now lived in the same street as the Czernys,[6] his teacher was able to see "Franzi" every evening. The boy almost became one of the family and was affectionately nicknamed "Puzzi" by them. Czerny, according to his own testimony, not only lent the boy large quantities of music, but taught him free of charge. This remarkable act of generosity was never forgotten by Liszt.[7] He was to repay Czerny a hundredfold in the years to come by introducing his works to the Parisians with stunning success.[8] And through his continual advocacy of Czerny's teaching ("my dear, revered master") he helped to smooth a path for his mentor when Czerny stayed for a time in Paris in 1837.

Liszt's other teacher was the great Italian composer and theorist Antonio Salieri. Born in Legnago, near Verona, he had picked up the rudiments of music as a boy from his elder brother Francesco, a pupil of Tartini. His parents having died while he was young, Salieri was befriended by Florian Gassmann, a Bohemian composer and a former Kapellmeister to the Emperor Joseph II of Austria. Gassmann treated the boy as his son, found teachers for him, instructed him in the craft of composition, and introduced him into Viennese court circles. When Salieri was only twenty-four, Gassmann was killed by a fall from his carriage. The young man immediately returned Gassmann's many kindnesses to him by looking after his family and educating his two daughters. Four years later, Salieri reached his definitive position, Court Kapellmeister to the Emperor of Austria, a prestigious job that he was to hold for thirty-six years. Salieri had a number of famous pupils. Schubert was his student for four years (1813–17), after his first teacher, Wenzel Ruzicka, had declared, "the boy knows everything already; he has been taught by God." Salieri, apparently, had no qualms about taking over from the Almighty.[9] Another pupil was the

---

6. Krugerstrasse 1014, on the second floor. (CEL, p. 28.)

7. We find an echo of it in his treatment of his own pupils, none of whom (after the mid-1850s) was charged a penny for his services, and one or two of whom (Tausig, for example) had the run of his home in Weimar. One of Liszt's earliest pupils, Hermann Cohen, was even dubbed "Puzzi" by his teacher. As Czerny's star began to decline, and his hundreds of keyboard works became relegated to the classroom as technical fodder for the young, Ramann thought it quite proper to describe him as "Der Mann der Mechanik und Form." (RLKM, vol. 1, p. 37.) In Liszt's personal copy of her book he struck out this phrase and wrote in the margin "Nicht ganz richtig" ("Not quite right").

8. LCRT, p. 242.

9. Schubert lived in Vienna for much of Liszt's stay there, a stone's throw away, at Göttweigerhof 1155. Surprisingly, the two composers never met. We have Liszt's own testimony for that. He later told his pupil August Göllerich: "Schubert . . . habe ich nicht persönlich gekannt." ("I never knew Schubert personally.") (GL, p. 20.) Such a categorical denial is worth stressing, since a rumour

famous pianist Moscheles, who left a touching account of his master in his diary. Even Beethoven occasionally sought Salieri's advice and was pleased to style himself "Salieri's pupil."

Hanging over Salieri for the last thirty years of his life was the slander of his having "poisoned" Mozart from feelings of professional jealousy. This mendacious story held the Viennese public in thrall, and it pursued Salieri to the grave. Moscheles, who visited Salieri in hospital during his last illness, relates that he tearfully protested his innocence to the last.[10] It is strange that the composer of so many operas and choral and instrumental works, highly regarded during his day, should now be remembered by this gruesome legend, which merely stains the reputation of its perpetrators. They appear not to have heard of Goethe's maxim "Eine neue Wahrheit ist nicht so schädlich als ein alter Irrtum."[11]

When Liszt became his pupil, Salieri was already past seventy. But he was an outstanding teacher, and since he was still the Royal Kapellmeister (he finally retired from that post on full salary in 1824) his name carried weight and authority—the very reasons why Adam chose him to be his son's mentor. Salieri showed great kindness to the young boy. He, like Czerny, taught Franzi free of charge, evidence of a rarely reported aspect of his character. A letter Salieri wrote to Prince Esterházy, in which the aged pedagogue expressed amazement at hearing Liszt sight-read and improvise, makes a number of facts clear. It reveals that Liszt commenced his lessons with Salieri in mid-July 1822 and that father and son used to walk from their temporary lodgings in the Mariahilf to Salieri's house three times a week. Because the journey was a long one, the boy used to arrive at Salieri's exhausted. The Royal Kapellmeister's voice was now added to the growing list of those who interceded with Prince Esterházy on Liszt's behalf.

> Vienna, August 25, 1822
>
> Your Highness,
>
> The most humble undersigned dares to ask a great favour of Your Highness's goodness.
>
> The young boy Francesco Liszt,[12] whom I heard by chance in a certain house while he was sight-reading and improvising on the piano, has left me so entranced that I actually believed I had been dreaming.

---

of a meeting with Schubert has haunted the Liszt literature for years. For example, it occurs in SL, p. 11, and SML, p. 125. The fiction is also entombed within *The New Grove* (1980), vol. 11, p. 29.

10. MAML, vol. 1, pp. 84–85.

11. "A new truth is not so harmful as an old mistake." See BSM.

12. Varied readings of this phrase have come down to us. The holograph has "il fanciullo Francesco Liszt."

I learned, after speaking to and heartily complimenting the father, that he is in Your Highness's service and that he had obtained permission to remain in Vienna for a year so that his son could study languages and could specialize in the study of his instrument with some of the best masters in this field. In addition, the father informed me that he had found all the tutors, with the exception of one, for the study of figured bass and composition.

When I finally realized that he intended to ask me to instruct his son, I immediately offered my services with great pleasure, motivated solely by friendship, as I have been wont to do these many years with poor students. Therefore, since the middle of last month, the father has been escorting his son to my home three times per week. The young man has been making extraordinary progress in singing, in figured bass, and in deciphering full scores of different genres, three disciplines in which I drill him during each lesson in order to introduce him gradually to composition and in order to maintain his sense of good taste.

On hot days the boy, accompanied by his father, always used to arrive about eleven at my home, perspiring heavily and overheated. It was as a result of this that I came to learn that they were lodging at Mariahilf. I pointed out to the father that on bad days this journey would be dangerous to the delicate constitution of his son and that it would be necessary to find accommodation in the city. The father answered that Your Highness had been beseeched so that this could be accomplished, but that an answer had not, as yet, been forthcoming. Lately, he has informed me that Your Highness has also accepted a petition concerning this matter.

So that this letter will not become any more tedious for Your Highness than necessary, I wish simply to add my most fervent entreaties to those of the aforementioned petition, and to promise Your Highness to double my zeal by having him come to my home every day, since I feel that his God-given musical talents are worthy of attention.

Humbly begging forgiveness for the liberty I have taken, I have the great honour of designating myself Your Highness's most humble, most devoted, and most indebted servant,

Antonio Salieri
Kapellmeister of the Imperial
and Royal Court of Vienna[13]

---

13. Acta Mus. no. 3325.

Neither Adam nor Liszt ever learned of the existence of this letter. Salieri's remarkable intervention remained an act of disinterested kindness, prompted only by admiration for the boy's "God-given" talent and a desire to see it prosper. After the Liszt family had finally managed to move to the city centre, the seventy-two-year-old composer generously saw his young pupil every day, continuing to teach him without payment. Liszt's first composition, a *Tantum Ergo* which has since been lost, was completed under Salieri's supervision. As with Czerny, Liszt never forgot the kindness of Salieri. Sixty years later Liszt remarked, "He still has my deep gratitude."[14]

II

It was while Liszt was studying in Vienna that he published his first extant composition. In 1822 Diabelli, the publisher, invited fifty-one of the most prominent musicians then living in Austria and Germany each to write a variation on a waltz he himself had composed. Everyone accepted, including Schubert, Czerny, Moscheles, Cramer, and the eleven-year-old Liszt, who was the youngest musician in the group. Everyone, that is, except Beethoven; he dismissed Diabelli's waltz as a "cobbler's patch." Shortly afterwards, however, he relented and composed not one but thirty-three variations on Diabelli's tune. Diabelli must have viewed the results, which immortalized his name, with mixed feelings. Not only had he now got two sets of variations on his hands, but a comparison between them was embarrassing. Beethoven's set is today ranked, together with Bach's *Goldberg* Variations, as a towering masterpiece, one of the greatest compositions of its genre. Diabelli's set, however, the one by fifty different composers, is a mere curiosity. The variations unfold not according to musical necessity but according to the alphabetical order of the composer's names. Assmayer, Bocklet, Czapek, Drechsler follow one another in stupefying succession. Certain individual variations do nonetheless stand out, including a particularly beautiful one by Schubert. Liszt composed his own variation in the style of a bold study in broken chords. It is clearly influenced by his master Czerny, and the crossing hands make a brilliant effect. On the manuscript is written, "Liszt, Franz (boy of eleven years), born in Hungary."

---

14. TLMF, vol. 2, p. 388. "[Salieri] had the great kindness of generously teaching me, in 1822 and

It makes no sense to play this little piece out of context, and the context itself is so strange that performances of the entire work are rare. And so the piece resides in oblivion. Its chief interest today lies in the fact that it gives us a glimpse into the future of Liszt's art, a future that was to become increasingly virtuosic.

III

Since playing in Pressburg two years earlier, Liszt had given no public concerts. Czerny had discouraged it; he was reluctant to have Franzi presented to the critical Viennese public before he was ready. Liszt's reputation grew, nonetheless, because of the private performances Adam arranged in the houses of the Austrian aristocracy. Soon pressure mounted for a public display of the boy's powers. Much of it came from Adam himself, and we shall shortly discover why. Czerny put Liszt through ten months' rigorous training before finally allowing the boy to face his critics. Liszt's first Viennese concert took place in the town hall on December 1, 1822, and he shared the billing with Caroline Unger, a nineteen-year-old Austro-Hungarian singer,[15] and Leo Lubin, a vio-

---

1823 in Vienna, not the art of composing—which can hardly be learned—but to become closely acquainted with the various clefs and procedures used in the scores of his time."

15. An interesting character sketch of Caroline Unger (1803–77) is preserved in LLF, pp. 74–80. Eighteen months after appearing in this concert, she sang the contralto part in Beethoven's Mass in D major under the composer's direction (May 1824). It was Unger who gently turned the deaf composer round to face the audience, so that he could see the applause he was unable to hear.

linist. Fräulein Unger sang an aria from Rossini's opera *Demetrio e Polibio,* while Liszt's contribution to the programme was Hummel's Concerto in A minor and a "free fantasy." The *Allgemeine Zeitung* carried a report of the concert.

> A young virtuoso has, as it were, fallen from the clouds, and compels us to the highest admiration. The performance of this boy, for his age, borders on the incredible, and one is tempted to doubt any physical impossibility when one hears the young giant, with un-abated force, thunder out Hummel's composition, so difficult and fatiguing, especially in the last movement.

The same notice referred to the "free fantasy" with lesser praise.

> We should prefer to call the fantasy a "capriccio," for several themes united by voluntary passages do not deserve that magnificent title, too often misused in our day. And yet it was really fine to see the little Hercules unite Beethoven's andante from the Symphony in A and the theme of the cantilena from Rossini's *Zelmira,* and knead them, so to speak, into one paste. *Est deus in nobis!*[16]

Liszt's success in Vienna was now assured. "Little Hercules," having "fallen from the clouds," appeared in several concerts thereafter, always in a supporting role, but always adding to his stature with each appearance.

Until recently, nothing whatever was known about the Liszt family's domes-tic circumstances during their stay in Vienna. But we can now fill in some details, thanks to the source material discovered in the Esterházy archives in Budapest. The background was depressing. The first few months were the worst. First, we learn that Adam's leave of absence from Raiding was not formally approved until April 9, 1822. Then he was unable to rent satisfactory accommodation in Vienna until May 8; a letter written to the manorial office in Eisenstadt on that date gives his address as Stiftgasse 92, at the house called Grüner Igel[17] (that is, the Green Hedgehog, possibly an inn or a hostelry). Finally, on May 16, Adam sent an urgent appeal to the prince for money. His funds were exhausted, he said, and he had spent his wife's dowry.[18] The prince remitted 200 florins in less than a week, an unusual display of haste, which indicates that Adam may have pulled some strings. By July he was desperate. His entire wealth now consisted of 162 florins. The family would soon have to move, he said, since Franzi's teachers would not travel out to the suburbs.

---

16. January 1823.
17. Acta Mus. no. 3531.
18. Acta Mus. no. 3279.

And then he added this revealing phrase: "the boy cannot cope with long distances, since he is often ill."[19] How the Liszts managed in the summer of 1822 is not yet known. We do know that by October they had moved to the centre of Vienna, for Adam then gave as his address Krugerstrasse 1014; they were now neighbours of the Czernys. The near-poverty of the Liszts helps to explain Adam's desire to see his son perform in public: he needed money urgently. It also explains Czerny's generosity towards Franzi; his philanthropy was an acknowledgement not only of Liszt's superb musical gifts, but also of the family's financial plight. The last straw for Adam was when he lost his job at Raiding, the prince appointing one Palisch to succeed him as intendant of the sheepfolds.[20] It was from this action that much of Adam's later bitterness towards Prince Esterházy stemmed.

Liszt's final Vienna concert took place in the famous Redoutensaal on Sunday, April 13, at midday.[21] The programme announced the event in the following manner:

With High Approval
the eleven-year-old youth

FRANZ LISZT

a native of Hungary
will have the honour of
giving

A CONCERT

in the small Imperial REDOUTENSAAL
on Sunday, April 13, 1823
at midday

Let us note the public acknowledgement that he was a native of Hungary. This assertion of his nationality recurred like a leitmotif in all his early concert

---

19. Letter of July 12, 1822. In 1823 the Esterházy Directorate, while considering a further request from Adam for a two-year leave of absence, came out with the phrase: "im Falle sein Sohn noch am Leben ist" ("in case his son is still alive"). (Acta Mus. no. 3550.)

20. Acta Mus. no. 3546.

21. Reports that Adam and his son journeyed all the way from Vienna to Arad (in Transylvania, several hundred miles away) in order to give a concert there in February 1823 must be discounted. They were circulated by the historian Sándor Márki towards the end of the last century (*Aradvármegye és Arad Szabad királyi város Története*, 1895) and were based on the unpublished diaries of a local Arad writer called János Vásárhelyi who claimed to have been present. The diaries have vanished and Márki's statements cannot be corroborated. It is unthinkable that Adam, who barely had the means to support his family in Vienna, would embark with his frail son on so arduous a journey for one concert, and there is no record of any other concerts being given in Transylvania at that time.

announcements. Soon it would become a battle cry, and the phrase "I am Hungarian!" would resound through the concert halls of Europe. Once again, the services of "assisting artists" were engaged. This was a usual practice; the sponsoring artist bore the expenses, but took the major billing. The supporting artists, on the other hand, helped to guarantee success: they lent variety, and often prestige, to the enterprise. Liszt played Hummel's Concerto in B minor and a set of Grandes Variations by Moscheles, and he rounded off the concert with his customary "free fantasy" on themes submitted by the audience. He was assisted by a group of singers from the Imperial Vienna Opera House, with an orchestra conducted by Herr Hildebrand.

Symphony in C minor (1st mov.)[22]	MOZART
Concerto in B minor for piano and orchestra	HUMMEL
Vocal Quartet (sung by singers from the Imperial Vienna Opera House)	CONRADIN KREUTZER
Grandes Variations for piano and orchestra	MOSCHELES
Aria (sung by Madame Schütz)	ROSSINI

Free Fantasy on the pianoforte from the concert-giver, on a written theme most humbly requested from Someone in the audience.

The inclusion of difficult works by Hummel and Moscheles, by common consent the two greatest pianists of the day, was a clever stratagem. A comparison to the young Liszt was here being openly invited. But it is the last item which calls for detailed comment. Behind its innocent formulation lies a minor musicological mystery which has vexed Liszt scholars for three generations. The deferential tone adopted in the announcement implies that the Someone in question was a figure of importance.[23] It was in fact Beethoven, who had twice been invited to the concert and who had only the previous day (April 12) been approached with an urgent request to provide this "written theme," but did not. Nor did he attend the concert; the fiction soon arose, however, that he did. Legend has it that as Liszt finished playing, Beethoven, amidst tumultuous applause, mounted the platform and kissed the young artist on the brow. Normally it would not matter two jots whether Beethoven was in the Redout-ensaal that day or not. But a set of circumstances later developed which appeared to suggest that Liszt might have deliberately put about this story from vainglorious motives. Because of the contradictory way in which the Liszt

---

22. Clearly a misprint; Mozart did not write a Symphony in C minor. The programme details are taken from the original handbill, now in the possession of the Vienna Historisches Museum.
23. "Freie Fantasie auf dem Pianoforte von dem Concertgeber, wozu er sich zum Sujet von Jemand der Zuhörer ein schriftliches Thema unterthänigst erbittet."

literature has dealt with this problem over the past one hundred and fifty years, we have a duty to try to set the record straight.

I V

The story of Beethoven's *Weihekuss*—his "kiss of consecration"—was reported many times during Liszt's lifetime and is now firmly embedded in the literature. It can be found in Ramann, Nohl, Kapp, Raabe, and others. The scene was even depicted in a commemorative lithograph published in Budapest in 1873 by István Halász to celebrate the jubilee (1823–73) of Liszt's Vienna début.[24] Halász's lithograph has been reproduced countless times as "proof" of Beethoven's public benediction, although it was brought out fifty years after the event it is supposed to portray. Liszt, who might have provided the correct information, chose not to do so. He must have known, however, that his biographers, Ramann and Ludwig Nohl in particular, both of whom were personally acquainted with him, were simply telescoping two quite different occasions.

What seems to have happened is this. A few days before the concert Liszt was taken to see Beethoven, who was by then totally deaf. It took considerable urging on the part of Schindler (his secretary) and Czerny to persuade the master to grant the interview at all, since Beethoven disliked child prodigies. The Conversation Books have a record of this authentic meeting.[25] The following entry was written either by Franz or by his father on his behalf.

> I have often expressed the wish to Herr von Schindler to make your high acquaintance, and I rejoice, now, to be able to do so. As I shall give a concert on Sunday the 13th, I most humbly beg you to give me your high presence.

The Conversation Books contain a series of entries in Schindler's hand, written sometime later. Beethoven's replies, of course, were spoken; but it is not difficult to read between the lines and guess that his reception of Liszt had been less than friendly. Schindler, probably feeling guilty about the outcome, approached Beethoven again, on Saturday, April 12, the day before Liszt's concert.

> "Little Liszt has urgently requested me humbly to beg you for a theme on which he wishes to improvise at his concert tomorrow.

---

24. BVL, p. 45 and p. 189.
25. BK, vol. 3, p. 168.

Ergo rogo humiliter dominationem vestrum, si placeat, scribere unum thema."[26]

"He will not break the seal till the time comes."

Beethoven did not provide this theme.

"The little fellow's improvisations do not amount to much."

"The lad is a fine pianist, but, so far as his fancy is concerned, it is far from the truth to say that he really improvises."

"Carl Czerny is his teacher."

"Just eleven years."

"Do come; it will certainly please Karl[27] to hear how the little fellow plays."

"It is unfortunate that the lad is in Czerny's hands."

"You will make good the rather unfriendly reception of recent date by coming to the little Liszt's concert."

"It will encourage the boy. Promise me to come."[28]

Schindler tells us categorically that Beethoven did not attend the concert.[29] This is corroborated by further entries in the Conversation Books themselves, which indicate that Beethoven merely heard about Liszt's concert from others. The Conversation Book for April 1823, for example, contains an exchange between Beethoven and his nephew Karl. Replying to his uncle, Karl reports that the concert was not full. Again, at the end of April 1823 Karl wrote, "Someone

---

26. "Therefore I humbly beseech your lordship, if it pleases, to write a theme." It is strange that Schindler switched to Latin here. Was he trying to cover his tracks? The craven tone of his request suggests that he was under intense pressure to get Beethoven to accede. It is well known that Schindler later put out two conflicting accounts: a false one, in which he said that Beethoven provided the theme, and, later, a true one, in which he said that Beethoven did not.

27. Beethoven's nephew Karl, not Carl Czerny.

28. BK, vol. 3, pp. 186–88. It is well known that Schindler tampered with the Conversation Books after Beethoven's death, and that he sometimes inserted entries for self-serving ends. Two such entries, posthumously "added" by Schindler, are given above: (1) "The little fellow's improvisations do not amount to much." (2) "It is unfortunate that the lad is in Czerny's hands." We do not require a great deal of insight to understand the motivation for these two entries. Schindler was ill disposed towards both Liszt and Czerny. We have reproduced his spurious entries here for a fairly obvious reason. Ever since the critical edition of BK, vol. 3, was launched in 1983, the knowledge of Schindler's editorial activities has raised doubts in the mind of the general reader about the authenticity of Liszt's meeting with Beethoven and about his request that Beethoven supply him with a theme on which to improvise. The omission of these two sentences, as we can see from a glance at the sequence of entries above, makes no difference to the situation as we have always understood it: the meeting between Beethoven and Liszt took place, and Liszt did request a theme.

29. BLB, p. 376. Schindler condemned Liszt's request for a theme from Beethoven as "thoughtless" and "unreasonable." He also observed that "the excessive enthusiasm for this boy exceeded the bounds of all reason."

from the Institute[30] was recently at the concert of the young List [*sic*], and said that he made many mistakes." All this is hearsay; Karl is telling Beethoven about an event neither of them had witnessed.

If, then, Beethoven was not there, who started the story that he was? It first turns up in Joseph d'Ortigue.[31] And as the years passed, it acquired some colourful embellishments. Schilling, for example, has Beethoven mounting the platform, taking the boy's hand, and pronouncing him "Artist!"[32] Ramann talks of Beethoven fixing him with his "earnest eye."[33] Corder even moves Beethoven to the front row of the audience—presumably out of consideration for his deafness.[34] Why did Liszt do nothing to deny the story? Because the essential part of it, for him, was true. There was indeed a *Weihekuss,* although it occurred in circumstances rather different from those invented by his biographers. Liszt himself left a record of his only meeting with Beethoven, giving this oral account to his pupil Ilka Horowitz-Barnay in 1875, more than fifty years after the event.

"I was about eleven years of age when my venerated teacher Czerny took me to Beethoven. He had told the latter about me a long time before, and had begged him to listen to me play sometime. Yet Beethoven had such a repugnance to infant prodigies that he had always violently objected to receiving me. Finally, however, he allowed himself to be persuaded by the indefatigable Czerny, and in the end cried impatiently: 'In God's name, then, bring me the young Turk!' It was ten o'clock in the morning when we entered the two small rooms in the Schwarzspanier house which Beethoven occupied, I somewhat shyly, Czerny amiably encouraging me. Beethoven was working at a long, narrow table by the window. He looked gloomily at us for a time, said a few brief words to Czerny, and remained silent when my kind teacher beckoned me to the piano. I first played a short piece by Ries. When I had finished, Beethoven asked me whether I could play a Bach fugue. I chose the C-minor Fugue from the Well-Tempered Clavier. 'And could you also transpose the fugue at once into another key?' Beethoven asked me. Fortunately I was able to do so. After my closing chord I glanced up. The great master's darkly glowing gaze lay piercingly upon me. Yet suddenly a gentle smile passed over his gloomy features, and Beethoven came quite close to me, stooped down, put his hand on

---

30. BK, vol. 3, p. 199. The reference is to the Blöchinger Institute in Vienna, a private school at which Karl was then a student.
31. OFL (1835).
32. SEW, p. 415.
33. RLKM, vol. 1, p. 47.
34. CFL, p. 13.

my head, and stroked my hair several times. 'A devil of a fellow,' he whispered, 'a regular young Turk!' Suddenly I felt quite brave. 'May I play something of yours now?' I boldly asked. Beethoven smiled and nodded. I played the first movement of the C-major Concerto. When I had concluded Beethoven caught hold of me with both hands, kissed me on the forehead, and said gently: 'Go! You are one of the fortunate ones! For you will give joy and happiness to many other people! There is nothing better or finer!' " Liszt told the preceding in a tone of deepest emotion, with tears in his eyes, and a warm note of happiness sounded in the simple tale. For a brief space he was silent, and then he said: "This event in my life has remained my greatest pride—the palladium of my whole career as an artist. I tell it but very seldom and—only to good friends!"[35]

According to this account, the *Weihekuss* took place in Beethoven's home, not in the concert hall. And Beethoven's Conversation Books corroborate that this is where a meeting actually did take place. There was, in fact, only one occasion when Liszt wrote about the kiss, in a letter to the Grand Duke of Weimar, at which time he merely says that Beethoven had on one occasion "consecrated my brow with a kiss."[36] He mentions nothing about the concert. Liszt may therefore be absolved from the charge of deliberately misleading his biogra-

---

35. *Neue Freie Presse,* July 7, 1898. See also FBLM, pp. 103–4. Felix Raabe (RLS, vol. 1, p. 230, fn. 12) describes this account as "unbelievable." It is true that Beethoven did not move to the Schwarz-spanier house until 1825; in April 1823 he was living in an apartment on Kothgasse and Pfarrgasse. But when Liszt made this slip he was relating an event which had taken place fifty-two years earlier.
36. LBLCA, p. 116. This letter deserves the closest scrutiny. Liszt is telling the Grand Duke about a new work of his, the *Vision à la Chapelle Sixtine,* and about a mystical experience surrounding it. He relates to the duke a story which is famous in the annals of musical history, in which the fourteen-year-old Mozart, having heard a performance of Allegri's *Miserere* in the Sistine Chapel, a secret piece performed during Holy Week whose circulation was strictly forbidden, then went back with his father to their lodgings and copied out the entire piece from memory. Liszt says that he himself has stood many times on that same historic spot where this remarkable event took place. He then makes the shrewd comment that Mozart had actually rescued Allegri's work from oblivion: hitherto one had to make a pilgrimage to Rome to hear it. Then he goes on: "It seemed to me as if I saw him [Mozart], and as if he looked back at me with gentle encouragement. Allegri was standing by his side, basking in the fame which his *Miserere* now enjoyed.
". . . Then there emerged from the background, next to Michelangelo's *Judgement Day,* slowly, unutterably great, another shadow. Full of inspiration, I recognized it at once; for while he was still bound to this earth *he had consecrated my brow with a kiss* [my italics]. He, too, had once sung his *Miserere,* and no human ear had ever heard such a deep and sublime sighing and sobbing. Strange! Three times has the genius of Beethoven made use of Allegri's style, even to employing the same intervals—an ever-returning dominant—in order that it may always leave an impression of his immortality. One should listen to the "Funeral March on the Death of a Hero" [*Eroica*], the Adagio from the *Sonata quasi una fantasia* [C-sharp minor], and the mysterious dance of angels and spectres in the Andante of the Seventh Symphony. Is not the relationship of these three motives with the *Miserere* of Allegri quite striking?"
Among the many aspects of this interesting letter which call for comment, two can be dealt with here. The *Weihekuss* is mentioned in a highly charged emotional context. Liszt is talking about a

phers. It is surely they who mixed up these two quite separate events: the visit to Beethoven's home on the one hand, and the concert in the Redoutensaal on the other.

Liszt treasured the memory of the *Weihekuss* all his life. He himself said that it set the seal on his career. When, in November 1873, the fiftieth anniversary of that career was celebrated in Budapest, the entire musical world knew that it was this Vienna concert, and the kiss of Beethoven in particular, which was deemed to have marked its true beginning. But more than that, the kiss was symbolic of Liszt's special relationship with Beethoven. He came to regard it as one of his artistic missions to promote Beethoven's cause. He became one of the greatest Beethoven interpreters of the nineteenth century, introducing such difficult works as the *Hammerklavier* Sonata to an unwilling public. He spent twenty-five years perfecting his remarkable series of piano transcriptions of Beethoven's nine symphonies, an artistic tribute par excellence and one of the grand peaks of the art of arrangement. He acquired Beethoven's death mask and his Broadwood piano, and regarded both as treasured relics.[37] For a brief time, he even possessed Beethoven's will. Finally, the statue honouring Beethoven's memory that today stands in Bonn could never have been erected in 1845, the seventy-fifth anniversary of his birth, without Liszt's initiative.

v

After Liszt's appearance in the Redoutensaal Adam could look back on their short stay in Vienna with considerable satisfaction. Every one of his objectives

---

metaphysical moment in artistic creation. If, as some scholars maintain, the story of the kiss is a fabrication, then it is Liszt who is fabricating, and in the most blatant fashion. But Liszt had no cause to invent the story. A kinder view sometimes encountered is that Liszt had a "faulty memory." It must be stressed that this letter of 1862 is the only occasion on which Liszt is known to have written about the topic. Incidentally, it requires no special insight to see that for Liszt, the shade of Beethoven stood in the same relationship to him as the shade of Allegri had to Mozart. Liszt's task was to "rescue" Beethoven from oblivion and to make him famous. If such a view sounds naive, we must remember that Beethoven was, a hundred and twenty years ago, by no means the universally admired figure that he has since become. Beethoven was Liszt's god; Liszt was Beethoven's prophet.

The other point concerns the shaft of musical perception which led Liszt not only to bring together Allegri's *Miserere* and Mozart's *Ave Verum Corpus* (that is basically what the "vision" is about), but to link them, in turn, to the three Beethoven pieces mentioned above. In strictly musical terms there is a relationship among all five works, and it was astute of Liszt to observe it. See LBW and NLB.

37. Liszt came into possession of Beethoven's death mask, executed by Joseph Danhauser, in 1840, while giving concerts in Vienna for the Beethoven Memorial Fund. It eventually passed into the possession of Marie von Hohenlohe, daughter of Princess von Sayn-Wittgenstein. It was from Marie that the mask was acquired by the Historisches Museum of the City of Vienna, where it can be seen today. Beethoven's Broadwood piano was given by Liszt to Hungary and is now exhibited in the Hungarian National Museum, Budapest.

Liszt's "farewell" concert in the Redoutensaal on April 13, 1823, incidentally, was reported in the *Wiener Allgemeine Musikalische Zeitung*, no. 34. It is worth pointing out that this notice carries no mention of Beethoven. Surely the presence of the most famous living composer would not have gone unremarked had he been there. (LFL, p. 19.)

had been achieved. His son was now the centre of attention in the capital. He had played before the most critical audiences and had brought honour to his family, his teachers, and his country. He had published his first composition. Above all, he had grown in artistic stature and stood on the threshold of a shining career. Adam now let his ambition grow. He had long nurtured a dream to take Franzi on a European tour, with France and perhaps England as their ultimate destination. What could be done in the Redoutensaal could be done elsewhere. Adam, as we have seen, had been deprived of his livelihood in Raiding, so Hungary seemed temporarily barred to him; Austria had nothing new to offer, and so he now looked westwards—to Munich, Stuttgart, Augsburg, and Paris. A great deal of money could be made from such a tour. Czerny protested that it was too soon to expose the boy to the rigours of concert life, and he feared that the experience might harm him. To uproot such a talent for money was to him inexplicable. He expressed himself candidly in his autobiography, accusing Adam of wanting "pecuniary gain" from his son's talent and making it clear that the boy was removed from his care just as that talent had reached its "most fruitful stage."[38] Whether he voiced these opinions openly to Adam is doubtful, for the two men exchanged a friendly correspondence over the next several years. If anyone had a right to utter such critical views, however, it was Czerny, who had never made a penny out of his famous pupil. It is a fact that wherever Adam now took his son, the charge of exploitation followed him. It was strictly untrue; Adam was a loving father, concerned for the happiness and welfare of his son. Yet the boy was now the breadwinner for both parents, and we have evidence that Adam was sensitive about this delicate situation. On at least two occasions he issued a public denial of the charge of exploiting his son.[39]

And so, after a mere fourteen months with Czerny, the boy embraced his master, whom he was not to see again for fourteen years, and took his leave of Vienna. Apart from his father, Czerny was the only piano teacher Liszt ever had, and he kept a lively remembrance of him. Adam summed up the feelings of his family when he later wrote, en route for Paris: "Together with my wife and child I kiss your hands with utmost gratitude for this good work which you have lavished on our boy. Never will you be able to escape our heartfelt thanks."[40]

V I

Before embarking on the journey to Paris, Adam decided to return briefly to Pest in order to show off his brilliant son to his fellow Hungarians. The

38. CEL, p. 29.
39. See pp. 109–111.
40. LCRT, p. 236.

"homecoming" concert took place on May 1, 1823. Placards were posted in the streets of Pest bearing the following announcement:

High and Gracious Nobility!
Estimable Officers of the Royal and Imperial Army!
Esteemed Public!

I am Hungarian, and I do not know a greater happiness than to introduce to my beloved country the first fruits of my education and studies—as the first expression of my gratitude. What is missing yet of my maturity I intend to acquire with lasting diligence, and perhaps then I will have the good fortune to become a small branch of my country's glory.

No original copy of this text survives. We know about it today purely by chance. When Liszt returned in triumph to the Hungarian capital seventeen years later, in 1840, an art dealer called Károly Miller came forward with a copy he had carefully preserved over the years. He offered it to the periodical *Der Spiegel* and it was at once reprinted.[41] The announcement had been worded by Adam and was clearly intended to appeal to the patriotism of the Hungarians and to arouse their pride in his son's achievements.

The concert took place in the halls of the Inn of the Seven Prince-Electors (Hét Választófejedelem). Liszt played, among other things, the set of Grandes Variations by Moscheles, with which he had aroused the enthusiasm of the Viennese, and some "free fantasies" on themes submitted by the audience. An interesting review of the concert appeared in the Hungarian journal *Hazai's Külföldi Tudósitások.*

The eleven-year-old boy from the District of Sopron has unfolded his talents on the Klavir [*sic*] to our astonishment. In all pieces the handsome blond youth has shown such a skill, lightness, accuracy, sentiment, pleasant strength, and masterful grip that the entire gathering was filled with joy and admiration. . . .

Because of his splendid playing everybody came to hope that he will bring glory to his homeland. . . . We wish to this beautiful soul health and long life . . . who with this concert wished to pay his respect to his homeland before he leaves for France and England, where he will certainly bring honour to the Hungarian name.[42]

41. *Der Spiegel,* 1840, pp. 7–8. See also Kálmán Isoz, "Liszt és Budapest," in *Liszt a miénk!* (Budapest, 1936), p. 71ff.
42. "Domestic and Foreign Reports," May 3, 1823.

Adam had scored an important coup. Young as he was, the boy was being publicly described as an ambassador of his country, someone who might one day "bring honour to the Hungarian name." This review, incidentally, also tells us that the first tour of England, which did not take place until the summer of 1824, had been planned by Adam at least a year in advance, since he here "leaks" it to the press as early as May 1823. The concert proved so successful that several others were quickly arranged, for May 10, 17, 19, and 24.[43]

Before the Liszt family took their leave of Pest, Adam paid a nostalgic visit to the Franciscan monastery in order to greet again the friends of his youth and to show them his remarkable son. He reminisced with his old companion and fellow novice Father Capistran Wagner. This monk made a profound impression on the mind of the young boy. Franzi played a number of pieces for the fathers, who were astonished at his genius. Adam was destined never to see any of the monks, nor indeed his beloved Hungary, again. When, seventeen years later, Franz Liszt returned to his native land and found himself in the midst of the wildest scenes imaginable, in celebration of the homecoming of the most famous living Hungarian, he did not forget the Franciscans. Recollections of this earlier visit came flooding back to him. He not only recalled everything he had seen as a boy in the monastery, but he asked after the monks by name; he even remembered the pieces he had played. So powerful was the pull of this childhood memory, in fact, that he consecrated an entire evening to the monks in order to revive the memories of his dead father and of his last visit to those cloisters.[44]

---

43. For further details see LFL, p. 20; LMZK, pp. 261–62 and 497. The details of the May 19 concert have been preserved in *Tudományos Gyüjtemény*, vol. 7, 1823, pp. 122–23. They are of great interest because they prove that the ten-year-old boy played the *Rákóczy* March and Weber's *Momento Capriccioso*, op. 12. Two pieces of misinformation current in the Liszt literature can now be corrected: Berlioz did not introduce Liszt to the *Rákóczy* March (Berlioz himself became acquainted with it, through Erkel, only in 1846), and von Lenz did not introduce Liszt to the piano music of Weber. (LGPZ.)

44. There is an absorbing account of this visit to the Franciscans in the contemporary journal *Társalkodó* (Pest), January 1840, p. 22. The church still stands in Budapest on the corner of Kossuth and Károlyi Mihály streets, although the Franciscan monastery which formerly adjoined it no longer exists.

Paris and the First World Tours

You can only guess at the acclaim he received
here; people spoke of nothing but wonders and
miracles.

ADAM LISZT[1]

I

In planning the boy's first world tour, Adam had very few precedents to guide him. Uppermost in his mind was the phenomenal success of the Mozart children, Wolfgang and Nannerl, who, sixty years earlier, had been taken on tour by their father and had set Europe by the ears. The fact that Adam followed a similar route—Munich, Augsburg, Strassburg, Stuttgart—should not surprise us. People were beginning openly to compare the young Liszt to Mozart, and it was typical of Adam to try to symbolize that fact publicly. Nonetheless, it was a formidable undertaking. Communications were poor. The railway system had not yet been introduced into Europe.[2] The roads were often little better than dirt tracks which, after a downpour of rain, either became impassable or developed potholes that could rip a wheel from a carriage moving at more than ten miles an hour. To travel a hundred miles under such conditions could be a major undertaking; Adam intended to travel a thousand.

Then there were the concerts themselves. Adam had to arrange each one personally. Sometimes he would do so with the help of powerful patrons; at other times the work would fall entirely on his own shoulders. The prospect of losing money was a real one. The modern reader is called upon to use his historical imagination and cast aside today's concept of a touring artist travel-

---

1. DM, p. 17.
2. The first public railway was opened in 1825, between Stockton and Darlington, in Durham. As for the continent of Europe, it was not until 1835 that the first railway line was built, in Germany, between Nuremberg and Fürth.

ling along a smooth, prearranged concert circuit consisting of a chain of musical centres professionally administered and with publicity and box office looked after in advance. The touring artist had not yet arrived; his parasites, the agent and the manager, were therefore scarcely imagined; the concert circuit did not exist. Adam would have to plan very carefully.

That he had a plan, and that he did not intend his son merely to drift on a haphazard tide of public acclaim, can be clearly demonstrated. As early as August 1823, before he left Vienna, Adam had approached Prince Metternich, the omnipotent Chancellor of Austria and former ambassador to Paris, for a letter of introduction. This document was released through the high office of the Vienna Chancellery and was signed by a top-ranking diplomat, Bretfeld, who was at that time the rector of Vienna University:

Letter of recommendation to the Royal Ambassador to
London and Paris and the Embassy in Munich

Vienna, August 8, 1823

The bearer of this letter, Mr. Adam Liszt, an official in the service of Prince Esterházy, who with his son intends to go on a tour through Munich and Paris to London, has asked me to write a letter recommending him to Your Excellency.

The musical talent of this boy is a really unusual, momentous phenomenon, and in every respect it deserves encouragement in order not to be frustrated in the development of its originality. So I have had no hesitation in agreeing to his request, and I recommend this promising young artist to Your Excellency for your kind acceptance and ask that you confer on him the patronage necessary for the fulfillment of his originality. I also ask you to arrange for those further dispositions which, in the case of famous and recognized artistry, every talented countryman of ours has, up to now, enjoyed on his journey through Paris, London, and Munich, even when he has not been invited.

I offer Your Excellency, on this occasion, the renewed assurance of my lasting devotion.

BRETFELD[3]

Munich, Paris, London. Adam's strategy was clear enough, and it would take at least a year to carry out. Behind the smooth, diplomatic surface of this letter two things can be perceived. First, we observe the regard with which Metternich held "Little Hercules," for the document would not have been issued

---

3. HLP, pp. 243–44. The holograph is kept in the Hof- und Staatsarchiv, Vienna.

without his sanction. Second, there is the phrase, "The musical talent of this boy . . . deserves encouragement in order not to be frustrated in the development of its originality." Liszt was now showing a flair for composition; a teacher had to be found to help him cultivate this gift. Metternich himself was to write the letter of introduction through which Adam started to nourish the hope of gaining entrée for his son into the Paris Conservatoire;[4] some of the best theorists in Europe were on its staff. And when this plan fell through, it was Metternich again who wrote to Ferdinando Paer about the young virtuoso, and who prevailed upon him to accept the boy as his composition student.[5] But all this was in the future. The tours still lay ahead.

I I

The Liszt family left Vienna on September 20, 1823. Their first stop was Munich, where they arrived on September 26. The city was full of visitors for the forthcoming Oktoberfest. Surrounded by a carnival atmosphere, the Liszts decided to prolong their visit and to stay in the Bavarian capital for a whole month. They were surprised to find that Moscheles was also in the city, and Adam wisely decided to postpone Franzi's concerts until the German master had played. Once more we observe Adam's sound instinct whenever his son's interests were at stake. He wanted the Munich public to draw the comparison; for Franz to appear immediately after Moscheles, one of the finest keyboard masters of the day, was a decided advantage. They heard Moscheles play one of his own concertos "in unrivalled fashion" with the excellent Munich Court Orchestra. His improvisation was a disappointment, however; Adam described it as "empty." Moscheles had other problems, too. He had attempted to capitalize on the presence of the Oktoberfest crowds by charging double prices, with the result that the hall was half empty.[6] It was now the boy's turn. Franz gave three concerts altogether,[7] two of them in the Court Theatre, for which Adam engaged the services of the same orchestra. Among the works Franz played was Czerny's Variations in E-flat major for piano and orchestra, a brilliant showpiece which, according to Adam, they had to repeat by popular demand. Adam had billed Franz as "a pupil of Carl Czerny." After the concert he was surrounded on all sides by admiring people wanting to know "whether Herr von Czerny had similar pupils." Adam later wrote a flattering letter to Czerny: "I gave them the reply that if pupils have talent and industry, they too can attain

4. OFL.

5. J.-G. Prod'homme, "Liszt et Paris," RM, p. 106.

6. LCRT, p. 237.

7. Two "solo" appearances took place on October 17 and 24. The third concert was shared with the violinist Karl Ebner, a youthful prodigy also from Hungary. (LCRT, p. 235.)

the same level of virtuosity from Your Excellency's wise and sound guidance."[8]
This lavish praise was Adam's way of repaying Czerny for his many kindnesses.
The royal family was present on two occasions, and the wunderkind was
presented to the king and the princesses. The king exclaimed, "Have you dared
come on the scene after Moscheles?," thereby revealing that he was well aware
of the comparison Adam had contrived. As the Liszts took their leave the king
embraced the boy and gave Adam various letters of introduction to Strassburg
and Paris.

The next step was Augsburg, where Franz gave three concerts in four days,
one of them in benefit of the poor. The Liszts' visit was clouded by rumours
of Salieri's attempted suicide. "God grant that it isn't true," Adam wrote to
Czerny. "Although I don't like being kept in suspense, I ask that you keep me
in the dark until we reach Paris."[9] After a brief rest the Liszts moved on to
Stuttgart, where two concerts had already been announced at the Court
Theatre, and then to Strassburg. From Adam's correspondence we gather that
he had made a "clean profit" of 921 florins from the first leg of the tour.

I I I

On December 11, 1823, the Liszt family at last arrived in Paris. Their post chaise
halted outside 10, rue du Mail, which in those days was the Hôtel d'Angleterre.
Here they disembarked after their tiring journey, unloaded their luggage, and
rented a suite of rooms.[10] Quite by chance, their hotel faced La Maison Erard,
the home of the celebrated piano manufacturer Sébastien Erard and his nephew
Pierre. This building housed the Erard workshops and a salon where public
recitals were held. Sébastien lived there with his two sisters, Catherine-Barbe,
and Elyse. We do not know the circumstances under which the Liszts and the
Erards first met, but the two families were soon on close terms. Liszt himself
later called the Erards his "adoptive family."[11] And in the case of Anna Liszt,
this friendship persisted for forty-three years. When she died in Paris in 1866,
at the venerable age of seventy-eight, the Paris press included the name of a

8. LCRT, p. 235.
9. LCRT, p. 236. In late 1823 false reports had begun to circulate that the seventy-three-year-old
Salieri had cut his throat in an attempt to commit suicide, and thus escape the campaign of vilification
mounted against him by those who believed he had poisoned Mozart. This campaign reached its
culmination at a performance of Beethoven's Ninth Symphony in Vienna on May 23, 1824, when
leaflets were circulated among the audience showing Mozart with his rival Salieri standing at his side
holding the poisoned cup. (BSM, p. 274.)
10. The accommodation at the Hôtel d'Angleterre, in the heart of the city, consisted of two reception
rooms on the ground floor and two adjoining drawing rooms above, with a pleasant view of the
street. A year later, the Liszts moved to 22, rue Neuve, St. Eustache, the old Hôtel Strasbourg.
11. RGS, vol. 2, p. 32; CPR, p. 40.

surviving Erard sister among the list of mourners attending the funeral service held at the Church of St. Thomas Aquinas on February 8.

Sébastien and Pierre Erard recognized the young Liszt's talent at once, opened many professional doors for him, and presented him with a new piano, one of their latest seven-octave models, which embodied their recently invented "double-escapement" action. This ingenious device allowed the player rapidly to repeat single notes before the key had fully rebounded, from a point midway between key bed and key surface, so that only the player's technique limited the rate of repetition. This was the instrument which Liszt subsequently took on tour with him and which, through his advocacy, was eventually introduced all over Europe. The high regard in which Adam Liszt held the Erard piano can be gleaned from his correspondence with Czerny.

> I believe this man [Sébastien] merits an important place in the field of piano manufacturers. . . . So far there are three pianos ready, and a fourth one is now being built for my son. After a time, we shall send it to Vienna. . . . The Erard piano reaches such a high level of perfection that it looks forward to the next century. It is impossible to describe it; one must see it, hear it, play it.[12]

Adam Liszt and Sébastien Erard seem to have worked out a business arrangement. Little Franzi would play on Erard pianos, providing Erard would ship them to their required destinations. Thereafter, the young Liszt was publicly advertised as an "Erard artist." For the next three years, Erard managed to have his new instruments waiting for Liszt at such scattered cities as London, Manchester, Bordeaux, and Geneva.[13] The advantage to Erard was obvious; he could sell without difficulty any piano this sensational boy had played on.

The day after their arrival in Paris, father and son presented themselves at the Paris Conservatoire. They arrived at the building at ten o'clock in the morning, accompanied by Erard. They were nervous and excited, and Liszt has described the awe he felt as he passed through the portals of the famous institution.[14] The director at that time was Luigi Cherubini, a stiff, formal, melancholy man. Cherubini, sixty-three years old, was a prolific composer of

---

12. LCRT, pp. 241–42, 254. Adam's letters to Czerny were published by La Mara in 1891. In her preface she claimed that it had been "a lucky chance" that had led her to discover the manuscripts in the archives of the Gesellschaft der Musikfreunde in Vienna. Alas, she was not as lucky as she thought. These letters had already appeared some twenty years earlier in the *Münchener Propyläen* of April 1869. Cosima Wagner, who was living in Munich at that time, subscribed to the *Propyläen* and was deeply moved by these long accounts of her father's childhood triumphs, written in such a glowing style by her grandfather. (WT, vol. 1, p. 81.)

13. See, for example, the public announcements of Liszt's Drury Lane concert on June 29, 1824, and his Manchester concert on August 4, 1824 (pp. 104 and 108).

14. RGS, vol. 2, p. 31; CPR, pp. 39–40.

operas (which were greatly admired by Beethoven) and of church music, and one of the most respected contrapuntists of his time. He had been in office for little more than a year when the Liszts arrived. As they were ushered into the director's presence, Liszt ran towards the old composer and kissed his hand, but then, thinking that he might have committed a faux pas, withdrew in confusion. Adam had met Cherubini twenty years earlier, it will be recalled, when the composer had visited Eisenstadt in 1805, and now hoped to make use of that connection. Cherubini gave no indication that he remembered their encounter. He received them politely, read their letters of introduction (one of them bearing the seal of Metternich), and then informed them that the present regulations forbade him to admit foreigners. This, in Liszt's words, came like a thunderclap. Cherubini himself was a foreigner. Blinkered by the rules of his office, this aging pedagogue refused to be moved by any of the arguments which Adam now brought to bear on him. The doors of the Paris Conservatoire remained shut.[15]

Other teachers had to be found. Adam's choice eventually fell upon Antonin Reicha for theory and Ferdinando Paer for composition. Both men had a fine reputation in their respective fields. Reicha was born in Prague in 1770. His early musical background had been varied and included a study of the violin, piano, and flute. In 1788 he went to Bonn and joined the orchestra as second flautist. There the eighteen-year-old musician met Beethoven, who played the viola in the same orchestra, and with whom he formed a friendship. This encounter awakened an interest in composition. Over the next two decades Reicha produced operas, symphonies, and a vast quantity of chamber music, on which his reputation still rests. Some of these works contain advanced harmonic combinations and are unusual also for their display of innovatory metres, characteristics which would later be taken up by the young Liszt. Reicha set great store by his *36 Fugues pour le piano,* which are dedicated to Haydn. In these works he deliberately set out to destroy the classical laws of fugue by placing his answers on any and every note of the scale, thus undermin-

15. OFL. D'Ortigue was the first writer to report this now-familiar story. Liszt himself left an emotional account of the event in RGS, vol. 2, p. 31, "On the Position of Artists" (1835). Despite the tendency among modern Liszt scholars to scoff at his account (including Haraszti, who discovered that a number of foreign students were enrolled at the Conservatoire at this time), Liszt's version is correct. On December 29, 1823, less than three weeks after Liszt and his father arrived in Paris, Viscount de la Rochefoucauld (Charles X's minister of fine arts) signed the following decree: "No applicant who is non-French will be able, by special dispensation or any other reason, to be admitted to the school in this branch of instruction"—i.e., the piano department (PCMHA, p. 307, doc. 471, article 4). The reason for the ban had nothing to do with Cherubini's "dislike of foreigners." It had to do with foreign *pianists,* who had descended on the Conservatoire in such large numbers that the piano department was in danger of collapsing, and the government decree, carried out with the full approval of the teaching faculty, was designed to stop it. Foreigners were never banned from other branches of instruction.

ing their tonal stability. Reicha also wrote a number of theoretical treatises, including his *Cours de composition musicale* (1818), which helped to gain for him, in the very year of its appearance, a professorship at the Paris Conservatoire. He became a naturalized Frenchman in 1829, and his achievements were crowned in 1831 when he was awarded the Legion of Honour.[16]

Paer stood in complete contrast. Born in 1771, in Parma, he had been appointed *maestro di capella* at Venice when he was only twenty. Thereafter he had composed a large quantity of church music and operas, which quickly made his name known beyond Italy. In 1798 he had moved to Vienna, where he met Beethoven. (It was Beethoven who, after hearing the Funeral March from Paer's opera *Achille* in 1801, came out with the memorable line: "I must *compose* that!"). In 1803 Paer was appointed Kapellmeister at Dresden. An important turning point came in 1806, when he accompanied Napoleon to Warsaw. The following year his position became unassailable: Napoleon appointed him his *maître de chapelle*. It was Paer who composed the bridal march for Napoleon's wedding to Marie Louise of Austria. Personally, Paer was greatly disliked. He grovelled before his superiors, and his penchant for stirring up intrigues among members of his own profession gained him enemies. But he had a strong capacity for survival, which was not seriously jeopardized even by Napoleon's downfall. In 1812 he succeeded Spontini and took charge of the Italian Opera, a post he retained until 1827. By the time of his death, in 1839, he felt overshadowed by Rossini; but posterity has assigned him a lasting, if modest, place in the history of opera.

These, then, were the two musicians whom Adam Liszt picked out to be his son's mentors. In the case of Paer, Adam received the powerful backing of Prince Metternich,[17] who had known the composer when he was Austrian ambassador to Paris. There was at least a year's delay before Franz started serious work with either teacher, and even then the arrangement was a loose one, punctuated by the boy's absences abroad. In retrospect, we can see that Cherubini's abrupt refusal to admit the boy to the Conservatoire ultimately worked to his advantage. His genius was allowed to develop unfettered. He was spared the rigours of institutional life, and with it much unhappiness. In this he enjoyed an advantage over his great contemporary Berlioz, for example, who at this very moment was being brought into sharp creative conflict with the Conservatoire's board of directors.

---

16. Excerpts from Reicha's unpublished autobiography appeared in MQLN, pp. 339–53.
17. Metternich's letter was reproduced by Prod'homme, RM, p. 106.

I V

Until comparatively modern times, little was known about Liszt's early years in Paris. We lacked even a rudimentary understanding of how the Liszt family managed to survive in this important and highly competitive metropolis. Liszt's "official" biographer, Lina Ramann, ignorant of Adam Liszt's letters and lacking any real first-hand documents, tells us nothing about Franz's daily life there during the three-year period 1824–27. Later biographers, taking their cue from her, assumed that there was, in consequence, nothing to tell. This was regrettable, since it was Paris that formed Liszt. He lived there for twelve years. He absorbed its culture and adopted its customs. He mastered its language and soon spoke French in preference to his mother tongue, which he quickly forgot. For the rest of his life he looked upon France with gratitude and affection. How, then, did he spend these early years?

According to a letter of Adam Liszt, his son played in public no fewer than thirty-eight times between December 1823 and March 1824.[18] The Paris newspapers first mentioned Liszt's appearance in the capital on December 22, 1823, when L'Etoile came out with a panegyric on him.[19] He first performed on New Year's Eve before the Duke of Orléans and the Duchess of Berry. The duke was so delighted with the boy's playing that he told him he could request any gift that he wished. With no thought to the incalculable wealth commanded by this aristocrat, to say nothing of the fabulous objets d'art with which he was surrounded, Franz, to the amusement of the other guests, cried out naively, "This clown!," pointing to a puppet on a string which was hanging from the wall.[20] On January 15, 1824, Le Corsaire reported that the boy had been elected an honorary member of the Société Académique des Enfants d'Apollon. An interesting account of this occasion is recorded in the minutes of the Société. Adam and Franz had been taken to one of its concerts to hear a local piano trio. The boy, unable to contain his excitement at hearing the music, ran to the keyboard and began improvising on themes he had just heard.

> The young Liszt, eleven years old,[21] was introduced to us by one of our composers, M. Chapellon. He was received as an interesting

18. DM, p. 16.
19. He is described in L'Etoile as being a year younger than he actually was. His spoken French is reported to be "fluent," which it wasn't. The author also succeeds in misspelling his name twice, referring to him first as "Leist" and then as "List." The French always had trouble in spelling Liszt's name and eventually settled for "le petit Litz," a title he came to abhor. In this, however, he had less to complain of than the violinist Rudolph Kreutzer, who, exasperated beyond endurance at the way in which the French mangled his name, eventually had his visiting cards inscribed "Bertrand."
20. "Diesen Hanswurst!," literally, a Merry Andrew doll. (SEW, p. 415.)
21. He was, in fact, twelve.

child. The concert began. The young visitor listened in silence and admiration, which didn't surprise us, to M. Baudiot (cello), M. Woest (piano) and M. Vogt (oboe). Liszt's natural impulses then took over, and he rushed towards the piano despite himself, took one of the motifs from the trio just executed, varied it, and gave it a new charm. At once one saw the renewal in him of the miracle that nature had produced in Mozart. Every transfixed listener thought himself transported by a dream into a place inhabited by the god of harmony. The clamour didn't stop until Liszt said that he wanted to rest. Then, by a spontaneous motion, Liszt was named a member of the Société. As a souvenir of this election, the Société had the prince make an engraving of the child.[22]

Thereafter *Le Corsaire* referred to the young Liszt as "the famous improviser" and led the way in the rush of critical eulogies that now rolled off the printing presses. *La Pandore, Le Journal des Débats, La Gazette de France, Le Diable Boiteux, Le Drapeau Blanc,* and *Le Moniteur Universel* were among those newspapers most vocal in their praise. It was not as if Paris were short of child prodigies. During the 1820s the young Larsonneur, the infant Léontine Fay, Anne de Belleville, the thirteen-year-old singer Euphémie Boyé, and the English child pianist George Aspull (born in Manchester) had been adulated by the public and duly celebrated by the press. But they all disappeared the moment the young Hungarian walked on the stage.

Adam now began negotiating for the rental of the Théâtre Italien so that his boy could appear before a larger audience. His letters, which were discovered in the archives of the Paris Opéra, reveal once again how capably he handled his son's affairs. After enlisting the support of Habeneck, the director of the Opéra, Adam elicited a favourable reply from the theatre management. The following letter of agreement was addressed to Habeneck.

From the Administration of the Royal Theatres

Paris, February 11, 1824

I have the honour of informing you that His Excellency the Minister of the Royal Household has, by a decision taken today, granted the use of the Salle de Louvois to the son of M. Liszt, so that he may give a concert there on Sunday evening for his own benefit, on condition that he play at one of the Concerts Spirituels.

By a letter written today, I have relayed this decision to M. Liszt,

---

22. DHEd'A, p. 137.

who must contact you so that you may converse together on the details pertinent to the execution of the concert.

In distinguished consideration,

Manager of the Royal Theatres,
BARON DE LA FERTÉ[23]

The use of the theatre, then, was given free, or rather the "fee" was to be a charity concert in the Concerts Spirituels series; these were favourable terms, and Adam readily agreed. The event was duly announced in *Le Corsaire* in its issue of March 1.

> The marvel of the day, the young Liszt, already famous at the age of eleven, and who has only been heard in Paris in certain circles, will give a public concert on Sunday next in which he will play and improvise on the piano. It is presumed that the Salle de Louvois will be too small to contain the crowd of music-lovers.

Although Liszt had already appeared in public numerous times during his childhood, it was this concert in the Théâtre Italien which represented his greatest public triumph so far, and which marked a turning point in his career. Most of Parisian high society was present for the first time, and many professional musicians were also in the audience; and since Adam had engaged a full symphony orchestra for the occasion, the spectacle inside the theatre resembled a gala occasion. Once again Liszt played Hummel's B-minor Concerto and also Czerny's Variations for piano and orchestra, works with which he had already achieved success in Vienna and Munich. Adam left a detailed account of the event.

> This concert was a public triumph for my boy. From the moment he appeared, the applause was almost without end; after every "passage" there was enthusiasm and the liveliest expressions of astonishment. After every piece he was brought back two or three times and applauded. The gentlemen of the orchestra relentlessly tapped their bows on the backs of their basses, cellos, violas, and violins, the brass players shouted themselves hoarse, and everyone was indescribably enchanted.[24]

The idea of an audience demonstrating its enthusiasm *during* the bravura passage-work of a performance strikes us as philistine today, and is an interesting social commentary on the times. Adam observed that he made 4,711 francs profit

23. HLP, p. 248.
24. DM, p. 17.

from the concert, and that "fourteen journalists competed with one another to write about the talent of my son."[25] One of these press notices, written by A. Martainville in *Le Drapeau Blanc* on March 9, has become a classic.

> I cannot help it: since yesterday evening I am a believer in metempsychosis. I am convinced that the soul and spirit of Mozart have passed into the body of young Liszt, and never has an identity revealed itself by plainer signs. The same country, the same wonderful talent in childhood, and in the same art. . . .[26]
>
> His little arms can scarcely stretch to both ends of the keyboard, his little feet scarcely reach the pedals, and yet this child is beyond compare; he is the first pianist in Europe. Moscheles himself would not feel offended by this affirmation.
>
> Mozart, in taking the name of Liszt, has lost nothing of that interesting countenance, which always increases the interest a child inspires us with by his precocious talent. The features of our little prodigy express spirit and cheerfulness. He comes before his audience with exceeding gracefulness, and the pleasure, the admiration which he awakens in his hearers as soon as his fingers glide along the keys, seem to him an amusement which diverts him extremely.
>
> It is a small thing for him, as Grimm said of Mozart, to execute an exceedingly difficult piece of music with the greatest precision, with assurance and unshakeable calm, with bold elegance, and yet with a feeling that brings out every shade; in a word, with a perfection that drives to despair the most skilful artists who, for the last thirty years, have studied and practised this beautiful and most difficult instrument.
>
> To give an idea of the impression he can make on his hearers, I will only mention the effect of his playing on the orchestra of the Italian Opera, the best in France and Europe. Eyes, ears, and soul were enchained to the magic instrument of the young artist. Meanwhile they forgot that they were also coadjutors in the concert, and at the return of the ritornello every instrument was dumb. The public, by their laughter and clapping, testified their hearty forgiveness of a distraction which was, perhaps, the most favourable acknowledgement the talent of the little prodigy has ever received.
>
> At first the instrument had been rather awkwardly placed, the end,

---

25. Ibid.
26. The article contains at this point a very long quotation from Grimm's account of the Mozart family's first visit to France in 1763—an account which enabled Martainville to develop his thesis that Liszt was really the reincarnation of Mozart. Ramann, too, omits this quotation, but fails to mention the fact—an indication that she had never read the original copy of *Le Drapeau Blanc*.

as usual, turned towards the public, and Liszt thereby quite hidden by the music stand. The audience expressed a wish to see the child; the direction of the instrument was changed so that he turned his back to the conductor. Without being put out of countenance by this new arrangement, he played, with the same composure he had already displayed during the concert, variations on a theme by Czerny, who is said to have been his teacher, if indeed it is true that he ever had a teacher. He scarcely looked at his notes, and then only at long intervals. His eyes wandered continually round the hall, and he greeted the persons he recognized in the boxes with friendly smiles and nods.

At last Liszt threw stand and notes aside, and gave himself up to his genius in a free fantasy. Here words are wanting to express the admiration which he excited. After a harmoniously arranged introduction, he took Mozart's beautiful air from *The Marriage of Figaro,* "Non più andrai," as his theme. If, as I have already said, Liszt, by a happy transmigration, is only a continuation of Mozart, it is he who has himself provided the text.

You have, no doubt, seen how a child plays with a chafer, which flutters unconsciously about, holding it by a silken thread or a long hair, following its rapid movements, letting the thread slip and then seizing it again; drawing the fugitive to him, only to let it fly again; only so have you any idea whatever of the way in which young Liszt plays with his theme, how he leaves it to take sudden possession of it again, and then loses it once more to find it again as quickly; how he leads it through the most surprising modulations, the happiest and most unexpected transitions through every key; and all this in the midst of the most astonishing difficulties which he seems to create in play, to have the pleasure of triumphing over them.

The warmest applause and repeated encores echoed through the hall. The proofs of delight and admiration were inexhaustible; even the tender hands of the fair female listeners were unwearied. The happy child returned his thanks with a smile.

Overnight "le petit Litz" had become the darling of Paris. A lithograph was made of him and displayed in all the print shops; the original was hung in the Louvre. Franz Gall, the founder of phrenology, took a cast of the boy's head in order to study it. Everywhere Liszt went, he was lionized and fêted. Whenever he appeared in the theatre, he "went the round of the boxes" during the interval, and was presented to admiring lords and ladies and petted by bejewelled dowagers. So many invitations were now showered on them that Adam set his son's minimum fee at 100 francs per appearance, and insisted that they be fetched and brought back again by carriage.[27] Whenever possible, Liszt played on Erard's new seven-octave piano, whose musical advantages were fast becoming obvious to everyone. This instrument produced a strong, full tone, and its "double escapement" made the faultless execution of trills and rapidly repeated notes a realistic possibility—perhaps for the first time in the history of the piano—which was a constant source of wonder and amazement.

There is no evidence that all this adulation spoiled the boy. Quite the contrary; he retained a childlike innocence which endeared him to all with whom he came into contact. Several thumb-nail sketches illuminate his character and appearance for us. He is described as possessing well-formed, regular features, and having a gentle manner.[28] His face, normally grave and meditative, would light up suddenly when registering an impression. He was as deeply religious as ever, and he and his father were regular worshippers at the Church of St. Vincent-de-Paul. The naiveté of the twelve-year-old Liszt is illustrated by the following anecdote. He was once walking down the Paris boulevards when he was stopped by a young street cleaner who begged him for a sou. Liszt, unable to deny the request, felt in his pocket but discovered that he only had a 5-franc piece. He asked the street cleaner whether he had any change. "No," came the reply, "but I can quickly get some." The street cleaner ran off, leaving his broom with the young artist. Liszt patiently stood there holding the broom. Only when he saw the astonishment of the passers-by did he realize how funny he looked, but he held on to the broom as his bounden duty, until its owner returned.[29] The newspapers reported that his conversation was animated and occasionally punctuated with both Italian and Latin; the former may have been acquired through his studies with Salieri, the latter through his father, who, we remember, read the classics and was fond of sprinkling his letters with judicious quotes from the Latin poets. Father and son frequently went to concerts, and during their first year in Paris they heard both Hummel and Anne de Belleville. Adam wrote critically of both artists, but especially of Belleville: "She did not play the piano, she bungled it through her ill-advised bravura runs and leaps."[30] What Czerny thought of this summary dismissal of his other famous prodigy pupil is not recorded. As for Hummel, they heard him four times in Erard's salon; Adam, after reporting on his thin audiences, observed that Hummel's improvisations were "dry." The prevailing view of Hummel, in fact, which was quickly relayed to Czerny, was that he was "half pianist and half organist":[31] the pianists thought he was an organist and the organists thought he was a pianist.

---

27. DM, p. 16.
28. *Le Moniteur Universel,* March 12, 1824.
29. OFL, p. 3.
30. LCRT, p. 256.
31. Ibid.

Music aside, this was the period during which the young Liszt absorbed French culture and laid the foundations for his knowledge of the French language. In March 1824, only four months after their arrival in Paris, Adam could write that Franzi already spoke French well, an observation readily confirmed by the fact that as a result of his recent success in the Théâtre Italien, he was now invited to compose an opera.[32] This was to be the one-act *Don Sanche,* first performed about eighteen months later on the stage of the Académie Royale, but already begun in the spring of 1824. Most important of all, perhaps, was the large network of artistic contacts the boy built up at this time, which was to serve him for the rest of his life and persuade him that Paris really was his second home.

It was the success of this trip to Paris which emboldened Adam to postpone taking his family back to Vienna after one year, as he had originally planned to do. He wrote to a friend in Eisenstadt that he did not now expect to return to the "Fatherland" until the summer of 1826, more than two years away.[33]

v

Meanwhile, what of Anna Liszt? Not once in the plethora of publicity surrounding the boy is she even mentioned at this time. Delighting in her son's success, she was nonetheless quite unable to participate in it; her plain manner, and perhaps the remembrance that not much more than a decade earlier she herself had been a chambermaid to that same class of family which was now celebrating her wunderkind, made her conscious of her station. Yet Anna loved Paris; in fact, she lived there for nearly forty years, longer by far than her famous son. As Adam's plans waxed more ambitious, it became impractical for Anna to accompany the family on the longer journeys, and she moved to her sister's in Graz, in the province of Styria, awaiting the end of the tours, at which time the family planned to be reunited. That, however, was not to be. The last time Adam saw his wife was probably in May 1824, shortly before he and Franz left for England. It is a very curious fact that although Adam lived for another three years, and although he brought his son back to France several times for extended stays, neither he nor the boy saw Anna on any of these occasions.

32. DM, p. 18.
33. Ibid.

V I

The Liszts now crossed the English Channel for the first time, arriving in London in early May. They were accompanied by Pierre Erard,[34] who shipped over with him one of his new pianos. The little party occupied lodgings at 18 Great Marlborough Street, where Erard's firm had its London branch. The very first mention of Liszt in a British newspaper was on June 7, 1824, when the *Morning Post* carried a brief item on the boy's London début, made two days earlier at a semi-private gathering in the Argyll Rooms[35] under the auspices of the Royal Society of Musicians. Surrounded by "eminent professors, amateurs and admirers of the fascinating science of music," Liszt created a sensation with the Erard piano. "To do justice to the performance of Master Liszt . . . is totally out of our power," wrote the *Post*. After appearing at a number of private soirées, the boy gave his first public concert on June 21, 1824, again in the Argyll Rooms. Although the concert clashed with one being given by the great Giuditta Pasta, it was well attended. Many pianists were there, including Clementi, Cramer, Ries, Kalkbrenner, Cipriani Potter, and other visitors to London, curious to observe the boy wonder and to hear Erard's new piano for themselves. Sir George Smart conducted the orchestra, and, as so often before, the chief work was Hummel's B-minor Concerto. According to the *Morning Post,* Sir George begged the audience for a theme on which "Master Liszt could work."[36] After a long pause, a lady called out "Zitti, zitti," from Rossini's *Barber of Seville,* and the young virtuoso at once improvised a fugue on this melody. A few days later, on June 29, Liszt gave a concert at the Theatre Royal, Drury Lane, where, according to the posters plastered outside the

---

34. Not Sébastien Erard. Liszt himself corrected this misconception in his personal copy of the Ramann biography. (RLKM, vol. 1, p. 69.)

35. These rooms were situated at the corner of Oxford and Argyll streets. They were destroyed by fire in 1830. (EOCR, pp. 115–22.)

36. June 23, 1824. Incidentally, it is evident from Adam's correspondence during this visit to England that the same sort of bargains were struck with the wealthy families of London as had been with their Paris counterparts the previous year. On one occasion the go-between was Cipriani Potter (MMR, October 1926):

The 26 May
18, Bentinck Street

Mons. Liszt,

Mr. Tunno much regrets that he cannot send his carriage for your son on Friday next, but as your son is somewhat delicate, Mr. Tunno will be very happy to pay the expense of a carriage. The address is No. 19, Upper Brook Street, Grosvenor Square, at 10 o'clock.

With the assurance of my esteem, I am your devoted servant,

CIPRIANI POTTER

Liszt in London, a playbill for Drury Lane Theatre, June 29, 1824.

theatre, "the incomparable Master Liszt has in the most flattering manner consented to display his inimitable powers on the New Grand Piano Forte invented by Sébastien Erard." The following month, the Liszts were received by George IV at Windsor Castle. The boy played before the royal family for over two hours and delighted the king with an improvisation on the Minuet from Mozart's *Don Giovanni,* which the monarch himself had suggested. An unexpected guest that evening was Prince Paul Esterházy, the son of Adam's former employer, and now the Austrian ambassador to London, who was hearing his famous compatriot for the first time.[37]

During Liszt's stay in London he somehow found time to compose several new pieces. One of his earliest extant letters, written in French when he was only twelve years old, mentions these works and is too humorous not to be included here. Its breathless grammar is reproduced intact.

> 18 great marlborought [*sic*]
> London, July 20, 1824
> Leap Year

Dear Sir!!

I would be greatly obliged to you if you would take the trouble of coming to see me today at a quarter past 3 having finished a few pieces and as I want have them engraved I am appealing to you to ask you to kindly hear them so that you don't buy the pig in the poke.

> Franz Liszt[38]

What were the works the young composer wished to play to his unknown buyer? We can only speculate. But already in this year of 1824 he had brought to completion an Allegro di bravura, a Rondo di bravura, and a set of Variations brillantes based on a theme from Rossini's *La donna del Lago.* The most notable composition was his set of Eight Variations in A-flat major, which was dedicated to Sébastien Erard. The second half of the theme discloses the young boy's propensity for "advanced" harmonic regions.

---

37. LCRT, pp. 245–46. See also the *Windsor Express* of July 31, 1824.
38. Hitherto unpublished. British Library, M.S. Add. 33965, fol. 229.

But it is in the variations themselves that we observe his unfailing skill in using the full resources of the new Erard keyboard. In variation 8 we hear a musical "salute" to Erard's "double-escapement" action, without which such a difficult figure would have been impossible to play.

Adam was soon to comment mockingly that Franzi already made Hummel and Moscheles "sit in the corner." His fatherly pride finds musical corroboration in the third variation, a brilliant example of the kind of passage-work for which both masters were so justly famed, and one in which the young Liszt so clearly excels them.

Liszt also gave two hastily arranged concerts in Manchester on August 2 and 4, 1824, in the Theatre Royal. Adam's correspondence with a Mr. Andrew

Ward, containing interesting details of these concerts, has been preserved. We learn that Adam insisted on a fee of 100 pounds, an astronomical sum in those days.

18 Gt. Marlborough Street
July 22, 1824

Mr. Liszt presents his compliments to Mr. Roe and begs to say, that the terms upon which he will take his son to Manchester to play at the concerts of the second and fourth of August next will be as follows:

Mr. Liszt is to receive one hundred pounds and be provided with board and lodgings in Mr. Ward's house during his stay in Manchester for his son and himself, and Mr. Liszt will pay the travelling expenses to and from Manchester.

London, July 29, 1824

Dear Sir:

In answer to your kind letter of the 27th inst. I beg to inform you that I wish my Son to play as follows: viz.:—At the first concert, a grand Concerto for the Piano Forte with orchestral accompaniment composed by Hummel, and the *Fall of Paris* also with grand orchestral accompaniment composed by Moscheles.

At the 2nd Concert—Variations with orchestral accompaniments composed by Charles Czerni [*sic*], and afterwards an Extempore Fantasia on a written Thema which Master Liszt will respectfully request any person of the Company to give him.

We intend to start to-morrow afternoon at three o'clock by the Telegraph Coach from the White Horse, Fetter Lane, and as we are entire strangers to Manchester it will be very agreeable to us if you will send someone to meet us.

Mr. Erard's pianoforte will be in your town on Sunday morning as I shall be glad for my son to play upon that instrument.

I remain, Dear Sir,

Yr. very humble Servant

LISZT[39]

Until Adam got to Manchester he did not know that his son was to have the dubious distinction of sharing the programme with a "baby harpist," the

---

39. HMR, p. 345.

SECOND GRAND CONCERT,
UNDER THE DIRECTION OF MR. A. WARD.

THEATRE-ROYAL, MANCHESTER,
WEDNESDAY, August 4th, 1824.

ACT FIRST.
OVERTURE............Zauberflöte............Mozart.
GLEE..................................." Go feeble Tyrant."
SONG............Mr. THORNE......Battle of the Angels............Bishop.
SONG............Miss D. TRAVIS............by desire............Donald.

THE INFANT LYRA,
Will have the honor of making her Second Appearance before the Manchester Audience, and play the following favorite Airs
ON THE HARP,
" Jessie, the Flow'r o' Dumblane,"—" Fresh and Strong the Breezes blowing,"—" My Love is but a Lassie yet,"—
and Grand Introductory March to the Air of " St. Patrick's Day," with Variations.
SONG......Miss SYMONDS......." My Henry is gone,"......Stevenson.
SONG................Mr. ISHERWOOD............Non Piu Andrai............Mozart.
THEMA, with GRAND VARIATIONS and ORCHESTRAL ACCOMPANIMENTS, composed by Charles Czerni,
will be performed by

MASTER LISZT,
ON ERARD'S NEW PATENT GRAND PIANO-FORTE OF SEVEN OCTAVES.
DUET............Mr. THORNE and Miss SYMONDS..........." Ma Braccia,"............Rossini.
GRAND SEPTETT..........Beethoven.
GLEE................." Chough and Crow,"............Bishop.

ACT SECOND.
OVERTURE............Prometheus............Beethoven.
GLEE............" When Winds breathe soft,"............Webbe.
SONG............Miss SYMONDS............" Bid me discourse,"............Bishop.
SONG......Mr. ROYLANCE............" A Lover's Eyes,"......Parry.

By Particular Desire,
The GRAND INTRODUCTION, and VARIATIONS to " ROY'S WIFE,"......on the HARP by

THE INFANT LYRA.
SONG..........Miss D. TRAVIS..........Vittima..........Pucitta.
SONG............Mr. THORNE............" The Sun his bright rays,"........Braham.
An EXTEMPORE FANTASIA on ERARD'S NEW PATENT GRAND PIANO-FORTE of 7 Octaves by

MASTER LISZT,
Who will respectfully request a written THEMA from any person present.
DUET............Mr. ISHERWOOD and Miss D. TRAVIS,............" Haste my Nannette,"............Travers.
FINALE..." God Save the King."

LEADER,................Mr. CUDMORE.
Principal First Violin,..Mr. BENNETT and four others. Principal Second,..Mr. WARD and five others. Principal
Tenor,..Mr. E. SUDLOW and three others. Principal Violoncello,..Mr. SUDLOW. Second Violoncello,..Mr. WHITTON.
Principal Double Bass,..Mr. HILL. Second,..Mr. WILKINSON. Flutes,..Messrs. KENNEY and PAIN. Oboes,..Messrs.
HUGHES and SMITH. Clarionets,..Mr. OWEN (Master of the Band of the Royal Scots Greys) and Mr. WILLIAMS.
Horns,..Messrs. WORNACHY and WADDINGTON. Bassoons,..Messrs. MONTAGE and BALL. Trumpets,..Messrs HYDE
and M'KINZIE. Trombones,..Messrs. ANSON, CAWSON, and CARTLEDGE. Drums,..Mr. JENKINSON.

Mr. R. Andrews will preside at the Piano-Forte.

MASTER LISZT being about to return to the Continent, where he is eagerly expected in consequence of his
astonishing talents, and the INFANT LYRA being on her way to London, the only opportunity which can occur for the
inhabitants of Manchester to hear them has been seized by Mr. WARD; and to afford every possible advantage to the
Voices and Instruments, he has so constructed the Orchestra, that the HARP and the PIANO-FORTE will be satisfac-
torily heard in every part of the house.

Tickets and Places may be had of Mr. ELAND, on Tuesday and Wednesday, at the Box-Office, from Eleven to Two;
and at ALL THE MUSIC SHOPS.
Doors to be opened at Six, and the Concert to commence precisely at Seven o'Clock.
Boxes, 5s.—Upper Boxes, 4s.—Pit, 3s.—Gallery, 2s.

ASTON, PRINTER, MANCHESTER

Liszt in Manchester, a playbill for the Theatre-Royal, August 4, 1824.

so-called Infant Lyra, "not yet four years old." In the event, the young Liszt was completely upstaged. A Manchester newspaper informed the amazed public that when the Infant Lyra walked on the platform

> she dropped a little short curtsey and kissed her hand to the smiling audience; and then *climbed* up to her chair, beside which stood a harp of a small size, but twice as big as herself. Her performance exhibited a proficiency which, in one who has not been in existence more than the time that might be required to learn, was surprising. The simple airs were given not merely with accuracy, but with feeling; and, though the physical exertion which was required to strike many chords afforded some amusement, the easier movements were elegantly executed, and the soft notes fell with a liquid sweetness from her tiny fingers. The whole performance gave the highest satisfaction.[40]

The Liszts left England a few days later with an invitation to return to both London and Manchester the following year. During the Channel crossing, on their way back to France, the twelve-year-old Liszt was seasick.[41]

Lina Ramann and her followers kept Liszt in England for the next six months "on holiday." We know from Adam's correspondence, however, that he took Franz back to Paris. He wrote to Czerny that his son had been composing industriously. By September 1824 the boy had already written two Rondos di bravura, a fantasy, several sets of variations, and various other things. Few of these juvenile works have survived. As for the piano, Adam assured Czerny that Franzi still adhered to the principles prescribed by his old master, and he disclosed the interesting fact that he made the boy practise with a metronome.[42] Adam's letters also reveal his obsession with money. His correspondence tells in detail of his son's concert fees, his family's living expenses, the cost of travel and clothing. His pleasure in the large profits he was now making from his son's public appearances is there for all to see. It was not simple greed on Adam's part that motivated his interest in money, however, but rather excessive caution born of a desire never to return to the old days when his family lived from hand to mouth; and it was natural that the old Esterházy bookkeeper should come out in him from time to time. Czerny was not the only one who thought that Adam was using his son for base motives. Some loose talk seems to have followed Adam which clearly disturbed him. It had already been brought into the open on March

---

40. *Cowdroy's Manchester Gazette,* August 7, 1824.
41. Letter to Pierre Erard, August 12, 1824, written from Calais. (Published in facsimile, BVL, p. 53.)
42. LCRT, p. 249.

18, 1824, by the critic of *La Pandore,* and Adam was forced to issue a rebuttal.

Paris, 1824

Sir:

The expressions which you frequently employed in speaking of my son have been so flattering, that I can not but be sensible of your kindness, and therefore take this opportunity of testifying my gratitude. I must say that I by no means anticipated the high degree of success with which he was honoured by the public of Paris, and, above all, was not prepared for the comparison, by no means advantageous, which they were pleased to draw between the rising talents of my son and those of our great Mozart. I recognize in this amiable exaggeration that spirit of French politeness, the boast of which I have all my life been accustomed to hear, and my son will think himself most happy if hereafter he shall have the good fortune to share some degree of celebrity with the masters of the German school, though he must remain at a very humble distance from him whom it glories in placing at its head.

You must however allow me, Sir, to make a few observations upon the following expression that occurred in one of your journals: "The parents of young Liszt are poor, and he supports them by the product of his talents."

Fortune, it is true, has not loaded me with her favours, yet I have no reason to complain of her neglect. For the space of twenty-three years I have been in the service of Prince Esterházy, where I filled the situation of steward of part of his sheep-farms. The immense income of this prince, and the noble and generous manner in which he acts towards those who have the good fortune to belong to any of his establishments, have long since placed me in that *aurea mediocritas* so happily described by the Latin poet.

Having observed in my only son, from a very early age, a decided predilection for music, and having from my youth cultivated the art as an amateur, I myself, for the space of three years, superintended his first musical education with that constancy and perseverance which form one of the characteristic traits of our nation. I afterwards placed him for eighteen months under the instruction of Messrs. Salieri and Czerny, from the first of whom he received lessons in harmony and counterpoint, and from the second, instruction on the pianoforte, and to both of whom he is indebted for their kind care and attention. I am happy to be thus able publicly to render them the homage of my grateful acknowledgements.

I came to Paris with the permission of the prince, and by the advice of my friends, in order to perfect my son's talents, by affording him an opportunity of hearing the numerous artists which this capital contains, and of cultivating the French language, of which he has already some general idea, a language which justly lays claim to the title of being that of Europe. At the same time, I have not neglected to take advantage of the eagerness testified by the Parisians to hear his performance, in order to indemnify myself for the expenses necessarily attendant upon a long journey, and the removal of my whole family.

Accept my best acknowledgements, and believe me, etc.,

ADAM LISZT[43]

This dignified response shows the level-headed approach of the father towards his gifted son. The generous praise of Salieri and Czerny, incidentally, is a clear indication that the boy had not yet commenced his studies with either Paer or Reicha, since Adam would certainly have mentioned it here.[44]

VII

During the spring of 1825 Liszt played several times in Paris, notably on the great stage of the Académie Royale in March 1825. Adam had been involved in protracted negotiations for this theatre since the previous December,[45] and the administration finally granted him permission to promote his son there. It is an indication of the thirteen-year-old boy's growing sophistication that we find him bypassing his father and writing to one of the directors himself on the subject of guest tickets.

---

43. The English journal *The Harmonicon* picked up Adam's letter and reprinted it in its June 1824 issue as a "news item," to coincide with the Liszts' first visit to London. One of the greatest difficulties that Adam Liszt faced was regular interference by well-meaning busybodies who thought that he was driving his delicate son too hard. In July 1824, during this same trip to England, Adam received a letter from a total stranger, one J. M. Raikes, an Englishman who lived in Ramsgate. Mr. Raikes informed Adam that his son's pale face gave the appearance of a too-protracted stay in the unhealthy climate of London. He offered Liszt a "paradise by the sea" at his Ramsgate hotel. "Think of the health of your son," urged the good Mr. Raikes, "as the most important goal of your life." Then he added gratuitously, "You are sacrificing your son's health on the altar of Plutus." And this to a man who had given up almost everything that he possessed for the sake of his child. (WA, Kasten 108, no. 1, unpublished.)

44. The first mention of Paer occurs in a letter Adam wrote to Viscount de la Rochefoucauld on November 5, 1824: "M. Paer . . . has been kind enough to take charge of the musical education of my son." (*Revue Musicale,* no. 11, 1911, p. 251.)

45. See Adam's letters to Viscount de la Rochefoucauld on this topic. (*Revue Musicale,* no. 11, 1911, pp. 251–53.)

to Monsieur de Bigarne
of the Académie Royale de Musique
rue Beaurépaire [sic] no. 24
Paris

March 13, 1825

Dear Sir:

I went to the office to speak to you, but since I did not have the pleasure of meeting you there, I am taking the liberty of writing to you.

I would like fourteen orchestra seats for the artists who will be singing in my concert, such as Messrs. Curioni, Pellegrini, Zucchelli, Bordogni and Mesdames Cinti, Pasta, Rossi, etc. I would be greatly obliged if you would send them at once.

Yours faithfully,

F. LISZT[46]

In June came a second visit to England. Liszt not only played again before George IV at Windsor Castle, and appeared several times in London, including at Drury Lane, but he also travelled up to Manchester and gave two further concerts at the Theatre Royal, on June 16 and 20, 1825, again under the aegis of Andrew Ward. The handbills show that Liszt shared the honours with Master Banks, a nine-year-old violin prodigy, and that he was advertised as being "only twelve years old" when in fact he was thirteen.

When father and son returned to London, an interesting artistic event took place, which throws light on Liszt's musical powers at this time. On one particular evening, Adam relates, he and Franz were invited to attend a musical soirée "in a stately home, where the top artists were gathered." Several people had already performed, including the Italian counter-tenor Velluti, for whom the piano had been tuned down a semitone in order to preserve his voice. It was now the turn of a flautist, Mr. Nicholson, who wanted to deliver himself of a Fantasy and Variations he had recently composed with "solo alternations" for the piano. His accompanist, Cipriani Potter,[47] seated himself at the piano. Nicholson's flute was now out of tune with the keyboard. At this point, the following dialogue took place.

"Your flute is too high."
"Good, you must transpose the piece, for I can't flatten my flute."
"What! The piece is in C major and I am supposed to play it in C-sharp major? I can't risk that, I can't consider it."

46. LLB, vol. 8, pp. 3–4.
47. Potter later became principal of the Royal Academy of Music, London, 1832–59.

A long argument ensued, and these gentlemen began to look conspicuous. Finally, Potter turned to the young Liszt, who had been standing to one side, and said:

> "Can you also transpose a little?"
> "Yes, sir."
> "Good, try it, because I won't risk it before such a distinguished gathering."

Whereupon Potter at once gave up his seat to Liszt, who transposed the work at sight, "solo alternations" and all, much to the astonishment of the other artists and the circle of onlookers. This episode, including the dialogue, was reported by Adam in a long letter to Czerny dated August 14, 1825.[48] While they were in London the Liszts also visited St. Paul's Cathedral. They were deeply impressed by the singing of massed choirs of seven to eight thousand children, scholars from the so-called Free Schools, which created an unforgettable visual and aural experience.[49]

Before returning to Paris, Adam arranged a short holiday for himself and his son at the fashionable bathing resort of Boulogne-sur-Mer, on the English Channel, in order, as he put it, "to wash away our English exhaustion." They bathed every day in the sea, walked along the beach collecting seashells, and admired the incoming and outgoing boats. In the evenings, they used to visit the large casino, a sea-bathing establishment built on the waterfront, owned by a M. Versial, where they would often take dinner. A large company of guests were assembled there, come to enjoy the sea baths, and word soon spread that the blond-haired youth was the prodigy Liszt. A piano stood in the middle of the salon, and requests began to come in for a concert. Adam, ever the professional, put the event on a proper footing, charging the wealthy guests a stiff admission fee. It not only covered all the expenses of their stay, but gave them a profit of 600 francs.[50]

VIII

Father and son arrived back in Paris in July 1825, wanting nothing more than to rest and to have a little time, in Adam's words, "in order to sort ourselves out." They had hardly unpacked when a letter arrived from the Ministry of Arts

---

48. LCRT, p. 257.
49. SEW, p. 416.
50. LCRT, pp. 258–59. The Liszts' arrival in Boulogne was announced in *L'Annotateur*, a local newspaper, on June 23, 1825. This same journal also reported that Liszt participated in a grand concert at the waterfront casino on July 8, culminating in a ball.

telling them that Liszt's opera *Don Sanche* was required within eight days for scrutiny by its jury. "Imagine the dilemma we were in," wrote Adam. "Nothing was copied, not a single singer was warned. I hoped for a postponement of fourteen days, which, however, was not forthcoming."[51] Somehow, the parts were got ready in time, and the distinguished jury (comprising Cherubini, Berton, Boieldieu, Lesueur, and Catel) listened to the opera in closed session. The verdict was unanimous: the opera was enthusiastically accepted for production later that year on the stage of the Académie Royale. Rehearsals began in October. "The young composer," wrote *Le Corsaire* two days before the premiere, "is always at his post. He goes, comes, listens, corrects, admonishes the orchestra, makes them begin again, throws himself about...."

The first performance of *Don Sanche, ou le Château d'Amour* took place on October 17, 1825, five days before Liszt's fourteenth birthday. It was conducted by Rudolph Kreutzer, music director of the Opéra. Adolphe Nourrit, the great tenor, was engaged to sing the title role, and his presence lent weight to the production. One or two of the Don's lyrical arias had been designed with Nourrit's voice in mind. The libretto was the collaborative effort of two minor contemporary writers, Theaulon and de Rancé, who had based their harmless plot on a medieval tale by the eighteenth-century poet Claris de Florian. Don Sanche, a courtly knight, seeks admission to the castle of love, the domain of Alidor the magician. Alidor's page informs him that only those who love, and are loved in return, may enter the castle. This disclosure brings Don Sanche to the brink of suicide: the object of his love, Princess Elzire, is destined to marry the Prince of Navarre. Through his magical art, Alidor conjures up a storm which brings Elzire's convoy to the castle in search of shelter. She, too, is refused admission when it is disclosed that she does not love her betrothed but is simply ambitious to become the Queen of Navarre. Various serenades, ballets, and interludes punctuate these proceedings. There is a duel between Don Sanche and one Romualde, who has threatened to abduct Elzire, during which Don Sanche is fatally wounded. Elzire's compassion is aroused, and then her love. She agrees to relinquish her hopes of a crown and enters the castle of love with Sanche, now miraculously healed. Romualde, it is helpfully revealed, was none other than Alidor in disguise. The opera ends with a general chorus of rejoicing.

In their preface to the score, Theaulon and de Rancé defend their ramshackle libretto thus:

> When we created this lyrical work our only consideration was to offer scenes of all the imaginable possibilities to the young prodigy to whose talent we owe the score. We therefore let the scene of jealousy be followed by the expression of nonchalant peace. Songs

---

51. LCRT, p. 259.

of joy and hymns of love are followed by the expression of deepest pain. We feel we owe these remarks to the high-minded people and members of society who might see little connection between some of the scenes of this humble opera. The demands of poetry were totally disregarded for the sake of the music. The interest that is already connected with the famous name of the young Liszt silenced our vanity as authors.

". . . Silenced our vanity as authors." Such a frank confession of guilt disarms criticism. *Don Sanche* was taken off after a run of only four performances and was not staged again for more than one hundred and fifty years.[52] The archives of the Paris Opéra reveal that the young composer received a mere 170 francs for his effort.[53] The reviews were mixed. Perhaps the general feeling was summed up by the *Almanach des Spectacles* of 1826, when it declared that "this work has to be judged with indulgence." Nonetheless, *Don Sanche* elicited some effective music from Liszt, including a beautiful aria, "Aimer, aimer . . . ," and some dramatic storm music. An opera by a thirteen-year-old boy had, after all, only one precedent: Mozart's *Bastien et Bastienne*.

For many years the score of *Don Sanche* was lost. Liszt himself believed that it had perished in the fire of 1873 at the Académie Royale. But in 1903 the French scholar Jean Chantavoine came across two beautifully bound volumes of the manuscript in the library of the Paris Opéra. They contained all the original rehearsal markings,[54] and most of our present knowledge of the work is obtained from this source. The score is not copied in Liszt's hand, and the music itself contains many passages which are reminiscent of the style of Paer, Liszt's composition teacher. This led Emile Haraszti to declare that *Don Sanche* was not by Liszt at all but by Paer himself. He could not accept that a boy of thirteen was capable of producing such a relatively polished work. However, Adam Liszt disclosed so many details about his son's opera-in-progress to Czerny[55] that he would have been perjuring himelf before his old friend if the opera had really been by Paer. Moreover, if we consult the programme of Liszt's second concert in Manchester, given on June 20, 1825, we learn that the orchestra led off with "A New Grand Overture, by Master Liszt." No other overture exists from this period than the one to *Don Sanche,* and it is certain that the boy was giving the Mancunians a preview of his new work.[56] For the

---

52. The first performance in modern times took place on October 20, 1977, at the Collegiate Theatre in London, as part of a London Liszt Festival held throughout that month.
53. HLP, p. 253.
54. CL, p. 18. Also *Die Musik,* no. 16, May 1904.
55. LCRT, pp. 259–60, letter dated August 14, 1825.
56. This "Grand Overture" caught the attention of Lina Ramann, who asked Liszt (in 1880) whether it might be the "missing" overture to *Don Sanche.* Liszt replied that it was, and that if the score ever came to light it ought not to be published, since no useful purpose could be served by

rest, the opera appears to have been ready, in all its essential details, as early as September 1824,[57] before Liszt became Paer's pupil. All that remained to be done on Liszt's return to Paris was to orchestrate the piece, an activity in which the boy may, admittedly, have had the guidance of Paer.

I X

At the beginning of 1826 Liszt and his father embarked on a tour of the French provinces. They visited Bordeaux, Toulouse, Nîmes, Marseille, Lyon, and other cities. A special honour was bestowed on the boy after his concert in Bordeaux when he was presented with the gold medallion of the Philharmonic Society. The inscription reads, "La Société Philharmonique de Bordeaux à Fçois Liszt XXV Janvier 1826."[58] He also visited Switzerland for the first time, playing in Geneva and Lucerne. An amusing story has been recorded in connection with the Geneva trip. A Genevan lady who had known Liszt as a nine-year-old child in Hungary when she had been governess to a wealthy family there went round to see him. Liszt recognized her at once and was overjoyed to meet her again. She could not help observing how much of a child he still was. During the concert the boy slipped out into the city streets between items in order to play a game of "mapis" with some small companions. A search party had to look for him so that the programme could continue.[59]

It is evident that Liszt's adolescence was lonely. We do not possess a single piece of evidence to suggest that the fifteen-year-old youth had any real friends of his own age. (Perhaps that is why he was so very convivial in later life.) He was constantly on the move. Everything he did was undertaken with a fanfare of publicity. His sole companion was his father. The relationship was close, but there were times when it was claustrophobic. He missed his mother, who was nearly a thousand miles away in Austria. Small wonder that this brilliant boy became withdrawn and introspective. He sought solace in reading. By nature deeply religious, even mystical, he gravitated towards Christian literature. He was already familiar with the *Lives of the Saints,* and he knew every page of the *Imitation of Christ* by the great mystic Thomas à Kempis, a work which illuminated his inner life.[60] Some of its aphorisms were elevated by him to the level of moral precepts, to be lived out in his daily existence:

resurrecting this juvenile composition: "Since it was nothing, it became nothing." (WA, Kasten 351, no. 1.)

57. LCRT, p. 253.

58. The medallion is now in the Liszt Museum (Hofgärtnerei) in Weimar.

59. KLG, February 14, 1897, p. 125. This concert took place in the newly completed Casino de Saint-Pierre.

60. This information derives ultimately from Liszt himself. (WA, Kasten 351, no. 1.)

Learn to obey, thou dust.

Learn to make thyself meek, thou earth and clay, and to bow thyself under the feet of all.

Dilate me in love that I may learn to taste with the inward mouth of mine heart how sweet it is to love and in love to melt and swim.

These are sombre thoughts which amount to morbidity in one so young. Yet they ran like leitmotifs through the heart and brain of the youthful Liszt. The fifteen-year-old boy kept a diary, which has never been published.[61] Containing quotations from St. Paul and St. Augustine, this journal also preserves Liszt's own thoughts.

Wasting time is one of the worst faults in the world. Life is so short, every moment is so precious; yet we live as if life will never end. [page 21]

God sees me and I could offend him in his presence. Am I capable of preferring to please a man, rather than God? [page 3]

There are few things which are impossible in themselves. We lack merely the application, not the means, to make them succeed. [page 5]

Who encouraged him to develop such stark ideas? Adam Liszt did, to whom they were familiar from his monastic background. Together with the boy's growing aversion to his life as a touring curiosity, they induced a severe mental crisis. He suffered a religious mania and experienced longings to become a priest. "In my early youth," he later wrote, "I often went to sleep hoping not to awake again here below."[62] He spent many hours in prayer, examining his conscience. Adam must have recalled his own past, when, as a young monk, he had prostrated himself in the cell at Tyrnavia. He was not about to allow his son to follow that same path. Father and son wrestled with the problem together. Liszt later told Lina Ramann that his father's view prevailed. "Your profession is music. To love something does not guarantee that one has a vocation for it. For music, however, you do have a vocation. The path of the true artist does not lead away from religion—it is possible to have one path for both. Love God, be good and upright, so that you will reach ever higher in your art." And Adam concluded, "You belong to art, not to the church."[63] Forty years later, Liszt revised that judgement. And anyone who is familiar with the minutiae of his daily existence during the last twenty years of his life will have no difficulty in perceiving the origin of that marked self-abnegation which

61. "Tagebuch des 15-jährigen Liszt, April–Juli 1827." BA, cat. no. HF, 51–IV.
62. WLLM, p. 384.
63. RLKM, vol. 1, p. 97.

was the dominant characteristic of his old age. Thomas à Kempis had already told him: "Love to be unknown, and accounted as nought."

X

A major artistic event for Liszt at this time was the publication of a set of twelve studies, the so-called Etude en douze exercices. These pieces are historically important, for they were later transformed into the Grandes Etudes of 1838 and later still into the Transcendental Studies of 1851. Liszt had begun work on these difficult pieces when he was only thirteen years old.[64] They were now published simultaneously by Boisselot of Marseille and Dufaut & Dubois of Paris. Although they were announced as "Forty-eight Exercises in All the Major and Minor Keys," only twelve studies appeared. The influence of his teacher Carl Czerny is evident, in particular of his *School of Velocity,* but they are an outstanding achievement for one so young. Their tonal connections reveal an adventurous outlook. Liszt unfolds the circle of fifths in a descending spiral, and every alternate study is linked to its predecessor by being in the relative minor. The resulting scheme—C major–A minor, F major–D minor, and so on—means that the collection of twelve pieces breaks off after B-flat minor. Obviously it was Liszt's intention to complete the sequence, but he never did. Liszt has not so far received the full credit he deserves for these juvenile pieces. They are worth any pianist's while to perform. Not only are they skilfully laid out across the keyboard, but they are musically interesting too. One of the most arresting of the set is the tenth, in F minor. The boy makes the keyboard sparkle from one end to the other, and the "crossed hands" effect is once more in evidence. The following passage spans fully six octaves.

---

64. LLB, vol. I, p. 189. Liszt himself tells us that they dated from his thirteenth year.

No pianist who plays the Transcendentals can afford to remain in ignorance of these juvenile pieces. Many of the most striking effects of the later studies started life here. Occasionally, however, the mature Liszt allows his early work to stand unadorned. The Study in A-flat major (later known as *Ricordanza*) reveals that the nocturne-like melody, which so many commentators familiar with the 1851 version assume to have been inspired by Chopin, was in fact the creation of the thirteen-year-old Liszt.

XI

In May 1827 Liszt paid his third visit to England. It was to be his last appearance in that country for many years. He and his father stayed in lodgings in Frith Street, Soho, at that time one of the more fashionable areas of London. On May 25 he again played at the Argyll Rooms. Charles Salaman, who was then a boy of fourteen, has left a lively pen-sketch of the occasion.[65] He was present at the morning rehearsal and reports that the seventy-five-year-old Muzio Clementi turned up unexpectedly and sat at the back of the hall, come to hear the young Hungarian. Liszt, mounting the steps leading to the platform, is described as "a pale-faced boy . . . slim and rather tall." He created a sensation with his performance of Hummel's A-minor Concerto, which Clementi listened to with intense interest, "his brilliant dark eyes glistening as he followed the marvellous performance." Shortly afterwards, the Liszts were invited round to the Salaman home for a family dinner. The young Charles never forgot Liszt's joyful exclamation, "O, gooseberry pie!" as his favourite dish was placed upon the table. After the meal, there was family music making, and the two boys played through some duets together. Salaman also discloses that Liszt then performed some of his recently published studies, gave him a presentation copy, and wrote out a specially amended version of the sixth study, Molto agitato in G minor. This was not the only account of Liszt playing his own music in London. Moscheles heard the boy play on June 9 and afterwards wrote in his diary of an A-minor Concerto which was full of "chaotic beauties."[66] This was almost certainly one of the two early piano concertos which, according to Adam Liszt, the boy had already written.[67]

During this visit to London Liszt gave further evidence of his growing facility as a composer. On May 27, within the space of a few hours, he wrote out a scherzo in G minor. It was never published during his lifetime. The manuscript was left behind in London and came into the possession of Busoni when he visited the city in 1909. He acquired it from the Danish pianist Frits Hartvigson, who was at that time on the teaching staff of the Royal College of Music. Nowhere does the title "Scherzo" appear on the

65. SPP, pp. 308 and 314.
66. MAML, vol. 1, p. 138.
67. LCRT, p. 260. These early concertos, as we have indicated, are lost. Nevertheless, this description by Moscheles misled Peter Raabe into speculating that the work was really an early version of the *Malédiction* Concerto for piano and string orchestra, first published in 1915. (RLS, vol. 2, p. 53.) *Malédiction* is in A minor; it begins with "chaotic" harmonies. One surely needs more evidence before jumping to so bold a conclusion.

manuscript itself. That was Busoni's description, and it eventually found its way into the *Collected Edition.*[68] The piece is totally forgotten today, but it offers evidence of the boy's awakening creative faculty, especially in the field of harmony.

Adam's correspondence at this time makes it clear that he pinned the highest hopes on his son's compositions. "He knows no other passion than composing," he wrote to Czerny; "only this brings him joy and pleasure."[69] Adam was not merely indulging in rhetoric when he added, "I hope he may later burn his piano." He had already written to grandfather Georg in the same vein, one of the few such letters to survive.

> Meanwhile, you will be pleased when I tell you that Franzi has not yet found his equal, and that Hummel and Moscheles have to sit in the corner because of him. His compositions surpass our under-standing.[70]

Although the manuscripts of a sonata for four hands, a trio, a quintet, and two piano concertos (all referred to in Adam's correspondence[71]) may never be found, a sufficient number of the young Liszt's works have survived to force us to revise the prevailing view that he was a late starter in the field of composition. True, he may not have found himself, creatively speaking, until

68. CE, II, vol. 9, p. 1. Unknown to Busoni when he announced its "first" publication in 1922, the piece had already been published in the *Allgemeine Zeitung* (nos. 22 and 23, 1896, p. 288).
69. LCRT, p. 260.
70. August 14, 1825; unpublished. (WA, Kasten 105, no. 3.)
71. LCRT, p. 260.

he was in his mid-twenties. But the repertoire of juvenile works composed between 1824 and 1827, that is, before his sixteenth birthday, reveals an uncommon grasp of composition, and it is worthy of comparison with any of the established minor keyboard masters of the 1820s—Clementi, Cramer, Czerny —lacking only their mature handling of large-scale forms.

The Death of Liszt's Father

*Up to now, your life was sweet. All you needed
to do was to obey, and you could rest blindly on
the care of your father.*

COUNT AMADÉ TO LISZT[1]

I

Franz and his father had been touring incessantly for three years, and it had begun to tax the boy's health. Adam decided that they should stay once more in Boulogne and "take the waters." That was to be a fatal decision. They arrived in mid-August 1827 and rented accommodation in the Hibernian Hotel at 36, rue Neuve-Chaussée, which was run by an Englishman, John Holt. Almost at once Adam fell seriously ill with typhoid fever and was obliged to take to his sickbed. His temperature rose; within a few days he had become delirious. The local doctor was called, and he told the boy, "It may be dangerous." Adam Liszt himself must have known that his end was near. In a lucid moment, he instructed his son to tell Anna of his plight and ask her to return to France. The following letter discloses the mature way in which the fifteen-year-old Liszt coped with his task.

Boulogne, August 24, 1827

Best of women, Mother!

At the very moment I write to you, I am anxious about my father's health. When we arrived here he was already feeling unwell, but it has got worse, and today the doctor told me that it may be dangerous. Father begs you not to lose courage. He feels very ill, and that is why he wants me to tell you in this letter that you may

---

1. LBZL, vol. 1, p. 5.

perhaps have to come to France. He thinks we can wait for a few days still, and he said to me: "You can write to her later on, once we know something definite."

He was very pleased to receive your letter. I thank you for your loving remembrance of me, and I will write to you again for sure in three or four days.

Farewell, we embrace you many times.

In haste,

F. Liszt[2]

The letter arrived too late. Adam Liszt died four days later, on August 28, 1827. This is confirmed by the death certificate, issued by the deputy mayor of Boulogne.

> In the year 1827, and on the 28th of August at 10:00 a.m., in our presence, Alexandre Gontran Lorgnier, deputizing during the absence of the mayor, in the office of the town of Boulogne-sur-Mer, in the district of Pas-de-Calais, the following witnesses were subpoenaed: Messrs Henry John Holt, innkeeper of this town, aged forty-four; Sylvain Bilot, clerk in the town hall of the said town and a resident, aged twenty-eight, both friends of the after-mentioned deceased, who declared to us that M. Adam Liszt, steward of the sheepfolds to Prince Esterházy, in Hungary, resident in Paris, a native of Eselsthal in Hungary, aged fifty-four years, husband of Anna Laagre (the names of the father and mother could not be transmitted to us), died this day at 8:30 a.m. at the home of the first witness, 36, rue Neuve-Chaussée.
>
> And the witnesses signed the present deed, after having perused it.
>
> HENRY HOLT
> BILOT
> LORGNIER[3]

This document, valuable though it is, contains several errors. It was written in haste, an hour-and-a-half after Adam Liszt had expired. Adam was fifty, not fifty-four, when he died. His native village was Edelsthal ("valley of the nobles"), not Eselsthal ("valley of the donkeys"), a hilarious slip of the pen. Anna's maiden name was Lager, not Laagre. We note, too, that the names of the grandparents could not be obtained. Haraszti interprets this as one more

---

2. LLBM, p. 9. This letter, which is in German, was written on Liszt's behalf and signed by him. The holograph is in Bayreuth. (BA, uncatalogued.)
3. Death notice no. 360. City Archives, Boulogne-sur-Mer.

example of Liszt's forgetfulness where family matters were concerned.[4] A more obvious inference suggests itself: Franz was not present when this document was drawn up. The boy would hardly have been mingling with city officials on the morning of his father's death, and less than an hour-and-a-half after that father had drawn his last breath. For the rest, he would surely have remembered his grandfather Georg; as for his grandmother, she had died in 1798, thirteen years before her famous grandson was born, and it is unreasonable to suppose that he should have known anything about her.

I I

Adam Liszt was interred the following day. After the burial service in the parish church of St. Nicholas, Boulogne-sur-Mer, the body was transported to the Cimetière de l'Est, about two miles away, on the outskirts of the old town. In the parish mortuary register there is a brief record of the ceremony.

> On August 29, 1827, was buried in the cemetery of this parish, by me, the undersigned vicar, the body of Adam Liszt, deceased the day before, aged fifty-four, husband of Anna Laagre. And also present were Simon Bazin and Pierre Caillier, undersigned.
> Signed:
>
> > PAQUE (Vicar)
> > BAZIN
> > CAILLIER

Franz was not present; otherwise Paque, the vicar, would have said so. Adam Liszt was therefore laid to rest by strangers, in a foreign land, far from home. It is a curious fact that his son did not once visit the grave, although he lived for nearly sixty years more and his tours often took him close to Boulogne.[5] Even more remarkable, Anna Liszt did not visit the cemetery either, and she lived for the next forty years in Paris, less than 150 miles away. News of Adam's death spread slowly. There was not a single mention of it in the Paris press. Tucked away on an inside page of an obscure Boulogne newspaper, however, we find this terse announcement: "The father of the young Litz [*sic*], the

---

4. HLP, part 2, p. 7.

5. Liszt actually passed through Boulogne on October 1, 1840, en route for Paris. The following year, on April 6, he stayed in Boulogne for one night at the Hôtel des Bains before continuing his journey to England. Liszt was by then world-famous, but the local newspapers do not even mention his visits. The facts came to light only after the embarkation and disembarkation registers at the port of Boulogne for those years were examined. Liszt could easily have visited his father's last resting place, but chose not to do so. Boulogne remained a painful memory.

celebrated pianist, died in Boulogne on Tuesday last, after several days of illness."[6] Three lines in a local journal: that is all Adam's life was deemed to be worth. His many friends in Paris were still hearing about his demise months later. Count Amadé, one of Liszt's Hungarian benefactors, did not learn of the tragedy until the following spring, and he at once wrote Franz a letter of condolence.

Vienna, May 1, 1828

to Monsieur François Liszt in Paris
38, rue Coquenard
Faubourg Montmartre

My dear Liszt,

I take a very sincere share in the misfortune that you have experienced. You have lost your first support, your best friend, him who concerned himself with your interests from your birth, and who loved you with the tenderest affection, long before you were in a condition to appreciate and deserve his love. Up to now, your life was sweet. All you needed to do was to obey, and you could rest blindly on the care of your father.

Now you have a more difficult task to fulfil. You have to acquire friends and become the support of your mother. You must thank heaven that it has saved for you the woman who, like your deceased father, will always be disposed to cherish and love you. It will not be the same of fresh acquaintances, whom your situation must now lead you to seek out; you will find in them neither that abnegation of self nor that disinterested affection that parents feel. But you must not rest content until you have succeeded in arousing their interest, and must do everything to obtain it. Do not get discouraged if the results do not immediately meet your expectations. With a firm resolve to succeed in the aim you have set yourself, with scrupulous observance of all the duties which propriety imposes, with simple manners and especially no presumptions as to your talents, you will sooner or later finish by acquiring public esteem and the affection of all men of merit.

This advice stems from my friendship for you, for I am keenly interested in your fate, and if I can be of some service to you, now or in the future, you may count on me, and address yourself to me with that sincerity that I have the right to expect from you by reason of the affection I bear you. Write to me from time to time, tell me

---

6. *Le Franc Parleur*, September 3, 1827.

about your affairs, your plans; in a word, consider me as the one who, after your parents, takes the keenest interest in everything that concerns you. My respects to your mother. Tell her that she was not mistaken in counting on the durability of my feelings for you.

Good-bye, dear Liszt, write to me soon, for all that concerns you is of infinite interest to me.

COUNT THADÉ AMADÉ[7]

This letter reveals the cordiality that existed between Amadé and Adam Liszt, and it is also an indication of the closeness with which Franzi's career was being watched by distinguished Hungarians at home.

Just before his death, Adam Liszt is supposed to have turned to his son and told him that he feared that women would hold sway over his life and trouble his existence. This is usually interpreted as a remarkable piece of clairvoyance on Adam's part. We do well to remember, however, that this "prediction" was first reported by Liszt himself, nearly fifty years after it was made, in a letter to Princess von Sayn-Wittgenstein (dated August 26, 1874), and long after the "prediction" itself had become a reality. The passage in question reads: "On his deathbed, at Boulogne-sur-Mer, [my father] told me that I was good-hearted and did not lack intelligence, but that he feared that women would trouble my existence and dominate me. This premonition was strange, for at sixteen years of age I had no idea of what a woman could be—and I naively asked my confessor to explain to me the Sixth and Ninth Commandments, fearing that I might perhaps have unwittingly transgressed them."[8]

I I I

Adam Liszt's grave is no longer to be found. A concession "in perpetuity" was granted on the burial plot, subject to renewal after eighty years at the request of the descendants. No such request was ever made. Adam's distinguished

---

7. LBZL, vol. 1, p. 5.

8. LLB, vol. 7, p. 82. What prompted this disclosure? By 1874 Liszt had known the princess for twenty-seven years, and it was the first occasion on which he had breathed a word of Adam's "prediction"—to her or to anyone. Its timing was no accident. A few weeks earlier, Liszt's pupil Olga Janina had published her bogus reminiscences *Souvenirs d'une cosaque* under the pseudonym "Robert Franz," which was designed to do him harm. Liszt wrote a number of letters to his friends about this scandal-monger, notably to Baron Augusz, to Robert Franz himself (who was disturbed to find his name appropriated by a common adventuress), and of course to Princess von Sayn-Wittgenstein. It is interesting to speculate that had Olga never published her libels, Liszt would have had no cause to report Adam's deathbed utterance to anybody, least of all to the princess, and posterity would consequently have lacked the evidence to attribute to the older Liszt any powers of prescience whatsoever.

progeny, with Cosima Wagner at their head, forgot the man who had sacrificed so much for his genius son. The concession therefore expired before World War I. Adam's remains must have suffered a common fate, quite usual in these circumstances. His corpse would have been exhumed, his burial plot reallocated, and his bones placed in their final resting place—an unmarked pauper's site in an obscure corner of the cemetery.[9] This total neglect of Adam Liszt spread to Liszt's biographers. He is always quickly glossed over. Yet this amateur musician and ex-Franciscan was by far the most powerful influence on Liszt during his formative years. Many times in the course of his long life, Liszt was to recall the sombre and mystical personality of his dead father, which would reach out even beyond the tomb and determine much of his future conduct.

---

9. All this happened long after Liszt himself had passed away. Liszt bought the concession on the family plot on February 28, 1832, more than four years after Adam's death. It was clearly his intention to perpetuate his father's memory. The transaction was carried out on Liszt's behalf by M. Obert, "a professor of music domiciled in Boulogne-sur-Mer." (BN NAF 16440, fol. 4.)

Obscurity in Paris

The truth is that in those days I completely ignored the world and concerned myself with nothing.

FRANZ LISZT[1]

I

We know virtually nothing of Liszt's movements during the autumn and winter of 1827. How did the boy get from Boulogne to Paris? Why, after Adam's medical bills and funeral expenses had been paid, was there so little money left that his son and widow found themselves temporarily in reduced circumstances? Why was there no will? And what became of Adam's personal possessions? The dutiful biographer is bound to raise questions. It is strange that Liszt appears to have neither inherited, nor retained, a single memento of his father. We know that Adam's diary survived, since, as we have seen, Anna Liszt was able to lend it to d'Ortigue in 1835. Adam's letters tell us that he had been paying sums of money to grandfather Georg through a bank in Vienna;[2] and a careful perusal of Franz Liszt's will, dated 1860, discloses the interesting fact that his father had invested some capital with Prince Esterházy in Vienna which was still yielding a modest interest nearly forty years later.[3] But the documents that would allow us to sketch in the details of Liszt's movements during the sad weeks following his father's funeral either have not yet come to light or have been destroyed.

Having arrived back in Paris, Franz installed himself and his mother (who had been living with her sister in Graz for the last three years) first at 38, rue

---

1. LLB, vol. 7, p. 240.
2. DM, p. 20.
3. LLB, vol. 5, p. 54.

Coquenard, and then at 7, rue de Montholon, opposite the Church of St.-Vincent-de-Paul in the Montmartre district. The sixteen-year-old youth assumed complete financial responsibility for himself and Anna, for he was soon able to establish himself as a fashionable young piano teacher. With his reputation, Franz did not have to seek out the sons and daughters of the aristocracy; they sought out him. Indeed, they were happy to own him as a teacher. Among his first pupils were the Countess Montesquieu and the daughters of Lord Granville, the British ambassador to France. We also know that he was appointed music teacher to a private school for young ladies run by one Madame Alix at 43, rue de Clichy. Why did not Liszt simply go on touring Europe? That would have been an easier way to solve the family's financial problems. The answer takes us to the heart of the boy's personality during this difficult period. Reflecting on his youth, much later on, Liszt witheringly likened himself to the performing dog Munito and complained bitterly about being "in the pay of the exalted." Although he did not commit these thoughts to paper until 1837, ten years after the death of Adam, they throw a flood of light on his feelings at this time and reveal the contempt in which he held his career as a wunderkind.

> When death had robbed me of my father . . . and I began to foresee what art *might* be and what the artist *must* be, I felt overwhelmed by all the impossibilities which surrounded me and barred the way which my thoughts indicated as the best. Besides, finding no sympathetic word from anyone harmonizing with me in mind, either among the contented leaders of society, or, still less, among the artists who were slumbering in comfortable indifference, knowing nothing of the aims I had in view, nothing of the powers with which I felt endowed, there came over me a bitter disgust against art, such as it appeared to me: vilified and degraded to the level of a more or less profitable handicap, branded as a source of amusement for distinguished society. I had sooner be anything in the world than a musician in the pay of the exalted, patronized and salaried by them like a conjuror, or the learned dog Munito. Peace to his memory![4]

Liszt's dislike of being a "performing dog" spread to performing dogs in general. His well-known aversion to infant prodigies requires no stressing.

---

4. RGS, vol. 2, pp. 127–28; CPR, p. 102. Munito (1820–30), a performing dog of unprecedented skills, had for long astonished the scientific community with his physical and mental tricks. This "matchless dog understands equally well French and Italian, works out the letters of the alphabet, distinguishes colours, plays dominos . . . and is acquainted with the principles of geography and botany." (TSCA, item 510. This source contains a three-page biography of Munito and provides a portrait of the clever canine.)

"Artists who *are* to be!" he used to call them scathingly. Was there a guilty recollection of his own past in his continual use of this phrase?

During his Paris years Liszt sowed the seeds of an irregular life-style which was to remain with him for the rest of his days. He kept uncertain hours, often leaving the house early in the morning and not returning until late at night. His pupils were scattered across the city, and he daily covered long distances. He barely left himself time for proper meals and would call at whatever café happened to lie in his path. By the end of 1829 we find him complaining that he had to teach "each day from 8:30 in the morning till 10:00 at night; I scarcely have time to breathe."[5] The young Liszt also took up smoking and drinking;[6] he became increasingly dependent on these stimulants in later life. Returning to the rue de Montholon long after dark, he sometimes found his mother already asleep, the evening meal that she had prepared for him spoiled. In order not to disturb her rest, he would sleep on the stairs (having first refreshed himself with a glass of wine or spirits), where he would be discovered by Anna the next morning, still fully clothed.[7] Adam's guiding hand had formerly directed every hour of every day. Left to himself, Franz failed at first to establish an orderly existence. The young Liszt was, in any case, an enemy of "structured time," and he lived somewhat impulsively. He neglected his piano practising, and it is a fact that we do not possess a single composition of his for the two-year period 1827–29.

II

It was at this time that Liszt experienced his first love affair. Among his aristocratic pupils was Caroline de Saint-Cricq, the beautiful seventeen-year-old daughter of Count Pierre de Saint-Cricq, minister of commerce in the government of Charles X.[8] Franz regularly visited their house on the rue de Lille in order to give the girl lessons. They soon formed a passionate attachment for one another. The lessons were chaperoned by Caroline's mother, who seems to have been sufficiently charmed by the young Liszt's personality to allow the couple to entertain thoughts of an early engagement. Within a few weeks, however, the mother fell ill and died.[9] On her deathbed she is supposed to have said to her husband, "If she loves him, let her be happy." If the count noticed these words, it was merely to attribute them to the delirium of a dying woman.

---

5. LLB, vol. 1, p. 5.
6. RLKM, vol. 1, p. 114; LGPZ, p. 9.
7. RLKM, vol. 1, pp. 113–14.
8. Pierre-Laurent-Barthélemy-François-Charles, Count de Saint-Cricq (1772–1854).
9. On June 30, 1828. Jeanne-Clémence Lenain de Tillemont, Countess de Saint-Cricq, was born in 1770.

The prospect of his daughter marrying a humble piano player did not arise. The Saint-Cricq household was shrouded in mourning and the lessons were temporarily abandoned, although Liszt called at the house every day to inquire after his pupil. When Liszt saw Caroline again after her mother's funeral, she was still dressed in black mourning garments. The reunion was highly charged, and they both wept bitterly. Since the count's ministerial duties kept him away from the house, he had no knowledge that Caroline and Liszt were seeing one another almost daily. Their conversations covered music, poetry, and religion and often lasted far into the night. On one occasion Liszt left the house after midnight and had to summon the hall porter to unlock the door and let him out of the building. Not yet sufficiently versed in the ways of the world, the young man failed to bribe this servant, and the count was duly informed of his daughter's nocturnal visitor. When Liszt reappeared on the doorstep of the Saint-Cricq house a few days later, the count was waiting for him. After reminding the young artist of his lowly station, he announced that the lessons with Caroline were terminated, and Liszt was shown the door. Caroline fell ill as a result of the enforced separation. For a time she was resolved to take the veil. She finally agreed to her father's plan for an arranged marriage with Bertrand d'Artigaux, the son of one of his fellow ministers, who owned a large estate near Pau in southern France. She was barely nineteen. This unhappy union was a long one, and Caroline bore it as a penance. As for Liszt, the consequences were more serious still. He suffered a nervous breakdown and succumbed once again to religious mania.[10] He spent long hours prostrating himself on the cold flagstones of St.-Vincent-de-Paul, and again experienced longings to become a priest. He begged to be allowed to enter the Paris seminary and hoped that it might be given to him to live the life of a saint and die the death of a martyr. Once again he was deflected from the church, this time by his confessor, Abbé Bardin, and by his mother.[11]

Liszt never forgot Caroline. In 1844, while he was on a tour of southern France and Spain, he passed through Pau and met her again. They reminisced about their sad love-affair and the bitterness it had caused them. Liszt also remembered Caroline in his will, bequeathing a signet-ring to her.[12] Since she died in 1872, fourteen years before he himself went to the grave, she never learned of this token of his feeling for her.

---

10. Liszt himself tells us that his illness lasted for two years (RGS, vol. 2, p. 128; CPR, pp. 102–3). See also KAS, p. 11.

11. RGS, vol. 2, p. 128. LLB, vol. 5, p. 52. LLB, vol. 7, p. 258. Abbé Jean Baptiste Edme Bardin (1790–1857), priest at St.-Vincent-de-Paul and Liszt's spiritual adviser, played an important role in the young man's life. During the years 1829–30 Abbé Bardin lived at 4, rue de Montholon, and Liszt saw him every day. In 1829 Bardin officiated at Liszt's confirmation. (DDP, p. 286.) Bardin remained the vicar of St.-Vincent-de-Paul for thirty-six years.

12. LLB, vol. 5, p. 60. See also the letters Caroline wrote to Liszt in 1853, LAG, pp. 56–58.

At the height of the Saint-Cricq affair Liszt gave two public concerts which have received scant attention. On April 7 he appeared at the Salle Chanterain, in the rue de la Victoire, where he improvised a fantasy on themes from a Beethoven symphony, Rossini's *Siège de Corinthe*, and Auber's *La Muette de Portici*.[13] The other concert took place a few days earlier. It was the opening Concert Spirituel, held at the Opéra, at which he played his old war-horse, Hummel's B-minor Concerto. This concert went badly. Fétis, the editor of *La Revue Musicale,* was present, and he published an extraordinary rebuke in the columns of his journal. He was particularly incensed at the speed with which Liszt took the Rondo finale. His long-forgotten article makes interesting reading today.

> What a pity that natural gifts such as those possessed by M. Liszt are employed solely to convert music into the subject for a thimble-rigger and conjuror. This is not for what this enchanting art is destined. . . . Profit from time where your still-virgin faculties permit your talent to change direction; take a step back and be the first among the young pianists, and have the courage to renounce brilliant frivolities for advances that are more substantial. You will reap the rewards.[14]

Such a candid assessment need occasion no surprise; Liszt's playing was ever the mirror of his emotional life. His spiritual desolation stood revealed. Fétis, of course, knew nothing of the anguish Liszt was undergoing. Anna Liszt was shortly to say that her genius-son had given up music altogether.[15]

III

The nervous breakdown occasioned by the Saint-Cricq affair, following so hard on the trauma of his father's death, brought gloom and despair to the rue de Montholon. His mother reports that she saw her son only at mealtimes, when he would sit opposite her as silent as a statue, staring at the table in complete apathy. Most of his time was spent in church, expiating his sins; he was a daily visitor to the confessional. In the autumn of 1828, reports of his death swept through Paris and were picked up by several French newspapers. A false

---

13. *La Muette* had received its première only five weeks earlier at the Paris Opéra.
14. 1828, vol. 3, pp. 253–54. One other public appearance by Liszt at this time deserves mention. On April 20, he took part in a performance of Beethoven's Symphony in A major, arranged for eight hands by Bertini. The other players were Sowiński, Schunke, and Bertini himself. See Prod'homme, RM, p. 110.
15. LGPZ, p. 8.

obituary notice was published by *Le Corsaire*[16] on October 23, 1828, under the sensational headline "Death of the Young Liszt."

Young Liszt has died in Paris. At an age when most children have not yet thought of school, he had already succeeded with the public. At nine years of age, when other children can scarcely stammer, he improvised on the pianoforte to the astonishment of masters, and yet they called him "le petit Litz," seeking to attach his name to that childish gracefulness from which he never passed. The first time he improvised at the Opéra, they made him go the round of the boxes and galleries, where he was caressed by all the ladies; in their naive admiration, suited to the age of the artist, they could think of no better reward than kisses and burnt almonds, and offered bonbons with one hand, while the other played with his fair silky hair.

This extraordinary boy increases the list of precocious children who appear on earth only to vanish like hothouse plants, which bear magnificent fruit but die from the exertion of bringing them forth. Mozart, too, who like Liszt astonished everyone by his precocity, died at the age of thirty-one,[17] but he bought some years of his life paid for with so many sufferings, and so much sorrow, that an earlier death would perhaps have been a blessing for him.

If we consider all the dangers to which talent is exposed, all the monsters which surround genius, persecute it incessantly, and accompany it to the last step, when we consider that every success awakens envy, and that while it makes mediocrity blush, goads on intrigue, we shall perhaps find that it was more fortunate for the flower to fade than to await the storms which might possibly later fall on and devour it.

Till now, young Liszt has had only admirers. His age was a shield which turned every arrow aside. "He is a child," they said at every success, and envy yielded to patience. But had he grown older, had the divine spark which inspired him been more developed, then they would have sought for failings, then they would have reviled his merits, and, who knows, might have poisoned his innermost life. He would have learned the caprices of power, the injustice of might; he would have been oppressed by the rough attack of unworthy and hateful passions; whereas now, wrapped in his shroud, he begins

---

16. Not by *L'Etoile,* as stated so frequently. In 1828 *L'Etoile* no longer existed, having ceased publication in August 1827.
17. Mozart was thirty-five when he died.

anew the sleep of childhood, and perhaps slumbers with the yearning
to continue the dream of yesterday.

The event is painful, not for his father, who went before him a
year ago, but for his family, whose name he had begun to make
famous, painful for us, for whom no doubt he would have opened
a new spring of musical impulse and joy. *We* too mourn his loss,
and unite with his family in lamenting his early death.

On the very day that Liszt was supposed to have died, he was at home in the
rue de Montholon quietly celebrating his seventeenth birthday. A swift denial
of this false report was issued by Madame Alix, of the rue de Clichy, at whose
school Liszt taught the piano, and it was published in *La Quotidienne* on
October 26.

> To the editor:
> Several people of the capital have just announced that the young
> Liszt, known equally as pianist and improviser, has just died in Paris.
> I am happy, sir, to be able to contradict an event that would be an
> affliction on all of the admirers of this young virtuoso. M. Liszt is
> in good health, and has not ceased teaching in the school for young
> ladies that I direct in the rue de Clichy.
> I cannot choose a better way than through your esteemed news-
> paper to give this happy news all the publicity it deserves.

Despite Madame Alix's assurances of his "good health," it is evident that Liszt
was still chronically ill. The journal *L'Observateur des Beaux-Arts* issued a report
that same day which openly declared that grief at the recent death of his father
had powerfully affected the young artist's health. Some of the shop windows
in Paris exhibited Liszt's portrait bearing the caption "Né le 22 Octobre, 1811,
mort à Paris, 1828." The Paris billboards, it is true, carried a large advertisement that Liszt would play Beethoven's *Emperor* Concerto on December 25,
but the concert was postponed when Liszt fell ill again, this time from the
measles.[18]

One of the best eyewitness accounts of Liszt at this time comes from
Wilhelm von Lenz. He was walking along the Paris boulevards one November
morning, he tells us, on his way to see Kalkbrenner, when one of those
billboards carrying the advertisement about Liszt's Beethoven concert caught
his attention. On a sudden impulse, he changed direction and went to see Liszt

---

18. We know this from the letter he wrote to his former master Carl Czerny on December 23. (LLB,
vol. 1, p. 3.)

instead; thus began an artistic encounter which had a colourful consequence, nearly fifty years later, in the famous opening chapter of von Lenz's book *Die grossen Pianovirtuosen unserer Zeit.*[19] Anna Liszt herself opened the door and showed von Lenz into her son's room. The visitor saw before him a "pale and haggard" young man "with unspeakably attractive features." He was reclining on a sofa and was smoking a long Turkish pipe, lost in meditation. His smile "was like the glitter of a dagger in the sunlight." The first thing that struck von Lenz was that Liszt kept three pianos in his studio, one of them with a specially strengthened keyboard built to his own specifications, on which he used to practise, and which von Lenz found virtually impossible to play. It is fashionable to discredit von Lenz today, since his monograph makes a number of claims which the modern Liszt researcher cannot entertain. He did not introduce Liszt to Weber's piano music.[20] Nor was he right to assert that he was Liszt's first piano pupil; Liszt had been teaching for at least eighteen months before he encountered von Lenz. Nevertheless, von Lenz is full of first-hand detail, with a penchant for memorable aphorisms; and he had many opportunities to hear Liszt, spanning nearly half a century. It was von Lenz who first said, "When Liszt appears, all other pianists disappear," and "Liszt is the past, the present, the future of the piano," phrases which have resounded through the Liszt literature. When Liszt received his personal copy of von Lenz's book in 1872, however, the thing that pleased him most was not the flattering remarks about his piano playing, but the author's perceptive comment on his religious calling. Seven years earlier, in 1865, Liszt had taken holy orders. Many sceptical voices were raised at the time, a fact which troubled him deeply. Von Lenz, viewing Liszt's life as a whole, wrote of his religious impulse: "His desire to become a priest came from the innermost core of his being. It was thematic." Liszt was grateful for that phrase, and picked it out for special mention in his letter of thanks.[21]

I V

One of the strangest companions of the eighteen-year-old Liszt was the Belgian-born musician Chrétien Urhan. Urhan had been the organist at St.-Vincent-de-Paul in the rue de Montholon, where Liszt had heard him daily.

---

19. LGPZ. Von Lenz (1809–83), who rose to become a Russian councillor of state, wrote about music in his spare time. He published several other books, the best known of which was his two-volume *Beethoven et ses trois styles*—the first time Beethoven's output had been analysed within these (by now) time-honoured divisions.

20. As a ten-year-old boy, Liszt had already played Weber's *Momento Capriccioso*, op. 12, in Pest. (*Tudományos Gyüjtemény*, vol. 7, 1823, pp. 122–23.)

21. LLB, vol. 2, p. 176. "Es war *thematisch.*" The italics are Liszt's.

He was a devout Catholic and his remote, mystical personality cast a spell over the young man. Urhan was also a gifted violinist and became leader of the Paris Opéra Orchestra. The historians have had a field-day with him. Urhan used to take communion at midday mass at St.-Vincent-de-Paul and fast every day until 6:00 p.m. Then he had dinner at the Café Anglais. He always began and ended his meal with the sign of the cross. He wore a light-blue frock coat, a colour he chose in honour of the Virgin, and was known locally as "the man in the blue clothes." For a time, this seraphic personality thought he was called to the religious life, and he left Paris for a Trappist monastery. The experiment failed after a week. Thereafter he was wracked with guilt and sought a special dispensation from the Archbishop of Paris before returning to his "worldly" position in the Paris Opéra Orchestra. Monsignor de Quélon replied that being a member of the opera orchestra did not necessarily constitute a hindrance to salvation. Nonetheless, Urhan made it a condition of his contract with the opera house that during the ballet he play his violin with his back to the stage lest, from his coign of vantage in the orchestra pit, he witness the abominations of the dancers disporting themselves before him and see the Devil. (It was common knowledge that in all the years Urhan played at the Opéra, he never saw a single ballet.[22]) Ernest Legouvé, who knew him personally, devoted a whole chapter to Urhan in his *Soixante Ans de souvenirs.*[23] Urhan often called on Madame Legouvé, sat with her for fifteen minutes without uttering a word, and then left, saying, "Good-bye, dear lady, I needed to see you!" Urhan's favourite instrument was neither the violin nor the organ, but the viola d'amore. He seemed drawn to its mournful, nostalgic sounds, in which he found the ideal counterpoint to his feelings. He was, in fact, a virtuoso on this seven-stringed instrument, which he rescued from oblivion and taught himself to play. He gave a number of concerts in the Paris Conservatoire which generated great interest. Urhan was also a composer. No one plays a note of his nowadays; indeed, copies of his music have become collectors' items. Liszt scholars are thereby denied the opportunity of exploring Urhan's musical influence on the younger composer. Urhan's compositions (typically, he preferred to call them "auditions") bore such fanciful titles as *Elle et moi, La Salutation angélique,* and *Les Regrets.* This music was anti-classical, highly subjective; it gave the young Liszt an early taste for musical romanticism. Equally important for him was Urhan's enthusiastic championship of Schubert. Urhan had already brought this neglected master to the attention of Paris within a year of the composer's death. Two of Urhan's string quintets are based on themes by Schubert, and he also composed some unusual piano studies based on the songs. Urhan's pioneer work

---

22. HLL, p. 86. Henri Doisy, an abbé of St.-Vincent-de-Paul, gives many interesting details of Urhan in his history of the parish. (DDP, pp. 289–91.)
23. LSS, vol. 3, pp. 168–77.

stimulated Liszt's own lifelong devotion to Schubert, which eventually resulted, among other things, in his arrangements for piano of more than fifty
of the songs.

v

The young Liszt developed into a voracious reader. A genuine thirst for
knowledge drove him to such diverse authors as Sainte-Beuve, Ballanche,
Rousseau, and Chateaubriand. His reading was, as yet, quite chaotic and lacked
the intellectual purpose of his later years. His bookshelves embraced both the
sacred and the secular. He filled his head not only with the "Defence of
Catholicism" by Lamennais, but also with the sceptical writings of Montaigne;
not only with the religious poetry of Lamartine, but also with the agnostic
prose of Voltaire. He often sat up half the night with such literature, looking
for some key with which to unlock the world. D'Ortigue once saw Liszt remain
motionless for four hours, sitting beside the chimneypiece, a volume of Lamartine in his hands. His soul, in Ramann's telling phrase, was full of presage. Only
eighteen years old, he could yet exclaim with René, "un instinct secret me
tourmente." Chateaubriand's romantic hero, in fact, had an intoxicating effect
on the whole of Liszt's generation. They were enslaved by this melancholic,
anguished character, steeped in the sorrows and disillusions of the world. So
completely did they identify with him that they aped his mannerisms and his
language, and "René fever" spread like an epidemic throughout Restoration
society. Too late came Chateaubriand's cry, as he saw himself surrounded by
ghastly parodies of his literary creation, "If it were possible to destroy René,
I would do it!" It was doubtless during an attack of René fever that the young
Liszt rushed up to the brilliant advocate Crémieux and cried, "Tell me everything about French literature!" The dumbfounded lawyer replied, "A great
confusion reigns in the head of this young man."

Liszt had also discovered the theatre. A favourite author was Victor Hugo,
whose *Marion Delorme* Liszt saw a number of times in the theatre of the Porte
St. Martin. The opera house, too, started to attract him, and during the winter
of 1829–30 he saw Rossini's *Guillaume Tell,* whose hero he admired for his
individual struggle against a tyrannical oppression, and also Auber's *La Fiancée.*
This latter work stimulated Liszt to produce his first composition in nearly two
years: the *Grande Fantaisie sur la tyrolienne de l'opéra "La Fiancée."* While not
particularly important musically, this operatic paraphrase is of documentary
interest because it fills a gap in our knowledge about Liszt's development as
a pianist. The opening pages, black with hemidemisemiquavers, confirm that
the tendency towards extreme virtuosity, so marked a characteristic of his music
in the late 1830s, was already formed within him.

When we hear this rarely played work today, we readily admit that Fétis's description of Liszt as a "thimble-rigger" was not unjust. The main purpose served by such pieces was to lead the young Liszt towards a deeper understanding of the resources of the modern keyboard and to prepare him for that technical breakthrough in the mid-1830s which is still described, a hundred and fifty years later, as "transcendental."

BOOK TWO

The Growing Virtuoso
1830 · 1834

After the July Revolution

He consumes himself, he feels everything too
deeply, the blade has worn out the scabbard. What
a pity!

COUNTESS AGÉNOR DE GASPARIN[1]

I

The last days of Restoration France were drawing to a close. Profound political and social changes were sweeping through the nation which culminated in the July Revolution of 1830. Charles X, who had been crowned at Rheims in 1825 with a pomp and ceremony unmatched since the coronations of the ancien régime, was a reactionary figure who hankered after a return to absolute monarchy—the old idea of "the divine right of kings," which Napoleon and the revolution of '89 had overturned. His difficulty was that the French people now had a charter which not only protected their freedoms, but which Charles was sworn to respect. When moderation was urged on him, and the throne of England held up as a model of how things should be in France, he made his classic remark, "I would rather hew wood." Opposition to Charles came to a head in March 1830, when the Chamber of Deputies addressed a firm resolution to the monarch expressing the fears of the nation. The king's reply was to suspend the chamber and, in effect, the constitution of France. During the next few weeks the political atmosphere in Paris was electric. People talked openly of civil war. Charles and his ministers ignored the warning signs. At a ball in the royal palace, while the highest aristocracy in the land pirouetted beneath the glittering chandeliers, heedless of the gathering storm outside, the politician Salvandy surveyed the scene and immortalized it with the comment, "We are dancing on a volcano."

---

1. BBAG, vol. 1, p. 150.

On July 27 the volcano erupted. Street barricades were raised and royalist troops under Marshal Marmont attacked them. It was the signal for a general conflagration. The following day, a group of young students from the Ecole Polytechnique unfurled the tricolour flag on the top of Notre Dame. Workers, artisans, and artists flocked to the side of the revolution, and soon the whole of the eastern side of Paris, including the rue de Montholon, where Liszt lived, was in the hands of the insurgents. After three days of bloody fighting—the "Three Glorious Days"—the French monarchy was again being brought to its knees. The effect on Liszt was immediate. Hearing the sound of gunfire, he rushed out of doors and witnessed hand-to-hand fighting in the cobbled streets of Montmartre. He joined the crowds shouting in support of General Lafayette, one of Napoleon's former officers who had taken up the people's cause. These experiences acted like a therapy and shook him from his lethargy. Anna Liszt, reflecting on these traumatic times, said, "The guns cured him."[2]

With the cannon of the "Three Glorious Days" booming in his ears, Liszt's creative energies were released, and he began to sketch out a "Revolutionary Symphony." Although Liszt never completed the work, it remains an autobiographical document of some interest. The sketch is headed "Symphonie" and is dated "27, 28, 29 juillet—Paris."[3] Programmatically conceived, the piece was to have been modelled on Beethoven's *Battle of Vittoria*. Liszt's idea was not to write a battle piece, however, but to express the glorious feelings aroused by revolution in general. Three themes were to have been worked into the fabric of the symphony: a Hussite song of the fifteenth century, the well-known German choral *Ein' feste Burg ist unser Gott,* and the rousing national march *La Marseillaise.* In the heat of the moment Liszt scrawled a number of words and phrases across the manuscript which can be deciphered with difficulty:

> indignation, vengeance, terreur, liberté! désordre, cri confus (vague bizarrcric) furcur . . . refus, marche de la garde royale, doute, incertitude, parties croisantes . . . 8 parties différentes, attaque, bataille . . . marche de la garde nationale, enthousiasme, enthousiasme, enthousiasme! . . . fragment de Vive Henry IV dispersé. Combiner "Allons enfants de la patrie."

Once the euphoria of the first heady days of the revolution had died down, Liszt set aside the score. Twenty years later, in response to the European uprisings in 1848–49, Liszt took up the project again, this time in the form of a five-movement symphony. Only the first movement was finished, and it later became known as the symphonic poem *Héroïde funèbre* (1854).

---

2. RLKM, vol. 1, p. 144.
3. WA. Facsimile reproduction in RLS, vol. 1, p. 327.

256   Zweites Buch.   Die Jahre der Entwickelung.

„Übrigens ist das alles nur konsequent und beweist auf das
klarste, wie sehr die Kunst beschützt wird und wie beneidens-
werth die Stellung der Künstler ist!"

Liszt's Antipathie gegen Bürgerkönigthum und Bourgeoisie
wurzelten in den Hindernissen, welche sie der Ausbreitung der
Kunst und der Verwirklichung der damaligen Humanitätsideale
entgegen trugen.   Seine Abneigung war eine konsequente und
äußerte sich unzählige Male, insbesondere aber in seiner Haltung
gegen Louis Philippe, dem er nicht nur zu begegnen auswich,
sondern vor dem er sich auch stets weigerte in den Tuilerien zu spie-
len.   Eine diese Haltung charakterisirende Anekdote dürfte hier Platz
finden.   Anfangs der vierziger Jahre war Liszt, in der Blüthe
seines Ruhmes stehend, gerade in Paris, als Pleyel eine Piano-
forteausstellung inscenirt hatte.   Eines Tages probirte Liszt die
Instrumente, als Louis Philippe mit einigen Herren in den
Saal trat, in dem er spielte.   Ein Ausweichen war unmöglich.   Der
König aber ging auf ihn zu und knüpfte eine Konversation an,
bei welcher Liszt, innerlich die Zähne knirschend, sich nur durch
stumme Verbeugungen und ein kurzes:
        „Ja, Sire —", betheiligte.
        „Erinnern Sie Sich noch, sagte endlich Louis Philippe,
wie Sie als Knabe bei mir, dem damaligen Duc d'Orléans,
spielten? — wie viel hat sich inzwischen verändert."
        „Ja", platzte Liszt los, „aber nicht zum bessern!"
        Die Folge hievon war, daß Louis Philippe eigenhändig
einen Strich durch Liszt's Namen zog, welcher auf der Liste
derer stand, die durch das Kreuz der Ehrenlegion ausgezeichnet
werden sollten. —

        Wie der Bourgeoisie, so stand Liszt auch zeitweise dem Adel
gegenüber.   Auch hier tritt uns manches Wort entgegen, das einer
inneren Feindseligkeit ähnelt und gleichsam in Opposition zu treten
scheint zu den Beziehungen, die zwischen ihm und der Aristokratie
bestanden.   Aber auch hier ist seine Gereiztheit keine, die dem
Stand als solchem gilt.   Es war gerade die Zeit, wo in Frank-
reich die „Aristokratie des Geistes" von der sie vertretenden Ge-
lehrten- und Künstlerwelt diskutirt, das Bestreben ihren Ver-
tretern im praktischen Leben Stellung und Geltung zu gewinnen von
den hervorragendsten Männern, unter ihnen von Guizot, welcher

*Another page from Lina Ramann's biography,
with Liszt's handwritten corrections.*

Victor Hugo described the Revolution of 1830 as "a revolution stopped halfway. Half progress, quasi right. Now logic ignores the quasi as the sun ignores a candle." There were many, like Hugo, who were critical of the political compromise which now emerged in France. Charles X had been banished only to be replaced by Louis-Philippe, the "Citizen King." Louis-Philippe, the former Duke of Orléans, had no claim on the throne of France. He was a bourgeois king, the creation of the middle classes, who disliked the notion of "divine right" but had no stomach for a republic. He had first been appointed lieutenant-general of the kingdom by Lafayette at the unlikely venue of the Hôtel de Ville. After the abdication of Charles, the Chamber of Deputies simply converted him into the new king, a move which meant that the French had to fight the revolution all over again in 1848. Meanwhile, Louis-Philippe, who had no pretentions to divinity, tried to be all things to all men. He often strolled about the streets, an umbrella over his arm. He called common workmen "my friends" and National Guardsmen "my comrades." Liszt, like Hugo and other radicals, detested Louis-Philippe and the compromise for which he stood, and his attitude never softened. Once in 1834 the "Citizen King" and his retinue visited a piano exhibition mounted in the Erard workshops. There he encountered Liszt, who was trying out the latest models. "Do you still remember," remarked the king, "that you played at my house when you were a boy and I was still the Duke of Orléans? Much has changed since then." "Yes, Sire," replied Liszt, "but not for the better." The remark cost Liszt the Legion of Honour; Louis-Philippe himself struck Liszt's name off the roll of nominees.[4] This people's monarchy, a contradiction in terms, could not survive. Louis-Philippe in turn was swept aside. In 1848 he fled Paris in a cab and arrived in England under the thoroughly bourgeois name of "Mr. Smith."

II

The liberal atmosphere released by the July Revolution acted like a catalyst on French creative thought. Writers, painters, musicians, and social reformers converged on Paris, and the capital fairly teemed with artistic and intellectual

---

4. RLKM, vol. I, p. 256; see also ACLA, vol. I, p. 68. In his personal copy of Ramann's biography (WA, Kasten 352, no. 1) Liszt, clearly aggrieved, jotted down a marginal note stating that the award of the medal was delayed for ten years as a result of his verbal exchange with the French monarch ("Erst 10 Jahre später erhielt ich la croix"; the facsimile is reproduced on p. 147). Liszt was not admitted to the lowest rank of the Legion of Honour, that of "chevalier," until April 1845. That he regarded the long delay as a blow to his pride is unquestionable, and he called it a "fiasco" (VFL, p. 70). Not until August 25, 1860, was he given the higher rank of "officer," through the intervention of Napoleon III. A year later, on May 31, 1861, he was elevated to the yet higher rank of "commander" by the same monarch. The certificates of both these latter titles are kept in Weimar. (WA, Kasten 123, nos. 3 and 4.)

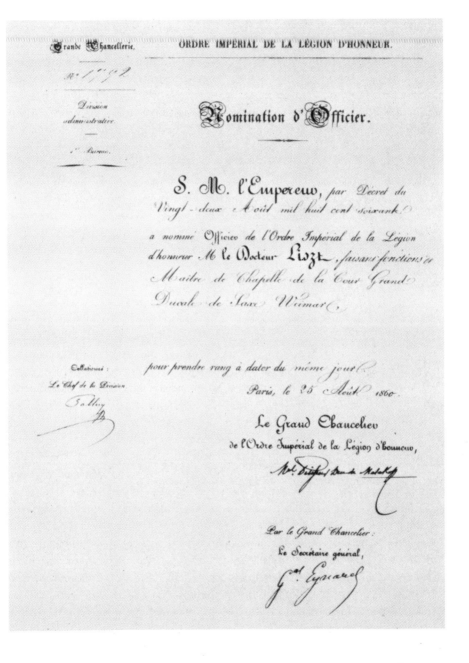

Liszt's certificate of nomination to the Legion of Honour, dated August 25, 1860.

activity. Among the writers and poets who lived and worked there were
Sainte-Beuve, Victor Hugo, Balzac, George Sand, and Heine. The painters
included Delacroix, Devéria, and Ary Scheffer, who bequeathed to posterity
the best portrait we have of the romantic young Liszt, with his pale profile and
his long "nervous" hands. As for the musicians, Hiller, Berlioz, Kalkbrenner,
and Alkan were long-time residents of the city. Soon this volatile mixture was
enriched by a flood of refugees from Warsaw, recently sacked by the Russians,
and Paris became the adopted home of a number of distinguished Poles,
including Chopin and Mickiewicz, the Polish national poet. Merely to list these
names is to call the roll of the very leaders of the Romantic movement itself.
Liszt was personally acquainted with every one of them.

All these artists came together in that most characteristic of Parisian institutions, the salon. Sponsored and organized by the wealthiest families in the
realm, the salons of the Faubourgs St.-Germain and St.-Honoré were the scenes
of dazzling assemblies of aristocrats, politicians, artists, and scientists. Here were
mixed and mingled all the radical ideas of the post-revolutionary years, producing a distillation that became the very embodiment of *haute culture*. These
sparkling occasions, renowned for their wit and polish, were presided over by
the most fashionable hostesses in the city, and included such flowers of the
aristocracy as the Countess de Montault, the Countess de la Rochefoucauld, and
the Duchess de Gramont. Each of these ladies vied with her rivals to capture
the most talented and interesting protégés. By far the most vivid description
of the Paris salon has been handed down to us by Countess Marie d'Agoult,
Liszt's future mistress, who once hired Rossini and the stars of the Italian Opera,
including the singer La Malibran, for the entertainment of her guests.[5] Her
circle also included Lamartine, Alfred de Vigny, and the novelist Eugène Sue,
whose books became best-sellers because they dealt with the seamy side of
Parisian life, a daring and original topic for those days, and one which held
the sheltered hostesses of St.-Germain in thrall. The salon was not without
humour either. On one occasion Countess d'Agoult invited Alfred de Vigny
to a literary evening in order to read his poem "La Frégate," which dealt with
the shipwreck of a frigate. The reading was a failure; hardly anyone could
understand it because the treatment was too technical. Halfway through, the
Austrian ambassador's huge moustache started to bristle, and he inquired gruffly
of his neighbour, "Is that gentleman a shipbuilder?" As de Vigny took his leave
he rose to the occasion; turning to the countess, he remarked with a smile, "My
frigate has been shipwrecked in your salon, madame."[6] Elegance, poise, *le bon
mot:* these were cherished qualities.

It was in the salons of the Faubourg St.-Germain that the young Liszt,

---

5. AS, pp. 301–13.
6. AS, p. 345.

hungry for whatever experiences life proffered, met the Countess Adèle La-prunarède, who later became the Duchess de Fleury. She was young and beautiful and, like many women of her social station, was married to an aging and neglectful husband. Adèle awoke a passion in Liszt, and he enjoyed his first extended love-affair with her. When the unsuspecting count announced that he and his wife were leaving Paris on a long trip to their castle at Marlioz in the Swiss Alps, Liszt was invited to accompany them. Surrounded by snow and ice, with the mountain roads impassable, Liszt and Adèle were marooned in the Castle Marlioz for the whole of the winter of 1832–33, with the count's elderly sister as chaperone. So secret was this attachment that no one in Paris seems to have known about it until much later, although Liszt's absence was observed by d'Ortigue.[7] When he finally returned to the capital Liszt kept up a clandes-tine correspondence with Adèle—an indiscretion that he later had cause to regret. Forty-five years afterwards he jestingly told Lina Ramann that with Adèle he had developed his first "exercises in the lofty French style."[8] The young dandy had other passing affairs too, most notably with the Polish-born Countess Pauline Plater. It was Countess Plater who, when asked to compare the merits of the three pianists who had played in her salon—Ferdinand Hiller, Chopin, and Liszt—said that she would choose Hiller as a friend, Chopin as a husband, and Liszt as a lover.[9] Not yet twenty-one, the young Liszt, it seems, already had a reputation with the hostesses of the Faubourg St.-Germain. He is known to have taken a trip to the Savoie in 1832 with one Mlle de Barré,[10] and two other young ladies who bestowed their favours on Liszt at this time, but about whom nothing is known save Liszt's solitary mention of them in his correspondence, were a certain Hortense and a Madame G——.[11] In a revela-tory letter Liszt tells us that in his twenty-first year his mother and a certain Madame D—— tried with all their might to arrange a marriage "in order to calm my excited nerves."[12] Another proposed bride was Mlle Charlotte Laborie.[13] Wisely, he resisted these family pressures. But it was for him "a time of struggle, of anguish, and of solitary torments."

Liszt still gave lessons at the school of Madame Alix, and he was now in

---

7. OFL.

8. RLKM, vol. 1, p. 317. This relationship with Adèle may have begun much earlier than anyone at the moment suspects. Liszt was in Geneva for an extended period in the spring of 1831, staying with his pupil Pierre-Etienne Wolff. From there he wrote to his mother that upon his arrival in Geneva he had found a letter waiting for him from Adèle, but that it had not yet been possible to see her and talk with her as as he wished. (LLBM, p. 18.) La Mara misdated this letter, attributing it to the year 1835. Yet the holograph, now in the Bayreuth archive, clearly bears the postmark "Geneva, May 1831." (BA, uncatalogued.)

9. RLKM, vol. 1, p. 229.

10. BLP, p. 90.

11. ACLA, vol. 1, pp. 83 and 89.

12. ACLA, vol. 1, p. 89. "Madame D——" was probably Euphémie Didier, the maternal grand-mother of the proposed bride. See ELP, p. 19.

13. ACLA, vol. 1, p. 83.

such demand among the daughters of the aristocracy that he became the subject of jealous bickering among them. Countess Agénor de Gasparin has left us some intimate descriptions of the grave young master. "He was so pale, this poor young man, that it grieved me. He consumes himself, he feels everything too deeply, the blade has worn out the scabbard. What a pity!"[14] Blond, tall, very thin, and with a distinguished bearing, Liszt at twenty-one was already a commanding presence. He had moved to 61, rue de Provence, where Countess de Gasparin sometimes met his mother. Nothing seemed more disparate to the countess than the contrast between Franz and Anna Liszt. The one was all emotion, the other all intelligence. The mother "does not have the appearance of having given life to this graceful young man, thin, pale, all soul, all spirit, all fire."[15] Countess Dash, who lived in the same building as Liszt, remembered him "coming down the steep stairs like a ghost."[16] Madame Auguste Boissier, whose daughter Valérie took lessons from Liszt during the winter of 1831–32, adds detail to the picture. She once spotted Liszt sitting in the audience at a *soirée musicale* organized by Erard, to which were invited such notables as Meyerbeer, Hérold, Nourrit, and Schunke. But it was Liszt who mesmerized Madame Boissier: "I perceived Liszt with his glasses on his nose, his face so pale, so sad, his expression so grave and remarkable, distinguished from all the others."[17] Later Madame Boissier chaperoned her daughter's lessons with Liszt and observed him at closer quarters. She reports that he disliked "civilized music," and would everywhere put in place of law and order revolution and strife: "He was able to reproduce all the passions at the keyboard—terror, fright, horror, despair, love."[18] Comparisons were made between a study of Kessler and Dante's *Inferno*. In order the better to play a study by Moscheles, the young master first made his pupil read *Jenny* by Victor Hugo.[19] These were unusual pedagogical conceptions. No wonder his students found him so stimulating. Madame Boissier aptly described these lessons with Liszt as "a course in musical declamation."

III

In the spring of 1832 Paris was struck by cholera. The life of the salons was temporarily halted. As the disease took hold, hundreds began to die every day. On April 10, when the scourge was at its height, two thousand people suc-

14. BBAG, vol. 1, p. 150.
15. BBAG, vol. 1, p. 151.
16. DMA, vol. 4, p. 149.
17. BLP, p. 10.
18. BLP, p. 39.
19. BLP, p. 23.

cumbed. The city ran out of coffins; the corpses were put into sacks and then placed on wooden carts which wended their way back and forth between the cemeteries. The wealthier classes left Paris, taking their doctors and well-stocked pharmacies with them. More than 120,000 passports were issued at the Hôtel de Ville, but many of the recipients never left the city, being caught up in the endless traffic jam of corpses which brought the boulevards to a standstill. Heine left a graphic eye-witness account of these macabre scenes in his *Letters from Paris.* Wishing to visit a friend one day, he arrived just as they were putting his corpse in the hearse. He caught a cab and followed the body to the Père-Lachaise cemetery. Outside the narrow gate he found himself trapped among hundreds of vehicles bearing the dead, and was obliged to pass several hours in these gloomy surroundings. One coachman tried to get before another. A disturbance broke out and the gendarmes came in with bared sabres. Some hearses were overturned, and the coffins fell to the ground and burst open. Heine wrote, "I seemed to see that most horrible of all *émeutes*—a riot of the dead."[20] Liszt remained in Paris throughout the epidemic. He was a frequent visitor to the home of Victor Hugo, where he used to play the Marche funèbre from Beethoven's Sonata in A-flat major "while all the dead from cholera filed past to Notre Dame in their shrouds."[21] This was not a rhetorical gesture. Liszt's obsession with the dead, the dying, and the damned was real enough and often provoked a musical response. There is a whole branch of his music dealing with death, and symbolized by such titles as *Totentanz, Funérailles, La Lugubre gondola,* and *Pensée des morts.* Countess Dash in her *Mémoires* recounts how she was once kept awake all night, together with the other tenants in the building in the rue de Provence, while Liszt played the *Dies Irae* from dusk to dawn in countless variations.[22]

Our picture of the young Liszt is rounded out in an unexpected way. We learn from the French newspapers that Liszt started visiting the hospitals of Paris. In "The Second Scrapbook of Marie d'Agoult," now in the Library of Versailles, a rare curiosity has been preserved. A newspaper cutting taken from the Paris journal *Le Pianiste* bears the striking headline "L'Idiote mélomane." It tells the strange story of a sixty-year-old woman who had been a patient in the Salpêtrière hospital for the insane from childhood. She was incapable of understanding anything, of dressing herself, of working, and even of speaking. When she wished to make her needs known, she could only do so by uttering

20. HSWMB, vol. 4, p. 121.

21. FJI, p. 133.

22. DMA, vol. 4, p. 149. According to Countess Dash, all the tenants in Liszt's building "joined together to ask for his expulsion. We would have got it, but he didn't put us to the trouble; he left of his own accord." Some idea of his irregular life-style at this time may be gained from his letters to Valérie Boissier. "I haven't had a *single free evening* for more than two months, which distresses my unfortunate porter, who is obliged to wait up for me (candle or taper in hand), and even more my too-kind mother, who is always so worried about my health and my future." (BDLL, p. 10.)

raucous cries, which she would repeat until her wishes were satisfied. It was noticed, however, that she responded at once to music. She was able to sing back melodies that were sung to her, and she could even recall them after a lapse of time. The hospital authorities invited Liszt to visit the institute and play for the *"idiote."* A piano was set up in her cell. The moment Liszt's fingers touched the keyboard, the old woman's eyes became fixated on them. Gnawing her fists, she appeared to enter a highly charged state, and she vibrated to every chord struck by the young musician. The passage he played produced a visible effect on her similar to that of an electrical discharge. More than twenty times this passage was repeated, and every time the old woman shook violently. It so happened that she was very fond of fruit, and her doctors now carried the experiment a stage further. Some apricots were placed before her, but as long as the music played she paid no heed to them. Only when Liszt ceased playing did she give her attention to the fruit.[23] This interesting report may well be one of the first recorded cases of what a later age would call music therapy. This visit to the Salpêtrière hospital for the insane fits in with everything we know of the young Liszt's sombre character. According to Madame Boissier, Liszt frequented "hospitals, gambling casinos and asylums." He even went down into prison dungeons in order to see those condemned to die.[24]

I V

In an attempt to find spiritual repose, Liszt had already been drawn to Saint-Simonism. The humanitarian ideals of the movement, which was just then enjoying a brief vogue in Paris, made a deep appeal to him. The Saint-Simonists attempted to combine socialism with the teachings of Jesus. Liszt attended the sect's revivalist meetings, led by Father Enfantin, and he familiarized himself with its literature. He immersed himself in Saint-Simon's *Lettres d'un habitant de Genève* (1803), later developed by its author into an ambitious "theory of life" whose main tenets can be summarized thus:

1. to improve the quality of human life through the dissemination of scientific knowledge;
2. to reorganize society in order that one's work, not one's birth, would determine one's place in the social hierarchy;
3. to work for the emancipation of women;

---

23. This story, as reported by *Le Pianiste* (February 5, 1835), was taken from the *Gazette médicale* (January 3, 1835). According to the Liszt-d'Agoult correspondence, however, Liszt had been visiting the Salpêtrière hospital since at least September 1833 (ACLA, vol. 1, p. 35).
24. BLP, pp. 39–40.

4. to prohibit idleness;
5. to distribute wealth equitably;
6. to "humanize" religion.

These ideals were to resonate in Liszt's mind for life, as his marginal notes to the first volume of Ramann's biography show.[25]

Claude Henri, Count de Saint-Simon, had been born in 1760 and died in 1825. From the start he had had a conviction of his own greatness. His valet had instructions to wake him up every morning with the words, "Have you forgotten, my lord, that you have great things to do?" Philosopher, social reformer, and political activist, Saint-Simon was to found one of the most vigorous intellectual movements in France. When he was only nineteen he became a volunteer in the American War of Independence and served in five campaigns. After his return to Paris he also took part in the French Revolution, on which he pinned great hopes for social reform. He lost a fortune as a result of some disastrous land speculations, became bankrupt, and was sent to prison. After his release he founded a "school" and attracted to his banner a number of disciples, of whom the most prominent were Fourier, Thierry, and later Michel Chevalier. Saint-Simon was not the first social reformer to become depressed because he failed to put the world to rights and create utopia in his lifetime. In 1823, worn out with struggles and sufferings, he gave up the good fight and attempted to blow out his brains. He failed, and lingered long enough to write his most influential book, *Le Nouveau Christianisme,* in 1825. That same year he died in the arms of his followers, a martyr to the cause.

Saint-Simonism enjoyed its greatest success after the demise of its founder. Through the press (the movement now controlled two newspapers, *L'Organisateur* and *Le Globe*) and especially through public meetings, the master's ideas took root and started to flower. In 1828 a complete exposition of Saint-Simon's views was given in a series of lectures in Paris by Amand Bazard, one of the leaders of the sect, and they aroused great interest. The members set up communes, the best known being at Ménilmontant, a property belonging to Enfantin, where they wore a distinctive garb, the *bleu-barbon* coat and a red beret, and shared all their worldly possessions. In 1832 the cult was investigated by the French courts. Chevalier, the manager of *Le Globe,* was arrested; he served six months in prison, and the sect was broken up. This merely served to provoke national interest in its activities. It is an indication of how fashionable Saint-Simonism became in the 1830s that in 1836, four years after he was jailed, Chevalier was awarded the Legion of Honour.

When Liszt clandestinely attended the Saint-Simonist meetings in their headquarters at 6, rue Monsigny, he was doing no more than other leading

---

25. WA, Kasten 352, no. 1, p. 154.

figures of the Romantic movement, including Heine, George Sand, Berlioz, and Sainte-Beuve, who actually drafted two of the society's manifestos for publication in *Le Globe*.[26] Félicien David even went into "exile" with Enfantin and forty of his most ardent disciples at Ménilmontant during the worst days of the inquisition and composed four-part choruses for the group to sing while waiting out the ordeal. We gather from d'Ortigue that Liszt sometimes played at the society's meetings. He once accompanied Malibran at a gathering held in one of its properties in the rue Taitbout and saw General Lafayette himself sitting in the congregation.[27] From another source, a leading Saint-Simonist, Hippolyte Carnot, we also learn that "Liszt would take his seat at the piano and abandon himself to his fantasy."[28] It is not hard to see what attracted these rising young Romantics to Saint-Simonism. Had not Emile Barrault, the movement's leading aesthetician and finest public orator, already placed art at the centre of life and elevated the artist to a new priesthood? The artist walked in heaven: he was the chosen vessel through which God transmitted divine fire.

After the police raided Ménilmontant and broke up the cult, Liszt's interest in Saint-Simonism waned. His biographers, led astray by some misleading comments of Heine, have placed too much stress on Liszt's connection with the organization. Liszt himself should be heeded on this point. He denied ever being a member of the society and expressed himself with humour on the topic: "Among my numerous tailors' bills, I can certify that there is not one to be found for a *bleu-barbon* coat."[29] Nevertheless, his brush with Saint-Simonism was a milestone in his psychological development. It not only stimulated his social conscience but, more important, it prepared him for an encounter with a man who symbolized all his youthful ideals, and whose teachings were beginning to exert a profound influence over the French Romantics generally: the Abbé Félicité de Lamennais.

V

Ordained as a priest in 1816, Lamennais had quickly risen to national prominence through his polemical writings. His *Essai sur l'indifférence en matière de*

---

26. It is possible to pin down the date of Liszt's first involvement with the Saint-Simonists fairly accurately. In a letter written on October 20, 1830, Father Enfantin recorded this observation: "Several artists, Liszt, Berlioz, Nourrit, are approaching us. Sainte-Beuve came to us by way of *Le Globe;* he attends our Thursday soirées." (*Oeuvres,* vol. 3, p. 49.) For more on Berlioz's involvement, see his unpublished letters to the journalist Charles Duvrier, in which he approves of the doctrine because it leads to "the betterment of the most numerous and poorest class, the natural ranking of talent, and the abolition of privileges of every kind." (BBRC, vol. 1, p. 136.)

27. OFL.

28. CSS, pp. 25–26.

29. LLB, vol. 1, p. 133.

religion (1817) won immediate praise. His position changed as he perceived that the only hope for France during the social upheavals of the post-Napoleonic era was the combination of a regenerated Catholic Church with political liberalism. He then struck out boldly against his own bishops and against the monarchy of France in his book *Des Progrès de la révolution et de la guerre contre l'Eglise* (1829), which drew upon him the wrath of the establishment. After the Revolution of 1830 Lamennais saw his chance and founded his controversial newspaper *L'Avenir,* which became a national mouthpiece for social reform. Many members of the literary intelligentsia wrote for its columns, including Sainte-Beuve, Hugo, and Balzac. *L'Avenir* advocated the separation of state and church, with democratic principles for the one and ultramontanism (papal supremacy) for the other. This was an inflammatory doctrine, calculated to antagonize both state and church. Publication of *L'Avenir* was suspended and Lamennais put on trial. He appealed to the Vatican and journeyed to Rome in order to plead his cause in person, but Pope Gregory XVI had no intention of playing the revolutionary role that Lamennais had advocated for him. The pontiff condemned the arguments of his rebel priest in the encyclical *Mirari Vos* (August 1832). Deeply embittered, Lamennais returned to France. Not only did he refuse to recant, but he launched a frontal attack on the Vatican in his famous *Paroles d'un croyant* (1834). This beautifully written book, couched in the ringing language of the Old Testament, has become a classic. Lamennais said that the printers who set the book could hardly wait to peruse each page as it came off the press. It provoked the encyclical *Singulari Nos* (July 1834), which describes the work as a "detestable production of impiety and audacity."[30] Lamennais now broke with the church. He retired to his country manor, La Chênaie, in Brittany, which he had inherited from his grandfather, and where he continued to write and reflect. His vigorous character, his mesmeric personality, and his uncompromising utterances turned him into a guru figure who attracted many disciples from across France. La Chênaie became a focal point of smouldering discontent. There Lamennais used to ramble through the grounds, dressed like a peasant in his straw hat, old woollen stockings, and tattered grey coat, holding forth to the young admirers who followed at his heels.[31]

Liszt first got to know Lamennais at the beginning of 1834. After reading

---

30. An English translation of the encyclicals *Mirari Vos* and *Singulari Nos* can be found in SPR, appendix C.

31. He was not excommunicated, as is sometimes stated. But he refused all his life to be reconciled with Rome, and after his death in 1854 he was buried, at his own request, in an unmarked grave, without the benefit of clergy. A big police guard attended his funeral, which attracted crowds of poor people. A gravedigger wanted to place a cross on his grave, but was prevented from doing so. Then somebody in the crowd shouted, "Everyone can go home, it's all over." (GVL, p. 170.)

Liszt, a lithograph by Devéria (1832).

the *Paroles d'un croyant* he wrote to Lamennais to tell him how much the book meant to him. Lamennais replied in detail[32] and invited Liszt to La Chênaie, where he spent most of the summer of 1834, in spiritual retreat, sitting at the master's feet. Lamennais was later to observe of his young disciple that he had "one of the most beautiful and noble souls that I have met on this earth."[33] Liszt in turn rhapsodized over his mentor.

> The abbé, our good father, takes his straw hat, completely worn out and torn in various places, and says in a *simpatica* voice, "Let's go, children, let's go for a walk," whereupon we are launched into space for hours at a time. Truly, he is a marvellous man, prodigious, absolutely extraordinary. So much genius, and so much heart. Eleva- tion, devotion, passionate ardour, a sharp mind, profound judge- ment, the simplicity of a child. . . . I have yet to hear him say: I. Always Christ, always sacrifice for others, and the voluntary accept- ance of opprobrium, of scorn, of misery and death.[34]

The fact is not sufficiently stressed that Liszt discovered himself as a composer at La Chênaie during that summer of 1834. Several compositions were born there which bear the unmistakeable imprint of his mature style, including the three *Apparitions, Harmonies poétiques et religieuses,* and the revolutionary piece *Lyon.* The first *Apparition*[35] is a miniature masterpiece, totally neglected today. No one who hears a passage such as the following can confound the authentic voice of Liszt with any of his Romantic contemporaries.

---

32. BL, vol. 3, p. 46, fn. 2.
33. BL, vol. 3, p. 101.
34. ACLA, vol. 1, p 120.
35. The title is derived from Lamartine's poem "Apparition" (1818).

During his stay at La Chênaie, Liszt worked daily at the keyboard, often with Lamennais within earshot.[36] Under these peculiar conditions was born the defiant composition *Lyon,* which emerged as a result of conversations the master had with his disciple about the five days' street-fighting in Lyon in April 1834, during which several workmen had been killed. Lamennais had defended some of the accused at their trial, appealing in court in their behalf. Liszt's revolutionary march bears the socialist motto "To live working or to die fighting," and is dedicated "to M. F. de L." This motto had been coined by a worker in the earlier Lyon uprising of 1831,[37] and Liszt's use of it here was deliberately inflammatory. His continuing interest in the plight of the silk-weavers of Lyon is borne out by his eloquent description of their squalid living conditions, based on his visits to that strife-torn city in 1835 and again in 1837 in order to give charity concerts for the poor.[38] Vianna da Motta has acutely observed that the rousing main theme with which *Lyon* begins is a musical setting of the motto itself.[39]

The march proper gets under way with a battle-song, cut from similar cloth to the *Marseillaise,* behind which we sense the ominous tread of a thousand feet. The din and clangour of armed conflict are never far distant, and it is not hard to imagine the whine of grapeshot, the muffled roar of cannon, puffs of smoke, and the cries of the wounded illuminating this vivid soundscape.[40]

---

36. ACLA, vol. 1, p. 119.
37. BLU, p. 207.
38. RGS, vol. 2, pp. 155–56; CPR, pp. 140–41.
39. CE, vol. 2, part 4, p. vi.
40. The actual date of *Lyon* is still in dispute. Liszt held back its publication until 1840, when he included it in his *Album d'un voyageur.* It has been suggested that this march dates from 1837 or even later, and that it arises from Liszt's traumatic contact with the weavers of Lyon in August of that

The most crucial ideas Liszt absorbed at La Chênaie concerned the role of the artist and his place in society. Lamennais expressed himself powerfully on such matters. Art, for him, was God made manifest; it ennobled the human race; insofar as the artist was a bearer of the beautiful, he was like a priest ministering to his congregation. These thoughts came to fruition in the last major work of Lamennais, his *Esquisse d'une philosophie* (1840), which was already foment-ing within him during the time he knew Liszt. There is nothing in these ideas that Liszt did not already dimly perceive. But it was left to Lamennais to sharpen and clarify Liszt's attitudes. The result was the composer's début as a polemical writer. In his very first article, "On Future Church Music" (1834), Liszt called for a new kind of music, one which would "unite on a colossal scale the Theatre and the Church," a remark worthy of Lamennais. A second article, "On the Position of Artists and Their Place in Society" (1835), ap-pealed to musicians to form among themselves "a holy bond, to stimulate the infinite spread of Music." It demanded that the status of artists be raised, "that measures be brought about to establish their dignity." Liszt then went on to unfold this manifesto:

In the name of all musicians, of art, and of social progress, we require:

(a) The foundation of an assembly to be held every five years for religious, dramatic, and symphonic music, by which the works that are considered best in these three categories shall be ceremonially

year. (MLL, p. 229.) When Liszt corrected his personal copy of Ramann's biography, however, he left untouched her notion that *Lyon* belonged to the period 1834–35, and both Raabe (R. 8) and Searle (G. 156) opted for this earlier date. In the absence of a manuscript, a letter, a diary entry, or a single piece of hard evidence in support of the later date, we have accepted Ramann's account—one which is silently endorsed by Liszt. For the details of Liszt's long association with the city of Lyon, see SLL.

performed every day for a whole month in the Louvre, being afterwards purchased by the government, and published at their expense. In other words, we require the foundation of a musical Museum.

(b) The introduction of musical instruction into the primary schools, its extension into other kinds of schools, and, at that point, the calling into existence of a new church music.

(c) The reorganization of choral singing and the reformation of plainchant in all the churches of both Paris and the provinces.

(d) General assemblies of Philharmonic Societies in the manner of the great musical festivals of England and Germany.

(e) Opera productions, concert and chamber-music performances, organized after the plan sketched in our previous article on the Conservatoire.

(f) A school of advanced musical studies, established quite separately from the Conservatoire by the most eminent artists—a school whose branches shall extend to all the provincial towns having a chair in the history and philosophy of music.

(g) A cheap edition of the most important works of old and new composers from the musical Renaissance to the present time. It will embrace the development of the art in its entirety, from folk song to Beethoven's Choral Symphony. This publication as a whole might be called the "Pantheon of Music." The biographies, treatises, commentaries, and glossaries which would have to accompany it would form a true "Encyclopedia of Music."[41]

This was the young Liszt's musical prescription for his times. It is a bold document, although one or two of its recommendations will strike the modern reader as naive. But let us not forget the bleak historical context which prevailed when Liszt drew up his seven-point plan. The radical notion of schools for advanced musical training going well beyond the level of education found in the conservatories has meanwhile become a reality. So, too, has the idea of cheap editions of music covering musical history from the Renaissance to the present day. During his Weimar years, when he finally had at his disposal the power and resources to implement his ideas, we shall find him returning to this youthful document and transforming some of its basic directives, with great political acumen, into musical reality. The ideals that it embodied sprang, after all, from his character.

41. A twelve-page holograph section of "On the Position of Artists," signed by Liszt, is in the British Library, M.S. Add. 33965, fol. 237–42. The manifesto was later incorporated into RGS, vol. 2, pp. 53–54. (CPR, pp. 71–73.)

A Riot of Pianists

When dear God is bored in heaven, he opens the
window and contemplates the boulevards of Paris.
HEINRICH HEINE[1]

I

Paris in the 1830s was the centre of the pianistic world. Dozens of steel-fingered, chromium-plated virtuosos played there, including Kalkbrenner, Herz, Hiller, Hünten, Pixis, Thalberg, Dreyschock, and Cramer. Some of these men spent their lives quite literally crouched over the keyboard, bringing their fingers to an unbelievable state of perfection. One or two of them even specialized in a particular branch of technique. There was Dreyschock with his octaves, Kalkbrenner with his passage-work, and Thalberg with his trick of making two hands sound like three. Nowadays we smile at such antics, but this generation of pianists solved some of the most intractable problems of piano technique and raised the general level of performance to hitherto unheard-of heights. They are still affectionately referred to in the profession as the "flying trapeze" school. Dreyschock appears to have had wrists of steel, for he could play octaves as fast as other pianists could play single notes. He used to amaze his audiences by performing Chopin's *Revolutionary* Study with the difficult left-hand part in octaves, a feat that had taken him many weeks of obsessive work to master. As for Kalkbrenner, the rapidity of his scale-work astonished everyone who heard it. Each note was crystal clear, each demisemiquaver individually polished until it shone like a jewel. He was a machine-tooled pianist who functioned with perfect precision down to his last finger-joint. According to Paer, he directed his fingers as if they were "a well-drilled company of soldiers," and

---

1. HSWMB, vol. 4, p. 89.

he would sit motionless at the keyboard like a general behind the front lines following the progress of a battle. Then there was Thalberg, who took Paris by storm in 1835. He was a master of the sustaining pedal and could make the piano glow with colour. His greatest speciality was to bring out the melody in the middle of the keyboard with alternating thumbs while surrounding it with cascades of arpeggios, making it sound as if he had three hands. Thalberg was more than a mere technician, however. At his best he was an outstanding artist who used the piano as a genuine means of musical expression. We shall hear more about Thalberg, for he was the young Liszt's only serious rival; on one occasion he nearly eclipsed him.

There was continual competition between these masters of the keyboard to gain popularity with the Paris audiences. Concert-goers watched with relish as one pianist attempted to outplay another—gladiators of the keyboard locked in combat, fighting it out in the open arena of the concert hall. There were, in fact, three arenas—the Conservatoire, the Salle Erard, and the Salle Pleyel —and the arenas themselves vied for the best attractions. Erard and Pleyel were business rivals. Their salons were conceived as miniature concert halls built to enshrine the "house piano." Every year the latest models rolled off the assembly-lines, bigger and better than ever—grand pianos, giraffe pianos, cottage pianos, square pianos—designed to fill the rapidly expanding domestic market created by the emergence of a wealthy middle class. Both Erard and Pleyel employed dozens of skilled carpenters, painters, turners, and metal-workers; and through the careful division of labour each of these firms was capable of creating a hundred or more pianos a year.[2] It was Erard's proud boast that he could ship a piano anywhere in Europe, and he made extensive use of the continent's canals and waterways to float his instruments to all parts of the civilized world. A concert in the Salle Pleyel or the Salle Erard, then, was much more than a purely musical affair: it was also a business convention in which the investors would gather to see some reigning virtuoso publicly endorse the latest model in front of an audience of four hundred or more connoisseurs. Kalkbrenner owned shares in Pleyel et Cie. When he gave a concert it ranked as activity on the stock-exchange. Henri Herz even opened his own factory; at a Herz concert one saw not merely the pianist Herz but the manager himself playing. When Chopin arrived in Paris he chose to make his début in the Salle Pleyel. Liszt, on the other hand, invariably appeared in the Salle Erard. And so the pendulum swung back and forth. As for the Paris Conservatoire, it too was a factory of sorts, turning out not pianos but pianists. The numbers alone are impressive. In 1822, when Cherubini was appointed director, he found no

---

2. An interesting history of the Erard factory, and one which gives an accurate chronology of the many improvements introduced into the instrument by this firm, was written by Pierre Erard himself and published in 1844 to mark the occasion of the Great Exhibition of Paris. (EPE.)

fewer than forty-one women and thirty-two men enrolled in the piano department. He described this number as "abusive and pernicious," but despite his
promise to "curb the pianists," that number had greatly increased ten years later.
The leading teachers were Pierre Zimmerman and Louis Adam (who wrote the
official *Méthode* for the Conservatoire), through whose studios passed a stream
of players, not unlike cars rolling off a modern assembly-line.[3] Marmontel's
book *Les Pianistes célèbres* says it all: the galaxy of talent he there reviewed
either came from the Conservatoire itself or had been attracted to France
because of the golden opportunities that country offered.[4] Paris was a riot of
pianists, and the noise they made was heard across the world.

II

Watching this Tower of Babel with his jaundiced eye was Heinrich Heine, who
immortalized the epoch in his *Musikalische Berichte aus Paris*. His pen earned
for him a reputation as the scourge of Europe. Wit was his deadliest weapon,
and he aimed it with lethal accuracy against the Paris Virtuoso School, which
he likened to "a plague of locusts swarming to pick Paris clean." Of Dreyschock
and his noisy octaves he remarked, "One seems to hear not one pianist Dreyschock, but *drei Schock* [i.e., three times three score] of pianists." And lest his
readers fail to grasp this pointed pun, he added, "On the evening of his concert
the wind lay in a southwesterly direction, so perhaps you could hear him in
Augsburg."[5] The powerful Kalkbrenner was dismissed in two sentences: "He
is like a sweet fallen in the mud. There is nothing wrong with it, but everybody
leaves it where it lies." Meyerbeer was a frequent target of Heine's poisoned
darts. When he heard of Meyerbeer's phobia about cats he observed, "That is
because in a previous incarnation he was a mouse!" Poets, playwrights, and
painters all feared Heine's banter. Alfred de Musset never forgave Heine for
calling him "a young man with a great future behind him." No wonder Heine
loved Paris. It offered him an unlimited supply of grindstones on which to
sharpen his literary blade. "If anyone asks you how I am," he once wrote to
Hiller, "tell him: 'like a fish in water,' or, rather, tell people that when one
fish in the sea asks another how he is, he receives the reply: 'like Heine in

---

3. See the official history of the Paris Conservatoire, PCMHA. Many details of the rigorous technical
requirements imposed on piano students enrolled in the Conservatoire during this epoch will be found
in the doctoral thesis of Frédéric de la Grandville, "Le Conservatoire de Musique de Paris et le piano"
(Université de Paris, Sorbonne, 1979, vol. 1). Cherubini's letter attacking the number of pianists
enrolled there was written to Viscount de la Rochefoucauld (the minister under whose jurisdiction
the Conservatoire fell) and is reproduced in PCMHA, pp. 306–8.
4. MPC. Marmontel was a pupil of Zimmerman and took his master's place at the Conservatoire
in 1848.
5. HSWMB, vol. 9, p. 275.

Paris.' "[6] In later life his wit turned to venom, his satire to gall, as he battled to survive against unimaginable odds. Even Heine's worst enemies would not have wished on him his twilight years, as this brilliant intellect lapsed into bedfast senility, enduring a seven-year ordeal on his "mattress grave," his palsied limbs held together by a monstrous conjunction of stays and wires, from which prison he continued to hurl invective at the world.

The relationship between Liszt and Heine was never easy. Heine's qualified admiration for Liszt the pianist was tempered by his dislike for Liszt the man. He suspected Liszt's instant enthusiasms and came to regard them as the expressions of a dilettante. "In what intellectual stall will he find his next hobby-horse?" he sneered. At the root of the antagonism lay Liszt's strong Catholic faith and his attraction to Lamennais, whose ideas the atheist Heine could not abide. Later it was whispered that Liszt had refused to pay the financially embarrassed Heine a bribe for a favourable review, and thus the two men parted company.[7]

III

Whatever conflicts and quarrels may later have coloured the lives of the early Romantics (historians are not wrong to call the maelstrom that emerged after 1850 the "War of the Romantics," a war which had its roots in the cornucopia of contradictory ideas from the 1830s), the degree of camaraderie they enjoyed in their youth was unmatched by anything from earlier epochs. Hiller tells of the time when he, Mendelssohn, Liszt, and Chopin were sitting outside a café in the boulevard des Italiens chatting noisily. Suddenly they saw the dignified figure of Kalkbrenner coming along. It was always Kalkbrenner's ambition to

---

6. Paris, October 24, 1832.
7. In April 1844 Heine wrote to Liszt warning him that he had prepared a newspaper article for publication *before* Liszt's second concert, and since there were things in it that might not please him, he offered to let him read it in advance ("I will expect you at my place between two and three o'clock tomorrow"). (LBZL, vol. 1, p. 68.) Liszt quite rightly ignored this veiled threat, and Heine's article duly appeared on April 25 in *Musikalische Berichte aus Paris*. (HMB, p. 404.) It attributed Liszt's success to lavish expenditures on bouquets and to the wild behaviour of his hysterical female "fans." After reading the offensive article Liszt broke off relations with Heine. Liszt was not the only musician to be blackmailed by Heine for the nonpayment of "appreciation money." Meyerbeer had both lent and given money to the rapacious wordsmith, but after refusing to hand over a further 500 francs was repaid by being dubbed "a music corrupter" in Heine's poem "Die Menge tut es." Old Salomon Heine, the Hamburg banker who supported his wayward nephew, was used to hearing Heinrich complain that he never had enough money. Once, during a visit to Hamburg in 1830, the young reprobate was told by Uncle Salomon: "If you are so short of money, why don't you threaten your friends? You have devices enough at your disposal." (DJE, pp. 330–31.) Heine seems to have taken this squalid piece of advice back to Paris with him and used it with devastating effect. For all his brilliance and insight, Heine's place in the history of music criticism is tarnished. He could be bought.

conduct himself in public like a perfect gentleman, with dress, cane, and top hat in proper alignment. Knowing how easily he lost his poise, and how embarrassed it made him to do so, the band of young bohemians surrounded him in the street and assailed him with a volley of loud banter as he hurried past, driving him to despair and his tormentors to laughter. "Jugend hat keine Tugend," quipped Hiller.[8]

Mendelssohn was making his first visit to Paris and had just become acquainted with Liszt. The two musicians went to Erard's showroom, where Mendelssohn showed Liszt the manuscript of his newly composed Concerto in G minor. Though it was hardly legible, Liszt sat down and played it at sight. Mendelssohn rushed back to Hiller and exclaimed, "A miracle, a real miracle!" He assured his friend that he knew of no one else who could have performed such a feat. There were frequent outings to the theatre and to the Opéra, and even jaunts into the surrounding countryside. "Dear Chopinetto," wrote Berlioz. "We're planning an excursion out of town. . . . I hope that Hiller, Liszt, and de Vigny will be accompanied by Chopin."[9] The use of the diminutive "Chopinetto" (an affectionate reference to Chopin's small stature) indicates the degree of informality which obtained among these young men, and a glance at the Paris concert programmes of those times shows that their fraternity extended to the concert platform. During the 1832–33 concert season Hiller, Liszt, and Chopin joined forces in a performance of the Allegro from Bach's Concerto for three pianos. Not long afterwards Jacques and Henri Herz came together with Liszt and Chopin in a concerto for eight hands on two pianos —rotating positions between movements, after the fashion of the day. This sort of thing reached a peak of absurdity in Milan when Liszt, Hiller, Pixis, Mortier la Fontaine, Schoberlechner, and Orrigi played a twelve-hand version of the *Zauberflöte* Overture, which one newspaper called, rightly if tritely, "a concert of sixty fingers." The musical merits of such extravaganzas aside, they symbolized the great hold the piano now had on the public imagination, a hold that assured the dominance of the instrument for a hundred years.

I V

Much of the piano's new-found glory was caught from opera, for the modern instruments of Pleyel and Erard yearned to sing. Bel canto became the watchword, and the piano was transformed into a master of musical illusion. The operatic idols Malibran, Pasta, and Nourrit, and the golden stream of cantabile they produced, served as models of melodic perfection for the essentially

---

8. "Boys will be boys." HMBE, pp. 22–23.
9. TBC, vol. 1, p. 262.

percussive keyboard to try to emulate. Thalberg, Chopin, and Liszt were all avid opera-goers. Not for nothing did Thalberg call his piano method "The Art of Singing on the Piano," a symptomatic title that was by no means unique. For years Friedrich Wieck had pursued the idea that in order to play the piano at all one must study singing, a notion which merits a lot of thought, and which was duly enshrined in his book *Clavier und Gesang,* to say nothing of the playing of his most gifted pupil, his daughter Clara. Chopin's near-idolatry of Italian opera, and the influence of Bellini on his melodic style, are well documented. When Nourrit died there was a national outpouring of grief, and Chopin played the organ at his funeral. Not enough attention has been paid to the creative links between opera house and recital hall, between the prima donna and the emerging generation of piano soloists. When Malibran walked across the stage a surge of electricity raced through the theatre. Every physical gesture was calculated to produce the greatest dramatic effect. Her interpretation of Desdemona in Rossini's *Otello* aroused real terror in the breasts of her audience as, endeavouring desperately to escape from Otello, advancing towards her with drawn dagger, "she ran to every window and every door, leaping through the room like a startled deer."[10] Pasta's interpretation of that same role had been to face death with pride; operatic, no doubt, but not so realistic. In a scene from Donizetti's *Maria Stuarda* Malibran ripped both handkerchief and glove to tatters, making her onlookers flinch at such an unexpected outburst. At the same time, she could so wring the hearts of her audience through her long-drawn arias that they wept openly. The message was not lost on the keyboard virtuoso whose stage presence hitherto had been, to say the least, lacklustre, and whose failure to realize that "body language" is an essential ingredient in performance—enhancing it when done well and harming it when done badly—had served to hold back his branch of the art. Liszt was Malibran's fervent admirer, and he esteemed her ability to play on the emotions of her audience. Quite by chance, while Liszt was on tour in Manchester in December 1840 he found himself staying in the very hotel room in which Malibran had died four years earlier at the tragically early age of twenty-eight, and the memory of her inimitable artistry once more rose before him.[11]

It was inevitable that pianists should attempt a final assault on the opera house and produce the "operatic paraphrase," a musical extravaganza which sometimes encapsuled whole operas for ten fingers and a seven-octave keyboard to delight in. By any other name it was plunder, but audiences revelled in these

---

10. LSS, vol. 2, p. 65. In Rossini's *Otello* Desdemona is stabbed, not strangled.
11. In a letter to Theresa von Bacheracht (December 4, 1840) Liszt wrote perceptively: "That [Malibran] should have gone so soon is perhaps better. Who knows? She might have ended with a journey to St. Petersburg and with singing out of tune, like Pasta." (MMR, March 1926.)

dazzling showpieces, which began to flood Europe by the thousand and made fortunes for their publishers. The day Liszt's "Réminiscences" of *Robert le diable* appeared it sold over five hundred copies and was at once reprinted.[12] At the heart of this massive sales effort stood Maurice Schlesinger, the proprietor of the *Gazette Musicale*, who founded his music-publishing house in Paris in 1821, and grew rich from the proceeds of such works. His brother ran the other half of the family firm, in Berlin, so Schlesinger automatically controlled the rights in Germany of anything he published in France, and vice versa; the *Gazette Musicale* was used as a mouthpiece for Schlesinger titles in both countries.[13] It was the growing monopoly of the *Gazette* in Germany, and its propaganda for Schlesinger's "lollipops," that prompted Robert Schumann to found the *Neue Zeitschrift für Musik* in Leipzig in 1834, and launch a series of critical assaults on the music of the Paris Virtuoso School. Although there was much dross in these compositions—an endless parade of variations, potpourris, fantasies, and "reminiscences"—the repertoire has an unassailable claim on our attention today: it tells the story of the birth of the modern piano. We know that Liszt did not disdain to make a thorough study of it, since he was able to play difficult pieces by Kalkbrenner and Herz from memory more than forty years later for the sheer amusement of it all, and without having so much as glanced at the music in the meantime.[14] Liszt's peculiar strength, both then and later, was that the individual branches of technique so assiduously cultivated and displayed on a selective basis by his contemporaries—octaves, scales, repeated notes, leaps— were all rolled into one in him. There was nothing they could do as a group that he could not do by himself.

---

12. *Gazette Musicale,* October 10, 1841. In a marginal note to his hand-corrected copy of Ramann's biography, Liszt observed that he was the first to use the titles "Paraphrase", "Transcription," and "Reminiscence." (WA, Kasten 352, no. 1.) These evocative terms have become widely accepted, and Liszt ought to be given proper credit for introducing them. The paraphrase, as its name implies, is a free variation on the original. The transcription, on the other hand, is strict, literal, objective; it seeks to unfold the original work as accurately as possible.
13. In 1834 Schlesinger purchased *La Revue Musicale* from F. J. Fétis and combined it with the *Gazette*. Under its enlarged title as *La Revue et Gazette Musicale* it became the most powerful musical organ in France, employing Berlioz, d'Ortigue, Fétis, Legouvé, and Liszt as contributing editors.
14. FMSG, p. 249.

Paganini

One hope still remains to me: it is that after my
death the calumny will have spent itself, and those
who have avenged themselves so cruelly for my
success will let my ashes repose in peace.

NICCOLÒ PAGANINI[1]

I

As it happened, the foremost virtuoso of the age was not Liszt. In fact, he was
not a pianist at all, but a violinist. Already, during his own lifetime, Paganini
had become a legend. He was the supreme artist who could do anything. His
virtuosity was such that in order to account for it at all, people supposed him
to be in league with the Devil. Rumour had it that his fourth string, from
which he could draw ravishing sounds, was made from the intestine of his
mistress, whom he had murdered with his own hands. It was whispered that
he had languished in jail for twenty years as a punishment for this crime, with
a violin as his sole companion, and, being uniquely isolated from the outside
world, had thus wrested from the instrument its innermost secrets. Paganini did
his best to deny these gruesome tales, and even sued some of the newspapers
for libel, but they pursued him to the grave.[2] Yet there was no doubting his

---

1. *Revue Musicale,* April 21, 1831.

2. The letter Paganini wrote to the *Revue Musicale,* April 23, 1831, in which he denied murdering
his mistress and being incarcerated, is graphic. Paganini even identified the source of his misfortune
in a vain attempt to silence his slanderers. It seems that a violinist called Duranowski, who was in
Milan in 1798, was induced to accompany a pair of ruffians to a nearby village where they proposed
to assassinate the local priest, who was reputed to be rich. One of their number shrank from
committing this crime and denounced his companions. The police arrived and arrested Duranowski
and his companions as they walked into the priest's house. For this attempted crime they were
condemned to twenty years in a galley-ship. Two years after receiving this sentence, Duranowski
was pardoned. "Will you credit it?" exclaimed Paganini. "Upon this groundwork they have constructed my history. It was necessary that the violinist's name end in 'i,' it was Paganini; the

virtuosity. He created and solved his own technical problems. Everywhere his works were regarded as unplayable, until Paganini turned up and played them. If a string broke, he could play equally well on three; if another broke, he could play equally well on two; in fact, his speciality was to play an entire piece on one string alone, with which he would bring the house down. Years of toil at his instrument had made it unnecessary for him to practise; thus his technical skills rested solely on his phenomenal public performances—each one of which kept him warmed up for the next. He rarely touched the violin in private, except to tune it, and when questioned about this he replied, "I have laboured enough to acquire my talent; it is time that I rest." Paganini guarded his secrets jealously. Whenever he rehearsed a concerto he would never allow the orchestral players a chance to observe what he did during the cadenza, for it was his habit to stop playing when this long-awaited moment arrived, give a nonchalant wave of the bow, and indicate that the passage was to be taken "as read." Paganini played his cadenzas once, and once only, and that was at the performance. These were moments of supreme virtuosity, when the man and his violin became one, and the hushed audience would witness such marvels of execution that it seemed, indeed, as if the very Devil had taken possession of him.[3]

It is easy to understand how the dark rumours about Paganini circulated when we consider his appearance. In his *Florentine Nights*[4] Heine has created the model for Paganini that will last for all time. He dressed from head to foot in black. His body, racked with pain, was slowly wasting away from syphilis.[5] He glided rather than walked across the stage—like a menacing vulture gently floating into position to consume its prey. His eyes had receded deep into their

assassination became that of my mistress, or my rival; and I it was who was sent to prison—with this exception, that I was to discover there a new school for the violin; I was not condemned to chains, in order that my arms might be at perfect liberty."

3. The young Charles Hallé used to see the silent figure of Paganini every afternoon sitting in the window of Bernard Latte's music shop in the Passage de l'Opéra, wrapped in a long cloak, absorbed in score-reading and acknowledging no one. Later Hallé was introduced to Paganini and played for him. "On one never-to-be-forgotten occasion, after I had played and we had enjoyed a long silence, Paganini rose and approached his violin case. What passed in me can hardly be imagined; I was all in a tremble and my heart thumped as if it would burst in my chest. . . . Paganini opened the case, took the violin out, and began to tune it carefully with his fingers without using the bow; my agitation became almost intolerable. When he was satisfied, and I said to myself, with a lump in my throat, 'Now, now, he'll take the bow!' he carefully put the violin back and shut the case. And that is how I heard Paganini." (HLL, p. 63.)

4. HSWMB, vol. 5.

5. The immediate cause of Paganini's death was tuberculosis of the larynx. A clinical diagnosis of his illnesses and a description of the medications and treatments prescribed for them was made by Dr. Francesco Bennati for the French Academy of Sciences during Paganini's lifetime, in March 1831 (*Histoire physiologique et pathologique de Niccolò Paganini*), a summary of which was published in the *Revue de Paris,* May 1831, vol. 11, pp. 113–16. Sections of Bennati's paper were republished in 1957 by de Courcy (CPG, vol. 2, pp. 36–41.)

sockets, and this, together with his waxen complexion, gave him a spectral appearance which was enhanced by the dark-blue glasses he sometimes wore. The mercury prescribed for his *morbo gallico* had attacked his stomach and rotted his jawbone, causing his teeth to decay and fall out and his mouth to disappear into his chin. When Paganini played, the macabre impression was that of a bleached skull with a violin tucked under its chin. His very name ("little pagan") symbolized the satanic aura which surrounded his personality.

Paganini was addicted to the gaming tables and would often gamble the night away in darkened, smoke-filled rooms with bizarre characters from the underworld as his opponents, making and losing whole fortunes on the spin of a wheel or the turn of a card. He would emerge from these hell-holes blinking in the morning sunlight, half drugged from alcohol and datura cigars, the only oral palliatives strong enough to dull the pain in his rotting jawbone, and go straight to the concert hall in the crumpled, stale-smelling evening suit he had worn all night. His violin was pawned several times in order to tide him over to his next concert receipts. The outcome of his passion for gambling was the Casino Paganini, a magnificent building in the rue de la Chaussée d'Antin which he and two other speculators bought from the Duke of Padua. Paganini lived there in a spacious suite of apartments with luxurious flannel-lined walls (to deaden the sound of his violin against eavesdroppers), surrounded by roulette wheels, dice tables, and various other games of chance. His paradise turned into purgatory when the French government refused to grant him a licence to operate the place, and he lost 100,000 francs.

Paganini did not begin his European tours until 1828, by which time he was already forty-six years old. That merely served to fuel the fires of speculation within the general public curious to know where he could possibly have spent the previous twenty-five years of his life. When he made his Vienna début he created a sensation, and the newspapers there talked of little else for two months. There followed a triumphal progress through Poland, Prussia, Bavaria, and England. Here Paganini got into difficulties with the authorities. He boarded with a certain Mr. Watson, an American singer who lived on Gray's Inn Road with his mistress, Miss Wells, and his sixteen-year-old daughter, Charlotte. The young Miss Watson became enamoured of Paganini, and when the violinist observed the harsh treatment to which she was subjected by her father's mistress, he rashly took it upon himself to intervene. The pair arranged a secret rendez-vous in Boulogne, from where, according to the young girl, they were to have proceeded to Paris in order to be married. Mr. Watson, alerted by a well-wisher, travelled ahead and intercepted the Channel boat when it docked at Calais, confronting his wayward daughter with the police. Paganini, who was waiting in Boulogne, was charged with abduction. A series of slanderous newspaper articles followed, in which Paganini was depicted as a kidnapper and lecher. He wrote two dignified replies to the editor of the Boulogne *Annotateur*

Paganini and the Philharmonic Orchestra, by Daniel Maclise.

(who, forsaking all pretence to impartiality, had taken up the cudgels for the father), in which he denied abducting Miss Watson, denied knowing that she was sixteen, denied proposing marriage, and claimed that Mr. Watson had been in debtors' jail four times in five years and might still be there had not he, Paganini, lent the scoundrel 45 pounds to secure his freedom. "I have long been accustomed to seeing the basest calumny provide an escort to all my tours, an essential accompaniment to the applause." This was too much for the anonymous editor, who retaliated with a ringing sermon on Paganini's morals. Paganini hit back the following week, concluding his letter with a telling flourish: "There is between the two of us one difference: it is that I have the courage to sign my letter—that courage you lack. I have the honour to salute you. Niccolò Paganini."[6] It is impossible today to disentangle fact from fiction; nor is it particularly important to do so. Paganini attracted this kind of notoriety all his life; for him it was one more example of the petty adversities that the world always flung in his face as a punishment for his "diabolical" talent.

Paganini's one solace throughout his long years of tribulation was his illegitimate son, Achille. Born in 1825 to Paganini's mistress Antonia Bianchi, the boy became the centre of his existence, the only stable relationship in his life. While Achille was still a child he broke his leg, and the pain was such that no one could keep the small boy still. Paganini held his son for eight days and nights until the broken bones had begun to knit together, and then collapsed from exhaustion. Later there was a touching reversal of roles. As Paganini's sicknesses gained dominion over his body, affecting both sight and speech, Achille became his eyes and voice, accompanying his father on his world tours. To compound his problems, a Prague surgeon had operated on Paganini's infected lower jawbone, making it difficult for him to swallow food and adding yet another indignity to what de Courcy aptly called the long Calvary of his later years.[7] Towards the end, Achille was Paganini's sole intermediary with the outside world, protecting him from unwelcome visitors, fetching and carrying, administering medicines. At his death Paganini left the bulk of his estate (about 2 million lire) to Achille, together with the title "Baron," which he had acquired on his journeys across Germany.

---

6. *L'Annotateur,* July 3 and July 10, 1834.
7. CPG, vol. 2, p. 36. The operation was carried out on October 10, 1828, under the direction of Dr. Julius Vincenz Edler von Kromholz, professor of surgery at the Prague General Hospital, assisted by three other doctors. Paganini himself described the nightmare scene in which he placed himself in a chair, "rigid as a statue, and they operated on me, armed with a huge needle, scalpels, and scissors." (Letter to Luigi Germi, October 20, 1828.)

11

On March 9, 1831, Paganini glided onto the stage of the Paris Opéra House and played to a packed audience. The event had been eagerly awaited for weeks by people agog to catch a glimpse of the living legend. Sitting in the glittering assembly that night were the violinists de Bériot and Ole Bull, the composers Meyerbeer, Cherubini, and Halévy, the pianists Kalkbrenner, Zimmerman, Adam, and Marie Moke, the poets Heine, de Vigny, and de Musset, the novelists George Sand and Victor Hugo, and a small army of newspaper critics, including Fétis, Legouvé, Jules Janin, and Castil-Blaze. It was, as Paganini's dry humour might have put it, a "well-tempered" audience. De Bériot sat with Legouvé, score in hand. "This man is a charlatan," he exclaimed. "He cannot execute what is printed here because it is not executable." The passage in question duly arrived and was duly executed. The solution then dawned on de Bériot—"He changed the tuning of his strings!"—and incredulity turned to admiration.[8]

A year later Paris heard Paganini again. It was April 1832, and cholera was raging through the city. The great violinist gave a benefit concert in the Opera House for the victims, and this time Liszt was present. In the lives of most great men there sometimes comes a blinding flash of revelation when they see their future destiny clearly marked out before them. Liszt's "blinding flash" occurred in response to hearing Paganini play. As he listened to the Italian wizard he experienced an artistic awakening. Paganini and his violin seemed indivisible. Here was a violinist who not only played the violin better than his rivals, but played it as well as it could be played—a somewhat different proposition. For all its dazzle and dash, the Paris Virtuoso School had failed to produce a comparable phenomenon among the pianists. The "Paganini of the piano" had still to appear. The galvanizing effect that this insight produced on Liszt is now a matter of history; that role he would carve out for himself. He wrote to his pupil Pierre Wolff:

Paris, May 2, 1832

For a whole fortnight my mind and my fingers have been working like two lost souls. Homer, the Bible, Plato, Locke, Byron,

---

8. DPG, p. 192. Ole Bull also left a detailed recollection. (BOM, pp. 369–76.)

Scordatura—a mistuning of the strings—was a favourite device of Paganini. A violinist's technical problems both wax and wane with the employment of this resource, which is therefore used with caution. When Paganini, after being lost in contemplation, used to leave his companions in order to tune his violin, he may well have been checking the technical consequences of such radical solutions. His early training on the guitar, whose strings are tuned differently from those of the violin, perhaps encouraged him to experiment with *scordatura*.

Hugo, Lamartine, Chateaubriand, Beethoven, Bach, Hummel, Mozart, Weber are all around me. I study them, meditate on them, devour them with fury; besides this, I practise four to five hours of exercises (thirds, sixths, octaves, tremolos, repetition of notes, cadenzas, etc.). Ah! provided I don't go mad you will find in me an artist! Yes, an artist . . . such as is required today.

"And I too am a painter!" cried Michelangelo the first time he beheld a masterpiece.[9] Your friend, though insignificant and poor, cannot leave off repeating those words of the great man ever since Paganini's last performance. René, what a man, what a violin, what an artist! Heavens! what sufferings, what misery, what tortures in those four strings!

Here are a few of his characteristics:

As to his expression, his manner of phrasing, they are his very soul![10]

---

9. The remark was actually made by Correggio when he first saw Raphael's painting of St. Cecilia.
10. LLB, vol. 1, pp. 6–8. It should be noted that this enthusiastic letter was provoked by Paganini's second visit to Paris, and not by his first. Where was Liszt in March 1831? There is circumstantial evidence that he was not in Paris at all, but in Geneva. (EDW, fn. 26.)

Four to five hours of exercises daily. It is a myth that Liszt never practised. He now set himself a titanic programme of work. Always the ideal of Paganini was before him. Liszt's immediate aim was to create a new kind of repertoire for the piano in which he could transfer to the keyboard some of the more spectacular of Paganini's feats—tremolos, leaps, glissandos, spiccato effects, bell-like harmonics. To this end he selected a group of Paganini's unaccompanied Caprices, notorious for their difficulties, and set about reproducing their complex problems on the keyboard. He brought forth the first fruits of these endeavours in 1838, the Paganini Studies, which represented a breakthrough in piano technique.[11] A more immediate result of the impact of Paganini, however, was the *Clochette* Fantasy (1832). This piece is really a gigantic working-out of the old Italian melody "La campanella," which Paganini had used in the finale of his B-minor Violin Concerto.

No one plays *Clochette* nowadays. The work contains intractable difficulties and has, in any case, been obscured by the more popular *Campanella* Study from the Paganini set, of which it is the early model. Yet if we wish to understand the young Liszt's individual brand of keyboard fireworks, *Clochette* proffers some important insights. The centrepiece of the fantasy is a "variation à la Paganini," whose first bars are given here.

---

11. These studies are discussed beginning on p. 308.

Demonic, mephistophelian, satanic: such words have often been used to describe Liszt's new style of keyboard diablerie. The emotional impact of his playing on the Parisians has been well documented. Storm and stress had entered the concert hall. The scene was sometimes like a séance in which some unknown spirit stirred and swept the audience with fear and ecstasy. Only Paganini had conjured up such a dark atmosphere before, and his influence on the history of virtuosity can never be eradicated.

III

The respect Liszt felt for the Italian master's "black art" came out strongly at the time of Paganini's death in 1840, the circumstances of which make horrific reading. The church, considering him an atheist, withheld the last rites and refused to allow his corpse to be buried on consecrated ground. A bitter quarrel flared up between Paganini's friends and the clergy. For a month the body remained unburied at Nice, where Paganini had died. Crowds of sightseers milled outside the house, crossing themselves, trying to catch a look at the unshriven corpse, which lay on a makeshift platform, its glassy eyes wide open. On its head a cotton nightcap was perched at a bizarre angle. Its sagging jaws were held together by a bandage. The stench given off by the decaying corpse made it imperative that a temporary abode be found for it, and it was placed by the authorities in an abandoned cement vat belonging to a nearby olive oil factory. When it was discovered that waste products from the factory were running into the vat and seeping into the coffin, Count de Cessole, one of Paganini's admirers, decided to defy the clergy and bury the body in secret on private property. A tomb of sorts was erected at Cap St.-Hospice, on the estate of Count de Pierlas, another of Paganini's friends. The body was carried by night along the deserted peninsula of St.-Jean–Cap-Ferrat to avoid the prying eyes of the scandal-mongers. The torchlight procession made slow headway along the difficult coastline, and the pallbearers sometimes found themselves knee-deep in water, floundering in the dark, the waves splashing over the coffin.[12] During the next two decades Paganini was exhumed and reburied several times. His posthumous to-ings and fro-ings shocked Europe. Finally,

---

12. An eye-witness to these macabre scenes was the painter Félix Ziem, who worked in the Nice studio of Alexis de Saint-Marc, a sculptor who had recently been commissioned to make a bust of Countess de Cessole. Ziem was one of the midnight pallbearers whom Count de Cessole pressed into service, and his memory of that nightmare journey was still vividly alive in 1892 when he related the story to Georges Maurevert. It was Maurevert who decided to publish Ziem's unique memoir (by then the other actors in this tragedy were all dead), and it appeared in *Le Petit Niçois*, March 30, 1905. See CPG, vol. 2, pp. 336–38, for the most reliable account of the necromantic fantasy that commenced after Paganini's death.

after more than forty years of wrangling, the body was lowered into a permanent grave at Parma, with the approval of the Vatican. The coffin was opened at least twice after this at the behest of people fascinated by the Paganini legend, the last time being in 1896.

One civilized voice to be raised in Paganini's defence was Liszt's. He was in London, in the middle of a British concert tour, when reports of Paganini's death reached him, and he wrote a generous necrology which was printed in the *Gazette Musicale* on August 23, 1840. After paying tribute to Paganini's dazzling virtuosity ("a miracle which the kingdom of art has seen but once"), Liszt felt it necessary to utter some reservations. Ten years had elapsed since his youthful wave of enthusiasm, and the times had changed. Paganini's artistry, for all its magic, had been flawed by his egotism: "His god was never any other than his own gloomy, sad 'I.' " Paganini, in short, was a negative model. Art was more than self-serving virtuosity, Liszt continued; it was a "sacred power" that exercised a beneficent influence on humanity. This perception led Liszt to formulate his characteristic imperative *Génie oblige!,* in which the possession of genius puts its owner under a special obligation to serve the rest of humanity not so fortunately endowed.

> May the artist of the future gladly and readily decline to play the conceited and egotistical role which we hope has had in Paganini its last brilliant representative. May he set his goal within, and not outside, himself, and be the means of virtuosity, and not its end. May he constantly keep in mind that, though the saying is *Noblesse oblige!,* in a far higher degree than nobility—*Génie oblige!*

Liszt was twenty-eight when he penned these lines. His own career, then and later, offered some telling examples of the good that can accrue when art is deflected from self and directed towards the welfare of mankind generally.

Friends and Contemporaries: Berlioz and Chopin

*When you have the misfortune, as I have, to be
both critic and creative artist, you have to put up
with an endless succession of Lilliputian trivia of
one sort or another, the most nauseating of all
being the cringing flattery of those who have or
are going to have need of you.*

HECTOR BERLIOZ

*I really don't know whether any place contains
more pianists than Paris, or whether you can find
anywhere more asses and virtuosos.*

FRÉDÉRIC CHOPIN[1]

I

Among Liszt's intimates during the post-revolution years was Hector Berlioz.
The two musicians first met on December 4, 1830.[2] The following day Liszt
attended the first performance of Berlioz's *Fantastic* Symphony at the Paris
Conservatoire and was struck with the power and originality of that semi-
nal work. Berlioz at this time was in the midst of his tempestuous love-affair
with Marie Moke, the concert pianist, whose infidelities were driving him
to the brink of suicide. No sooner was this affair terminated than he picked
up the threads of an earlier romance with the Irish actress Harriet Smithson.
Berlioz himself has told the story of the comedy of errors that constituted
his courtship of Harriet so unforgettably that no later commentator can improve upon it. Liszt, a confidant of Berlioz and privy to his innermost thoughts,
felt constrained to utter some reservations about "Henrietta" which
Berlioz proceeded to ignore—to his later regret. The ill-fated marriage was

---

1. BM, p. 239; SCC, vol. 2, p. 39.
2. Berlioz wrote to his father on December 6, "Liszt, the well-known pianist, literally dragged me
off to have dinner at his house and overwhelmed me with the vigor of his enthusiasm."

solemnized at the British Embassy on October 3, 1833, and Liszt, attempting to repair whatever damage his remarks may have caused Miss Smithson, closed ranks behind his friend and took part in the ceremony as an official witness.[3]

During the years that followed, Berlioz suffered grinding poverty (Henrietta brought little to the marriage except her debts), and he was forced to undertake hack journalism in order to survive. In January 1834 Paganini commissioned him to write a new work so that he might show off his recently acquired Stradivarius viola. The result—*Harold in Italy*—did not please the virtuoso ("I am not given enough to do"), and the first performance was given with Urhan as the soloist.[4] It was not until the winter of 1838 that Paganini first heard the work that he had inspired. Deeply moved, he declared Berlioz to be the successor to Beethoven. Berlioz has related in his *Mémoires* how Paganini approached him in the company of his twelve-year-old son, Achille. The violinist was already suffering from the tuberculosis of the larynx which was to kill him two years later, and he could barely whisper. He signalled to Achille, who climbed onto a chair and placed his ear close to his father's mouth. After listening intently the boy climbed down again and addressed Berlioz: "My father bids me tell you, sir, that never in all his life has he been so affected by any concert. Your music has overwhelmed him. . . ."[5] A few days later Paganini sent a gift of 20,000 francs to the impoverished Berlioz by the hand of Achille in recognition of the composer's genius. The rumour was later put about by Paganini's detractors that this gift was really from Armand Bertrand, the wealthy proprietor of the *Journal des Débats,* who wished to do good by stealth and used Paganini as his cover, but the tale is now discredited.[6] (Berlioz's *Mémoires* do not lack imaginative touches, but neither do they create deliberate falsehoods.) After Achille had left his bedside (Berlioz had collapsed with influenza immediately after the concert) the astonished composer summoned his wife, and together they knelt down and gave thanks. It is extraordinary to think that Berlioz heard the great violinist who played such an important role in his life on only one occasion, at a chamber-music concert.

In his *Mémoires* Berlioz invariably speaks of Liszt with warmth and affection. At their first meeting Berlioz introduced Liszt to Goethe's *Faust,* a book "which

3. Liszt's reservations about Harriet were as old as marriage itself. See TBC, vol. 1, p. 240, for Berlioz's response, written four days after the wedding night.

4. November 23, 1834, at the Paris Conservatoire.

5. BM, p. 248.

6. One of the chief culprits was Ferdinand Hiller, who claimed to have received the story from Rossini. (HK, p. 89.) Paganini's original credit note, drawn on Rothschild's bank in Paris, is now in the Liceo Musicale Niccolò Paganini in Genoa. It was reproduced by de Courcy (CPG, vol. 2, p. 185) and is proof positive that the account of this episode that Berlioz left in his *Mémoires* is absolutely correct. It never seems to have occurred to those who want to rob Paganini of this magnanimous gesture that they are virtually accusing Berlioz of forging the letter he claimed to have received from Paganini, telling him of the gift of 20,000 francs, which he published for all the world to see in his *Mémoires.* (BM, p. 248.)

he had not read but which he soon came to love as much as I."[7] As their friendship ripened they came to address one another with the familiar *tu* (apart from d'Ortigue and later J. W. Davison, the critic of *The Times,* Liszt was the only nonrelative whom Berlioz allowed himself to address in the intimate form). For twenty years Liszt remained Berlioz's strongest advocate. After Liszt had settled in Weimar, and attempted to give modern music a new direction, he did not forget his old friend. In 1852, and again in 1855, he arranged week-long Berlioz festivals in the presence of the composer at which such works as *Benvenuto Cellini, Lélio,* and the *Fantastic* Symphony were performed. Shortly afterwards their friendship cooled, owing to the mercurial Frenchman's antipathy towards Wagner, whose cause Liszt also championed at Weimar. Here Berlioz found an unexpected ally in Princess von Sayn-Wittgenstein, Liszt's mistress during the Weimar years, whose dislike of Wagner surpassed his own and who took over more and more of the correspondence with Berlioz. It was the princess who sustained Berlioz in his efforts to complete his magnum opus *The Trojans* (the opera is dedicated to her), a work which she regarded as driving the last nail into the coffin of Wagner and music drama.

But all this lay in the future. And nowhere did the future shine more brightly than in Paris, on December 5, 1830, when the world first hearkened to the strains of the *Fantastic* Symphony. Is there more idiosyncratic orchestral music anywhere? Despite the technical difficulties, Liszt contrived to transfer this unique work to the piano and render its complex textures playable by ten fingers. His chief motive was to help the poverty-stricken Berlioz, whose symphony remained unknown and unpublished.[8] Liszt bore the expense of printing his keyboard transcription himself, and he played it in public mainly to popularize the original score. Not the least remarkable aspect of this mammoth undertaking was that Liszt was only twenty-one years old when he completed it, in September 1833.[9] Sir Charles Hallé heard him play the "March to the Scaffold" in 1836, at a concert in Paris, and wrote:

> At an orchestral concert given by him and conducted by Berlioz, the "March to the scaffold" from the latter's *Fantastic* Symphony, that most gorgeously instrumented piece, was performed, at the conclusion of which Liszt sat down and played his own arrangement, for the piano alone, of the same movement, with an effect even surpass-

---

7. BM, p. 139. It was entirely appropriate that in the years ahead their mutual admiration for *Faust* would be expressed through reciprocal dedications of works inspired by Goethe's masterpiece: Berlioz dedicated to Liszt his *Damnation of Faust,* while Liszt dedicated to Berlioz his *Faust* Symphony.
8. The score was finally printed in 1845 by Schlesinger.
9. "The *Fantastic* Symphony will be finished on Sunday evening. Say three 'Pater' and three 'Ave' on its account." (ACLA, vol. 1, p. 36.)

ing that of the full orchestra, and creating an indescribable furor. The feat had been duly announced in the programme beforehand, a proof of his indomitable courage.[10]

One can well believe that passages such as the following would have rolled across the hall like peals of thunder when drawn from the keyboard by Liszt's hands.

Schumann's detailed review of the *Fantastic* Symphony was written with Liszt's piano transcription at his side (he was unable to consult the orchestral score).[11] It has been remarked that such a feat has few parallels in the annals of criticism. In fact, Schumann's feat was made possible by an even greater one: the fidelity to Berlioz's score of Liszt's transcription, which, at times, approaches the accuracy of a mirror held up to the object it seeks to reflect.

---

10. HLL, p. 38.

11. NZfM, no. 3, 1835, pp. 1–47. Since Liszt cues in the orchestral instruments—a lifelong practice with him in this sort of work—his transcription can also serve the mundane purpose of a conductor's "piano reduction." Both Liszt and Berlioz (who checked the proofs of Liszt's transcription) are caught snoring in the first movement: bar 401 is missing. Schumann's favourable review was written partly as a retaliation against the hostile one supplied by Fétis for the *Revue Musicale,* in which that intrepid critic of all things new (Fétis had a nearly unblemished record of going wrong whenever called upon to express an opinion on the modern music of his day) had labelled the symphony "flat and monotonous" and had dismissed its harmony as "bunches of notes simply thrown together." Even

Apart from anything else, Berlioz and Liszt were drawn together by the uncommon breadth of their artistic tastes, which did not stop at music but ranged across poetry, drama, and painting. Another quality they shared was a lifelong dislike of academicism, and their reckless disdain for narrow pedantry brought them early into conflict with the establishment, as punishment for which they suffered the slings and arrows of stupid enemies; but each assault only forced them to become more original. As true children of the July Revolution they were both caught up in the spiritual regeneration of Jeune France, whose cultural horizons now seemed limitless, and the maelstrom of ideas which whirled about Paris in the 1830s swept them both towards that brief flirtation with Saint-Simonism which has already been observed. Shakespeare, Byron, and Beethoven were particular heroes, masters who illuminated the stony path which destiny would oblige both men to tread in the years ahead. To have heard Beethoven's *Emperor* Concerto performed by this pair of Dionysian spirits (Berlioz conducted the concerto with Liszt as soloist in Paris in April 1841) must have been an unforgettable experience, an occasion to make one regret that Edison had not yet invented the phonograph.[12]

Like everyone else, Berlioz had quickly succumbed to Liszt's piano playing, and particularly to his playing of Beethoven. They were once invited to the home of the critic Ernest Legouvé, together with Eugène Sue and the playwright Prosper Goubaux, and in the course of the evening a typically Romantic scene ensued. The group had moved into Legouvé's drawing room, which possessed a piano, only to discover that there were no lights and that the fire had burned low. Goubaux brought in a lamp while Liszt seated himself at the piano. "Turn up the wick," said Legouvé, "we can't see," whereupon he accidentally turned it down, plunging the room into almost total darkness. Doubtless prompted by the gloom, Liszt began playing the Adagio of Beethoven's *Moonlight* Sonata while everyone remained rooted to the spot. Occasionally the fire's dying embers spluttered and cast strange shadows on the wall as the music unfolded its mournful melody. The experience was too much for Berlioz, who could not master his emotions. As Goubaux lit a candle, Liszt pointed to his friend, who had tears streaming down his cheeks, and murmured, "See, he has been listening to this as the 'heir apparent' of Beethoven."[13] As it happened, Beethoven's mantle fell on neither of them, but the fact that the remark was uttered at all indicates the central position that the Viennese master, who had died barely four years earlier, already occupied in their young uni-

---

Mendelssohn called the work "a deadly bore." (Letter to Moscheles, April 1834.) In the controversy that swirled around this composition from its very beginning, Liszt stood out as its first and most consistent champion.

12. Liszt and Berlioz came together again on the platform in the first performance of Liszt's E-flat major Piano Concerto on February 17, 1855, during the second Berlioz week at Weimar.

13. LSS, vol. 2, pp. 144–45.

verse. It must be remembered that Beethoven was still viewed with suspicion by the ordinary music lover. Paris audiences in particular were convinced that his late works were the product of a deranged mind. (When the C-sharp minor Quartet was performed there in the late 1820s, most of the audience walked out.) It was not until the second half of the nineteenth century that a more favourable climate prevailed. Seen in this context, Berlioz's short study of Beethoven, published in 1829, and Liszt's public performance of the *Hammer-klavier* Sonata in 1836 were acts of courage matched by few other musicians of the day.

I I

By 1832 Paris had become a city of émigrés. Italians, Poles, and Austrians who had escaped political oppression at home flocked there and formed communities in exile in a society which was now regarded as the most tolerant in Europe. The Polish insurrection of 1831, especially, drove large numbers of refugees from Warsaw to the French capital, including the poet Mickiewicz, the dramatist Słowacki, and Chopin, where they added yet more colour and variety to this cosmopolitan city. Chopin was in the midst of a tour of Austria and Germany when he heard of the fall of Warsaw, and he found himself abruptly cut off from his native land. More by accident than design, he wandered into Paris in the autumn of 1831, in a mood of bitter despair. He was destined to remain there, except for brief intervals, for the rest of his life. Chopin's fierce patriotism (his exile made him more Polish than the Poles), his intensely nationalistic music, his aristocratic aloofness, and his utterly original approach to the keyboard set him apart from the Paris Virtuoso School, and with the passing years has transformed him into a unique figure. As his frame was slowly ravaged by tuberculosis, all thoughts of a performing career were abandoned. (Chopin played in public fewer than a dozen times in his life; the very rarity of his appearances made them events to cherish.) His contemporaries had at first little idea of the importance and originality of Chopin's music, and most of them would have found it unbelievable that this frail, pale-faced young man, who stood less than five feet, two inches tall and weighed a mere ninety pounds during his final years, would one day be placed among the musical giants of his age. John Field described him as "a sickroom talent," and both Rellstab and J. W. Davison (critics for Berlin's *Iris* and London's *Times,* respectively) did their best to obstruct Chopin's career by issuing a series of carping criticisms against him over the years.[14] As late as 1841 Davison could write that "the entire

---

14. When he first observed Chopin's finger-twisting Studies, op. 10, Rellstab sarcastically warned his readers not to play them. "Those who have distorted fingers may put them right by practising

works of Chopin present a motley surface of ranting hyperbole and excruciat-
ing cacophony,"[15] a phrase which serves to remind us that musical criticism,
then as now, was helpless when confronted by the new and unexpected.

Almost as soon as Chopin entered Paris, Liszt made his acquaintance. He
attended Chopin's début at the Salle Pleyel on February 26, 1832, and he
appeared on the same platform as Chopin on April 3 and December 15, 1833.
Chopin cemented these early connections by dedicating to Liszt his newly
published set of Twelve Studies, op. 10. What Chopin thought of Liszt's performance of these pieces was expressed in a letter to Ferdinand Hiller the following year.

> I am writing without knowing what my pen is scribbling, because
> at this moment Liszt is playing my studies and putting honest
> thoughts out of my head. I should like to rob him of the way he
> plays my studies.[16]

Although the names of Chopin and Liszt are frequently linked in the popular
imagination, the notion of a romantic friendship is a legend fostered by the
nineteenth-century biographies. Chopin frankly disliked Liszt's theatricality, his
playing the *grand seigneur,* and he came to regard Liszt the composer as a mere
striver after effects. (Liszt, it should be remembered, had not yet found his true
direction and hardly came into his own until after Chopin's early death.) The
question of Chopin's influence on Liszt has often been debated. Anyone who
is even remotely familiar with the general style of both composers knows that
they lie far apart and are connected through externals only. For a time, though,
Liszt lay under the spell of certain individual compositions of Chopin; in
particular, the ghosts of Chopin's A-flat major Polonaise (op. 53), the F-minor
Study (op. 10), and the Berceuse later turned up to haunt some of Liszt's
middle-period works.[17] A close inspection of Liszt's F-minor Transcendental
Study reveals some intriguing similarities to Chopin's own F-minor Study,
which Liszt is known to have played. The opening themes of both works appear
to have been cast from the same mould.

---

these studies; but those who have not should not play them, at least not without having a surgeon
at hand." Rellstab then published a spurious letter, a "reply" to such criticism, purporting to come
from Chopin but which may have been forged by Rellstab himself. (*Iris,* vol. 5, 1834.) Chopin could
only look on in bewilderment. Eventually Rellstab realized that his attacks on Chopin were making
him look foolish. In 1843 he turned up in Paris bearing a diplomatically worded letter of introduction
from Liszt ("however hard it may usually be for artists and critics to agree," etc., SCC, vol. 3, pp.
128–29), which served to heal the breach. Rellstab may well have been the only music critic in history
to go to jail for his views: a criticism of Henrietta Sontag in 1826 in which he satirized a respected
diplomat earned him a three-month stretch in Spandau prison.

15. *Musical World,* October 28, 1841.
16. SCC, vol. 2, p. 93.
17. For a fuller discussion see WL, pp. 58–65.

At such moments as these (and there are dozens from which to choose), the two composers seem to be interchangeable. Yet it is precisely on such occasions that we must exercise the most caution if we wish to avoid becoming ensnared in a historical trap. The F-minor Transcendental Study as we know it today is an outgrowth of the juvenile version that Liszt composed as a youth of fifteen, long before he had heard a note of Chopin. Liszt, in other words, often received more from himself than he received from others. This topic of influence may be a paradise for historians, but it is full of pitfalls for those who do not know their Liszt in toto.

A rift arose between the two composers in early 1835. The apparent cause was Marie Pleyel, the recently estranged wife of Chopin's friend Camille Pleyel.[18] Liszt is said to have used Chopin's apartments in the rue de la Chaussée d'Antin for a tryst while Chopin was out of Paris, and on his return Chopin felt compromised. While the story is basically unprovable, certain pieces of circumstantial evidence do support it.[19] By the late spring of 1835 Liszt had moved to Geneva, and thereafter to Italy, so the two musicians rarely met. Liszt, for his part, never lost interest in Chopin's music and often included it in his programmes, particularly the polonaises, studies, and mazurkas.[20] In his Weimar masterclasses, held during the 'seventies and 'eighties, Liszt constantly encouraged his pupils to play Chopin, and his remarks on this repertoire show that his admiration for it remained undiminished.[21] After Chopin's death in 1849 Liszt conceived the idea of writing a biography of

---

18. Marie Moke had married Camille Pleyel in 1832, almost immediately after her stormy engagement to Berlioz had been broken off. There was a twenty-five-year difference in their ages, and Marie was persistently unfaithful to her elderly husband. They lived together for barely three years, although Marie continued to use her husband's name for her professional career as a concert pianist, which spanned the next forty years. Camille Pleyel later repudiated his wife for her conduct and cut her out of his will (1855).

19. ACLA, vol. 1, p. 313. In 1839, four years later, Liszt met La Pleyel again in Vienna and wrote about their chance encounter to Marie d'Agoult: "She asked me if I remembered Chopin's room. . . . Of course, madame, how to forget?"

20. ACLA, vol. 2, p. 379.

21. GLK, pp. 48, 75–76.

him. He sent a questionnaire to Chopin's sister Louise in order to acquire some basic information for his book; she regarded Liszt's approach as tactless, however, and the questionnaire was filled in by Chopin's pupil Jane Stirling. Liszt's book, a pioneering study of the Polish master, was eventually written in collaboration with the Princess von Sayn-Wittgenstein and was published in 1852.[22]

Among Liszt's other acquaintances in Paris, two call for special mention. The stature of that strange, enigmatic figure Charles-Valentin Alkan[23] has undergone a radical transformation in our time. Still not enough is known about his personal relationship with Liszt, but for a brief period in the 1830s the two pianists were friendly. Alkan was the only composer of his time to write transcendental keyboard music to approach that of Liszt. His *Douze Etudes dans tous les tons mineurs,* op. 39, which includes the four-movement Piano Symphony and the variations called *Festin d'Esope,* are among the most difficult and original compositions of the century. (How ironical that these modern-sounding pieces are dedicated to the arch-conservative Fétis!) Like everything else Alkan wrote, this music was badly neglected by his contemporaries and remained little known except to a small circle of devotées. In our own century Busoni, Petri, Sorabji, and Isidore Philipp were consistent champions of his compositions, but a correct evaluation of his oeuvre remains one of the more urgent priorities facing musical criticism. The very titles of some of his compositions indicate how utterly different and unconventional they are. The man who wrote *Fire in the Neighbouring Village, Funeral March for a Dead Parrot,* and the very first musical illustration of the newfangled railway-engine, *Chemin de fer,* was a pioneer, and the trail he blazed still beckons.

Alkan had been a child prodigy, enrolling in the Paris Conservatoire as a pupil of Zimmerman when he was only six. By the time he was fifteen he had walked off with all the major piano prizes at the Conservatoire, assisted Zimmerman in his piano classes as *répétiteur,* and stood on the brink of a shining career. Like Liszt, Alkan went the rounds of the Paris salons. At one of these soirées, given by Princess de la Moscova, his natural pleasure at his success turned to humiliation when a tall young man with a grave countenance was invited to the piano and played so brilliantly as to make Alkan feel like a beginner. He tells us that he returned home, wept tears of frustration, and spent

---

22. RGS, vol. 1. Liszt's questionnaire was reproduced in *Souvenirs inédits de Frédéric Chopin, recueillis et annotés par Mieczyslaw Karlowicz* (Paris, 1904). Louise received it less than three weeks after her brother's funeral (Liszt's covering letter is dated "Pilsen, November 14, 1849"), so the timing could hardly have been worse. Also, it contained intimate inquiries about the relationship between Chopin and George Sand which Louise regarded as both irrelevant and impertinent. Jane Stirling fielded Liszt's questions in such a masterful way that her responses, while true, are virtually useless for biographical purposes.

23. His real name was Charles-Valentin Morhange. Alkan was his father's first name, a Hebrew word meaning "the Lord has been gracious."

a sleepless night. It was his first encounter with Liszt.[24] During the 1830s, Alkan moved into the fashionable Square d'Orléans, where Chopin and George Sand became his next-door neighbours, and set up as a teacher. (When Chopin died many of his pupils went over to Alkan; Chopin also left to him the manuscript of his uncompleted piano method.) Liszt, too, was a frequent visitor at this time. Alkan dedicated to Liszt his *Trois Morceaux dans le genre pathétique*, op. 15,[25] and in April 1837 the two pianists appeared on the same concert platform together in Paris. In later life Liszt told Frits Hartvigson that Alkan had the finest technique of any pianist that he knew, and when we inspect some of Alkan's more problematic keyboard works we must acknowledge that Liszt's remark may not have been the sort of idle compliment in which he was wont to indulge in his old age.

Alkan's performing career was blighted by an introverted personality which forced him to withdraw from public life while still relatively young. For his last forty years he lived like a hermit, shut off from the world, and even close friends had difficulty in gaining access to him. The concierge had strict instructions never to let anyone pass. Alkan rented two apartments, one above the other, the better to encapsule himself from the rest of mankind, and it was not unusual for visitors who had somehow penetrated the front line of defence and reached the lower set of rooms to wander around confirming for themselves that they were empty. When Frederick Niecks visited Paris in 1880 he tried to call on Alkan, only to be told by the well-drilled concierge that he was "not at home." Niecks persisted and asked when he would be at home. The concierge rose to his duties superbly and replied, "Never."[26] The cause of Alkan's withdrawal into solitude may never be fully known, but it dates from 1848. That was the year he was manoeuvred out of a piano professorship at the Conservatoire by the joint efforts of Auber and Marmontel, after months of bitter wrangling, and although Marmontel's interesting character-sketch of Alkan in *Les Pianistes célèbres,* written thirty years later, holds out an olive branch in its closing paragraph, Alkan experienced a lifelong sense of betrayal. His letters to his old friend George Sand, whom he asked to intercede in his behalf, make sad reading. When he died in 1888 he was all but forgotten; only a small handful of admirers remained. *Le Ménestrel* carried an obituary notice which summed up his unusual fate: "Charles-Valentin Alkan has just died. It was necessary for him to die in order to suspect his existence. 'Alkan,' more than one reader will say, 'who is Alkan?' " The cause of his demise was unusual: he was trying to

---

24. BAEP, p. 136.

25. The individual titles of these pieces are "Aime-moi," "Le Vent," and "Morte." Schumann wrote a blistering review of the work for the *Neue Zeitschrift für Musik* (no. 8, 1838) in which he described it as "false, unnatural art," an early indication of the slow headway this music would make across the century.

26. NPR, pp. 4–7.

reach for his copy of the Talmud on the top shelf of a bookcase which toppled over and crushed him to death.[27]

The name of Ferdinand Hiller rarely receives more than passing mention in books about Liszt, yet his path never ceased to cross Liszt's in an amazing series of coincidences. Pianist, teacher, composer, conductor, and writer, roles in which he industriously attempted to outmatch his contemporary, Hiller even contrived to be born in the year of the comet, 1811, only two days after Liszt. A pupil of Hummel in Weimar (a privilege vainly coveted by the young Liszt), Hiller had arrived in Paris aged sixteen, four years after Liszt, with the same reputation of having been presented to Beethoven. He met Marie d'Agoult long before Liszt himself was introduced to her (Marie and Hiller were both born in Frankfurt-am-Main), and he later followed them to Italy, becoming one of Marie's closest confidants. Their correspondence suggests that Hiller saw in Liszt not a friend but a rival. Hiller, who conducted the Gewandhaus Concerts in Leipzig in 1843–44, became jealous of Liszt's direction of the German festivals during the 1850s and launched a series of intrigues against him. At the Aachen Music Festival, which Liszt directed in 1857, Hiller created a disturbance during the rehearsals and had to be ejected. His subsequent criticism of Liszt in the Cologne press was damaging enough to provoke a public rebuke from Liszt's pupil Hans von Bronsart.[28] Even the honorary doctorate bestowed on Hiller by the University of Bonn in 1863 only served to remind him that a similar honour had already been extended to Liszt by the University of Königsberg more than twenty years earlier. Hiller's *Künstlerleben* contains an "Open Letter to Franz Liszt" written in 1877, in which he reviews their long connection in flattering detail and dwells on their youth in Paris with particular pride. This document should mislead no one; it is merely a diplomatic smokescreen behind which Hiller continued to work against Liszt to the end.[29] The story of their declining relationship

---

27. The ultimate source for this familiar story was Isidore Philipp, who claimed to have been present when Alkan's body was pulled from under the bookcase. Philipp was one of the four solitary mourners who witnessed Alkan's interment in the Montmartre Cemetery on April 1, 1888. His description of Alkan's death has been challenged, but never disproved. (See SA, pp. 73–75.)

28. LLB, vol. 2, pp. 333–34, and vol. 3, p. 91.

29. What was the real cause of Hiller's jealousy? Marie d'Agoult often unburdened herself to Hiller and disclosed details of her relationship with Liszt that amount to a breach of loyalty. To conclude on the basis of their correspondence (some of which was published in *La Revue Bleue,* November 1913; see also pp. 261 and 264 of the present work) that there had been a great intimacy between Hiller and Marie d'Agoult is perhaps dangerous, but there was enough gossip about their friendship (which persisted into the 1870s) to make it possible for Olga Janina to work this triangle into one of her satirical novels, *Le Roman du pianiste et de la cosaque* (ZRPC). Behind the masks of "Nélida" (Marie), "Bernheim" (Hiller), and "François-Xavier" (Liszt), Marie and Hiller are made to cuckold Liszt. Marie lived long enough to read this humiliating parody of her friendship with Hiller; she died the following year. Hiller's "Open Letter to Franz Liszt" was written a few months later. (HK, pp. 204–12.)

happens to be of more than anecdotal interest: it presents a visible example of the fate suffered by so many of the musical relationships Liszt formed during his halcyon days in Paris, a fate which will already have struck the reader with force. One by one his early acquaintances either abandoned him or turned against him—Berlioz, Chopin, Mendelssohn, Hiller, Heine, Schlesinger—and this pattern was later repeated with Schumann, Joachim, von Bülow, and Wagner. In view of the many personal kindnesses extended by Liszt to all these colleagues over the years, their rejection of him is bewildering, and it tinged his life with sadness. When we read today that Liszt was "one of the leaders of the Romantic movement," the phrase, however true, has a somewhat hollow ring to anyone familiar with the minutiae of his life; the fact is that for much of the time there was no one willing to be led by him at all, and for the last twelve years of his life he resigned himself to artistic isolation. This wholesale refusal by most of the great names of the Romantic movement to take Liszt seriously, let alone recognize his fundamental contribution to their cause, must await its explanation in a later volume of this work. Meanwhile, these musicians were young, their horizons seemed limitless, and their world was full of promise.

Enter Marie d'Agoult

I

At the beginning of 1833 Liszt was introduced to the woman who changed the
course of his destiny. When he first met Countess Marie d'Agoult she was
twenty-eight years old, unhappily married to a man fifteen years older than
herself, and the mother of two children. She was beautiful and elegant, with
"a profusion of blond hair that fell over her shoulders like a shower of gold."[2]
Despite the difference in their ages (Liszt was twenty-one), and still more the
difference in their backgrounds, the couple were drawn violently together. The
story of their ill-starred romance (which appeared to the world like a brilliant
liaison, but which in reality bore all the marks of classical tragedy, generating
untold misery in its wake) has been related so often that the reader may well
ask if there is anything left to say. During the past thirty years or so, however,
sufficient new material has come to light to call for a fresh examination of this
turbulent relationship.

The first meeting between Liszt and Marie d'Agoult was carefully documented by Marie herself. It took place in the salon of the Marquise Le Vayer,[3]
who liked to surround herself with writers, artists, and "women of the world"
in her spacious apartments in the rue du Bac. Her niece was Charlotte Talley-

---

1. AS, p. 349.
2. RLKM, vol. 1, pp. 322–23.
3. AM, pp. 21–24. As the Marquise Le Vayer died in February 1833, Marie's encounter with Liszt
must have occurred no later than January of that year.

rand, whose love of music had led her to become a pupil of Liszt and who lost no time in telling her aunt of the phenomenal talents of her young mentor. One afternoon the marquise gathered together a female choir to perform a piece by Carl Maria von Weber. Marie d'Agoult was asked to participate because of her agreeable mezzo-soprano voice. The guest of honour was Liszt. Although Marie arrived late, Liszt arrived even later, and so she chatted to her hostess until the proceedings could begin. Marie herself picks up the story.

> Madame L. V. was still talking when the door opened and a wonderful apparition appeared before my eyes. I use the word "apparition" because I can find no other to describe the sensation aroused in me by the most extraordinary person I had ever seen. He was tall and extremely thin. His face was pale and his large sea-green eyes shone like a wave when the sunlight catches it. His expression bore the marks of suffering. He moved indecisively, and seemed to glide across the room in a distraught way, like a phantom for whom the hour when it must return to the darkness is about to sound.[4]

Madame Le Vayer came forward and introduced the young man to her distinguished friend. Liszt seated himself next to the blond-haired beauty, and they began to talk as if they had known one another for a long time. The effect that this first encounter with Liszt had on Marie d'Agoult is evident from her *Mémoires,* in which she writes in romantic vein of "his flashing eyes, his gestures, his smile, now profound and of an infinite sweetness, now caustic," which "seemed to be intended to provoke me either to contradiction or to intimate assent." Suddenly the spell was broken. The piano was opened and the candelabra were lighted at each end of the music desk. Madame Le Vayer approached and whispered some words in Liszt's ear that he did not let her finish. He rose abruptly and walked impatiently towards the piano, around which was grouped the small chorus of singers. Marie followed and took her place among the mezzo-sopranos. After the piece was finished, Marie joined the others in offering some complimentary remarks on Liszt's accompaniment. He replied with a silent bow. Marie went home rather late, and that night, she tells us, her sleep was troubled by strange dreams. Prompted by Madame Le Vayer, who called on her the next day, Marie wrote to Liszt inviting him to visit her. She tore up three drafts of this troublesome note before getting it right—an indication of her confused state. Liszt did not reply. He turned up in person, and the instant he entered her salon she felt again his magnetic attraction. From that day he became a frequent visitor. After six years of marriage, as Marie points out, she enjoyed complete independence, and there were no barriers to their meetings.

---

4. AM, pp. 21–22.

From the begining our conversations were very serious and, by common accord, quite free from anything banal. Without hesitation, without effort, by the natural inclination of our souls, we embarked at once upon elevated subjects, which alone had any interest for us. We talked of the destiny of mankind, of its sadness and incertitude, of the soul and of God. . . . Franz spoke with a vivacity, an abundance, and an originality of impressions that awoke a whole world that had been slumbering in me; and when he left me I was sunk in reveries without end. The voice of the young enchanter, his vibrant speech, opened out before me a whole infinity, now luminous, now sombre, forever changing, into which my thoughts were plunged and lost. . . . Nothing of coquetry or of gallantry was blended with our intimacy, as so often happens between fashionable persons of opposite sexes. Between us there was something at once very young and very serious, at once very profound and very naive.[5]

In order to understand the origins of this love-affair, to say nothing of its tempestuous development, we must explore Marie d'Agoult's personality and family background in greater depth than is usual in a biography of Liszt. Who was this woman, about to throw away every social advantage in order to link her life with his? She remains a stranger to most musicians, even to those who have a right to claim some acquaintance with the minutiae of Liszt's daily life, being known mainly by her mundane title of "first mistress." Yet the force of their initial encounter and their subsequent love-affair, followed by the violence with which they ultimately rejected one another, left them emotionally drained and produced psychological scars which they carried to the tomb.

I I

Marie d'Agoult was descended from the powerful Bethmann family, one of the wealthiest banking dynasties in Germany. The enterprise on which the family fortunes were built had been founded by the brothers Simon Moritz and Johann Philipp Bethmann during the first half of the eighteenth century in Frankfurt-am-Main. In 1793 Johann died, leaving his massive inheritance to his Swiss-born widow, Katherina, and their two children, Moritz and Marie-Elisabeth. The family lived in a palatial mansion in Frankfurt called the Baslerhof, a name which emphasized the Swiss connection, where they were surrounded by servants and luxuries of all kinds. Frau Bethmann ruled over this household with a rod of iron. Although her son now ran the business, he was dominated

5. AM, pp. 25–27.

by his mother. Her daughter, Marie-Elisabeth, had been married off at sixteen to her father's elderly business partner, Jacob Bussmann, but within two years he had died and left his child-bride a widow. Frau Bethmann used to entertain lavishly at the Baslerhof; her business connections were worldwide and her dinner parties became famous. In the 1790s Frankfurt harboured large numbers of French émigrés, officers in the French army who were still loyal to the toppled monarchy and who were prepared to restore it by force of arms if necessary. Among these officers was the dashing young Viscount de Flavigny. In due course he received an invitation to one of the Baslerhof dinner parties, and when the eighteen-year-old widow Marie-Elisabeth met him she fell in love with him.

Frau Bethmann heard of the affair and was determined to stop it. It was easy for her to arrange for the authorities in Frankfurt to find something wrong with the papers of this young officer-refugee, and he was promptly sent to jail. But the old matriarch reckoned without the intransigence of her stubborn daughter. Marie-Elisabeth bribed her way into the prison and spent the night in her lover's arms, under the watchful eye of his jailor. The next morning she returned to the Baslerhof, happily compromised, and confronted a horrified Frau Bethmann with reality: either allow the wedding to take place or face the unfortunate consequences. The young viscount was hastily released from jail and a wedding arranged. Three children were born of the marriage. The first was a son, Eduard, who died in infancy; then in 1799 came a second son, Maurice; six years later their daughter was born, and they gave her the grandiloquent name of Marie-Catherine-Sophie de Flavigny. Since the viscount refused to return to France while Napoleon ruled, Marie was brought up in the ancestral home of her grandmother in Germany. Marie's childhood memories were dominated by Frau Bethmann dressed in black, sitting bolt upright in her enormous thronelike chair in the vast drawing room of the Baslerhof, from where she issued her orders to servants and family alike. Marie hated and detested her.

III

When Viscount de Flavigny led his eighteen-year-old bride to the altar, she was not only a widow but the mother of a small daughter, Augusta, Marie's half-sister. Augusta was mentally unstable. Her new stepfather was unable to control her. She was allowed to grow up quite wild and several times amazed Frankfurt by her eccentric behaviour. When she was still in her mid-teens, and inspired by her mother's example, she compromised the poet Clement Brentano, who was obliged to marry her. This disastrous match ended in divorce, but not before Augusta twice attempted suicide (once by stabbing herself with a penknife and once by drinking poison).[6] A second marriage was no more successful, although it produced four children, about whom Marie writes in her *Souvenirs*. After a public quarrel with her husband in a Frankfurt restaurant, Augusta flung herself into the river Mainz and drowned. Marie knew well the instability in her family and sometimes feared that she herself might go mad. She became a lifelong victim of depression and psychosomatic illnesses, for which she regularly sought treatment in Paris at the clinic of Dr. Emile Blanche. In the spring of 1869 her private nightmare became reality: her reason snapped and she temporarily turned into a raving lunatic. Her son-in-law Emile Ollivier witnessed a dreadful scene in which Marie was forcibly put into a straitjacket and removed to Dr. Blanche's clinic for observation.[7] Not a word of this has crept into Marie's biography, let alone the various accounts of Liszt's own life. But enough is now known of her violent attacks of spleen, which contrast so sharply with the refined image of marbled beauty handed down to us, to make us wonder how Liszt was able to endure their ten years together. Her early childhood was tranquil enough, however. Though feeling little affection for her mother she adored her father, who brought her up on Horace, Ovid, and Voltaire. Her literary tastes were acquired early; she was familiar with Greek myths long before she knew her Bible. She never forgot that warm Sunday afternoon in September when, as a little girl, she was walking in the garden with a cousin and company unexpectedly arrived. Her mother called her indoors. A kindly old gentleman caressed her golden hair and spoke a few words of greeting to her. It was Goethe, whose ardent admirer she later became, and whose profile is today carved on her tombstone.

When Marie was thirteen years old her father died. She had been playing in the woods around her home and when she returned was told that he had fallen ill. She ran to his bedside and he asked her where she had been. "For a beautiful walk," she replied. "I'm glad you have enjoyed yourself," he said; "I'm in pain." The remark was not intended to wound, but it cut the child to the heart; and when her father died three days later without having spoken to her again, Marie was devastated. Unable to confide in her mother, she hugged this private grief to herself throughout her adolescence. It was the first great trauma of her life, and she learned to handle it with the same self-restraint she exhibited in later life in times of stress. Her inability thereafter to find her "great

---

6. VCA, vol. 1, pp. 18–19.
7. OJ, vol. 2, p. 362. As early as 1852 Marie's medical condition had been diagnosed as "spleen," an umbrella term which, in nineteenth-century parlance, covered a wide range of emotional disorders. "What is spleen?" wrote Marie in her unpublished "Journal." "Can one see it as a gush of blood which leaves the brain, or else floods in in too great a quantity? (VCA, vol. 4, pp. 11–12.) She described her recurrent illness, which sometimes lasted for three months at a time and rendered her incapable of all physical activity, as "a bankruptcy of the nerves," and she feared that it made her "the victim of stupidity and imbecility." Her only remedy was to shut herself away in a darkened room in complete silence until the depression lifted.

man," and the evident difficulty she had in choosing a husband, can be traced to the irreparable loss of her father during her formative years. Those who did not know her well thought her cold and heartless. But the icy exterior was a mask whose rigidity stood in inverse ratio to the boiling emotions it held in check. She was aptly portrayed in her womanhood as "six inches of snow covering twenty feet of lava," a description she quotes in her *Souvenirs* without disapproval.[8] When she was sixteen Marie was sent to a fashionable convent school in Paris, the Sacré-Coeur, which was run by Jesuits, in order to finish her education. As the heiress to the Flavigny fortune she was treated with deference, being allowed the privilege of her own room and a piano, which enabled her to continue the music lessons she had begun in her early teens. This was a consolation to her. Nonetheless, her years of adolescence were lonely. She writes with distaste of this period, hating the stifling routine and "the odour of sanctity." One story stands out from this time. She befriended a younger pupil, an ugly and awkward child who was further handicapped by her slow intelligence. The other pupils cruelly tormented her until Marie, goaded beyond endurance at the young girl's distress, rushed into the fray, scattering her tormentors in all directions.[9] From that day no one dared touch the girl, and Marie was treated with new respect. It was an early indication in her of Flavigny chivalry. When she became "Daniel Stern" and developed Republican sympathies, she would break many a lance for the underprivileged and distressed.

In due course Marie, like other young ladies of her social class, "came out." It was now expected of her that she marry. Such matters were usually negotiated by the families of the interested parties, and Madame de Flavigny and Marie's brother, Maurice, who had entered the diplomatic service, proceeded to screen some possible candidates. Marie was now a dazzling blonde beauty, one of the most desirable debutantes in society. There was no shortage of suitors. Chaperoned meetings were set up, but the young Lorelei found no one with whom she felt compatible. Shy and reserved, Marie had come to resemble George Sand's later description of her as "straight as a candle, white as a sanctified wafer," and her suitors found her aloof. After three or four seasons had slipped by and Marie was still unmarried, her mother and brother began to worry. At last she showed an interest in a certain Count de Lagarde, aide-de-camp to the Duke of Richelieu. Lagarde was forty-five, more than twice Marie's age, but after several visits she felt that he might offer her paternal affection. Unfortunately, Lagarde was as shy as Marie, and he found himself unable to express his feelings. The silence dragged on for several months. Lagarde finally decided he must end it. He paid one last visit to the salon of

---

8. AS, p. 349.
9. AS, p. 173.

Marie d'Agoult, an oil portrait by Henri Lehmann (1839).

Madame de Flavigny, resolving that if Marie herself asked him to stay he would remain, the happiest of men; if not he would leave, never to return. Here is how Marie continues the story.

> M. de Lagarde had been in the salon with my mother for nearly an hour before I could bring myself to enter it. I had needed all this time to pluck up my courage. As I opened the door M. de Lagarde was on the point of leaving. I went towards him and held out my hand. "You're going then?" I said, with tears in my eyes. "Yes, I'm going," he said, as his eyes met mine. And as I could say nothing, "I'm going," he repeated, emphasizing his words, "unless you your-self order me to stay." Stay! . . . This short little word, which would have changed my whole existence, came to my lips more swiftly than thought; I felt it vibrate and tremble there . . . and die . . . in an incredible weakness of my love and my will-power. . . . Someone else came in; M. de Lagarde went.[10]

The departure of Count de Lagarde changed the course of her life. Marie relates in her *Souvenirs* that she was so upset that she resolved to marry the next suitor to present himself and told her family to arrange a suitable match. Their choice fell upon Count Charles d'Agoult. Born in 1790, and therefore fifteen years Marie's senior, the count belonged to one of the oldest families in France. A distinguished military career lay behind him. He had joined the French army at seventeen and had risen to the rank of colonel. During the Battle of Nangis he had led a cavalry charge against Russian infantry and was shot in the left leg. Thereafter he always walked with a limp. Marie quickly perceived that Count d'Agoult was a man of great kindness and integrity. Although she did not love him, she came to respect him, and when he proposed to her she accepted. He told her that he would willingly give her back her freedom should she ever regret her decision. And eight years later, when that crisis came, he kept his word. The wedding took place on May 16, 1827, in the fashionable Church of the Assumption. A glittering assembly of aristocratic families gath-ered to mark the event. The marriage contract was witnessed by Charles X himself, and the dauphin and the dauphine. According to Count d'Agoult, his wife brought 300,000 francs to the marriage as her dowry.[11] Shortly afterwards Marie was presented at court, where she created a sensation with her train of white silk and gold brocade, adorned with diamonds. The honeymoon was spent in London. The Channel crossing was rough, and the count retired below, indisposed. Marie stayed on deck throughout the voyage, however, admiring

---

10. AS, pp. 232–33.
11. ACS, p. 14.

the turbulent seas. The event was symbolic of the manner in which their independent relationship was to unfold.

IV

The unpublished memoirs of Charles d'Agoult offer us some rare insights into the character of his wife. She never travelled anywhere without trunkfuls of writing paper, which even accompanied the newlyweds on their honeymoon, to the count's evident exasperation. Stranger still is the story the count relates concerning his wife's experiment in transvestism. "One day," he writes,

> Madame d'Agoult came into the drawing room (where I was alone) wearing my military cap, dressed in my greatcoat, wearing a pair of my trousers, my boots with spurs, and my riding crop. At first I was somewhat taken aback. Then I hastened to tell her that the costume suited her very well—it was true—and that she even had the swash-buckling air of a musketeer. She looked at herself in the mirror, swished the air with her crop, and went out saying, "That's what I needed, a pair of trousers and a crop!"[12]

As Marie d'Agoult scribbled away, covering reams of paper with her daily jottings about other people, memorabilia that she would one day incorporate into the account she gave of herself to the world, she had no idea that she herself was being closely observed—by her husband. Count d'Agoult had no literary talent; nor did he have any interest in "setting the record straight" (neither his wife's *Mémoires* nor her correspondence with her lover were published during his lifetime). But he understood his wife's difficult character through and through. His unpublished account is a straightforward description of their years together. It differs in detail from the received picture of Marie d'Agoult—calm, poised, unruffled—which was painted largely by herself.

After their return to France, Marie and Charles d'Agoult installed themselves in a mansion on the Left Bank of the Seine, almost opposite the Tuileries Palace. It was here that the countess held her first salon, scoring her greatest success with Rossini and his troupe of singers. From her balcony she witnessed the violent clash between workers and soldiers during the July Revolution. She recalled seeing soldiers running in all directions across the Tuileries and heard gunfire,

---

12. VAMA, p. 14. When Barbey d'Aurevilly launched his savage attack on "Daniel Stern," calling her not merely a bluestocking but a "blue-trousers" as well, he had no idea of the existence of this unpublished document, which, as Jacques Vier points out, lends unexpected weight to his description. The holograph of Charles d'Agoult's "Souvenirs" is today in the possession of his descendant Count Saint Priest d'Urgel.

screams, and breaking glass as furniture was thrown out of windows. Finally, to her astonishment she saw the tricolour flag run up over the Clock Pavilion. The monarchy had collapsed. It was Marie's first encounter with "the people."

Two children were born of the marriage: Louise in 1828, and Claire in 1830. In 1832 Marie d'Agoult bought a permanent home for her family: the Château de Croissy, a palatial residence built in the time of Louis XIV. Situated six miles from Paris and set in beautiful grounds, Croissy offered Marie an ideal retreat from the social whirl of the city. Her husband was frequently absent from Croissy for long periods of time. Posterity has not treated Count d'Agoult kindly. He is usually depicted in biographies of Liszt as an insensitive husband and an indifferent father, giving Marie ample reason to leave him. It is time to set this canard aside: Charles d'Agoult held his wife and small daughters in great affection. He had feared for the stability of his marriage from the start, rightly pointing out that in her youth Marie had been surrounded by bad models. The marriage was scarcely a year old when they had their first serious quarrel. Charles felt instant remorse and wrote Marie a soothing letter. Three years later a more serious rift occurred, resulting in a temporary separation. In one of his rare letters to Marie, Charles wrote:

> I'm longing to hear from you, for the thought that you or my children are far away from me gives me no peace. I reproach myself for my last letter; it will have hurt you when you were ill, and that is far from my intentions! I was wrong to be so hard, forgive me that fit of bad temper. As you say, who among us does not have reproaches to make against themselves? It's that sometimes I have moments which are a little sad, for my wife and children are everything to me and nothing can replace them.[13]

This was Marie d'Agoult's background when the twenty-one-year-old Liszt entered her life. Her marriage was strained, her adolescence had contained many frustrations, her half-sister was suicidal, and Marie herself was neurotic and liable to bouts of depression and melancholia. It is a less flattering account of her personality than the one we are used to reading. Since her wedding day, she confessed, she had not enjoyed a single happy hour.

v

By the summer of 1833 the Liszt–d'Agoult affair had begun to develop rapidly. Liszt sometimes travelled out to Croissy, and Marie occasionally came to Paris,

---

13. January 31, 1831. VAMA, p. 21

where they met secretly in his mother's apartment (referred to jocularly as the *Ratzenloch,* the "rat hole"). That fact alone makes it obvious that Marie was a willing partner in the liaison.[14] In order to avoid detection, they resorted to elaborate subterfuge, writing to one another through intermediaries. As early as December 1833 Marie was urged by Liszt to forward her letters to one Madame Vial ("I am completely certain of her"). He, in turn, sometimes addressed his envelopes to "Marquise de Gabriac at the Château de Croissy," and would then begin the letter in English (a language Marie could read), "This is not for the marquise. Do you understand?" His letters are studded with German and English phrases to obscure the time and place of their next tryst.[15] At first their correspondence was formal and correct. But as the couple saw more of one another, their letters acquired intimate overtones. By January 1834 at the latest there was an open declaration of love. In the early summer Liszt spent an idyllic week at Croissy. On his return to Paris he wrote, "How ardent, how glowing on my lips is your last kiss!" And a short time later: "Write to me often. You write so divinely, so straight from the heart; your every word burns with an inner flame. There is only one name now that I repeat every hour." Marie, for her part, had long since declared herself; although many of her letters are missing from the *Correspondance,* she had written as early as May 1833, "Sometimes I love you foolishly, and in these moments I comprehend only that I could never be so absorbing a thought for you as you are for me."[16] She had already addressed one of her letters "To a genius."[17]

Even in these early days the course of their love-affair did not run smoothly. It seems that Marie had come into possession of some old letters that Liszt had written to Adèle Laprunarède and others. All of them dated from 1831, but her jealousy was aroused and she confronted him with them. He explained that these affairs were over long before he had met her. That did not satisfy Marie.

---

14. Liszt's "seduction" of Marie d'Agoult is another canard that has become so deeply entrenched in the literature that it may never be eradicated. It has long been assumed, even by those biographers who are in other respects sympathetic to Liszt, that his "pursuit" of the countess wrecked her life by placing her in an impossible social position, and they hold him largely responsible for her plight. Yet even Marie's own family, who knew her better than anyone, and who had had first-hand experience of her instability, never took such a position, holding her chiefly to blame for the liaison and its radical consequences on her life. In this connection see the letter from Maurice de Flavigny which not only virtually clears Liszt of the charge of "seduction" but makes allowance for his youth (p. 225). In old age, Liszt grew tired of defending himself against gossip and wrote his last word on this subject to Lina Ramann: "Madame d'Agoult was never seduced by me, and both her husband, Count d'Agoult, and her brother, Count de Flavigny, eventually held this to be true. 'Liszt,' they said, 'is a man of honour.'" (WA, Kasten 327, unpublished letter dated November 14, 1880.)

15. "Ich werde ganzen Tag auf Sie warten, hier, 21 in der Strasse von Erard, zweiten Stock, die Türe rechts—ich bin immer allein" ("I will wait here all day for you, number 21 in Erard's street, second floor, the door on the right—I am always alone"). (ACLA, vol. 1, p. 29.)

16. ACLA, vol. 1, p. 57.

17. ACLA, vol. 1, p. 53.

She required him to confess to her in the greatest detail all the indiscretions of his past. He appears to have done so, but protested that he was not ashamed of these love-affairs and would never deny them.[18] Marie "forgave" him, but the episode rankled. It was a dress-rehearsal for the many lovers' quarrels that would typify their relationship in the years to come.

It is entirely in keeping with what we know of Marie d'Agoult's character that she now consulted a clairvoyant to predict her future. The name of this fortune-teller was Mlle Lenormant, and she lived in the rue de Tournon, then one of the seamiest quarters in Paris. At the height of her fame Mlle Lenormant had numbered among her clients Alexander I of Russia and the Duke of Wellington, who consulted her in 1818 in order to discover who had attempted to assassinate him. She was now old, fat, and ugly, and she held her consultations in a dark, stuffy room, seated in a leather armchair in front of a table on which she shuffled some cards, while a black witch's cat circled at her feet. So deeply did this eerie scene affect Marie's impressionable mind that she was able vividly to recall the details even after a lapse of many years.

> Your destiny [Mlle Lenormant told Marie] will be changed completely two or three years from now. What seems impossible today will come to pass. You will change your way of life entirely. Later you will even change your name, and your new name will become famous not only in France but in Europe. You will leave your country for a long time. Italy will be your country of adoption; there you will be loved and honoured. You will love a man who will make a sensation in the world and whose name will cause a great stir.[19]

This prophecy became true in all the essential details.

Throughout the summer of 1834 Marie had ample time to dwell on her destiny. Liszt was 200 miles away with the Abbé Lamennais at La Chênaie, where he remained for three months. It seems that the separation was planned in order to give the couple time to reflect on the consequences of their relationship. Whether Marie, under normal circumstances, could ever have mustered the courage to leave her home and husband in order to link her life with Liszt's is uncertain. But the hand of fate now intervened. In October Marie's elder daughter, Louise, fell ill; by December she was dead. Marie has left a moving account of this tragedy. The six-year-old child apparently contracted a fever at Croissy which turned into inflammation of the brain. She

---

18. ACLA, vol. 1, pp. 72 and 83.

19. AS, p. 386. This consultation with Mlle Lenormant took place on June 23, 1834, at the very time that Marie came into possession of the Adèle Laprunarède letters.

A facsimile of a letter from Liszt to Marie d'Agoult,
written in the spring of 1834.

became delirious and went into long fainting fits. Marie took her to Paris for expert medical treatment, and did not leave her daughter's bedside. Just before the end, and after three nights without sleep, it seemed to Marie that the crisis had passed, and she retired to the next room to tidy herself.

> Hardly had I gone when some instinct drew me back to her bed. How terrible! The child was bolt upright, her eyes open and haggard. I rushed towards her. She threw her arms round my neck in terror as though to escape an invisible hand. I clasped her to me. She uttered a cry; I felt her body sag and hang limp against my breast.[20]

Prostrate with grief, Marie became severely depressed. Liszt called at the house every day for news, but she refused to see him. Nearly six months had elapsed since the pair had last seen one another, and we have a number of Liszt's letters to Marie which tell of his anxiety and despair; they remained unanswered. Marie returned to Croissy in a suicidal frame of mind, threatening to drown herself.[21] She had hardly any recollection of the days and weeks that followed. A sad footnote to the tragedy was that she was quite unable to bear the presence of her younger daughter, Claire, whose innocent laughter and playfulness during this period of mourning so jarred on her nerves that she placed the child in a convent. One morning, Marie relates, after she had begun her convalescence, she was given a pile of letters that had arrived at Croissy during her illness. Among them was one from Liszt announcing his intention of leaving France and expressing a desire to see her one last time before his departure. No such letter exists in the Liszt-d'Agoult *Correspondance*; Marie merely cites it in her *Mémoires*. Whatever the cause, Marie's resistance crumbled. She travelled to Paris to see Liszt, and their emotional reunion took place in his apartment in the rue de Provence. That must have been no later than March 1835: their first child, Blandine, was born the following December.

VI

It was now impossible for the lovers to remain in Paris. In order to avoid a scandal, they planned an elopement to Switzerland. The arrangements were made in absolute secrecy.[22] The only two people Liszt confided in were his

---

20. AM, pp. 36–37.
21. ACLA, vol. 1, p. 133.
22. The following month, April 1835, Liszt gave a concert in Paris. It is an indication of the physical and mental strain under which he was labouring that he collapsed at the keyboard and had to be carried off the platform. This dramatic scene was witnessed by Henry Reeve, who left the following description: "Liszt had already played a great Fantasia of his own, and Beethoven's 27th Sonata, in

mother and his spiritual adviser, Abbé Lamennais, who hurriedly left his retreat in Brittany and travelled to Paris in an attempt to dissuade Marie from pursuing so radical a course. Their discussion lasted more than an hour, but Marie remained obdurate. She set out from Croissy at the end of May in the company of her mother, Countess de Flavigny, who had as yet been told nothing about the reasons for the journey. Liszt delayed his own departure until June 1, for appearance' sake, having arranged to rendezvous with Marie in Basel a few days later. [23] Just before leaving Croissy for the last time, Marie wrote a letter to Charles d'Agoult, perhaps the most difficult lines she ever penned.

May 26

I am going to leave, after eight years of marriage. . . . Whatever you may think, I have not been able to make such a decision without a cruel struggle, without bitter tears. I have no wrongs to reproach you with, you have always been full of affection and devotion for me; you have thought always of me, never of yourself, and yet I have been truly unhappy. I am not blaming you for this unhappiness. Perhaps (and I cannot reproach you for this opinion) you think that the blame for it lies solely in me. I do not think so. When fate has joined two people as dissimilar as we are in temperament and mind, without their knowing one another, the most constant efforts and the most painful sacrifices from both sides only serve to deepen the abyss which separates them. . . . I ask for your forgiveness on Louise's grave. . . . Your name will never leave my lips except when it is uttered with the respect and esteem which your character deserves.

---

the former part of the concert. After this latter piece he gasped with emotion as I took his hand and thanked him for the divine energy he had shed forth. . . . My chair was on the same board as Liszt's piano when the final piece began. It was a duet for two instruments, beginning with Mendelssohn's 'Chants sans paroles' and proceeding to a work of Liszt's. We had already passed that delicious chime of the 'Song written in a Gondola' and the gay tendrils of sound in another lighter piece. . . . As the closing strains began, I saw Liszt's countenance assume that agony of expression, mingled with radiant smiles of joy, which I never saw in any other human face, except in the paintings of our Saviour by some of the early masters; his hands rushed over the keys, the floor on which I sat shook like a wire, and the whole audience were wrapped in sound, when the hand and frame of the artist gave way; he fainted in the arms of the friend who was turning over for him, and we bore him out in a strong fit of hysterics. The effect of this scene was really dreadful. The whole room sat breathless with fear, till Hiller came forward and announced that Liszt was already restored to consciousness, and was comparatively well again. As I handed Mme. de Circourt to her carriage, we both trembled like poplar leaves, and I tremble scarcely less as I write." (RML, vol. 1, p. 49.)

The episode was later confirmed by Hiller, who described it in his *Künstlerleben* as a "catastrophe." (HK, p. 206.) He had great difficulty in dispersing the audience, some of whom were fearful that Liszt had expired. From Hiller we also learn that the concert took place in the assembly hall of the Hôtel de Ville.

23. Details of Liszt's journey from Paris to Basel will be found in his unpublished Pocket Diary for this period, recently discovered in the Bibliothèque Nationale. See EDW.

As for me, I ask only for your silence in the face of the world, which is going to overwhelm me with insults.

M.[24]

Henceforth Charles d'Agoult's lot was not easy. He continued to live at Croissy, cared for his daughter, Claire, and bore stoically the humiliation that Marie brought on him and his family. Not once did he attempt to deflect his wife from her purpose. And when, five years later, she returned to Paris, her illusions shattered, it is a measure of his devotion that he offered to take her back into the conjugal home.[25]

---

24. VAMA, pp. 22–23.

25. In 1849 Charles d'Agoult was forced to leave Croissy when Claire, who had married Count Guy de Charnacé earlier that year, claimed her inheritance and took over the château as her matrimonial home. Charles moved into modest lodgings in the Batignolles and eked out his declining years on a small pension. Marie carried her guilt and remorse with her to the grave. That she never lost her respect for Count d'Agoult is borne out by a letter she wrote forty years later, on April 5, 1875, a few days after hearing of his death: "M. d'Agoult passed away on the 18th of last month, in his eighty-fifth year. He had foreseen his end for a long time, and waited for it with a soldier's simplicity and a gentle Christian philosophy. But the agony of the last hour was spared him. Neither he nor even the doctor had foreseen the danger near. He had no apparent suffering or death agony. He leaves in the memory of those who knew him the image of a most gallant man. In the most delicate relations I found him constantly loyal, impartial, generous. I wear mourning for him with respect, and the regret of having been unable to equal him in the spirit of abnegation and devotion. . . ." (VAMA, p. 16.)

BOOK THREE

The Years of Pilgrimage
1835 · 1839

Elopement to Geneva

> *Ramparts of granite, inaccessible mountains now
> arose between ourselves and the world as if to
> conceal us in those deep valleys, among the shad-
> owy pines, where the only sound was the mur-
> muring of waterfalls, the distant thunder of unseen
> precipices. . . .*
>
> MARIE D'AGOULT[1]

I

Marie arrived in Basel, in the company of her mother, at the beginning of June 1835 and took rooms at the Drei Könige hotel. She had not yet summoned up the courage to tell her family about her future plans, let alone her present condition. That fact stands revealed in a letter she wrote to Liszt shortly after her arrival in Switzerland.

> Wednesday, Drei Könige
> Basel, June 5, 1835

> Let me know at once the name of your hotel and your room number. Don't go out. My mother is here; my brother-in-law has left. By the time you read this, I will have told her. Up to now, I haven't dared say anything.
> It is the last, difficult trial, but my love is my faith and I am avid for martyrdom.

Liszt had arrived in Basel after Marie, on June 4, and had registered at a different hotel in order to avoid meeting her relatives. The last sentence of his reply was written in English, presumably to avoid detection.

---

1. AM, p. 42.

Basel, June 1835

Since you called for me, I am here.

I shall not go out till I see you—My room is at the Hôtel de la Cigogne number twenty at the first *étage*—go at the right side.

Yours[2]

It used to be a commonplace of the Liszt literature that he had gone to Basel for no other purpose than to escape the clutches of Marie d'Agoult, and that she, on finding that her young lover had fled Paris, pursued him to Switzerland, there to throw herself on his charity.[3] The facts speak differently. We have a letter from Liszt, written to his mother, in which it becomes abundantly plain that the elopement to Switzerland was planned in Paris, that Basel was merely a temporary solitude, and that Liszt was far from unhappy at the hand fate had dealt him.

---

2. ACLA, vol. 1, p. 136.

3. The story was put about by Göllerich, among others. (GL, pp. 89–90.) It achieved total fantasy in Schrader: "Liszt, warned by Berlioz, maintained an attitude of reserve towards her; but when he seemed in danger of succumbing, his friends advised him to leave Paris and so avoid a scandal. Liszt, therefore, went in the spring of 1835 to Switzerland. One day when he was sitting at his writing table in Berne [*sic*] the door flew open and the countess burst in, followed by her servants, who deposited her numerous trunks in the room." (SFL [2], pp. 29–30.) William Wallace (WW, p. 130) went further, calmly asserting that Marie used the weapon of divorce to bring Liszt to heel, then, "having obtained her decree was after him with tons of portmanteaux and hat boxes." Marie and Charles d'Agoult were never divorced. On the question of who followed whom to Switzerland, Liszt's unpublished Pocket Diary proves that he arrived there after Marie. (EDW.) So much for the "chase" theory.

Two other troublesome errors can be disposed of here. Ramann wrongly reported the location of the tryst as Berne instead of Basel. Ernest Newman, in his one-man crusade against Liszt (NML, pp. 51–53), huffs and puffs his way across three pages in an attempt to show that the substitution of Berne for Basel was symptomatic of a plot by Liszt's official biographer (with Liszt's own connivance) to cast a smokescreen over his elopement with Marie d'Agoult. Such zeal is worse than useless, since it becomes necessary for later biographers to clear up the mistakes it generates in its wake. In Liszt's personal copy of Ramann's biography (WA, Kasten 352, no. 1) the composer himself struck out Berne wherever it occurs and substituted Basel. Ramann's innocent blunder is one more proof that the first time Liszt ever saw his official biography was when a printed copy was handed to him. The other error stems from the same source. "She was without revenue," wrote Ramann (RLKM, vol. 1, p. 333), the implication quite clearly being that the countess arrived in Basel penniless and that the twenty-three-year-old Liszt was henceforth expected to shoulder a heavy financial burden, keeping his titled mistress in the luxurious style to which she was accustomed, in addition to coping with all his other cares. This is a romantic notion, designed to make him look chivalrous, but Liszt corrected his copy of Ramann's book and wrote in the margin the terse comment "nicht richtig" ("not true"). He was the first to acknowledge that during their early years together the countess, who was in receipt of a regular income from her share of the Bethmann fortune, bore most of their expenses.

Basel, spring 1835

Dear Mother,

Beyond all expectations, we arrived in Basel at ten o'clock this morning. . . . Longinus [one of Liszt's pet names for Marie] is here, also her mother. I don't know anything definite yet, but we will probably leave here in four or five days' time, taking her *femme de chambre* with us. We are both in fairly good spirits, and have no intention of being unhappy.

I am well, the Swiss air strengthens my appetite. . . .

Adieu. . . . I will write to you again soon.[4]

The Viscountess de Flavigny now learned for the first time of the crisis through which her daughter was passing. The countess returned to Paris alone in order to break the sensational news to the rest of the family. The attitude of Maurice, Marie's elder brother and head of the family, appears to have been both generous and forgiving. He wrote Marie a letter full of tender and affectionate understanding, and thoughtfully enclosed a little note from Marie's daughter, Claire, then five years old: "I embrace you. Will you come back soon?"[5] Marie had expected reproaches. Had her family's attitude been harsh and uncompromising, it would have been easier to bear. But this letter from Maurice, who had not been trained as a diplomat for nothing, nearly broke her heart.

The lovers tarried at Basel for a week. It was during this trying time that they decided on Geneva as their ultimate refuge. This French-speaking city was a quiet backwater, far enough away from Paris for the couple to feel reasonably insulated against the scandal their elopement would provoke. Moreover, Liszt had useful connections there; he had made at least two previous visits to the city in earlier years. Thanks to the good offices of the parents of his pupil Pierre-Etienne Wolff, who now lived there, Liszt was able to rent an apartment in the city at 1, rue Tabazan. On June 14 the couple set out for Geneva, making several excursions into the Swiss countryside along the way. They arrived at Lake Constance on the 16th. A few days later they were at Lake Wallenstadt, which Liszt immortalized with his piano piece of that name. Marie d'Agoult later wrote in her *Mémoires,* "The shores of Lake Wallenstadt detained us for a long time. Franz wrote for me there a melancholy harmony, imitative of the sigh of the waves and the cadence of oars, which I have never been able to hear without weeping."[6] By the 23rd they had made the ascension of St.-Gothard.

---

4. LLBM, pp. 16–17. The original copy of this letter was not dated. We know it to be June 4, however, from collateral evidence in Liszt's unpublished Pocket Diary. (EDW.)

5. AM, p. 49.

6. AM, p. 45. A detailed itinerary of the excursion from Basel to Geneva can be found in Madame d'Agoult's "Unpublished Notebooks" (AC).

Following the Rhône Valley, they were at Martigny by July 1. After sojourn-
ing at Bex for a few days, they continued their journey, finally arriving in
Geneva on July 19.

The house on the rue Tabazan in which the lovers installed themselves still
stands today. It occupied the corner site next to the rue des Belles-Filles.[7] Liszt
wrote to his mother, describing it as "a magnificent residence," and asked her
to send from Paris his manuscripts, his library of books, his piano, and other
personal possessions.[8] Although he and Marie lived there for only thirteen
months, it was clear that they at first regarded it as a permanent home. News
of the distinguished couple's arrival spread swiftly. They were pleased to receive
some unexpected visitors from Paris—Prince Belgiojoso, Countess Potocka,
Mallefille, and Ronchaud. Among the habitués of the rue Tabazon were the
doctor Coindet, the botanist Pyrame de Candolle, the politician James Fazy,
the orientalist Alphonse Denis, and the economist Simonde de Sismondi. One
of the best accounts of Liszt's first few weeks in Geneva comes from the journal
of Madame Auguste Boissier, then living in Geneva. Ever since their lessons
in Paris in 1832, Valérie Boissier had showered Liszt with invitations to visit
her family in Switzerland.[9] Little could she have imagined the circumstances
of the reunion when it finally took place. It was in their imposing house (called
Le Rivage) that the twenty-three-year-old Liszt presented his runaway countess, "without blushing," and apparently shrugging his shoulders "at the blessing
of marriage and similar bagatelles," to the honest burghers of this straitlaced,
Calvinist community.[10]

II

Marie idealizes this "honeymoon period" in her *Mémoires*. For her, the rue
Tabazan seemed at first a paradise, a perfect setting for the realization of a
cherished dream. Here, in this isolated retreat, she would become Liszt's Egeria,
his inspirational guide. And through the stream of masterpieces that would now
pour from his pen, her "great man" would be revealed to the world—together
with the true nature of her sacrifice. Not for a humdrum piano player had she
callously abandoned hearth and home, but for a shining genius whose matchless
art would one day vindicate her choice. Meanwhile, the world had to be helped.
It is no accident that on June 14, just two weeks after their elopement to

---

7. Today the house bears the address 22, rue Etienne-Dumont, and carries a memorial plaque to Liszt,
unveiled in 1891.
8. LLBM, pp. 20–22.
9. See Liszt's letters to Valérie Boissier. Eight of these rare items were preserved by the Boissier family
and published for the first time in 1928. (BDLL.)
10. BRRS, pp. 29–30.

Switzerland, the *Gazette Musicale* came out with Liszt's first "official" biography, by Joseph d'Ortigue. The timing was perfect; the word "genius" appears frequently. On May 3, that same journal had published the first part of Liszt's literary effort "On the Position of Artists"; and the following December the *Gazette* carried his first *Bachelor of Music* essay, "To George Sand." Whether written by Liszt or by Marie, or more likely by them both, these articles served to burnish Liszt's image and present him to the public as a philosopher and a seer.[11]

Marie's horizons could not remain cloudless for long. Her elation was diminished by the sudden arrival in Geneva that August of Liszt's fifteen-year-old pupil Hermann Cohen.[12] This gifted youth, having been Liszt's student in Paris for the past two years, was now inseparable from him. "Puzzi" had become a familiar sight in the Faubourg districts, accompanying Liszt to his concerts. George Sand had already immortalized his name in one of her *Lettres d'un voyageur,* in which she gives a memorable depiction of the boy standing by his master's side, turning the pages.[13] Puzzi had started pining for Liszt almost as soon as his teacher had left France, and Liszt now gave him permission to come to Geneva. Cohen arrived in the company of his elder brother and their mother. Madame Cohen had been obliged to place her young daughter in a Paris boarding school and undertake the journey to Switzerland at a financial loss, and the family took up residence near Liszt so that Puzzi might resume his daily lessons. It was entirely characteristic of the fatherly attitude Liszt adopted towards his pupils that he thought it quite normal to see them every day, and even have them move into his home and live with him *en famille*;[14] and it was equally characteristic of Marie d'Agoult that she should object. In her *Mémoires* she makes heavy weather of Hermann's abrupt appearance in Geneva. She was piqued that Liszt had not properly discussed the matter with her before bringing an "intruder" into the house. "Six days later," she wrote, "a resounding hammer blow fell on the outside door of the house. Somebody ran up the stairs, four at a time, brushed past the servant, and threw himself around Franz's neck. It was Hermann."[15] Puzzi stayed in Switzerland for almost a year. His name appeared in the Geneva concert programmes several times

---

11. Liszt was already working on four articles for the *Gazette Musicale* by November 1835. (LLBM, p. 24.)
12. According to Marie d'Agoult's "Unpublished Notebooks," Hermann arrived in Geneva on August 14, less than a month after she and Liszt got there. (AC, folio 63.)
13. SLV, p. 45.
14. Liszt referred to his Paris pupils of this period as "my children." See his letters to his mother, LLBM, pp. 24 and 27. Later, during his Weimar years, pupils such as von Bülow and Tausig had the run of his home in the Altenburg—the latter living under Liszt's roof for months at a time.
15. AM, pp. 57–58. Young Hermann was certainly a boisterous youth. Countess Dash dreaded his coming to 61, rue de Provence, for his lessons with Liszt. She describes him as "a rowdy little boy, dressed in overalls, running about the stairways and in the courtyard." (DMA, vol. 1, p. 149.)

during the 1835–36 season, and we shall find him adding some unexpected colour to Liszt's life during this period.[16]

III

The event for which Liszt and Madame d'Agoult had eloped to Geneva duly presented itself. Their first child, Blandine-Rachel, was born there on December 18, 1835. The birth certificate, filed at the Geneva registry office three days after the delivery, contains some interesting details.

> On Friday, December 18, 1835, at 10:00 p.m. was born in Geneva, 8, Grande Rue, Blandine-Rachel Liszt, the natural daughter of François Liszt, professor of music, aged twenty-four years and one month, born at Raiding in Hungary, and of Catherine-Adélaïde Méran, a lady of property, aged twenty-four years, born at Paris, neither parent being married and both domiciled in Geneva. Liszt has freely acknowledged that he is the father of the child and has made the declaration in the presence of Pierre-Etienne Wolff, professor of music, aged twenty-five years, and Jean James Fazy, proprietor, aged thirty-six years, both domiciled in Geneva.
> Witnessed in Geneva, this 21st day of December 1835, at 2:00 p.m.
> [Signed]
>
> > GOLAY, civil servant
> > F. LISZT
> > J. J. FAZY
> > P. E. WOLFF[17]

The three witnesses signed this document without turning a hair, but they all knew that they had perjured themselves by bearing false testimony. Catherine-Adélaïde Méran was none other than Countess Marie d'Agoult, married; she was not twenty-four but thirty years old; and she was born at Frankfurt-am-

---

16. Puzzi's subsequent career may be briefly summarized here. After returning to Paris he fell in with bad company and lost huge amounts of money at the gambling tables. Liszt took him in hand, and in 1841 entrusted him with some private business affairs. Puzzi repaid Liszt by swindling him out of 3,000 francs. (ACLA, vol. 2, p. 183.) He later defended himself by saying that "a plot, prepared with the most diabolical cunning," had succeeded in estranging him from Liszt, but his explanation (SLFH, p. 32) does not ring true. After drinking the cup of worldly pleasures to its dregs, the dissipated young man was converted from the Judaism of his forefathers to Christianity. In 1850 he became a Barefoot Carmelite priest and was henceforth known as Father Hermann. During the Franco-Prussian War of 1870 he ministered to the prisoners in Spandau jail, where he caught typhoid fever. He died in Spandau on January 20, 1871, aged fifty. (See E. von Asow's "Hermann Cohen: Ein Lieblingsschüler Franz Liszts," *Oesterreichische Musikzeitschrift*, no. 9, September 1961.)
17. Register of Births, vol. 38, no. 651, State Archives, Geneva.

Main, not Paris. Moreover, she did not live at 8, Grande Rue. The civil servant Golay knew two of the witnesses very well. James Fazy was the celebrated publisher of the *Journal de Genève*; it is amusing to see the future mayor of Geneva putting his hand to this document. Pierre Wolff was a respected professor at the newly opened Geneva Conservatoire. Many years later Marie d'Agoult herself explained why this document was fabricated. It was not possible to disclose her identity, she said, without making Blandine the legitimate child of Count Charles d'Agoult. "Liszt and I had but one thought: to avoid this monstrosity."[18]

Blandine was handed over to a local wet-nurse, Mlle Churdet. A few months later, when Liszt and Marie left Geneva, the child was left behind with a certain Pastor Demelleyer and his family until Marie could send for her. This arrangement, made with good intentions, was to lead to many complications later on.

I V

Liszt's arrival in Geneva coincided with an important musical event: the founding of the Geneva Conservatoire of Music. For years the city had needed an institution of higher musical learning; its best talent usually defected to Paris or Brussels. Thanks to the efforts of a newly formed board of directors, and encouraged by the generous patronage of François Bartholoni, its first president, Geneva's Conservatoire opened its doors in the autumn of 1835. The institution offered courses in solfège, piano, singing, violin and cello, and wind instruments. At first the piano students were split into two groups. Madame Henri was appointed to teach the ladies, Pierre-Etienne Wolff the gentlemen.[19] The unexpected arrival of Liszt in Geneva threw these plans into disarray. Liszt offered his services to Bartholini, proposing to give lessons to the advanced students "on condition that the course be free." He further offered to prepare for the Conservatoire a "piano method." Such an opportunity could not be lost. Unfortunately, Madame Henri did not relish the thought of working with a celebrity, and she resigned her appointment. A further complication arose when the Conservatoire admitted no fewer than thirty-three piano students—twenty-eight ladies and five gentlemen—at the start of the first term. Liszt was asked to take on ten students; Wolff was given thirteen. Liszt suggested that the remaining ten be taught free of charge by his young pupil Hermann Cohen,

18. Unpublished letter to Dr. Guépin (Archives Daniel Ollivier), VCA, vol. 1, pp. 393–94.
19. BRRS, pp. 44–51. See the Minutes of the Directorate of the Conservatoire, August 5, 1835, Geneva Conservatoire Library. See also Henri Bochet, *Le Conservatoire de Musique de Genève, 1835–1935* (Geneva, 1935), pp. 17–22.

"for whose talents and morals he would be answerable."[20] The board of directors accepted the offer, but decided that Hermann should be remunerated in the same way as Pierre Wolff.

We still have Liszt's "class book" in which he notated various comments on the progress of his students.[21]

Julie Raffard	Remarkable musical feeling. Very small hands. Brilliant execution.
Maric Demelleyer[22]	Vicious technique (if technique there be), extreme zeal but little talent. Grimaces and contortions. Glory to God in the Highest and Peace to All Men of Good Will.
Ida Milliquet	An artist from Geneva. Languid and mediocre. Fingers good enough. Posture at the piano good enough. Enough 'enoughs,' the grand total of which is not much.
Jenny Gambini	Beautiful eyes.

By January 1836 Wolff had left Geneva for Russia. Liszt therefore proposed that Wolff's position be offered to Alkan (nothing came of this interesting idea); in the meantime, he and young Hermann would take on Wolff's pupils as well as their own. The directors turned down this proposal; Liszt's multifarious interests, they thought, would not allow him to do justice to so many students.[23] Liszt himself then left the Conservatoire, in the summer of 1836. Bartholini presented him with a gold watch and chain as a token of their esteem. As a further mark of recognition, Liszt was given the title "Honorary Professor of the Geneva Conservatoire."

And what of the "piano method" which Liszt had promised to prepare? It is mentioned several times in the Minutes of the Directorate meetings. On July 13, 1836, for instance, Bartholoni was recorded as saying, "Liszt has confirmed his intention of offering the rights of his method to the Conservatoire, on condition that the latter pay the costs of engraving and printing." A few months later, on October 12, Bartholoni informed his colleagues that "Liszt himself has decided to carry out the engraving at his own expense. He has requested permission to dedicate his oeuvre to the Geneva Conservatoire and to offer it some copies." These copies never arrived. Nothing more is known of Liszt's "method," which appears never to have existed.[24]

---

20. Minutes of the Directorate, November 4, 1835.
21. Geneva Conservatoire Library.
22. We surmise that this pupil was the daughter of Pastor Demelleyer, Blandine's foster parent.
23. Minutes of the Directorate, March 16, 1836.
24. Despite all the rumours to the contrary which have dogged the Liszt literature for years, one

V

It was while he was living in the rue Tabazan that Liszt brought to fruition some of the pieces in his *Album d'un voyageur,* which later found their way into the "Swiss" volume of that great three-part collection of works he called *Années de pèlerinage.*[25] Liszt's life was ever reflected in his art. These pieces, distinctly impressionistic in character, are filled with the sights and sounds of the Swiss countryside, whose natural beauty enchanted him. Earth and air, rain and storm are all represented here. Distant churchbells, cascading falls, mountain echoes, and the cries of Swiss yodellers are among the charming repertoire of effects Liszt incorporates into these soundscapes.

The titles of the "Swiss" volume are:

> *Chapelle de Guillaume Tell*
> *Au Lac de Wallenstadt*
> *Pastorale*
> *Au Bord d'une source*
> *Orage*
> *Vallée d'Obermann*
> *Eglogue*
> *Le Mal du pays*
> *Les Cloches de G . . .*

One of the more forward-looking items is *Au Bord d'une source,* a piece of "water music" prophetic of Ravel's *Jeux d'eau* in its evocation of splashing fountains. It is prefaced with a quotation from Schiller: "In murmuring coolness the play of young nature begins."

---

of which even has Olga Janina running off with the still-unpublished manuscript of Liszt's "method" to America in the 1870s and losing it there, we can now say with certainty that it was never written. We have Liszt's own word for that. When the story of the missing method reached Lina Ramann's ears nearly forty years later, she asked Liszt point-blank for information about it. His reply was unequivocal: "I have never written such a work, and will never think of writing one. . . . The only *methodisches* opus I have committed to writing is a series of technical studies." (Unpublished letter dated August 30, 1874, WA, Kasten 326.) This refers to the twelve volumes of Technical Studies, a product of Liszt's maturity published by Alexander Winterberger in 1887 (WTS), a quite different work from that intended for the Geneva Conservatoire in 1836.

25. Liszt's first title, *Album d'un voyageur,* was possibly derived from George Sand's *Lettres d'un voyageur,* which she had begun in 1835. The "Swiss" volume was originally divided into three parts, called *Impressions et poésies, Fleurs mélodiques des Alpes,* and *Paraphrase.* For the genesis of these early pieces, and for their transformation and condensation into the *Années de pèlerinage: "Suisse"* a decade or so later, see SML, pp. 23–29.

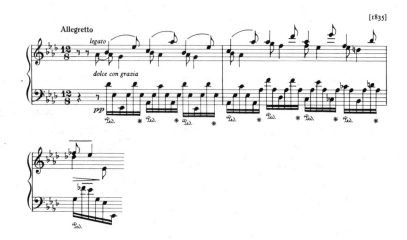

The nearly twenty years which elapsed between the first and second versions of *Au Bord d'une source* saw great changes in Liszt's handling of keyboard texture. He took immense strides forward during that period, and by the time the piece had reached its definitive form, in 1855, he had discovered a way of unfolding the same music by means of crossing hands, in a much less cumbersome way.

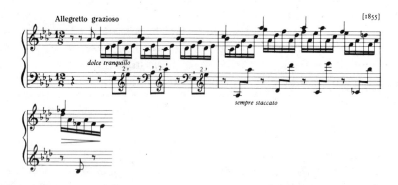

Perhaps the most topical piece in the collection, an evocative testimonial to Liszt's stay in Geneva, is *Les Cloches de G . . . ,* which the composer dedicated to his daughter Blandine in commemoration of her birth in that city. It bears a quotation from Byron's *Childe Harold:*

> I live not in myself, but I become
> Portion of that around me.

The opening page attempts to capture distant churchbells drifting across the Swiss valleys. At one point we hear a bell strike ten, perhaps in symbolic depiction of the hour of Blandine's birth. As the piece gathers momentum, Liszt skilfully combines his bell effects with the main theme of the work, and actually draws attention to them with the word *cloche*.

When *Les Cloches de Genève* was drastically revised in the 1850s, Liszt abandoned these programmatic aids along with much of the original musical material. Indeed, the earlier version is so radically different from its "revision" that it ought to be regarded as a separate work and brought back into the repertory.

In a revelatory letter to Ferdinand Hiller, written from Geneva in November 1835, Liszt disclosed his creative intentions thus.

> The game I am playing now will take three years to win or lose. Afterwards I will begin again with another; and then yet another, because, thank God, I am only twenty-four years old—the same as you. Three long-winded works, which I hope to have finished by the spring of 1837, and which will be published at that time, will vindicate me, I hope, in the eyes of you other unyielding people.
>
> As for the title, for better or worse, for now:
>
> 24 Grandes Etudes
>
> Marie, Poem in six melodies for piano
>
> *Harmonies poétiques et religieuses*, complete (that is, five or six new items).
>
> What has become of Chopin? Tell me about him, because frankly, I don't believe I will ever receive two lines from him. Embrace him for me. Also tell him, in order to amuse him, that yesterday evening I played his Etude in E-flat major [opus 10, no. 11] and one of the

most eminent artists in Geneva noticed a great analogy with the
romance of *La Folle*! I could tell you a thousand such tales![26]

What was the three-year "game" that Liszt declared himself to be playing?
Nothing less than total dominion over the piano and a repertoire to embody
that fact. As early as 1835, it seems, the twenty-four-year-old Liszt was working
on two major piano compositions normally attributed to a later period: the
Transcendental Studies (first called Grandes Etudes) and the ten-part collection
of pieces called *Harmonies poétiques et religieuses.* Both collections were to point
the piano in a new direction.[27]

VI

As the summer of 1836 approached, Liszt and Marie planned to explore the
Swiss valley of Chamonix, which was dotted with picturesque hamlets and
villages and dominated at its southwesterly end by Mont Blanc and its glaciers.
They invited George Sand to accompany them. At that moment Sand was
detained at La Châtre, a chief witness in the divorce proceedings she had
brought against her husband, Casimir Dudevant. The case was a seamy one
(involving assault, lesbianism, and the division of property, as well as good
old-fashioned adultery) and it dragged on for three months. Judgement was
finally given in her favour at the end of July,[28] and possession of her family
home at Nohant was restored to her control. It was in a mood of elation that
Sand, at the end of August, set out for Geneva to meet her old friends.

By the time Sand and her retinue arrived in Geneva (she had brought along
her two children, Maurice and Solange, as well as Ursule Josse, her maid), Liszt
and Marie d'Agoult had already set out for Chamonix. Liszt had left a note
for her at the Geneva hotel where they were all supposed to rendezvous,
explaining that their good friend Major Adolphe Pictet would act as her
travelling companion. The major (so called because of his pioneering work on
percussion shells for the Swiss federal army) sported a fierce beard and a military
cape. He reminded Sand of Mephistopheles dressed as a customs official. He was
a voracious debater, and within five minutes he and Sand were in the middle
of a heated argument about the merits of Swiss democracy. Sand won this
particular round by handing the major one of her famous "poetic cigars"
(obtained from an obscure source in the Middle East, and wrapped in datura
leaves), which left him feeling dizzy.

---

26. UB, p. 45.
27. See the chapter "Liszt and the Keyboard," where works from both collections are discussed.
28. The details were reported in the July 30–31 issues of *Le Droit.*

Posterity owes a debt of gratitude to Pictet and to Sand for leaving such vivid accounts of the Chamonix episode. Pictet's *Une Course à Chamonix* and Sand's tenth *Lettre d'un voyageur* make mandatory reading for the events which followed.

Arrived in Chamonix, Sand and the major tracked down Liszt and Marie at the Hôtel de l'Union. As Sand looked through the hotel register she saw that Liszt had signed himself in with a series of extravagant flourishes.

Place of birth:	Parnassus
Profession:	Musician-Philosopher
Coming from:	Doubt
Journeying towards:	Truth

Sand, rising to the occasion, picked up her pen, and wrote:

Names of travellers:	Piffoël family
Domicile:	Nature
Coming from:	God
Journeying towards:	Heaven
Place of birth:	Europe
Occupation:	Loafers
Date of passport:	Eternity
Issued by:	Public opinion

The hotel lobby was full of staid Englishmen with prim wives who gave Sand's party some glacial looks. At first the hotel proprietor mistook Sand for a page-boy and the military Pictet for a policeman. "Have you come to arrest them, sir?" the proprietor anxiously inquired. "Arrest whom?" "That band of Gypsies upstairs with long hair and smocks." From this point the Chamonix episode degenerated into low comedy. It was by now dark. Sand and her exhausted party were led upstairs by a nervous maid holding a flickering candle. They stopped outside room number 13. The maid opened the door, but in the dim light Sand tripped over Puzzi Cohen, who was resting on the floor in a sleeping-bag. Pandemonium broke out. Marie d'Agoult was seized by the "page," who in turn was seized by the long-haired Liszt in a three-way embrace. The maid, who could not grasp this confusing picture, dropped her candle and rushed downstairs to tell the kitchen staff that the hotel had been overrun by Gypsies. Major Pictet joined them shortly afterwards and found Marie at one end of the sofa clasping a bottle of perfume, her sole defence against Sand, who was sitting at the other puffing clouds of smoke from her long Turkish pipe. Liszt was sitting on the floor between them. The atmosphere seemed sufficiently informal to encourage the major to embark on one of those long philosophical discussions of his (he had journeyed to Berlin to study philosophy with Hegel, and was now not only immersed in the work of Schelling but insisted on immersing everyone else in it as well), and he took as his text "The Absolute Is Identical with Itself." After a few minutes of this Sand picked up her candle and retired to her room. The argument was interrupted by the sound of violent swearing from the street below. Liszt opened a window to find out what was going on. Three Englishmen were gesticulating angrily upwards. Sand had absent-mindedly aimed a large jug of water at her window box, missed, and drenched the three Britons instead. Liszt went downstairs to placate them, and they finally dispersed when Sand peered over her flower box and apologized for her error.

The following evening the motley group created a mild sensation as they entered the crowded dining room. They were shown to a table in a far corner and found themselves sitting opposite a fat Englishman who stared at them in disbelief. "Who are these fellows?" the Englishman kept asking. A Frenchman nearby told him that the man in military uniform (Pictet) was fluent in Sanskrit, that the pale young fellow (Liszt) could play any instrument, and that the young boy with the dark hair (Sand) was a juggler. The Englishman, his curiosity thoroughly aroused, peered at them through his pince-nez. George Sand retaliated by focusing her lorgnette on him and peering back. "My God, he's ugly," she exclaimed, forcing the Englishman to look hastily the other way. It so amused Liszt to be referred to as "that fellow," he adopted the term as a pseudonym. He and Marie were called "Mr. and Mrs. Fellows" for the rest of their stay at Chamonix. At this point the major handed out various nick-names of his own derived from Sanskrit literature. George became "Kamporoupi," who could change her sex at will; Liszt became "Madhousvara," the melodious one; and Marie was known as "Arabella," the thoughtful one.[29] In high good humour, the party now retired to their rooms. Liszt had ordered a bowl of hot punch and it was brought in flaming. George Sand handed out more of her "poetic cigars," which almost certainly contained opium. What happened next was observed by Marie d'Agoult, who, as the only non-smoker in the company, did not succumb to euphoria. When last observed, Liszt was conducting the chairs with a candle snuffer, angrily silencing those who were singing out of tune; Pictet had launched himself into a deep philosophical debate with an imaginary audience somewhere in the ceiling; and George Sand

---

29. Liszt had a lifelong fondness for nicknames. In his correspondence he often refers to Marie d'Agoult as "Longinus" or "Zio." She in turn dubbed him "Crétin," a mock tribute to his sharp intelligence. Their three children came to be affectionately known by them both as "les Mouches" (the flies), because as infants they crawled all over one. Hermann Cohen, as we have seen, was known to everyone as "Puzzi," a houseboy. During the Weimar period Liszt invented a whole battery of nicknames for his pupils, including "Ludwig II" for Anton Rubinstein, who had a striking facial resemblance to Beethoven. The reader who works his way diligently through Liszt's correspondence will soon conclude that he requires a veritable *Who's Who* to keep him on the right track.

Liszt, Marie d'Agoult, and Major Pictet, a caricature by George Sand (1836).

was dancing about the room in fits of laughter. Sand later produced a caricature. "Arabella," Liszt, and the major are sitting on a sofa. Hanging over them like a black cloud is the notorious caption: "The Absolute Is Identical with Itself." Liszt, his hair standing on end, asks, "What exactly does that mean?" Pictet admits: "It's a bit vague." Arabella, her head buried in the cushions, sighs, "I've been lost for ages."[30]

The travelling circus now took to the road. There was Liszt, his long hair streaming in the wind, and at his side the major, wearing his military cloak, arguing and gesticulating. Then came Sand in her male attire, smoking a cigar, and Arabella, mounted demurely on a donkey. Gambolling at their heels were Solange and Maurice Sand, and Puzzi Cohen, with his long hair dressed in imitation of his revered master, making him look like a young girl; the maid Ursule brought up the rear. They looked like a strolling band of vagabonds. It is not difficult to imagine the astonishment they aroused at some of the small mountain inns. One of the first stops was Martigny. It was very late when they arrived at the local hotel, and a disgruntled maid let the bedraggled party in. Ursule, who had never been out of France, was sobbing uncontrollably, think-

---

30. PCC, p. 144.

ing that the party had arrived at Martinique by mistake. Exhausted, they fell into their beds, only to be awakened by the sound of the major giving Puzzi (with whom he had been obliged to share a room) a good thrashing to stop him from snoring. At Lucerne, "Arabella" and "Kamporoupi" contracted food poisoning, with its attendant consequences. To crown everything, it rained solidly for the rest of the trip.

The most memorable excursion was to Fribourg, where Liszt wanted to see the newly installed Mooser organ in the Church of St. Nicholas. This huge instrument had been fitted out with sixty-three stops and four thousand pipes. As they entered the church an organist was demonstrating its capabilities, simulating, in Sand's words, "a complete storm, rain, wind, hail, faraway cries, dogs in distress, and thunderbolts." "It was not what I had expected," Marie remarked, registering her disappointment. Liszt seated himself at the organ and began an extended improvisation on the *Dies Irae* from Mozart's *Requiem*. As the music rang throughout the church, the full magnificence of the instrument stood revealed. Both Pictet and Sand later wrote of it as an apocalyptic vision, and Sand could not rid herself of the sombre, funereal words of the text:

Quantus tremor est futurus,
Quando judex est venturus.

Suddenly the organ gave up the ghost between Liszt's hands. The vesper bell had begun to ring. Mozart himself, wrote Sand, could not have persuaded the organ blower to postpone the ritual of his office. "I felt like beating him. . . ."[31]

The party spent their last few days in Geneva before finally dispersing. The lights burned into the small hours at the rue Tabazan. Liszt used to play the piano in those convivial surroundings with George Sand sitting underneath the instrument, the only place, she claimed, where she felt "enveloped" by the sound. Inspired by Liszt's performance of his newly completed rondo *El Contrabandista,* Sand stayed up the whole of one night and, in a furious burst of creative energy, wrote her short story "Le Contrabandier"—an amplification of Liszt's rondo. On September 26 they all attended a concert given by young Hermann Cohen in the Casino, at which Liszt and some of his pupils at the Geneva Conservatoire assisted.[32] Then, with embraces and kisses all round, and with promises to meet again in Paris, Sand and her group returned to France. The Chamonix holiday was ended.

---

31. SLV, p. 309; PCC, pp. 102–3.
32. *Le Fédéral* printed an appreciative review of Hermann's playing in its issue of September 30, and drew attention to the presence of Sand in the audience. See KLG, p. 325, where the programme is reproduced in full.

VII

Liszt and Marie stayed on in Geneva for only two or three weeks. It is clear that they felt they had no permanent future in that provincial capital. They missed Paris and badly wanted to return, but they were uncertain as to the kind of reception that might await them. Barely sixteen months had elapsed since their sensational elopement, and the scandal still smouldered. Marie's family, in particular, had to be spared further embarrassment. In May 1836 Liszt had made a brief return to Paris in order to meet Marie's brother, Maurice. Liszt gave an account of this interview in a letter to Marie.[33] He made it clear to Maurice that his intentions towards Marie and their child were entirely honourable. Maurice had appeared to be mollified; the professional diplomat in him told him to accept reality. While he thought that Liszt lacked the means to support Marie, he was forced to acknowledge: "Liszt is a man of honour."[34] When the Countess de Flavigny had written to him the previous summer to tell him of Marie's conduct, Maurice had come back with a remarkably objective letter, full of sympathy for the plight of the runaway couple.

> Dear Mother,
>   All the sad details that you give me on Marie's misguidedness have profoundly touched my heart and proved to me more and more clearly that no human agency could have saved her. We can only hope that God and the course of time will bring her back. There is absolutely nothing to be done with Marie at the moment, and only in two or three months' time will you be able to show her how far your maternal devotion goes. . . .
>   As for Liszt, you can be completely at rest. I feel very certain that no vengeance or violence on my part would improve the situation at present. I even believe that he is not altogether to blame: he says that he asked Abbé Lamennais to help him. It is true that he did so only after having pretty well set the house on fire, but I feel that we should make allowances for his being only twenty-two years old; only the future can prove what there really is in this man and what consideration he may merit. . . .[35]

At this same time Liszt had discreetly sounded out old friends and acquaintances and was relieved to learn that he and Marie would not be unwelcome in Paris.

---

33. ACLA, vol. 1, pp. 159 and 172.
34. WA, Kasten 327.
35. AMA, p. 79.

He had also talked frankly to his mother about their situation, and had written back to Marie, "My mother accepts everything."[36]

The pair arrived in Paris on October 16[37] and installed themselves in the fashionable Hôtel de France at 23, rue Lafitte. Everything went better than they had dared hope. Lamennais came to see them; so did Rossini and Meyerbeer. Hard on their heels followed Berlioz and Chopin. Soon the couple were surrounded by a host of old companions. Among the brilliant men of letters who called on them to pay their compliments were Sainte-Beuve, Balzac, Heinrich Heine, and Victor Hugo. Marie gave a number of soirées and it must have seemed as if she and Liszt were about to be rehabilitated in the eyes of Parisian society. The bevy of artists which surrounded Marie was totally different from the one that she had entertained during her days as a society hostess in the Faubourg St.-Germain. In the Hôtel de France she mixed as an equal with some of the greatest poets, musicians, and novelists of the time. Quick to seize the advantage, she now started to forge that powerful network of connections which would one day be so valuable to her when she turned herself into "Daniel Stern." Marie wrote enthusiastically to George Sand, now back in Nohant, about her latest circle of literati and invited her to join them. Sand arrived at the Hôtel de France at the end of October and occupied rooms on the floor immediately below Liszt and Marie. They shared a common sitting room where they entertained mutual friends. "Those of mine you don't like," wrote Sand, "will be received on the landing." It was in the Hôtel de France that George Sand was introduced to Chopin and heard him play for the first time. Chopin appears at first to have been affronted by her cigars, her mannish dress, and her flamboyant manners. "What an antipathetic woman that Sand is!" he exclaimed to Hiller as they walked home after the party. "Is it really a woman? I am ready to doubt it." And to his family in Warsaw he wrote that there was "something about her that repels me."[38] From such unlikely seeds blossomed a *grande passion* which perplexed even their closest friends, so mismatched a pair did they seem to be. Shortly afterwards (probably in early November) Liszt and Marie took Sand to see Chopin in his apartments in the rue de la Chaussée d'Antin. After some behind-the-scenes prodding, Chopin invited Sand back to his apartments on December 13, when he gave a large soirée. The company included the pianist Pixis, the tenor Adolphe Nourrit, and a number of Polish exiles, led by Albert Grzymala, who had been wounded by the Russians in the winter campaign of 1812. Sand was determined to make a better impression this time and turned up wearing white pantaloons and a

---

36. ACLA, vol. 1, p. 163.
37. Not in December 1836, as wrongly reported by Daniel Ollivier (ACLA, vol. 1, p. 180). For the true sequence of events consult Vier (VCA, vol. 1, p. 233).
38. SCC, vol. 2, p. 208.

scarlet sash—the colours of the Polish flag. Marie d'Agoult served tea and helped pass round ices; Nourrit sang some Schubert songs, with Liszt accompanying. The highlight of the evening was a performance by Chopin and Liszt of Moscheles's Sonata in E-flat major for four hands, with Chopin playing the secondo part and Liszt the primo. The Sand-Chopin affair, so important in the annals of Romantic music, was aided and abetted in its beginnings by Marie d'Agoult, who was doubtless glad to shift the spotlight from herself and give Paris a different scandal to gossip about.

Liszt gave very few public concerts in Paris during the winter of 1836–37. On December 18 he played at a Berlioz concert and performed his Fantasy on Berlioz's *Lélio*. In January and February 1837 he appeared in a series of chamber-music concerts with Urhan and the cellist Batta, featuring the piano trios of Beethoven, which were then totally unknown in Paris.[39] At the concert on February 4 an innocent hoax was perpetrated on the unsuspecting Paris public. In order to make a better effect the programme was turned around, the Beethoven trio changing places with a trio by Pixis. No announcement was made. The audience applauded vigorously after the Pixis trio, thinking it to be by Beethoven; the Beethoven trio drew a lukewarm response, everybody assuming it to be by Pixis. Not a word of all this can be found in the contemporary press. The critics of the day, apparently, could not hear the difference.[40] (A notable exception was Berlioz, who spotted the switch at once.) The episode merely served to strengthen Liszt's resolve to insist on "peer criticism," the right of every artist to be criticized by his equals, and it does not surprise us to find him developing this central theme in his writings.

The ceaseless commotion at the Hôtel de France, and the perpetual discussions among the intellectuals who congregated there about politics, society, Saint-Simonism, and all the other issues then agitating the left-wing liberals of Paris, led the locals to dub the group "the Humanitarians." It was a good label, and it stuck. A contemporary periodical[41] has left a satirical description of one of their gatherings under the title "An Evening with the Gods."

> "Coachman, rue Lafitte, number . . ." You pay him 32 sous, you knock, then you go up to the porter's lodge.
> "Porter, is Providence at home?"
> "Third floor on the mezzanine, the door on the right."
> You climb fifty-seven steps and ring at the gate of Paradise. The

---

39. All these concerts took place in the Salle Erard on January 28 and February 4, 11, and 18, respectively. They attracted widespread attention. Berlioz devoted no fewer than three articles to them, published in the *Gazette Musicale* on February 5 and 19 and March 12, 1837.
40. ACLA, vol. 1, p. 187. The event was later incorporated into Liszt's *Bachelor of Music* essay "To George Sand." (RGS, vol. 2, pp. 139–40; CPR, pp. 118–19.)
41. *Vert Vert*, December 15, 1836.

bell rope is an old belt which might formerly have been suitable for a lady-in-waiting.

It isn't Saint Peter who opens the door. Every religion has its retainer. At the Humanitarian Divinity's establishment it's a maid who opens Heaven's gate; she's a redhead from Picardy.

For we're at the Humanitarians'. You introduce yourself as an Apostle, you hand in your references from two or three saints, and you are admitted. The Goddess [Marie d'Agoult], who is blonde and cultivated, greets you charmingly.

The Goddess is dressed in Spanish style, with a lace veil on her head, open-work stockings, and pink shoes. She offers you a cigarette. You light up and watch.

All the Gods are gathered together, all the prophets are present. Four old Gods are playing a hand of whist in a corner. Don't pay any attention to these Ancients.

Behold instead the young Gods; they show great promise, and there are several about whom one can say: Theirs is the Kingdom of Heaven.

Some of the other Gods are bursting with wit and talent and could have been very distinguished men if they had not been summoned to the eternal spheres.

Here's one who deigns to be famous in our corrupt society; he's fat and well fed; he's a strong melodious Divinity [Adolphe Nourrit]. Another God moves towards him. What a contrast! This second God is as thin as a rake: it's the God Franz; he's indignant.

"O Sublime Intelligence," someone says to him, "what is troubling you? Is it, by chance, Dantan's sacrilegious caricature? Should we strike the blasphemous one with lightning?"[42]

"No," replies Franz, "I'm too great a God and too great a Pianist not to be above that. Besides, plaster makes one popular. But my thinness has been insulted in quite another way."

"What's that, my God?"

"Listen! Just now, I walked on the boulevard past the Jockey

---

42. Dantan's famous statuettes, depicting Liszt in agonized caricature at the keyboard with a proliferation of fingers at the ends of his hands, had appeared earlier that year (1836). *Charivari* had actually carried a picture of one on July 11, 1836, shortly before this particular "evening with the Gods." It was well known that Liszt disliked these statuettes, which, paradoxically, have always been admired by everybody else. Léon Escudier casts an interesting sidelight on Liszt's reaction to Dantan's work in his *Souvenirs*. When Liszt saw the first caricature in Dantan's studio he complained that the sculptor had exaggerated the length of his hair. After he had left, Dantan started work on a second statuette in which one sees nothing *but* a head of hair (Liszt is viewed from behind, still seated at the keyboard). That is what one gets, punned Escudier, for "splitting hairs" with a man whose wit extended to the point of his chisel. (ES, p. 341.)

Liszt at the piano, a statuette by Dantan (1836).

Club. Four dandies converged on me and offered me magnificent emoluments if I would be willing to become a racing jockey. As they scrutinized me through their lorgnettes, they said, 'That fellow doesn't weigh anything!' "

"What a humiliation!"

"What does it matter to me how much I weigh? What annoys me is that these people don't recognize me, so there are still some people to whom I am unknown and when I pass by them not everybody says admiringly: It is He! . . ."

"Oh, the futility of celebrity!"

"Suppose we have some music."

"Puzzi [Cohen], open the piano!"

At that command the God Puzzi springs up, passes over the heads of three Goddesses, and opens the piano. The God Franz seats himself; his mass of hair flows down to the parquet floor; he parts the curtain of his tresses to reveal his face.

Inspiration comes, the God's eyes light up, his hair quivers, he clenches his fingers and strikes the keys fervently; he plays with his hands, his elbows, his chin, his nose. Every part that can hit, hits. Finally, to end the piece with a dazzling effect, Franz soars up and falls back to earth with his seat on the keyboard.

"It's sublime!" they exclaim.

"That will cost me 20 francs in repairs," says the Goddess of the house.

The God Puzzi says nothing, but swoons away.

"Franz, Thou art Thou!" says a deep-throated voice.

"Thank you," replies the God, "thank you, George."

The God thus named [Sand] is dressed in Turkish costume. As a turban he has a floss-silk shawl; he wears bombazine trousers and Turkish slippers of hardened leather. He is smoking cheap tobacco in a clay pipe.

The Turkish God's posture is completely oriental; the puffs of smoke he blows out create a divine cloud around him; he's at the centre of conversation. Some people say, "Hello, George!" and others "How are you, madame?"

"Well, Major" [Pictet], the God George says to another God, "how do you think I look in this outfit?"

"You look like a camel-dealer."

"That lovely major, always so frank, so natural: but what are you doing rumpling my trousers?"

"Don't pay any attention, I'm seeking the meaning of life."

"That's the spirit!" George replies . . . "but I'm thirsty."

"Arabella, have them pour me a glass of the blood of the grape."

Then a little weasel-faced God, spruced up and hopping about, whom they call Monsieur l'Abbé [Lamennais], unfurls a piece of paper; they form a ring around him. "It's a speech against the Pope," they say. "You'll see how the abbé has dealt with him."

The abbé reads; they applaud; midnight strikes; it's time to retire. The Gods don't like to stay up too late. They have chatted, played cards, made music, smoked, drunk, read; it has been a delightful evening. Franz sits down at the piano again and plays the popular song "Allez-vous-en, gens de la noce!" You take your hat and withdraw from Olympus, swearing that they'll never get you back there again. . . .

These "evenings with the Gods" were terminated only when the "Gods" themselves dispersed. George Sand left for Nohant in January 1837 and persuaded Marie d'Agoult and Liszt to join her there. Marie arrived in February; Liszt, however, lingered at the Hotel de France for a few more weeks, finally setting out for Nohant in April. The reason for this delay is not hard to find. A new star had recently arisen in the firmament of pianists: Sigismond Thalberg, whose famous "duel" with Liszt was about to be fought out in the full glare of the Paris arena. This colourful episode, possibly without parallel in Liszt's early career, is of such absorbing interest that it has been allotted a chapter to itself.

The Lion Shakes His Mane:
Liszt's Duel with Thalberg

Liszt . . . is the pianist of the future.

HECTOR BERLIOZ[1]

THAT man is Thalberg.

FRANÇOIS FÉTIS[2]

I

Sigismond Thalberg was born in Switzerland in 1812. He was reputed to be the illegitimate son of Prince Moritz Dietrichstein and Baroness von Wetzlar. Shortly after his birth, so we are told, his mother wrote to the prince suggesting that their child be given the name "Thalberg"—"May this child be a peaceful valley [*Thal*], but may he someday become a mountain [*Berg*]." These tales have become deeply entrenched in the literature. The facts are somewhat less impressive. According to Thalberg's birth certificate, he was the legitimate son of Joseph Thalberg and Fortunée Stein, both of Frankfurt-am-Main, and he was born in Geneva on January 8, 1812.[3] Thalberg, then, was his real name. The famous letter from Baroness von Wetzlar is now considered to be a fabrication. Who wrote it, and for what purpose, we shall probably never know. But the possession of princely forbears, even imagined ones, was never a hindrance to a successful musical career, and Thalberg himself must bear a share of the responsibility for keeping this colourful legend alive.

When Thalberg was ten years old his mother took him to Vienna. He was

---

1. *Gazette Musicale*, June 12, 1836.
2. *Gazette Musicale*, January 8, 1837.
3. Register of Catholic Baptisms, 1804–19, no. 4, p. 154; State Archives, Geneva. "A search of the archives at Geneva revealed the fact that the birth was never registered," asserted *Grove V* (1954). But the birth certificate had already been published in 1912, Thalberg's centenary year. Even during his lifetime, there were many who doubted his claim to aristocratic lineage, among them Marmontel (MPC, p. 165), whose pioneering book *Les Pianistes célèbres* deserves to be better known.

at first intended for a diplomatic career and was placed in the prestigious Polytechnic School. One of his fellow students was the Duke of Reichstadt (Napoleon's fourteen-year-old son, the so-called King of Rome), who filled Thalberg with military ardour and nearly persuaded him to join the army. Thalberg did, in fact, become a skilful horseman and fencer. His musical talent prevailed, however. His principal teachers were Hummel and Moscheles for the piano and Sechter for composition. Within a short time the boy was making phenomenal headway; we learn that he often rose at 3:00 a.m. in order to practise. In 1826, when he was only fourteen, he made a brilliant début in the home of Prince Metternich. Two years later he started to compose the first of that steady stream of fantasies and operatic paraphrases on which his reputation ultimately rested. A successful tour of England, undertaken in 1830, brought Thalberg to the forefront of his profession. Tours of Holland, Belgium, and Germany followed. His early career was crowned in 1834 when he was appointed *Kammervirtuos* to the Emperor of Austria. He was still only twenty-two years old.

II

There have been many attempts to describe Thalberg's piano playing. All are agreed that it was "poetic," "aristocratic," "refined." He possessed a quiet demeanour at the keyboard and produced his glittering technical effects while seeming to remain motionless. That always startled his audience. Thalberg appeared, said one writer in a particularly happy phrase, "to realize the Zen ideal of central peace with peripheral combat."[4] One of his cherished attributes was a fine singing tone, and through the judicious use of the pedal he could send delicate washes of colour to the back of the concert hall. In an age of piano thumpers, these were uncommon qualities. His passage-work was legendary. It inspired one critic to see "handfuls of pearls" escaping from beneath his fingers.[5] This phrase became a cliché. To "pearl" one's passages was now an ideal towards which all students of the piano were encouraged to strive. Thalberg's greatest speciality, however, was his "three-handed" effect, which brought out the notes of a melody in the middle of the keyboard with alternating hands, the "free" hand at any given moment providing a soft accompaniment of arpeggio-like figuration. This beautiful and original effect depended, to a large extent, on Thalberg's skilful use of the sustaining pedal to "hold the line," so creating the

---

4. LMWP, p. 372. An interesting memoir of Thalberg was left by Charles Salaman (SPP, pp. 322–24), who met the pianist when he visited London in 1836. "When Thalberg, with amazing skill, made a hurricane of arpeggios sweep over the keyboard, he never lost in the effort his tranquil ease of manner."

5. Henri Blanchard in the *Revue et Gazette Musicale de Paris*, May 8, 1838, p. 153.

magical illusion of a singing third hand. A typical example may be found in his Fantasy on Rossini's *Mosè in Egitto*.

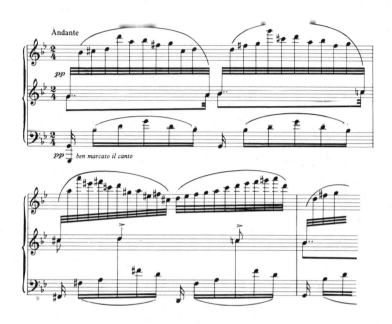

Thalberg did not invent this "three-handed" texture, although he is usually given the credit for it.[6] He did, however, give it visual prominence by printing it on three staves (as if to enshrine the melody within the very heart of his swirling arpeggios), an unusual procedure in the piano music of the 1830s. We have already observed Thalberg's passion for singing, and for bel canto in particular. It was inevitable that the man who composed more than sixty operatic paraphrases, married the daughter of the great bass singer Lablache, and eventually bought a retirement home near Naples should regard it as his sacred mission to sing on the piano. So advanced were the new Erards and Pleyels that the cantandos they produced could indeed create the illusion of song. And here we have a clue to Thalberg's success: the man and the instrument came together at just the right moment in history. The ideals of the one found a perfect vehicle of expression in the other.

When Thalberg arrived in Paris in the autumn of 1835 he created a furor. The Parisians recognized in him the most polished representative of the Classical

---

6. Its originator was the English harp virtuoso Parish-Alvars (1808–49), whom Berlioz described in his *Mémoires* as "the Liszt of the harp." Thalberg was so impressed with Parish-Alvars that he transferred his "three-handed" effects to the piano. His *Moses* Fantasy is, in fact, a partial copy of Parish-Alvars's own paraphrase of that same opera, which the Englishman played with spectacular success on his European tours.

School, a natural descendant of Hummel and Moscheles. He was taken up by Kalkbrenner (whose pupil he became for a time) and by the powerful Fétis, who started to publish a series of laudatory articles about him in the French press. That winter the Parisians divided into two camps: the "Thalbergians" and the "Lisztians." The comparisons were not always flattering to Liszt, who, it will be recalled, had already left the capital for Switzerland and knew nothing of these developments at first hand. He received random reports about the *königliche Kammervirtuos* through his network of friends, however, and we know that they aroused his curiosity. We find him writing to Anna Liszt from Geneva that all the music of Thalberg he had so far seen had struck him as being "so-so."[7] Later he asked her to get hold of a copy of Thalberg's *Huguenots* Fantasy so that he could study it.[8] There is nothing here to suggest that Liszt saw in Thalberg a rival. Least of all did he "rush back to Paris, nostrils dilated, to defend his crown," as one modern journalist has put it. When Liszt made his first trip outside Geneva in April 1836 it was primarily to give concerts in Lyon. Before returning to Switzerland he made a detour to Paris, not in order to "seek out Thalberg," but, as we now know, for the all-important interview with Marie d'Agoult's brother, during which the delicate family situation was discussed. In the event, Thalberg had left the city before Liszt arrived. Had the two pianists met then, the world might well have been spared the prospect of their ivory duel the following year.

III

If we wish to understand the reasons for the Liszt-Thalberg battle we must look elsewhere—to the French press. As early as October 1835 the Paris journals were spoiling for a fight. On October 25 the *Gazette Musicale,* taking note of the unusually large contingent of pianists in Paris, talked of that "special corps of distinguished artists who are going to wrestle zealously and with talent for our winter pleasures." These "winter pleasures" had turned into a veritable carnival, with pianists lining up to play in the Erard and Pleyel showrooms; more than two hundred concerts were held in those establishments during the 1835–36 season alone. Thalberg had soon "wrestled" his way to the top, become the man of the hour, and departed. By the late spring of 1836 Fétis had already emerged as his literary champion, lauding him in the journals. At this moment Liszt arrived in Paris. It was May, the concert season had ended, and the "special corps" of pianists, including Thalberg, had dispersed for the summer. Liszt was prevailed upon to give two semi-private performances for his friends (who had

7. LLBM, p. 31.
8. LLBM, p. 32.

not heard him for more than a year) in the Salle Erard. His programmes were severe and included a performance of Beethoven's *Hammerklavier* Sonata, possibly the first time that difficult work had been heard in Paris. Berlioz was in the audience, score in hand, and came out with a glowing review in the *Gazette Musicale* in which he hailed Liszt as "the pianist of the future." He was deeply impressed with Liszt's fidelity to the text of this sonata, which he dubbed "the riddle of the Sphinx." Warming to his metaphor, Berlioz went on:

> A new Oedipus, Liszt, has solved it, solved it in such a way that had the composer himself returned from the grave, a paroxysm of joy and pride would have swept over him. Not a note was left out, not one added . . . no inflection was effaced, no change of tempo permitted. Liszt, in thus making comprehensible a work not yet comprehended, has proved that he is the pianist of the future.[9]

The phrase "the pianist of the future" rankled with Fétis. Was Thalberg now the pianist of the past? At this point, an unfortunate sequence of events occurred. In the autumn of 1836 Liszt persuaded Maurice Schlesinger to allow him to review Thalberg's music for the *Revue Musicale*. Liszt, we recall, was now living at the Hôtel de France with Marie d'Agoult, who had surrounded herself with literary admirers and wanted to flex her muscles as a writer. It was a simple act of folly on Liszt's part that he allowed Marie to write this particular article for him.[10] The review is condescending and dismisses Thalberg's music as worthless. At first Schlesinger was reluctant to publish it. He then allowed a compromise, expressing his editorial reservations in a footnote. The article duly appeared on January 8, 1837.[11] There was an immediate outcry. Fétis published an open letter against Liszt in April in which he bluntly declared: "You are a product of a school that has outlived itself and has nothing to look forward to. You are not the creator of a new school. *That* man is Thalberg; this is the whole difference between you two."[12] Liszt hit back the following month in his "Letter to Professor Fétis," in which he dismissed Fétis's views as "much ado about nothing." The newspaper war expired a few days later, with Fétis (generously allowed a final word by Schlesinger) publishing a defence of his article against Liszt.

This, then, was the background against which the Thalberg-Liszt duel was

---

9. June 12, 1836.

10. This is beyond dispute. In "The Second Scrapbook of Marie d'Agoult" (ASSV) there is an entry in the hand of her daughter Claire, the Countess de Charnacé, which states categorically, "Madame d'Agoult told me that the articles from the *Gazette Musicale* signed Liszt were by her; article under Thalberg, p. 17 of the scrapbook."

11. RGS, vol. 2, pp. 67–73.

12. RGS, vol. 2, p. 87.

fought. Such a war of words had not been seen in Paris since the *guerre des bouffons* eighty-five years earlier. Fétis's attitude towards Liszt was part of a perfectly logical process: the struggle of a dying art against a new one. None of the onlookers understood this at the time. The confrontation was seen by everyone simply as a gladiatorial combat, fought out on a personal plane. Today we can view it differently. The "battle" was a perfect illustration of that deeper historical process which governs change throughout all human activity: the Old had to defend itself against the New, and the New won. If history had not brought Liszt and Thalberg together during that spring of 1837, and turned them into symbols of her purpose, she would doubtless have found other pianists through whom to work out her age-old dialectical ritual.

I V

Liszt heard Thalberg play for the first time in February at the Paris Conservatoire. He wrote to Marie d'Agoult, "I have just heard Thalberg: really, it is absolute humbug." He then went on to describe the *Kammervirtuos* as "a failed nobleman and a failed artist."[13] Friends tried to bring them together. When it was suggested that they should give a joint concert, Thalberg was supposed to have remarked, "I do not like to be accompanied." Shortly afterwards, Liszt was asked his opinion of Thalberg's playing and retaliated, "He is the only man I know who plays the violin on the piano." Such comments set the whole of Paris laughing. They were merely preliminary skirmishes, however, meant to herald the main event. Thalberg fired his opening shot on March 12. He appeared in a Sunday afternoon matinee at the Conservatoire and played his newly composed Fantasy on "God Save the King" and his old war-horse the *Moses* Fantasy. Liszt's "reply" was to rent the Paris Opéra House the following Sunday afternoon and play his Fantasy on Pacini's opera *Niobe* and Weber's Concertstück. This great auditorium held about three thousand people—nearly ten times the number that could be squeezed into the Conservatoire. Liszt and his piano were dwarfed by the size of that vast stage.

> When the curtain rose [wrote Ernest Legouvé] and we saw this slender young man appear, so pale and so thin, paler and thinner through the distance and the lights, alone with his piano on this immense stage, . . . a kind of fear came over us. Our whole sympathy was with this madness, for only madness can bring forth great things. The whole audience shared this uneasiness, and each one listened for the first tones with an anxious ear. After the opening bar the victory

13. ACLA, vol. 1, p. 190.

was half won, the piano vibrated under Liszt's fingers like the voice
of Lablache.[14]

Thalberg and his supporters could not ignore such a challenge for long. An open
trial of strength between the two pianists was inevitable.

   The spectacle presented itself on March 31, 1837, in the salon of Princess
Cristina Belgiojoso-Trivulzio. Shrewdly observing the mounting tension between the Liszt and Thalberg factions, she invited both pianists to play in her
home, together with other artists, in aid of the Italian refugees. Everybody in
Paris saw through this piece of diplomatic bluff. The princess had scored the
social coup of the season.

                                    V

Who was Cristina Belgiojoso? Often called the "revolutionary princess," she
was a friend of both Garibaldi and Mazzini, and she supported them in their
struggle for the independence and unification of Italy. Charged with high treason by a criminal tribunal in Milan, she escaped arrest and fled to Paris. In her
beautiful home in the rue d'Anjou she gathered around her a distinguished circle of artists including Bellini, Meyerbeer, Dumas, de Musset, and Heine. She
was a keen lover of music (Bellini had once given her some piano lessons and
she had been a singing pupil of Pasta) and an ardent opera-goer. Italian opera
affected her so strongly, in fact, that it was not unusual to observe her leaving
her box in the theatre and being helped into her carriage weeping. Estranged
from her husband, Prince Emilio Belgiojoso, who had eloped to Switzerland
with the beautiful young Duchess de Plaisance, she now took a series of lovers,
including the seventy-three-year-old Lafayette and the young Heine. In December 1838 she gave birth to a daughter of unknown paternity. For a time she
was interested in "table-tapping" and held séances in her country home which
were attended by Bellini and Heine, among others. Because of the princess's
political affiliations she was under constant observation by the Austrian secret
police[15]. Forced to flee Europe, her properties sequestered, Belgiojoso lived in

14. *Gazette Musicale,* March 26, 1837.
15. When they eventually searched her palace at Locate in northern Italy in September 1848, they
made a gruesome discovery. Hidden inside the villa was the cadaver, fully preserved in evening
dress, of one of her young lovers, a twenty-eight-year-old revolutionary named Gaetano Stelzi,
whom she had employed as a secretary. According to the parish register, Stelzi had died the previous June and had been laid to rest in the churchyard at Locate. So what was his body doing in the
palace, and who had had it transported there? These questions, which had an innocent if somewhat
unusual explanation, became the starting point of some sinister stories that still stain the princess's
reputation. Her biographer, Carlo Barbiera, embellished the Stelzi episode and had the corpse em-
balmed. Popular imagination then moved it to a closet in Cristina's bedroom. By 1926 Augustin

exile in Constantinople, where she picked up first-hand knowledge for her book on oriental harems. Here fate dealt her a cruel blow. She was accosted by a former manservant whom she had dismissed from her service. He stabbed her in the neck, causing her permanent injury. For the rest of her life she carried her head bent on her breast, as if in mourning.[16] She liked to drape herself in the ashen-hued shroud of the "Gray Sisters," a religious order founded in Paris in 1617, and would sometimes decorate it with pond lilies, which helped to obscure her deformity. This colourful and unusual figure was finally granted an amnesty, her properties were returned to her, and she ended her days by Lake Como in 1871.

At the time of the Liszt-Thalberg duel, Princess Belgiojoso's overriding concern was the Italian refugees. Towards the end of March 1837 she conceived the idea of an extravaganza, a great three-day charity bazaar in her salon, the climax of which would be the long-awaited confrontation between the two pianist-rivals. The following advertisement appeared in the *Gazette Musicale* on March 26.

> The greatest interest . . . will be without question the simultaneous appearance of two talents whose rivalry at this time agitates the musical world, and is like the indecisive balance between Rome and Carthage. Messrs. Listz [*sic*] and Thalberg will take turns at the piano.

So fierce was the demand to see Liszt and Thalberg "take turns" that the princess was able to charge 40 francs a ticket. A number of other musicians took part in this lavish entertainment—including Massart, Urhan, Pierret, Matthieux, and the singers Taccani and Puget—but they might as well have stayed at home. All eyes were on "Rome" and "Carthage." Thalberg played first, giving another performance of his *Moses* Fantasy. Then Liszt appeared and played his

---

Thierry had Cristina garlanding Stelzi's remains with flowers, a necrophilic pastime that led to a rash of horror stories about her. The spurious *Souvenirs* of the "Marquis de Floranges," a hoax perpetrated in 1906 by the popular writer Marcel Boulenger, provided details of her inner sanctum in Paris—a gallery decorated with skull and crossbones, a bedroom draped with white silk, a magnificent ebony bed inlaid with elephant tusk on which she received her lovers. Had Cristina known what a ghoulish fate posterity planned for her, she would surely have abandoned her perfectly legitimate wish to build a monument for Stelzi in the graveyard. His remains had been temporarily brought inside the palace grounds (with the full approval of the parish priest) while work on his sepulchre was completed. The recapture of Lombardy by Austrian troops in the summer of 1848 forced the princess into exile and left poor Stelzi's corpse to be discovered by the authorities who now persecuted her. To the charge of treason posterity added the infinitely more damaging accusation of necrophiliac, which unjustly clings to her to this day. MCPB, vol. 3, pp. 162–72.
16. WRP, p. 256.

Niobe Fantasy. Thanks to the critic Jules Janin, a detailed description of this historic encounter was preserved for posterity in the *Journal des Débats* of April 3.

> Never was Liszt more controlled, more thoughtful, more ener-
> getic, more passionate; never has Thalberg played with greater verve
> and tenderness. Each of them prudently stayed within his harmonic
> domain, but each used every one of his resources. It was an admirable
> joust. The most profound silence fell over that noble arena. And
> finally Liszt and Thalberg were both proclaimed victors by this
> glittering and intelligent assembly. It is clear that such a contest could
> only take place in the presence of such an Areopagus. Thus two
> victors and no vanquished; it is fitting to say with the poet ET AD
> HUC SUB JUDICE LIS EST.

"Two victors and no vanquished." It is not true, then, that Liszt emerged as the undisputed champion on that Sunday afternoon, although his biographers, almost to a man, have him trampling Thalberg in the dust. Even the *Gazette Musicale,* normally so favourably disposed towards Liszt, produced an even-handed criticism of the "duel."[17] When asked to sum up the verdict, Princess Belgiojoso came out with a diplomatic aphorism that has found a permanent niche in the literature: "Thalberg is the first pianist in the world—Liszt is unique."[18]

VI

In an attempt to keep the flames of battle burning, La Belgiojoso had meanwhile produced another masterstroke of showmanship. She invited six of the leading pianists in Paris to write a variation each on the march theme from Bellini's *I puritani.* The proceeds of the publication were destined, once again, for the Italian refugees. Liszt, Thalberg, Pixis, Herz, Czerny,[19] and Chopin were all sent the theme. Thus were the so-called *Hexaméron* (= six) Variations born.[20] Such pieces always capture the public imagination, and this one turned out to

---

17. April 9, 1837.
18. LLF, p. 42. Liszt, in short, could not be compared.
19. Czerny had moved to Paris from Vienna (partly at Liszt's prompting) just in time to take part in *Hexaméron.* For years, Liszt had wanted his old master to settle in the piano-playing capital of Europe in order fully to enjoy the reputation as the doyen of piano pedagogues now rightfully his. Liszt had written long before to his "dear and beloved Master" that "if you ever entertain this idea . . . *I will do for you what I would do for my own father*" (his emphasis). (LLB, vol. 1, p. 5.)
20. The first mention of this audacious work occurred in an announcement in the *Journal des Débats,* March 21, 1837.

be a real winner. Liszt ruefully remarked that it was a pity there was this time no Beethoven among the six composers to reject the princess's quack idea and go on to produce a mighty set of variations of his own—as Beethoven had done with Diabelli's theme fourteen years earlier in Vienna. *Hexaméron,* nonetheless, has become one of the curiosities of that age, providing the modern scholar with a useful conspectus of the contrasting piano styles of the 1830s. Princess Belgiojoso's choice of theme was quite deliberate: the March was a revolutionary call to arms. The words which accompany Bellini's rousing tune mean "Sound the trumpet for liberty."

This tune, incidentally, retained its political flavour until modern times: it was used as an anthem by the Sicilian Independence Movement after World War II. (Bellini himself was a Sicilian.) The variations range in character from a brilliant presto by Thalberg to a beautiful larghetto by Chopin, the undisputed gem of the set. Liszt himself composed the introduction, the interludes, and the virtuosic finale.

La Belgiojoso evidently hoped to have all six composers present in her salon on March 31 to give a combined performance of this unusual work and thus turn *Hexaméron* into the highlight of her charity bazaar. The title page bears this tell-tale inscription:

HEXAMÉRON
Grandes
Variations de Bravoure
pour piano
sur la
Marche des Puritains de Bellini
composées
pour le concert de Mme la Princesse Belgiojoso
au Bénéfice des Pauvres

Perhaps it was that inscription, together with a false report in the *Neue Zeitschrift für Musik,* which gave rise to the story that all six composers had in fact been physically present, each one playing his own variation. History, regrettably, must record that no such gathering took place. The reason is simple:

Hexaméron was not finished in time. This is made clear by a letter Cristina wrote to Liszt on June 4, 1837, two full months after the bazaar.

> Here, my dear Liszt, are the variations of M. Herz and the others, which you already know. No news from M. Chopin, and since I am still proud enough to fear making a nuisance of myself, I do not dare ask him. You do not run the same risk with him as I, which prompts me to ask if you would find out what is happening to his adagio, which is not moving quickly at all. It will be one more kindness on your part, for which I shall be as grateful as for the others. You know, I hope, that this implies a great deal. Try also to work seriously on the overture and finale of the piece, as though it were something that had to be completed at once. You will think no more of it afterwards, and I will remember it only to thank you and no longer to torment you.[21]

The work was published by Haslinger in Vienna, in 1839, with a dedication to the princess. A perusal of Liszt's concert programmes over the next few years shows that he played *Hexaméron* all over Europe, sometimes as an encore piece, with great popular success. He even had a set of orchestral parts made so that he could play the work with orchestra to better effect. The first performance was given by him in Italy at the end of December 1837, and it was also at that time that he gave "the monster work," as he dubbed it, its definitive title.[22]

VII

Thalberg traditionally disappears from Liszt's life at this point. As it happened, his greatest triumphs were still to come. He extended his tours and played his way through Germany, Poland, and Russia, reaching that closed continent in 1839, two years before Liszt himself arrived there. In 1845 he embarked on a tour of Spain, overlapping with Liszt's own visit. Everywhere he created new admirers. And since he always seemed to arrive just before his old rival, he succeeded in keeping the comparison alive. The Liszt-Thalberg hubbub, in fact, was still echoing through the European press ten years after the duel itself had taken place. Thalberg undertook a marathon tour of Brazil and America in 1855–56 (a pioneering effort that Liszt, for all his years of wandering, never matched) and made a great impact in such cities as Boston and New York. His two operas—*Florinda* and *Cristina di Suezia*—produced in London and Vienna,

21. OAAL, pp. 135–36.
22. OAAL, p. 141.

respectively, were failures; and his more than sixty fantasies on operas and popular tunes of the day have not survived. Nevertheless, Thalberg remained the measure by which Liszt was judged as a pianist and he is still regarded as an important figure in the world of piano playing. Liszt, unlike his biographers, did not lose interest in Thalberg the moment he left Princess Belgiojoso's salon in March 1837. With true generosity of heart Liszt featured some of Thalberg's music in his later concerts,[23] and he renewed his acquaintance with the *Kammer-virtuos* when he visited Vienna in 1838. Twenty-eight years later we find him writing to Thalberg and addressing him as "illustrious friend." And two or three days after Thalberg's death at Posilipo in 1871, Liszt wrote to his widow a touching letter of consolation.[24]

---

23. ND, p. 78. At Liszt's London concert on June 12, 1841, for example, he played Thalberg's *Norma Fantasy* for two pianos with Julius Benedict.
24. LLB, vol. 8, pp. 172 and 223.

Switzerland and Italy

*Mighty artist! Sublime in great things, superior
in small. . . . When Franz plays the piano, the
burden is lifted from my heart.*

GEORGE SAND[1]

I

Liszt gave his "farewell" concert on April 9, 1837, in the Salle Erard. He played
a group of Chopin's newly composed Studies, op. 25 (which are dedicated to
Marie d'Agoult), and his arrangement of Hummel's Septet.[2] He then set out
for Nohant, George Sand's country house, where Marie had awaited him since
February. The next three months were spent as Sand's house-guests. The lovers
of Geneva occupied quarters on the ground floor, immediately below Sand's
bedroom. An Erard piano was installed there in advance of Liszt's arrival. A
stream of friends and acquaintances passed through Nohant. Didier, Michel de
Bourges (Sand's current lover), the actor Bocage, and Mallefille were among
the occasional visitors who came and whiled away their time with the distinguished trio. The warm summer evenings at Nohant were superb. After dinner
everybody would gather on the terrace, and once the post-prandial discussions
had subsided, Liszt would move indoors, open the French windows, and begin
to play. With the old house bathed in moonlight, and the pine trees swaying
gently in the perfumed air, the music began to drift over the grounds. He played
mostly Beethoven and Schubert. Marie had recently preoccupied herself with
making French translations of the Schubert song texts in order to help him
towards a fuller understanding of their meaning. Long after the other guests
had retired to bed, Liszt, absorbed, would continue to play, occasionally stop-

---

1. SJI, pp. 45–46.
2. NZfM, no. 34, 1837.

ping to try out a passage in a variety of ways. Sand, who used to scribble the night away by candlelight in her room upstairs, in silent counterpoint to Liszt's nocturnal playing, was enthralled, as her diary entries show.[3]

On July 24, 1837, Liszt and Marie left Nohant and embarked on their journey towards Italy. George Sand and Mallefille accompanied them on horseback as far as La Châtre, the next town. They then travelled to Lyon, where Liszt, moved by the plight of the starving workers and their families, gave a benefit concert with the tenor Nourrit. The weavers of Lyon had been on strike for months, had clashed with the police at the street barricades, and were now in a desperate situation. "The elderly were without peace, the young without hope, the children without joy," wrote Liszt.[4] Before leaving this unhappy city, Liszt raised several thousand francs for the relief committee. The young poet Louis de Ronchaud, whom Liszt and the countess had first met in Geneva, two years earlier, was in the audience and firmly attached himself to them;[5] at Liszt's invitation he travelled with them to Chambéry. After making a detour to Saint-Point in order to visit Lamartine, they continued through Geneva. Their itinerary was not without purpose: in nearby Etrambière they saw Blandine and were relieved to find her in perfect health. On August 10 Marie wrote in her diary:

> I saw Blandine at Etrambière; she is very lovely. Her high forehead, her serious and intelligent air indicate that she is an exceptional child. She has a passion for flowers and already practises charity, putting coppers in the hat of her favourite beggarman. She has a temper and is also sensitive; while I was there she pinched her nurse and then immediately kissed her to show how sorry she was. What holy joys for us are enclosed in this little bud who is still so frail and so incomplete![6]

Marie determined to be reunited with her daughter as soon as possible, but her itinerant life placed one obstacle after another in the way of this resolution. By August 17 Liszt and Marie had reached Baveno and were enjoying the spectacular scenery of Lake Maggiore. The couple then followed the same "grand tour"

---

3. SJI, pp. 45–47. Liszt's long series of Schubert song transcriptions began life at Nohant. According to a letter he wrote to Massart (VFL, p. 30), Liszt had already transcribed the first group of seven songs by July 29, 1837. Raabe (cat. no. 243) wrongly assigns them to 1838.

4. RGS, vol. 2, p. 155; CPR, p. 140.

5. Louis de Ronchaud (1816–87) was now twenty years old. After Marie's final rupture with Liszt, in 1844, Ronchaud became one of her intimates, and he remained a lifelong friend. Marie dedicated her *Souvenirs* to him, and Ronchaud published them in 1877, a year after Marie's death. As Marie's literary executor, Ronchaud had access to all her personal papers, including the hundreds of letters Liszt wrote to her over the years. (See n. 12 on p. 8.)

6. AM, pp. 106–7.

as Montesquieu in 1728, since immortalized in the travel essays of Goethe, Madame de Staël, and Chateaubriand. By early September, having explored the entire eastern coastline of Lake Como, they were resting at Bellagio.

Following Ramann, every major Liszt biography detains Liszt and Marie at Bellagio for nearly five months, there to await the birth of their second daughter, Cosima. Ramann wanted to give Liszt a proper setting for his work. She therefore had him rent the Villa Melzi, overlooking the lake, its beautiful gardens filled with flowering oleanders and scented magnolias. Every day she sent the couple into the Villa Melzi park in order to rest at the foot of the marble group *Beatrice Leading Dante,* sculpted by Comolli in 1810. There, under the shade of the trees, she had them read the *Divine Comedy,* and there, too, in these inspirational surroundings, Ramann decided that one of Liszt's earliest masterpieces, the *Dante* Sonata, must have first seen the light of day. In every one of these particulars Ramann is wrong. Liszt did not rent the Villa Melzi. He and Marie did not make repeated pilgrimages to Comolli's statue. There is only one recorded instance of their ever having visited the Villa Melzi park, on August 20, when Marie noted in her diary that "the Dante in particular is a common and deplorably vulgar piece."[7] Liszt did not compose his *Dante* Sonata at Bellagio; least of all was he inspired to do so while reading the *Divine Comedy* under the trees. Finally, Cosima was not born at Bellagio. Such a catalogue of errors deserves wide exposure. In reality, Liszt and Marie changed residences several times, and they were beset by mundane problems. Marie's passport was confiscated by the police, and she was detained at Sesto-Calende for two days. She then had to bribe the customs officials for the release of her belongings. Shortly afterwards, she developed a severe toothache.[8] These may have been petty harassments, but they did nothing to enhance that lovers' idyll that Marie and Liszt are popularly supposed to have enjoyed at this time. (Ramann described their days by Lake Como as "cloudless." In Liszt's annotated copy of her book, he struck out this word and replaced it with a diplomatic question mark.) From September 6 to November 5, they were definitely back in Bellagio, making their home in "a delicious little inn."[9] What Liszt really thought of Marie's romantic attempts to play the role of Beatrice to his Dante during these honeymoon years later emerged with vehemence. "Bah, Dante! Bah, Beatrice! The Dantes create the Beatrices, and the real ones die at eighteen!" When, after their final rupture in 1844, Marie kept referring to the Beatrice-Dante model, to which she was clearly attached, Liszt put it more cogently: "It is only the poets who create and deify their Beatrices—not the Beatrices who create or deify the poets."[10]

---

7. AM, p. 109.
8. AM, p. 117.
9. VFL, pp. 36–37.
10. RLKM, vol. 1, p. 546; LLB, vol. 4, pp. 223–24.

II

Liszt usually spent his afternoons composing at the piano, while Marie worked on her journal or read "topical" books such as Goethe's *Lettres sur l'Italie*. In the evenings they often went out on the lake in a gondola, fishing by torchlight. On October 22 Liszt and Marie celebrated his twenty-sixth birthday by taking a mountain excursion. They set out at nine o'clock in the morning, with Marie mounted on a donkey, led by their guide, Buscone, a local gondolier. Soon the whole of the surrounding countryside was spread out below them like a map. They saw the distant chateaux, a magical view of Lecco, and Bellagio itself covered in a thousand tints of brightly coloured foliage. After dark, they sat on the balcony of their inn with a bowl of flaming peaches, while Buscone lighted a resin torch in the prow of his boat and speared the mesmerized fish with a long harpoon. Marie summed up their existence thus:

> A bad piano, a few books, the conversation of a serious-minded woman suffice for him. He renounces all the pleasures of pride, the excitement of the battle, the amusements of social life, even the joy of being useful to others and of doing good; he has given them all up without even realizing, apparently, that he has done so![11]

When Marie d'Agoult's confinement became imminent, the couple moved to Como and took up residence at the Hotel dell'Angelo. And it was here, on December 24, at two o'clock in the afternoon, that Marie gave birth to a daughter. They called her Francesca Gaetana Cosima, and she was baptized in the Cathedral of Como on December 26.

III

Until modern times the details of Cosima's birth were obscure. She herself always celebrated her birthday on Christmas Day. Richard Wagner, her second husband, naturally took to recording this date in his correspondence,[12] and from there the error spread rapidly through the Liszt-Wagner literature. The latest victim (though surely not the last) is the English translator of the recently published *Diaries* of Cosima Wagner, who flatly asserts that she "was born on Christmas Day 1837, in Bellagio, Italy, on Lake

---

11. AM, p. 119.
12. See, for example, Wagner's letters to Judith Gauthier (TRW, p. 340) and Albert Niemann (SLWB, vol. 5, p. 232, fn. 3). He told Niemann that he must finish the newly completed score of *Parsifal* "in time for the birthday of my wife, December 25."

Como"[13]—yet it would have been the work of a moment to look up the letter Marie d'Agoult wrote to Liszt on Christmas Day 1840, in which she gives the true date of Cosima's birth as December 24.[14] Moreover, Cosima's birth certificate, apart from confirming the correctness of the latter date, furnishes absolute proof that Cosima was not born at Bellagio at all, but in the city of Como. The parish records of the Basilica Cathedral of Como reveal this entry:

> Francesca Gaetana Cosima Liszt, illegitimate, born on December 24, 1837, baptized on the 26th by the priest Pietro Cavadini, the daughter of Caterina de Flavigny, residing at the Hotel dell'Angelo in Como, room 614, and of Franz Liszt, also residing in the same hotel; both Catholic, her father a professor of music and landowner, her mother of noble birth. The godfather was Luigi Mortier of Milan, residing in Brussels, professor of music. The godmother was Eufrasia Mortier.
>
> [Note] Franz Liszt has declared in the presence of the undersigned priest and witness that he is the father of the girl, whose name is hereby recorded.
> [Signed]
>
> LUIGI MORTIER, godfather and witness
> AMBROGLIO SALA, witness
> BARTOLOMO CASATI, priest
> MARIA RODANI, midwife[15]

Cosima's unusual name has posed another puzzle for Liszt-Wagner sleuths across the years. The favoured theory is that she was named after Lake Como, but this makes no sense, etymologically speaking. Cosima happens to be the feminine form of St. Cosmas, the patron saint of physicians, and when we recall that Blandine and Daniel, Liszt's other children, also bear the names of saints, the difficulty vanishes. It has hitherto escaped attention that in Cosima's *Diaries* she frequently refers to September 27 as "my name day"—the day on which the church celebrates the martyrdom of Cosmas.[16] At home Cosima was known by the unique diminutive "Cosette," an affectionate nickname by which her father addressed her all his life. When Victor Hugo called the heroine of *Les Misérables* (1862) Cosette, he could only have borrowed the name of Liszt's daughter.

---

13. WT, vol. 1, p. 11.
14. ACLA, vol. 2, p. 85.
15. From the Baptismal Register of Como Cathedral for 1837, sec. 88, item 133.
16. WT, vol. 1, p. 577. Cosmas was tortured and beheaded in A.D. 303. Because he and his brother Damian gave their medical services to the poor, they became known as "the silverless ones." See their entry in Butler's *Lives of the Saints*.

Marie d'Agoult was absent from the ceremony. As on the occasion of Blandine's baptism two years earlier, she was still convalescing after a difficult birth. The fact that Liszt officially acknowledged himself to be the father of Cosima, as he had previously acknowledged himself to be the father of Blandine, was later to assume importance. In French law it made Liszt the legal guardian of these illegitimate children and left Marie d'Agoult (improperly identified on both baptismal certificates[17]) with few if any rights. After their rupture, Marie was to fight Liszt for the custody of their children, but the flimsiness of her legal position soon became apparent, and Liszt was able to remove them not only from her immediate sphere of influence but from France itself.

It appears that the arrival in Como of two such distinguished visitors attracted the attention of the local police. A report written by an agent of the Italian secret intelligence, which was prepared for one Count Hartwig in Milan, sheds further light on the circumstances surrounding Cosima's birth.

A lady with a passport under the name of Countess d'Agoult has been staying in this city for some time. She is believed to be the wife of the French minister d'Argoult.[18] This same person lives in the Hotel dell'Angelo with the celebrated pianist Liszt. On December 24, at two in the afternoon, and assisted by the midwife Maria Baino [*sic*], she gave birth to a little girl who is commonly thought to be the consequence of her relationship with the famous player mentioned above.[19]

I V

While staying at Como, awaiting the birth of Cosima, Liszt paid regular visits to Milan. The city lay 35 miles to the south and was within easy reach. Liszt's first encounter with it was entirely characteristic.

Strolling through the streets early one morning, Liszt passed the music shop of Ricordi, the publisher. He walked in, saw an open piano standing in the middle of the room, and began to improvise. Ricordi, sitting in his office, heard the music ringing through the building and rushed out exclaiming, "This must be Liszt or the Devil!" Ricordi then overwhelmed the young virtuoso with

---

17. "Catherine-Adélaïde Méran" was now transformed into "Caterina de Flavigny," a lighter camouflage, but a camouflage nonetheless, consisting of a simple combination of her second Christian name and her maiden name—a styling she adopted on no other occasion.

18. Count d'Agoult was here confused with the Minister of France d'Argoult.

19. Doc. no. 1676, p.r., Milan City Archives.

hospitality, opening for him his villa in the Brianza, lending him his box at La Scala, and placing at his disposal his library of fifteen hundred scores.[20] Liszt also met Rossini, who was likewise living in Milan and was in the middle of that famous forty-year retirement from the operatic stage. Although Rossini had composed nothing for the opera house since *Guillaume Tell* (1829), he was still at the very centre of Italian musical life, and giving elaborate dinner parties to which opera singers, literati, and Milanese society were all invited.

The musical taste of the Milanese was poor. They were interested only in opera. There was no enthusiasm for pianists. Very few of the European virtuosos had ventured south of the Alps. Italy had never heard Moscheles, Hummel, Kalkbrenner, or Chopin. The last great pianist to play there had been John Field, who met with no success. Even the compositions of Beethoven and Mozart had little standing in Milan. The most acceptable form of piano music was the operatic fantasy, during the playing of which the Milanese would unabashedly join in, whistling and singing the familiar tunes as they went along. Liszt had few illusions about what he was up against when, on December 10, 1837, with the influential backing of Ricordi and Rossini, he took over the Scala opera house, placed his solitary Erard piano in the centre of that vast stage, and gave a solo recital. But even he must have received a jolt when, in the middle of a performance of one of his studies (duly announced beforehand), a gentleman called out from the stalls, "Vengo al teatro per divertirmi e non per studiare!"[21] This comical incident set the tone for Liszt's two other Milan concerts, given in the Assembly Rooms on February 18 and March 20, 1838. On one occasion he placed a silver urn, recently presented to him by a group of admirers, in the foyer of the concert hall to receive suggestions for themes on which he might improvise. The urn was then ceremoniously borne onto the stage so that Liszt might read the suggestions aloud from the platform. He had reckoned without the wry humour of the Milanese, however. The first slip of paper read "The Milan Cathedral," the next "The Railway Station." The pride of the collection carried this conundrum: "Is it better to marry or remain a bachelor?" Liszt rose to the occasion and recalled to his audience the words of the sage: "Whatever conclusion one comes to, whether to marry or remain single, one will always repent it."[22] The Milanese appreciated his ready wit more than his piano playing.

This first encounter with Milan produced an artistic consequence. Rossini had recently broken his long silence and had published a dozen songs called *Les Soirées musicales*. In order to please the Milanese, Liszt decided to transcribe these little gems for the piano and feature them in his concerts. They were

---

20. RGS, vol. 2, p. 168; CPR, p. 160.
21. RGS, vol. 2, p. 209; CPR, p. 213. "I come to the theatre to enjoy myself, not to study!"
22. RGS, vol. 2, p. 211; CPR, pp. 215–17.

published by Ricordi in 1838. Today they are hardly known by pianists but ought to be brought back into the repertory. Their titles are

La promessa	*La partenza*
La regata veneziana	*La pesca*
L'invito	*La danza*
La gita in gondola	*La serenata*
Il rimprovero	*L'orgia*
La pastorella dell'Alpi	*Li marinari*

V

Liszt and the countess left Milan in mid-March 1838 and made their way to Venice. They took the conventional route, travelling via Verona, Vicenza, and Padua. Marie's *Mémoires* are filled with observations about the works of art they observed as they passed through these ancient cities. Nothing seemed to please her, and she confessed that she found the journey exhausting.[23] They arrived in Venice during the last week in March. Liszt fell in love with this magical city at first sight. He was absorbed by its canals, its bridges, and the play of light across its unique architecture. He hired a gondolier, Cornelio, to row them along the narrow waterways. Marie, however, disliked Venice intensely. She called it "a modern Carthage,"[24] false and materialistic. The bookstores, according to her, sold books fit only for chambermaids. A mood of uncontrollable depression swept over her. The innate differences in temperament between her and Liszt flowed over into daily disagreements, which in turn developed into major quarrels. Venice was a turning point. For the first time, Liszt appreciated the full consequences of being linked to such a joyless, brooding personality. It seems clear that Marie fell victim to another nervous breakdown in Venice.[25] Her diary entries are full of despair and lamentations.

> Sometimes I am afraid that I am going mad, my brain is tired; I have wept too much.
>
> My heart and spirit are dry. It is an ailment I must have been born with. For an instant, passion elevated me, but I feel that the principle of life is not within me. . . .

---

23. AM, p. 131.
24. AM, p. 138.
25. The first, it will be recalled, was in 1834, shortly after the death of her eldest daughter, Louise, when she had contemplated suicide. For a detailed account of Marie's mental problems, which dogged her for life, see VCA, vol. 4. See also p. 194 of the present volume.

And then, with a shaft of true insight, she added:

> I feel myself an obstacle to his life, I'm no good to him. I cast sadness
> and discouragement over his days.[26]

Liszt tried to encourage her, but it was uphill work. Once, from Milan, he had
sent her a note: "Love me always, and most of all try to be a little satisfied,
a little gay, a little happy if possible."[27] She merely sank further into gloom
and despondency. The relationship between Liszt and the countess was, in fact,
approaching its dénouement. They had reached that most mournful of all the
conditions that can afflict two lovers: they were unhappy together and unhappy
apart. As so often before in Liszt's life, destiny now intervened. A short time
earlier he had written to Lamennais and asked, "Will my life be forever tainted
with this idle uselessness which weighs upon me? Will the hour of . . . *virile
action* never come?"[28] He did not then suspect that this hour had almost struck,
and that his life was about to be changed by events of the first magnitude.

---

26. AM, p. 140.
27. ACLA, vol. 1, p. 203.
28. LLB, vol. 1, p. 17.

After the Flood in Hungary, 1838–1839

*O my wild and distant homeland, my unknown
friends, my great family! Your painful cry calls
me back to you, and deeply moved I bow my head,
ashamed that I could forget you for such a long
time.*

FRANZ LISZT[1]

I

In March 1838, after an unusually severe winter, the frozen Danube melted and overflowed its banks. Within seventy-two hours the water-level rose to a record 29 feet above normal, and the tidal wave that rolled across western Hungary was unstoppable. Entire villages were swept away, and the crops of the Hungarian peasants were ruined. Pest, the low-lying city of the Magyars, stood in the path of the oncoming waters. It was completely inundated; almost the entire city was destroyed. Nearly three thousand houses collapsed in the water; about half again that number were seriously damaged. More than one hundred and fifty people were drowned, fifty thousand were made homeless, and thousands more faced disease and famine. Small boats threaded their way through the streets of Pest, searching for stranded survivors. It was the biggest natural disaster to strike Hungary in modern times. The Hungarian government, sitting in the ancient capital of Pressburg, launched an international appeal.[2] Liszt was still in Venice when he heard about the flood. He was sitting

---

1. RGS, vol. 2, p. 224; CPR, p. 234.
2. The sum of 1 million forints was eventually raised. It enabled the Hungarians to start work on the reconstruction of their city. New houses were built on a massive new base whose ground-level was raised many feet above that of the Danube. The banks of the river were likewise strengthened. This feat of engineering laid the foundations for the modern city of Budapest. The statistical details of the 1838 flood, from which the above figures are extracted, are preserved in the Record Office of the Hungarian Legislature, Budapest.

in the Café Florian, in St. Mark's Square, taking his morning coffee, when he noticed a German newspaper bearing news of the catastrophe. He had last seen Pest, and his native Hungary, in 1823, as a boy of ten, and his childhood memories came rushing back to him. He hurried to Vienna, arriving there in mid-April, and at once arranged to give a series of charity concerts for the victims. Liszt had not been heard in the Austrian capital for fifteen years. His presence there generated immense excitement. Between April 18 and May 25 Liszt gave eight concerts[3] which raised the colossal sum of 24,000 gulden, the largest single donation the Hungarians received from a private source.

Liszt's Vienna concerts are traditionally interpreted as "marking his official return to the stage." But they have a deeper meaning: Liszt's swift response to the catastrophe in Hungary is an indication of his latent patriotism. Fifteen years of residency in France had obscured his remembrance of his native land. It is a fact that in all the years he had spent with Marie d'Agoult, he scarcely mentioned his boyhood in Hungary and could write to her, "Childhood memories, as you know, have little attraction for me."[4] The disaster in Hungary changed all that. Hungary, and Hungary alone, was the reason why Liszt found himself in Vienna. In a self-revelatory passage written in May 1838, he tells how the catastrophe shook him, awakened in him the concept of the "homeland," and gave back to him a sense of national identity which he never lost. He looked into his heart, he says, and "found the treasury of memories from my childhood intact."

> I was badly shaken by that disaster. . . . And the surge of emotions revealed to me the meaning of the word "homeland." I was suddenly transported back to the past, and in my heart I found the treasury of memories from my childhood intact. A magnificent landscape appeared before my eyes: it was the Danube flowing over the reefs! It was the broad plain where tame herds freely grazed! It was Hungary, the powerful, fertile land that has brought forth so many noble sons! It was my homeland. And I exclaimed in patriotic zeal

---

3. Raabe stated that six concerts were given (RLS, vol. 1, p. 236, fn. 55). Kapp mentioned ten (KFL, p. 103). The true number is eight, as was shown when the diary of Therese Walter (1819–66) was published in 1941. Miss Walter, who attended every one of Liszt's concerts, provides all the dates, as well as a complete record of the works he played. The daughter of a wealthy Viennese banker, she was a gifted amateur pianist and used to arrange musical soirées in her house every Thursday evening. It was here that she met Liszt and jotted down her personal impressions of the pianist. (See WLCC.) The financial accounts drawn up by Tobias Haslinger for Liszt's Vienna concerts, and preserved in the Weimar archives (WA, Kasten 133, nos. 1–8), likewise prove that Liszt gave eight concerts.

4. ACLA, vol. 1, p. 391.

that *I,* too, belonged to this old and powerful race. I, too, am a son
of this original, untamed nation which will surely see the dawn of
better days. . . .[5]

I I

Also in Vienna at this time was Clara Wieck, giving concerts of her own. She
wrote in her diary:

> We have heard Liszt. He can be compared to no other player
> . . . he arouses fright and astonishment. His appearance at the piano
> is indescribable. He is an original . . . he is absorbed by the piano.[6]

Clara and her teacher-father, Friedrich Wieck, found themselves staying by
chance in the same hotel as Liszt, the Zur Stadt Frankfurt,[7] and after dinner
they occasionally made music together. Liszt formed a high opinion of this
nineteen-year-old girl's piano playing ("everything concerned with her art is
noble and without pettiness").[8] She in turn lost no time in introducing Liszt
to two works by her husband-to-be, Robert Schumann, whom Liszt did not
at that time know: *Carnaval* and *Fantasiestücke.* The initial outcome of this
encounter with Clara was Liszt's dedication to her of his newly composed
Etudes d'exécution transcendante d'après Paganini, a fitting tribute to her powers
as a pianist.

Liszt was reunited in Vienna with a number of old friends, including his
former master Carl Czerny, the tenor Randhartinger (with whom he had
studied theory under Salieri), and his early benefactor Count Amadé. Czerny's
comments on Liszt's playing are interesting. He always listened to his greatest
pupil with a critical ear. He tells us that when he had heard Liszt play in Paris
a year earlier, his performances had seemed monstrously complex, overgrown
with technical difficulties. Now he reversed that judgement and subsequently
recorded that Liszt's genius had "received a new impetus" and that he had
"developed that brilliant and more limpid style of playing for which he has
now become so famous throughout the world."[9] Liszt's Viennese audiences of

---

5. RGS, vol. 2, pp. 223–24; CPR, p. 233.
6. LCS, vol. 1, p. 199. See also an important letter from Friedrich Wieck to his wife in which he
describes Liszt's inaugural concert on April 18 in detail (WFWB, pp. 93–94).
7. ACLA, vol. 1, p. 217.
8. Ibid.
9. CEL, p. 29. Czerny's move to Paris in the spring of 1837, made partly at Liszt's prompting, was
short-lived. He returned to Vienna after less than one year.

1838 were among the first to witness the transformation, and those audiences, in fact, were highly distinguished. On the musical side they contained the Wiecks, Czerny, Kalkbrenner, Haslinger, Thalberg, and some of the leading professors of the Vienna Conservatory.[10] On the social side Liszt played before Metternich, Prince Dietrichstein, and Emperor Ferdinand and Empress Anna-Carolina of Savoy.[11] The musical statistics are impressive. Liszt played more than forty compositions in Vienna, all of them from memory, including Beethoven's *Moonlight* and *Funeral March* Sonatas, and works by Weber, Chopin, Scarlatti, Handel, Moscheles, and others. He also accompanied Randhartinger in performances of some Schubert songs. The sixth concert, given on May 14 under the auspices of the Vienna Musikverein, is typical.

Sonata in C-sharp minor	BEETHOVEN
Songs (including "Die Forelle") sung by B. Randhartinger, tenor, Director of the Viennese Court Orchestra. Piano accompaniment—F. Liszt	SCHUBERT
Study in A flat	KESSLER
Fugue in E minor	HANDEL
"Cat's Fugue"	SCARLATTI
Two Songs	RANDHARTINGER

Hexaméron: Variations on a duet from Bellini's *I puritani*
by Liszt, Thalberg, Chopin, Herz, and others

The Scarlatti item aroused interest. Liszt introduced this "antique" composer, whom he had discovered in Italy, to the Viennese public for the first time. Other pianists now hastened to find their own "old masters," and it suddenly became fashionable to include "historical pieces" in concert programmes.[12] Shortly after Liszt's visit to Vienna, in fact, Tobias Haslinger opened a subscription for the first "complete" edition of Scarlatti's sonatas, edited by Czerny, who acknowledged in his preface, *"It was Liszt* who gave the first impulse to this undertaking." The Schubert items, too, were to have important consequences. It is no accident that almost as soon as Liszt had entered Vienna, the city of Schubert's birth, Schubert song transcriptions had started to pour from his pen; his first attempts included "Auf dem Wasser zu singen," "Erlkönig,"

---

10. ACLA, vol. 1, p. 216.
11. Something of the feverish excitement generated at these gatherings is glimpsed in the diary entries of Baron von Neumann, Austrian ambassador to the Court of St. James. "April 23rd: Liszt . . . played in an electrifying manner. He is a meteor. Under his touch the piano becomes an altogether different instrument." (ND, p. 78.)
12. This vogue for old music among the Romantics reached a culmination of sorts in the celebrated "historical recitals" given by Anton Rubinstein in the St. James Hall, London, in 1886.

"Ständchen," and "Ave Maria"—twenty-eight songs altogether. He introduced groups of them into four of his eight charity concerts, and they became overnight successes. Some were immediately published by Diabelli; others were brought out by Haslinger, who sold his stocks so quickly that he at once commissioned more. By 1839 Liszt had produced no fewer than thirty-eight transcriptions, and we find him complaining, "Haslinger overwhelms me with Schubert. I have just sent him twenty-four more new songs . . . and for the moment I am rather tired of this work."[13]

These transcriptions served a triple purpose. First, they promoted the name of Schubert, still little known outside Vienna. Second, they advanced the field of piano technique, posing special problems of layout and timbre which had never before been solved. Third, they widened Liszt's own repertoire. The main technical problem facing Liszt was obvious: how to incorporate the vocal line into Schubert's piano accompaniment, thereby making a self-contained keyboard work with no loss of musical substance. Some of Schubert's accompaniments, after all, are very difficult, and themselves demand a virtuoso technique. To reproduce the vocal line as well seems an impossible feat. But Liszt always succeeds in finding a solution.

The great favourite with the general public was "Erlkönig," a model of its kind. Liszt played it not only in Vienna but in Leipzig, Prague, London, Berlin, and St. Petersburg. This powerful arrangement, with its reiterated octaves, makes heavy demands on the pianist, taxing muscle and sinew to their limits. Liszt's version of the song does not contain a single bar that Schubert himself did not write. Only the occasional octave doubling has been allowed.

This merely serves to enhance the drama as the father (in Goethe's poem), riding swiftly through the night, his horse's hooves pounding beneath him, draws his terrified son ever closer to him, with the sinister erlking in relentless pursuit. Liszt even contrives to bring out the four characters who play a role in this

---

13. LLB, vol. I, p. 29. Altogether Liszt published fifty-six transcriptions of Schubert songs, including twelve from *Winterreise* and a group from *Die schöne Müllerin*. They remain among his most neglected arrangements. All fifty-six transcriptions were excluded from the thirty-four-volume *Collected Edition* published during the years 1901–36.

unique song—father, son, erlking, and narrator—through skilful changes of melodic register, a technique not available to Schubert. There is one giddy moment in the headlong rush of this song in which Liszt calls for the pianist to play the following passage with a repeating fifth finger. Goethe's line says: "I will play beautiful games with you." The passage discloses a sly sense of humour on Liszt's part at which only the erlkings of the keyboard can afford to smile.

Liszt, incidentally, always took the trouble to incorporate the words within the musical text, so that the pianist has the poem constantly before him. He considered it vital that the player be familiar with the poetry. When the first batch of twelve transcriptions was brought out in 1838, Haslinger printed the poems separately, inside the front covers. Liszt at once protested that this was useless and that the transcriptions must be reprinted with the words underlying the notes—exactly as Schubert himself had set them—a request that was eventually carried out.[14]

III

It is entirely characteristic of Liszt that while he was in Vienna, enjoying one of the most glittering receptions ever accorded an artist by that city, he established contact with his aunt Therese Lager, Anna Liszt's younger sister, who had nursed him back from death in his childhood[15] and now lived in the vicinity. We know that Liszt gave her material help, for in a letter to his mother

14. LLB, vol. 2, p. 212. Liszt continued to play his arrangement of "Erlkönig" into old age. One of his Weimar pupils, Anton Strelezki, left an eye-witness account of such a performance, which throws light on Liszt's approach to the piano generally: "I was surprised to note that as he left the piano, not a trace of fatigue was noticeable on his face or hands. Only a few weeks after this I heard the same piece played by [Anton] Rubinstein. From his outward appearance, at the close, you would imagine that he had just walked out of a shower bath, taken with all his clothes on. And yet Liszt's rendering was just as vivid as Rubinstein's, and his fortissimo was as tremendously powerful." (SPRL, p. 7.)
15. See pp. 56–57.

he wrote, "I am certainly sending a little something to Therese, whom I like best of all our family. Do you think that 400 francs will be sufficient?"[16] There was also a meeting with another family member, his "cousin" Eduard, the twenty-one-year-old half-brother of Adam Liszt, who was studying jurisprudence in Vienna.[17] This relationship became very dear to Liszt. After 1869 (by which time Eduard occupied the powerful position of Imperial Public Prosecutor in Vienna), Liszt always stayed at the family home in the Schottenhof district of the city, where a room was kept in readiness for him. To judge from Liszt's correspondence, we surmise that he was approached by other family members, both Lagers and Liszts, many of whom lived in Vienna and its environs, and who simply wanted money from their famous relative. Liszt sent them all packing, considering most of them layabouts who had "compromised the family name."[18] On his many subsequent visits to Vienna he always avoided them, choosing to stay with Eduard. It is an interesting commentary on his "thirty or forty uncles and aunts, nephews and nieces" that he once wrote to his mother, "I am glad that Eduard does not ask me for money."[19]

Liszt would have liked to stay longer in Vienna. He even intended to travel on to Pest to see the devastation in Hungary for himself. These plans were abruptly changed when he heard from Marie d'Agoult that she had fallen seriously ill and was unable to leave her room.[20] So after giving his last concert in the Musikverein on May 25[21] and attending a farewell banquet given in his honour, Liszt set out for Italy and rejoined Marie in Venice at the very end of May. He made the 350-mile journey, much of it over mountainous terrain, in four days.

IV

Ever since the publication of Marie d'Agoult's *Mémoires* in 1927 it has become fashionable to compare her account of the Vienna episode with Liszt's. When

16. LLBM, p. 46.

17. DLFW, p. 1ff.

18. See n. 19 on p. 35.

19. LLBM, p. 41. See also the first known letter Liszt wrote to Eduard, dated Milan, December 17, 1837. He praised Eduard for overcoming the poverty of his family background and acquiring an education. "You have done well to learn French," Liszt wrote. "This language is necessary today for anyone who does not want to remain buried in his own village." And he added, "If I can be useful to you in some way, that would bring me great joy." (Friedrich Schnapp, ed., "Briefe Franz Liszts und seiner Familie." *Die Musik*, vol. 28, no. 9, June 1936, p. 663.)

20. ACLA, vol. 1, p. 233. Her illness was not disclosed. She wrote urgently on May 24: "I am waiting for you, I am still unable to leave my room. In the name of heaven, delay no more."

21. WLCC, pp. 58–59. Before he left Vienna Liszt was elected an honorary member of the Vienna Musikverein. His letter of acceptance is dated Venice, June 1, 1838. The postmark helps us to pin down the date of his reunion with Marie. (LLB, vol. 1, p. 21.)

the *Mémoires* were first presented to the world they aroused widespread interest in Lisztian circles. Of particular fascination was Marie's account of the course of their estrangement, the roots of which can be traced back to Liszt's departure for Vienna in April 1838. This side of the story had never before been properly told, and its timing was perfect. In the post-Ramann years, it was becoming evident that an incomplete picture of Marie d'Agoult was being presented to the world, and that this part of Liszt's life would one day have to be rewritten. Suddenly, some fifty years after Marie had died, here was her own account, a factual document no less, which purported to give a blow-by-blow description of the entire episode. It was as if Marie herself had returned from the grave to act as a witness in her own behalf.

Marie always insisted that Liszt was not driven to Vienna by humanitarian considerations for the victims of the Danube floods, least of all by a sense of patriotism. Rather was he drawn there by the prospect of cheap salon successes, newspaper glory, and the applause of the multitude. According to her, Liszt callously abandoned her in Italy in pursuit of an unworthy cause. History must judge whether the suffering of Liszt's native Hungary, to which he responded in such generous measure, is best described as "unworthy." Marie was ill at the time, and this may have clouded her judgement. She reports that although she lay at death's door for several days, Liszt turned a deaf ear to her urgent appeals to return to her side. So well does Marie tell this particular tale in her *Mémoires*[22] that almost every subsequent Liszt biographer has been swayed by the eloquence of her testimony, which certainly places Liszt in a questionable light. Here are the celebrated passages in question.

> One day Franz burst into my room, contrary to his custom, holding a German newspaper. He had just read of the horrible flood of the Danube. The suffering was intense. Public charity was doing its best. "What a desperate situation," he said. "I would like to send them every penny I possess." Then he added, with a bitter smile: "But I possess nothing but my ten fingers and my name! What do you think? If I suddenly arrived in Vienna, the effect would be prodigious. The whole city would want to hear the little prodigy it had

---

22. From the moment of their first appearance Madame d'Agoult's *Mémoires* received more critical acclaim than they really deserved. The *Mémoires* were published incomplete (a fact not recorded by Daniel Ollivier, her grandson–editor) from a compilation of rough notes that Marie had not properly revised. We have no means of knowing what material Marie would have worked up for publication and what she would have suppressed had the *Mémoires* appeared during her lifetime instead of fifty years after her death. Moreover, Ollivier cut certain passages from the text. Add to that the facts that several unpublished sections reside in the Bibliothèque Nationale (NAF 25179) and that yet another fragment has turned up in the Versailles Library, and it will be readily understood that the published *Mémoires* do not constitute a particularly satisfactory document on which to base firm conclusions about the personal relations between Marie and Liszt.

last seen as a young child! People are enthusiastic and generous in Vienna. I would earn a fantastic sum. . . ."[23]

This dialogue, which Madame d'Agoult puts into the mouth of the twenty-six-year-old Liszt, is so unlikely that it reads like fiction; and that, as we shall discover, is what it originally was. She goes on to tell us that Liszt left her the very next day, entrusting her to the care of one "Count Theodoro" (his real name was Count Emilio Malazonni), a young Venetian aristocrat whom they hardly knew.[24] Although Liszt promised to return in a week, he was absent for nearly two months.

> One day a letter came for me sealed with a female coat of arms. The thought crossed my mind that this letter must have been written at a lady's house. I tore it up.[25]

Marie is now consumed with jealousy and falls ill with worry. She asks "Count Theodoro" to write to Liszt and entreat him to return to Venice. Liszt's callous reply is that he is busy, and he requests that Marie be brought to Vienna instead. On hearing this news Marie promptly faints, and "Theodoro" rushes for the doctor. Marie tells us that she spent a week between life and death, almost unconscious, calling Liszt's name in her delirium. Then comes her *cri de coeur*:

> Franz had abandoned me for such small motives! It was not to do a great work, not out of devotion, not out of patriotism, but for salon successes, for newspaper glory, for invitations from princesses.[26]

---

23. AM, p. 143.
24. AM, p. 144. This is confirmed in Marie's correspondence with Ferdinand Hiller. (RB, p. 578.) "You must know that Liszt has suddenly been overwhelmed by strong patriotic feelings, and right now he is practising his octaves for the citizens of Pest. He'll be back in two weeks. I've been left in the care of a charming, extremely witty twenty-five-year-old youth. I flatter myself that appalling things might have come of this, but, as in the cheap novelettes, I said *"Piu tosto morir"* ["Death before dishonour"], and things are just the same. . . ." Later her letter lapses into sarcasm. "[Liszt] tells me very naively, and I'm telling you even more naively, that everyone fell into raptures at a little gathering of artists when he did his tricks." (April 20, 1838.) "Did his tricks"—that is all that Marie can find to say of the man who, at that moment, was being hailed by the Viennese as the greatest pianist of his time. A little-known letter from Marie to Ronchaud contains further disclosures about her relationship with Count Emilio Malazonni (FFDS, p. 526), whom she openly identifies here as the "twenty-five-year-old youth." Fleuriot de Langle was not the first to ask: "Were there two suitors then? . . . Unless Count Theodoro of the *Mémoires* is the same as Count Emilio cited in the letter (hardly likely), Marie revenged herself on the countesses, duchesses, and princesses fighting over the master by the number of her devoted escorts." The confusion stems from the *Mémoires* themselves, in which Marie, for reasons which remain obscure, masks a friend with a pseudonym.
25. AM, p. 145.
26. AM, p. 147.

Not one of Liszt's modern biographers has questioned the veracity of Marie's account. It so happens that the first time she told this tale was not in her *Mémoires* at all. She had already bequeathed it to posterity in a highly charged, and purely fictionalized, account of the affair in what appears to be the sketch of an unpublished novella, "Episode de Venise." An eleven-page holograph fragment of this novella, which exactly covers the Venice period, is preserved in the Library of Congress.[27] Written some time after the events it purports to portray, this piece of fiction was later worked up by Marie for inclusion in the "factual" *Mémoires*. A comparison between the *Mémoires* and the holograph fragment offers some revelations. The scene depicted in the holograph is the same as the one Marie later made famous in her *Mémoires,* but the names of the leading characters have been disguised—after the fashion of a cheap romance. Liszt is referred to as Wolfram; Count Theodoro is called Tibaldi; Marie herself plays the part of Lucy. It is "Lucy" who falls into a dead faint, "Tibaldi" who rushes for the doctor. And in her delirium it is the name "Wolfram" that Lucy cries out. One cannot escape the conclusion that at the very time these harrowing events were taking place (harrowing, that is, according to Marie), she was busy turning life into literature and already had one eye on her future career as an author. As it happened, the novella got nowhere. But since the story was too rich in detail to waste entirely, Marie could not resist the temptation to incorporate the narrative into her *Mémoires,* modifying it here and there, in which form it became a part of the "authorized" version of her life with Liszt.

There is some evidence, in fact, that the "Episode de Venise" was never intended for the *Mémoires* at all. Daniel Ollivier must bear the final responsibility for including this story. At the very point of the sojourn in Venice, Ollivier brings Marie's narrative to a halt and inserts the following editorial announcement.

> We interrupt the journal here in order to make way for a fragment of the *Mémoires* which is devoted to the period of the stay in Venice. This fragment, very short, is in reality only an assembly of notes. It gives an interesting synthesis of the reasons that were weakening a union over which was already hanging the threat of an estrangement.[28]

With these words we are pitched straight into the drama, with Liszt bursting in at the door, brandishing the German newspaper containing news of the flood in Hungary. Seen in this light, the entire "Episode de Venise" appears incongru-

---

27. AJF.
28. AM, p. 141.

ous and suspect. *Ubi est veritas?* The existence of a fictionalized scenario, complete with dialogue, already more than twenty years old when the *Mémoires* were being updated and prepared for publication, and on which scenario Marie's account is almost exclusively based, undermines this particular chapter and renders it unreliable as a scholarly source. As if to confirm our suspicions, Madame d'Agoult's biographer Jacques Vier has dealt with yet another novella fragment which was later rewritten by Marie for inclusion in her "factual" *Mémoires*. This one, the so-called "Palma-Wolfram" episode, deals with the period 1834–35 and the emotional events leading up to her elopement with Liszt.[29] To bend life into literature is one thing; to bend literature back into life is quite another.

It is clear that when Liszt finally returned to Venice there was a quarrel. Tormented by jealousy, Marie could not forgive what she termed his neglect of her. "I took on all my pride as a woman, as a *grande dame,* as a Republican, to judge him from above," she wrote. And she hurled at him her final epithet. "I called him a Don Juan parvenu,"[30] a phrase that has become a *locus classicus* in the Liszt literature. Liszt never forgot this insult. One of the cruellest aspects of the quarrel, and one that casts a strange light on their relationship at this time, is that Marie gave Liszt the "Episode de Venise" to read.[31] Small wonder that when, in the 1860s, Liszt heard that Marie was preparing her *Mémoires* for publication, he provided posterity with a *locus classicus* of his own and dubbed them "poses et mensonges"—postures and lies.[32]

---

29. VAMA, pp. 25–33; VCA, vol. 4, pp. 263–64.

30. AM, p. 147. Peter Raabe, one of Madame d'Agoult's severest critics, has this to say about the phrase. "A lady who 'took on all her pride as a woman' in order to judge him 'from above' would be unable to possess the heart of the charitable, philanthropic, beneficent Liszt for long. That is self-evident." (RWL, p. 27.)

31. This act of spite took place on June 20, 1840. Marie and Liszt were by that time in London. They had quarrelled once more (ACLA, vol. 1, p. 450),on the self-same issue of Liszt's absences from her. She showed Liszt her manuscript, which she must have brought with her from France for that purpose. He appears to have been stunned and wrote beneath her text the following observation: "You have remembered my words to you, but perhaps those you said to me on various occasions have left no trace in your memory. As for me, I haven't forgotten them, however hard I have tried to do so. When you are able to remember them, they will explain to you many things which seem inexplicable because of some unfathomable misunderstanding which has existed between us right up to this point." (AM, pp. 149–50.)

There is an ironical footnote to all this, having to do with the authorship of Liszt's writings. Were it true that Marie d'Agoult was the sole author of the disputed *Bachelor of Music* essays, then she would clearly be guilty of providing the world with two quite separate and conflicting accounts of the enna episode: the one in her *Mémoires* and the one attributed to Liszt in the *Bachelor* essay of May 1838, "To Lambert Massart" (RGS, vol. 2, pp. 223–24; CPR, pp. 232–34). Either Marie is being hypocritical, which is unlikely, or we must restore to Liszt the credit for writing the particular article from which we have quoted on pp. 254–55. We cannot repeat too often that there is no ready solution to the problem of the authorship of these articles. Each one must be considered on its merits.

32. LLB, vol. 6, p. 111.

v

As soon as Marie was well enough to travel the couple left Venice and moved to Genoa, where Liszt had rented a villa in which she might complete her convalescence. He even hired a carriage and horses and took her for daily drives. Then they moved up to Lake Lugano, by whose shores they languished for the rest of the summer. They continued their readings of Dante and Petrarch, and made frequent trips into nearby Milan, exploring its famous art galleries and museums.

The summer of 1838 was enlivened for Liszt by the appearance of some anonymous articles published in the Milanese press. They were full of personal invective against him, and Liszt, who had never enjoyed a happy relationship with the Milanese public, felt obliged to reply. The newspapers mainly responsible for stirring up the trouble were *Il Pirata, Figaro,* and *Il Corriere dei Teatri.* They were incensed by the latest *Bachelor of Music* essay, which had recently appeared in the *Gazette Musicale* over Liszt's signature, and in which he had criticized Italian musical taste and had attacked the management of La Scala.[33] This essay had actually been published by Marie d'Agoult during Liszt's absence in Vienna.[34] Polemical in tone, it set out to deflate the vanity of the opera singers and the gullibility of their mindless admirers. By the time Liszt got back to Italy, the damage had been done. The Milanese felt insulted and were now hitting back.[35] They launched a frontal attack under the headline "War on Franz Liszt." As the newspaper battle heated up, a shower of "poison-pen" letters arrived at Lugano, and Liszt's life was even threatened. Liszt offered to meet his detractors in public and wrote a letter to the editor of the *Glissons.* He then drove through the streets of Milan in an open carriage, defying his anonymous accusers to show themselves.

---

33. RGS, vol. 2, p. 182ff.; CPR, p. 177ff. "La Scala (March 1838)," first published in Schlesinger's *Gazette Musicale* on May 27, 1838.

34. The proof that Marie was part author may be found in her correspondence with Ferdinand Hiller (RB, pp. 578–79). She writes: ". . . When he went off he left me to finish a letter on La Scala and *le facciade musicale di Milano* in general. So I went to it with a will. . . . When it arrives in the capital of Lombardy I hope that this letter will create a loud *oh oh.*" (April 20, 1838.) Was Marie venting her spleen against Liszt by writing a letter in his name which she knew would cause him problems? It certainly seems so. What she really thought of the Milanese can be read in her journal dated January 29 to March 16, 1838 (AM, pp. 126–32), where she deprecates the social frivolities surrounding the Scala productions: "I found in Milanese society the same silliness and the same empty-headedness as elsewhere . . . but there is a good side to this habit of daily meetings at La Scala. It is useful for the men to get all their social duties over in a couple of hours, and the sight of all those little salons with their adjacent rivalries is quite amusing. They would certainly not gossip more loudly elsewhere, and the talking of a lot of nonsense to a musical accompaniment has a certain charm."

35. See *Il Pirata* (July 17), *Il Corriere dei Teatri* (July 18), and *La Moda* (July 19). *La Moda* also carried a letter from Liszt, published in both French and Italian, on July 19.

Friday morning, July 20 [1838]
Hotel de la Bella Venezia

Sir:

The invectives and insults of the papers continue. As I have already said, I shall certainly not engage in a war of words. To judge by the tone of the *Pirate* and the *Courrier des Théâtres,* this could only be an exchange of scurrilities. Still less can I reply to *anonymous* insults. Therefore I declare, for the hundredth and last time, that my intention has never been, and never could be, to insult Milanese society. I also declare that I am ready to give, to whosoever should come to ask it of me, all the necessary explanations.

Accept, sir, the assurance of my most distinguished consideration.

F. LISZT

Of course, no one turned up. The issue was a nine-day wonder and fizzled out as rapidly as it had erupted. But the breach with Milanese society remained. When, a few months later, Liszt attempted to arrange a concert in Milan, he had to cancel his plans for lack of public support.

As the autumn approached, Liszt and Marie left Lugano and returned to the Italian towns. Liszt gave concerts in Florence, Bologna, and Pisa, in order, as he wrote to Berlioz, "not to forget my trade entirely." The winter of 1838 was spent mainly in Florence. Here they met the young painter Henri Lehmann, a German Jew who had settled in Italy. Lehmann admired them both and painted their portraits. He became closely attached to Marie and was to prove himself a staunch ally in the troubled years ahead. Liszt and Marie also met the sculptor Lorenzo Bartolini and sat for him.[36]

In January 1839 Blandine was delivered to them in Milan. This child, it will be recalled, had been brought up in Geneva by a Protestant pastor, one Demelleyer. Marie had had difficulty in recovering her daughter from Demelleyer, who not only refused to travel to Milan with his small charge (Marie had explained that her health would not permit her to make the return journey to Geneva in the middle of winter) but now started to express his moral concern at the libidinous conduct of the adulterous parents and to entertain doubts about their fitness to bring up their infant daughter. Marie had been compelled to write to Adolphe Pictet in Geneva and charge him with the invidious task of retrieving Blandine from the clutches of Demelleyer and then despatching the child to Milan without delay. In her letter to Pictet, written from Florence on December 8, 1838, Marie had witheringly described Demelleyer as "a minister of the Protestant cult, the most stupid

---

36. These likenesses by Lehmann and Bartolini, among the best known in the Liszt iconography, are reproduced in BVL, pp. 88 and 89.

man in the republic of Geneva. There is nothing more harrowing than dealing with a fool."[37]

Blandine was now three years old. She had golden hair reaching down to
her shoulders and large blue eyes. Liszt, who had not seen his elder daughter
for more than eighteen months, was enchanted with her. Marie's emotions were
reflected in her diary.

> Tomorrow Blandine will be in Milan: profound emotion; memories
> of Louise. I feel that I shall love this child immensely, that my life
> is going to change, improve. I do not know if it will last, but I feel
> a great peace; I do not want to lose it.[38]

Marie had good reason to fear losing her tranquillity. She was pregnant again,
expecting her third child in less than four years. Now thirty-four, she was
showing signs of physical and mental exhaustion, and she began to suffer from
those violent attacks of spleen for which in later years she was forced to seek
medical help. She may also at this time have been suicidal.[39] The general air
of depression was darkened still further when she and Liszt heard of the suicide
of their old friend Adolphe Nourrit, who had flung himself from the balcony
of his hotel window in Naples while still at the height of his career.

Liszt and Marie moved to Rome in the spring of 1839 to await the birth.
They took apartments at 80, via della Purificazione, which then, as now, opens
from the Piazza Barberini, dominated by the famous fountain of Giovanni
Bernini. Rome cast a spell over Liszt. He saw St. Peter's and the Vatican for
the first time, and visited the Sistine Chapel. After contemplating the great
masters of the Italian Renaissance he wrote to Berlioz that the various arts were
really unified, that "Raphael and Michelangelo make Mozart and Beethoven
more easy for me to understand."[40] Herein lay the germ of Liszt's theory of
programme music, developed during his Weimar years. Although he had no
inkling of it at the time, the Eternal City was to dominate his old age and for
the last twenty-five years of his life draw him constantly back. In Rome Liszt
became acquainted with Ingres, the director of the French Academy at the Villa
Medici, whose knowledge of the city's art treasures was unrivalled. Liszt's
friendship with Ingres almost amounted to a bargain, for Ingres was a music-
lover, and in return for being shown round the galleries and churches, Liszt
would play to him and even listen to Ingres play his violin. A lasting testimonial

37. BRRS, pp. 85–88.
38. AM, p. 161.
39. A short time earlier she had written to Ronchaud, "If I ever fall in the water, let me go to the
bottom without trying to save me; it would be a greater proof of friendship than anything else."
(FFDS, p. 528.)
40. RGS, vol. 2, p. 253; CPR, p. 261.

to their encounter was the famous drawing of Liszt that Ingres made at this time.[41] Liszt's first visit to Rome was further enlivened by the unexpected appearance of Sainte-Beuve, en route from Milan to Genoa and Pisa. The distinguished literary critic spent a few days in Liszt's company, and together they visited the gardens of Tivoli and explored Hadrian's magnificent Villa.[42] Sainte-Beuve enshrined his impressions in a poem, "La Villa Adriana," which he dedicated to Liszt.

On May 9, 1839, Marie gave birth to their son, Daniel, in their apartments in the via della Purificazione. At the moment of his birth cannon-shots boomed across Rome. It was the feast day of the Ascension. Liszt observed that his son had chosen a singular moment to make his entrance into the Eternal City. And he added, amusingly: "Nothing has changed, there is only one Roman more."[43] The boy was handed over to a wet-nurse, a woman from the village of Palestrina, to enable Marie to convalesce. Neither parent saw Daniel again until the autumn of 1841.[44] In a letter to George Sand, written from Albano on June 9, Marie confided:

> I have had the caprice to bring into the world a *little fellow* of the greatest promise who, from his first hour, was suckled on the milk of the most beautiful woman of Palestrina. . . . [Liszt] is melancholy at the thought of being the father of three small children.[45]

If Liszt, in Marie's words, was melancholy, it had nothing to do with his children, who were always a perpetual delight to him. In her neurotic state Marie was incapable of diagnosing the truth. Here was one of the outstanding artists of the age, the greatest pianist the world had yet seen. Irresistible forces were stirring within him, demanding their total expression. In all the years that Liszt had known Marie, he had yielded to her romantic wish to live in semi-seclusion. For her sake he was denying his vocation. His rare public appearances had been a source of discontent for Marie, and merely served to

---

41. See p. 268. This drawing was inscribed by Ingres for Marie d'Agoult, who later gave it to Cosima. Today it forms part of the Wagner holdings at the Villa Wahnfried in Bayreuth.

42. S-BC, vol. 3, p. 111. In 1831 Sainte-Beuve had published a set of poems, *Les Consolations*. This was to be the origin of the title Liszt later gave to six of his best-known piano miniatures.

43. This was a witty allusion to the words of Count d'Artois, who, on making his entry into Paris in 1814, declared, "Nothing has changed, there is only one Frenchman more." (Letter to Hortense Allart de Meritens, dated May 11, 1839; VFL, p. 54.)

44. The proof that Marie d'Agoult waited for nearly two and a half years before sending for Daniel is furnished by Marie herself. On September 21, 1841, she was staying on the island of Nonnenwerth and casually told her neighbour Baroness Czettritz: "The youngest child is still with the wet-nurse in Italy." (JFL, p. 93.)

45. SCC, vol. 2, p. 342. Sand would have been the first to appreciate the family joke behind the phrase "little fellow." Liszt and Marie, it will be recalled, had styled themselves "Mr. and Mrs. Fellows" during their Chamonix holiday in the summer of 1836. (See p. 222.)

Liszt in Italy, a drawing by Ingres (1839).

widen the cracks in their relationship. All the while, Liszt's art was maturing and developing. He was now nearly twenty-eight years old and approaching the height of his powers. His frustration is revealed in a rare personal outburst, recorded in the couple's joint diary, the so-called Journal des Zyi.[46]

> There is thunder in the air, my nerves are irritable, horribly irritable. I need a prey. I feel the talons of the eagle tearing at me. Two opposing forces are fighting within me: one thrusts me towards the immensity of space, higher, ever higher, beyond all suns, up to the heavens; the other pulls me down towards the lowest, the darkest regions of calm, of death, of nothingness. And I stay nailed to my chair, equally miserable in my strength and my weakness, not knowing what is to become of me.

It required only one event of any significance to trigger another quarrel between them, and this duly presented itself.

V I

In June 1839, shortly after Daniel's birth, Liszt and Marie left Rome in order to avoid the stifling summer heat, and travelled to the fashionable watering place of Lucca, staying at the Villa Massimiliana, about 2 miles outside the town. After lingering there for a few weeks, the lovers of Geneva moved on to the little fishing village of San Rossore. They spent the month of September living in what Marie d'Agoult disdainfully described as "a small wooden hut"[47] overlooking the Mediterranean. Actually it was a secluded twelve-room house, located a short distance from the beach on the *tenuta del Gombo*. It belonged to one Gaetano Ceccherini and his family, from whom Liszt rented the entire second floor. The lovers' apartments were reached via a separate, outside wooden staircase.[48] At San Rossore the couple passed their days walking along the beach, watching the fishermen mending their nets, bathing, reading. Liszt spent much of the time in meditation, sitting under the shade of a juniper tree, puffing on his pipe, gazing out to sea towards Elba, which jutted out of the blue waters about 40 miles away.

It was while he was in San Rossore, virtually cut off from the world, that news reached him which was to change the course of his career. The Beethoven Memorial Committee in Bonn had just announced that their international

46. AM, p. 174.
47. AM, p. 168.
48. SSR, pp. 27–28.

appeal to raise funds for the erection of a monument to the master at the place of his birth had collapsed through lack of public support. The French section, in particular, had disgraced itself by contributing the paltry sum of 424 francs, 90 centimes. Liszt was incensed at what he considered to be an insult to his idol. He wrote to Berlioz, "Such a niggardly almsgiving, got together with such difficulty and sending round the hat, must not be permitted to help towards building our Beethoven's monument!"[49] Rather than see the scheme collapse, Liszt offered to take it on single-handed. He first contacted Bartolini in Florence to find out the cost of a statue in marble. He then set out his terms to the Memorial Committee in the following manner, posting the letter in Pisa.

Pisa, October 3, 1839

Gentlemen,

As the subscription for Beethoven's monument is only getting on slowly, and as the carrying out of this undertaking seems to be rather distant, I venture to make a proposal to you, the acceptance of which would make me very happy.

I offer myself to make up, from my own means, the sum still wanting for the erection of the monument, and ask no other privilege than that of naming the artist who shall execute the work. That artist is Bartolini of Florence, who is universally considered the first sculptor in Italy.

I have spoken to him about the matter provisionally, and he assures me that a monument in marble (which would cost about fifty to sixty thousand francs) could be finished in two years, and he is ready to begin the work at once. I have the honour to be, etc.,

FRANZ LISZT[50]

The Bonn committee's reply has been preserved. They accepted Liszt's generous offer and acquiesced in his choice of Lorenzo Bartolini as sculptor, but requested that the statue be in bronze, not marble, since it would be situated out-of-doors and exposed to the elements.

Bonn, December 1839

Sir,

We have received the letter, dated the 3rd of October last, that you did us the honour of sending us, on 12 inst.

The gracious offer that you make in it is the most convincing

49. RGS, vol. 2, p. 256; CPR, p. 265.
50. LLB, vol. 1, pp. 30–31.

testimony to your noble sentiments and to your piety towards the celebrated deceased. Only an artist of a fame that the whole of Europe admires is capable of so profound a veneration for an illustrious predecessor, and that artist deserves to see his name perpetuated with him whose memory will be preserved forever.

Please, sir, do not doubt our feelings of deep gratitude, and be persuaded that your munificence has so much exceeded our expectations that we do not hesitate for a moment to conform as far as is possible with the realization of your proposals.

Consequently, we willingly renounce the plan we had of initiating a public competition to choose the model most worthy of its subject, and we accept the condition attached to your offer, all the more so in that the renown of M. Bartolini gives us sufficient guarantee of his superiority.

But, sir, we are compelled to point out to you that very serious considerations have determined us to prefer, for the construction of the statue, bronze to marble, although of course the latter looks more beautiful and would have a more brilliant effect; but, forced as we are to erect the monument in one of the public squares of this town, where we could not shelter it from the weather and other damage, and seeing that in these circumstances marble does not offer the necessary strength, we were obliged to choose bronze. We do not doubt that you, sir, as well as M. Bartolini, will share our opinion about this, all the more so as M. Bartolini is taking charge not only of the making of the model (in connection with which we reserve only our approval) but also of the casting and every other aspect of the construction. It is also in this way that, recently, M. Thorwaldsen enriched Germany with several bronze monuments, among others the town of Mainz with that of Gutenberg, and as, according to the opinion of experts, the cost of a monument in bronze is not greater than that of a similar work in marble, the above-mentioned monument at Mainz, for example, not having cost more than the sum indicated by M. Bartolini for a statue in marble, we are persuaded, sir, that in every respect you will approve our reflections.

The sum that we have at our disposal at the moment amounts to about 40,000 francs, and would no doubt be further augmented if your generous proposition had not been known so early and so widely.

Please therefore, sir, take into consideration the observations that we have just made to you and give us your opinion thereof. Once the matter is decided, we shall not fail to get directly in touch with

M. Bartolini in order to obtain the model from which the monument is to be executed and to give him the observations that its
positioning requires.

Yours very sincerely, etc.

The Committee for the Monument:　　　　BREIDENSTEIN

VON SALOMON

DE CLAR

CLOGGERON

KREISEL

WALTER

GERHARD[51]

This committee had been in existence for years, and it was clearly incompetent.
The alacrity with which it handed over its responsibilities to Liszt, after having
failed to reach its target, is, for all the fine-sounding phraseology, a sufficient
commentary on its effectiveness. And the idea expressed by the committee that
it might actually have been hindered from raising money by Liszt's generous
offer is a wonderful example of inverted logic, a self-protective ploy typical
of group thought. In three months Liszt was able to achieve what the committee
had failed to bring about in three years. The German nation, and the wider
world of music, has Liszt to thank for the statue that stands in Bonn today.[52]

The only way that Liszt could raise such a large sum was to return to the
concert platform. Marie objected to his decision but was powerless to prevent
it; she genuinely believed it to be against his best interests as a composer. By
mid-October Liszt had announced his opening concerts in Vienna, and Marie,
deeply embittered, made arrangements to return with her small family to Paris.
Liszt has often been blamed for his "abandonment" of Marie d'Agoult. His
subsequent pianistic career vindicated it, however. Raabe was surely right when
he said that "in her doubtless strong love for him Marie had never considered
that so magical a genius as the young Liszt belongs to the whole world, not
to one woman."[53] There was, in any case, no question of a permanent break.
That was still more than four years away. Marie d'Agoult was not yet "Daniel
Stern"; *Nélida* was not yet written.

There was an emotional farewell in Florence, just before Liszt's twenty-

---

51. ACLA, vol. 1, pp. 334–36. Liszt did not receive this reply for more than two months, at which
point the Beethoven memorial concerts were already behind him and he was in Pressburg, en route
to Pest. On December 19 he enclosed it with a letter to Marie, who was by now back in Paris. She
had it published in the French newspapers, where it drew some vitriolic criticism, presumably because
it exposed French apathy towards Beethoven. See ASSV.

52. Lorenzo Bartolini (1777–1850) was never commissioned. The statue that was unveiled in Bonn
(August 1845) was sculpted by Ernst-Julius Hähnel (1811–91). See n. 14 on p. 422 for the reasons
behind this turn of events.

53. RLS, vol. 1, p. 52.

eighth birthday. Liszt then left for Trieste, where he was to give one or two concerts en route to Vienna. Marie embarked at the little Italian port of Livorno, taking ship for Genoa, with her three-year-old daughter Blandine and their maids. While they were crossing the Mediterranean a storm broke out. The sad little party was buffeted by a howling gale, and Marie wished that the waters would engulf her.[54] At Genoa they were joined by Cosima and her nurse. Daniel, who was only four months old and still being suckled by his wet-nurse in Palestrina, was placed in the care of Miss Lehmann, the painter's sister. Lehmann himself had promised to bring the infant to Paris as soon as the boy was strong enough to face the journey.

V I I

It was in the midst of these many distractions, both public and private, that Liszt brought to fruition some of the best music of his younger years. By his own admission he worked immensely hard in Italy, "writing four to five hundred pages of piano music."[55] Between the spring and winter of 1838 he completed the first versions of the *Grandes Etudes de Paganini* and the *Etudes d'exécution transcendante* and most of the "Italian" volume of the *Années de pèlerinage*. Such a remarkable achievement ought not to go unacknowledged. By universal consent some of these pieces occupy a central place in the history of piano playing. The titles of the *Années de pèlerinage* volume clearly reflect Liszt's sojourn in Italy:

Sposalizio	*Sonetto 104 del Petrarca*
Il penseroso	*Sonetto 123 del Petrarca*
Canzonetta del Salvator Rosa	*Après une lecture du Dante:*
Sonetto 47 del Petrarca	*Fantasia quasi sonata*

Although some of these pieces were later revised, and the finished cycle witheld from publication until 1858, the creative impulse behind this music sprang from Liszt's first contact with Italian art—its painting, sculpture, and poetry. *Sposalizio* ("Betrothal") was inspired by Raphael's painting *The Marriage of the Virgin,* which depicts the wedding of Joseph and Mary and hangs in the Brera Gallery in Milan. The incentive for *Il penseroso* ("The Thinker") came from the famous Michelangelo statue of the same name which contemplates the tomb of Lorenzo de' Medici in the San Lorenzo Church in Florence. An aura of foreboding hangs over this composition, which exploits the sepulchral tones

54. AM, p. 183.
55. LLB, vol. 1, p. 32.

of the extreme bass register of the piano and closes in a remarkable series of chromatic harmonies, well in advance of its time.

Liszt requested that *Sposalizio* and *Il penseroso* both be illustrated with drawings by Kretschmer of the Raphael painting and Michelangelo sculpture on the inner title page, as if to emphasize their origins in these masterpieces of Italian art.

The three Petrarch sonnets were first composed as songs, in 1838. Immediately afterwards Liszt transcribed them for piano solo, in which form they have become widely admired. The best-known of the group is *Sonetto 104*. In its original 1838 version this *Sonetto* retained the long introduction (originating in the song) and enunciated the first verse in the left hand alone, a beautiful device which is rarely found in Liszt's keyboard works.

The crowning achievement of the "Italian" volume of the *Années de pèlerinage* is the so-called *Après une lecture du Dante: Fantasia quasi sonata*. This work is one of Liszt's more formidable keyboard compositions. Inspired by Dante's *Divine Comedy,* Liszt set out to encompass in music that world of "strange tongues, horrible cries, words of pain, and tones of anger" which Dante describes in his *Inferno.* Confusion and error surround the genesis of the *Dante* Sonata. Following Ramann, most Liszt scholars continue to regard the composition as a product of that earlier, idyllic period in 1837 when the lovers of Geneva were living at Bellagio by the shores of Lake Como, supposedly reading Dante together in pastoral seclusion at the foot of Comolli's statue *Beatrice Leading Dante.*[56] In fact, the *Dante* Sonata was not even begun until September 1839, by which time Liszt was already living in the village of San Rossore, a fact we glean from a letter Marie wrote to Lehmann on September 26: "The *bravo suanatore* began this morning a *fragment dantesque* which is sending him to the very Devil. He is so consumed by it that he won't go to Naples, so as to complete this work."[57] She added gratuitously that it was "destined to remain in his sketch portfolio," but here she was mistaken. Liszt gave the first public performance of his *"fragment dantesque"* less than six weeks later in Vienna, during November 1839.[58] The manuscript of this early version has disappeared. Only after 1849, when Liszt had settled in Weimar, did he revise the work (together with the others in the volume) and give it its present title, which he incorrectly derived from Victor Hugo.[59] The introduction begins with a musical portrayal of hell evoked by a descending series of tritones ("Abandon hope all ye who enter

56. Raabe (RLS, vol. 2, p. 246) and Searle (SML, p. 29) both err in their accounts of the dating and origins of the sonata. So too does the *New Liszt Edition* (NLE, 1/7, 1974). For a correct account see Sharon Winklhofer (WLA).

57. JCR, p. 35.

58. Announced in the *Allgemeine Musikalische Zeitung* for January 1840, reviewing the last quarter of 1839. See "Wien: Musikalische Chronik des vierten Vierteljahres, 1839," *Allgemeine Musikalische Zeitung,* ser. 1, vol. 42, pp. 91–92.

59. "Après une lecture *de* Dante," the twenty-seventh in a collection of thirty-two poems by Hugo called *Les Voix intérieures* (1837). This title had already been borrowed by Liszt to describe the sonata by July 1853, when Liszt played the still-unpublished composition to Ede Reményi, who later wrote: "This scribbler allows himself to address a great man—after having heard the *Fantaisie d'après Dante.*" (LBZL, vol. 1, p. 283.)

here"), that timeless symbol of the Devil which musicians still call *diabolus in musica.*

The first subject depicts the souls of hell wailing in anguish. They wail in D minor, a key that has often symbolized the underworld in music.[60] Dante's "horrible cries and words of pain" are worked up into a spectacular conflagration. Here is music to match the poet's apocalyptic vision of the Inferno.

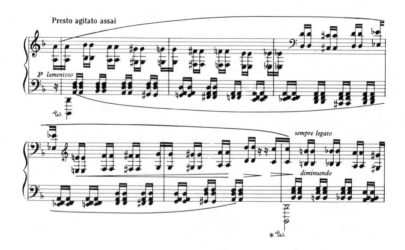

As the fires of hell subside, a second subject, a chorale-like theme, emerges in F-sharp major, another symbolic key in which much of Liszt's "beatific" music unfolds.[61]

---

60. Liszt's *Dante* Symphony and his *Totentanz* both unfold in D minor. Among the many other examples that could be cited at random are the statue scene from Mozart's *Don Giovanni,* the Queen of the Night's aria ("Der Hölle Rache kocht in meinem Herzen") from the same composer's *Zauberflöte,* and Schubert's "Der Tod und das Mädchen."

61. Including *Bénédiction de Dieu* and *Les Jeux d'eaux à la Villa d'Este.*

It would be difficult to think of a more powerful thematic contrast, yet Liszt has skilfully derived one theme from the other through a technique of unification which he relied on increasingly during his middle years, and which became universally known as the metamorphosis of themes. The following example compares the outlines of these "contrasting" subjects and makes the connection clear.

Liszt left no official clues to the programme of this work aside from his tersely worded title "After a Reading of Dante," a phrase which can mean all things to all men. Since every other composition in the collection refers to a specific work of Italian art, this lack of precision is a curious exception and raises the question: *which* readings of Dante? In Walter Bache's personal copy of the music, which he appears to have bought in Weimar in 1883, there existed pencilled annotations which link the three themes we have just cited to certain passages from the *Inferno*. Bache, who was a pupil of Liszt in the 1880s, may have received the information directly from the composer himself. At any rate, Bache's copy confirms that the tumultuous first subject was inspired by Canto 3:

> Here sighs, with lamentations and loud moans,
> Resounded through the air pierced by no star,
> That e'en I wept at entering. Strange tongues,
> Horrible cries, words of pain,
> Tones of anger, voices deep and hoarse,
> With hands together smote that swelled the sounds,
> Made up a tumult, that for ever whirls
> Round through that air with solid darkness stained,
> Like to the sand that in the whirlwind flies.

The chorale-like theme, in its first violent presentation,

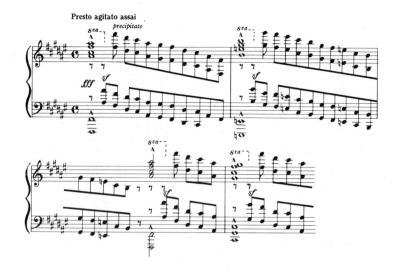

is nothing less than a musical depiction of Lucifer, described by Dante in Canto 34 as "the creature eminent in beauty once."

> "The banners of Hell's Monarch do come forth
> Towards us; therefore look," so spake my guide,
> "If thou discern him." As, when breathes a cloud

Heavy and dense, or when the shades of night
Fall on our hemisphere, seems viewed from far
A windmill, which the blast stirs briskly round;
Such was the fabric then methought I saw. . . .
. . . To the point we came,
Whereat my guide was pleased that I should see
The creature eminent in beauty once.

As if to confirm this interpretation, the theme of "Hell's Monarch" is used by Liszt in a final transformation of great beauty to suggest the scene where Dante gazes up to heaven and hears in the distance the music of Paradise. Hell and heaven, it tells us, are but different sides of the same coin: Lucifer himself once sat at the right hand of God, and his power and ostentation are here revealed to have their origins in a divine source.

The *Dante* Sonata remains one of Liszt's unique creations, little played and little understood for over half a century after its initial publication in 1858. Its fate in England was typical of the general neglect it endured until modern times. Walter Bache gave the first British performance, in London in February 1887; there is no other record of a performance in Britain until well after the turn of the century.

---

62. BBM, p. 312. See also GLD, p. 39.

VIII

Liszt's solitary trip back to Vienna took him through Venice and Trieste. In Venice he explored St. Mark's Cathedral and visited Byron's house. He took a gondola down the Grand Canal and was astonished to discover that his gondolier had once rowed Byron fifteen years earlier. "What! Byron?" exclaimed Liszt. "Yes, sir. I served him for five days because one of his *bateliers* was ill."[63] The gondolier then recited to Liszt two poems that he had learned by heart as Byron rode on the Lido, and gave him news of Byron's mistress Teresa Guiccioli, who now owned a small shop at Dolo where one could take coffee and liqueurs. By October 26 Liszt had arrived in Trieste. Here he gave a concert in the Marino Faliero Theatre with the singer Caroline Unger, whom he had last seen seventeen years ago when he was a boy in Vienna. He gave Marie d'Agoult an extremely detailed account of their conversations (he spent a fortnight in Caroline's company), apparently to allay her jealousy.[64]

After travelling for three days and nights, Liszt arrived in Vienna in the early hours of the morning of November 15. His concerts had been sold out days in advance. (Tobias Haslinger acted as his impresario.) Between November 19 and December 14 Liszt gave six matinee recitals in aid of the Beethoven Memorial Fund. The opening concert on November 19 was a gala affair attended by the dowager empress, at which Liszt played his transcription of Beethoven's *Pastorale* Symphony for the first time. A newspaper article proclaimed him "Protector of Beethoven." This set the tone for the Viennese public, with whom he was immensely popular. Total strangers applauded him in the hotel lobby. Prints of him were sold in the shops, and the ever-resourceful Viennese confectioners sold biscuits in the shape of a grand piano iced with the word "Liszt." The critic Saphir wrote a perceptive article in *Der Humorist.*[65] In an

---

63. ACLA, vol. 1, p. 267.

64. Résumé de nos conversations avec La Ungher [*sic*]," ACLA, vol. 1, pp. 278–80.

65. November 22, 1839. Moritz Gottlieb Saphir's brilliant satirical articles about Liszt in the Viennese press did much to establish the image of him as a heaven-storming, long-haired virtuoso in the eyes of the general public: "After the concert Liszt stands there like a victor on the battlefield, like a hero at a tournament. Daunted pianos lie around him; torn strings wave like flags of truce; frightened instruments flee into distant corners; the listeners look at each other as after a cataclysm of nature that has just passed by, as after a storm out of a clear sky, as after thunder and lightning, mingled with a rain of flowers and a snow of petals and a shimmering rainbow; and he stands there, leaning melancholically on his chair, smiling strangely, like an exclamation point after the outbreak of general admiration. This is Franz Liszt." Saphir's humour, which represents one of the brighter patches in nineteenth-century music criticism, is well documented in *Saphiriana,* a collection of jokes, anecdotes, and puns directed against friend and foe alike, the product of thirty years or more of journalism in Vienna. (SAW.) Liszt retained a friendly connection with Saphir, who visited him in Weimar during 1855. (LLB, vol. 3, p. 5.)

amusing letter to Marie, Liszt observed that he had become so famous that even
the doctor treating him for a cold—he had arrived in Vienna with a fever—
had suddenly been inundated with new patients requesting not treatment but
news of the great pianist.[66]

That was the public side of Liszt's life. The private side was different. For
most of his month-long stay in Vienna Liszt was treated by Dr. Loewe, who
specialized in homeopathic medicine. Liszt reports that Loewe prescribed tiny
doses of powders, which made him sweat, and put him on a severe diet. He
felt so wretched that he regarded his concerts as "a diversion" from his illness.
From his sickbed Liszt wrote, "My doctor has finally given me permission to
play on Wednesday. I don't really know whether I shall be able to do it, for
my hand trembles fearfully."[67] The symptoms so alarmed Marie that she wanted
to leave Paris and come at once to Vienna. For the next three years Liszt was
unable to shake off this fever, which attacked him in Leipzig, Berlin, and
southern England, where he started taking quinine. Meanwhile, he was confined
to his hotel room, utterly miserable and besieged by a host of visitors. Haslinger,
Dessauer, Saphir, and Krauss (a local musician who was arranging the *Grand
Galop chromatique* for orchestra) walked in and out to consult him on a thousand
matters. Dr. Loewe finally signed a notice forbidding further visitors, which
was displayed at the bottom of the staircase. All the more remarkable, then, was
Liszt's public bearing. Few people in his audiences suspected that he was ill. The
range of his repertoire was enormous. It included not only such popular pieces
as the *Hexaméron* Variations and the paraphrases on *La sonnambula* and *Lucia*
but serious works like Beethoven's *Appassionata* and *Pastorale* sonatas and his
C-major Piano Concerto. Then Liszt volunteered his services to appear in a duo
concert with the violinist Bériot at forty-eight hours' notice. Another surprise
appearance was with the pianist Marie Pleyel, whose formidable talent had led
Der Humorist to dub her "the female Liszt." Madame Pleyel had arrived in
Vienna in early December to give some concerts of her own, and when she
discovered that she was staying in the same hotel as Liszt, she approached him
with a request that he present her to the public. Liszt gallantly obliged by taking
her arm, leading her onto the platform, and introducing her with a speech from
the piano.[68] The *Allgemeine Musikalische Zeitung* was not wrong to describe him
as "the hero of the day."[69]

Liszt was now approaching his halcyon years. His *Glanzzeit,* or "splendour
period," was almost upon him. No artist in history had ever received the

---

66. ACLA, vol. 1, p. 293.

67. LLB, vol. 1, p. 32.

68. ACLA, vol. 1, pp. 332–33. See also "Liszt und Madame Pleyel in Wien" by Arnold Winkler,
Der Merker, no. 12, 1912, p. 472.

69. January 1840, p. 91.

acclaim and honours about to be showered on him in such profusion. The eight gruelling years through which his concert tours would lead him might have broken a lesser man. On occasion they came close to laying him low. But he emerged, transformed by the experience, having made a contribution to the history of piano playing that will last as long as the instrument itself survives.

BOOK FOUR

The Years of
Transcendental Execution
1839 · 1847

Liszt and the Keyboard

Liszt knows no rules, no form, no dogma;
he creates everything for himself.

M. G. SAPHIR[1]

I

The years 1839–47 are still described by Liszt scholars as his "years of transcendental execution," when he embarked on a virtuoso career unmatched in the history of performance. Liszt's recitals have never been properly chronicled. He visited, among other countries, Spain, Portugal, Germany, Austria, France, England, Poland, Rumania, Turkey, and Russia. Since he often gave three or four concerts a week,[2] it is safe to assume that he appeared in public well over a thousand times during this brief, eight-year period. His legendary fame as a pianist, which he continued to enjoy long after his official retirement from the concert platform, aged thirty-five, rested mainly on his accomplishments during these fleeting years. That is a remarkable fact, and before unfolding a detailed account of Liszt's concert tours the biographer has a duty to stand back and take stock of his achievements. Merely to list them is to observe musical history in the making.

Liszt's career remains the model which is still followed by pianists today. The modern piano recital was invented by Liszt. He was the first to play entire programmes from memory. He was the first to play the whole keyboard repertory (as it then existed), from Bach to Chopin. He was the first consistently to place the piano at right angles to the platform, its open lid reflecting the

---

1. *Der Humorist,* November 22, 1839.
2. ACLA, vol. 1, p. 405.

sound across the auditorium.[3] He was the first to tour Europe from the Pyrenees to the Urals, and that at a time when the only way to traverse such distances was by post-chaise, a slow and often uncomfortable mode of travel. The very term "recital" was first he introduced it in London on June 9, 1840 for a concert in the Hanover Square Rooms. In Milan and St. Petersburg he played before audiences of three thousand people or more, the first time a solo pianist had appeared before such vast assemblies. His Berlin recitals of 1841–42 are worth special mention: in ten weeks he gave twenty-one concerts and played eighty works—fifty of them from memory.[4] Few pianists today could match that feat. It was not merely that he could learn so much, but that he could learn so quickly. One example can stand for the others. When he was in Vienna in December 1839 he was asked to play Beethoven's C-minor Concerto, which he did not at that time know. Less than twenty-four hours later he played it in public, with an improvised cadenza.[5]

The pianos which greeted Liszt as he arrived at the smaller provincial towns of Europe give us pause for thought. Liszt played on Broadwoods, Streichers, Pleyels, and Erards—still the last word in piano manufacture. For his tour of Spain and Portugal in 1844–45 Liszt played on a Boisselot which travelled around the country with him, but that was exceptional; he usually played on whatever instrument each town and hamlet could best provide. The results were occasionally unsatisfactory. In Ireland, at the little market town of Clonmel, Liszt played on a small Tompkinson upright which rattled and shook as he performed. Most of those instruments had a restricted compass and a delicate tone best suited to the salon; their light materials made them inadequate for Liszt's bigger works. Some of the older models which confronted him were little better than boxes of wood and wire, and they sometimes collapsed beneath the strain. Perhaps his worst experience occurred in 1840 at Ems, where he gave a command performance before the Tsarina Alexandra of Russia and her retinue. The piano was old, and as Liszt played the strings started to snap one after another. Bound by strict court etiquette, everyone sat stiff and erect, watching in consternation as the disaster unfolded before them. The instrument might have literally broken to pieces under Liszt's powerful playing had not the empress finally thought of a way out of the ghastly predicament into which

---

3. Tomášek, in his autobiography, claimed that Dussek had already positioned his piano in this way, the better to show off his beautiful profile. Dussek did not do this consistently, however, and in any case his career had no lasting impact on the history of piano playing. Liszt appears to have been unaware of Dussek's tentative reforms when he came to the conclusion that one must not only play the piano but "play the building," and to that end he experimented with the placement of the instrument until he got it right. Martainville's press notice of the young Liszt's Paris concert in 1824 is worth re-reading, since the disadvantage of having the end of the piano pointing towards the public (its usual position) is there made plain. See p. 100.
4. RFL, p. 41ff.
5. ACLA, vol. 1, p. 311.

she had plunged her circle, by declaring herself to be ready for a cup of tea. Clara Schumann once described Liszt as "a smasher of pianos." It is a false image. Even Clara snapped a string or two in public. Most pianists in the first half of the nineteenth century regarded it as a normal hazard of their profession. Liszt's practical solution was occasionally to have two pianos standing on the platform simultaneously, and he would make a point of moving from one keyboard to the other several times in the course of a recital.[6] Not until the great firms of Steinway and Bechstein produced their powerfully reinforced instruments in the 1860s did Liszt's repertoire of the 1840s come into its own. Necessity was the mother of invention.

No artist before Liszt, not even Paganini, succeeded so completely in breaking down the barriers that traditionally separated performing artists from those who were then grandly called their "social superiors." After Liszt, all performers began to enjoy a higher status in society. Haydn and Mozart had been treated like servants; whenever they visited the homes of nobility they had entered by the back door. Beethoven, by dint of his unique genius and his uncompromising nature, had forced the Viennese aristocracy at least to regard him as their equal. But it was left to Liszt to foster the view that an artist is a superior being, because divinely gifted, and that the rest of mankind, of whatever social class, owed him respect and even homage. This view of the artist who walks with God and brings fire down from heaven with which to kindle the hearts of mankind became so deeply entrenched in the Romantic consciousness that today we regard it as a cliché. Nonetheless, the cliché is important, since it explains much about Liszt that would otherwise remain a mystery. When he walked on stage wearing his medals and his Hungarian sword of honour, it was not out of vanity but rather to raise the status of musicians everywhere. It was the most telling gesture he could make to show the world that the times had changed. Here, he seemed to say, was an artist with as many titles and medals as a monarch. It would be tedious to list all those titles, but four can be mentioned here. He received the Cross of the Lion of Belgium. The title Cavalier of the Order of Carlos III was bestowed on him by Queen Isabel of

6. See, for example, Buchner (BLB, p. 93) on his Prague recitals of 1846 and Stasov (SSEM, p. 121) on his St. Petersburg recital of 1842. At his inaugural concert in Vienna on April 18, 1838, Liszt had the misfortune to wreck three pianos in succession. He had borrowed Thalberg's Erard grand for this important occasion but strained the action during a performance of Weber's Concertstück. A Viennese Graf was then pushed into position for him. Less than a quarter of the way through the *Puritani* Fantasy, two brass strings snapped. Liszt, by now exasperated, personally dragged a third instrument (another Graf) from a corner of the stage and plunged into a performance of his Transcendental Study called *Vision*. Before he had reached the closing chord, two more strings had snapped beneath his powerful fingers. (WFWB, pp. 93–94.) During Liszt's stay in London in the summer of 1840, the periodical *John Bull* (May 3) carried an advertisement informing its readers that "each piece" to be heard in Liszt's first concert on May 8 "will be played on a separate Grand Piano, selected by himself from Erard's." Since he played at least four solo items on that occasion, the stage must have been jammed with keyboards.

Spain, who had the order's cross encrusted with diamonds. The Sultan of Turkey, Abdul-Medjid Khan, also decorated him in diamonds with the Order of Nichan-Iftikar. Finally, Wilhelm Friedrich IV of Prussia elevated him to the Ordre pour le Mérite, a purely military distinction normally gained on the field of battle. Inevitably it was said of these decorations that Liszt had manoeuvred to get them. The French newspapers, as usual, were the most vocal in their condemnation and fabricated some strange stories. One of their best efforts deserves to be better known. In 1845 they circulated a false report that Liszt was planning to marry the Queen of Spain and that the queen had given him the title of the Duke of Pianozares.[7] How could anyone take such a report, to say nothing of such a title, seriously? The general public did, however, since Liszt received a number of letters of congratulation.

If we wish to know what Liszt himself thought about the propriety of public recognition for services rendered towards art, the evidence lies to hand. In 1840 the *Gazette Musicale* claimed that Liszt had been angling for the Legion of Honour. Liszt at once wrote a strong denial to the editor, Maurice Schlesinger.

London, May 14, 1840

Sir,

Allow me to protest against an inexact assertion in your last number but one:

"Messieurs Liszt and Cramer *have asked for* the Legion of Honour," etc. I do not know if M. Cramer (who has just been nominated) has asked for the cross.

In any case I think that you, like everyone else, will approve of a nomination so perfectly legitimate.

As to myself, if it be true that my name has figured in the list of candidates, this can only have occurred entirely without my knowledge.

It has always seemed to me that distinctions of this sort could only be *accepted,* but never "asked for."

I am, sir, etc.,

F. LISZT[8]

That Liszt would have felt contempt for any artist who requested a formal distinction is beyond question. He himself occasionally went out of his way to make an enemy of powerful aristocrats if he thought that his dignity as an artist

---

7. RLL, pp. 87–88.

8. LLB, vol. 1, pp. 35–36. As we have seen, Liszt did not receive the Legion of Honour until five years later (n. 4 on p. 146). Concerning the French love of decorations generally, he later wittily observed, "In France one *must* go about with a decoration. One is less noticeable on the boulevards." (*Le Moniteur à Paris,* March 19, 1886.)

had suffered. Into this category falls his chilling reply to Tsar Nicholas I of Russia, who arrived late and then started talking during one of Liszt's recitals in St. Petersburg. He stopped playing and sat at the keyboard with bowed head. When Nicholas inquired the cause of the hushed silence, Liszt replied, "Music herself should be silent when Nicholas speaks." This public rebuke may well have cost Liszt a medal. It was, as Sacheverell Sitwell pointed out, the first time that "music herself" had answered back. Tsar Nicholas later made it known that he wanted Liszt to give a benefit concert for the survivors of the Battle of Borodino. It was a tactless idea and Liszt refused. "I owe my education and my celebrity to France," he said. "It is impossible for me to make common cause with her adversaries." When the tsar heard that, he remarked to one of the ladies of the court, "The hair and political opinions of this man displease me." This was promptly reported to Liszt, who retorted, "I let my hair grow in Paris and shall cut it only in Paris. As for my political views, I have none and will have none until the day the tsar deigns to put at my disposal three hundred thousand bayonets."[9] A similar scene took place in the drawing room of Princess Metternich in Vienna. After keeping Liszt waiting while she chatted idly with her other guests, she suddenly turned to the pianist and said, "You gave concerts in Italy—did you do good business?" Liszt bowed stiffly and replied cuttingly, "Princess, I make music, not business," and left.[10] Thanks to Liszt, artists soon became the new aristocracy, and the great public was quick to recognize it.

After 1842 "Lisztomania" swept Europe, and the reception accorded the pianist can only be described as hysterical. Admirers swarmed all over him, and ladies fought over his silk handkerchiefs and velvet gloves, which they then ripped to pieces as souvenirs. Sober-minded musicians like Chopin, Schumann, and Mendelssohn were appalled by such vulgar displays of hero-worship and gradually came to despise Liszt because of them. Was Liszt to blame for the unrestrained conduct of his audiences? That is rather like asking whether Niagara Falls is to blame for so many suicides. Liszt was a natural phenomenon, and people were swept away by him. The emotionally charged atmosphere of his recitals made them more like séances than serious musical events. With his mesmeric personality and long mane of flowing hair, he created a striking stage-presence. And there were many witnesses to testify that his playing did indeed raise the mood of the audience to a level of mystical ecstasy. In 1840 Hans Christian Andersen, a close observer of men and manners, happened to

---

9. RLKM, vol. 2, p. 186. Stasov dismissed this anecdote as "a ridiculous fairy-tale." The tsar, he said, never arranged concerts. (SSEM, p. 136.) Liszt's first visit to St. Petersburg, however, did coincide with the annual Lenten Concert for the veterans of 1812. He did not participate in that concert, but pointedly gave other charity concerts while in Russia. For further comments of Liszt on Tsar Nicholas, whom he grew to detest, see LLB, vol. 2, p. 335, and LLB, vol. 3, p. 129.

10. BALV, vol. 3, pp. 405–6. This amusing exchange was confirmed by Felix Lichnowsky, who later told Liszt, "The whole city is in a flutter, people speak only of this affair." (LBZL, vol. 1, p. 33.)

be present at one of Liszt's Hamburg recitals. He recorded his impressions in his travel book *A Poet's Bazaar.*

> As Liszt sat before the piano, the first impression of his personality was derived from the appearance of strong passions in his wan face, so that he seemed to me a demon nailed fast to the instrument whence the tones streamed forth—they came from his blood, from his thoughts; he was a demon who would liberate his soul from thraldom; he was on the rack, his blood flowed and his nerves trembled; but as he continued to play, so the demon vanished. I saw that pale face assume a nobler and brighter expression: the divine soul shone from his eyes, from every feature; he became as beauteous as only spirit and enthusiasm can make their worshippers.

Not only artists but hardened critics were shaken by Liszt's magnetic playing. The Russian critic Yuri Arnold once heard Liszt play in St. Petersburg. "I was completely undone by the sense of the supernatural, the mysterious, the incredible," Arnold wrote. "As soon as I reached home, I pulled off my coat, flung myself on the sofa, and wept the bitterest, sweetest tears."[11]

In former times the old aristocracy had had a motto: *Noblesse oblige!* The new aristocracy, the men of genius, Liszt resolved, should have a motto too: *Génie oblige!*[12] Much of the fortune Liszt accumulated during these years of travel he gave away to charity and humanitarian causes. His work in behalf of the Beethoven monument and his support of the Hungarian National School of Music are well documented. Less well known are his generous gifts towards the building fund of Cologne Cathedral, the establishment of a *Gymnasium* at Dortmund, and the construction of the Leopold Church in Pest. There were also many private donations to hospitals, children's schools, and charitable organizations such as the Leipzig Musicians Pension Fund.[13] When he heard of the Great Fire of Hamburg, which raged for three weeks during May 1842 and devastated much of the city, Liszt at once gave concerts in aid of the thousands of homeless.[14] Never before had an artist given so liberally of his time and his talent. Inevitably his goodness was sometimes abused. He became the target of petty vindictiveness when he was unable or unwilling to help. In Halle he was sued by a local music teacher who claimed that Liszt owed him 4 louis d'or for advance publicity. Liszt fought and won the case. He then felt sorry for the man's wife, who was in childbed, and sent her 8 louis d'or.[15]

---

11. SSEM, pp. 127–28.
12. "Genius has obligations."
13. CMGM, vol. 2, p. 245. See also Archives of the Grand Duchy of Thuringia, vol. 13, p. 304.
14. See the letter of thanks from the Hamburg City Council (WA, Überformate 129, 1M).
15. ACLA, vol. 2, p. 246.

History has not always been kind to Liszt when reviewing his *Glanzzeit.* Whatever the final verdict, one thing seems sure. He will never be freed of the charge of not doing more to raise the level of public taste, through his enormous prestige, instead of pandering to its base desires for pyrotechnics and an endless stream of such trifles as his operatic paraphrases, "reminiscences," and popular arrangements. The low quality of his programme-building is a matter of record. What are we to make of the following, a recital he gave at Kiev in 1847?

Hexaméron Variations	LISZT
Concertstück	WEBER
"The Trout"	SCHUBERT–LISZT
A Study	CHOPIN
Invitation to the Dance	WEBER

It is eccentric by modern standards. Yet to accuse Liszt of poor taste shows a lack of historical imagination. In 1847 he had nothing to guide him. Indeed, he felt it quite proper to let others plan his programmes for him. "I seldom . . . planned them myself, but gave them now into this one's hands, and now into that one's, to choose what they liked. That was a mistake, as I later discovered and deeply regretted."[16] By leaving the organization of his concerts to others, Liszt sometimes fell victim to amusing errors. He once played in Marseille and included in the programme his arrangement of Schubert's "La Truite" ("The Trout"). Owing to a printing error the piece appeared as "La Trinité," and the unsuspecting audience sat through this bubbling music with quasi-religious reverence. When Liszt realized the mistake he got up from the piano and made an impromptu speech, asking the audience not to confuse the mysterious idea of the Trinity with Schubert's trout, a helpful interjection which caused great hilarity.[17]

Génie oblige! Liszt's motto still exacts a posthumous penalty. It was very easy for a later generation of pianists to avoid his mistakes while criticizing him for having made them. By 1860, in fact, long after Liszt had retired from the concert platform, a legend in his lifetime, scores of long-haired, champagne-sodden virtuosos (often with a mere half-dozen pieces in their briefcases) were roving around Europe, vainly trying to emulate his triumphs. Even the greatest pianists of the second half of the nineteenth century—men of the calibre of Tausig and von Bülow, both pupils of Liszt who, at their best, may have equalled him—did not come close to matching his public impact. The reason was simply that Liszt was there first. History does not enshrine the names of those who follow the pioneers.

---

16. LLB, vol. 1, p. 257.
17. *Le Nouvelliste,* Marseille, July 31, 1844.

Liszt's Years of Travel
(1838–47: A Summary)

LISZT'S YEARS OF TRAVEL, 1838–1847

Liszt's fame as a performer rested mainly on the great tours of Europe and Asia Minor undertaken by him during the years 1838–47. His marathon journeys, which spanned thousands of miles, ranged from Lisbon in the west to Constantinople in the east, from Gibraltar in the south to St. Petersburg in the north. The map shows only the main towns and cities in which Liszt played during this remarkably brief period. The list that follows adds more details of his itinerant life. Naturally, he often visited certain places more than once. And in some cities (for example, in London, Berlin, and Vienna) he appeared before the public many times.

Aachen, Germany	1841, 1842	Cologne, Germany	1841, 1842, 1843
Agen, France	1844	Constantinople, Turkey	1847
Alicante, Spain	1845	Copenhagen, Denmark	1841
Altenburg, Germany	1841	Córdoba, Spain	1844
Amsterdam, Holland	1842	Cork, Ireland	1840, 1841
Angers, France	1845	Coventry, England	1840
Angoulême, France	1844	Cracow, Poland	1843
Antwerp, Belgium	1841	Crefeld, Germany	1841
Arad, Rumania	1846	Czernovtsy, Ukraine	1847
Augsburg, Germany	1843	Darlington, England	1841
Avignon, France	1845	Darmstadt, Germany	1845
Baden-Baden, Germany	1840, 1841	Derby, England	1840
Barcelona, Spain	1845	Dessau, Germany	1843, 1844
Basel, Switzerland	1845	Detmold, Germany	1841
Bath, England	1840	Dijon, France	1844, 1845
Bautzen, Germany	1844	Doncaster, England	1840
Bayonne, France	1844	Douai, France	1845
Belfast, Ireland	1841	Dresden, Germany	1840, 1841, 1844
Berdichiv, Ukraine	1847	Dublin, Ireland	1840, 1841
Berlin, Germany	1841, 1842, 1843	Durham, England	1841
Bernburg, Germany	1844	Düsseldorf, Germany	1841
Besançon, France	1845	Edinburgh, Scotland	1841
Beziers, France	1844	Eisenstadt, Austria	1840
Bielefeld, Germany	1841	Elberfeld, Germany	1841
Birmingham, England	1840	Elisabetgrad, Ukraine	1847
Blandford, England	1840	Ems, Germany	1840, 1841
Bologna, Italy	1838	Erfurt, Germany	1842, 1844
Bonn, Germany	1840, 1845	Eszék, Yugoslavia	1846
Bordeaux, France	1844	Exeter, England	1840
Boston, England	1840	Exmouth, England	1840
Boulogne, France	1841	Florence, Italy	1838
Braunschweig, Germany	1844	Frankfurt-am-Main,	
Breslau, Germany	1842, 1843	Germany	1841, 1842
Bridgwater, England	1840	Freiburg, Germany	1845
Brieg, Germany	1843	Fürstenwalde, Germany	1843
Brighton, England	1840	Galatz, Rumania	1847
Bristol, England	1840	Gibraltar	1845
Brünn, Czechoslovakia	1846	Glasgow, Scotland	1841
Brussels, Belgium	1840, 1841, 1842, 1845	Glogau, Poland	1843
		Gotha, Germany	1841, 1842, 1844
Bucharest, Rumania	1846, 1847	Gottingen, Germany	1841
Bury St. Edmunds,		Granada, Spain	1845
England	1840	Grantham, England	1840
Cambridge, England	1840	Graz, Austria	1846
Cassel, Germany	1841	Grenoble, France	1845
Cadiz, Spain	1845	Hague, Holland	1842
Cette, France	1844	Halifax, England	1841
Châlons-sur-Marne, France	1845	Halle, Germany	1841
Chalon-sur-Saône, France	1845	Hamburg, Germany	1840, 1841, 1843
Chelmsford, England	1840	Hannover, Germany	1844
Cheltenham, England	1840	Harborough, England	1840
Chester, England	1840	Hechingen, Germany	1843
Chichester, England	1840	Heidelberg, Germany	1843
Clifton, England	1840	Heilbronn, Germany	1843
Clonmel, Ireland	1841	Hermannstadt, Rumania	1846
Coblenz, Germany	1841, 1845	Horncastle, England	1840
Coburg, Germany	1842	Huddersfield, England	1840
Colchester, England	1840	Hull, England	1840
Colmar, France	1845	Huntingdon, England	1840

II

Whatever else the world may debate about his life and work, one thing is generally conceded: Liszt was the first modern pianist. The technical "breakthrough" he achieved during the 1830s and '40s was without precedent in the history of the piano. All subsequent schools were branches of his tree. Rubinstein, Busoni, Paderewski, Godowsky, and Rachmaninoff—all those pianists who together formed what historians later dubbed "the golden age of piano playing"—would be unthinkable without Liszt. It was not that they copied his style of playing; that was inimitable. Nor did they enjoy close personal contact with him; not one of them was his pupil. Liszt's influence went deeper than that. It had to do with his unique ability to solve technical problems. Liszt is to piano playing what Euclid is to geometry. Pianists turn to his music in order to discover the natural laws governing the keyboard. It is impossible for a modern pianist to keep Liszt out of his playing—out of his biceps, his forearms, his fingers—even though he may not know that Liszt is there, since modern piano playing spells Liszt. When he was already thirty years old, Busoni began the study of the piano afresh in order to remedy what he considered to be defects in his own playing. He turned to Liszt's music. Out of the laws he found there Busoni rebuilt his technique. "Gratitude and admiration," wrote Busoni, "made Liszt at that time my master and my friend."[18]

In his younger days Liszt's total absorption with the piano provoked comment even from his friends and supporters. Why not branch out into the larger orchestral forms, like Berlioz, instead of wasting time at a keyboard? Liszt reflected carefully on his position and produced his "Letter to Adolphe Pictet," an autobiographical document of some importance. His abiding love for the piano, and his unshakable belief in its future, shine forth.

> You do not know that to speak of giving up my piano would be to me a day of gloom, robbing me of the light which illuminated all my early life, and has grown to be inseparable from it.
>
> My piano is to me what his vessel is to the sailor, his horse to the Arab, nay even more, till now it has been myself, my speech, my life. It is the repository of all that stirred my nature in the passionate days of my youth. I confided to it all my desires, my dreams, my joys, and my sorrows. Its strings vibrated to my emotions, and its keys obeyed my every caprice. Would you have me abandon it and

---

18. BEM, p. 86.

strive for the more brilliant and resounding triumphs of the theatre or orchestra? Oh, no! Even were I competent for music of that kind, my resolution would be firm not to abandon the study and development of piano playing, until I had accomplished whatever is practicable, whatever it is possible to attain nowadays.

Perhaps the mysterious influence which binds me to it so strongly prejudices me, but I consider the piano to be of great consequence. In my estimation it holds the first place in the hierarchy of instruments. . . . In the compass of its seven octaves it includes the entire scope of the orchestra, and the ten fingers suffice for the harmony which is produced by an ensemble of a hundred players. . . .[19]

III

According to his own testimony, Liszt sometimes practised for ten or twelve hours a day, and much of this labour was expended on endurance exercises—scales, arpeggios, trills, and repeated notes. He set great store by the absolute independence of each finger. Every scale was practised with the fingering of every other scale (using, say, C-major fingering for F-sharp major, and D-flat major fingering for C major). No pianist can afford to neglect Liszt's fingering. It is both imaginative and original and often looks far into the future of the keyboard. Here are three ways in which he tackled scale-building:

five-finger scale *(Rhapsodie espagnole)*

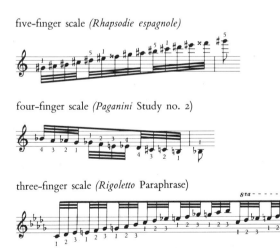

four-finger scale *(Paganini Study no. 2)*

three-finger scale *(Rigoletto Paraphrase)*

---

19. RGS, vol. 2, p. 151; CPR, p. 135.

Particularly intriguing is Liszt's solution to the problem of how to produce a chromatic glissando scale, which is not strictly possible on a piano keyboard.

The second finger of the right hand, nail down, plays C-major glissando. Simultaneously the five fingers of the left hand play every black key. When both hands move at the same speed, the result is a chromatic scale, glissando.[20]

Such solutions as these, utterly bold and original as they are, bring home a central truth about Liszt's technique. He did not conceive of a pianist's hands as consisting of two parts of five fingers each, but as one unit of ten fingers. From his youth Carl Czerny had instilled into him the doctrine of finger equalization. But Liszt far outstripped his old mentor in the wholesale application of this philosophy. The interchangeability of any finger with any other became an ideal towards which he constantly strove. Many of the models in Liszt's twelve volumes of Technical Studies[21] are obsessed with the problem. They reached a peak of audacity in this kind of passage.

Until the hands are truly "interlocked," such fingerings will seem perverse. The difficulty is mental, not physical. Once the pianist has grasped the notion that he does not have two separate hands, but a single unit of ten digits, he has made an advance towards Liszt. In this radical approach to the keyboard, there might be something to be said for numbering the fingers from one to ten. Incidentally, the logical outcome of the interlocking two-fingered scale shown above appeared in this shining passage from *La campanella,* which unfolds two dovetailed chromatic scales.

20. Liszt once told Olga von Meyendorff, "For your glissando exercises I once again advise you to use only the nail, either of your thumb or of your index or third finger, *without even the tiniest area of flesh*" (Liszt's emphasis). (WLLM, p. 390.)
21. WTS.

Liszt's contemporaries were constantly amazed at his finger dexterity. He could apparently respond to any emergency. Joachim never forgot the manner in which Liszt accompanied him in the finale of Mendelssohn's Violin Concerto, all the time holding a lighted cigar between the first and middle fingers of the right hand.[22] Lina Ramann relates a similar story. She once told Liszt that Ludwig Böhner had played fugues on the organ, in spite of two lame fingers. Liszt pondered this problem for a while, then, "with a certain tension of the muscles of the face, he seated himself at the piano and began to play a difficult fugue by Bach, with *three fingers* of each hand."[23] Liszt's playing of Beethoven's *Emperor* Concerto in Vienna on the fiftieth anniversary of the composer's death was the occasion for an equally impressive feat. Sometime before the performance he cut the second finger of his left hand.[24] He played the concerto without using that particular finger, redistributing the notes among the remaining ones in such a way that no one was aware of the injury he had sustained.

Wherever Liszt has left us his own fingerings, then, the modern pianist does well to consider them before exhausting himself on all the alternatives. The reason is really quite simple: all the alternatives were known to Liszt and rejected by him. Consider this double-thirds passage from the sixth Paganini Study.

22. MJ, p. 70.
23. RLKM, vol. 1, p. 166. Ludwig Böhner was the eccentric real-life model on whom E.T.A. Hoffmann based his character "Kapellmeister Kreisler," later to become a source of musical inspiration to Schumann in his *Kreisleriana*.
24. Not the right hand, as the earlier biographies have it. Liszt corrected this mistake in his own copy of RLKM, vol. 1, p. 166 (WA, Kasten 352). The cut occurred while Liszt was being shaved by his valet, Spiridon Knézéwicz. It was "completely my own fault," wrote Liszt. "I was recommending something to Spiridon while he shaved me and, stupidly, raised my left hand too high—and have learned to esteem even more the excellence of his razor." (LLB, vol. 7, p. 168.)

Its fingering is unorthodox. Yet how much simpler it is than the official conservatory fingering for such passages. The left hand forms itself into a fork, or two-fingered prong, shaking its way up the keyboard. It happens to be such a natural solution to the problem that even mediocre pianists can play the passage well. A similar procedure was followed in the first Hungarian Rhapsody, this time in the right hand.

The technique reached its apogee in such passages as the following (also in the First Rhapsody), which unrolls a pair of interlocking, double-third chromatic scales, spread across two hands. Any other fingering than that proposed by Liszt would hamper the mercurial progress of this inventive texture.

It is easy to understand why Liszt was accused of "destroying the true art of piano playing." Old Marmontel, the doyen of piano teachers at the Paris Conservatoire, charged Liszt with "striving too much after eccentric effects." In general, teachers were always Liszt's enemies. He disturbed their fixed ideas, and his free, creative approach to the keyboard terrified them.

The concept of "interlocking" hands led Liszt to discover one of his most sensational effects. Known to this day as "Liszt octaves," it symbolized clearly the difference between the old and the new schools of playing. Liszt worked up some spectacular storms with this effect. It is achieved by interlocking two sets of octaves, with the thumbs as pivots. A favoured way of practising such passages, in fact, is with the thumbs alone. A typical passage comes from the Paganini Study no. 2, in E-flat major.

For the rest, in all his technical discoveries Liszt appears to have heeded Quintilian's maxim: *Si non datur porta, per murum erumpendum* ("If there is no doorway, one must break out through the wall").

I V

Liszt's hands were long and narrow, and his fingers were notable for their low-lying mass of connective tissue, which gave them the appearance, in Edward Dannreuther's graphic phrase, of being "the opposite of webbed feet." Because his finger-tips were blunted, not tapered, they gave him maximum traction on the surface of the keyboard. These were distinct advantages. The lack of webbing between the fingers allowed of wide extensions. Liszt could take a tenth with ease. The following passage from the first version of "Gondoliera" in *Venezia e Napoli* (1839) was not uncomfortable under Liszt's hand, although he later modified these stretches.

Liszt's fourth fingers were unusually long, and that, too, encouraged him to employ fingerings difficult for normal hands. Consider this stretch between fourth and fifth fingers in *Au Lac de Wallenstadt.*

Almost equally difficult is the right-hand accompaniment at the beginning of *Bénédiction de Dieu*.

It would be a mistake, however, to assume that Liszt's keyboard writing is idiosyncratic. He had an unerring sense of the "topography" of the piano. There is not a passage in Liszt, however difficult, that is truly unpianistic. Even Schumann and Chopin occasionally lapsed here: both wrote passages against, rather than for, the piano, passages in which the limitations of the fingers are ignored while purely musical considerations prevail. Liszt's passage-work is often simpler to play than Chopin's, although it may sound more brilliant. Busoni is of interest here. He wrote, "An eye-witness relates how Liszt—pondering over a cadenza—sat down at the piano and tried three or four dozen variations of it, playing each one through until he had made his choice." The secret of that choice, Busoni concluded, was symmetry.[25] A good example may be found in the opening cadenza of *Totentanz*. Once the basic pattern (X) has been grasped, the rest must follow.

It is often said that Liszt frowned on the use of "mechanical aids" to develop the hands. This was true only in later life. A wealth of testimony from his Weimar master classes held during the 1870s and '80s suggests that he was bored by technique, never taught it, and was singularly unimpressed when his young "matadors of the keyboard" displayed it. In his youth Liszt's attitude was different. As early as 1828 Liszt's Paris studio, as we have seen, contained a piano with a specially strengthened keyboard on which it was impossible to play without effort. In 1832 he recommended to Valérie Boissier that she practise her octaves "on the brace,"[26] a mahogany handrail which

---

25. BEM, p. 155.

26. BLP, p. 65. Symbolic of the piano's increased popularity during the 1820s and '30s was the meteoric rise to prominence of J. B. Logier and his invention of the "Chiroplast"—a complex

could be attached to each end of the keyboard and which ensured smooth lateral movements of the arms. He also suggested to the same pupil that repetitive exercises be mastered while reading a book, in order to avoid boredom. As late as the 1840s, during his European tours, Liszt was still using a dumb keyboard on long journeys.

V

Leaps were a particular speciality. Liszt himself clearly enjoyed taking risks, and there are times when he asks the pianist to perform some difficult feats. The following passage comes from the first version of *Au Bord d'une source* (1835).

Textures such as these led Henry Chorley to observe that Liszt appeared to take up more space on the keyboard than any other pianist he knew.[27] Contemporary caricatures show Liszt seated at the piano with a multitude of hands and fingers jostling for a place on the keyboard. "See, he has three hands!" they used to exclaim of Thalberg. With Liszt it sometimes seemed like ten. A notorious example of rapid leaps, and one which has brought about the downfall of many a pianist, occurs in *Campanella*. It is not so much the distances to be traversed (at most two octaves) as the fact that the player must endure the ordeal of leaping back and forth across the void at speed for extended periods.

---

mechanism of brass rods and rails for disciplining 'prentice hands at the keyboard—which ruined many a promising career before it had properly started. Logier subsequently developed a system of mass piano teaching based exclusively on its use, which allowed him to coach up to a dozen beginners simultaneously. Since they all paid him simultaneously as well, Logier soon became rich and opened "Chiroplast instruction centres" in most of the large cities of Europe (including Berlin, Paris, London, and Dublin), laying the foundations of a reputation as a piano teacher which the results hardly seemed to justify: not one pianist of stature was produced by this method. Among the advocates of the Chiroplast was Kalkbrenner, whose notorious handrail was clearly modelled on Logier's invention. Even the young Liszt was swept up by the handrail and recommended it to his pupils, although he later abandoned such advice, once he understood the harm that could flow from it.

27. Chorley left a compelling account of Liszt's total command of the keyboard in CMM, pp. 45–51.

In order to play such a passage with security, the player must feel that the piano is an extension of his own body. You do not need your eyes to tell you that your limbs are attached to your torso. Likewise, this passage can be played blindfold by the pianist who has "internalized" the topography of his instrument. Again, the caricaturists of the time drew truer than they knew when, inspired by Greek mythology, they depicted Liszt as a piano-centaur—half man, half piano—a unique amalgam in which the instrument and the player had become indissolubly merged.

Note-repetition was another branch of keyboard technique that Liszt made his own. Ever since Sébastien Erard had perfected the double escapement, which made rapid note-repetition easy, pianists had been looking for an opportunity to explore the mechanism to the full. Liszt found it in *La campanella,* a piece containing quick-fire note-reiteration such as the piano had never been challenged to play before. Another splendid summit of this branch of Liszt's art is displayed in the Tarantella from *Venezia e Napoli.*

Liszt here produces a magical illusion. Like some latter-day Merlin, mixing potions and casting spells across the keyboard, the wizard deludes us into thinking that the piano has been metamorphosed into a sustaining instrument of radiant beauty.

It was Liszt's view that all keyboard configurations, however complex, could be reduced to a small group of elements—scales, octaves, leaps, repeated notes, etc.—and that if the student worked at them consistently, he could meet any challenge. Trills and tremolos Liszt placed under the category of repeated notes: a trill, that is, is merely two repeated notes alternating with one another. A method Liszt used to make his trills more brilliant was to finger them not with two, but with four fingers.

VI

The first indication of Liszt's technical "breakthrough" at the keyboard had come in 1838–39 with the appearance of the twelve Transcendental Studies and the six Paganini Studies. These eighteen pieces represented a treasury of keyboard resources not found in any earlier work. Such is their historical position in the world of piano music that some account of their genesis is called for.

As we have seen, Liszt was only thirteen years old when he composed the first version of the Transcendentals, in 1824.[28] He now took these juvenile exercises and transformed them into works of towering difficulty. It is not clear why he chose to revise his 'prentice pieces, rather than to compose a completely fresh set of works; the transformations doubtless came into being gradually, as a natural result of his improvising increasingly complex variations over the first models. Whatever the reason, twenty-four studies were announced; once again, only twelve appeared. They were published by Haslinger of Vienna in 1839 with a dedication to Carl Czerny, and were called Grandes Etudes. A review copy found its way into the hands of Schumann, who astutely observed their connections with the juvenile pieces, overlaid though they are with monstrous technical complexities, and described them as "studies in storm and dread for, at the most, ten or twelve players in the world."[29]

It was partly as a result of playing his Grandes Etudes in public, under widely varying circumstances, that Liszt revised them yet again (after his official "retirement" from the concert platform in 1847), smoothing out their more intractable difficulties. He brought out this third version in 1851, under the generic title Etudes d'exécution transcendante, and again dedicated them to his old master Carl Czerny, "from his pupil, in gratitude and respectful friendship."

28. See pp. 118–19.
29. NZfM, no. 11, 1839.

At the same time Liszt added programmatic titles to all but two of the individual numbers. The original tonal connections (first laid down in the juvenile set) were meanwhile preserved.[30]

1. *Prelude* (C major)	7. *Eroica* (E-flat major)
2. Molto vivace (A minor)	8. *Wilde Jagd* (C minor)
3. *Paysage* (F major)	9. *Ricordanza* (A-flat major)
4. *Mazeppa* (D minor)	10. Allegro agitato (F minor)
5. *Feux-follets* (B-flat major)	11. *Harmonies du soir* (D-flat major)
6. *Vision* (G minor)	12. *Chasse-neige* (B-flat minor)

Modern scholarship has done a disservice to Liszt by suppressing the two earlier versions, arguing that they do not represent Liszt's final thoughts.[31] For Liszt, however, a composition was rarely finished. All his life he went on reshaping, reworking, adding, subtracting; sometimes a composition exists in four or five different versions simultaneously. To say that it progresses towards a "final" form is to misunderstand Liszt's art. Entire works are "metamorphosed" across a span of twenty-five years or more, accumulating and shedding detail along the way. The famous F-minor Study, for example, originally (1824) took this form.

In the second (1838) version it has been transformed into a work of prodigious complexity.

---

30. See p. 118. It is not generally known that Liapunov, a Liszt admirer, also composed a set of Transcendental Studies, which complete Liszt's key-scheme, starting in F-sharp major (the next key in Liszt's descending spiral). He dedicated his pieces to the memory of Liszt.

31. See, for example, the editorial preface to NLE.

Later still (1851), Liszt reformulated the texture of bar 3 (and all the others modelled on it) and notated it thus:

The transformations in *Feux-follets* are equally remarkable. Compare the juvenile model with the highly developed concert study which later sprang out of it. The one version shimmers behind the other, and the moment the player knows it his performance is bound to be affected.

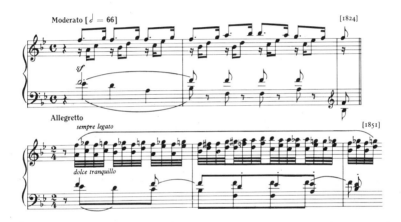

In the Transcendentals Liszt really unfolds a part of his musical autobiography in public: Liszt the supreme virtuoso openly reminisces about Liszt the youthful prodigy. It may not be essential to learn the early models before one plays the Transcendentals well. But it will certainly colour the player's attitude towards them, in a positive sense, and will bring him more closely into line with Liszt's own attitude towards them, if he hears the Transcendentals over that same musical background against which Liszt himself composed them.

The modern pianist may disparage Liszt's studies, but he should be able to play them. Otherwise he admits to having a less than total command of the keyboard. Paradoxically, the biggest enemy of the Transcendentals is not the pianist whose technique is too bad to play them, but the pianist whose technique is only just good enough to do so. The former is instantly exposed for what he is: incapable. The latter, however, gamely attacks all the difficulties but leaves behind him a battlefield in which the piano and the pianist have totally exhausted themselves in physical combat. Such pianists give the Transcendentals a bad name. They create the impression that Liszt has demanded too much of the piano when he has merely demanded too much of them. All they succeed in doing is to communicate the music's difficulties. What the Transcendentals require, above all, is a pianist whose technique is so advanced that he succeeds in communicating their simplicities.[32] Only then will their musical attractions stand revealed. True, we are describing a pianist who not only commands all branches of keyboard technique, but has absorbed them deeply into his second nature and so placed distance between himself and the keyboard. We are describing a pianist who negotiates all difficulties with magisterial ease. We are describing a pianist for whom all things are easy, or they are impossible. We are describing the twenty-eight-year-old Liszt. What harsh words have been uttered against Liszt's virtuosity, usually by those who could not match it! How strongly has it been attacked in the name of Art! Yet virtuosity is an indispensable tool of musical interpretation. One recalls Saint-Saëns's telling aphorism: "In Art, a difficulty overcome is a thing of beauty." Henri Maréchal once informed Liszt (who was by then an old man living in Rome) of the disgust he had felt at seeing an "imbecile pianist" play the *Rigoletto* Paraphrase in a difficult arrangement for the left hand. This showman had had the nerve to take out his silk handkerchief with his right hand and blow his nose in the middle of the piece, so that the audience might see that only the left hand was working. As Maréchal was telling Liszt that such antics were fit only for the fairground, Liszt gently squeezed his arm and said with a smile, "My dear child, for a virtuoso that is necessary! It is absolutely indispensable."[33]

The background to the six Paganini Studies is less complex. Liszt wrote these pieces under the influence of the great violinist whose name they bear. Five of them are transcriptions from Paganini's Twenty-four Unaccompanied Caprices, epoch-making works which raised violin playing to a new level. (It was no accident that Liszt turned to these particular pieces for his transcriptions, which were a constant reminder of the sort of goals he had set himself on the piano.) The remaining item is *La campanella,* a set of variations on the well-known tune of that name which Paganini had used in the Rondo of his Violin Concerto in B minor. When Liszt first published these six studies, in 1840, he gave them the title "Etudes d'exécution transcendante d'après Paganini." Eleven years later he revised them, together with the Transcen-

---

32. Friedheim once reported Liszt as having remarked, "To be able to play Beethoven well, a little more technique is required than he demands." Liszt might well have been speaking of his own music.

33. MRS, pp. 111–12.

dentals, and provided a new title, Grandes Etudes de Paganini. The six items
are:

1. G minor (tremolos)
2. E-flat major (scales and octaves)
3. G-sharp minor, *La campanella* (leaps and repeated notes)
4. E major (arpeggios)
5. E major, *La Chasse* (thirds and sixths)
6. A minor (theme and variations)

Again, a comparison between the two versions is instructive. The conscientious
player, moreover, will want to consult Paganini's violin originals and see for
himself how Liszt has achieved his transfers. Typical of his procedure is the
Study in E-flat major. Paganini's original is an exercise in scales and double-
stops. The problem posed by Paganini is how to switch effortlessly from the
one technique to the other.

Liszt does far more than transfer these notes to the keyboard. He transfers the
problem as well, reformulating it in pianistic terms.

How to jump from the last note of the scale to the chord immediately following? That is not Liszt's problem; it is Paganini's. Liszt has simply incorporated
it into his transcription as faithfully as he can, placing physical obstacles on the
keyboard which match the ones experienced on the violin. By handicapping
the pianist's right hand with double-thirds and a flying leap to the other end
of the keyboard, Liszt is attempting to translate an essential technical point in
Paganini's music. When Liszt revised this study he introduced many simplifica-
tions which, on the whole, make it "speak" more effectively. The same passage
in the final version (1851) unfolds thus.

V I I

During the 1830s and '40s Liszt developed some unconventional marks of expression, presumably because the ones currently in use were not subtle enough for his needs. Thus a single straight line over a group of notes (———) indicated a ritenuto. An oblong box (⬚) indicated an accelerando. Both symbols were used in the first version of *Ricordanza* (1839).

Another symbol was the double line with open ends (═══), which stood for an agogic accent. The piece called *Lyon* (1834) contains many examples of this expressive device.

Although these symbols, which have the merit of simplicity, gave Liszt exact control over tempo rubato, he later formed the view that such decisions are best left to the player, and dropped them. They are of interest chiefly because they tell us how Liszt himself may have played. Equally indicative of his personal interpretations are his unusual dynamic markings. Liszt often placed a single stress mark over two or more notes simultaneously. These "multiple accents" are found, for example, in *Venezia e Napoli.*

Even a simple crescendo or diminuendo could be transformed by Liszt into a vehicle of great expressive power. He once told Valérie Boissier to practise crescendos like this:

This telling effect is captured to perfection by the symbol that represents it, and renders descriptive comment superfluous.

Closely allied to Liszt's expression marks is his pedalling, which is occasionally both daring and futuristic. At a time when his contemporaries still regarded the sustaining pedal as a special effect, to be used with caution, Liszt perceived in it the very soul of the piano, without which the instrument dies. He realized the great advantage the pedal gives to the player in freeing his hands to do other things. Not least was he intrigued by the endless possibilities of mingling "foreign" harmonies in new combinations. Ever since Debussy and the Impressionists it has been accepted that clarity in piano texture is not always a virtue, that deliberate blurring and clouding of the harmonies is a genuine musical effect. In Liszt's day this was a novel attitude. Accordingly, such pedal markings as we see at the beginning of *Funérailles* were without precedent; there is nothing to match them in Chopin or Schumann. The player who lacks the courage to keep the pedal down may produce a "cleaner" sound, but he will lose the noise and clangour of funeral bells which build up to a deafening roar. If he loses that, he loses the piece.

Unlike his contemporaries, Liszt was interested in the use of the soft pedal as an expressive device. In his early paraphrase on Auber's *La Fiancée* he even indicates that both pedals are to be used simultaneously, casting a soft veil over the timbre.

Liszt's notation is worth special study; it is often highly original. Since his compositions frequently arose from his improvisations, his notation occasionally assumes a spontaneous, almost wayward appearance. It must sometimes have been a problem for him to find a form of notation that perfectly matched his free-ranging creations. In the first *Apparition* (1834) a temporary lull in the music produces a similar lull in the notation.

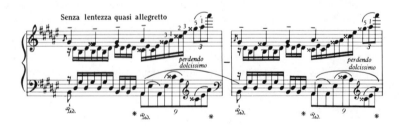

Liszt heard, and he wrote what he heard. Likewise, he frequently unfolded his keyboard music on three (sometimes four) staves in order to avoid overcrowding and make his intentions clearer. His arrangement of Schubert's *Mélodie hongroise* in E-flat major contains a typical example, whose left hand, incidentally, offers an object lesson in note-distribution.

By contrast, Liszt unfolded an entire piece on one stave alone, without ambiguity, in his E-major Paganini Study.

In his visionary *Harmonies poétiques et religieuses* (1834) the young Liszt produced an advanced, asymmetrical effect worthy of Bartók. The numerical divisions are Liszt's own, and he clearly thought them essential for a correct rendering of this problematic passage.

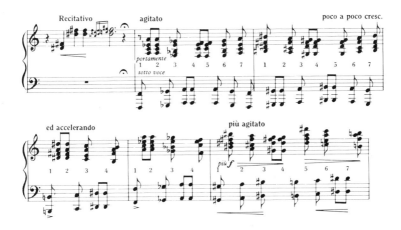

What is the true time signature of the first bar? It is characteristic of Liszt to leave the question open. For the rest, notation does not produce music; music produces notation. Notation's sole function is to symbolize the "sonic surface"

of the composition which lies behind it; and even when it functions well, it needs must carry out its task imperfectly. The evidence lies everywhere to hand. How often have we heard performances (especially of Liszt's music) in which the notes are all there but the piece is missing?

Liszt's operatic paraphrases happen to be important in the history of keyboard notation. To condense an operatic score (soloists, chorus, and orchestra) into a viable piano texture need not be difficult. To transform that texture from a dull piano reduction (a dead copy of the original) into a living composition calls for a touch of the magician's wand—with poetic licence, roulades, diamond-bright cascades, and even the occasional eruption of flame and fire—to cast a spell over the keyboard and persuade it to illuminate by suggestion the creative spirit of the original. A perennial problem in this kind of work is the clear separation of melody and accompaniment. Liszt's favoured solution was to print his notation in two different shades of typeface—light and bold—so that the player is at once informed how to distribute his tone. Nowadays this is commonplace, in Liszt's day it was new. The *Rigoletto* Paraphrase offers a good example.

This separation of melody and accompaniment was perfectly understood by Liszt. However complex the ornamentation, it was subordinated to the composition as a whole. His great pupil Moriz Rosenthal has told us that under Liszt's hands, "the embellishments were like a cobweb—so fine—or like the texture of costliest lace." The same cannot be said of Liszt's would-be imitators, who frequently vulgarized these compositions by "bringing out" the difficulties inherent in the embellishments in a misdirected effort to score a public ovation. After Liszt's death the operatic paraphrases fell into neglect for fifty years. There were good historical reasons for this. The operas that they had so bravely pioneered, even popularized, were by now well known; the original, crusading impulse for playing such compositions in public was therefore diminished. But a deeper reason prevailed. The early twentieth century saw the rise of musicology, with its emphasis on "authenticity," in which the composer's original thought was perfectly preserved, in which every note was sacrosanct, in which the "sonic surface" of the music was reproduced as nearly as he himself envisaged it. The crime of the paraphrase now was that it *was* a paraphrase. It was not interested in preserving the "original thought"; it changed music's notation with impunity; it lacked reverence for the "sonic surface" of a work; indeed, it often flitted about, chameleon-like, donning the most far-flung acoustic disguises, lording it over territory it had no business to occupy. Liszt's sixty-odd paraphrases, out of temper with the times, were hushed up and forgotten. An inimitable treasury of piano music was silenced by prejudice. It never seemed to occur to our forefathers that every opera has an overture. And what are the best overtures but arrangements of the themes of the operas they precede? Brahms, no Liszt admirer, used to maintain that in Liszt's old operatic fantasies was to be found "the true classicism of the piano." It is in this spirit that they have been revived in modern times, and the best of them—*Norma, Rigoletto,* and *Faust*—are likely to remain in the repertoire for as long as the operas after which they are modelled.

The bigger effects in Liszt's music called for a large hall to contain them. We recall that it was Liszt who took the piano out of the salon and placed it in the concert hall. When, as early as 1837, he gave a recital before three thousand people in the Scala opera house, he was democratizing the instrument. Strange to say, in order to achieve this worthy end he had to overcome much prejudice. There were many musicians whose thinking was rooted in the eighteenth century and who regarded the piano—much as they had regarded the harpsichord before it—as a chamber instrument meant to be played only before a small circle of connoisseurs. Chopin, Hummel, and Moscheles had all made their reputations in that way. When Chopin played in the salons of Paris before a select audience drawn from high society, it was on the silvery-toned Pleyel with its light action that he gave his incomparable performances. Liszt had often played the Pleyel and found it wanting: he scathingly described the instrument as "a pianino." The seven-octave Erard, with its heavier action and larger sound, was more congenial to him. The morning after his Scala recital, the twenty-six-year-old pianist wrote a letter to Pierre Erard expressing his satisfaction with the instrument.

Como, December 11, 1837

Let them not tell me any more that the piano is not a suitable instrument for a big hall, that the sounds are lost in it, that the nuances disappear, etc. I bring as witnesses the three thousand people who filled the immense Scala theatre yesterday evening from the pit to the gods on the seventh balcony (for there are seven tiers of boxes here), all of whom heard and admired, down to the smallest details, your beautiful instrument. This is not flattery; you have known me too long to think me capable of the least deception. But it is a fact, publicly recognized here, that never before has a piano created such an effect.[34]

VIII

This raises the question of Liszt's own interpretations. By all accounts they were unfettered by "performing tradition," especially during his days as a touring virtuoso. He continually sought out new ways of playing old works. "The letter killeth but the spirit giveth life" was his watchword. He would try to penetrate to the very heart of a composition, playing it through in a variety of different ways until he thought that he had divined its true meaning. This sometimes led him into exaggeration and made him the target of criticism. Once, during a performance of Beethoven's *Kreutzer* Sonata (with Ole Bull), such liberties were taken with the interpretation as to "call forth the disapprobation of the audience."[35] One wonders what exactly took place. We do well to put such matters into historical perspective. "Classical" playing was a discovery of the Romantics. Beethoven, that is to say, did not play his music classically.[36] What in the profession is nowadays called fidelity to the text was hardly fostered until the second half of the nineteenth century, when it became associated with the "restrained" performances of such artists as Clara Schumann and Joachim. Today, of course, it has become dogma. Liszt was deeply con-

---

34. BQLE, p. 10. See also PMPE, p. 97, in which Liszt expresses himself vehemently against the Pleyel pianos provided for his concerts in Bologna and Florence in 1838: "The keyboard is prodigiously uneven, and the bass, middle, and upper registers are all terribly muffled." The Bologna instrument he described as "despicable." In despair, he borrowed a Streicher from Prince Hercolami, on which he completed his concert engagements in Bologna. Erard, it seems, could not always keep up when Liszt set out on his travels.

35. *Musical World,* London, June 9, 1840. A few days earlier (June 1) Henry Reeve had heard Liszt play the same sonata with Batta at a private gathering in London "en doublant les passages." (RML, vol. 1, p. 117.)

36. SBLB, p. 413. Ries, Cramer, Tomášek, and others all testified to Beethoven's unpredictable performances of his own music. Cherubini characterized his playing as "rough."

cerned by this trend, which he regarded as a denial of the player's artistic personality. He aptly called it the "Pilate offence"—washing one's hands of musical interpretation in public[37]—and he would have nothing to do with it. There is no doubt that in his youth his performances were often considered unconventional, and he may well have played fast-and-loose with the text when the Gypsy in him stirred. We know from the lessons he gave to Valérie Boissier that he viewed the entire question of tempo in a liberal light. "I don't play according to measure," he once told her. "One must not imprint on music a balanced uniformity, but kindle it, or slow it down, according to its meaning."[38] It was the same during the Weimar years with conducting. He considered it demeaning for the conductor "to function like a windmill." Liszt indicated phrasing and tempo through very general gestures. He was fond of making a nautical analogy: "We are helmsmen, not oarsmen."[39] Sometimes his helmsmanship led him to chart a dangerous course and sail his ship towards treacherous waters. Charles Hallé once heard him tack the finale of Beethoven's C-sharp minor Sonata (op. 27) onto the Variations of the one in A-flat major (op. 26), without any break, and was offended by such a disrespectful approach to the classics.[40] But as Liszt matured, his attitude towards interpretation modified. We have the testimony of such witnesses as Berlioz, Wagner, and von Bülow that once Liszt was out of earshot of the great public, his Beethoven performances were faithful marvels of re-creative beauty.[41] When von Bülow dedicated his edition of the Beethoven sonatas to Liszt (the results of "the fruits of his teaching"), he was not merely paying his respects to his former master; he was also acknowledging Liszt's supremacy as an advocate and interpreter of Beethoven. But even in Liszt's twilight years his playing was not entirely predictable. He lived by the maxim "Tradition is laziness." Whatever doubts

---

37. LLB, vol. 1, p. 258.
38. BLP, p. 35.
39. RGS, vol. 5, p. 232. "Wir sind Steuermänner und keine Ruderknechte."
40. HLL, p. 38.
41. Count Apponyi, who was present at Wahnfried in the 1870s when Liszt performed the slow movement of the *Hammerklavier* Sonata, has described the impact his playing had on Wagner: "When the last bars of that mysterious work had died away, we stood silent and motionless. Suddenly, from the gallery on the first floor, there came a tremendous uproar, and Richard Wagner in his nightshirt came thundering, rather than running, down the stairs. He flung his arms round Liszt's neck and, sobbing with emotion, thanked him in broken phrases for the wonderful gift he had received. His bedroom led onto the inner gallery, and he had apparently crept out in silence on hearing the first notes and remained there without giving a sign of his presence. Once more, I witnessed the meeting of those three—Beethoven, the great deceased master, and the two best qualified of all living men to guard his tradition. This experience still lives within me, and has confirmed and deepened my innermost conviction that those three great men belonged to one another." (AAM, pp. 100–101.)

Liszt tells us, incidentally, that he had played the *Hammerklavier* Sonata from the age of ten, "doubtless very badly, but with passion—without anyone being able to guide me in it. My father lacked the experience to do it, and Czerny feared confronting me with such a challenge." (LLB, vol. 7, p. 164.)

still linger today about Liszt's cavalier attitude towards the printed page are largely dispelled the moment we consult his editions of Bach, Beethoven, Schubert, Chopin, and others. There is not a single case of bowdlerization. All adhere faithfully to the basic text,[42] and the degree of "touching up" which Liszt allows (e.g., in the domain of dynamics, phrasing, and pedalling) is not extreme by nineteenth-century standards. Those who object to *any* licence in this field are free to dispense with Liszt's editions altogether, but they should not forget that after a hundred years these volumes have themselves become important tools of research, offering one of the few direct insights into how Liszt might have interpreted the classics. After all, each piece is different and makes different demands. Liszt's saying, "There is music which comes of itself to us, and there is music which requires us to come to it,"[43] is illuminating, since it lays down a central distinction of use both to editors and players alike. The important thing, of course, is to get the distinction right.

---

42. See, for example, Liszt's preface to his performing edition of the Schubert sonatas (1870), which is a model of correct musicological practice, placing before the player the various typographical symbols used to distinguish Schubert's original text from Liszt's (comparatively few) editorial suggestions.
43. RC, p. 27.

A Prodigal Returns to Hungary, 1839–1840

> *Of all living artists, I am the only one who can proudly exhibit a proud Fatherland. While the others paddle about miserably in the shallow waters of a mere public, I sail forward freely on the open sea of a great nation. My North Star constantly shows that Hungary will one day point proudly towards me.*
>
> FRANZ LISZT[1]

I

While Liszt was in Vienna in December 1839, raising funds for the Beethoven monument, a deputation arrived from Pest to invite him back to Hungary. Liszt had not seen his native land for sixteen years. He was now the most famous living Hungarian. Hungary, in turn, regarded him as its greatest son. The previous year, it will be recalled, his patriotism had been stirred by the disaster at Pest. The Hungarians had, as yet, found no adequate way of acknowledging his generosity to them on that occasion. This invitation was an expression of national appreciation. More than that, it was a first step towards bringing Liszt home. During the first week of December 1839, Liszt informed Marie d'Agoult that he expected "to spend a fortnight in Hungary."[2] With this simple announcement, Liszt embarked on a journey that changed the course of his life and had important consequences even for Hungary itself.

Few other episodes in Liszt's long career have resulted in so many distortions and misconceptions as his return to Hungary. The national acclaim with which he was greeted had no precedent. To the outside world it remained incomprehensible that an entire nation could rally to a pianist. That fact still strains the

---

1. CLBA, p. 36.
2. ACLA, vol. 1, p. 310

credulity of the modern biographer and imposes on him an obligation to try to explain it. Let us recall the historical context in which Hungary found herself in 1839. For one hundred and fifty years she had been oppressed by Austria. Her language was banned, her culture undervalued, her material resources plundered. Every important aspect of the nation's life was administered by Vienna. A great tide of national fervour was sweeping the country as Hungary struggled for its independence. At the very moment that Liszt stepped onto Hungarian soil, his compatriots were searching for Magyar heroes, ambassadors who might make Hungary's plight better known abroad. What followed—the near-idolatry with which Liszt was worshipped, the search for his "aristocratic descent," the presentation of the bejewelled "Sword of Honour," the national cry of "Éljen! Liszt Ferenc!" ("Hail! Franz Liszt!")—all the things, in fact, that brought him criticism in the years to come—can only be understood once we see them as part of that general striving for a nation to assert itself through its leading individuals.

Liszt himself always saw the matter in its proper perspective; his correspondence proves it. The same cannot be said of his critics, who have generally missed the significance of the honours which were now showered on him and have attributed them (with no proof) to his personal pride and arrogance.[3] But let the facts speak for themselves.

II

The first stop was Pressburg, where Liszt had first played as a child of nine. He travelled overnight from Vienna, arriving in this ancient capital, the seat of the Hungarian Diet, at five o'clock in the morning on December 18, and stayed for a few days as the guest of Count Batthyány. His first matinee concert was fixed for the following day. It aroused so much interest that the Palatine of Hungary was forced to postpone a reception he was giving in order to allow the Magnates to go and hear Liszt instead. "Enthusiasm impossible to describe," wrote Liszt after the concert.[4] Since the applause showed no sign of diminishing, Liszt returned to the piano and played his arrangement of the *Rákóczy* March, a melody which was banned by the Austrians because of its revolutionary associations. From the first bar, the performance was punctuated with cries of "Éljen! Éljen!" This spontaneous demonstration of patriotism, which was reported back to Vienna by the secret police, was only a prelude to more dramatic things to come.[5]

---

3. NML, pp. 90–91, for example.
4. ACLA, vol. 1, p. 336.
5. We have already seen that Liszt had played the *Rákóczy* March as a child (n. 43 on p. 87). This ancient melody was part of his musical autobiography. Yet Haraszti falsely asserts, "Towards the end

Liszt travelled in triumphant progress, from Pressburg to Pest, in the carriage of Count Casimir Esterházy. Three other carriages followed, carrying Baron Wenckheim, the two Counts Zichy, and Count Leo Festetics. Liszt described the procession as "une caravane aristocratique."[6] The party arrived in the Hungarian capital on Christmas Eve 1839. Liszt stayed as a guest in the home of Festetics, much to the annoyance of the Pest hotel-keepers, several of whom had made elaborate preparations to welcome him to the city. On his arrival, Liszt was serenaded by a small choir, and a military band played Hungarian airs in the courtyard below. Festetics then led Liszt onto the balcony to present him to the crowd. Liszt stood in the biting cold, like a general reviewing his troops, while the band played an overture. Returning to the drawing room, Liszt found that music desks had been set up, and the best amateurs in Pest now treated him to a performance of Beethoven's Septet. Then, exhausted after the long journey, Liszt retired for the night. The following day, Christmas Day, he wrote a letter several thousand words long describing to Marie d'Agoult all these events in great detail.[7]

In Pest talk was of nothing but Liszt. After his concerts were announced, hundreds of people travelled in from the provinces, some of which were four or five days distant, in order to hear him play. Print sellers were despatched to Vienna for engraved likenesses of their famous compatriot. Even the pastry-cooks excelled themselves by producing a new type of biscuit, in the shape of a grand piano, inscribed with the name "Liszt" in icing sugar.[8] At a banquet given in his honour, someone got up and proposed a subscription for his bust; in less than ten minutes 1,500 francs was raised. Liszt describes how these brilliant dinners lasted until the small hours of the morning, an unheard-of thing in a city where even the nobility were usually in bed by 10:00 p.m.

Among the politicians whom Liszt met was István Széchenyi. This legislative genius was even then in the midst of a struggle to bring to fruition his dream of building a great bridge across the Danube, thus uniting the twin cities of Buda and Pest, and creating a future Magyar capital in the very heart of Hungary. His scheme had encountered much opposition in the Hungarian Diet.

---

of 1839 Liszt was in Vienna, where he for the first time heard the 'Rákóczy' March which thrilled him to the marrow." ("Berlioz, Liszt and the 'Rákóczy' March," *Musical Quarterly*, April 1940.) It was Liszt's famous piano arrangement, incidentally, with its sequence of startling chords, that influenced Berlioz when he came to orchestrate the march for his *Damnation of Faust* during a visit to Pest some six years later. Liszt held back his own orchestration of the march out of deference to his colleague. In 1882, after Berlioz's death, Liszt wrote: ". . . one of my earlier transcriptions served as the chief basis for his harmonization, which differs strikingly from the rudimentary chords generally used by the Tzigane and other small orchestras when playing this march. Without the slightest vanity I am simply pointing out a fact which any musician can easily verify." (LLB, vol. 2, p. 336.)

6. ACLA, vol. 1, pp. 340–44.
7. Ibid.
8. PCM, p. 345.

Why build a bridge when Hungary did not even have proper roads? The nobles refused to pay for it. Széchenyi then forced through the legislature a law obliging nobles and peasants alike to submit to the paying of tolls. It was regarded as a major victory for the reform movement over feudalism. Széchenyi had many links with England, and he particularly admired the old Waterloo Bridge which spanned the Thames. He brought to Hungary the English engineer Adam Clark, who began work on the famous Budapest suspension "chainbridge" which still bears Széchenyi's name.[9] Liszt came to admire Széchenyi and other liberal politicians, such as Ferenc Deák and József Eötvös.[10] These were the men who, under Lajos Kossuth, were to lead Hungary in the Revolution of 1848, and eventually win for her a measure of freedom from Austria. The politicians, in turn, saw in Liszt an ambassador of Hungary, an international celebrity who could bring honour and prestige to the liberal causes they espoused.

III

It was in this nationalistic atmosphere that the question of bestowing on Liszt a Hungarian title was first broached, a topic which has already been dealt with elsewhere in this book.[11] Two points remain to be clarified here. First, Liszt neither sought nor expected a title of nobility. This was the idea of Count Festetics and his aristocratic friends, and it was politically motivated. Second, the strange notion that he might *actually* be descended from the Hungarian nobility had not yet entered Liszt's head. That thought was put there in 1839 by his Hungarian well-wishers and backed by a vigorous press campaign. The three newspapers principally involved were *Társalkodó, Buda-Pesti Rajzolatok,* and *Pesther Tageblatt.* They drummed up much popular support for Liszt in a series of articles published between December 17, 1839, and January 8, 1840. Liszt, they asserted, was of aristocratic descent anyway; it was therefore unnecessary to approach Vienna for a fresh title. They then published diplomas and other "original" documents in support of their claim. A favourite theory circulated by them was that Liszt was descended from the noble sixteenth-century Listhi family, an idea that was quite bogus. Liszt may well have been sceptical about what he read in the press concerning his "nobility," but he lacked the means to disprove it. The truth about his family background existed

9. BSS, pp. 275–77. The bridge was opened in 1849.
10. An interesting product of Liszt's old age was his set of seven *Hungarian Historical Portraits*. Three of these portraits commemorate Széchenyi, Deák, and Eötvös. As if to symbolize their political unity, all three movements are thematically linked. The other four pieces bear the names of the poets Petöfi and Vörösmarty, the composer Mosonyi, and László Teleki, the politician.
11. See pp. 30–33.

only in the church and parish registers scattered throughout western Hungary, and those registers remained unknown to scholars until modern times. Today, however, it is still a commonplace of the Liszt literature that Liszt was brought up to believe in his aristocratic descent from childhood.[12]

Liszt first disclosed that he was about to be offered a title by the Hungarians in a letter to Marie d'Agoult, written in Pressburg on December 19, 1839.[13] He described the affair as "an eight-day wonder," which tells us all we need to know about what he really thought of their offer. Nonetheless, he was unsure how successfully Festetics might press the case, and he had to be prepared. He asked Marie for help in designing a suitable coat of arms.

Pressburg, December 19, 1839

It is probable that, within a month, I shall be given a title by the Hungarian Diet. As it is a national thing that I neither sought, nor asked for, nor coveted in any way, I confess that it will please me. I didn't want to mention it to you until the matter had been decided. But there is a little difficulty, which isn't one at all, really. If I am given letters of nobility, I must also be given a coat of arms. Now I'd like you to design some arms for me. Up to now Festetics has found only the owl admissible, since the lyre, harp, and scroll would be absurd. But we should need something to go with the owl, and something significant.

Try to work something out and write and tell me about it immediately.

Within three days of Liszt's having written this letter, Festetics had submitted a formal petition to King Ferdinand V in Schönbrunn. Ferdinand was in no hurry to reply to such a strange request. Six months elapsed before he rejected the petition, on June 20, 1840. By then Liszt was in London, his life had taken a new direction, and he had lost interest in the issue.

I V

The climax of Liszt's return to his native land occurred on January 4, 1840. On that evening Liszt gave a historic recital in the old Hungarian National Theatre, at the close of which he was presented with the famous "Sword of Honour"

---

12. See NFL (1855), where the seeds of this false information were first implanted, and compare with RLKM, vol. 1, p. 4; SL, p. 5; and LAFB, p. 1ff., among many others, where the legend took root and flourished.

13. ACLA, vol. 1, p. 331.

by a group of Hungarian noblemen. This symbolic event has been consistently misrepresented in the Liszt literature. It became the source of so many later misunderstandings, and Liszt himself became the butt of so many jokes, even among his biographers, that the occasion merits the fullest examination. There is, in fact, a wealth of testimony which enables us to re-create an accurate picture of the event and weigh its significance. Two of the most reliable witnesses, both of them sitting in the audience that night, were Franz von Schober and the English writer Julia Pardoe, who happened to be on a visit to Pest collecting material for her book *The City of the Magyar* at the very time of Liszt's visit. Each left a separate description of the recital, and of the presentation ceremony itself, and the following account is based largely on what they saw and heard.[14]

The Hungarian National Theatre, for whose benefit Liszt gave the concert, was brilliantly lighted and packed to capacity. So dense was the audience that it overflowed onto the wings of the stage, and the back of the theatre had to be converted into boxes. Crowds milled outside the building for hours in the bitter winter cold in the vain expectation of procuring even standing room. Liszt then walked onto the platform wearing Hungarian national costume. As the tumultuous applause died down Liszt seated himself at the piano and commenced his advertised programme, which included his paraphrase on Donizetti's *Lucia di Lammermoor* and his own *Grand Galop chromatique*. Since the tumult which followed his performance showed no signs of diminishing, Liszt returned to the piano and struck up his arrangement of the *Rákóczy March*. The furor was "almost enough to have awakened the dead." At the height of the demonstration, with Liszt still standing by the piano, a group of six high-ranking Hungarians, all dressed in glittering national costume, walked onto the stage and advanced towards him. They were led by Count Leo Festetics bearing a jewel-encrusted sabre.[15] The blade bore the following inscription:

> To the great artist Ferenc Liszt,
> for his artistic merit and
> for his patriotism, from his
> admiring compatriots.

---

14. PCM, pp. 349–55; SB, pp. 36–45. One of the most trustworthy accounts of Liszt's stay in Hungary, and the events leading up to it, will be found in "Liszt Ferenc magyarországi hangversenyei, 1839–40" (Franz Liszt's Concerts in Hungary, 1839–40), by Zsuzsa Dömötör and Mária Kovács (LT, pp. 9–75). The authors base their account on the newspapers, diaries, and letters of the day.

15. The others were Count Domokos Teleki, Pál Nyáry (chief notary of Pest County and director of the Hungarian National Theatre), Baron Pál Bánffy, Antal Augusz (chief notary of Tolna County), and Rudolf Eckstein (sheriff of Pest County).

Count Festetics then drew the sword from its case, delivered a speech in which he addressed Liszt as a patriot, and presented the pianist with this priceless token of his nation's esteem and affection. The vast audience was turned to stone by these proceedings, and in the total stillness which prevailed throughout the theatre, every word of Festetics's address was clearly heard. "It was probably the most perfect drama ever enacted on that stage."[16] Liszt appears to have been unprepared for so magnificent a gift. There was a pause while he collected his thoughts. Then his strong emotions got the better of him, and he wept openly on the stage, holding his face in both hands, the tears streaming through his fingers, while the audience looked on in painful silence. Liszt then rallied, accepted the sword, and delivered the following speech, in French.

> My dear compatriots! (for it is not possible for me to see here merely a public). The sabre that is offered to me by the representatives of a nation whose bravery and chivalry are so universally admired I shall keep all my life, as the most precious and dearest thing to my heart.
>
> To express in words, at this very moment when the strongest emotion weighs on my breast, how deeply touched and grateful I am for this token of your sympathetic esteem and warm affection, that, in truth, I cannot do. Forgive my silence on this point, therefore, and believe that I shall make every effort to prove to you (and soon, I hope) all my gratitude by deeds and actions, such as behooves a man who prides himself on having been born among you.
>
> Allow me, nevertheless, to say a few words this very day.
>
> This sabre, which has been so vigorously brandished in former times in the defence of our country,[17] is placed at this moment in weak and pacific hands. Is that not a symbol? Does it not seem to say, gentlemen, that Hungary, after having covered herself with glory on so many fields of battle, today asks the arts, literature, and science, those friends of peace, for new illustriousness? Does it not say, gentlemen, that men of intelligence and industry have also a noble task, a high mission to fulfil among you?
>
> Hungary, gentlemen, must not remain a stranger to any glory. She is destined to march at the head of the nations, by her heroism as by her genius in peaceful pursuits.

---

16. PCM, p. 350.

17. Here Liszt was mistaken. The sword was made in 1839, and had never been used in battle. Nor had it ever belonged to Stephen Báthory, a romantic idea fostered by Julia Pardoe (PCM, p. 350) which later found its way into the literature.

And for us artists, this sword is also a noble image, a shining symbol.

Precious stones, rubies, diamonds, adorn the scabbard; but they are merely accessories, brilliant futilities.

The blade lies within. Thus let there always be in our works, under the countless capricious forms with which our thought invests itself—as the blade in this scabbard—that love of humanity and of country which is our very life.

Yes, gentlemen, let us pursue by every legitimate and peaceful means the work for which we must all strive, each according to his strength and his means.

And if ever anyone dares unjustly, and with violence, disturb us in the accomplishment of this task, well! gentlemen, if it must be, let our swords be drawn again from the scabbard (they are not tarnished, and their strokes will still be terrible as in former times) and let our blood be shed to the last drop for freedom, king, and country.[18]

In view of the strained political relations then obtaining between Pest and Vienna, Liszt's demand that blood be spilled "for freedom, king, and country" amounted almost to insurrection, and the wonder is that he was not arrested on the spot.

Antal Augusz and Pardoe wrote down the speech as Liszt delivered it. Augusz at once translated it into Hungarian and read it from the platform for the benefit of that large section of the audience who did not understand French.[19] The demonstration of enthusiasm prompted by these sentiments was now impossible to quell. As Liszt left the theatre, the audience streamed out into the street, where it swelled the crowd still waiting in the freezing cold outside. Liszt and Festetics were forced to descend from their carriage and march at the head of a torchlight procession of five thousand people, complete with a band, back to the Festetics residence about a mile away.[20]

This scene could only have taken place in Hungary. In London it would have provoked mirth, in Paris sarcasm. Only in Hungary was it absolutely right. It was a genuine manifestation of a country's pride in one of its greatest sons.

---

18. SB, pp. 40–43.
19. Augusz later published the speech in Hungarian in *Századunk* (Pressburg), vol. 3, Jan. 16, 1840. It was also published that same year in English by Julia Pardoe (PCM, pp. 351–53). Three years later it was issued by Franz Ritter von Schober in its original French (SB, pp. 40–43), from which the present translation was made.
20. The old Hungarian National Theatre, where these events took place, was demolished in 1913. It occupied the site on the corner of Rákóczi and Múzeum streets.

V

None of this was understood beyond Hungary's borders. The press of Europe broke into a peal of laughter whose echoes were to mock Liszt to the grave. Cartoons appeared depicting him as a "piano hussar," decked out in full Magyar regalia, wearing his sword at the piano in a variety of more or less ridiculous postures. The Paris newspapers were the worst. They published some biting personal attacks on him, predictable enough in a country that had twice overthrown its own monarchy and was well on its way to becoming the most egalitarian society in the world, but still offensive to Liszt, coming as they did from his adoptive city. The following well-known quatrain was typical of the lampoons of the time.

> Entre tous les guerriers, Litz est seul sans reproches,
> Car malgré son grand sabre, on sait que ce héros
> N'a vaincu que des doubles croches,
> Et tué que des pianos.[21]

Attacks were also made in the columns of the professional journals. In October 1840, for example, *La Revue des Deux Mondes* ridiculed the sabre, likening its presentation to the bouquets carelessly tossed at the feet of ballerinas. Liszt felt that Hungary had been insulted and addressed a reply to this journal. His letter puts the case so well that it need not be embellished.

Hamburg, October 26, 1840

Sir,

In your musical review for October my name was mixed up with the outrageous pretensions and exaggerated success of some executant artists; I take the liberty to address a few remarks to you on this subject.

The wreaths thrown at the feet of Mlles Elssler and Pixis by the amateurs of New York and Palermo are striking manifestations of the enthusiasm of a *public;* the sabre which was given to

---

21. Liszt alone among all warriors is without reproach,
 For despite his big sword, we know that this hero
 Has vanquished only semiquavers,
 And slain only pianos.

These satirical lines were penned by A. J. Lorentz and were first published in the *Miroir Drolatique* (July 8, 1842). They accompanied a cartoon of "Litz" in full Hungarian regalia, bestriding a charger, with his sabre absent-mindedly buckled to his right side—that is, the wrong side for fighting.

me at Pest is a reward given by a *nation* in an entirely national form.

In Hungary, sir, in that country of antique and chivalrous manners, the sabre has a patriotic significance. It is the special token of manhood; it is the weapon of every man who has a right to carry a weapon. When six of the chief men of note in my country presented me with it among the general acclamations of my compatriots, whilst at the same moment the towns of Pest and Oedenburg conferred upon me the freedom of the city, and the civic authorities of Pest asked His Majesty for letters of nobility for me, it was an act to acknowledge me afresh as a Hungarian, after an absence of fifteen years; it was a reward of some slight services rendered to Art in my country; it was especially, and so I felt it, to unite me gloriously to her by imposing on me serious duties, and obligations for life as man and as artist.

I agree with you, sir, that it was, without doubt, going far beyond my deserts up to the present time. Therefore I saw in that solemnity the expression of a hope far more than of a satisfaction. Hungary hailed in me the man *from whom she expects* artistic illustriousness, after all the illustrious soldiers and politicians she has so plentifully produced. As a child I received from my country precious tokens of interest, and the means of going abroad to develop my artistic vocation. When grown up, and after long years, the young man returns to bring her the fruits of his work and the future of his will, the enthusiasm of the hearts which open to receive him and the expression of a national joy must not be confounded with the frantic demonstrations of an audience of amateurs.

In placing these two things side by side it seems to me there is something which must wound a just national pride and sympathies by which I am honoured.

Be so kind as to insert these few lines in your next issue, and believe me, sir,

Yours obediently,

FRANZ LISZT[22]

Liszt also wrote to his friend Franz Ritter von Schober to try to enlist his help in clearing up the distorted newspaper stories. Schober, who was an eye-witness,

---

22. This letter was translated into Hungarian and published in the magazine *Regélö* on January 3, 1841. By then it had already drawn a sarcastic rejoinder from the editor of *La Revue des Deux Mondes* (November 5, 1840), who stooped to a personal attack and sneeringly observed that Liszt's Hungarian nationality was clear to everybody from the style of his French prose.

later did so in the form of his *Briefe über F. Liszt's Aufenthalt in Ungarn,*[23] although it did not appear until 1843.

It has to be observed here, especially in view of the direction in which the posthumous Liszt literature unfolded, that not only the newspapers but also some of his biographers started to believe the myth they had created. It became mandatory to call Liszt at this juncture of his life an actor, a poseur, a vulgar charlatan, even. How sincerely the myth was held to be true was borne out in 1933 when the Liszt-d'Agoult *Correspondance* was published for the first time. It contains a number of very long letters by Liszt which tell Marie about his stay in Hungary in the greatest detail and which were, of course, written under the immediate impact of the events themselves. They describe the honours showered on him, the adulation of the crowds, the homage paid him by titled aristocrats, the large fees earned, and the sum of money (a thousand francs) he had to pay for the privilege of decking himself out in Magyar costume. When the *Correspondance* appeared, these letters were at once held up as proof positive of the pianist's love of the limelight, a supreme example of his egotism and his insufferable conceit.[24] And yet, when we examine them and compare what he wrote with the impartial testimony of those who were close to the events, Liszt's descriptions seem like a model of restraint. We remarked that there were two eye-witness accounts of the "Sword of Honour" ceremony. There were, of course, three. The third came from Liszt himself. Here is what he wrote to Marie d'Agoult the evening after the sword had been presented to him.

Pest, Midnight
Tuesday, January 6, 1840

> I spoke to you of a splendid day. This word is not exaggerated. I will not write to anybody about it, and to you yourself I will write very badly about it, because these things cannot be written about. On January 4 I played in the Hungarian Theatre the Andante from

---

23. SB. The first hint that Liszt was going to have trouble with the French press came in a letter from Marie d'Agoult on January 28, 1840 (ACLA, vol. 1, p. 369). She told Liszt that she had already sent details of the presentation ceremony to Berlioz, in the reasonable expectation that he might write an article on the topic for the *Gazette Musicale.* The plan misfired. An unsigned article meanwhile appeared in the *Gazette* (January 26) which said sarcastically that the sword made "a flattering present, but a very strange one for a man of peace." The next day, January 29, Marie wrote a second letter (ACLA, vol. 1, p. 369), in which she reported that another article had appeared, in *Le Journal des Débats,* adding ominously that the details diverged widely from the ones she had sent to Berlioz, but that they were excellent for the general public. The anonymous author had bestowed the title "Monsieur *de* Liszt" on the pianist. There was now a landslide, with journals merely quoting from each other, culminating in the October issue of *La Revue des Deux Mondes* in which the sword was likened to a bunch of flowers. It was in this context that Liszt wrote to the editor of the *Deux Mondes* and later to Franz von Schober.

24. NML, pp. 90–91.

La Lucia, the *Galop,* and, as they would not stop applauding, the *Rákóczy* March (a kind of aristocratic Hungarian *Marseillaise*). Just as I was about to leave the platform, in came Count Leo Festetics, Baron Bánffy, Count Teleki (all Magnates), Eckstein, Augusz, and a sixth whose name I forget—all in full Hungarian costume, Festetics carrying a magnificent sabre (worth 80 to 100 louis) adorned with turquoises, rubies, etc., in his hand. He addressed a little speech to me in Hungarian before the whole audience, who applauded frantically, and then he buckled the sword on me in the name of the nation. I asked permission, through Augusz, to speak to the audience in French. In a grave and firm voice, I delivered the speech that I shall send you tomorrow, printed. It was punctuated several times by applause. Thereupon, Augusz advanced and read the same speech in Hungarian.

You cannot imagine the seriousness, the grave and profound impression of this scene, which, anywhere else, would have been ridiculous, and which could easily have become so here, at least for a certain malicious minority that one finds everywhere, but for the "aplomb" and that "something" that I have when I speak, which animated and sustained the others.

It was magnificent. It was unique. But that wasn't all. When the ceremony was over, we got into our carriage, and there was an immense crowd filling the square, and two hundred young people, with lighted torches and the military band at their head, shouted, "Éljen! Éljen! Éljen!"

And notice what admirable tact. We had scarcely gone 50 yards when a score of young people rushed forward to unharness our horse. "No! No!" shouted the others, "that's been done for wretched dancers, for Elssler, but for this one we must celebrate differently!" Isn't that remarkable!

The house of Festetics, where I am staying, is quite a distance from the Hungarian Theatre. When we were about a third of the way, I said to Festetics, "I can't stand it any longer, let's get out. Let's not act the aristocrats in your carriage." I opened the door, and the shouts, which had not ceased for ten minutes, redoubled with a sort of fury. They immediately drew back, and we all three walked— Festetics, Augusz, and I in the middle in Hungarian costume (mine, by the way, cost me a thousand francs, and it is only very simple: it was a necessary expense).

Impossible to give you an idea of the enthusiasm, the respect, and the love of this population! At eleven o'clock in the evening

all the streets were full. At Pest, everyone, and even the most elegant society, goes to bed at ten o'clock, except perhaps five or six
people.

The shouts did not cease. It was a triumphal march such as
Lafayette and a few men of the revolution have experienced.

At a street turning I asked Augusz, who has a great habit of
speaking in public (he is protonotary of an extremely active committee) to address those young people; and he acquitted himself admirably. I had given him for a theme "that I could in no wise have
deserved, nor do I deserve now, the reception that they were giving
me in my country. But I accepted this more than flattering reception
as imposing on me new duties to fulfil, etc. . . . !"

At the first words, they replied by the most formal, the most
unanimous, the most noisy denial. . . . Yes, you do, they all shouted.
You deserve it, and much more still.

It's wonderful, isn't it?

The military band stopped at the door of my house, but thirty-
odd young people conducted me with their torches to the entrance
of my apartment. It was nearly half-past eleven. The military band
played a few more pieces. I was called back twice, and at last
Festetics harangued them from the balcony to dismiss them. I was
exhausted.

It is half-past one in the morning. My head is burning, my heart
full of sadness and love.

Wherever you are, whatever you are doing, whatever you are
dreaming of, I am yours alone.[25]

It is instructive to compare this letter with the independent accounts later
published by Augusz and Julia Pardoe. Liszt's letter was written within twenty-
four hours of the events it so strikingly portrays. It was meant for Marie's eyes
alone. He could not possibly have known that his letter would one day be
published for all the world to see, be read out of context, and held up to ridicule
for its artistic arrogance. His critics, presumably, would have preferred him to
keep silent, or modestly to underplay, the remarkable events now shaping his
life. They would not dream of imposing similar constraints on the other great
artistic personalities of the century. Here was a young man of twenty-eight,
and the world was at his feet. Nothing could be more natural than to want to
share his reception with the woman who was still the dearest person in the
world to him. Only in comparatively modern times has it become possible to

---

25. ACLA, vol. 1, pp. 351–52.

examine the letter in the light of contemporary evidence. Not one word is an exaggeration; every sentence can be objectively confirmed. Liszt is not being sensational; he is merely reporting sensational events.[26]

VI

Liszt stayed in Pest for a further ten days. On January 11 he gave another concert in the National Theatre to raise funds for the foundation of a newly proposed National Conservatory of Music, the idea for which was just then starting to gather momentum and was about to be debated for the first time in the Hungarian Diet. Liszt made his début at this concert in the unfamiliar role of conductor (one which was to assume increasing interest for him as the years passed). The main work was Beethoven's Choral Fantasy, and the concert raised the large sum of 12,000 francs.[27] A magnificent ball was afterwards held in Liszt's honour by the ladies of Pest, followed by a banquet attended by two hundred people. He met the poet Vörösmarty, who later wrote his famous "Ode to Franz Liszt," a ringing tribute which has become part of Hungary's literary heritage and is still taught to Magyar schoolchildren. Liszt rounded off his visit to Pest by hosting a farewell supper-party to which he invited some of the "richest and most elegant people" in the city, including members of the Wenckheim, Szapáry, and Zichy families. The supper lasted until 2:30 in the morning, and the guests were serenaded by a small chorus from the National Theatre.[28]

In the midst of his triumphs Liszt did not forget the Franciscan monks whom he had last seen in 1823 as a boy of eleven in the company of his father. He slipped quietly away in order to visit them in their monastery in Pest and revive the memories of his youth. Adam's old friend and fellow novice at Tyrnavia,

---

26. The subsequent history of the "sword of honour" is soon told. It was sent first to Paris (ACLA, vol. 1, p. 397) and stored with all the other treasures Liszt had collected on his tours—including Beethoven's death mask and his Broadwood piano of 1817. After 1848 it was sent on to Weimar and kept at the Altenburg. Liszt included the sword in his will (1860) and bequeathed it, together with other objets d'art, to Princess von Sayn-Wittgenstein. In 1874, rather against the wishes of the princess, Liszt gave the sword, and several other valuable relics, to the Hungarian National Museum, Budapest. The correspondence confirming his bequest was published in GLMM, pp. 121–25. Today the sword is permanently exhibited in the National Museum.

27. A copy of this rare programme is reproduced in LT, p. 55. It reveals that Liszt also conducted performances of the overtures to Mozart's *Zauberflöte* and Weber's *Oberon*. Thanks to Liszt's generous initiative, the National Conservatory opened its doors five years later, in 1845. It played an important role in Hungary's musical life until modern times. (The Liszt Academy of Music, incidentally, which is world renowned for the training of its performers, was not founded until 1875—again with generous support from Liszt.) There was a disturbing discrepancy between the sum Liszt raised and the sum actually handed over to the organizing committee. Liszt suspected that he might have been swindled by his Pest impresario, Joseph Wagner. (PBUS, p. 49.)

28. ACLA, vol. 1, p. 356.

Capistran Wagner, was still the father superior. It was a moving reunion, and Liszt spent an entire evening in the company of this priest who had made such a powerful impression on him during his childhood. We learn about the episode from the Hungarian Journal *Társalkodó*. [29] Liszt, who remembered all the monks by name, became sombre as Capistran reminisced about his dead father; "the name of him who was decaying in the grave had touched his soul." Liszt took an emotional farewell of the monks, and they gathered round to wish him Godspeed and to urge him not to delay returning to his homeland.

V I I

Liszt left Pest at the end of January 1840, and travelled back to Vienna via Pressburg. His journey took him through western Hungary, the land of his childhood, and stirred his early memories. After spending two weeks in Vienna he arrived in Oedenburg, the capital city of Sopron County, where his father had first presented him to the public as a nine-year-old prodigy. On February 18 he gave a recital for the poor in the Great Casino. A rare copy of this programme has survived. [30]

Fantasy on Motifs from *I puritani*	BELLINI–LISZT
"Ständchen"	SCHUBERT–LISZT
"Erlkönig"	
Hungarian Melody and March	transc. LISZT

A few days later, a public banquet was arranged in his honour, and the freedom of the city of Oedenburg was bestowed on him. His native village of Raiding lay less than 12 miles away, and the temptation to make a pilgrimage to his birthplace proved irresistible. As he travelled towards Raiding, in the company of his friends Schober and Count Alberti, he recognized every village and church steeple along the route, and even recalled the names of individual houses. About two miles outside Raiding he was met by a group of peasants on horseback, gaily attired, who escorted his carriage to the home of the local judge. The entire population of Raiding—about a thousand people altogether —turned out to greet Liszt. [31] A crowd of well-wishers accompanied him to the old whitewashed house in which he was born. It was now the home of a gamekeeper. Liszt had last seen this humble cottage eighteen years earlier, as

---

29. January 1840, p. 22. The author of the report was a Franciscan monk called Kilit Gasparich. He was a gifted orator and Hungarian patriot. During the 1848 Revolution he served as an officer, was later persecuted, and in 1853 was hanged by the Austrians.
30. In the City Museum of Sopron.
31. ACLA, vol. I, p. 391. Also SB, pp. 57–58.

a child of ten, when he had set out for Vienna to begin his studies with Czerny. The wooden fence was still there; so were the orchard and the primitive well in which Anna had nearly lost her life. Inside the house, nothing had changed. Schober tells us that even the furniture was the same.[32] Liszt recognized Adam's old piano, and remarked that the same pictures of Haydn and Beethoven were still hanging on the wall. He then walked along the narrow path to the tiny village church where he had worshipped as a boy, and attended mass. The church was filled to overflowing. Afterwards he returned to the home of the judge, where a meal had been prepared. Although it was freezing outside and there was snow on the ground, open-air dancing and merrymaking followed. Liszt called it "a ball in the snow."[33] Among the people he met that day was his old schoolmaster Johann Rohrer, who still ran the village school. Rohrer delivered a moving speech, and afterwards gave the manuscript to Liszt as a souvenir.[34] Before going back to Oedenburg, Liszt settled a sum of money on Rohrer and left a hundred ducats for the repair of the church organ and for the poor of Raiding.[35]

Liszt made two other nostalgic trips at this time. The first was to Eisenstadt, where he saw again the Bergkirche where his father had once played under Haydn. The other trip was to the village of Pottendorf, where his eighty-five-year-old grandfather Georg Liszt still conducted the church choir.

VIII

An important highlight of this first return to Hungary was Liszt's renewed contact with the Gypsies and their music. Ever since his childhood this dark, nomadic race had held him in thrall. The memory of the Gypsy bands, and particularly of the violinist Bihari, was ineradicable. It was entirely in keeping with the spirit of this return to his native land that Liszt should now seek out a Gypsy encampment and relive these early experiences.

Liszt has left a graphic description of this visit.[36] The Gypsies had pitched their tents in the middle of a colonnade of ash trees. Liszt was led to a pile of fur skins out of which a kind of seat-of-honour had been built for him. The men warmed themselves by the fire, eating meat and honey. They resembled

32. SB, p. 58.
33. ACLA, vol. 1, p. 391.
34. RGS, vol. 6, p. 140.
35. *Társalkodó*, vol. 3, no. 25 (1840). The modest two-manual organ was retrieved when the Raiding church was rebuilt in 1924. It is now exhibited in the Geburtshaus.
36. RGS, vol. 6, pp. 135–37.

one another like the sons of one mother. The women were dancing, crashing their tambourines and uttering little cries of mimicry as they swayed back and forth. Metal rings and coins dangled from every finger and glinted in the firelight. The brandy started to flow, and the dance became ever more animated. In the background could be heard the squeaking of badly greased axles as the wagons were pushed back to make more room for the dancers. Added to this were the wild cries of the youngsters, who turned somersaults, cut capers, and fought frantically over a bag of nuts, the ownership of which was in dispute. They uttered frantic shouts in the Romany tongue, translated for Liszt as "Éljen! Liszt Ferenc!" Squatting by the fire were some shrewish old women with hair erect, inflamed eyes, distended nostrils, and toothless jaws, adding further colour to the scene. Liszt continues:

> After examining some horses which had recently been given them, the men put on a heavenly smile, showing off to advantage their teeth, which were as white as snow. After that they started imitating castanets by cracking the joints of their fingers, which are always long and charged with electricity. They began throwing their caps into the air, following this by strutting about like peacocks. Then they examined the animals again. Suddenly, as if inspired by a gratitude which they had all the while been trying to express, and the true manifestation of which had only just occurred to them, they had recourse to a nobler medium. Flying to their violins and cymbals, they began a real fury of excitement. The *friska* was not long in rising to a frenzy of exultation, and then almost to delirium. In its final stage it could only be compared to that vertiginous and convulsive writhing motion which is the culmination point in the Dervish ecstasy.[37]

Liszt's special interest in the Gypsies now had an important creative consequence. In 1840 he produced a series of pieces called Magyar Dallok ("Hungarian National Melodies") based on material he heard the Gypsies play. They were later revised and published under the generic title Hungarian Rhapsodies (1851–53). The inspiration of the Gypsy bands, with their colourful improvisatory effects—now languishing, now wild and orgiastic—is omnipresent. The rhapsodies, in fact, preserve the two main elements which make up the "struc-

---

37. RGS, vol. 6, p. 137. No one who reads such passages will be left in any doubt about the hypnotic hold that Gypsy music had on Liszt. He once wrote to Edmund Singer, "This sort of music is, for me, a kind of opium, of which I am sometimes in great need." (LLB, vol. 1, p. 205.) He wrote to Princess von Sayn-Wittgenstein in a similar vein: "You know what a special attraction this music exerts over me." (LLB, vol. 4, p. 316.)

ture" of a typical Gypsy improvisation: the *lassan* ("slow") and the *friska* ("fast"). At the same time, they incorporate a number of special effects unique to the "sonic surface" of the Gypsy band. Chief among them is the sound of the cimbalom, which can be heard shimmering at the opening of the Eleventh Rhapsody.

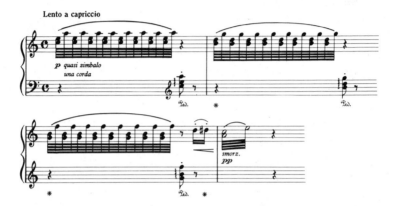

The "Gypsy scale" is also much in evidence, with its mournful augmented fourths. Perhaps the most heart-wrenching examples are to be found on the first two pages of the Thirteenth Rhapsody.

The Fourteenth Rhapsody quotes a Hungarian popular song "Magasan repül a darú, szépen szól" (as it was played to Liszt by Gypsies), in the form of a majestic funeral lament for a dead hero, with muffled drums in the background.

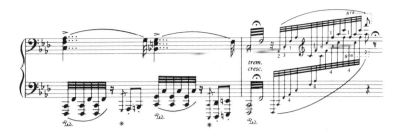

This particular rhapsody has a very effective *friska,* marked by Liszt "à la zingarese"—"in the Gypsy style."

Liszt has told us that as he transcribed and arranged all this material it dawned on him that he was not really dealing with separate pieces at all, but with a single, epic work. Here is how he described it.

> After I had submitted a fair number of these pieces to the process of transcription it began to dawn on me that I should never finish. . . . A mountain of material was before me. I had to compare, select, eliminate, elucidate. I gradually acquired the conviction that in reality these detached pieces were parts of one great whole—parts disseminated, scattered, and broken up, but lending themselves to the construction of one harmonious ensemble. . . . Such a compendium might fairly be regarded as a National Epic—a Bohemian Epic— and the strange tongue in which its strains would be delivered would be no stranger than everything else done by the people from whom it emanated.[38]

---

38. RGS, vol. 6, pp. 388–89.

Such a concept cannot fail to interest both scholars and performers. For what Liszt here implies is that the whole is greater than the sum of the parts; that the spirit of an individual rhapsody will not be grasped until that of the entire collection is grasped; that because each and every rhapsody is simply a facet of the whole, broken off and offered for separate scrutiny, so to speak, it needs must throw light on that whole. And we note once more Liszt's flair for descriptive titles. The term "rhapsody" was absolutely right for such pieces. Liszt recalled that the ancient Greek orator was called a *rhapsode,* and in his "rhapsody of words" he enshrined the history and the epic deeds of his people. By setting himself up as a national bard, however, Liszt, as we shall shortly discover, demonstrated that he misunderstood the nature of Gypsy music, and he subsequently created grave problems for himself among the Magyars.

From the start, Liszt was worried about the way the rhapsodies might be received by "cultivated" musicians, and later events were to justify this fear. It was not the first time in history that a great composer had descended to the "ethnic" level in search of material, but it had never before been attempted on such a bold scale, and never in connection with the Gypsies. Liszt therefore decided to "explain" the rhapsodies to the world by publishing an introduction to them. But it grew to such massive proportions that the first fifteen rhapsodies were already in print before the "introduction" appeared, in 1859, almost twenty years after his first return to Hungary, in the form of the two-volume *Des Bohémiens et leur musique en Hongrie.* Though this book is a pioneer work, it is, alas, defective from both the ethnomusicological and the anthropological standpoints (as any such book was bound to be, written as it was in the 1850s, without the benefit of modern techniques of scientific inquiry). But it is so rich in autobiographical asides, and so densely packed with first-hand accounts, that it remains an indispensable guide.[39]

Liszt's interest in Gypsy music cannot be explained on artistic grounds alone. He was drawn to the Gypsy race—to its origins, its migration patterns, its folklore, its contribution to Western culture; his interest in its music was a symptom of this absorption. Liszt admired the independence of the Zigeuner, who had survived unimaginable persecutions across the centuries, had been driven out of practically every "civilized" country in Europe—save Hungary, where the Gypsies have always been tolerated—and yet somehow managed to preserve his cultural identity intact. Liszt marvelled at the musicality of the Zigeuner, whose intuitive grasp of the art called for an explanation. Here was a nomad, with a history stretching back into antiquity, who actively shunned

---

39. The two Hungarian "experts" whom Liszt consulted in the writing of this book during the 1850s were Gábor Mátray (1797–1875) and István Fáy (1809–62). It is impossible to know, at this late stage, just how much false information they fed him, but neither Csermák nor Lavotta was a Gypsy violinist, although Liszt implied that they were.

all formal education. Yet, without the benefit of conservatory teaching, music sprang up spontaneously within him and gushed forth like a fountain. The typical Zigeuner could not even read music notation, yet his repertoire was all-embracing. He seemed to possess total musical recall. And in the art of improvisation he had no peer. It was not simply that he made up music as he went along. What excited Liszt was that ten or more players made it up, each one in telepathic communication with all the others, and they would steer their joint improvisation, with somnambulistic certainty, towards its goal. The Zigeuner transformed everything he touched, and his melodies were decorated with exotic ornamentation. Through music he expressed all his joys and sorrows. His violin was an instrument of mourning and of jubilation. It was the proud boast of the Zigeuner violinist that he could match his performance to any mood, and to that end he would approach his listener, look him straight in the eyes, and try to drain the emotion from him by osmosis.[40] A perfect embodiment of this notion was found in the Gypsy violinist Patikárus. His name, which means "chemist," was bestowed on him for curing, through his violin playing, a Hungarian nobleman of melancholia.[41]

It is easy to see the attraction in all this for Liszt. It confirmed his own view of music as a natural force, a universal language of the soul. The Gypsy proved conclusively that music was innate, like eating and breathing, and that it was not "put there" by civilizing influences. Liszt's attraction to this idea was so firm that it had an amusing outcome. One day, while still in Hungary, he was speculating aloud on the challenge of attempting to give a formal education to a Gypsy musician. His words, uttered casually, were taken seriously. Liszt has told us how Count Sándor Teleki later turned up in Paris saying, "Look, I've brought you a present!"[42] There stood "Josi" Sárai, a twelve-year-old Gypsy violinist dressed in Hungarian costume. Teleki had discovered Josi on his estates in Hungary and, recalling Liszt's words, had bought him from his Gypsy parents in order to give him to Liszt. The education of Josi (an attempt to civilize a savage) failed. True to his childish nature, he stole any object he fancied, broke any mechanism he did not understand. Liszt gave him money. He spent it all on a colourful wardrobe of waistcoats and cravats, and on the latest coiffure, in order to attract the eyes of the passing ladies. When Liszt left Paris on his Spanish tour in 1844 he placed Josi in the hands of the violinist Lambert Massart, who found him uncontrollable and unteachable.[43] Josi was

---

40. Even today this tradition is kept alive by the *primás* of the Gypsy bands in the restaurants of Eastern Europe, who walk from table to table playing to the expression on their listeners' faces.

41. SC, p. 133.

42. RGS, vol. 6, p. 165.

43. It appears that Josi may for a time have been brought up with Liszt's own children, or at any rate may have been allowed by Massart to mix closely with them. Years later Cosima recalled that during her childhood in Paris the boy violinist "was always fiddling to us children." (WT, vol. 1, pp. 315–16.)

finally sent back to Hungary and reunited with his tribe. In the first edition of *Des Bohémiens* Liszt wondered what had become of him. To his delight, Josi replied with a letter. He was now playing in a Gypsy band in Debreczin, he told Liszt, and was happily married to a Gypsy woman. He had a son called Ferenc, named after Liszt, who had been made the child's godfather in absentia. Liszt was pleased by this remembrance and sent the little boy a miniature violin on which to continue the family tradition. To Josi, now a man of twenty-eight, he wrote:

> I could almost envy you for having escaped from the civilized art of music making, with its limitations and constrictions. . . . No prattle and jargon from pedants, cavillers, critics, and all the nameless brood of such can reach you; with your fiddle bow you raise yourself above everything miserable in the world and play away defiantly.
>
> You have done well, my dear Josi, not to engage in concert-room torture, and to disdain the empty, painful reputation of a *trained* violinist. As a Gypsy you remain lord of yourself, and are not reduced (as is now the case with civilized artists) to ask other people for forgiveness when you are only doing right.[44]

The case of Josi Sárai taught Liszt an important lesson. One of his chief concerns in *Des Bohémiens* was the harmful consequences of civilization on Gypsy culture. He lamented the fact that even in his day the process of corruption had already begun.

> Nowadays, Bohemian musicians, instead of the nomads they formerly were, have become commercial travellers. Instead of moving off with their tribe, folding their tent and lifting their cooking vessels into the dusty wagon, they go from one capital to another by railway, in order to carry on their business in European style. Ever since they began to smell a new musical atmosphere, causing art to become to them less of a joy and more of a trade, . . . they have devoted themselves to speculation and now seek a reputation in order to find money. Preoccupied with that mammon-worship, which is especially hideous when artists engage in it, they now forsake art for gain.[45]

The dispute which the Hungarian Rhapsodies subsequently engendered is now a matter of history. In his book *Des Bohémiens* Liszt made a gift of this

---

44. The correspondence between Liszt and Josi is not to be found in RGS, vol. 6. It was published only in the first German edition of Liszt's book, translated by Peter Cornelius (*Die Zigeuner und ihre Musik in Ungarn* [Pest, 1861], pp. 147–50).

45. RGS, vol. 6, p. 373.

epic work to the Gypsies, even though it contained Hungarian melodies, and by so doing caused offence in his native land. To the world at large it appeared that the Gypsies were the true representatives of Hungarian music, and the Hungarians violently objected.[46] Liszt subsequently became a victim of history. At the turn of the century Kodály and Bartók produced their monumental studies in Hungarian folk song. They demonstrated that the genuine folk music of Hungary originated in the remote Hungarian-speaking villages and hamlets of the hinterland, of Transylvania and Rumania, kept alive by an oral tradition stretching back hundreds of years, and that it had nothing whatever to do with the Gypsies. For a long time the rhapsodies fell into disrepute. It seemed that they were "corrupt," and musicologists wanted nothing to do with them. This was a foolish attitude: the value of music is inherent and has nothing to do with how close it remains to, or how far it departs from, an ethnomusicological standpoint. Moreover, as the discipline of ethnomusicology itself advanced, the scientific case against the rhapsodies started to collapse. For what Liszt in his book called Gypsy music turned out to be Hungarian music after all, albeit composed largely by members of the Hungarian upper middle classes and appropriated by the Gypsies for their own purposes.[47] As we now know, the Gypsies had no real creative tradition of their own. They took music wherever they found it and fashioned it in their own image. Liszt knew nothing of all this in 1840—the science of ethnomusicology did not yet exist—and it shows a lack of historical imagination to condemn him for not behaving like a twentieth-century scholar. Nor would it have made sense for him to abandon his infinitely more important activities as a pianist and disappear into the Hungarian hinterland, to re-emerge after several years with a folk-song collec-

---

46. The chief criticism came from Ritter von Adelburg, who, within weeks of the appearance of Liszt's book in 1859, published a polemic against it (AE). The journal *Hölgyfutár* (August 11) also published a critical article, by Simonffy. That same journal (September 15) then carried a correspondence between Liszt and Simonffy debating the issues. After two years of almost continuous public acrimony, the composer Mihály Mosonyi weighed in with two defending articles (*Zenészeti Lapok,* August 17 and October 17, 1861).

47. The identity of these composers has long been known; they include József Kossovits, Márk Rózsavölgyi, and Béni Egressy. A comprehensive table of the true sources of these melodies, improvised almost beyond recognition by the Gypsies and innocently transcribed by Liszt, was drawn up first by Ervin Major (MLMR) and completed by Zoltán Gárdonyi (GP).

It is worth observing that the Hungarian Dances of Brahms, quite illogically, have not suffered the same criticism as the rhapsodies of Liszt, even though Brahms, like Liszt, used "corrupt" material. Brahms was accused by the Hungarian bandmaster Béla Kéler of having published under his own name two Hungarian Dances composed by Kéler himself—nos. 5 and 6. In fact, Brahms's Fifth Hungarian Dance is based on Kéler's *csárdás Bártfai emlék.* Brahms defended himself by arguing that no greater compliment could be paid to a composer than to find his melodies being sung in remote country villages by the peasants; Brahms had simply taken Kéler's melodies for genuine folk songs. (KJB, vol. 1, pp. 64–68.) Ervin Major also provided a list of Brahms's "plagiarisms" in his article "Brahms és a magyar zene," *Fejezetek a magyar zene történetéből* (Budapest, 1933). See also Bartók's classical defence of Liszt in *Liszt a miénk!* (Budapest, 1936), pp. 55–67.

tion of unimpeachable authenticity. In 1840 such conduct would have been regarded as insane, even by the Hungarians themselves.[48] Happily, more musicians are today returning to the Hungarian Rhapsodies and, unencumbered by the scholarly dispute which has for so long surrounded them, are finding in these works a genuine source of musical pleasure and enjoyment.[49]

---

48. Nevertheless, Liszt had already come close to expressing some such wish when, as early as 1838, he wrote that he wanted "to explore the Hungarian hinterland alone, on foot, with a rucksack on my back." (RGS, vol. 2, p. 225; CPR, p. 235.)

49. This account of Liszt's complex relationship to Hungarian and Gypsy music is necessarily suspended here. The discussion will be resumed in Volume II, where Liszt's book *Des Bohémiens,* and the causes of its hostile reception in Hungary after 1859, will be considered in detail.

The World Tours I:
Prague, Leipzig, and London,
1840–1841

Le concert, c'est moi!

I

Liszt left Vienna at the beginning of March 1840 in order to continue his tours. The immediate plan was to visit three major cities where he had not yet been heard—Prague, Leipzig, and Dresden—and then to travel on to Paris, where he would be reunited with Marie d'Agoult and the children. News of his sensational appearances in Vienna and Pest had gone before him, and he was now awaited everywhere with mounting excitement.

Liszt's Prague concerts were surrounded by administrative confusion. The newspaper *Bohemia* reported on February 11, 1840, that Liszt would arrive in Prague on February 18 "in order at last to fulfil the long-cherished wish of many music-loving Czechs to make acquaintance with and admire his genius." The arrangements were handed over to one Jakub Fischer, who ran a music shop in the Carolinum, the heart of Old Prague, and who promptly doubled the price of all tickets. Public posters were plastered throughout the city, announcing Liszt's first concert for February 27. Unfortunately, Liszt did not arrive in Prague until March 3.[2] The posters then advertised his first concert—a matinee

---

1. LLB, vol. 1, p. 25.
2. We now understand why, although the Prague newspapers made no mention of it at the time. After leaving Vienna in mid-February, it will be recalled, Liszt had made an unscheduled detour to see his natal village and receive the freedom of the city of Oedenburg. On the very day on which he was supposed to be in Prague (February 18), Liszt was in Oedenburg giving a concert for the poor. This put back his itinerary by at least ten days, and he never did succeed in making up the lost time. His concerts in Leipzig and Dresden were also held later than expected.

—for March 5 in the Salle zum Platteis at half-past eleven. Early on the morning of the recital the time was abruptly changed to half-past twelve, and the long-suffering Jakub Fischer came out with more posters bearing the correction. The result was that most of the audience assembled a good two hours before Liszt walked onto the platform, the real enthusiasts having been in position since 9:00 a.m.

A report in *Bohemia* described the occasion as follows:

> Imagine a pale young man, with a striking and pleasant countenance, with long, smoothly dressed chestnut-brown hair, and with a bearing which does not betray, either in mimicry or gesture, artistic pride, but testifies to sincere modesty and kindliness, and you have a picture of Liszt's appearance before he sits down to the piano. Once he has struck the first chord, however, he forgets the concert hall and has neither awareness of, nor interest in, even his immediate surroundings. A deep earnestness comes over his features, and his fervour seems to grow in the breathless silence which his magic tones create around him. . . . When the last chords die away or boldly conclude the work, this outstanding genius suddenly steps out of the magic circle of his poetic vision and is delighted, like a good and modest companion, that the public has listened to him attentively and without interruption.[3]

Two singers from the Ständetheater, Katerina Podhorska and Karel Strakaty, also took part. Strakaty sang Schubert's "The Pilgrim," and he was accompanied at the piano by Liszt's pupil Hermann Cohen, who, having heard that Liszt was due to play in Prague, had travelled from Paris in six days to be with his master. (Cohen remained with Liszt for several weeks. He followed him to Dresden and Leipzig, where, as we shall presently discover, he became embroiled in a libel action and caused Liszt some embarrassment.) Two other concerts followed, on March 6 and March 7; the proceeds of the latter (2,218 francs, 40 kroner) were donated by Liszt to a local hospital and institute for the blind. The final concert was supposed to have been given on Monday, March 9, but two further concerts were hurriedly arranged to satisfy public demand.

Liszt developed a great liking for Prague and did some sight-seeing while he was there. He toured the old part of the city, built in medieval times, and visited the Loretto Church, where he rang the famous seventeenth-century carillon. A number of aristocratic families invited him into their homes, notably the family Schlick,[4] and he gave one or two private recitals. Among the musical

---

3. BLB, pp. 67–68.
4. It was in the home of Countess Eliza Schlick that Liszt heard a number of Hussite songs. Unwittingly, he took them to be genuine fifteenth-century melodies, as did many Czechs. He later

acquaintances Liszt made in Prague were Tomášek[5] and his pupil Johann Kittl (who later became director of the Prague Conservatory), Johann Hoffman the publisher, and Sigmund Goldberg the composer. All of them urged Liszt to return soon, and he promised to do so, although it was not until 1846 that the city would see him again. Before he left Prague the poet J. L. Horner composed an acrostic poem in his honour. It contains twenty lines, and the first letters of each line read downwards form the greeting "Lebe wohl an Franz Liszt."[6]

I I

After giving six concerts in eight days in Prague, Liszt journeyed to Dresden. A distinguished audience, which included several members of the royal family, had gathered for his opening concert on March 16. Sitting in the audience that night was Robert Schumann, who had travelled from Leipzig to cover the concert for the *Neue Zeitschrift für Musik*. His pieces on Liszt's concerts in Dresden and Leipzig are among the classics of nineteenth-century criticism. All eyes were turned expectantly towards the door through which Liszt would make his entrance, wrote Schumann. As Liszt walked to the piano there was a roar of acclaim.

> I had already heard him, but privately. It is one thing to hear an artist playing for a few friends, quite another to hear him before an audience. It is a different occasion—and a different artist. The beautiful bright rooms, illuminated by candlelight, the bejewelled and decorated audience, all stimulate the giver as well as the given. The

---

arranged one of them as a piano fantasy (R. 100). This melody had actually been composed by a local singer called Josef Krow. Because his song dealt with national sentiments, it was banned by Austria, so Krow had it published in Mainz under the pseudonym "Workowsky" (Work = Krow backwards). Copies were then smuggled back into Prague, and the tune was circulated anonymously.

5. Tomášek left an interesting account of his meeting with Liszt in *Ost und West* (1840). See BLB, pp. 76–77.

6. *L*iebend drücken DICH ans Herz die Musen,
*E*inen sich um DICH im trauten Kreis,
*B*leibe ihnen hold, wahr' sie im Busen,
*E*wig grünt DIR dann der Lorbeerreis.

*W*enn an DICH der Freigeist stellt die Bitte
O dann biet' DEIN „Ave Maria" dar,
*H*ehr erhellst DU seines Zweifels Schritte,
*L*eitest ihn zur Andacht wunderbar.

*A*chtung hegt DEIN Geist für Schuberts Manen,
*N*imm DEIN teif' Gemüth "Erlkönig" auf,

*F*ern auf nie geahnten Künstlerbahnen
*R*agt hervor des Kunstkometen Lauf.
*A*usdrucksvoll Beethoven zu erfassen,
*N*imm aus DEINEM Spiel der Kenner wahr,
*Z*auber sprudelt aus den Tönemassen,

*L*iegt sein Geist vor uns so groß—so klar.
*J*ubelnd feiert DICH der Völker Menge,
*S*o auch scheiden wir mit feuchtem Blick,
*Z*ieh mit Gott! Beglück'die Welt durch Klänge,
*T*raulick denk'—auch fern—an uns zurück.

demon began to flex his muscles. He first played along with them, as if to feel them out, and then gave them a taste of something more substantial until with his magic, he had ensnared each and every one and could move them this way or that as he chose.

It is unlikely that any other artist, excepting only Paganini, has the power to lift, carry, and deposit an audience in such high degree. A Viennese writer has celebrated Liszt in a poem consisting of nothing but adjectives beginning with the individual letters of his name. It is a tasteless thing as poetry, but there is something to be said for it. Just as we are overwhelmed in leafing through a dictionary by an onslaught of definitions, so in listening to Liszt are we overwhelmed by an onslaught of sounds and sensations. In a matter of seconds we have been exposed to tenderness, daring, fragrance, and madness. The instrument glows and sparkles under the hands of its master. This has all been described a hundred times, and the Viennese, in particular, have tried to trap the eagle in every possible way—with winged pursuit, with snares, with pitchforks, and with poems. It simply has to be heard—and seen. If Liszt were to play behind the scenes, a considerable portion of poetry would be lost.

He played the whole programme alone, including the accompaniments for Madame Schröder-Devrient, probably the only artist who could survive in such company. They did the "Erlkönig" and a few smaller songs by Schubert. Mendelssohn once had the notion of composing a whole concert programme, including an overture, vocal offerings, and all the usual trappings. Liszt has something of the same idea. He gives his concerts pretty much alone.

I am ill-qualified to appraise the impression this great artist made in Dresden, having no experience with the local applause thermometer. The enthusiasm was described as extraordinary. The Viennese, among all Germans, is the least sparing of his hands, and treasures as a souvenir the slit glove with which he applauded Liszt. In northern Germany, as I have said, it is different.

Early Tuesday morning Liszt continues on to Leipzig. About his appearances there, more in our next.[7]

This historic encounter between Liszt and Schumann requires some amplification. In 1837, long before the two composers met, Liszt had published a long and highly favourable article about Schumann's keyboard works in *La Revue*

---

7. NZfM, no. 12, 1840, pp. 102–3; PMW, pp. 157–58.

et Gazette Musicale.[8] Schumann, who was then still struggling for recognition, was deeply appreciative (he was far better known in Germany as the editor of the *Neue Zeitschrift für Musik* than as a composer). He sent Liszt more of his compositions, and the pair struck up a friendly correspondence. In April 1838, Clara Wieck, Robert's future wife, visited Vienna and heard Liszt for the first time. When, a few weeks later, Liszt dedicated to Clara his Paganini Studies it was clear to Schumann that some kind of reciprocal gesture was called for. Schumann invited Liszt to Leipzig, but Liszt was unable at first to accept.[9] Meanwhile, Liszt's commitment to the idea of a Beethoven memorial statue aroused Schumann's admiration still further. Schumann had in manuscript at that time a number of compositions (including *Kreisleriana, Kinderszenen,* and the great *Humoreske*), any one of which could have been dedicated to Liszt. His choice, however, fell on the C-major Fantasy, a work which was itself intended to raise funds for the Beethoven monument and which was supposed to be "about" Beethoven. The Fantasy was eventually printed in the spring of 1839 bearing an inscription to Liszt. Liszt and Schumann had still not met. They were finally united in Dresden, on or about March 14, 1840, two days before Liszt's first concert there. They travelled back to Leipzig together, where Liszt was already billed to appear at the Gewandhaus in less than forty-eight hours' time. He electrified Schumann with some private performances of the latter's *Novelletten* and the Fantasy,[10] and told him, "I feel as if I had known you twenty years."[11] Schumann, for his part, wrote an appreciative review of Liszt's Gewandhaus concerts, the musical highlight of which was Liszt publicly sight-reading Mendelssohn's Piano Concerto in D minor.[12] Given such favourable beginnings, why did this promising artistic friendship deteriorate so sharply?

The causes were complex, the consequences simple. At the heart of the problem lay Leipzig itself. Liszt never had any lasting success there, although that at first had little to do with Schumann. Leipzig was one of the most conservative cities in Europe. A hundred years earlier Bach had lived and worked there. The great Bach revival would soon sweep across Europe and

---

8. "Robert Schumanns Klavierkompositionen, opp. 5, 11, und 14." RGS, vol. 2, pp. 99–107.

9. LLB, vol. 1, p. 20.

10. In 1869 Liszt gave an interesting oral account of Schumann's reaction to his performance of the Fantasy: "I remember the first time I played it to the great composer; he remained perfectly silent in his chair at the close of the first movement, which rather disappointed me. So I asked him what impression my rendering of the work had made upon him, and what improvements he could suggest, being naturally anxious to hear the composer's ideas as to the reading of so noble a composition. He asked me to proceed with the 'March,' *after* which he would give me his criticism. I played the second movement, and with such effect that Schumann jumped out of the chair, flung his arms round me, and with tears in his eyes, cried 'Göttlich! our ideas are absolutely identical as regards the rendering of these movements, only you with your magic fingers have carried my ideas to a realization that I never dreamt of!'" (SPRL, pp. 4–5.)

11. LCS, vol. 1, p. 413.

12. NZfM, no. 12, 1840.

confirm Leipzig as the most traditional of German cities. The important printing house of Breitkopf & Härtel had its home there, and had already started to grace the libraries of the world with its collected editions of the older masters. But the pride of Leipzig was its Gewandhaus concerts. Subsidized by the city's linen merchants and held in their ancient market-hall, these concerts had a distinguished history stretching back to the first half of the eighteenth century. Presiding over Leipzig's musical life was the young Felix Mendelssohn. He had been appointed the conductor of the Gewandhaus concerts five years earlier, when he was only twenty-six but already a composer of European stature. Under his inspired leadership the Gewandhaus had become an artistic shrine at which the faithful gathered regularly to hear the masterpieces of Bach, Beethoven, and Schubert brought to life under his incomparable baton. Schumann once described Mendelssohn as "the Mozart of the nineteenth century."[13] Already there was talk of founding a Conservatory of Music. Within three years a group of wealthy merchants had put up the required capital and had appointed Mendelssohn its first director. He in turn had put conservatives like Hauptmann, Rietz, and David on its teaching staff. Liszt dubbed them "little Leipzigers" and their music "Leipzigerisch." He later formed the view that Leipzig was holding back the progress of nineteenth-century music. After he was placed in charge of Weimar's musical activities, in 1842, and turned that city into a centre of modern music, the resulting conflict between Leipzig and Weimar took on all the trappings of a classical drama: the old versus the new, the past versus the future, reaction versus revolution. The "War of the Romantics," as this conflict has been called, was one of the major cultural struggles of the nineteenth century, and its complex exegesis will be dealt with in a later volume. Meanwhile, Leipzig was proud of its musical past. A success in Vienna, Paris, or Prague counted for nought. The only success that meant anything in a city run by middle-class linen merchants was one in the Gewandhaus.

In 1840, when Liszt first stepped onto that august stage, he had no notion of this. He was, in fact, preoccupied with more immediate problems. Schumann was at that time in the midst of a lawsuit against Friedrich Wieck, the object of which was to force Wieck to show cause why the twenty-year-old Clara should not be allowed to marry Schumann. Liszt took Schumann's side. He snubbed Wieck by refusing to send him press tickets for his Dresden concerts. This garrulous old man, who lived in Dresden and was a respected musical figure there, was outraged and started to slander Liszt and his pupil Hermann Cohen in the Leipzig papers. Liszt shrugged off his attacks. Cohen, however, took Wieck to court and eventually won substantial damages against him.[14] Clara now sprang to her father's defence, turned against Liszt, and wrote to

13. NZfM, no. 13, 1840, p. 198.
14. LLB, vol. I, p. 256.

Robert: "This has cost me bitter tears and it is not right of you at all."[15] To add to Liszt's troubles, the Leipzigers were also annoyed because the "free list" of complimentary tickets traditionally distributed on such occasions was suspended. Then Liszt developed a severe fever, which put him to bed for two days. He was already unwell at the time of his opening concert on March 17, facing an unfriendly audience. He began with his transcription of the Scherzo and Finale of Beethoven's *Pastorale* Symphony, and failed to do himself justice. "It was a wilful choice," wrote Schumann,

> and unfortunate on many grounds. In private, in a small room, this otherwise ultimately decent transcription may well let one forget the orchestra. In a large hall, and one, moreover, where we have heard the symphony played by the orchestra so often and so perfectly, the weakness of the instrument was painfully evident, especially where it was called upon to reproduce the big effects. A more modest arrangement, a mere suggestion might have been more effective. One was aware, of course, that the instrument was presided over by a master. One was satisfied. We had at least seen the lion shake his mane.[16]

Liszt cancelled his second concert, scheduled for the next day. The story was inexplicably put about by Schumann that Liszt had retired to his hotel with a "diplomatic cold,"[17] offended by the cool reception he had received. Liszt's correspondence with Marie d'Agoult tells a different story.

> Leipzig, Friday evening
> March 20, 1840
>
> I was supposed to have given my second concert the day before yesterday, Wednesday, but around three o'clock I was seized with such violent shuddering that I was forced to go to bed. Today the machine is perfectly in order, although I am still not going out, because of the terrible weather. Do not be in the least anxious, you know that towards the spring I am always obliged to spend a day or two in bed. The fever completely left me yesterday. The boring part of all this, coming at such a bad time, is that I am obliged to remain here three days more.[18]

---

15. LCS, vol. 1, p. 418.
16. NZfM, no. 12, 1840, pp. 118–20; PMW, p. 159.
17. LCS, vol. 1, p. 414.
18. ACLA, vol. 1, p. 414.

Mendelssohn, Hiller,[19] and Schumann visited Liszt in his sick-room. Liszt was particularly impressed with Mendelssohn, describing him to Marie d'Agoult as "a man of remarkable talent and very cultivated intelligence. He draws marvellously, plays the violin and viola, is currently reading Homer in Greek, and speaks four or five languages fluently."[20] Mendelssohn generously arranged a private concert in Liszt's honour (for which he rented the Gewandhaus, engaged the services of two hundred and fifty singers and players, served mulled wine and cakes, and invited special guests). The idea was to compensate for the negative impression left by Liszt's opening concert and heal the breach with the public.[21] Mendelssohn deliberately chose works unfamiliar to the pianist, including Schubert's C-major Symphony (which was still in manuscript), three choruses from St. Paul, and Bach's Concerto in D minor for three keyboards, played by Liszt, Mendelssohn, and Hiller. Schumann described it as "a musical festival unlikely to be forgotten by Liszt or anyone else who was present . . . three hours of the most beautiful music, the sort of thing one might not hear in years."[22]

Liszt's second Gewandhaus concert took place two or three days later. Determined to reverse the negative impression he had created, he summoned all his resources and made an overwhelming impact with Weber's Concertstück. Schumann called the performance "extraordinary."

> Both artist and audience appeared to be in a particularly lively mood, and the enthusiasm during the playing and at the close surpassed just about anything ever experienced here. And how Liszt went at the piece, with a strength and grandeur as if it concerned a battlefield manoeuvre, increasing the tension from minute to minute until it seemed as though he were at the head of an orchestra and jubilantly directing it himself! At this moment he seemed, indeed, that field commander to whom, in outward appearance, at least, we have previously compared him [Napoleon], and the applause was mighty enough to have been a Vive l'Empereur! . . .
>
> Whose idea it was to have a favourite singer present him with a bouquet of flowers at the close of the concert I do not know. Certainly it was not unearned. How mean and spiteful to carp at such attentions, as one of our local papers has seen fit to do! The pleasure that he gives is an artist's lifelong goal. You listeners know little of

19. Hiller had travelled to Leipzig for a performance of his oratorio The Destruction of Jerusalem, which took place the following week.
20. ACLA, vol. 1, p. 416.
21. See Mendelssohn's letter to his mother (MB, vol. 2, March 30, 1840), which provides some background to the difficulties Liszt experienced with the Leipzig public.
22. NZfM, no. 12, 1840, p. 118.

all the pains his art costs him. He gives you the best that is in him, the full flower of his life, even perfection. Should we then begrudge him a simple floral wreath? Liszt was graciousness itself. Visibly pleased by the glowing reception accorded his second concert, he declared himself prepared to give a third for the benefit of any appropriate charity, leaving the choice to those acquainted with local circumstances.[23]

This promise was fulfilled the following Monday, March 30, when Liszt gave a benefit concert for the Pension Fund for Aged and Ailing Musicians. Since Liszt had earlier pledged himself to be in Dresden over the weekend (in order to give another benefit concert), he had to make the four-hour trip back to Leipzig on the morning of the concert. Spontaneously he decided to feature music by his three friends Mendelssohn, Schumann, and Hiller. Mendelssohn's Concerto in D minor had been handed to Liszt only four or five days previously, so he walked onto the platform and played it through virtually at sight. The other pieces consisted of some studies by Hiller and ten numbers from Schumann's *Carnaval,* a work Liszt knew (Clara had introduced him to it in Vienna in 1838) but had had no time to prepare. This was a musical tour de force which those in the know were quick to admire. Yet the pressure of so many concerts in such a short time, combined with illness, had started to take its toll. "No man is a god," Schumann wrote, "and the visible strain under which Liszt played on this occasion was the natural consequence of all that he had been through." The chief purpose was fulfilled, however; Liszt's concert raised the tidy sum of 643 taler, 2 groschen for the musicians' pension fund.[24]

Liszt left Leipzig on Tuesday evening, March 31, in order to join Marie d'Agoult in Paris. Six months had elapsed since they had last seen one another, and Marie, overjoyed at the prospect of greeting Liszt, came to meet him. The lovers embraced at Meaux, a small town about 30 miles outside the French capital.

III

Liszt spent the whole of the month of April in Paris. He made no public appearances, but did give two private soirées in the salon of Sébastien Erard. Most of his time was spent mending fences. His liaison with Marie d'Agoult

---

23. NZfM, no. 12, 1840, pp. 118–20; PMW, p. 160. The *Allgemeine Musikalische Zeitung,* the old rival of Schumann's magazine, reviewed Liszt's Gewandhaus concerts (April 1840, no. 40, pp. 298–99) in greater depth than did Schumann himself. The editor, G. W. Finck, provided many details about Liszt's programmes not reported by the *Neue Zeitschrift.*
24. DGG, p. 213.

was still a lively issue in the salons of the Faubourg St. Germain, and Liszt paid a number of diplomatic calls on old friends and acquaintances, including Schlesinger, Berlioz, and Princess Belgiojoso, who left a detailed account of their meeting in her *Souvenirs*.[25] He also met again Chopin and George Sand, whose liaison was attracting some notoriety of its own. Liszt's most notable encounter was with an impoverished twenty-seven-year-old composer named Richard Wagner, who called on him at his hotel one morning. Liszt, surrounded by friends, scarcely noticed his visitor and later had no recollection of this meeting. Neither musician had any inkling that theirs would develop into one of the great artistic friendships of the nineteenth century.

Above all, Liszt was now obliged to resolve some serious family matters. Marie, who was anxious to rehabilitate herself with Parisian society, had moved into spacious apartments in the rue Neuve des Mathurins, situated in the heart of the Faubourg St.-Honoré. Since her return to Paris the previous November she had cultivated her social and literary connections. She now numbered among her friends Sainte-Beuve, Balzac, Eugène Sue, and Emile de Girardin, the powerful editor of *La Presse,* who was to help her to lay the groundwork for her literary career and her transformation into "Daniel Stern." Neither Liszt nor Marie could be sure of their uncertain future. Meanwhile, Liszt had to shoulder the burden of looking after their three young children. The long and complicated story of their childhood in Paris, of Marie d'Agoult's new career as a writer, and of her reconciliation with the Flavigny family has been reserved for a later chapter. The point to observe here is that Liszt was now faced with the prospect of earning sufficient capital to pay for the upkeep and education of his family, and we know from his correspondence that he was short of money. He was in the paradoxical position of having handed out vast sums to

---

25. BSE, pp. 132–34. According to Princess Belgiojoso, Liszt, who was about to set off for London, took his leave of her in her garden on the rue d'Anjou. They strolled through the shrubbery for almost an hour before he could bring himself to the point. He was there for one reason: to ask her to pay some social calls on Madame d'Agoult during his absence in England, since she had been "cut" by a number of former friends. "He spoke of the sadness, the loneliness, the suffering of that charming woman." Paris was too selfish a city, he continued, in which to be alone and ill. Marie needed female companionship. "Be kind, madame, go to her, open your heart and mind to her." With some misgivings La Belgiojoso, who on her own admission hated "scenes," agreed to do Liszt's bidding and a few days later called on Madame d'Agoult. Ushered into the drawing room by a liveried servant ("I wouldn't swear that his hair wasn't powdered"), she was asked to wait while the mistress of the house completed her toilette. Marie finally entered wearing a black velvet gown, with her hair dressed in the style of Catherine de' Medici. The encounter was stiff and formal, the princess having great difficulty in reconciling the regal figure before her with the crushed and broken Marie d'Agoult of Liszt's description. After they had talked about Marie's newly acquired collection of precious minerals, the conversation slid to a halt, and Princess Belgiojoso fled, never to see Marie d'Agoult again. The story is trivial, but it indicates that Liszt's efforts at behind-the-scenes diplomacy in Marie's behalf, born of his well-justified fears for her welfare during his trips abroad, were sometimes brought to nought by Marie herself, whose glacial reserve could freeze the warmest approaches.

charitable causes while having given no thought to his immediate needs or to the needs of those who were dependent on him.

It was against this background that Liszt turned his eyes towards England, the scene of so many of his youthful triumphs. The prospect of making money seemed real. He had last been heard there in 1827 as a boy of fifteen. To revive those early successes would be easy, he probably thought. In this he was to be sadly mistaken.

Since the trip to England looked like becoming an extended one, it was agreed that Liszt would proceed at once and Marie would join him in London for a holiday in June.

I V

Altogether, Liszt travelled to England no fewer than three times during 1840. In May and June he played mainly in London and its environs. After a brief absence he was back again in August and September in order to tour the southern provincial towns of Chichester, Exeter, Bath, and Plymouth. A third and more extended visit was arranged in November and embraced the north of England, Scotland, and Ireland. In sum, Liszt spent nearly six months in Britain, from May 1840 to the end of January 1841. It is one of the least documented periods of his career.

He set out from Paris on the evening of May 5, 1840, and travelled overnight towards the English Channel. The journey was not without incident. His route took him past a small village near Beauvais. It was dark, and as his carriage approached he was horrified to see the entire village engulfed in flames. Stunned villagers stood by helplessly and watched their neighbours perish in the inferno. Within an hour the village was burnt out. Shortly afterwards, Liszt was on board a steamship, crossing the Channel and writing about the drama to Marie d'Agoult.[26] He finally set foot on British soil for the first time in thirteen years on May 6.

Two days later Liszt gave his first London concert at the Hanover Square Rooms. He played his newly composed Reminiscences on Bellini's *I puritani,* his Fantasy on Donizetti's *Lucia,* the *Rákóczy* March, and the perenially popular *Grand Galop chromatique.* The hall was full to overflowing, and at the end of his performance "the room rang with acclamations from all sides."[27] But English audiences were one thing; English critics were another. Shortly after he had been engaged for two Philharmonic Society Concerts (May 11 and June

26. ACLA, vol. 1, p. 419.
27. *Morning Chronicle,* May 9, 1840.

8), the *Musical World* came out with what appear to have been the worst press notices of Liszt's career. The anonymous reporter was "unable to detect an atom of genuine feeling" in his playing. Liszt was accused of turning "elegance into ugliness." Finally, our scribe observed that "Liszt employs his acquirements on some of the ugliest and least artistic combinations of sound that ever found acceptance in a concert room."[28] The *Musical Journal* was even less polite. After his second appearance it reported that Liszt was presented by the directors of the Philharmonic with an elegant silver breakfast service "for doing that which would cause every young student to receive a severe reprimand — viz., thumping and partially destroying two very fine pianofortes."[29] Liszt appears to have met his first serious artistic defeat in England. In an attempt to explain this interesting phenomenon, Sitwell suggested that it was all due to an outbreak of Victorian morality. The English "took such a stern view of the pianist and his irregular union with Madame d'Agoult that his concert tour was a failure."[30] The truth was simpler. The English critics did not appear to care for Liszt's music, and they disliked what they regarded as his swashbuckling approach to piano playing. This is borne out by the satirical tone taken by the periodical *John Bull*.

> The musical town have gone mad about Mr. Liszt, the pianoforte player, or rather the pianoforte tyrant; he has no mercy; he rattles his keys like a jailor, and the people cry, and shriek, and shudder in wonder and astonishment while he is at it. "List, oh List!" should be his motto.[31]

He was, in fact, very well received by English society. He was summoned to Buckingham Palace to play before Queen Victoria and the Prince Consort.[32] Lady Blessington invited him to Gore House, where he met Lord Castlereagh, Lord Canterbury, and Lord Chesterfield. He was also introduced to Benjamin Disraeli. Count d'Orsay painted his portrait and took him to dine with the Duke of Beaufort. Lady Blessington, the famous author of the *Confessions,* whose own *ménage à deux* with Count d'Orsay was the talk of the town, was much taken with the force of Liszt's personality, which she likened to that of both Napoleon and Byron. She has found a niche for herself in the Liszt literature by uttering the timeless remark: "What a pity to

---

28. *Musical World,* June 1840, pp. 305, 361–64.
29. *Musical Journal,* July 14, 1840. The inscribed silver breakfast service is now on display in the Liszt Museum (Hofgärtnerei), Weimar.
30. SL, p. 97.
31. *John Bull,* May 24, 1840.
32. ACLA, vol. 1, p. 444. According to Queen Victoria's *Journal* (RA[a]), the concert took place on the evening of May 25, 1840.

put a similar man to the piano!"[33] It was meant as a compliment. The English aristocracy have never regarded music as a suitable profession for a "gentleman."

In mid-May we find Liszt looking for lodgings in Hampstead so that Marie can join him there. He writes to her about the purity of its air, its marvellous views over London, and the excursions they could make to Richmond and Greenwich. Marie, full of enthusiasm about such a romantic idea, writes back in light-hearted vein in English

> Let us buy a maisonette
> Let us far idyll [*sic*].

She sets sail from Le Havre on the steamship *Britannica,* disembarking at the Tower of London on June 6. Liszt sends a servant, Ferco, to meet her, since he himself has been detained at a rehearsal.[34] The search for lodgings in Hampstead having failed, Liszt and Marie stay at a small hotel in Richmond. It is clear that they have missed one another, yet they quarrel almost at once. Marie protests against his continual absences in London, where he is engaged on an endless round of professional calls. She refuses to accompany him, preferring to remain in seclusion in Richmond. She is again unwell, and a recurrence of an old inflammation in her leg, possibly phlebitis, is causing her pain.[35] They visit the races at Ascot. Liszt writes to her from London, "Yesterday, all the way from Ascot to Richmond, we drove along without your saying a single word to me that was not a wound or an insult."[36] The "far idyll" has dissolved, in less than a fortnight, into a series of pointless recriminations. They leave England during the first week of July. Never again will Liszt have Marie join him while he is on tour.

V

During this visit to England, Liszt broke new ground by giving a series of historic concerts which were announced in the London press as "Piano Recitals." The solo recital, which is now a musical institution, was invented by Liszt

---

33. ACLA, vol. 1, p. 433. See also the diary of William Macready, the actor, who later became the manager of Drury Lane Theatre. He reports a second visit to Gore House on May 31, 1840, during which Liszt played several times: "The most marvellous pianist I ever heard; I do not know when I have been so excited." (MD, vol. 2, p. 64.)

34. Liszt had brought this servant to England from Paris. Ferco remained in London for more than six months while Liszt toured the English provinces, Scotland, and Ireland, looking after his master's interests during his absence.

35. ACLA, vol. 1, p. 450.

36. Ibid.

and first introduced by him on June 9, 1840, at the Hanover Square Rooms. The advertisement read:

Liszt's Pianoforte Recitals

M. Liszt will give, at Two o'clock on Tuesday morning [*sic*], June 9, 1840, RECITALS on the PIANOFORTE of the following works:

1. Scherzo and Finale from Beethoven's Pastorale Symphony
2. Serenade by Schubert
3. Ave Maria by Schubert
4. Hexaméron
5. Neapolitan Tarentelles [*sic*]
6. Grand Galop Chromatique

Tickets 10s 6d each. Reserved Seats, near the Pianoforte, 21s.[37]

Note the plural form of the term "Recitals"; each piece, apparently, was to be "recited." The general public was at first bewildered. "How can one recite on the piano?" people asked. It was Liszt's way of proclaiming the new direction his concerts had recently taken. A year earlier, in June 1839, he had written to Princess Belgiojoso, "I have ventured to give a series of concerts all by myself, affecting the style of Louis XIV and saying cavalierly to the public: *Le concert, c'est moi!*"[38] These first recitals were informal affairs. At the conclusion of each piece, Liszt would leave the platform and descend into the body of the room, where the seats had been arranged in such a way that he could move about and chat with the audience. A number of distinguished musicians were present, their curiosity thoroughly aroused, including Salaman, Moscheles, Benedict, and Cramer. And in the *Memoirs* of Henry Reeve we read the intriguing diary entry, "I took Mme d'Agoult to his recital on June 9th."[39] According to the memoirs of Willert Beale, it was his father, Frederick Beale (a partner of J. B. Cramer, the pianist and publisher), who first suggested to Liszt the term "recitals." Liszt used to visit the Beales at their home in Albion Street, London. Willert was then a young boy, and he recalled being very frightened by Liszt's long hair and his wild appearance. "Franz Liszt, as I afterwards learned, gave performances at the Hanover Square Rooms, which my father for the first time called Recitals. The title

---

37. *Athenaeum*, June 6, 1840.
38. LLB, vol. 1, p. 25. This was in Italy, where the only suitable term he could think of to describe what were already his solo recitals was "musical soliloquies."
39. RML, vol. 1, p. 117.

was much discussed, G. F. Graham being the only one of our home circle who supported my father in approving it."[40]

Although the *Musical World* dismissed these recitals as "this curious exhibition,"[41] there was sufficient general interest in them to encourage Liszt to put on a second series. It was the *Athenaeum* which rightly gauged the historic importance of what was happening, and which seized on the essential point.

> We cannot call to mind any other artist, vocal or instrumental, who could thus, by his own unassisted power, attract and engage an audience for a couple of hours. The critics may not understand M. Liszt, but the musicians crowd to listen to him.[42]

The anonymous writer of this article was the noted English journalist and art critic Henry Chorley. About his last point there was no doubt. Moscheles, a fair and dispassionate observer, attended every one of Liszt's London recitals, and recorded his impressions of his fellow pianist in his diary.

> At one of the Philharmonic Concerts he played three of my studies quite admirably. Faultless in the way of execution, by his talent he has completely metamorphosed these pieces; they have become more his studies than mine. With all that, they please me, and I shouldn't like to hear them played in any other way by him. The Paganini Studies too were uncommonly interesting to me. He does anything he chooses, and does it admirably; and those hands raised aloft in the air come down but seldom, wonderfully seldom, upon a wrong note.[43]

When, the following year, Liszt returned to London, he became a regular visitor to Moscheles's house and took part in several performances of the latter's *Preciosa* Variations for four hands. Moscheles summed up the experience thus: "It seemed to me that we were sitting together on Pegasus."[44] And he was astonished when Liszt picked up the music of two intricate studies he had just written for Michetti's *Beethoven Album* and played them straight off at sight.

The opening concert of the second series of recitals contained a special highlight: a performance of Beethoven's *Kreutzer* Sonata in which Liszt was

---

40. BLOD, vol. 1, pp. 16–17.
41. *Musical World,* June 11, 1840, p. 361.
42. *Athenaeum,* July 4, 1840.
43. MAML, vol. 2, p. 49.
44. MAML, vol. 2, p. 77.

joined by the Norwegian violinist Ole Bull. This was fully reported in *The Times* on July 2, 1840.

LISZT'S RECITALS

On Monday morning Mr. Liszt commenced his second series of pianoforte recitals at Willis's Rooms.[45] Nothing can have been better than the music selected on this occasion for displaying the extraordinary versatility of Liszt's talent. The programme contained the names of Handel, Rossini, and Beethoven, as if to refute the often-repeated but unjust opinion that the great pianist excels only in the performance of his own compositions or those in which mechanical dexterity of execution is the chief characteristic. His performance commenced with Handel's Fugue in E minor, which was played by Liszt with an avoidance of everything approaching to meretricious ornament, and indeed scarcely any additions, except a multitude of ingeniously contrived and appropriate harmonies, casting a glow of colour over the beauties of the composition, and infusing into it a spirit which from no other hand it ever received. The next piece was the overture to *William Tell,* which brought all the performer's power at once into action. In this overture, as in the fugue, Liszt with exquisite taste and tact continued his additions to the harmonies; and though this composition is probably one of the fullest scores that Rossini ever wrote, yet the most complete orchestra by which we have ever heard it performed never produced a more powerful effect, and certainly it was very far behind Liszt in spirit and unity of execution. How all this is accomplished with ten fingers we confess ourselves unable to guess; and even could description convey any idea of Liszt's performance, its possibility would still appear incredible, except to those who have heard it. The overture to *William Tell* was succeeded by one of Beethoven's sonatas (violin obligato [*sic*]), the violin part being performed by Ole Bull and the pianoforte by Liszt. During the performance of this sonata we were forcibly struck with the truth of an observation made by Schindler, in his memoirs of Beethoven, recently published in Germany. Schindler, who is a most enthusiastic worshipper of his departed friend, and who condemns with inflexible severity all erroneous and imperfect interpretations of the great master's ideas, emphatically says that "Franz Liszt has contributed more than almost

---

45. One of London's chief concert halls, situated at 55 St. James's Street. It belonged to the music publisher Willis and Company. The building was destroyed during World War II. See EOCR, p. 74ff.

any instrumentalist of the present day to the just comprehension of Beethoven's music." Liszt gave decided proof of the accuracy of this observation by his performance of the sonata yesterday. There was not a note to which he did not give meaning, and passages which in the hands of other performers would have fallen, as it were, dead on the ear, were prominently brought out by Lizst [*sic*], and the hearers felt their connexion with, and importance to, the beautiful whole. This sonata of Beethoven, and Schubert's songs, appeared to us to be the masterpieces of Monday's performance. In Schubert's songs it is no exaggeration to say that he made the instrument sing. The soft whisperings of the piano passages seemed to compete with the tones of Rubini's voice, and the showers of light notes which he scattered through some of the variations realized every idea that can be formed of fairy music. In fine, we have no hesitation in saying that Liszt leaves every other performer, whether on the pianoforte or any other instrument, at an immeasurable distance behind him.

V I

Liszt meanwhile agreed to tour the south of England in August and September. He signed a contract with the entrepreneur Louis Lavenu[46] for the astronomical sum of 500 guineas a month. Lavenu wanted to take a small troupe of performers on the road (including the singers Miss Steele and Miss Louisa Bassano, and the Welsh harpist and composer John Orlando Parry, best known for his humorous songs "A Wife Wanted" and "The Musical Husband") with Liszt as the star attraction. The tour opened in Chichester on August 19 and then proceeded along the south coast through Portsmouth, Exeter, Plymouth, and Exmouth, pausing at Bath. On September 3 it branched out to include Cheltenham, Cambridge, Ipswich, and Colchester, finishing at Brighton on September 28. Liszt writes with humour about this travelling circus. The audiences were small—fifty or sixty people at most—and there were moments of low comedy mingled with periods of boredom which he whiled away by playing whist. He was impressed with a visit to Stonehenge, however, and retained a lively remembrance of Newstead Abbey.

Although the tour was losing money, the intrepid Lavenu now planned an ambitious itinerary. In November he took his little party to the industrial north

---

46. Louis Henry Lavenu (1818–59) was a cellist and a composer of light music. His opera *Loretta, a Tale of Seville* was produced at Drury Lane in 1846. When he met Liszt, Lavenu had already succeeded to his father's music publishing business at 28 Bond Street, London, and had established himself as an entrepreneur. Frustrated with his career in England, Lavenu eventually emigrated to Australia, where he was appointed director of music at the Sydney Theatre. He died there aged forty-one.

of England (Manchester, Halifax, Preston, Rochdale, and Liverpool), across the Irish Sea to Dublin, Cork, and the small market towns of Ireland, and back again to Scotland. A particularly inane announcement heralded the adventure:

> Mr. Lavenu with his corps musicale will enter the *lists* again on the 23rd instant, when it is to be hoped the *list*less provinces will *list*-en with more attention than on his last experiment, or he will have en*list*ed his talented *list* to very little purpose.[47]

The tour was dogged by ill-fortune. Liszt's Channel boat was delayed by contrary winds and he arrived in England two days late,[48] having missed the opening concert in Reading on November 23. Parry noted mournfully in his diary:

> Went to Town Hall—140 people—when they heard Liszt was not come a great many left! We were obliged to go on with concert to only a few persons—Everything went flat.[49]

Liszt caught up with the group at Oxford. Misfortune struck again when Liszt developed toothache and had to have a tooth extracted by a dentist in Liverpool.[50] By the time they reached Dublin, in mid-December, the group was dejected and Lavenu's concerts had degenerated into farce. We get an idea of the ramshackle organization from Parry's diary. It was in the Dublin Rotunda that

> Liszt played for the first time . . . extemporaneously, and a most wonderful performance it was. When Lewis asked the audience if they had any themes ready written—one was handed only—but Mr. Pigott gave him the Russian Hymn in addition. This was not enough —so after *talking to the audience in the most familiar manner and making them laugh* very much because he had got no lively air to work on —he turned round suddenly and said—"I play de Wanted Governess!" And off he started with the Irish air and then the Russian Hymn and last my song, which he played most wonderfully. Not all the way thro'—but the waltz part in the first symphony. He

---

47. *Musical World,* November 12, 1840.
48. He had meanwhile been giving a series of concerts in Hamburg.
49. PD, November 23, 1840. The diaries of John Orlando Parry contain a faithful account of Liszt's tour of Britain in which visits to every town and village are carefully documented. Lavenu's group covered 3,389 miles (by road, rail, and sea) in four months.
50. ACLA, vol. 2, p. 63.

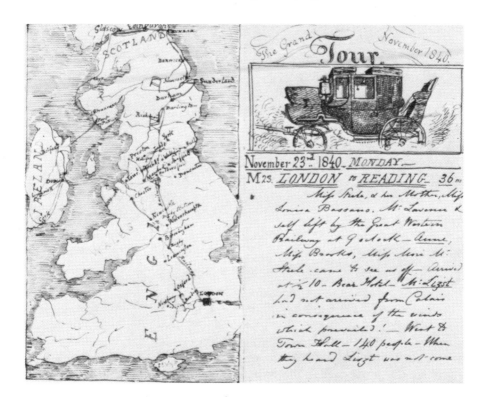

An extract from the unpublished diary of John Orlando Parry, November 23, 1840.

played it at least 12 different ways and then wound up with the 3 together in a manner truly extraordinary!—'Twas received as it deserved with tumultuous applause.[51]

After Christmas the party was based at Cork,[52] the low point of the tour. They once travelled through the night from Cork to the little market town of Clonmel, a distance of about 50 miles over rough roads, only to discover that the concert had been forgotten. Liszt insisted that the programme be given in their hotel sitting room, which possessed a small Tompkinson square piano.

---

51. PD, December 23, 1840.
52. The editor of ACLA, Daniel Ollivier, made an elementary mistake in transcribing the name of the Irish city of Cork as York. (See ACLA, vol. 2, pp. 83–90, where a short exchange of letters between Liszt and Marie d'Agoult has been misattributed.) Liszt spent Christmas 1840 in Ireland.

> We went through the whole programme to 25 Ladies and Gentle-
> men—'twas like a private matinee—So funny to see Liszt firing
> away at *Guillaume Tell* on this little instrument, but it stood his
> powerful hand capitally.[11]

The journey back to Dublin was marked by a blizzard during which Liszt sat
outside the crowded coach all night, through driving snow. When he eventually climbed down he resembled a snowman.

Limerick lay ahead. The *Limerick Standard* had proudly announced on
Christmas Eve that "M. List" would give "a Grand Concert on Tuesday 29
December 1840 in the Northumberland Rooms." This was wishful thinking.
Parry's diary tells us that his brave little party did not even arrive in Limerick
until January 9, 1841, at seven o'clock in the morning. The concert took place
that very lunchtime in Swinbourne's Room. By now Parry's outlook was
jaundiced.

> A poor, dirty place. There were about 100 people present, not more.
> These were almost more than had been expected, for the Concert had
> been much postponed—They were uncommonly lively for a morn-
> ing concert and gave everything applause. I had a double encore.
> Joey not well—out in the cold all night—played very queer and
> threw his Flute down and nearly broke it after missing a passage in
> "Rousseau's Dream"—Liszt was encored once.[54]

Back across the Irish Sea to Scotland, the plucky pioneers now landed at
Portpatrick and travelled on via Stranraer through deep snow to Ayr. "At Ayr,"
wrote Parry,

> the carriage was brought to the door with Liszt asleep in it, and
> having got all our own things we prepared for a start. 'Twas now
> half-past three and a fine starlight morning! Freezing very hard. As
> the Quay was very near (that is a quarter of a mile) the ostlers and
> boots, etc., put a rope to the carriage and proceeded without horses
> to the Quay, but as our carriage was very heavy we lent a hand,
> and a funny procession it was, Miss Steele carrying a lantern and
> we all tugging the carriage and the great pianist, who was fast
> asleep all the while and knew nought of the honours being con-
> ferred on him.[55]

---

53. PD, January 2, 1841.
54. PD, January 9, 1841.
55. PD, January 18, 1841.

The concluding concerts took place in Glasgow and Edinburgh, where the tour came to a muted close at the end of January. The *Scotsman* carried a strangely worded advertisement on its front page which declared that "at the suggestion of many families of distinction Liszt will give positively his last concert in Edinburgh on Saturday, January 23." It could have been better phrased, but everyone knew what was meant. The public's desire was duly realized in the Hopetoun Rooms, in Queen Street, Edinburgh, and Liszt never did return to Scotland. The unfortunate Lavenu lost more than a thousand pounds on the tour and returned to London with an empty purse. With typical generosity Liszt released Lavenu ("the poor devil") from all his contractual obligations before returning to the Continent. From the financial standpoint, Liszt's tour of Britain had been ruinous.[56] There is a footnote to this unhappy story. Liszt made a fleeting return to London in June 1841 in order to fulfil a last engagement for the Philharmonic Society, at which he played the piano part in Hummel's Septet. Shortly before the concert he was thrown from a carriage and sprained his left hand. He gave the concert but his playing was impaired.[57] The accident was somehow symbolic of his entire encounter with England. He did not return to Albion's shores until 1886, the last year of his life.

---

56. MAML, vol. 2, p. 77. See also ACLA, vol. 2, p. 116, where Liszt writes of the disasters: "For my part I leave it with all the honours of warfare."

57. See Chorley's generous review in the *Athenaeum*, June 19, 1841. On June 4, *The Times* reported the cancellation of a concert Liszt was to have given in His Majesty's Theatre two days earlier, stating that he had met with "a serious accident." The accident occurred on the night of June 1, returning from Norwood. Baron von Neumann was in the coach, and he reported that Liszt, as well as injuring his hand, also suffered a contusion on the head. The coachman's shoulder was dislocated. (ND, pp. 168–69.) Such incidents serve to remind us yet again of the primitive travel conditions under which Liszt's European tours unfolded, and make us wonder how he was able to endure eight years of ceaseless travel in a post-chaise, much of it at night.

The World Tours II:
Berlin and St. Petersburg,
1841–1842

*Liszt has created a madness. He plays everywhere
and for everyone.*

ALEXIS VERSTOVSKY[1]

I

With the first leg of his European tours behind him, Liszt reflected on three
salutary experiences. First, it was possible to lose large sums of money as a
pianist. Second, it was not always wise to rely upon local amateurs to administer
one's concerts. Poorly tuned pianos, inadequate concert halls, bad advertising,
chaotic travel and hotel facilities—these were mundane matters, but they could
mean the difference between success and failure. Third, and perhaps most
important, Liszt (as his correspondence amply testifies) was lonely on his tours
and felt the need for a convivial travelling companion. A solution to all three
problems had to be found if the tours were to continue. As far back as
November 1839 he had foreseen the necessity of appointing a personal secretary
and had given the job to a certain Mihály Kiss (recommended to him in Pest),
who had proved to be incompetent.[2] His trusted pupil Hermann Cohen temporarily took over the running of Liszt's affairs and vanished with 3,000
francs.[3] We then find Liszt writing to his Austrian friend Franz Ritter von
Schober:

---

1. VET, vol. 7, 1912.
2. LLB, vol. 1, p. 34; ACLA, vol. 1, p. 407; PBUS, p. 50. See also the *Pesther Tageblatt* of January
10, 1840.
3. ACLA, vol. 2, p. 183. See pp. 213–14.

Would you see any great difficulty in joining me somewhere next autumn—at Venice, for example—and in making a European tour with me? Answer me frankly on this matter. And once more the question of money need not be considered. As long as we are together (and I should like you to have at least three free years before you) my purse will be yours, on the sole condition that you undertake the management of our expenses. . . .[4]

Schober, who would have made an ideal secretary, was unable to accept. It was Marie d'Agoult who finally solved the problem. In August 1840 she wrote to Liszt from Paris saying that she had just interviewed someone whom she thought ideal. His name was Gaëtano Belloni, and he entered Liszt's service in February 1841. For the next six years Belloni travelled the length and breadth of Europe with Liszt. He became the chief architect of Liszt's performing career. The huge success of the visits to Berlin and St. Petersburg, and of the great tour of 1844–45 across the Iberian Peninsula, was due largely to Belloni's efforts. Heine dubbed him "Liszt's poodle,"[5] but he was much more than that. Manager, secretary, and general factotum, Belloni also became a close friend. Liszt frequently charged him with delicate family commissions, involving the welfare of his children, his mother, and his financial investments. It is one of the minor ironies of Liszt biography that while so many people who scarcely knew Liszt rushed into print with their fleeting impressions, Belloni, his inseparable companion for six years, never kept a diary and never wrote his memoirs. The loss of such a priceless wealth of detail as only Belloni could have bequeathed to posterity has to be lamented.[6]

Liszt arrived back in Paris from his tour of Britain in mid-March 1841, and remained in the French capital throughout April. He made several concert appearances during this time. The most noteworthy occurred on March 27, when he gave a solo recital in the Salle Erard and played his newly composed *Reminiscences* on Meyerbeer's *Robert le diable*. Such was the success of this work that it led to the famous incident on April 25 at a fund-raising concert for the Beethoven memorial. This all-Beethoven programme featured the *Emperor* Concerto with Liszt as soloist and Berlioz conducting. The audience would not allow the concert to proceed, and noisily clamoured for a repetition of *Robert*, leaving Liszt with no alternative but to oblige while Berlioz and the orchestra stood idly by. Richard Wagner was at this concert, reviewing the event for the Dresden *Abendzeitung*,[7] and he was offended by the abrupt insertion of this flashy work. "Some day," he wrote, "Liszt in heaven will be summoned to play

---

4. LLB, vol. 1, p. 34.
5. HSWMB, vol. 9, p. 394.
6. See the appreciative words Liszt wrote about Belloni in his will (1860). (LLB, vol. 1, pp. 367–68.)
7. May 5, 1841.

his Fantasy on *The Devil* before the assembled company of angels." The very next day, April 26, Liszt attended a recital given by Chopin in the Salle Pleyel. For months Chopin's admirers had been urging him to make one of his rare, reluctant appearances, and he had finally agreed.[8] Chopin played, among other things, his F-major Ballade, his C-sharp minor Scherzo, and some studies. The event should have been covered by Ernest Legouvé, the regular critic for the *Gazette Musicale,* but Schlesinger allowed Liszt to write the review instead. When Chopin heard this news he was apprehensive. Legouvé told him not to worry, adding, "He will make a fine kingdom for you." "Yes," replied Chopin, "in his empire." Chopin's fears were groundless. Liszt's long article[9] was highly flattering and full of admiration for Chopin's playing.

II

One of Liszt's close companions during 1841 was Count Felix Lichnowsky, an idealistic young man of twenty-six and the nephew of Beethoven's famous patron. Lichnowsky had come forward after one of Liszt's concerts in Brussels in February of that year and had attached himself to the famous pianist. Later he had accompanied Liszt on his travels through the Rhineland, where Liszt had given concerts to raise more money for the Beethoven statue. Lichnowsky, who was heir to vast domains in Silesia and East Prussia, with a fortress castle at Krzyzanowitz, had been cut off by his family for his liberal political views and was now in financial difficulties. Liszt generously helped him out with a loan of 10,000 francs and felt amply rewarded by the friendship of such a warm and cultivated man. During their trip through the Rhineland, Liszt and Lichnowsky came across a near-deserted island in the Rhine called Nonnenwerth. Located in the Siebengebirge district, near Bonn, Nonnenwerth was steeped in romance and mystery. According to an old German legend, Roland of Roncevaux had died of love there. A half-ruined convent, a chapel, and a few fishermen's huts were now the only dwellings. The convent was run as a small hotel, but there were hardly any guests. It was an ideal summer retreat. Here Liszt could compose, practise, and plan the next phase of his concert tours in tranquillity.[10] He negotiated a lease on the island, entitling him to live on

---

8. George Sand is amusing on this topic. She referred to the forthcoming recital as "this Chopinesque nightmare," and went on, "He will have nothing to do with posters or programmes and does not want a large audience. He wants to have the affair kept quiet. So many things alarm him that I suggest that he should play without candles or audience, and on a dumb keyboard. . . ." (Letter to Pauline Viardot, April 18.)

9. *Gazette Musicale,* May 2, 1841.

10. The care with which Liszt now planned his tours after the debacle in the British Isles is evident in his correspondence. In a little-known letter to Princess Belgiojoso, written from Nonnenwerth in October 1841, Liszt declared, "I have come to the Rhine in order to have a rest and to

Nonnenwerth for three years. A piano, manuscripts, and furniture were floated across by ferryboat. Liszt then wrote to Marie telling her of this Rhineland paradise. She was not at first enthusiastic. Their "reconciliation" in England the previous year had ended unhappily. "I'll doubtless come to the Rhine," she wrote cautiously, "if it's the only way of seeing you, but it's the worst arrangement for me because it's the one which will cause the most repercussions and I'll look as if I'm running after you or Felix."[11] Nevertheless, she travelled from Paris and arrived at Nonnenwerth in August 1841. She registered at the hotel under an assumed name, calling herself Madame Mortier-Defontaine, and occupied the quarters formerly belonging to the abbess of the convent. The lovers also spent the summers of 1842 and '43 on the island. Marie wrote to Sainte-Beuve in Paris:

> Every day I see from my window ten or twelve ships passing up and down the river. Their smoke fades away in the branches of the larches and poplars. None of them stops! Nonnenwerth and its island recluses have no business with the rest of humanity![12]

Nonnenwerth was to be their last home together. Neither entertained any illusions about their dying love-affair. Baroness Czettritz, their nearest neighbour, painted a touching portrait of the old lovers. "Liszt is able to compose only when Madame d'Agoult is near him. He seats himself by her, sings or plays to her the notes he has scattered on paper. When he gets up he beseeches her to be diligent, then she writes until one o'clock in the morning."[13] It is the old picture of Marie as Liszt's muse. George Sand's description of the couple was truer. Her phrase "the galley slaves of love" had taken on a grim new meaning. The bonds which formerly drew them together were now transformed into chains which prevented them from drawing apart. Marie d'Agoult summed up Nonnenwerth as "the tomb of my dreams, of my ideals, the remains of my hopes."[14]

Felix Lichnowsky became a frequent visitor to Nonnenwerth. He wrote a poem called "Die Zelle in Nonnenwerth," inspired by one such visit, which Liszt set to music. A more telling souvenir of Nonnenwerth was the song "Die Lorelei," a setting of words by Heine, which Liszt dedicated to Marie d'Agoult. The Lorelei is a steep rock that rises perpendicularly on the right

---

take a breather before my voyage to Russia." That voyage was still six months distant. (OAAL, p. 180.)

11. ACLA, vol. 2, p. 153.

12. Published by Claude Aragonnès in the *Mercure de France*, July 1935. "You see that I am here under a pseudonym," wrote Madame d'Agoult. "It is the beginning of fame."

13. JFL, p. 98.

14. VCA, vol. 2, p. 70.

bank of the Rhine. It is located at a point on the river which is difficult to navigate and is celebrated for its echo. Legend has it that a beautiful siren sits on the rock and lures mariners to a watery death with her enchanted song. Liszt must have sailed past the Lorelei many times, and he found the old legend impossible to resist. It drew from him a setting which now ranks with the finest of his seventy songs. The introduction contains a striking allusion to the opening bars of *Tristan,* not the first time that Liszt had stolen from the future of music.

There were occasional forays from Nonnenwerth into the nearby cities of Bonn and Cologne. At Cologne Liszt caught his first glimpse of the great, unfinished cathedral and pledged himself to raise money for its building fund.[15] One of these excursions was of more than passing interest. In mid-September Liszt visited Frankfurt-am-Main and became a member of the Freemasons Lodge there. His sponsor was one Wilhelm Speyer.[16] Liszt signed the formal document of enrolment on September 18, 1841.[17]

In October Liszt and Marie left their island sanctuary. They were not to meet again for eight months. She returned to Paris, while Liszt struck out across Germany in pursuit of his performing career—to Cologne, Cassel, Leipzig, Dresden, and Weimar, a city in which he had not yet been heard and which

15. His first concert for the *Dombau* took place on August 22, 1841, and raised 380 thaler, 1,110 marks. (See Henseler, *Das musikalische Bonn im 19. Jahrhundert,* p. 178.)

16. Wilhelm Speyer (1790–1878) was a composer and violinist who had settled in Frankfurt and now owned a business there. He had founded the local Mozart Stiftung and ran a popular series of *Liederkranz* evenings for the performance of male-voice choruses. Liszt composed several works for Speyer in this genre (including his vocal quartets "Rheinweinlied," "Studentenlied," and "Reiterlied," R. 542) and published them in 1843 "for the benefit of the Mozart Institute."

17. Reproduced on p. 369. For more information on Liszt and Freemasonry, and his induction into the *Zur Einigkeit* Lodge in Frankfurt, see his correspondence with Wilhelm Speyer published in SWS, pp. 228–35. The entire question of Liszt's connection with the Freemasons has been ably dealt with by Philippe Autexier in AML. On February 22, 1842, he was admitted to the *Zur Eintracht* Lodge in Berlin (WA, Überformate 120, 1M). Eighteen months later, on September 23, 1843, he was made an honorary member of the Freemasons Lodge in Iserlohn (WA, Überformate 130, 1M). Finally, on July 15, 1845, he joined the Lodge *St. Johannes Modestia cum Liberate* in Zürich (WA, Überformate 179, 1M). Even after he received the tonsure in 1865, Liszt retained his links with the Freemasons, and he was elected to the *Zur Einigkeit* Lodge in Budapest in 1870. After his death the *Freemason's Journal* published an obituary notice in which it referred to "Brother Franz Liszt, on whose grave we deposit an acacia branch."

Liszt and Freemasonry, a document of enrolment into the Zur Einigkeit *Lodge,*
Frankfurt-am-Main, September 18, 1841.

was to change the whole direction of his career. The season would be crowned with triumphal visits to Berlin and St. Petersburg.

III

Liszt gave his first concert in Weimar at the Court Theatre on November 29, 1841.[18] The *Weimarische Zeitung* provided no hint of the importance of the occasion, reporting merely that "the famous pianoforte player Liszt gave . . . a concert that fully justified the call that went out for him."[19] Afterwards Liszt met the hereditary rulers of Sachsen-Weimar, Grand Duke Carl Friedrich and Grand Duchess Maria Pavlovna, the rich and powerful sister of the tsar. Maria Pavlovna, who was to become one of Liszt's staunchest allies during his Weimar years, was very musical; she sang and even composed. Liszt's first impressions of his future benefactors, and of the city of Weimar itself, with which his name was soon to be inextricably linked, may be found in his letter to Marie d'Agoult dated December 7, 1841.[20] More important was the friendship he formed with their twenty-three-year-old son, Carl Alexander, the Grand Duke Apparent, who, as Raabe points out, at once recognized in Liszt not only "a famous pianoforte player" but someone who might help in the spiritual and artistic regeneration he planned for Weimar—a noble aspiration he was to pursue throughout the nearly fifty years of his distinguished reign. Carl Alexander wanted nothing less than the restoration of the once-proud city of Goethe and Schiller to its former glory, achieved under the benevolent rule of his illustrious grandfather Carl August, and through his vision he persuaded a number of eminent men in the arts and sciences to settle there. Could Liszt too be tempted to regard Weimar as his home? The opportunity to ask him did not present itself until the following year. Liszt passed through Weimar again in October 1842 and played to the royal family in the castle and once more in the Court Theatre. The occasion was a particularly joyous one, since Carl Alexander had just married Princess Sophie, the eighteen-year-old daughter of King Wilhelm II of the Netherlands, and the young couple were still on honeymoon. With the full approval of his parents Carl Alexander offered Liszt the title of Court Kapellmeister in Extraordinary,[21] a position that for

18. See the diary of M. S. Sabinina, *Zapiski,* Russkii arkhiv, vol. 1 (Moscow, 1900), p. 530, for an eye-witness account of the concert. Also MFL, vol. 1, p. 768, fn. 98.
19. December 1, 1841.
20. ACLA, vol. 2, p. 182.
21. The decree is dated November 2, 1842. Although the document was issued under the direct command of the reigning Grand Duke, Carl Friedrich, the subsequent correspondence makes it clear that it was the son, Carl Alexander, who initiated this appointment, and it was to Carl Alexander that Liszt always pledged allegiance.

the time being carried with it few duties, demanded Liszt's presence in Weimar for only two or three months of each year, and left him free to follow his virtuoso career wherever it led him. The arrangement was mutually advantageous: Carl Alexander had bound Liszt's name and fame to his court, while Liszt now had an artistic haven to which he might return at will. As it happened, he did not take up full-time residence there until 1848, but even as his world tours unfolded, Weimar became for him an artistic Camelot, constantly beckoning, and his plans for its musical future were never far from his thoughts.

Some of Liszt's concerts during the 1841–42 season were given in collaboration with the Italian tenor Giovanni Rubini, an uneasy alliance about which little is known except that it was punctuated by outbreaks of artistic temperament on both sides, and that it hardly survived the first few weeks. Having parted in Prussia, for example, Rubini and Liszt came together again for a joint appearance at The Hague before the Dutch royal court. At the conclusion of the concert the royal chamberlain presented each of them with a snuffbox. Liszt was taken aback to discover that his own was of less value than Rubini's. "It does not suit me," he wrote to Marie d'Agoult, "not to be put on the same level as he," and he gave his snuffbox to Belloni.[22] Perhaps he felt the snub more keenly because it followed so hard on the heels of the wild demonstrations his playing had provoked in Berlin and St. Petersburg just a few months earlier, and which should now command our attention.

I V

Liszt arrived in Berlin just before Christmas 1841 and took up residence at the Hôtel de Russie. Mendelssohn, Meyerbeer, and Spontini were there to greet him.[23] Word of Liszt's arrival spread quickly, and that same evening a group of thirty students turned up and serenaded him with a performance of his part-song "Rheinweinlied." No one could have foreseen from this harmless reception that a storm was to break loose. His first recital took place in the Berlin Singakademie on December 27. It included several old favourites— the overture to *Guillaume Tell, Robert le diable,* and "Erlkönig"—works which had been near-failures in England the previous year. This time it was different. The clamour which erupted shook the Singakademie to its foundations and set the tone for the rest of his stay. It was at Berlin that "Lisztomania" swept in. The word was coined by Heine. The symptoms, which are odious to the modern reader, bear every resemblance to an infectious disease, and merely to call them mass hysteria hardly does justice to what actually took place. His

---

22. ACLA, vol. 2, p. 240.
23. ACLA, vol. 2, p. 189.

portrait was worn on brooches and cameos. Swooning lady admirers attempted to take cuttings of his hair, and they surged forward whenever he broke a piano string in order to make it into a bracelet. Some of these insane female "fans" even carried glass phials about their persons into which they poured his coffee dregs. Others collected his cigar butts, which they hid in their cleavages.[24] The overtones were clearly sexual. Psychologists may have a wonderful time explaining such phenomena, but they cannot change the facts: Liszt had taken Berlin by storm, and for a pianist that was unprecedented. Liszt remained in Berlin for ten weeks. His feat of playing eighty works in twenty-one concerts has already been noted. In no other city did he make so many appearances in so brief a time.[25] The Prussian royal family attended most of them. As a mark

24. A. Brennglas, *Franz Liszt in Berlin: Eine Komödie in drei Acten* (Berlin, 1842). This singular practice was even transported to the marble halls of the court of Weimar. Liszt once threw away an old cigar stump in the street under the watchful eyes of an infatuated lady-in-waiting, who reverently picked the offensive weed out of the gutter, had it encased in a locket surrounded with the monogram "F.L." in diamonds, and went about her courtly duties unaware of the sickly odour it gave forth—to the mystification of the rest of the royal household, who could not wait to get beyond range whenever she appeared. (BKMM, vol. 1, p. 42.)

25. The statistics may be found in Rellstab (RFL, pp. 41–44) and in the Berlin press. Nine of the twenty-one concerts were for charitable causes, including the building fund of Cologne Cathedral and the University of Berlin. Since it is of historical interest, and since it represents a major musical feat usually lost in the hullabaloo surrounding his appearances in Berlin, the repertoire *Liszt played from memory* during his ten-week sojourn is preserved here.

BACH	Chromatic Fantasy and Fugue in D minor; Organ Prelude and Fugue in A minor; Organ Prelude and Fugue in E minor; Prelude and Fugue in C minor (Bk. 1, "48")
BEETHOVEN	Sonata in C-sharp minor; Sonata in D minor; Sonata in F minor *(Appassionata)*; Sonata in A-flat major *(Funeral March)*; Sonata in B-flat major *(Hammerklavier)*; Concerto in C minor; Concerto in E-flat major *(Emperor)*; Choral Fantasy
BEETHOVEN–LISZT	Scherzo, Storm, and Finale from the *Pastorale* Symphony; Funeral March from the *Eroica* Symphony; Song Cycle: *Adelaïde*
CHOPIN	Studies; Mazurkas; Waltzes
HANDEL	Fugue in E minor; Theme and Variations (D-minor Suite)
HUMMEL	Septet; *Oberons Zauberhorn*
MENDELSSOHN	Capriccio in F-sharp minor
MOSCHELES	Studies
PAGANINI–LISZT	*La campanella; Carnival of Venice* Study
ROSSINI–LISZT	*William Tell* Overture; *Tarantella; La Serenata e l'Orgia*
SCARLATTI	Sonatas
SCHUBERT–LISZT	"Erlkönig"; "Ave Maria"; "Ständchen"; "Lob der Thränen"
LISZT	
Paraphrases	*Don Giovanni* (Mozart); *Robert le diable* (Meyerbeer); *Lucia di Lammermoor* (Donizetti); *Niobe* (Pacini); *La sonnambula* (Bellini); *I puritani* (Bellini); *Norma* (Bellini); *Lucrezia Borgia* (Donizetti); *Les Huguenots* (Meyerbeer)
Original works	Valse à capriccio (no. 3); "Heil im Siegerkranz" ("God Save the King"); Grande Valse di bravura; Grand Galop chromatique; *Au Lac de Wallenstadt; Au Bord d'une source;* Hungarian Rhapsodies; Hungarian March; *Mazeppa* (Transcendental Study); *Hexaméron* Variations

of appreciation, King Wilhelm IV bestowed on Liszt the Ordre pour le Mérite. In mid-February Liszt was elected a member of the Prussian Academy of Fine Arts.

Liszt was now accused of "playing to the gallery," of lapsing into vulgarity. But what was he supposed to do? Cease playing? He had suddenly become the victim of his own success and hardly knew how to cope. His correspondence discloses that he was as surprised as anyone at the furore surrounding him. The fuss was entirely the fault of the Berliners. If proof be sought, it will be found in their reaction to Liszt just one year later when he returned to Prussia. Ashamed of their initial emotional outburst, they all but shunned him and turned his second visit to their city into one of the low points of the year. Yet the Liszt of 1843 was no different from the Liszt of 1842. By then, however, "Lisztomania" had moved on and was sweeping southern France. Heine saw in it the deft hand of Belloni. He spread the story that Liszt's manager was importing the claque and paying for "ovation expenses."[26] There is no evidence for this tale, but it was too good to suppress and persists in the Liszt literature to this day.

Liszt's sojourn in Berlin was marked by close friendships with two women of distinction. One of them was Charlotte von Hagn, the finest actress in Germany and one of the great beauties of her time. A typical Bavarian, with blond hair and blue eyes, Charlotte was twenty-one years old. She spoke excellent French, and Liszt found in her a warm and delightful companion. Vulnerable to Liszt's chivalrous attentions, Charlotte scribbled a love-poem on the corner of her fan for him. Liszt carried it off and set the words to music.[27] Seven years after their brief encounter, Charlotte, who was now married, wrote to Liszt, "You have spoiled all other people for me. Nobody can stand the comparison."[28] Liszt's other friendship was with the formidable Bettina von Arnim, who had known both Goethe and Beethoven. Bettina was now fifty-seven years old and reflecting on her past life. Liszt had many conversations

---

The contemporary newspapers of Berlin do not always give keys and numbers. For example, it is impossible to say precisely which works of Scarlatti were featured. Likewise, we cannot be certain about the identity of the Chopin groups.

The strain of so much playing took its toll once again. As in Leipzig the previous year, and under somewhat similar circumstances, Liszt fell ill. He wrote to Marie d'Agoult, "You cannot imagine how I live! I have been ill for two days. Sometimes I feel as if my head and my heart would burst." (ACLA, vol. 2, p. 191.)

26. HMB, p. 397.

27. See his song "Was Liebe sei," R. 575(a).

28. LLF, p. 113. By 1849 Liszt was Kapellmeister to the Weimar court. Did Charlotte hope to resume their friendship? Her letter contains this pointed pun: "Sie müssen ja schon als Kapellmeister ungemein viel Takt haben!" ("As a conductor you must of course have exceptional tact." In German *Takt* also means "beat" or "measure.") Four of Charlotte's unpublished letters to Liszt are kept in the Weimar archives (WA, Kasten 24, no. 19).

with her about these two men of genius and treasured her recollections of them.[29]

When Liszt finally left Berlin he was driven out of the city in a coach drawn by six white horses. Thirty other coaches followed in stately procession along the Unter den Linden. Prince Felix von Lichnowsky rode at Liszt's side as his aide-de-camp. An escort of Prussian students, bedecked in colourful uniforms, accompanied them as far as the Brandenburg Gate. The University of Berlin suspended its sittings for the day as a mark of respect. It was a bright sunny morning on March 3, and multitudes stood in the Schlossplatz and the König-strasse shouting "Vivat!" as Liszt drove past. King Wilhelm IV and his queen stood at the palace windows waving the procession farewell. It was as if a reigning monarch were taking leave of his people. "Not *like* a king, but *as* a king," in Rellstab's happy phrase.[30] From Berlin Liszt proceeded to Königsberg. After giving a concert for the university, he was awarded the honorary degree of Doctor of Philosophy. "A slap in the face for the Berlin professors who, in their stupid pride, had denied it to him," wrote Varnhagen von Ense.[31] Concerts in Mittau and Riga followed. Liszt finally reached St. Petersburg, by way of Warsaw, in April 1842.

v

Liszt's first visit to Russia could not have taken place in more favourable circumstances. He was there under the direct patronage of Tsarina Alexandra, to whom he had been presented two years earlier at Ems. There were other Russian well-wishers too. During the winter of 1839, in Rome, Liszt had played in the home of Prince Galitzine, the governor-general of Moscow, who had also pressed on him an invitation to visit Russia. Meanwhile, the Berlin newspapers had travelled ahead of Liszt, spreading news of his latest conquests. By the time he entered the imperial city of St. Petersburg his success was virtually assured. The day after his arrival, on April 4 (Old Style), he was presented to Tsar Nicholas I, who, on seeing Liszt enter the audience chamber,

---

29. See Liszt's letter to Bettina, written on March 15, 1842, after his departure from Berlin, in which he poetically describes their friendship as "a magnetic force of two natures which will, I believe, increase with distance." ("Unbekannte Briefe Franz Liszts, veröffentlicht von Friedrich Schnapp," *Die Musik,* vol. 18, no. 10, July 1926, p. 720. See also La Mara's sketch of Bettina in LLF, pp. 119–37.
30. Eye-witness reports of the scene may be found in RFL, p. 37, and VT, vol. 2, p. 30.
31. VT, vol. 2, p. 30. The investiture was carried out by Professors Jacobi and Rosenkranz of the Faculty of Philosophy. During the ceremony Jacobi delivered a fulsome address, part of which is reproduced in KFL, pp. 160–61. See the letter of thanks Liszt wrote from Mittau, dated March 18, 1842, addressed to "The Faculty of Philosophy at the University of Königsberg." (LLB, vol. 1, p. 46.)

broke away from his generals and court officials, and advanced on him. The following dialogue ensued:

> "We are almost compatriots, Monsieur Liszt."
> "Sire?"
> "You are Hungarian, are you not?"
> "Yes, Your Majesty."
> "I have a regiment in Hungary."[32]

The dislike that soon arose between the military-minded Nicholas and Liszt has already been remarked. But even Liszt must have been rendered speechless by this tactless comment.

On April 8 Liszt gave his first concert in the great Assembly Hall of the Nobles, before an audience of three thousand people. No artist had ever played in Russia before such a vast throng. A small stage had been erected in the middle of the hall "like an islet in the middle of an ocean." Two pianos stood on it, turned in opposite directions, so that Liszt could move from one to the other and thus face each half of the huge audience in turn. The occasion was enshrined in the reminiscences of Vladimir Stasov, the Russian critic, who attended the concert in the company of his friend the composer Alexander Serov.

> As people began streaming into the hall, I saw Glinka for the first time in my life. He was pointed out to me by Serov, who had met him not long before and, of course, rushed up to him all smiles, handshakes and questions. But Glinka did not spend much time with Serov. A shrivelled old lady, Mme. Palibina (who, by the way, was an excellent pianist) began calling him. . . .
>
> Suddenly there was a commotion in the crowded Assembly Hall of the Nobility. We all turned around and saw Liszt, strolling arm in arm through the gallery behind the columns with the potbellied Count Mikhail Vielgorsky. The Count, who moved very slowly, glowering at everyone with his bulging eyes, was wearing a wig curled à l'Apollo Belvedere and a large white cravat. Liszt was also wearing a white cravat and over it, the Order of the Golden Spur which had recently been given him by the Pope.[33] Various other orders dangled from the lapels of his frock coat. He was very thin and stooped, and though I had read a great deal about his famous "Florentine profile," which was supposed to make him resemble

---

32. ACLA, vol. 2, p. 211.
33. Stasov was mistaken. Liszt was never given the Order of the Golden Spur.

Dante, I did not find his face handsome at all. I at once strongly disliked this mania for decorations and later on had as little liking for the saccharine, courtly manner Liszt affected with everyone he met. But most startling of all was his enormous mane of fair hair. In those days no one in Russia would have dared wear his hair that way; it was strictly forbidden.

Just at that moment Liszt, noting the time, walked down from the gallery, elbowed his way through the crowd and moved quickly toward the stage. But instead of using the steps, he leaped onto the platform. He tore off his white kid gloves and tossed them on the floor, under the piano. Then, after bowing low in all directions to a tumult of applause such as had probably not been heard in Petersburg since 1703, he seated himself at the piano. Instantly the hall became deadly silent. Without any preliminaries, Liszt began playing the opening cello phrase of the *William Tell* overture. As soon as he finished, and while the hall was still rocking with applause, he moved swiftly to a second piano facing in the opposite direction. Throughout the concert he used the pianos alternately for each piece, facing first one, then the other half of the hall. On this occasion, Liszt also played the Andante from *Lucia,* his fantasy on Mozart's *Don Giovanni,* piano transcriptions of Schubert's "Ständchen" and "Erl-könig," Beethoven's "Adelaïde" and in conclusion, his own *Galop chromatique.*

We had never in our lives heard anything like this; we had never been in the presence of such a brilliant, passionate, demonic temperament, at one moment rushing like a whirlwind, at another pouring forth cascades of tender beauty and grace. Liszt's playing was absolutely overwhelming. . . .[34]

After the concert, Stasov reports, he and his friend Serov "were like madmen." They rushed home to capture their impressions in writing. "Then and there, we took a vow that thenceforth and forever, that day, 8 April 1842, would be sacred to us, and we would never forget a single second of it till our dying day."

Altogether Liszt gave six public concerts in St. Petersburg during April and May. One of them was for the victims of the great fire that had devastated Hamburg. In addition he played many times at receptions given by the nobility —including Grand Duchess Elena Pavlovna, Prince Peter of Oldenberg, Prince Yusupov, and Count Benkendorf. He also met the great pianist Adolf Henselt, who had lived in St. Petersburg since 1838 and was now the Imperial Court

34. SSEM, pp. 120–21.

Pianist. Von Lenz was present at this meeting and reports that at Liszt's request, Henselt played Weber's *Polacca* in E major. Liszt was stunned by the polished performance, given in Henselt's inimitable fashion, sitting motionless at the keyboard, impervious to technical difficulties. "I, too, could have had velvet paws if I had wished," Liszt remarked.[35] The friendship formed on this occasion, based on mutual respect for one another's musical gifts, survived until Liszt's death. Liszt's farewell concert took place in the home of Count Vielgorsky on May 16. Afterwards there was a banquet in Liszt's honour. Among the guests were Glinka, Henselt, and von Lenz. Liszt delivered a speech of thanks, promised to return to Russia next year, and that same evening boarded ship for Lübeck.

Altogether Liszt visited Russia three times. He returned there in 1843 and again in 1847. Neither occasion matched the triumphs of his first visit. Stasov suggests that the fickle Russian public was by then under the spell of Italian opera. A more compelling reason was that on his way through Warsaw in 1843 Liszt was charged with expressing support for the Poles in their struggle for national independence from the Russian yoke, in consequence of which the great aristocratic families of St. Petersburg could not afford to be closely associated with him.[36] It is a fact that on his next visit to that city Liszt was obliged to hire the small Engelhardt Hall, since he could not fill the Assembly Hall of the Nobles. His radical views were documented by Eva Hanska, the Polish mistress of Balzac, who met Liszt in St. Petersburg. He went several times to her home and she left a detailed description of the great pianist.

> One day the servant walked in and announced "M. Liszt" with no more ceremony than if M. Liszt had simply been the owner of the coat he was wearing. . . . I rose and went towards him, stammering a few words of conventional greetings. Liszt is of medium height, thin, pale, and drawn. He has the bilious complexion belonging to people of great talent and personality. His features are regular. His forehead is less high than they show it in his portraits. He is furrowed with lines. . . . His eyes are glassy, but they light up under the effect of his wit and sparkle like the facets of a cut diamond. . . . His best feature is the sweet curve of his mouth, which, when it smiles, makes heaven dream. . . .[37]

---

35. LGPZ, p. 104. The details of five of Liszt's St. Petersburg recitals, incidentally, were published in MFL, vol 2, pp. 434–37.

36. According to Liszt, the chief of police in Warsaw sent false reports to St. Petersburg about his "Polish sympathies" and these were distorted by the Polish press. (RL, p. 401; WA, Kasten 351, no. 1.)

37. Letter dated April 13, 1843; Spoelberch de Lovenjoul collection, Chantilly.

Their conversation led them inevitably to Balzac, with whom Liszt had already become acquainted in Paris. Balzac's novel *Béatrix* was then being published by instalments. The book is beyond question a fictionalized account of the love-affair of Marie d'Agoult and Liszt. Did Liszt recognize himself in this novel? Madame Hanska could not forgo the opportunity of asking him. "They wanted to break our friendship," Liszt told her. "They tried to insinuate that he had dressed me up in a far from flattering manner under the name of Conti . . . but since I didn't recognize myself in it, I didn't accept the portrait."[38]

The next stop was Moscow, where Liszt had agreed to give one concert under the aegis of the governor-general, Prince Galitzine. He was obliged to give eight, so tumultuous was his reception.[39] The Moscow concerts of 1843, in fact, fared much better than the ones in St. Petersburg, possibly because Liszt was being heard there for the first time. The Muscovites also appreciated the

---

38. The first two parts of *Béatrix* were published in *Le Siècle* in April and May 1839. They then appeared in book form in 1842, just before Liszt met Madame Hanska. Part 3 appeared in *Le Messager* between December 24, 1844, and January 23, 1845. In the novel Marie is portrayed as Marquise de Rochefide and Liszt as Count Gennaro Conti, an Italian musician. The marquise deserts her husband for Count Conti, just as Marie had done for Liszt. She wants to be Conti's inspiration, to play the Beatrice to his Dante, just as Marie had wanted to do for Liszt. First-hand material about the lovers of Geneva had been fed to Balzac by George Sand while he was her guest at Nohant in the early part of 1838. As early as March 2, 1838, Balzac had written to Madame Hanska from Nohant: "Apropos of Liszt and Madame d'Agoult, she [Sand] gave me the subject of *Les Galériens ou Les Amours forcés* which I am going to treat, for in her position she cannot do so herself. Keep this secret."

After the publication of *Béatrix* the close relationship between Sand and Madame d'Agoult was irreparably broken. Why, it may be asked, should Sand betray her old friend and behave in Balzac's presence like a cheap gossip? It was Marie herself who brought about her own downfall. During the period 1837–39 she wrote a number of indiscreet letters to their mutual friend Countess Carlotta Marliani, the wife of the Spanish consul in Paris, in which she referred to Sand's affairs with Mallefille and Chopin as a comedy. Carlotta showed these letters to Sand, who lost no time in punishing Marie through Balzac for her presumptuous remarks. Not content with punishment by proxy, Sand struck a blow for herself when she placed Marie in her novel *Horace* (1841) as Viscountess de Chailly. The portrait she painted there was a personal insult: ". . . she had, indeed, a nobility as artificial as everything else—her teeth, her bosom, and her heart." Marie was deeply humiliated by the publica- tion of *Béatrix,* followed so hard by that of *Horace.* According to Janka Wohl, Marie wept tears of rage and humiliation over *Béatrix* and demanded that Liszt seek satisfaction on her behalf, something he refused to do. "Is your name in it? Did you find your address in it, or the number of your house? No! Well then, what are you crying about?" (WFLR, pp. 67–68.) We may be sure that such galling experiences shook Marie's pride and gave her the idea of later creating a pen-portrait of her own —in *Nélida.* And Liszt? He made the wise and sensible decision of always denying that he was the model for any fictionalized portrait whatsoever. Four years before she raised the question, then, Madame Hanska knew the answer.

39. The Moscow concerts of 1843 have never been well documented. Liszt's opening concert took place on April 13 (Old Style) in the Bolshoi Theatre. The others occurred in swift succession on April 15, 17, 20, 22, 27, 30, and May 4. Substantial articles appeared in the Moscow press, including *Severnaya Pchela, Moskvityanin, Russkii invalid,* and *Biblioteka dlya Chteniya.* The scholar V. Khvos- tenko compiled a useful assembly of press notices from Liszt's tours of Russia in 1842 and 1843, which appeared in the November and December 1937 issues of *Sovietskaya Muzyka.* From this source we learn that for his Moscow concerts Liszt played on a newly invented "orchestral piano" by Lichtental, which achieved massive effects by means of octave couplings.

pianist's generosity towards them. He gave an organ recital for charity in the Protestant Church of St. Peter and Paul, raising 13,000 roubles for the Orphans Fund. And when he learned of the difficult situation of Fyodor Usachov, an actor in the Moscow theatre, he volunteered his services at a benefit concert.[40] These acts were widely reported in the press and endeared Liszt to the Russian public. The climax of the visit came at the beginning of May, when he made his first contact with the Moscow Gypsies. He was utterly fascinated by the Eastern flavour of their melodies and their wild Asiatic rhythms, and he was swift to compare them with their Hungarian counterparts.[41] On one occasion he became so absorbed by their performance that he forgot about his own concert that day and arrived at the hall very late. By the time he walked onto the platform, the audience had become restless. Liszt seated himself at the piano, amidst loud applause, but instead of beginning the first item on the printed programme he fell into a reverie. Then there emerged from the piano an improvisation on themes Liszt had just heard the Gypsies sing. The audience was at first puzzled, then captivated by the inspiration that flowed from the keyboard. Word soon spread that Liszt had been detained by Gypsies and had left them deeply stirred.

During this visit of 1843 the Muscovites entertained Liszt lavishly. One of these gala dinners was reported in the journal *Moskvityanin* in amusing terms. Liszt seemed bored by the orchestral overtures played in his honour. Then several men entered the banquet hall bearing a sturgeon almost seven feet long and weighing a hundred pounds. Liszt had never seen anything like it. He started to applaud the sturgeon, and everybody else followed suit. "The applause grew so lively that the chef, who had walked out on the stage behind his enormous artistic creation, was obliged to take bows for the insensible fish."[42]

V I

Liszt's visits to Russia were historically important. When he first arrived there musical culture was in its infancy and run by dilettantes. This was long before the great conservatories at St. Petersburg and Moscow were established. Russian musicians had nowhere to go for their training. Glinka, Russia's leading composer, was neglected and his epoch-making opera *Russlan and Ludmilla* criticized on all sides by blinkered amateurs who preferred to import Rossini. Glinka

---

40. DFL, vol. 4, 1911, p. 81; vol. 7, 1912, p. 65.
41. Liszt mentions this visit to the Moscow Gypsies in his book *Des Bohémiens* (RGS, vol. 6, pp. 145–51).
42. *Moskvityanin* pt. 3, no. 5, 1843; SSEM, p. 133.

himself writes well about the undeveloped state of music in Russia during the 1840s in his memoirs. So too does Stasov, a more objective chronicler; surveying the bleak landscape that passed for culture in those days, he could only exclaim, "What a time, what people!" Liszt showed a keen interest in Russian folk song and actively encouraged Russian musicians to break away from the European yoke and develop their own language. He declared *Russlan and Ludmilla* to be a masterpiece and pleased Glinka immensely by playing through the score at sight on the piano. Liszt's visits served as a catalyst to the Russians, who were reeling under their impact years after he left. Two generations passed and some of Russia's best pianists were still travelling to Weimar—Siloti, Friedheim, and Vera Timanoff, among others—to join his master classes. In later years few things gave Liszt greater pleasure than the emergence of "the mighty handful," with its distinctive nationalistic speech.

Liszt left Russia in early May 1842. His sojourn had lasted four weeks. He had made large sums of money (in one week alone he earned more than 40,000 francs;[43] one-quarter of this was immediately despatched to Anna Liszt in Paris for the care of his children), but the constant round of concerts, coupled with the wear and tear of travel, was taking its toll. "I feel a great tiredness of life and a ridiculous need of rest, of languor," he wrote.[44] This theme recurs with increasing regularity in Liszt's correspondence. He was only thirty years old and already burning himself out. Nonetheless, he was back in Paris by mid-June (travelling through Central Europe at the rate of 50 or 60 miles a day), where he gave a charity concert and directed a male choir in performances of his "Rheinweinlied" and "Reiterlied" settings. The following month he went to Liège to attend the unveiling of a statue to Grétry, and then to Brussels to participate in the Grétry festival. At the end of the unveiling ceremony Liszt was publicly invested with the Cross of the Lion of Belgium.[45]

Liszt's return to France did not go unnoticed by the local press. Since his departure from Paris a year earlier, the French had witnessed the amazing spectacle of "Lisztomania," and they were determined to cut the pianist down

---

43. The difficulty of translating Liszt's concert fees (which he earned in a variety of different currencies —pounds, francs, gulden, thaler, roubles, etc.) into sums comprehensible to the modern reader is impossible to resolve. The twin phenomena of inflation and floating exchange rates will forever mask the true value of money in times past. Some social historians have dealt with this sort of problem via concordance tables which convert money into goods (e.g., 100 pounds equals a house, 500 francs equals a field of barley) in an attempt to produce an "absolute" standard, but this only leads to further complications, as the cost of goods differs from country to country. The biographer is wise to follow the example of the legendary Scots divine who, confronted by a fatal flaw in the logic of his sermon, told his congregation to "stare this difficulty in the face and pass by on the other side."

44. ACLA, vol. 1, p. 213.

45. The ceremony took place on July 18, 1842, in the main public square of Liège. It is amusing to note that Liszt received the cross in company with his old critic Fétis, who was now a director of the Brussels Conservatoire of Music.

Liszt in Berlin, a silhouette by Varnhagen von Ense (1842).

to size. He became the object of a scurrilous attack in the columns of the *Sylphide*.

> For a long time M. Liszt has been merely ridiculous. We laughed at his long hair and his great sabre. His last trip to Germany begins to make him odious. Today, this Word of the piano is vainly trying to change into a man, growing a body, hat, cane, boots, like every Tom, Dick, and Harry, sticking a pince-nez to his eyebrows and deigning to watch the crowd pass by on the boulevard.[46]

This notice was calculated to wound. Its wicked references to a carriage "drawn by six coal-black horses" and a bared sabre brandished before "a flock of duchesses" were thinly disguised variations on past scenes in Berlin and Hungary. They had nothing to do with anything in Paris. Paris laughed anyway. Liszt had become the butt of much satire in his adopted city.

46. *La Sylphide,* vol. 6, 1842, p. 59.

Marie d'Agoult Becomes "Daniel Stern": Nélida versus Guermann

> *It is to* him *that I owe everything. He aroused in me a great love, he turned me away from trivialities, cruelly but for my own good he thrust me from himself. If he made me suffer, let him have no regrets, feel no remorse. If he had been what he should have been, I would have remained with him. My name would never have emerged from obscurity.*
>
> MARIE D'AGOULT[1]

I

Liszt's biographers, following the model first laid down by Lina Ramann, traditionally push Marie d'Agoult into the wings at this stage of his life. His career, it is true, had taken on such spectacular proportions that the mere act of reporting them overshadows Marie's subsequent activities. The many "standard" lives of Liszt produced over the past century, however, have been uninterested in her to the point of professional neglect. This is a pity, for Marie stood on the brink of a brilliant literary career which deserves to be more widely known. In any case, her life was still closely bound up with Liszt's. There was, as yet, no question of a permanent break between them. They were still in love; their voluminous correspondence proves it. There were also frequent reunions; as we have seen, Marie had visited Liszt during his stay in London in 1840, and for three consecutive summers, from 1841 to 1843, they had spent their holidays together at Nonnenwerth. They were united, above all, in the love they bore their three children, whose interests dominated most other considerations. It was only after Marie had transformed herself into

---

1. AM. p. 184.

382

"Daniel Stern" and published her novel *Nélida,* with its unflattering portrait of Liszt, that their relations became poisoned. We must now see how that transformation came about.

I I

Marie had arrived back in Paris at the beginning of November 1839 and had taken up residence at 10, rue Neuve des Mathurins, situated in the heart of the Faubourg St.-Honoré. This imposing home comprised a large salon, two reception rooms, a library, and living quarters for her household staff—a cook, a valet, and a groom. Marie's return to Paris had led to a swift rapprochement with her brother, Maurice, and her mother, Countess de Flavigny. The embarrassment of the three illegitimate children was easily solved: in the eyes of Countess de Flavigny these children simply did not exist. She never once acknowledged them.[2] Within the Flavigny circle it was taken for granted that, in return for being received back into the family bosom, their errant daughter would behave with tact and circumspection as far as the welfare and education of her three illicit offspring by Liszt were concerned, and do nothing further to compromise the family name. Happily, this delicate problem resolved itself. The children were brought up in Paris by their grandmother Anna Liszt, who loved them as her own, and was loved by them in return. Blandine and Cosima had been taken to Anna almost as soon as Marie had returned to Paris. Daniel was still in Italy and did not join his sisters until the autumn of 1841. When Henri Lehmann was finally instructed to bring the two-year-old boy home, he found him in a badly neglected state, starving, and as he later told Marie d'Agoult, "all skin and bone." Anna Liszt nursed the child devotedly until he regained his strength, and probably saved his life. She was delighted to have her grandchildren around her, and this arrangement was sanctioned by Liszt, who regularly sent his mother large sums of money, often in excess of 15,000 francs, for their upkeep and education. According to his will (1860), Liszt

---

2. In a revealing note to Georges and Emma Herwegh, inviting them to dinner, Marie cautioned them: "When my mother is there, please do not mention Blandine. She *protests* against the existence of these children by her constant silence, and becomes terribly embarrassed if they are even mentioned." (HPD, p. 64.) Some indication of just how strained Marie's relations with her mother had become may be gleaned from her unpublished correspondence with Ronchaud. Shortly before returning to Paris she had written, "It has been three years now since [my mother] has given me, or asked for, a sign of life." And she added bitterly, "It is the second time in her life that she has shown proof in this way of the nobility of her feelings and the superiority of her intelligence." (FFDS, p. 529.) What was the first "proof" to which Marie refers? She has nothing less in mind than Countess de Flavigny's icy reserve towards her eldest daughter, Augusta Bussmann (Marie's half-sister), whose divorce from Clement Brentano and subsequent suicide had also stained the family's name.

succeeded in amassing a capital fund of 220,000 francs, most of it raised during his European tours in the 1840s, which was invested for his family with Rothschild's bank in Paris. Marie d'Agoult did not pay a penny for the welfare of the children, even after she came into possession of the Flavigny fortune following the death of her mother.

On the d'Agoult side of the family, matters were still more delicate. Charles d'Agoult had borne the scandal of his wife's elopement with dignity and forbearance. He still lived at their country château, Croissy, with their daughter, Claire, now ten years old. It says much for d'Agoult's character that when he learned of Marie's return to Paris, he uttered not one word of acrimony or reproach. He not only gave Marie complete access to their daughter, but offered to forgive and forget if she would return to Croissy as his wife. Marie reported this magnanimous gesture to Liszt, who, thoroughly alarmed, spoke out strongly against it.

> No and no again. If your husband wishes to go to extremes, I shall come to Paris immediately and we will put a stop to it, once and for all. Come what may, I am absolutely determined on it, and even you will not make me change my mind.
>
> Without doubt, in the eyes of the law you belong to him body and soul, but matters do not always turn out like that in this world below. One temporizes, one arranges things, one agrees as one has to when each detests the other. Let us be confident, as in the past. The hardest part is over, without doubt.[3]

This letter reveals Liszt's practical, common-sense approach to life. It was good advice, which, as it happens, Marie had no need to accept, since she had not the slightest intention of returning to live under Charles d'Agoult's roof. It was a thinly veiled attempt to make Liszt jealous, one of several similar ploys she used to keep Liszt's interest in her alive. A few weeks later we find her writing to him about a new admirer, Henry Bulwer-Lytton, a diplomat attached to the British Embassy in Paris. Bulwer became enamoured of Marie, and would certainly have proposed marriage had she been free to accept. He even made the extraordinary suggestion that he should adopt one of Liszt's daughters,[4] an idea that Liszt sharply rebuffed. Marie, playing her cards with all the skill she could muster, wrote to Liszt about Bulwer and asked him for "une petite permission d'infidélité." Liszt gave Marie a worldly-wise reply which, in effect, called her bluff.

---

3. ACLA, vol. 1, p. 295.
4. ACLA, vol. 1, pp. 361–62.

You ask me for permission to be unfaithful! Dear Marie, you do not give me any name, but I suppose it is Bulwer. It does not matter. You know my way of looking at that kind of thing. You know that for me the facts, the deeds, are nothing. The feelings, the ideas, the shades of meaning, especially the shades of meaning, are everything. I want and I wish you always to have complete freedom, because I am convinced that you would always use it nobly, tactfully. . . .

If you feel the need to, or if it gives you pleasure, or even distracts you to talk to me about Bulwer, do so. I shall be satisfied and flattered; otherwise I will never mention the matter.[5]

Marie was completely disarmed and could only reply lamely:

What you say about the *permission d'infidélité* . . . is full of feeling and fills me with respect for you, although your way of looking at it will always be completely incomprehensible to me. It is as impossible for me to conceive of it as it is for a fish to fly in the air, and I can only accept it as an inexplicable fact.[6]

It was all a ruse. She was amused by Bulwer, but she did not love him. In any case, she would hardly have made a satisfactory lover. Racked by guilt over her abandoned husband, Marie found the stresses and strains of her private life and the psychological pressures under which she laboured during this difficult period of her social rehabilitation to be too much for her. She again fell victim to bouts of severe depression, and suffered from neurasthenia. Over the years her "nerves" became so poor that she sought medical advice and became a regular patient of Dr. Emile Blanche,[7] a Paris nerve specialist who ran a private clinic in Passy. Marie also suffered a great deal of pain in one of her legs, possibly from phlebitis, which for a time made it difficult for her to get about.[8] By the spring of 1840 this condition had become so distressing that Liszt and Maurice de Flavigny had been forced to carry Marie, arm in arm, from one room to another.[9] To add to her other discomforts, she contracted erysipelas.[10]

---

5. ACLA, vol. 1, p. 357.

6. ACLA, vol. 1, p. 365.

7. VCA, vol. 3, p. 194.

8. ACLA, vol. 1, p. 366.

9. LLB, vol. 7, p. 303.

10. ACLA, vol. 1, p. 349. It would be misleading to suppose that Marie d'Agoult was henceforth condemned to a life of chastity, however. On the basis of unpublished letters, we believe that she took two lovers after her return to France. The first was Emile de Girardin, and the other was Charles

Marie's salon soon attracted some of the best-known names in politics and art. Her circle now included Lamartine, Victor Hugo, Georges and Emma Herwegh and the critic Théophile Gautier. A frequent visitor was Emile de Girardin, the editor of *La Presse;* his wife was Delphine Gay, the poetess, who had known Marie long before her liaison with Liszt had begun and now smoothed the path for her return into fashionable society. Girardin was a notoriously taciturn man who never took part in after-dinner conversations but would silently withdraw, leave his loquacious wife in charge of the field, wrap himself in an enormous shawl, and doze quietly in a corner of the room until it was time to go back to his office. His newspaper was his life, and he was one of the best editors in France. He had a flair for discerning the major issues of the day and for spotting new writing talents to treat them. Girardin became deeply interested in Marie d'Agoult and in the story of her years of "exile" with Liszt in Italy. When he discovered that she had already dabbled in writing, he promised that he would publish in *La Presse* anything she cared to give him. One day she happened to mention that she had visited an exhibition of paintings by Delaroche in the Ecole des Beaux Arts and had written down her impressions of each picture. Girardin insisted that she read him the piece aloud. When she had finished he said: "It is excellent. I know nothing about art, I don't know if you are right, but your article is written as few people can write, and you give the impression of someone with a right to form an opinion."[11] He took the pages from her and promised to return the next day with the proofs. As he was about to leave he noticed that they were not signed.

"I can't sign it," Marie said.

"Why not?"

"I can't use a name that doesn't belong to me alone, and I have no intention of asking permission to use it. If I am going to be criticized for what I have written, I don't want anyone to have to defend my honour."

This was not a romantic delusion. Journalism could be a dangerous profession in those days for a writer with outspoken views, and it was not unusual to be challenged to a duel. Girardin himself had been challenged just four years earlier and had killed his opponent—a tragedy that still caused him remorse.

"You are right," said Girardin. "In which case, why not take a pseudonym?"

"But what name can I take?" asked Marie.

She walked over to her writing-desk and jotted down a name on the blotting pad at random: Daniel. It was the name of her son, and the name of her

---

Didier. In his unpublished *Journal,* Didier hints that Marie submitted to him on the night of January 30, 1842, after an evening at the Opéra. (See also VCA, vol. 2. p. 281.)

11. AM, pp. 211–12.

favourite biblical prophet, who had bravely entered the lions' den. The surname eluded her for a moment. Girardin was still waiting at the other side of the room. She wanted above all to write the truth, and suddenly thought in German, "Daniel Wahr" ("True"), but it did not look right. Perhaps as a writer she would have a lucky star *(Stern)*. "Daniel Stern." The name was found.[12] The next day *La Presse* carried Marie's article,[13] her first under this pseudonym, and launched a distinguished literary career which is still not forgotten in France. One of the things that helped to catapult "Daniel Stern" to fame was her clear and incisive way of writing. She excelled at the feuilleton—short, hard-hitting pieces which often dealt with sensitive political issues and broke a lance for the underprivileged—and gained for herself a wide following. As the years passed, Marie found herself at the centre of a growing circle of political admirers for whose revolutionary ideas she was often the mouthpiece. She discovered that she had a flair for historical objectivity, and this reached its natural outcome in her three-volume *Histoire de la Révolution de 1848,* which is still regarded as the best account of that event in any language. Other historical works included *Marie Stuart: Trois Journées historiques* and a play, *Jeanne d'Arc: Drame historique,* which was produced with great success in Italy, though never in France. The actor Bocage gave a reading of it in Marie's salon before a distinguished gathering. Michelet, the French historian, was present and paid her the perfect compliment: "You carry the burden of history with a light touch."

III

In two respects must posterity find Marie culpable. First, she appears to have shown not the slightest interest in Liszt's creative activity; at any rate, she disdained writing about it. One can search her voluminous correspondence in vain for all but a few scraps of information about his work, and these are totally lacking in detail about his composing and his playing. This is truly extraordinary when we recall that she lived on terms of daily intimacy with Liszt for over five years. On those rare occasions when she deigns to mention his work at all, it is either in passing ("to go through life with a woman like me, one needed something more than being able to play the piano well"[14]) or it is to make some self-pitying observation to the effect that his professional interests are taking him away from her side. Contrast that with the detailed observations left by Clara Schumann, or of Liszt's own daughter

---

12. AM, p. 212.

13. "La Nouvelle Salle de l'Ecole des Beaux-Arts peinte par M. Paul Delaroche," December 12, 1841.

14. VFL, p. 152.

Cosima, both of whom bequeathed to posterity diaries and letters which are an unfailing source of illumination about the respective geniuses with whom they lived. The second matter, though not so important, is equally symptomatic. Marie showed scant interest in Liszt's childhood and early background. It is as if he simply did not exist for her before his twenty-first year, when he walked into Marquise Le Vayer's drawing room in 1833 and Marie set eyes on him for the first time. In grooming him for the sophisticated world outside, it would not do to dwell on Liszt's lowly origins, which she accordingly thrust from her. It is significant that after the break had come, Marie flung his origins in his face: "Beneath the French veneer one still detects in you the Hungarian peasant."[15] Contrast that with the attitude of the Princess von Sayn-Wittgenstein, who, soon after uniting her life with his, in the winter of 1847, went on a pilgrimage with him to his natal village of Raiding and thereafter became an assiduous collector of Liszt memorabilia—so much so that she turned their home in Weimar into a veritable Liszt museum, a shrine to his memory even during his lifetime.

One clue to such studied neglect suggests itself. In Marie's quest for her "great man" it was clearly implied that she, and she alone, would be his guiding light, his inspiration. Liszt soon made it plain that she was to be nothing of the sort. Whatever the reasons that made him love her, she was dispensable as far as his art was concerned. (It is a demonstrable fact that among the voluminous body of compositions that poured forth during their tempestuous relationship, only three are actually dedicated to her. Of these, "Die Lorelei" and an arrangement of Schubert's "Ave Maria" form an ironic coupling, which unconsciously marks the poles of her character.) For all this Marie could not forgive him. Some way had to be found to punish him for his creative independence. She subsequently accused him, through her novel *Nélida,* of artistic impotence. No more logical argument existed for her than to assume that the reason she did not inspire him was because there was nothing in him to inspire. He was therefore unworthy of her love. Her invention of Guermann, the painter who suffers from a "creative block" (and who represents Liszt in her novel), was a masterpiece of self-deception. But it served Marie's purpose: it did Liszt harm.

We shall come to understand Marie's growing hostility towards Liszt only if we continue to look at the situation through her eyes. During the years 1840–44 she was forced to follow Liszt's career from afar, after having been an intimate part of it for five years. She had at first consoled herself with the thought that he would soon return to Paris in order to resume their life together. But as the years rolled by it became obvious that no such reconciliation would take place. His rare visits to France were merely brief respites for fresh conquests abroad. That she was still vitally interested in everything Liszt

---

15. GL, p. 93.

did is borne out by her scrapbook,[16] which contains hundreds of newspaper cuttings, in several languages, carefully arranged in chronological order, documenting his successes all over Europe. Soon rumours began to reach her about his encounters with the opposite sex—Marie Pleyel, Charlotte von Hagn, Eva Hanska. All her old jealousies returned to torment her. There is no doubt that Marie suffered intensely from these stories of his flirtations, and she taxed him about one or two of them. About Charlotte von Hagn he told her obliquely: "I have told you the truth and nothing but the truth about the person in question."[17] Later it came to Marie's attention that Liszt had written to the actress, and Marie demanded that he recover his letters. "It will be very difficult for me to get back the letters from La Hagn," he replied, "since she will scarcely relinquish them to me."[18] As for Marie Pleyel, Liszt had been obliged to write Madame d'Agoult a long letter of explanation about their encounter in Vienna,[19] and he had every reason to suppose that she had accepted it. Early in 1844, however, Liszt's *Norma* Fantasy was published with a dedication to La Pleyel, and a flattering letter which Liszt had addressed to her, in which he referred to her as "my dear and ravishing colleague," adorned the first edition as an engraved facsimile for all the world to see—a sharp piece of salesmanship by the publisher, Schott, who could only have received this letter from Marie Pleyel herself. It was picked up by the Paris journal *Le Ménestrel* and reprinted on February 4, 1844. Madame d'Agoult angrily demanded that the dedication be withdrawn. At first Liszt prevaricated,[20] but, as Marie kept insisting, he told her curtly, "The dedication to *Norma* must be left as it is."[21]

More than one hundred and fifty years have elapsed, and not a single piece

---

16. ASSV.
17. ACLA, vol. 2, p. 224.
18. ACLA, vol. 2, p. 257.
19. ACLA, vol. 1, pp. 331–33.
20. ACLA, vol. 2, p. 323.
21. ACLA, vol. 2, p. 332. Since the letter to La Pleyel remains obscure, never having found its way into the main collections, it is reproduced here in full.

Weimar, January 1844

Madame,

Here, my dear and ravishing colleague, is a fantasy loaded and overloaded with arpeggios, octaves, and those dull commonplaces supposed to be brilliant and extraordinary, with which many of our other colleagues, not very ravishing besides, have been bludgeoning and assassinating us for a long time, so much so that we're all up to our ears in it.

Nonetheless, such is the magic of your personality and talent that, if you are willing to go over these few pages of reminiscences with your matchless fingers, I have no doubt that they will seem new and will produce the most magnificent effect.

Schott, whom our mutual friend Berlioz likens quite ingeniously to the Sleeping Beauty, for certainly he scarcely sleeps when it is a question of publishing a mass of good and bad things, agrees with me in this instance.

of solid evidence has ever come to light to prove that Liszt's connection with any of these women was sexual. Liszt was human, and there were times when he doubtless succumbed to the temptations that his erratic life-style occasionally strewed across his path. But he was not the sexual predator that some of his earlier biographers have claimed him to be. Unlike the true Don Juan, Liszt genuinely liked female company, and he had a great respect for female intuition and intelligence. Perhaps that is why he was surrounded by so many female admirers, both young and old, throughout his long life. Liszt treated them as his intellectual equals (which again sets him apart from the real Don Juan, who, because he sees women simply as his sexual prey, has no female admirers at all), and this must have made his companionship not merely refreshing but prized in those socially bigoted times.[22] One other point requires attention. Liszt remained free of the *morbus gallicus,* a disease that laid waste so many artists of the nineteenth century—Schumann, Heine, Paganini, Smetana, and Hugo Wolf among them—which suggests that he was at the very least a more selective lover than they were. Those biographers who insist on following the old line that Liszt led a life of sexual recklessness during these turbulent years must be invited to produce the evidence—or drop the claim. Chivalry and adoration of the fair sex were ever Liszt's portion, especially where intelligence happened to be clothed in beauty, but we are not aware that this calls for a defence, even in this plebeian age. Typical of his chivalrous attitude was his innocent attachment to Marie Duplessis (who was later immortalized by Alexandre Dumas in his novel *La Dame aux camélias*). This beautiful twenty-one-year-old girl, who had been loved by many men, was already dying of con-

---

The composer and publisher therefore humbly request your patronage for this extremely mixed composition, laying it at your feet and in your hands: the latter begging you to let the public hear it often, since it will never tire of admiring you, and I asking to be pitied a little for not knowing how to spend my time better than by writing this sort of banality.

Many renewed regards,

F. LISZT

It is difficult for the detached reader to see anything more in this letter than a harmless piece of flattery, a puff of prose meant to swell the artistic pride of Madame Pleyel. Why Marie d'Agoult chose to translate it into a public humilation remains a mystery. Julien Tiersot (TLMF, vol. 2, pp. 355–56) rightly draws attention to Liszt's deadpan humour. The phrase "our mutual friend Berlioz" is addressed to the former Marie Moke, over whom Berlioz, as we have observed, had nearly committed suicide after she had rejected him.

22. As Liszt grew older, his mesmeric charm for women seemed to become stronger. Berthold Kellermann, a Weimar pupil who knew Liszt well during the 1870s, was one of the few observers to keep a level head when addressing this topic. "The insistence of some Liszt biographers that Liszt was a great Don Juan is untrue and has its origin chiefly in the vanity of certain women who, because they were jealous of one another, used to boast that the Master loved them. . . . How seriously Liszt thought about matters of love is indicated by his noble behaviour towards Countess d'Agoult. That he did not marry the mother of his children, despite their long years of life together, was not his fault." (KE, pp. 51–52.)

sumption when Liszt was introduced to her in Paris, in November 1845, by her physician, Dr. Koreff.[23] The last time Liszt visited her bedside she begged him to take her away with him. "I won't bother you," she pleaded. "I sleep all day. In the evening you can let me go to a show and at night you can do what you like with me."[24] There was something deeply affecting about this frail girl's desperate bid to cling to life through Liszt. In order to calm her agitated nerves, Liszt promised to take her to Constantinople, but she carried this unfulfilled dream to an early grave. "And now she is dead," wrote Liszt. "I do not know what strange chord of elegy vibrates in my heart in memory of her." When Liszt told Madame d'Agoult that Marie Duplessis was the first woman he had loved who now lay dead in a cemetery, he was saying that women who were attracted to him were not usually harmed by the experience. Such fine points were lost on Madame d'Agoult, however; she was the mother of his children, and infidelity was infidelity, whether conducted on a spiritual or physical plane. Even so, and despite the casuistry of which she often accused him, she still loved him and would have been willing to forgive him his transgressions, real or imagined. But then something happened that she found impossible to accept.

I V

Early in March 1844 Liszt passed through Dresden and met Lola Montez, the flaming, flamboyant "Spanish dancer." The couple were spotted in public, and rumours of a liaison got into the European newspapers. For several years Lola

---

23. Both Anna Liszt and Marie d'Agoult had been patients of Dr. David-Ferdinand Koreff (ACLA, vol. 1, pp. 300–301). A "society doctor" who prescribed dubious cures for his wealthy female clientele, Koreff was described by André Maurois, the biographer of Marie Duplessis, as resembling "a strange figure out of Hoffmann, half charlatan, half genius." The letter Liszt wrote to Koreff on February 12, 1847, sheds light on this obscure relationship. (*L'Intermédiaire des Chercheurs,* August 20, 1913.) After the death of Mlle Duplessis, it appears that Koreff sued her executors for unpaid medical bills, amounting to 1,400 francs, and turned to Liszt for support in his case against them. Liszt refused to be drawn, reminding Koreff that he did not even know Mlle Duplessis during the period of medical treatment in dispute (May–June 1845), having been introduced to her in November of that year. Apparently Mlle Duplessis, sensing that Koreff's remedies were useless against her illness and that her end was near, had dispensed with his services and had called in the most reputable medical specialists in Paris. It transpired that Koreff had been slowly killing his delicate patient with one centigramme of strychnine per day. (GCR, p. 240.)

In his preface to Alexandre Dumas's novel, Jules Janin insisted that it was he who introduced Liszt to Marie Duplessis in the foyer of a small boulevard theatre, the Ambigu, during the intermission of a new play. Although Janin's account does not tally exactly with Liszt's recollection of his having been first taken to Mlle Duplessis's home by Koreff, the discrepancy is a small one and is understandable, given the hectic social whirl in which Liszt lived at this time. A chance meeting, such as Janin describes, could very well have taken place in the Ambigu's foyer, to be followed up a day or two later with a more formal introduction by Koreff.

24. ACLA, vol. 2, p. 379.

had trailed scandal and gossip in her wake, and Marie d'Agoult felt betrayed. She wrote Liszt a sharp letter "five times sealed," to which he responded:

> After having thought matters over for a long time, deeply and sorrowfully, I feel that it is impossible for me to justify myself or to answer in any way your letter. . . . So I am simply enclosing with this letter the broken sphinx you gave me in Rome.[25]

Of all Liszt's passing *galanteries,* this one attracted the most attention. Let us attempt to jettison some of the gossip and establish some of the facts. Her name was not Lola, she was not Spanish, and, if her critics are to be believed, she was not a dancer either. Everything about Lola Montez was false—except perhaps her ample bosom, which she once bared before King Ludwig I of Bavaria. Her real name was Eliza Gilbert, and she was born in Limerick, Ireland, in 1818. Even more prosaic was her family background. Her father was Ensign Edward Gilbert, a young army officer who had seduced her mother, a certain Miss Oliver, while she was still a girl of fourteen; Lola was born at the Limerick army barracks before the honeymoon period had expired.[26] Not long after this calamitous beginning, Ensign Gilbert was despatched to Calcutta with his child bride and baby daughter. Ordered into the Indian hinterland, he contracted cholera and died. The young widow soon acquired a new husband, Captain Patrick Craigie, who sent his small stepdaughter back to Scotland to be brought up by his relatives. Her childhood and adolescence were spent in Montrose and Bath. When Lola was eighteen her mother returned from India and announced that she had arranged for her daughter to wed a sixty-year-old judge, Sir Abraham Lumley. Lola flatly refused to entertain the idea of reclining in the bosom of "a gouty judge," and she eloped instead with her mother's travelling companion, Lieutenant Thomas James. They were married in Dublin in 1837 and moved in with Lieutenant James's relatives, who lived in a small village on the edge of a peat bog. In these salubrious surroundings Lola first began her long repentance of her precipitous marriage. Lieutenant James was now posted back to India, where he joined the Twenty-first Bengal Native Infantry. Life in the Punjab was not to Lola's liking either, and she started to quarrel violently with her husband, alleging among other things that he "slept like a boa-

---

25. ACLA, vol. 2, p. 335.
26. The literature on Lola Montez is filled with confusion and error, most of it sown by Lola herself. *The Times* printed a letter from her (March 31, 1847) in which she claimed to have been born in Seville in 1823, to be the daughter of a Spanish envoy in the service of Don Carlos, and to be called Maria Dolores Porres Montez. This tissue of lies found its way into many books about her. Lola Montez is buried in New York, and her tombstone bears the inscription "Mrs. Eliza Gilbert." Perhaps the most painstaking account of her life is by Horace Wyndham (WMM), from which the present summary of her activities has been drawn.

constrictor." Captain James (he had meanwhile been promoted) took his revenge by running off with the wife of his adjutant, Mrs. Lomer. Lola travelled back to England in 1840 on board H M S *Larkin*. To protect her "good name," she put out the story that her departure from India had been occasioned by "an equestrian accident": in short, that she had been thrown from a horse. Once on board the *Larkin* she was touched by scandal again. During the long voyage she met a Captain Lennox, and when the ship docked in London she stayed with him at the Imperial Hotel in Covent Garden. The resulting court case, *James v. Lennox*, was reported in *The Times* on December 7, 1842.

Lola now decided to become an actress. She enrolled in the drama school of Fanny Kemble, but was so bad that Miss Kemble advised her to take up dancing instead. In June 1843 she pounded the boards of the Haymarket Theatre, dressed in purple and red petticoats and with castanets, performing under the name of Doña Lola Montez, and was booed off the stage. For eighteen months she toured Europe in this ridiculous guise. It was a fact that she could scarcely keep time, and whenever she appeared on stage the musicians were instructed simply to "follow Lola." With very little money, with her body as her chief asset (and with a succession of managers who were her lovers—the only way, in the absence of talent, to keep her career afloat), she openly proclaimed it to be her ambition "to hook a prince." She succeeded beyond all her expectations in 1846, when she hung up her dancing shoes and became the mistress of Ludwig I.

When Liszt arrived in Dresden at the end of February 1844, the twenty-six-year-old Lola was already in the city. Her career was going badly; she needed a benefactor. Nothing is known of their first meeting, but she quickly latched on to the famous pianist. We do not have a single piece of documentary evidence to suggest that she became Liszt's mistress—not one letter, not one diary entry, not one confession from either side. Strangely enough, Lola, who was never reluctant to name her other lovers, was silent on the subject of Liszt.[27] He took her to a performance of *Rienzi,* and during the interval they went round to the artists' dressing room to congratulate the tenor Tichatscheck. They bumped into Richard Wagner, who was repelled by the painted lady on Liszt's arm, with her insolent eyes, and who hastily withdrew. Lola is rumoured to have followed Liszt to several German towns, where her presence became an embarrassment to him. Julius Kapp even has Liszt bribing the hotel porter to lock Lola in her room for twelve hours so that he might make his escape, having already paid in advance for the damage the infuriated woman would do to the furniture when she discovered she had been duped.[28] This story has been

---

27. Her nine volumes of memoirs, for example, make but passing mention of him.
28. KFL, p. 177. Kapp describes this as an "authoritative episode." We take leave to doubt it. Much of the information for Kapp's generally reliable biography (1909) came from Liszt's own pupils and disciples. But the Lola Montez episode was more than fifty years old when Kapp began his inquiries. There was no one among the survivors of Liszt's last circle who went back that far. This harmful

repeated many times, but there is no proof that it is anything more than a colourful concoction. Of far more interest are the dates. Since the performance of Wagner's *Rienzi* took place on February 29, and since Lola was already in Paris by March 30 to make her dancing début in Halévy's *Le lazzarone,* the Liszt-Montez encounter could not have lasted for more than three weeks. Lola could not possibly have "pursued Liszt to Paris," as so many of his earlier biographers have asserted, for we now know that he himself did not arrive there until April 5,[29] one week after her début. To suggest, as Huneker and others have done, that Liszt was touring Europe with Lola, and even went to Constantinople with her, is irresponsible and indicates that they had no knowledge of Lola's itinerary, which took her almost at once to Warsaw and St. Petersburg while Liszt went on to Spain. Moreover, the torrid affair she began with the Paris journalist Dujarier (whose death through duelling resulted in a trial at which she was a prosecution witness) kept Lola in France for much of 1845.

By the time Liszt got back to Paris, the press had had a field-day with Lola. Her début at the Paris Opéra had been a fiasco. Halfway through a dance routine a slipper fell off. She picked it up and threw it into the boxes, where the "gentlemen of fashion" brandished it as a trophy. Jules Janin wrote an offensive article in the *Journal des Débats,* while Théophile Gautier tore her to tatters with rapier-like thrusts:

> The only thing Andalusian about Mlle Lola Montez is a pair of magnificent black eyes. [She] . . . has small feet and shapely legs. Her use of these is quite another matter. . . . We suspect, after the recital of her equestrian exploits, that Mlle Lola is more at home in the saddle than on the boards.[30]

It is only in this wider context that we can understand Madame d'Agoult's decision to make her break with Liszt irrevocable. Lola Montez was now in Paris dancing at the Opéra, less than half a mile from Marie's apartments in the rue Neuve des Mathurins. She had every reason to suppose, even though it was not true, that Liszt had brought this strumpet to Paris himself and secured engagements for her at the Opéra. Marie and Liszt dined together almost as soon as Liszt got back to Paris, but the occasion was a melancholy one. A day or two later she wrote Liszt a sad letter in which she described herself as "a cause

---

anecdote, which Kapp has the dubious distinction of having launched, has meanwhile been stolen from his original German and given wider circulation by Lola's French and English biographers, whose books appear to "corroborate" the very incident in dispute. It is one more example of the readiness of biographers to take in one another's washing, irrespective of the condition of the garments.

29. ACLA, vol. 2, p. 335.
30. ALM, p. 66.

of sorrow and useless strife" in his life. She told him that she was parting from
him "in the deepest sadness of my soul."[31] Liszt replied with two or three short
notes, but they remained unanswered. He then learned that Marie was planning
to leave Paris for a while, and insisted on seeing her again. There was a violent
quarrel, in which Marie cried that she did not object to being his mistress but
she objected to being *one* of his mistresses.[32] The quarrel was reported to
Georges Herwegh, for on May 17 he replied:

> The news you give me was not unexpected; I knew that Liszt
> would make another attempt before your departure, and I was not
> sad without reason when I heard, during the course of the day, of
> the scene between you and him.
> Liszt remains entirely faithful to his nature. Just as it is impossible
> for him to shake off the present and the thousand *good-for-nothings*
> who dog his footsteps, so he will never shake off his past, and scenes
> like the one on Monday between you and him will recur as long
> as you and he find yourselves in the same place.[33]

Marie had good reason to want to leave Paris for a few weeks. Her final rupture
with Liszt, painful though it was, could never by itself have driven her away
from her home and her friends. Deeper motives were at work. On March 22,
two weeks before Liszt got back to Paris, she had written to Herwegh: "I will
send you tomorrow the plan of the novel that I have begun."[34] The novel was
Nélida, the literary tombstone beneath which she now planned to bury her dead
hopes. It had always been assumed that Marie d'Agoult began *Nélida* after her
final break with Liszt, but we now know that she had first conceived the idea
for this strange book as early as November 1843, more than six months before
she and Liszt parted company.[35] When Liszt and Marie met for the last time,
in early May 1844, not only were the details of the novel planned, but a
preliminary draft was already in the hands of Georges Herwegh. Marie's chief
reason for leaving Paris stemmed from her desire to complete the book as
speedily as possible, free from interruptions.

Nélida was finished during the summer of 1844 while Marie d'Agoult was
on holiday in the village of Herblay, where she had rented a small house with
a view of the Seine and the forest. In these inspirational surroundings she
reflected on her years with Liszt and offered the world her fictional account

---

31. ACLA, vol. 2, p. 337.
32. VFL, p. 152.
33. HPD, p. 71.
34. HPD, p. 62.
35. VCA, vol. 2, p. 141. "Began *Nélida* with extreme enthusiasm," Marie recorded in her unpublished
"Agenda" on November 3, 1843. (Bibliothèque Nationale, Archives Daniel Ollivier, NAF 25179).

of their romance. Marie wanted *Nélida* to be perceived not so much as a novel than as a barely disguised autobiography, and anyone remotely familiar with the main outlines of Liszt's life cannot doubt that Marie generated much of her narrative from reality. She even appears to have used their correspondence as source material. Even so, it would be absurd to regard *Nélida* as a historical document. It is mostly the product of Marie's fantasy. Its chief interest to the Liszt scholar is the light it throws on Marie herself. The book possesses scarcely any literary merit. Why, then, deal with it at all? Because the world, recognizing that parts of it were true, had every reason to suppose that all of it was. In order to disentangle fact from fiction, it is necessary to know something of the story.

V

The heroine of the novel is Nélida[36] de la Theiellaye, a young woman of high breeding and noble aspirations, and the heiress to a fortune. As a young child she is brought up on the estates of her aunt, Viscountess d'Hespel. Adjoining the d'Hespel estates is a humble little house in which lives a widow, Madame Regnier, and her young son Guermann. Nélida and Guermann become play-mates; Guermann rows her on the lake, walks with her through the woods, and steals cherries for her from the orchard of a local farmer. Nélida tells him that it is wrong to steal, but Guermann only laughs and tells her to eat them. When they return home they are reprimanded for their escapade. Already in this opening chapter the authoress has sharply delineated their personalities, insisting on Guermann's plebeian birth and his lack of moral scruples, the twin "defects" she henceforth hammers at in her dealings with Liszt. Nélida is sent to complete her education at the Convent of the Annunication, where she remains for several years. The mother superior, Mère Elisabeth, dotes on her and convinces her that she has a religious vocation. Nélida's only true friend is a fellow pupil, Claudine, whom she has rescued from the taunts and teasings of her school-mates. These episodes are drawn straight from Marie's adolescence at the Sacré-Coeur, and their real-life counterparts will be found in her *Souvenirs*.[37] The day dawns when the viscountess comes to fetch Nélida away from the school and arrange for her début in the world of fashionable society. She makes a great impression at a ball given by the Austrian ambassador and becomes one of the most eligible débutantes of the season. Not long afterwards, Nélida meets Count Timoléon de Kervaens, a young aristocrat who has recently returned

---

36. The name Nélida is, as pointed out earlier, an anagram of Daniel. From the beginning, then, the world had no difficulty in recognizing in the book's leading character the personality of Marie herself.
37. AS, pp. 164–65, p. 173.

from a tour of Asia Minor. Nélida and Timoléon dance together. Since it is the first time a man has held her in his arms, she almost faints as her emotions overwhelm her. Timoléon, however, is more attracted by her wealth than by her beauty, and he confides to one of his mistresses, Mlle Hortense Langin, his intention of marrying the girl. Hortense reports his passion to Nélida, who, tricked into believing that he loves her, accepts his proposal of marriage.

Shortly after her engagement to Timoléon a young man calls at the d'Hespel residence. It is Guermann Regnier, whom she has not seen since her childhood. They stroll in the garden and Guermann tells Nélida that he has become a painter. He has always loved her, he says, ever since he stole cherries for her, a misdemeanour for which he had been forbidden to see her again. He had decided to become an artist in order to win fame for her sake; the social barriers that separated them made no other course possible. "Art," Guermann later declares, "is great, holy, immortal. The artist is the first, the most noble among men, inspired by the Creator." Guermann tells Nélida that he has painted her portrait from memory, a task which has occupied him for seven years. Impressed by this declaration of love, and flattered to think that she has become the source of his inspiration, Nélida begins to visit Guermann in his studio. They discuss art and religion, and they share one another's lofty ideals. Guermann declares that Nélida has become for him as perfect an image of womanhood as Beatrice was for Dante. In the middle of one of these blissful exchanges, Nélida receives a letter from Timoléon informing her that the legal business which took him away from Paris is settled and asking her to fix a date for their marriage. The letter falls from her fingers; Guermann picks it up and reads it. There follows a passionate scene in which Nélida and Guermann declare their love for one another. Again, all this has an autobiographical flavour. In view of the contents of the *Correspondance*[38] we would expect her to lose no time at this stage of the drama in introducing a "betrayal scene," and sure enough that is the very next episode in the novel. One day Nélida arrives at the studio while Guermann is out. She is admitted by a pretty model who, knowing nothing about Nélida, naively informs her that she lives there as Guermann's "wife." Nélida rushes from the house, sobbing bitter tears, utterly shocked by Guermann's duplicity and by her own folly. She attempts to commit suicide by throwing herself into the Seine but is deterred by a passerby, "an ordinary workman." For forty-eight hours she is in a delirium, but she recovers to find Timoléon at her bedside, overjoyed that she recognizes him. She resolves to turn her back on Guermann, and a few months later is married to Count Timoléon de Kervaens in a lavish wedding which is the highlight of the season.

For the next few months the couple live in Timoléon's splendid castle in Brittany, where they receive many distinguished guests. Timoléon quickly

---

38. Compare ACLA, vol. 1, pp. 72 and 82.

becomes bored with his intellectual young wife and starts an affair with one of his guests, Marquise Zepponi. Nélida learns of her husband's infidelity from an elderly cousin of his, who, wishing to open the young woman's eyes to the true nature of the rake to whom she is married, tells her of Timoléon's earlier affair with Hortense Langin as well. Timoléon blithely informs Nélida that he is going to spend the day in the nearby town. Instead he elopes with Marquise Zepponi to Italy. Nélida and Timoléon never see one another again. Betrayed by Guermann, deserted by her husband, Nélida withdraws into solitude and spends her time reading and studying elevated subjects.[39]

One day a visitor appears with a painting which Count de Kervaens had commissioned for his private chapel before fleeing with his mistress. It is Guermann, who uses the opportunity to ask Nélida for her forgiveness. At first she resists his entreaties, but because she still loves him she gradually yields. Since their last meeting Guermann has had his paintings exhibited in Paris, and he is now widely regarded as a genius. Nélida tells Guermann that she is prepared to sacrifice her place in society by going away with him.

The lovers elope to Geneva, just as Marie and Liszt had done.[40] At first they are blissfully happy, and Guermann paints his great picture *The Trial of John Huss*. Their happiness is clouded when word reaches Guermann that his reputation in Paris is threatened by an upstart rival, the painter D——, whose picture *Savonarola* is the talk of the town, and that he must return at once to defend his honour. This is an unmistakable reference to the Thalberg-Liszt "duel," and Marie makes the most of it. "The thought of such a check was more than his lofty *amour-propre* could bear," she writes. Guermann went to Paris "with his heart ulcerated, dreaming of nothing but success, triumph, and revenge." Once there, Guermann secures a victory over his rival. He is fêted and lionized by society, but success goes to his head. He now sees Nélida as a shackle on his life and is slow to rejoin this "obstacle to his career" in Geneva. Without doubt, Marie's *Mémoires* and her letters to Liszt provided the raw material for this part of the novel. It is almost as if these documents were open before her as she wrote. She had found the prolongation of Liszt's stay in Paris (in the spring of 1837) unbearable. In turning life into literature, however, she makes rather

---

39. It never occurred to Marie that if she wanted the world to recognize Liszt in the character of Guermann Regnier, she could hardly be surprised if they also saw Charles d'Agoult in the character of Nélida's husband, Count de Kervaens, whom she depicts as a liar and a lecher. Throughout the novel there is the implication that her husband has done her an unspeakable injustice, the chief reason why she flees with Guermann. In real life, of course, it was different. But Charles d'Agoult has never been able to shake off this cruel pen-portrait. In modern times there was even a play by René Fauchois (*Rêves d'amour,* 1943) which put him on the stage in the grotesque role created for him by his wife.
40. Life is here bent into literature again. Neither in *Nélida* nor, more interestingly, in her *Mémoires* does Marie reveal the true reason why she left Paris: she was pregnant. One cannot blame her for her discretion on such a difficult topic, but it serves to remind the reader that *Nélida* is full of pitfalls for anyone wishing to regard it as a mirror of reality.

heavy weather of it all. She portrays herself as harrowed and suffering, and writes of Guermann:

> He arrived in Geneva with his heart more full of rage than of love. But when he saw Nélida's hollow cheeks, her listless eyes, her pale lips, saw that she was still of an incomparable majesty in her sorrow, his worse nature was vanquished. He fell at her feet, clasped her to him with more ardour than on the first day, and in the madness of his transports soon made her forget all she had suffered during his cruel absence.

The lovers now proceed to Milan, as Liszt and Marie had done, on pain of a solemn promise from Guermann that he will henceforth shun the world and devote his energies to artistic elevation. But again he lapses. He is attracted to society like a moth to a candle; he attends late-night balls and becomes drunk on his own fame. Money pours in from his paintings, which are in great demand in Milan, and he becomes dissolute through indulging himself in high living. Eventually he becomes entangled in the web of a coquette, Marquise Zepponi, the very same adventuress who had run off with Nélida's husband. At this Nélida's fury becomes ungovernable. In righteous anger she parades before him all the sacrifices she has made for him, and demands that he now make a sacrifice for her in return. His cynical reply is to tell her that Malibran could not have acted the scene better. It is the parting of the ways for them both.

The novel now moves towards its true message. Guermann becomes a painter-in-residence attached to the court at W——, a small duchy in Germany. (Liszt, we recall, had been appointed to the court at Weimar just four years earlier.) The grand duke, his patron, has commissioned him to paint a huge fresco in the central hall of the local museum, and Guermann resolves to deliver himself of a masterpiece. Then he catches his first glimpse of the huge walls.

> At the sight of this enormous gallery Guermann's heart suddenly contracted; a cold perspiration moistened his brow. He stood silently, contemplating with startled eyes the dazzling whiteness of the huge domed ceiling bathed in light. . . . At that moment he suffered a horrible sensation. His soul was filled with doubt; he felt himself unequal to his task; he was aware of the appalling discrepancy between his abilities and his ambition. . . .

This passage is the crux of the novel. The white walls of W——'s huge gallery stare back at Guermann mockingly. They defy him through their sheer size, and Guermann's artistic impotence stands revealed. The twofold meaning is clear: without Nélida, Guermann lacks inspiration; also, his small-scale talent is unequal to the large-scale demands now placed on it. The remainder of the novel collapses into banality. Shortly after discovering his creative limitations, Guermann falls ill. He sends for Nélida, who arrives just in time to forgive him for his infidelities before he dies in her arms. Nélida then returns to France, where she devotes the rest of her life to good works.[41]

When *Nélida* was finished Madame d'Agoult submitted the manuscript to Lamennais for criticism. Perceiving the novel's potential for trouble, he refused to be drawn. "It seems very distinguished to me," he replied cautiously, "but I am not competent to judge this kind of thing." He went on to recommend the critic Béranger, "whose judgement in these matters is infallible." Béranger read it and turned it down. "The Abbé Lamennais has told me that you are a woman to whom one can speak the truth. . . . I would advise you not to publish this novel."[42] This was sound advice which Madame d'Agoult did not heed. *Nélida* was published by instalments in the *Revue Indépendante* in 1846. It aroused so much speculation that it was quickly issued in book form. Within a year it had become a best-seller.

Liszt always refused to recognize himself in *Nélida*. At first he was merely curious about the book and wrote Marie a complimentary letter on the "aristocratic manner" of its style.[43] Marie must have been relieved; the full consequences of her allegory had only dawned on her slowly. But when the *Journal des Débats* came out with an article of no less than ten columns by the critic Gachons de Molènes,[44] she knew that she had a runaway success on her hands. She wrote to Liszt, trying to excuse herself, apologizing if his feelings had been hurt. His reply was one from which he never wavered.

> . . . In reply to the torrent of questions, insinuations, condolences and every kind of meanness that has descended on me as a result of *Nélida*, I have always replied imperturbably that never in my life did I wish to become a painter, nor to dine at the table of any Highness, and finally that, so long as I am not mentioned by my full baptismal name and address, I shall always refuse definitely and absolutely to recognize myself in the articles and books whose authors have had the kindness to concern themselves indirectly with my poor person. . . .[45]

---

41. Liszt's good works are not mentioned. The fictional Guermann is never allowed to portray Liszt's highly ethical achievements in behalf of the Beethoven Memorial Fund, the victims of the Danube floods, the charity concerts for the starving silk workers of Lyon. That would have compromised Madame d'Agoult's case against him.
42. AM, pp. 214–15.
43. ACLA, vol. 2, p. 348.
44. May 19, 1846.
45. ACLA, vol. 2, pp. 371–72.

Liszt was totally silent, then and later, about the scene in which Guermann faces the bare walls of the gallery and experiences fears of inadequacy. By 1846 he had created the Transcendentals, the Paganini Studies, the Hungarian Rhapsodies, two volumes of the *Années de pèlerinage,* and a host of other compositions. Did these achievements signify nothing? "Why have you been so hard on poor Lehmann?" Liszt once quipped.[46] Such a question must have rankled with Madame d'Agoult, for the full extent of her blind fixation on the importance of her own role in Liszt's life was revealed twenty years later when she brought out a second edition of *Nélida* unaltered. The fuss created by the first edition had largely died down. *Nélida* was almost forgotten, except by Marie. In 1866 Liszt returned to Paris for a performance of his *Graner* Mass, and she took the opportunity to republish her novel. Liszt now stood for everything Marie had said he could never achieve. His great Weimar accomplishments of the 1850s were behind him. Here was the inventor of the symphonic poem, the creator of the *Faust* Symphony, the B-minor Sonata, and other large-scale compositions, and she depicts him still staring at his empty walls! It was at this point that Liszt called Guermann "a stupid invention."[47] Posterity has meanwhile been obliged to concur.

---

46. WFLR, p. 126. By presenting her "hero" as a painter, Marie d'Agoult had only herself to blame if Liszt jestingly insisted that she had pilloried her admirer Lehmann instead. He repeated the joke to George Eliot when the novelist visited him in Weimar in the summer of 1854 and the topic of *Nélida* was broached. (EGEL, vol. 2, p. 109.)

47. LLB, vol. 6, p. 111. It is amusing to observe that within a few months of the appearance of *Nélida,* George Sand had produced her novel *Lucrezia Floriani,* in which Chopin is depicted as Prince Karol, a weak and unstable neurotic. Was this a coincidence? Hardly. The astonishing parallels between Marie d'Agoult and George Sand must be remarked. Within a year of Marie's elopement with Liszt, in 1835, Sand has "acquired" Chopin. Both ladies stay with their paramours on romantic islands—Nonnenwerth and Valldemosa, respectively. Both live there in deserted monasteries. Both leave their sanctuaries disillusioned. Both quarrel with their pianist-lovers. Both then pick up their pens and write novels about them, taking care to position themselves in a favourable light. Both write memoirs in later life which tell history that they were wronged. And the paramours themselves? Both refuse adamantly to recognize themselves in these novels. It is as if there were two different pairs of actors but only one script.

This was not the only time that Sand made literary capital out of a dead love-affair. Flushed with the success of *Lucrezia Floriani,* she now picked over the bones of her old romance with the poet Alfred de Musset, and in 1859 published her novel *Elle et lui.* This time it rebounded on her. The dead poet's brother published a rebuttal called *Lui et elle.* None of this was of more than passing interest to Liszt, of course. But the modern reader should be aware when considering *Nélida* that not only is it not a unique document, but it is a fairly common example of its kind. Disraeli, Stendhal, Madame de Staël, and others all based novels on living people. And hovering over the roman à clef was the giant shadow of Balzac, whose *Béatrix* had struck sparks from both Sand and Marie d'Agoult.

VI

During most of 1844–45 their go-between was Lambert Massart, Liszt's violin-playing colleague, who was on the staff of the Paris Conservatoire. Of immediate concern was the future of the three children. It was agreed that Blandine, who was now eight, would be sent to the boarding school of Madame Bernard and educated there; Cosima and Daniel would join their sister when they were a little older but would meanwhile continue living at their grandmother's. Liszt undertook to pay Madame d'Agoult a thousand francs a month for Blandine's upkeep. In the course of their long years together the couple never thought that the matter of their children's illegitimate births might one day become a problem. But it now emerged as an important issue as these young offspring found themselves the object of a tug-of-war between their parents. The arrangements negotiated through Massart at first worked well. But soon Liszt heard of personal attacks Marie was publicly making against his character in Paris (he appears to have known nothing yet of *Nélida,* whose publication was still a year away). By itself this would have caused him no lasting concern, but it then reached Liszt's ears that Marie was planning to remove Blandine from Madame Bernard's boarding school and take her home until the school holidays. Liszt felt that he owed it to himself to protest; if Marie blackened his name with his friends, she might also do so with his children. The severe tone of his letter is a measure of the distance which now separated them.

Marseille, May 2, 1845

I always thought, madame, that there was no need of a third party between you and me, and, by accepting those people you chose, my intention was simply to show deference to you. However irritated you are by me now, I am addressing myself directly to you so as to conclude reasonably a debate which is as painful as it is futile. Massart and my mother have written to me that you wish to keep Blandine in your home until the holidays. This arrangement, which seems to me to be of no real value for Blandine, is not the sort to please me very much either.

About a year ago, madame, I was able to think that the incredible opinion you held of me, and expressed to me in several letters, remained a secret between us. I was even obliged to conclude from your past, full of ardent devotion for me, that you would keep the same reserve towards others as I had imposed on myself with regard to you. Now this illusion is no longer tenable, for I can no longer remain in ignorance of the fact that you are going about telling all comers the craziest and most foolish things about me. If it suited you to reflect for a minute, you would easily realize that it is absolutely impossible for anyone to discover the slightest foundation for the accusations you make against me. But it is no longer my task to get into this argument again, and that is not why I am writing these lines to you. They have no other purpose than to ask you if you seriously imagine that it would suit me for Blandine to be raised in your home as long as you remain armed for battle at any price against me.

Obviously not; and without uselessly lengthening my letter, let me hope that you would be willing not to change anything by force in a situation which is, if not good, at least acceptable to us both, and that you will spare me the pain of having to have recourse to unfortunate necessities.[48]

This last line was a veiled threat. Since Liszt did not trust Madame d'Agoult to heed his warning (by this time he had been out of Paris for eight months), he wrote to Massart the same day urging him to take whatever action was necessary to ensure that the children did not fall into her hands. Liszt's anxiety is apparent in every sentence.

May 2, 1845

I want absolutely nothing to be changed in the present situation of the children. Therefore, let Blandine stay at Madame Bernard's and Cosima with my mother. My firm intention is to refuse completely to pay for other arrangements. If, despite that, Madame d'A were to push things to their limits and take the children by force to her home, *I should not consent to it!* and would come to Paris to put an end to all these struggles *some way* or another. I know Madame d'A well enough to make her realize that my refusal to continue to pay Blandine's boarding fees (in the event that Blandine should be withdrawn from Madame Bernard's) will exasperate her enough to make her want to take her to her home at any price, with Cosima too . . . but however painful and disagreeable this resolution of hers would be to me, it would scarcely stop me, and since she has no rights over the children, I myself would have no scruples either in taking all three of them away from her without considering anyone or anything. If, however, it is possible for you to circumvent this unfortunate extremity, do it. Try

---

48. VFL, pp. 77–78.

to get a reasonable decision out of her; the children cannot be raised at her home as long as we two are on the present terms with each other. She would, indeed, have too much the air of a beautiful victim, and I have no desire to give even the appearance of a decision in favour of the many foolish things she is pouring out about me. It is impossible in any case.

Since the mail is leaving at once, it is too late for me to reply to Madame Bernard. You can and indeed you should keep her informed of my relations with Madame d'A. I don't know if she will be able to refuse to give her Blandine without causing a scandal; in any case, *I would approve of her doing this* and would not fail to take responsibility for the consequences. I will reply to Madame Bernard and my mother by tomorrow's post. If things reach the point at which a scene is necessary, I'll come to Paris. I promise you that the affair would be ended in three days. Meanwhile, take heart and be patient. Try to keep the peace, if it is possible, but without making any concessions, because Madame d'A has called upon me no longer to grant her any.

Did Ciabatta give you the thousand francs? Reply at once to Benacci's address, rue St.-Côme, no. 2, Lyon.

Yours affectionately,

F. LISZT[49]

There are few sadder spectacles in Liszt's life than the one of him quarrelling so bitterly with his old lover over their children, the finest fruits of their love. These three infants became the innocent victims of their parents' wrath, and with the passing years they were made miserable by the utter futility of this seemingly endless strife. Liszt was no more suited to the role of tyrant and despot than Madame d'Agoult was suited to the role of a latter-day Niobe gathering her children about her in righteous anger. Both were defensive postures; but they led to terrible consequences, climaxing in Liszt's removing the children not merely from Marie d'Agoult's immediate sphere of influence, but from France itself. The key to the situation lay in the citizenship of the children. Under French law they were regarded as foreigners. Not only had they all been born on foreign soil, but they were also illegitimate. This left Marie d'Agoult with no legal rights whatsoever. Since Liszt had always admitted paternity, and since these offspring openly bore his family name, as far as the French were concerned his children had inherited his nationality: Hungarian. But what about Austro-Hungarian law? Liszt consulted a Marseille lawyer and set about amassing a dossier of family documents which would

---

49. VFL, pp. 78–80.

prove the lineage of his children to be Hungarian.[50] By May 1845 it was completed and despatched to Vienna and Pest for notorization. When Madame d'Agoult learned of the full extent of Liszt's legal authority over their children, and discovered that she had few if any rights other than the ones Liszt chose to grant her, her anger spilled over into a letter which is probably without parallel in their entire correspondence.

Paris, June 3, 1845

A year ago, sir, you said to me: *"Be careful, you don't know what I am capable of."* Now I know.

You are capable of trampling an honourable agreement underfoot, of imposing on a woman to whom you owe every respect humiliating conditions when she wants to exercise her sacred rights, recognized by you.

Finally, you are capable of the worst cowardice: of threatening *from a distance,* and *on grounds of a legality,* a mother who claims the fruit of her womb!

You refuse to come to Paris to hear an impartial judgement in the interests of your daughters; you are playing with their whole future without bothering to put yourself to the trouble of replying to my reasonable requests and without examining with mutual friends the decisive stand you have taken with unparalleled brutality.

I admit, sir, that I have lost a desperate skirmish in which I had nothing to invoke except your heart, your reason, and your conscience. But I protest before God and mankind, I protest before every mother against the brutality that has been meted out to me.

The respect I feel for these poor children compels me not to make a scandalous public scene and not to make them the witnesses and victims of the *extreme stand* with which you are threatening me.

From now on, sir, your daughters no longer have a mother; that is what you wanted. Their fate lies in your hands; no amount of

50. This dossier (Bibliothèque Nationale, Archives Daniel Ollivier, NAF 25179) contains copies of the birth certificates of grandfather Georg, and of Adam and Anna Liszt; Adam and Anna's marriage certificate; Liszt's own baptismal certificate; and the baptismal certificates of his two daughters, Blandine and Cosima. We may surmise from his correspondence with Massart (VFL, pp. 82–84) that Liszt pinned his hopes on a direct appeal to Hungary. He cited the precedent of Paganini, who had obtained the legitimization of his son Achille by petitioning the court in Sardinia. An important letter to Lamennais should also be considered in this context: "It is evident that my children can in no way be considered French. . . . They are, willy-nilly, Hungarian. . . . What I must do is to ask for full legitimization from the emperor, through the intermediary of the Palatine of Hungary." (May 18, 1845, LLB, vol. 8, pp. 40–42.)

Blandine, Cosima, and Daniel Liszt,
a water colour by Amélie de Lacépède (1843).

heroic devotion will ever be strong enough to fight against your madness and your wild egotism.

Be good enough to give your orders directly to Madame Bernard. Tomorrow I will go to say good-bye to Blandine, praying God to leave the impression on her forehead of her last kiss from her mother.

One day, perhaps, your daughters will ask you: where is our mother? You will reply: it did not suit me for you to have one.[51]

This devastating letter accuses Liszt of brutality, cowardice, and emotional blackmail. From Marie's standpoint she doubtless felt justified in whipping up this hail of words to shower down on his head. On the other hand, she had shown scarcely any interest in these children when they were born, and had been quite willing to leave them in the hands of total strangers for the first two or three years of their infancy, an arrangement that had nearly resulted in Daniel's death. Now that she was about to lose them, her maternal instincts were aroused. Both she and Liszt, so highly intelligent in other matters, seemed blind to the fact that they were reducing their children to hostages in a cruel game of blackmail.

VII

It was with a heavy heart that Liszt embarked on his six-month tour of the Iberian Peninsula. Between October 1844 and January 1845 he appeared in Madrid, Seville, Córdoba, and Cádiz. He then moved on to Portugal, arriving about mid-January in Lisbon, where he stayed for six weeks. Liszt was the first and certainly the greatest virtuoso to roam freely through Iberia. Others would one day follow him, including Thalberg, Gottschalk, and Henri Herz, but it is a measure of Liszt's impact that he became the standard by which all the others were judged. In retrospect his tour of Spain was probably the high point of his *Glanzzeit,* but for much of the time he was preoccupied with family problems and concerned for the future of his children. On October 9 he wrote a farewell letter to nine-year-old Blandine:

Pau, October 9, 1844

Dear child,

In three or four days I shall leave for Spain. Look up on your map *Madrid, Cádiz*—and *Lisbon.* The memory of you will follow me everywhere there, in the depths of my heart. Give me news of yourself, through the intermediary of grandma; tell me about your

---

51. VFL, pp. 154–55.

mother; and pray God to accord me patience and the constant wish for good.

I am pleased with your progress and the happiness you give Madame Bernard. It would be a pleasure to see you again, but I really do not know when it will be possible for me to pass through Paris. Good-bye, dear child. Be happy and don't be concerned about me now; but later—and may it be as late as possible—when chagrin and sadness come to you, then think of your father, who, at the cost of his life, would have liked to avoid them for you.

F. LISZT[52]

It was in Pau, near the Spanish frontier, that Liszt had a nostalgic reunion with Caroline de Saint-Cricq, the first love of his youth. The previous day, October 8, he had given a recital in the Salle de Spectacle; afterwards he learned that the Erard piano on which he had played had been lent for the occasion by one Madame d'Artigaux.[53] Liszt at once sought out his benefactress. He and Caroline had last seen one another in 1828, before her forced marriage to Bertrand d'Artigaux. Caroline now had a small daughter, Berthe, with whom she lived in a mansion with a magnificent view of the Pyrenees. M. d'Artigaux was rarely in evidence, and it was common knowledge in Pau that her marriage had brought Caroline much unhappiness. Liszt visited her several times during his two-week stay in Béarn, and they reminisced about their love-affair and the hand that fate had dealt them. In memory of their reunion Liszt composed one of his best songs, "Ich möchte hingehn wie das Abendroth." It is a song of farewell; neither would ever see the other again. The yearning *Tristan* motif which the song embodies was written ten years before Wagner started work on that masterpiece.

On a manuscript copy now in the Weimar archives, Liszt has scribbled the words: "This song is the testament of my youth—therefore no better, and also

52. OCLF, pp. 24–25.

53. Why was Liszt in Pau? Madame Molina, a former student, was vegetating there, her talents unrecognized, unable to find any pupils. Liszt's concert was given for her benefit, and he had her appear on the platform and play with him. She had no further trouble finding students. (LEL and BCLP; see also *Mémorial des Pyrénées*, October 11, 1844.)

no worse." After leaving Pau, Liszt sent Caroline a talisman bracelet containing a valuable turquoise which he had brought back from his trip to St. Petersburg the previous year.[54]

VIII

Liszt arrived in Madrid on October 22, 1844, his thirty-third birthday. His travelling companions were Louis Boisselot (the elder son of the Marseille piano manufacturer) and the baritone Ciabatta, who acted as Liszt's secretary throughout his tour of Iberia.[55] He gave four concerts in the Teatro del Circo (on October 31 and November 2, 5, and 9), the first time a solo pianist had been heard on that great stage, and was paid the vast sum of 2,000 francs per concert. His repertory consisted largely of operatic arrangements—*Don Giovanni, Norma, I puritani*—with such equally popular showpieces as the *Rákóczy* March and the *Grand Galop chromatique,* culminating at his concert on November 9 in "Improvisaciones al piano por el señor Liszt." Liszt played on a Boisselot piano, a powerful instrument especially brought in from Marseille by Louis Boisselot, which accompanied him on his journey across the Iberian Peninsula.[56] Spain was at that time ruled by the fourteen-year-old Queen Isabella II. Far from being forbidden by court etiquette to play before this sheltered monarch (a story still current in the literature), Liszt appeared at the royal palace on November 7, and the queen invested him with the Cross of Carlos III and presented him with a diamond-studded pin.[57] Liszt's four remaining concerts in Madrid were for charity, the one on November 14 being in the hall of the society that had sponsored his visit to Spain, the Liceo Artistico y Literario.[58] Liszt left Madrid on December 4 and travelled to Córdoba. He was met by a deputation of Liceo members who honoured him with a hearty

---

54. LLBM, p. 60.

55. Ciabatta had joined Liszt in Paris and remained with him for six months. "He accompanied me throughout my entire tour of Spain and Portugal and can give you all the news about it." (LLB, vol. 1, p. 54.)

56. Liszt had had friendly connections with Boisselot et Fils for years. It will be recalled that his Twelve Studies, op. 1, had been published by Boisselot *père* in Marseille in 1826. The Boisselot piano on which Liszt played was presented to Queen Maria II of Portugal at the end of his tour and remains in Portugal to this day. The queen gave it to the royal princes' music teacher, Manuel Inocência dos Santos, who later bequeathed it to the National Conservatory of Music. The instrument is now exhibited in Lisbon's State Museum and bears the inscription "No. 2027, Boisselot et Fils à Marseilles." See also SLML. For further information on Liszt and the Boisselot pianos, see the interesting booklet by Marcel Carrières, *Franz Liszt en Provence et en Languedoc en 1844* (Beziers, 1981).

57. *Revista de Teatros,* November 18, 1844.

58. *Revista de Teatros,* December 17, 1844. At the close of this concert two four-year-old girls ran onto the stage and presented Liszt with a floral wreath. He took them both in his arms, and someone shouted over the applause: "Hail artist, favoured by fortune, your triumph in Spain has no equal!" (*Allgemeine Musikalische Zeitung,* no. 5, January 1845.)

breakfast, after which he was installed with his host, Diego Pérez de Guzman. The enthusiasm was such that Liszt wrote a witty letter from Córdoba in which he remarked, "Only one thing remains to be done—to plant myself in person in some public square instead of a statue."[59] By December 17 he had moved on to Seville, where he was overwhelmed by the grandeur of the cathedral. He spent ten days in this city and went to gaze at the towering edifice daily. He described it as "an epic in granite, an architectural symphony."[60] While wandering beneath its vaulted roofs, "nose in the air and mouth open," Liszt heard the cathedral organist Eugenio Gómez. Gómez showed Liszt a group of pieces from his *Melodias armonizados* and asked for his frank opinion. Liszt, who was full of praise for these colourful gems, replied, "One defect, and a very grave defect, which I have discovered in your *Armonizados* . . . is that there are only twelve instead of twenty-four or forty-eight, as all true music-lovers will wish. Make haste, my dear M. Gómez, to repair this unpardonable defect as quickly as possible."[61] Gómez took Liszt's advice and composed twenty-four additional numbers for his collection.

From Seville, Liszt wended his way to Cádiz and Granada. He visited the Alhambra and years later recalled seeing the Spanish Gypsies gathered at nightfall around that "enchanting marvel."[62] A few days later he arrived at the British colony of Gibraltar.

Liszt now turned his eyes towards Lisbon. He boarded the British steamship *Montrose* at Gibraltar on January 12 and with his Boisselot piano sailed up the coast of Portugal, docking at Lisbon on January 15. On the very evening of his arrival he attended a performance of Donizetti's *Lucrezia Borgia* at the San Carlos Theatre, the site of some of his own triumphs. Liszt stayed for six weeks in Lisbon and gave twelve concerts. His repertory included Weber's *Invitation to the Dance*, the operatic fantasies on Bellini's *Norma* and *La sonnambula*, the ever-popular *Robert le diable*, a "Hungarian melody," and a Chopin mazurka (unidentified); he also appeared with the theatre orchestra in a performance of Weber's Concertstück. The Portuguese press hailed him as "The God of the Piano" and called him "the most marvellous thing in Portugal."[63] He was taken up by Lisbon "high society" and attended private receptions given by such notables as the queen's chief minister, Costa Cabral, Viscount de Cartax, and the papal nuncio.[64] He stayed at the nuncio's mansion until three o'clock in the

---

59. PBUS, p. 54.

60. LLB, vol. 2, p. 397.

61. LLB, vol. 2, pp. 396–97.

62. RGS, vol. 6, p. 229.

63. *O Patriota*, January 24, 1845.

64. Many doors were opened to Liszt because of his friendship with Prince Felix Lichnowsky, who had paid an extended visit to Portugal in 1842 and to some extent paved the way for him. Lichnowsky mentions Liszt in his book *Portugal: Erinnerungen aus dem Jahre 1842.*

morning, and as he was about to leave he noticed that he had misplaced his glasses. There was a general search for them, and Liszt joked, "I need my glasses to look for my glasses." Behind the witticism lay a serious observation: after twenty-five years of sight-reading and composing at all hours of the day and night, he was now quite myopic. The high point of his sojourn in Lisbon was his appearance at the royal palace, where he played before Queen Maria II. She created Liszt a Knight of the Order of Christ and presented him with a gold snuff-box encrusted with diamonds, which he described as "the most magnificent royal gift that I have ever received."[65] Liszt in turn presented Queen Maria with a dedicated copy of his "Marche funèbre" from Donizetti's *Dom Sébastien*. This was a composition over which Liszt had taken immense pains, and it could not have been more apt. The opera itself had been dedicated to Queen Maria and was now awaiting its first performance at the San Carlos Theatre. When Donizetti heard Liszt's arrangement he wrote to a friend, "Buy Liszt's arrangement of the March; it will make your hair stand on end."

With typical generosity Liszt also gave a charity concert for an orphanage, the Asylo de Mendicidade. Unfortunately, after the grasping theatre management had subtracted half the box-office receipts for its "fee" and the orchestra had been paid, the sum handed over to the orphanage was so small that Liszt made up the balance from his own pocket.[66] While in Lisbon Liszt befriended the Portuguese pianist João Guilherme Daddi. He invited Daddi to share the platform at one of his concerts, and together they played Thalberg's two-piano arrangement of themes from *Norma*. This episode, too, brought out one of Liszt's best character traits. Forty-one years later, when he was in London, he met the Portuguese ambassador and inquired whether Daddi was still alive. When Liszt's friendly concern was reported to Daddi in Lisbon, he was overcome to think that he was still remembered after so many years. Daddi had been made to suffer after Liszt's departure from Lisbon by the petty intrigues of local musicians who resented the special favour Liszt had shown him.

Liszt's stay in Lisbon ended on a controversial note. He offended the directors of the Philharmonic Society by at first refusing to accept from them a citation of membership. Once, after reluctantly accepting an invitation, he cancelled it on the very day of the ceremony. Another date was set, but Liszt turned up an hour late, the concert already in progress. More than three hundred Society members were present. Liszt took his seat only to walk out again after twenty minutes in the middle of a performance by one of Lisbon's prima donnas. He was later discovered outside the hall reading a newspaper. This act of disrespect cost him some goodwill and was adversely reported in the press.[67]

65. Letter to Prince Lichnowsky, May 14, 1845. (*Bayreuther Blätter*, vol. 30, 1907, p. 34.)
66. *Revista Universal Lisbonense*, vol. 4, no. 31, p. 378.
67. *Revista Universal Lisbonense*, vol. 4, no. 30, pp. 365–66. Family problems may well have been responsible for Liszt's uncharacteristic prevarications. By mid-February 1845, Madame d'Agoult had

Liszt left Lisbon on February 25. He boarded the British steamship *Pascha* and sailed back to Gibraltar. From here Liszt wrote a letter to his old friend Franz Ritter von Schober which disclosed the depths of his unhappiness at this time.

Gibraltar, March 3, 1845

What precisely is going to become of me this coming spring and summer I do not exactly know. In any case, I will not go to Paris. You know why. My incredibly wretched connection with —————— has perhaps indirectly contributed more than anything to my Spanish-Portuguese tour. I have no reason to regret having come, although my best friends tried to dissuade me from it. Sometimes it seems to me that my thoughts ripen and that my troubles grow prematurely old under the bright and penetrating sun of Spain. . . .[68]

Liszt was torn by his family troubles. He could not stay in Spain; he would not return to Paris. In fact, it was to be eight years before he saw his children again. Two days after his letter to Schober, he wrote to seven-year-old Cosima:

Gibraltar, March 5, 1845

Dear child,

Grandmother writes that you often talk about me and that you remember me every day. That's a really nice thought for me, I assure you, and I don't want to miss telling you that I will see you again in a few months. Even if I couldn't come back to Paris, grandmother would take you somewhere where I was, either in France or Germany. This little trip will improve your health, which I would like to see more robust. But meanwhile you can give me great pleasure. Listen children. On April 2 it is St. Francis, my saint's, day, and I want you to celebrate it. Try to get Blandine a day off from Madame Bernard's, and all three of you go to morning mass. If the Church of St.-Vincent-de-Paul, rue de Montholon, is still open, go there. I prayed a great deal there in days gone by. For the rest of the day, go for a ride in a carriage and play as much as you want. Grandmother will give you flowers and toys; and in the evening invite

---

already begun spreading the slander about which Liszt complained to her in the letter already cited (VFL, pp. 77–78), and he knew that he might have to return to Paris at a moment's notice, albeit unwillingly, in order to deal with it. Was he culling the French newspapers for evidence of the false statements he alleged her to be circulating? Paris certainly dominated his thoughts at this time.
68. LLB, vol. 1, p. 51.

Madame Seghers to dinner and whoever else you like, and then write to me, or have a letter written for you if you are still not advanced enough in handwriting, telling me about your day.

Look for Gibraltar on your geography map; I am writing to you from there. On April 2 I will be in Granada.[69] May your thoughts reach me there and may a reflection of mine shine softly on your innocent celebration!

Good-bye, dear child; kiss Dumdum,[70] and may you be happy and always stay sweet and kind.

With much love,

F. LISZT[71]

From March until mid-April we find Liszt travelling up the east coast of Spain, with stop-overs at Malaga, Valencia, and Barcelona. While in Valencia he played the organ to the monks in the cathedral. An eyewitness reported that

> . . . the canons all remained in their seats, respectfully silent. The afternoon sun played through the cathedral windows, lighting up the gilded altar furnishings. Liszt sat next to me, listening attentively while Pérez Gascón played a fugue on the organ. When it was done, he rushed to the organ and fervently kissed Pérez Gascón's hands. Small hands, yes, but capable of playing marvellous music. Next, Liszt himself must play the organ. When he finished, the canons could hardly restrain themselves from applauding.[72]

The following day Liszt was taken to the home of Antonio Ayala, an important civic official, who lay on his sickbed. Thirty years later Ayala still vividly recalled that visit.

> A mutual friend brought him to our house on April 2, his saint's day, San Francisco de Paulo. Beside my bed, where I lay prostrate, was placed the sweetest-toned grand piano. What did he play? Schubert's celestial "Ständchen." I cannot describe my emotion. His playing revived me, brought me back to myself, restored me to health. He embraced me before departing, like an angel of the resurrection.[73]

---

69. By April 2 Liszt was already in Valencia.
70. A nickname for Daniel.
71. HSD, pp. 133–34.
72. RMV, pp. 199–200.
73. Letter to Francisco Asenjo Barbieri, May 1872.

Liszt left Spain and re-entered France during the second week of April 1845. He never returned to Iberia, yet the memory of his visit lingered on for two generations. Several of the peninsula's finest pianists eventually followed Liszt to Weimar and began their higher keyboard studies with him, the most prominent being the Portuguese virtuoso Vianna da Motta, who later became the director of the National Conservatory in Lisbon. Although Liszt languished in Iberia for six months, he composed only three works during the entire period, a symptom of his unsettled frame of mind. On February 12 he completed in Lisbon "Le Forgeron," a setting for male voices and piano of a text by Lamennais.[74] He also left behind in Spain the manuscript sketch of a brief *feuille d'album,* which turns out to be an early waltz version of a theme later incorporated into the Ballade in D-flat major.[75]

His most striking creation was the *Grosse Konzertfantasie über spanische Weisen,*[76] a shining display piece which introduces variations on three Spanish dances— a fandango, the famous jota aragónese, and a cachucha—and combines the last two of them in a remarkable climax. The *Grosse Konzertfantasie* has meanwhile been totally eclipsed by the better-known Spanish Rhapsody (completed much later, in 1863), which has no direct connection with the Spanish tour at all.

---

74. See Liszt's letter to Lamennais (LLB, vol. 1, pp. 54–55), in which he talks about "Le Forgeron" ("The Blacksmith") at length. According to Göllerich, Wagner got the idea for Siegfried's Forge Song from this chorus.
75. It was given to Nunes dos Reis and published in facsimile in 1945 by his great-grandson Pedro Bathala Reis (see RLL, p. 56), marking the centenary of Liszt's sojourn in Lisbon.
76. R. 89. Published posthumously in 1887.

I X

On May 24, 1845, Liszt gave a recital in Mâcon, in the heart of Burgundy. The following day Lamartine unexpectedly appeared, and the local officials hurriedly proceeded to lay on a banquet in honour of their town's most distinguished son. The great poet was serenaded far into the night. Liszt was present, and it doubtless made a pleasant change for him to fête rather than to be fêted. The two men exchanged toasts. Liszt's speech, delivered impromptu at the banquet table, referred to Lamartine as an artist "who firmly holds the threefold sceptre of rhetoric, history, and poetry." Lamartine replied that Liszt was a genius whose generosity was extended towards "the suffering masses of the people."[77] A day or two later Liszt and Lamartine made the 40-mile journey back to Lamartine's château at Monceau, where Liszt stayed as his guest. This visit to Monceau was to have unusual consequences.

Living in Lamartine's household was his young niece, Countess Valentine de Cessiat. She was twenty-four years old, and despite the thirty-one-year difference in their ages, she was devoted to her uncle. Her feelings were reciprocated. (A year earlier she had joined Lamartine and his wife[78] for an extended holiday in Ischia, Venice, Rome, and elsewhere, and thereafter hardly left his side.) Liszt himself may have been blind to the true nature of their relationship, which, admittedly, was obscured for many years from the outside world. This unusual *ménage à trois* had, in fact, just been formed when Liszt ran into it. He saw in Valentine only a gentle, talented, and resourceful young woman.[79] She was an excellent pianist and was already helping to manage the Lamartine household, a duty she eventually took over completely. Liszt had been on the road for six years; he had given hundreds of recitals all over Europe; he was emotionally and physically exhausted. And now, at Monceau, he paused for thought.

What happened next has always perplexed Liszt's biographers. Liszt proposed marriage to Valentine, and Valentine turned him down.[80] He broached this delicate question through Madame Alix de Pierreclos, an elder married sister of Valentine, who told him plainly that she did not think he was suited for matrimony. Liszt reminded her that he had been "worse than married," having

---

77. Both toasts were printed in the *Journal de Saône-et-Loire*, May 28, 1845.

78. Mary Ann Birch, an Englishwoman. She had borne Lamartine two children: a son, Alphonse, who died in infancy, and a daughter, Julia, who died when she was ten.

79. Her photograph is reproduced in Luppé, *Les Travaux et les jours d'Alphonse de Lamartine* (Paris, 1942), p. 374.

80. Paul Fleuriot de Langle, "Liszt et Lamartine: Documents inédits," *Le Figaro*, February 16, 1929. See also HL, p. 45. Liszt had visited Lamartine in July 1844 at the poet's Saint-Point home, on his way to Spain (SLL, p. 42). Did he meet Valentine on that occasion? It is also possible that she accompanied her uncle when he attended a concert Liszt gave in the vicinity on August 6, 1844 (*Le Sémaphore* nos. 5060 and 5069).

remained attached to Madame d'Agoult for ten years. Madame de Pierreclos undertook to intercede with her sister but treated her responsibilities lightly. Liszt had hardly left Monceau before his place was taken by Louis de Ronchaud. The Lamartine household was still agog with gossip about Liszt's marriage proposal, and Ronchaud, fed directly by Madame de Pierreclos, reported every detail back to Marie d'Agoult.[81] In the event, all speculation was made redundant by Valentine's attachment to Lamartine, from whom she refused to be parted. We see in this episode, however, a genuine desire on Liszt's part to give up his life as a wandering minstrel, settle down in a home of his own, and find a mother for his three children.

Valentine's subsequent history indicates that Liszt may have had a lucky escape. That same year, 1845, she turned down another offer of marriage, from one Guige de Champvans. And in the spring of 1847 two further suitors were also despatched. Marriage negotiations were then begun in 1849 with Count Ferri-Pisani; but the count, not unreasonably, refused to live with the Lamartines, and so the negotiations were broken off. Valentine's obsession with her uncle was left to run its natural course. The *ménage à trois* became, through attrition, so to speak, a *ménage à deux* when Madame Lamartine died in 1863. In September 1867 Lamartine and his niece were married with the special dispensation of Pope Pius IX. It was not a moment too soon: Lamartine had been enfeebled by a severe stroke. He died eighteen months later, in February 1869. Valentine survived him by twenty-five years, dying in 1894, aged seventy-three.[82]

---

81. Ibid. Ronchaud, who was now one of the closest confidants of Marie d'Agoult, indulged in much idle chatter on this topic. After one session with Madame de Pierreclos he told Marie that Liszt had made "endless recriminations and accusations against you." It was the kind of talk calculated to stir "Nélida's" anger. Ronchaud had a vested interest in the matter, since he was infatuated with Marie, who, it should be added, while flattered by his attentions, did not return his feelings. His hostility towards Liszt, who had always shown friendliness towards him, is explained by that simple fact. Viscount Fleuriot de Langle expressed a forceful view of Ronchaud when he declared that by putting together his harmonious rhymes he had tried to redeem the insult to the French ear his name represents (*ronchonner* = to gripe; *le ronchot* = the griper). After 1845 Ronchaud's persistent criticism of Liszt more than justified Fleuriot de Langle's devastating observation.

82. Liszt saw Valentine again at least once. In 1860 she was struck down by typhoid, and the Lamartines moved to Paris. Liszt was there in 1861 and played in their home. *Dwight's Journal of Music* (July 13, 1861) carries a long report about this visit, including a letter from Lamartine, who refers to Liszt as "the old prodigy of Orpheus."

The Beethoven Monument
Unveiled in Bonn, 1845

*For us musicians, Beethoven's work is like the
pillar of cloud and fire which guided the Israelites
through the desert—a pillar of cloud to guide us
by day, a pillar of fire to guide us by night, "so
that we may progress both day and night."*

FRANZ LISZT[1]

I

The Beethoven Memorial Festival now loomed large. Nearly six years had
elapsed since Liszt had inaugurated his Beethoven concerts in Vienna. The
number of recitals he had meanwhile given for this cause has never been
properly calculated. Suffice it to say that the bronze statue of Beethoven
sculpted by Hähnel that now stood in Bonn's Dom Platz, patiently awaiting
its unveiling, would never have been brought into existence without his help.
Many of the supplementary expenses generated by the festival were also paid
for by Liszt.

In accordance with his published declaration, Liszt had perceived it to be his
chief function to raise money,[2] and his contributions had flowed into the coffers
of the festival committee in Bonn in ever-increasing abundance. But as the
months slipped by, and then the years, it must have dawned on Liszt that the

---

1. LLB, vol. 1, pp. 123–24.
2. LLB, vol. 1, pp. 30–31. The long-standing mystery of how much money Liszt handed over to
the committee can now be cleared up. Liszt contributed 10,000 francs towards the direct cost of the
statue (we learn this from his unpublished reply to one of Ramann's questionnaires, WA, Kasten 351,
no. 1). This sum is considerably lower than the figure of 50,000 francs which has passed back and
forth across the literature. But since Liszt underwrote the cost of the specially constructed *Festhalle,*
and guaranteed the deficit the festival was expected to generate as well, his contribution became the
largest made by any individual. In the event, there was no deficit. Years later he modestly told La
Mara, "There was no loss, but a surplus of 1,700 thalers." (LDML, vol. 1, p. 113.) Nonetheless, a
good part of Liszt's capital was tied up in escrow until the festival's accounts were closed. By the
autumn of 1845 he was almost bankrupt.

committee was riddled with incompetence. One deadline after another had been missed. The original appeal had appeared in the newspapers almost ten years earlier.[3] A second appeal had followed in November 1838. Both appeals had foundered; much more was required than an occasional announcement in the press. The following year, in October 1839, the newspapers had reported that the drive was about to collapse, and it was at that point that Liszt had stepped in. The year 1845 was finally chosen for the Beethoven Festival, since it marked the seventy-fifth anniversary of the master's birth. If this target-date was meant to be more stimulating than the others, the committee showed no signs of it, as it lapsed once more into the arms of Morpheus. As the year moved inexorably towards the festival date, Bonn seemed unaware that within a few weeks it was to host more than five thousand guests, hundreds of musicians, and two of the most important royal households in Europe. Headed by Professor H. K. Breidenstein, a Bonn musician, this committee had never grasped the complexities of the event for which it had made itself responsible. One of the problems was that its membership was far-flung and could meet only rarely. Liszt also was for much of the time performing in remote corners of Europe. In any case, he had no cause to assume that the organizational aspect of the festival would be left to him as well. He was in Spain until April 1845; he then progressed through France, gave concerts in Zürich, and proceeded towards Bonn. He was totally unprepared for the confusion that greeted him as he entered the city.

In the middle of July, just four weeks before the festival began, it was discovered that Bonn had no suitable auditorium in which to hold the concerts. In consternation, the festival committee toured the city, unsuccessfully trying out one hall after another. When Liszt heard of this latest debacle he expressed the view that a *Festhalle* should be specially constructed. The committee balked at the idea on the grounds of expense. Liszt then offered to pay for the construction costs out of his own pocket. In the face of such magnanimity the committee was shamed into silence.[4] Bonn in those days was only one hour's distance from Cologne. In this city lived the architect Zwirner, whose firm was involved in the construction of Cologne Cathedral. Fired by Liszt's enthusiasm, Zwirner and his team of devoted workmen set to work. A site was found, trees were felled, earth was levelled, and one of the great

---

3. Entitled "Aufruf an die Verehrer Beethovens" ("An Appeal to the Admirers of Beethoven"), it bore the dateline "Bonn, on Beethoven's birthday, December 17, 1835."

4. CMGM, vol. 2, pp. 251–52. Some idea of the crass intelligence of the committee may be gleaned from its proposal (quashed by Liszt) to save money by not engaging woodwind and brass players for the orchestra. Since it still expected the remaining players to perform Beethoven's C-minor Symphony, it must have hoped for a miracle equivalent to that of the loaves and the fishes. As it was, the orchestra was badly balanced. Berlioz speaks of "eight or nine cellists trying to compete with a dozen double-basses." (BSO, p. 320.) According to the diary of Sir George Smart (SLJ, p. 301), conditions were so poor that less than a week before the festival, Liszt was rehearsing the orchestra in the arena of a local riding school.

Rhine rafts was broken up for timber. Interior decorations were made in Cologne and transported to Bonn. Slowly the *Festhalle* rose like a mirage. Nearly 300 feet in length, it resembled a great oblong box and could seat three thousand people.[5] The nave comprised two rows of fourteen arches each. To offset the crude effect of exposed timber beams, the roof was painted pale blue. Trimmed fir trees formed the central pillars; since there was no time to plane them, they were festooned with hanging ivy. The walls were hung with pale red paper which, from a distance, took on the hue of marble. It was a masterpiece of improvisation. More remarkable still, everyone agreed that the acoustics were excellent. The builders worked round the clock, and by August 9 the edifice was ready. The city meanwhile started to fill up with visitors. Among the celebrities were Meyerbeer, Spohr, Sir George Smart, Moscheles, Berlioz, Marie Pleyel, Jenny Lind, Charles Hallé, and Manuel Garcia. An army of newspaper critics was in attendance, including Fétis, Rellstab, Jules Janin, Léon Kreutzer, and Henry Chorley. Thousands of other guests poured in from all over Europe. Some stayed at the Golden Star Hotel; others found private lodgings. They were the lucky ones; it was a common complaint that there were not enough rooms in the city. Henry Chorley wrote at length about the difficulties of making the pilgrimage to Bonn[6]—unreliable trains, unfriendly customs officials at the Belgian border, and the spectacle of guests walking about the streets with luggage and no-where to stay. And every two or three hours yet another boat would dock and disgorge more visitors into the overcrowded city. Although Bonn had been decked out in festival garlands, not even a coat of paint had been spared to make Beethoven's birthplace in the Rheingasse look more presentable, and the neglect of this "forlorn and grim mansion" stood in contrast to the gay colours paraded by the rest of the town.

Many of the visitors were disgruntled at the poor facilities. As each day passed and some new imperfection revealed itself in the ramshackle organiza-tion, people could be seen standing in angry little knots on landings, or gathered in doorways, letting their resentment simmer. It was as if, in Moscheles's words, they had gathered in Bonn for the express purpose of arousing hostility and seeing the festival fail. The weather did not help matters, and Bonn sweltered under 90 degrees of heat, its inhabitants unable to sleep. Since the committee wisely kept out of sight, all the invective was now directed towards Liszt. The injustice of this was not lost on Léon Kreutzer, who wrote a masterly article in the *Gazette Musicale*.

---

5. ACLA, vol. 2, p. 350, and CMGM, vol. 2, p. 252. A rough sketch of the *Festhalle* was drawn by Sir George Smart and published in his diary (SLJ, p. 313). The dimensions given by Smart differ from those of Chorley: "two hundred feet long and seventy-five feet broad. . . . They say it will hold four thousand persons." (SLJ, p. 310.)

6. CMGM, vol. 2, p. 255.

The organization was deplorable. Liszt was not able to patch up all the foolish mistakes of the old committee; he could not prevent vain and inept people from bearing him a grudge because he established a bit of order among the chaos; he could not stop men with no talent from being formally invited while great artists were disdainfully rejected; he could not stop a ridiculous musician coming to inflict on Beethoven's statue the martyrdom of such loathsome music that it must have shuddered even though it was made of bronze; he could not prevent lists of invitations being lost, nor correct the curious ineptitude of a committee which did not even concern itself with finding lodgings for the guests, calmly abandoning them to the streets of a town bursting with inhabitants. Anxiety and confusion reigned everywhere. One was suffocated in the hotels, the halls, the square, and around the statue. A crowd of Englishmen, usurping all the seats with their gold, occupied those of the real artists and relegated them to the most inferior rows among the soldiers, the valets, and the horses.[7]

Then came the unkindest cut of all: Liszt was accused of putting on a one-man show, of organizing the Beethoven Festival around his own personality. This was the classical defence of little men who have shirked their responsibilities. Where were they when they were needed, during the long years of public indifference? No one had robbed them of the limelight then. The charge, in any case, was untrue. Liszt had asked Spohr to share the artistic direction of the festival and to do most of the conducting. Liszt himself took part in three works only: he conducted Beethoven's C-minor Symphony, appeared as soloist in the *Emperor* Concerto, and directed his own Festival Cantata. For the rest of the time he was consumed with anxiety lest the organizing committee commit some new blunder and push the festival from the precipice on which it was so precariously balanced into the abyss below. He was also privately disappointed at the conduct of friends and colleagues of whom he had a right to expect more. Moscheles, for example, was asked to accompany a singer in a performance of Beethoven's "Adelaïde," but when he learned that Madame Pleyel was to play a concerto in the same programme, he refused "to perform an inferior service."[8] The attitude of Anton Schindler, who at that time had the unique distinction of being Beethoven's only biographer, was still more perverse. Schindler had publicly protested in the columns of the *Kölnische Zeitung* at the choice of Liszt to conduct the C-minor Symphony, asserting that

7. "Grands Festivals de Bonn à l'occasion de l'inauguration de la statue de Beethoven," August 17, 1845.
8. MAML, vol. 2, p. 142.

as a mere pianist, Liszt lacked the necessary experience.[9] This provoked a polemical reply whose anonymous author pointed out that Liszt had already directed the A-major and C-minor symphonies in Weimar, and the *Coriolan* Overture in Berlin.[10] The writer urged Schindler, in effect, to "put up or shut up." Schindler evidently decided to shut up, and although he attended the festival it was in the capacity of a private citizen with no official status whatsoever. Hiller, Mendelssohn, and Schumann stayed away from the festival altogether. This powerful boycott raised a number of eyebrows. The criticisms Liszt subsequently endured from the "Leipzig School" after he had settled permanently in Weimar showed him that he was not wrong to regard the boycott as an early expression of hostility towards himself. Such conduct hurt him deeply, coming from colleagues whose interests he had so often placed above his own.

This was the background of contention and dispute against which the Beethoven Festival now unfolded. Queen Victoria and Prince Albert were expected daily, and their royal hosts, the King and Queen of Prussia, had promised to participate in the unveiling ceremony. The eyes of the musical world were turned on Bonn. And the worst was yet to come.

11

On August 11, the first day of the festival, a new steamboat was launched called the *Ludwig van Beethoven*. Amid a salvo of cannon shots the vessel made its way down the Rhine to Nonnenwerth with a party of festival guests on board. A banquet lay in readiness on the island, and this was followed at dusk by a brilliant fireworks display. On the journey back Moscheles observed, "Pickpockets active. We escaped untouched."[11] The evening in Bonn was marked by what *The Times* called "a public ball for the lower classes."[12] The following day, August 12, was selected for the unveiling of the monument. By 8:00 a.m. the streets were bustling with activity: bands marched, students paraded, the guilds were out in force. Every building flew a flag. The public thronged around the cathedral for a performance of Beethoven's *Missa Solemnis* conducted by Spohr. Afterwards people streamed towards the great wooden dais in the Dom Platz which stood next to the statue and formed the centrepiece

9. *Kölnische Zeitung*, no. 179, June 1845.

10. "Ad Vocem Beethoven-Fest," Bonn, June 29, 1845, WA, Kasten 261, no. 8. A nervous editorial note was appended to this polemic: "The name of the author of this article has been forwarded to Herr Schindler at the request of this newspaper." It was in an effort to avoid further public acrimony that Liszt yielded the baton to Spohr.

11. MAML, vol. 2, p. 141.

12. August 13, 1845.

for the unveiling ceremony. It was now noon. The royal guests were late, and people started to swelter under the hot sun. Berlioz, who later wrote a long account of the festival, was very amusing at this juncture.[13] In order to find a seat in the reserved enclosure he had to vault a fence and then use his fists. He observed, "Taking all in all, the invitation I received from the committee in charge of the Bonn festival did not positively prevent me from witnessing it." At last the shriek of a train whistle was heard in the distance, and a peal of bells announced the arrival of their majesties Queen Victoria and her cousin King Wilhelm IV of Prussia, together with their royal retinues. As soon as they had taken their places on a draped balcony opposite the statue, Professor Breidenstein advanced towards the covered monument, delivered an oration,[14] and pulled on the cord. What should have been a hallowed moment was characterized by yet another blunder. With a roar of cannon and cheers from the crowd, the covers parted to reveal Beethoven's statue with its back to the assembly. Various dignitaries made their way around the monument in order to admire Hähnel's work from the front. One of the first was Liszt, who stood for a moment before the statue, his hair streaming in the light breeze. "I think that I have never seen an expression so nobly and serenely radiant on any face," wrote Chorley.[15] Liszt then signed the book of commemoration and withdrew. As dusk descended, the Dom Platz became deserted. Nobody had thought to illuminate the monument, which was abandoned to the darkness while the crowd celebrated in other parts of the city. The royal party, including Queen Victoria and Prince Albert, now took up residence in the castle at Brühl, and a number of the festival's celebrities shuttled back and forth to give command performances there, including Liszt. According to London's *Morning Post* a "scene" took place during his recital, which was reported in this inimitable way:

---

13. BSO, p. 423.

14. See the *Festgabe zu der am 11. August 1845 Stattfindenden Inauguration des Beethoven-Monuments* (Bonn, 1845) by H. K. Breidenstein. This festival booklet, which is now a rare item, contains a wealth of information about the events surrounding the Beethoven celebrations. It prints a full list of private donors to the monument, and the text of Liszt's unpublished Festival Cantata, as well as details of all the programmes. The latter, incidentally, were affected by the general chaos surrounding the festival, and they do not always reflect reality. The diaries of Chorley, Smart, Moscheles, and others who were there, and personally endured the purgatory, form a more reliable source. Breidenstein put himself forward as a composer and inflicted on the audience his Festival Chorus for men's voices, which he himself conducted. It was undoubtedly Breidenstein's offering which prompted Léon Kreutzer to protest against music fit to make Beethoven's bronze statue shudder. A further mystery is clarified by the festival booklet. The reason why Hähnel and not Bartolini sculpted the monument emerges on pages 6 and 7 of Breidenstein's introduction. Bartolini was a "foreigner." How would it have looked, asked Breidenstein, for an outsider to have built such a statue? What Liszt, himself a foreigner, thought of this comment has not been recorded.

15. CMGM, vol. 2, p. 269.

Liszt . . . being interrupted by some little chattering from an exalted quarter, he, in vain, made his terrible instrument roar under
his discontented hand, the harmless chat continuing, the artist, in
impatient anger, stopped short without even finishing his commenced melody. A second attempt did not command more silence,
and he, again, forthwith silenced his unacknowledged notes. None
in Court had taken offence at this lawful pride of so eminent an
artist, but, indeed, he surpassed himself. These whims of great artists are liked; to command respect they must respect themselves. I
forget the name of the poet who, when he read anything at the
Duke of Orleans', demanded that all the clocks of the Palace be
previously stopped, and the Duke of Orleans willing assented to
these minute precautions.[16]

Royalty had been chastized; artistic honour had once again been saved.

The last morning of the festival began with a great memorial concert in the
Festhalle. This "artists' concert" was far too long, consisting of no fewer than
fourteen items, and featuring a galaxy of soloists including Marie Pleyel, Jenny
Lind, and Liszt himself in a performance of the *Emperor* Concerto. Liszt was
now to conduct the Festival Cantata he had composed for the occasion.[17] As
he approached the rostrum he was greeted with an orchestral fanfare and an
ovation from the public. Unfortunately, the royal party was once more late,
and since Liszt was reluctant to commence the Cantata without them, there was
a long delay during which the audience grew restless. Liszt finally decided to
begin and had just reached the closing bars of this somewhat long work when
the court arrived. The audience was then treated to a second performance, a
licence which some took amiss.[18] King Wilhelm made a selection of items he
wanted to hear, after which the royal party left, abandoning the audience to
the gargantuan programme still to follow.

---

16. August 29, 1845.

17. *Festkantate zur Enthüllung des Beethoven-Denkmals in Bonn;* text by O. L. B. Wolff. The second
half of the cantata contains an orchestral arrangement of the Adagio from Beethoven's Trio in B-flat
major, op. 97. The manuscript of this work, which has never been published, is in Weimar.

18. In order to console Liszt for its rather cool reception, Jules Janin took the Cantata back to Paris
and arranged a further performance there. (See Paul Smith's review, "Liszt et sa 'Cantata,'" *Revue
et Gazette Musicale,* January 18, 1846.) This performance, too, met with a poor reception and initiated
a heated exchange of letters between Liszt and Marie d'Agoult. (ACLA, vol. 2, p. 349.) Marie referred
maliciously to the Paris performance as a "failure" (she was not present) and drew Liszt's attention
to the crushing article published against him in the *Morning Post* (Monday, August 18, 1845), in which
his handling of the Bonn festival had been criticized (it referred to "the Beethoven Festival in honour
of Liszt"). In his reply, Liszt takes Marie's letter apart, paragraph by paragraph, and answers each
one of her charges, an indication of the injustice he felt he had been subjected to by the European
press. See also Liszt's letter about the Festival Cantata to Jules Janin (VFL, pp. 145–46).

About four hours later the ordeal was over. The audience poured into the Golden Star Hotel for the ceremonial banquet which was supposed to bring the festival to a close. Karl Schorn has left us a detailed account of the disgraceful scenes at this banquet, attended by more than four hundred guests, which hardly brought honour to Beethoven's name.[19] Hand-to-hand fighting broke out for the seats: occupied or reserved, they were taken by assault by last-minute invaders. Lola Montez was seen elbowing her way through the crowd, claiming to be "a guest of Liszt."[20] The champagne flowed too freely, and many of the guests became intoxicated. As the chief guest of honour, Liszt was called upon to make a speech. Because the assembly represented many different countries, Liszt thought that it would be appropriate to take as his theme the universality of Beethoven's music. He spoke in German, and it was soon apparent from his halting delivery that he was not used to expressing himself publicly in this language. He got to his feet and began, "Here all nations are met to pay honour to the master. May they live and prosper who have made a pilgrimage here—the Dutch, the English, the Viennese." There was a moment's pause. Then the French representative Hippolyte Chélard leapt to his feet in a rage and shouted at Liszt, "Vous avez oublié les français." Immediately there was an uproar. Some guests tried to calm the Frenchman down. Others applauded him. Beneath the din, Liszt tried vainly to extricate himself from the consequences of his gaffe. He explained that he had lived in France for fifteen years and would not deliberately insult his adopted country. Nobody listened. Dr. Wolff, the author of the insipid words to the cantata, valiantly mounted the table and tried to restore order. He was howled down. The climax came when Lola Montez jumped on the table, knocking over the glasses and champagne bottles, and executed a pirouette, exclaiming, "Speak up, Mr. Wolff, pray speak up!" The drunken dancer was in turn howled down. Fortunately, Divine Providence intervened. The heat-wave which had plagued the festival broke, and a violent cloudburst drenched the town in water, to the spectacular accompaniment of forked lightning and rolling thunder. The banquet broke up in disarray, and the guests re-formed themselves into tight little groups of partisans, all arguing simultaneously about the shortcomings of the festival. It later transpired that the French delegation was sensitive about its poor contribution to the memorial fund, as well it might have been, and it had mistaken Liszt's omission of them as a rebuff.

---

19. SLE, vol. 1, pp. 193–216. See also MAML, vol. 2, pp. 142–44, and CMGM, vol. 2, pp. 272–75.
20. Lola Montez had not been invited to Bonn. She was, in Chorley's words, doing some "promiscuous gambling up and down the Rhine" when she decided to gate-crash the festival. The Golden Star Hotel refused her accommodation. Liszt avoided her, but her appearance in the hotel banquet room was enough to link their names once more in the press.

Liszt, a daguerreotype (c. 1845).

III

In retrospect the Bonn festival was a personal triumph for Liszt. Yet the immense strain made inroads into his health. After the noisy crowds had departed, and Bonn had lapsed once more into somnambulistic indifference, Liszt dropped the diplomatic mask he had been forced to wear while the festival was in progress. Kreutzer observed him in a state of near-collapse. "The artist had disappeared, and I no longer saw anyone but the man exhausted by work, by pressure, and perhaps by the warring factions he had endured in Bonn."[21] Fétis also commented on Liszt's low morale: "I met him a few days after the festivities, in Coblenz, tired, discouraged, and nearly bankrupt."[22] But the most astonishing thing about the festival was still to emerge: the aftermath of burning resentment it created in the hearts of the city fathers. It did not matter to them that they now had a monument to their greatest son. All they recalled was the licentious conduct of some of the visitors, the Lola Montez fracas, and the endless squabbles, many of which merely exposed their own ineptitude. No matter. Everything was heaped on Liszt's shoulders—the only official thanks he got for his magnanimity. (To be entirely fair, it must be recorded that they later named a street after him.) Liszt was great-hearted enough to accept the situation, and not once did he utter a word of recrimination. Some measure of the bad feeling generated in Bonn may be gauged by the fact that when, in 1870, twenty-five years after these events, the Beethoven centenary celebrations were mounted there, Liszt was not invited.

---

21. *Gazette Musicale,* September 7, 1845.
22. *Biographie universelle des musiciens,* vol. 5, 1875, p. 321.

The World Tours III:
Transylvania, Russia, and Turkey,
1846–1847

Away, away, my steed and I,
Upon the pinions of the wind,
All human dwellings left behind.
LORD BYRON, "Mazeppa"

I

During his long tours of Europe the thought of retiring from the concert platform was never far from Liszt's mind. He had many times expressed the wish to settle down and give up his life as a wandering virtuoso,[1] but events had kept him bound to his piano "like Mazeppa bound to his horse," condemned to a headlong flight towards disaster. "Away! Away!" became a favourite motto as he likened his fate to that of Byron's hero, whose nightmare journey ended only when his half-crazed steed dropped dead beneath him and deposited the rider's naked and bleeding body on the ground. Nor was Liszt's simile merely poetic. His career had by now taken on such colossal proportions that it was virtually impossible for him to sustain it. Countless demands were made on his time and his purse. Each new concert generated a demand for several more, leading to the prospect of compound growth so horrendous in its implications that even Liszt shrank from it. One last tour still beckoned him and it was to prove by far the longest and most arduous of his career. For long he had nourished the dream of travelling to Asia Minor and visiting Constantinople. In those days Turkey was a land of fable and mystery; few Western travellers ventured so far. Liszt and Marie d'Agoult had actually planned such

---

1. See, for example, his letters to István Fáy (PBUS, p. 51) and Franz Schober (LLB, vol. 1, p. 51), in which we find Liszt planning the end of his European tours as early as 1845.

a trip ten years earlier, but the idea had lapsed together with their relationship. The long journey through Transylvania, Rumania, Russia, and Turkey with which Liszt now intended to crown his virtuoso career eventually led him to the fairyland palace of Sultan Abdul-Medjid Khan, at the very heart of the old Ottoman empire. Today we have almost forgotten this epic journey. At times it is as if Liszt had disappeared from the map without trace. For that reason we shall attempt to follow him with care, basing our observations on contemporary documents. Liszt's trek from Translyvania to Asia Minor was eventful, and the record of this pioneering journey deserves a better fate than to moulder in the newspaper archives of Eastern Europe.

I I

After the stresses of the Beethoven Festival in Bonn, Liszt temporarily lost his bearings. He was taken ill at Cologne and went to Baden-Baden in order to enjoy the "water cure."[2] In the autumn of 1845 he gave a few sporadic concerts in Freiburg and eastern France, but his main concern was to recover his strength for the crushing work-load planned for the following year. No one could have withstood the constant round of concerts, speeches, balls, and banquets by day, often followed by travel to the next town by night—year after unremitting year—without suffering injury to his health, and Liszt's was often near breaking-point. His letters are full of references to the illnesses and indispositions he endured as he attempted to cope with the pressures of his itinerant existence.[3] He had taken opium, quinine, and a variety of homeopathic medicines, and had even dieted in an attempt to "keep the machine running," as he put it. Thanks to the strains of public life he was also heavily dependent on tobacco and alcohol; cigars and cognac were constant companions, and he occasionally indulged in them to excess. One such occasion was in the spring of 1846. Berlioz met Liszt in Prague. An official banquet had been laid on in Berlioz's honour, and Liszt was adopted as the speaker because his French was more fluent than that of the president. "Unhappily," wrote Berlioz, "if he spoke well, he drank likewise. That fatal cup set such tides of champagne flowing that all Liszt's eloquence was shipwrecked in it." At two o'clock in the morning Belloni and Berlioz were propelling Liszt towards his hotel and away from a drunken Bohemian with whom he wanted to fight a duel. He was supposed to give a

2. Liszt wrote that he was suffering "mit einer eclatanten Gelbsucht" ("from a brilliant jaundice") and was forbidden to exert himself. (LLB, vol. 8, p. 44.)
3. "I forgot to tell you what my illness was," he once wrote to Madame d'Agoult. "I don't know its exact scientific name, but here are the symptoms. A raging fever for five or six hours a day. Shivering, heat, profuse sweating, delirium." (ACLA, vol. 1, p. 303.) These symptoms were chronic and tended to be worse in the spring and autumn.

concert at noon. By half-past eleven he was still asleep. The hotel staff finally roused him and he climbed into a waiting carriage, "arrived at the hall, entered to a triple-barrelled broadside of applause, sat down, and played as I do not believe he has ever played in his life. Verily," Berlioz concluded, "there is a God—for pianists."[4] Nor was this a solitary lapse. The diaries of John Orlando Parry suggest that Bacchus was rarely absent during the six-month tour of the British Isles that he and others made with Liszt in 1840–41. At two o'clock in the morning Parry rounded off one diary entry: "Whiskey triumphant!"[5] No better impression of Liszt's vagabondage may be gained than by scrutinizing his itinerary for the eighteen-month period of March 1846 to September 1847.[6] The wonder in all this is that he still found time to compose.

1846

VIENNA	March 1–April 4: ten concerts.
BRÜNN	March 12–24: three concerts.
PRAGUE	April 13–19: three concerts in the Platyz.
PEST	April 30–May 14: five concerts. Raises a total of 1,800 forints for the National Conservatory of Music. Also gives a benefit concert for the József orphanage.
GRÄTZ	May 26–June: guest of Prince Lichnowsky at the Castle Grätz.
ZAGREB	July 27: concert in the city theatre. Is made an honorary member of the city music society.
OEDENBURG	August 3: concert in the Great Hall of the Casino. Raises 400 forints for the poor. Is made a magistrate of the County of Oedenburg and is presented with a solid silver baton. Visits Raiding.
KÖSZEG	September 27: benefit concert for the city music society. Is made an honorary burgher at a general sitting of the city council on September 25, the eve of his arrival.
DÁKA	October 6–10: guest of Count Leo Festetics.
PEST	October 10–12: benefit concert for the József orphanage, at which he gives the first performance of his paraphrase on Erkel's opera Hunyadi László.
SZEKSZÁRD	October 13–24: guest of Antal Augusz. October 18: concert in the city hall.
HÖGYÉSZ	October 15: visits Count Georg Apponyi.

---

4. BM, pp. 411–12.
5. PD, December 31, 1840.
6. The details, as given here, are drawn from Liszt's correspondence, the newspapers of the day, printed concert programmes, and Liszt's passport for 1846–47. (WA, Kasten 137, no. 5.)

NÁDASD	October 24–25: guest of Bishop Scitovszky of Fünf-kirchen.
FÜNFKIRCHEN	October 25–27: two concerts in the city hall. October 27: plays the organ in the Cathedral of Fünfkirchen.
MOHÁCS	October 27.
ESZÉK	October 28: en route.
ZIMONY	October 29.
BÁNLAK	October 29–30: guest of Count Guido Karácsonyi.
TEMESVÁR	Liszt's tour of Transylvania begins. November 2: concert in the Great Hall of the Prefecture. November 4: benefit concert in the city theatre for the Temesvár music society.
ARAD	November 7–11: two concerts in the ballroom of the White Cross Inn. Receives the freedom of the city.
TEMESVÁR	November 13: concert.
LUGOS	November 15: concert.
TEMESVÁR	November 17: benefit concert.
HERMANNSTADT	November 20: concert in the Salle des Redoutes.
KLAUSENBURG	November 26–December 3: three concerts in the city theatre. November 28: is made an honorary member of the city music society. December 6: visits the Conservatory of Music and gives a concert in the city theatre.
NAGYENYED	December 8: benefit concert which raises 400 forints for the city's kindergarten.
BUCHAREST	December 16–31: resides in the city for two weeks. December 21, 23: two concerts in the Ieronim Momolo Theatre. December 31: plays in the home of Prince Georg Bibesco.

1847

JASSY	January 1–13: resides in the city for two weeks. January 5–8: concerts in the home of State Treasurer Alex Bals. January 11: concert in the Nouveau Théâtre.
KIEV	Three concerts. February 2 (Old Style): concert in the Great Hall of the University of Kiev.
WORONINCE	February: guest of Princess Carolyne von Sayn-Wittgen-stein for ten days.
LEMBERG	April 13–27 (New Style).
CZERNOVTSY	May 19–26: resides in the city for one week. Two concerts in the Hotel Mikuli.
JASSY	May 27.
GALATZ	In quarantine.

CONSTANTINOPLE	June 8–July 13: resides in the city for five weeks. Several concerts in the Russian Embassy. Plays twice to the Sultan Abdul-Medjid Khan. Receives the order of Nichan-Iftikhar.
GALATZ	In quarantine.
ODESSA	July–August: resides in the city for six weeks. Ten concerts in the Hall of the Stock Exchange.
ELISABETGRAD	September: gives his last public recital.

As we can see from this punishing schedule, Liszt spent much of 1846 in his native Hungary (the concerts he gave there for charity and various educational causes will not go unobserved), where he consolidated old friendships with such figures as Antal Augusz, Count Teleki, and Count Festetics. During this period, too, he received some important civic honours: he was made a magistrate of the County of Oedenburg on August 3 and appointed an honorary burgher of the city of Kőszeg on September 25. These honours were bestowed not merely because Liszt was an outstanding pianist. Hungary was bracing itself for national independence and the bloody Revolution of 1848; it would do the country no harm to have a Hungarian world figure on its side.[7] The famous oil portrait of Liszt by Miklós Barabás, in which he is depicted in Hungarian national costume with the manuscript of the Second Hungarian March lying open on the piano beside him,[8] dates from May 1846, and when seen in the context of the times becomes highly symbolic.

In October 1846 Liszt went down to Szekszárd, in southern Hungary, to spend a few days in the home of Antal Augusz. Augusz organized an excursion for his guest which nearly ended in disaster. Returning from a visit to Counts Ficzai and Apponyi, who lived nearby, Liszt and Augusz were travelling in their carriage at dusk when one of the wheels struck a pothole and the carriage toppled into the ditch. According to the local newspaper, "our nocturnal adventurers" were not injured, but since it was nightfall and the carriage could not be repaired, they had to borrow an old farm-cart from a local miller, in which they were unceremoniously jolted all the way back to Szekszárd.[9] On the evening of October 22 a banquet was given to celebrate Liszt's thirty-fifth birthday. A crowd of well-wishers gathered outside the Augusz residence, and in response to their greetings Liszt had the piano pulled to the open windows and played to them his arrangement of the *Rákóczy* March. Accompanying Liszt on his Hungarian tour was the editor of *Honderü*, Lázár Petrichevich

---

7. By 1846 Liszt had become the best-known Hungarian on the international scene. His name was far more familiar to the man in the street in England and France than that of Kossuth or Széchenyi —the leaders of the Hungarian nation.

8. The March is dedicated to Count Sándor Teleki, "in Freundschaft und Bruderschaft." See p. 438.

9. *Életképek,* October 24, 1846; CLFB.

Horváth, and it is from his reports that many of the following details have been culled. While Liszt was in Szekszárd a delegation of fourteen citizens arrived from the nearby city of Fünfkirchen, inviting him to play there. Liszt agreed, and in the company of Augusz and Horváth drove first to Nádasd, where he stayed for one day at the summer residence of Bishop János Scitovszky. During dinner a vocal quartet from Fünfkirchen, especially brought in to serenade the guests, complained to Liszt that they were unable to get any songs in Hungarian from Pest. Whereupon Liszt composed on the spot, during the course of the dinner, a vocal quartet for which Horváth selected a poem by Garay entitled "To the Brook." It was at once rehearsed, and even before the dinner was over the work was sung to the other guests.[10] The party travelled on to Fünfkirchen in the bishop's carriage. That same evening Liszt gave a recital in the city theatre. It was symptomatic of the times that all the German signs and inscriptions in the theatre had been taken down and Hungarian ones put up.[11] Even Liszt's programme was printed in Hungarian (a patriotic gesture he repeated throughout this tour of Hungary and Transylvania, and one that the ordinary Hungarians deeply appreciated). This was highly appropriate when we recall that sitting in the audience that night were two of Hungary's leading fighters in the 1848 Revolution, Counts Batthyány and Perczel. Before leaving Fünfkirchen Liszt went to the cathedral, on the morning of October 27, at Bishop Scitovszky's invitation, and played the organ for about forty-five minutes. Among the works he performed were the "Ave Maria" from his *Harmonies poétiques et religieuses* and the Funeral March from *Dom Sébastien*. It was from this time that the long friendship between Liszt and Bishop Scitovszky began. Liszt promised the bishop that he would compose a mass for the festivities following the restoration of the cathedral. Because the building was so long delayed, this idea did not come to fruition. Soon the bishop himself was elevated to cardinal and moved to Gran, in western Hungary. In 1856, when the new basilica at Gran was about to be consecrated, Cardinal Scitovszky asked Liszt to redeem the pledge made ten years earlier and compose a ceremonial mass for the occasion. The result was the so-called *Graner* Mass, one of Liszt's undoubted masterworks.

---

10. CLFB. The manuscript remained in Bishop Scitovszky's archives for many years. It was eventually published in the Hungarian musical journal *Apollo,* vol. 3, 1874.

11. In this same year, 1846, a city law was passed restricting the use of the theatre to Hungarian companies. Since its opening in 1840, only German-speaking companies had appeared there. Belloni, Liszt's manager, apparently paid a pittance for the rental of the hall simply because Liszt was a Hungarian, a concession which stirred up criticism in the columns of the *Temesvári Hirlap* (no. 384, 1846). Horváth defended the arrangement in the newspaper *Honderü* (December 8, 1846), saying that without Liszt's concert the hall would have been unused. It was a storm in a teacup, but it indicated that even trivial issues could now be worked up into epic proportions when nationalistic differences were at stake.

III

Liszt's migration through Transylvania began in early November 1846 and took him through such cities as Temesvár, Arad, Klausenburg, and Nagyenyed, culminating in his visit to Bucharest. His wanderings through the vast hinterland of Hungary, a region steeped in legend and romance, are barely remembered today. Yet the enthusiasm his appearances aroused matched anything in his career. It must not be forgotten as we follow Liszt that his journey took place in the hypercharged atmosphere preceding the Revolution of 1848. The countryside, especially, was seething with discontent. When Liszt played the *Rákóczy* March in the Transylvanian town of Hermannstadt, there was an ugly scene as the Hungarians applauded enthusiastically while the Saxon aristocrats, who supported the status quo, expressed their hostility. When Liszt arrived in the town of Lugos the peasants considered him a harbinger of justice. The newspaper *Honderü* reported:

> While we were near the coupé prepared for Liszt, some peasants approached with petitions in their hands and absolutely refused to go away, insisting that they had been waiting for a long time for the arrival of such an important gentleman who could help them get satisfaction for their just claims.[12]

Difficult as it is for a modern reader to grasp the fact, Liszt symbolized to these simple people hope and freedom. His playing expressed to them a message that went beyond mere keyboard virtuosity. Metternich's agents watched the pianist closely and sent regular despatches back to Vienna.[13]

Liszt's tour of Transylvania began in Temesvár on November 1, 1846. The local newspapers had anticipated his arrival for several days, and by the time he got there large crowds were gathered in the streets to greet him. After his first concert, given the following day in the Great Hall of the Prefecture, a torchlight procession accompanied him home, and a composition for male voices, composed in his honour by the orchestral leader Franz Limmer, was sung in front of his house.[14] These spontaneous demonstrations were the first indications Liszt had of the outpouring of feeling he was to encounter as he progressed through the Hungarian hinterland. He wrote to Antal Augusz:

---

12. *Honderü,* December 15, 1846.
13. The Austrian consul to Jassy, one Eisenbach, sent a long despatch to Metternich on January 25, 1847, which reviewed Liszt's contacts with "progressive circles" in Bucharest and, in effect, gave him a testimonial for his good behaviour. (See HNTR, pp. 118–19.)
14. HNTR, p. 110.

It is the most fantastically glorious journey that an artist could ever have dreamed of, and without my having suspected any of it in 𝑎𝑑𝑣𝑎𝑛𝑐𝑒. The cold laurel wreath that about twenty of the most notable people of Temesvár gave me after my second concert is admirably made and will figure brilliantly among the five or six things which mark the principal dates of my career.[15]

Liszt reached Arad on November 7 and took rooms in the White Cross Inn. The local newspaper *Aradi Hirdető* carried a vivid description of his arrival in the city. His carriage was met by Mayor Ferenc Schärfeneder, the chief constable, and a group of Hussars carrying flaming torches, who escorted him to his lodgings. The crush of sightseers was so great that the pianist's carriage was nearly overturned, and its shaft bar snapped. "It was not a bad omen," the newspaper reported, "but *felix quem Dii favore!*"[16] Later that evening the military band of the Royal Schwarzenberg Lancer Regiment serenaded Liszt outside his hotel. A Gypsy band then came to his room and improvised for him. The *primás* advanced and kissed his hand respectfully, and Liszt ceremoniously kissed the *primás* on his forehead.[17] The following day, November 8, Liszt gave his first concert in Arad in the "winter room" of the White Cross Inn. During the recital some enthusiasts scattered a batch of poems in honour of Liszt from the gallery into the stalls, and the leaflets rained down on the audience like confetti. Liszt picked up a copy which had landed on the piano and read that the poet wished him not only a happy life, but a second life. Whereupon Liszt got up and made a public speech declaring that if he was indeed granted a second life, it would be dedicated to Hungary. A storm of applause greeted this popular sentiment. By now such scenes, quite amusing by modern standards, were part and parcel of the Liszt mythology, and Liszt took them in his stride. A second concert followed on November 10, in aid of local charities. Once again it was given in the "winter room" of the White Cross Inn:

Andante from *Lucia di Lammermoor*	DONIZETTI–LISZT
Norma Paraphrase	BELLINI–LISZT
Magyar Dallok	LISZT
"Ave Maria"	SCHUBERT–LISZT

---

15. CLBA, p. 36.

16. "Happy is the man whom the gods favour!"

17. Liszt met a number of Gypsies on this tour of Transylvania, also in Jassy and Bucharest, and he recorded his observations in his book *Des Bohémiens*. (RGS, vol. 6, pp. 160–62.) A short time earlier he had written to Count Leo Festetics in connection with the publication of his growing collection of Hungarian melodies, Magyar Dallok, and had jokingly described himself as "the first Gypsy in the Kingdom of Hungary." (PBUS, p. 57.) Throughout his Transylvanian journey Liszt carried a sketchbook (later found in Weimar) in which he jotted down the popular melodies he heard along the way.

"Erlkönig"   SCHUBERT–LISZT
Fantasy on *Robert le diable*   MEYERBEER–LISZT

According to *Der Spiegel*,[18] Liszt used two pianos for his concert, specially brought from Vienna. Before his departure from Arad on November 11 he received the freedom of the city.

Twelve days later Liszt was in the old city of Klausenburg, where he lingered for two weeks.[19] He gave four recitals in Klausenburg, the most important being on November 29, in the theatre on Farkas Street, an auditorium which held one thousand people. Liszt gave the proceeds of that concert to charity.[20] Despite the heavy downpour of rain, two hundred torchbearers escorted Liszt home, and the military band gamely trudged through the mud in sodden uniforms. It was in Klausenburg, incidentally, that Liszt composed his First Hungarian Rhapsody. Count Teleki, whom he met there, has told us how this came about. One evening they were chatting when Liszt turned to Teleki and said, "I would like to hear some good Gypsy music. Tell me, who is the best Gypsy musician in Hungary now?"

"Károly Boka in Debrecen, or Laci Pócsi at Sziget," Teleki replied.

"But isn't there anyone here?"

"Of course. They are very good, but they are German Gypsies playing from the notes, and you are already familiar with them. You need the "uncivilized" sort, because the Gypsies who play from notes are partly *Künstler.*"

"When I visit you at Koltó will you send for an "uncivilized" band there? I would very much like to hear them."

"It isn't necessary to bring one from Koltó."

Among the persons present listening to this conversation was Teleki's good friend Viktor Harai, with whom he shared accommodation.

"Viktor, would you like to do Liszt and me a favour? Go home, harness the horses to a carriage, and bring back Laci Pócsi and his band. But be careful, don't smash him to pieces on the way."

Harai took off at once for Sziget. A week later, Pócsi and his entire troupe arrived and performed for Liszt. Teleki reports that Liszt's eyes were burning during the playing; he snapped his fingers and shouted to the music. Then, while everyone was dancing, Liszt sat down at the piano and composed his First Hungarian Rhapsody.[21]

---

18. November 25, 1846.
19. The letters of Lajos Pákei (a local government official) to his sister Krisztina are full of first-hand information about Liszt's concerts in Klausenburg. They were published by István Lakatos in his article "Kolozsvári Liszt-emlékek," *Musicological Studies to the Memory of Liszt and Bartók,* ed. Szabolcsi and Bartha (Budapest, 1955).
20. *Erdélyi Hiradó,* no. 799, 1846.
21. TE, vol. 1, p. 58–59.

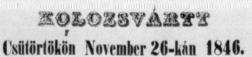

A Liszt recital in Klausenburg, Transylvania (1846).

From Klausenburg to Bucharest Liszt was accompanied by Count Teleki and Count Bethlen, both of whom had recently been named deputies of the Diet of Transylvania. There were now four coaches in the caravan, each drawn by eight horses, and the colourful procession attracted much attention as it proceeded along the dusty roads. Belloni and Parray (Bethlen's secretary) occupied one of the coaches and at every station would get out and prepare food and drink for the rest of the party. Liszt and his travelling companions whiled away the time by smoking a *chibouk* (a long Turkish pipe) and playing *taroc*.[22] They arrived in mid-December in Bucharest, the capital of Walachia, where a villa had been put at Liszt's disposal by Prince Michael Ghika.

Altogether Liszt gave three concerts in Bucharest.[23] One of his most popular items, presented during his last recital, was an improvisation on two Rumanian melodies which he combined in such an ingenious fashion that a murmur of approval swept throughout the hall while the performance was still in progress. This was the origin of the so-called Rumanian Rhapsody, which remained unpublished until 1936. According to Bartók, Liszt used themes that he had heard in the district of Szatmár.

The eagerness with which Liszt was "taken up" by high society made it easy for him to establish contact with Bucharest's leading artists and intellectuals. The air buzzed with talk of the impending struggle against Austria. Among the nationalistic writers with whom Liszt mixed were César Bolliac, C. A. Rosetti, Enric Winterhalder, and Ioan Catina. Grouped around an official Literary Society (whose patriotic secretary, Nicolae Balcescu, played a prominent part in the 1848 Revolution), their aim was nothing less than the creation of a Rumanian national literature. Liszt sympathized with their aspirations, but he restrained himself from making public utterances. Mindful of his experience in Poland in 1843, which had created difficulties for him in Russia, he was not about to repeat that mistake now. Liszt also met the artist Károly Pap Szathmáry, who painted a portrait of him improvising at the piano.[24]

Liszt's wanderings through the old Danube principalities ended at the ancient Moldavian capital of Jassy.[25] At the last of his three concerts, on January 11, 1847, he shared the platform with Alexander Fechtenmacher, one of the founders of Rumanian music. Fechtenmacher conducted his *Moldavian* Overture, which proved to be so popular that the large audience demanded its immediate encore. As a finale to the concert, Liszt improvised on the *hora* (a national dance) and cleverly combined it with themes from the *Moldavian* Overture,

---

22. LLB, vol. 8, p. 46.

23. On December 21, 23, and 31. These concerts were reported in the local newspapers *Curierul romîn* and *Vestitorul romînesc.*

24. HNTR, p. 114.

25. Details of Liszt's sojourn in Moldavia, and reports on his concerts there, are found in *Albina Romîneasca,* vol. 19, January 9 and 16, 1847.

Liszt in Hungarian national costume, an oil portrait by Barabás (1846).

thus, in the words of the local press, "rendering formal homage for the elegant welcome he had been given, in public and private, from all the people of our capital."[26] This concert is still regarded as a watershed in the history of Rumanian music because of the encouragement it gave to aspiring native composers to cast aside their Austro-German straitjackets and realize their national aspirations.

IV

Towards the middle of January 1847, Liszt crossed into Russia. It was the depths of winter, and the Ukraine was a frozen wasteland. Wrapped in thick furs to shield them from the searing wind, he and Belloni travelled across miles of snow-covered steppes in a sleigh hauled by dog teams. This was Liszt's third visit to Russia, and it was to be his last. His intention was to play in cities that had not so far heard him—Kiev, Lemberg, and Odessa—and then push south to Constantinople. As Liszt's sleigh slid to a halt in Kiev, he could not know that fate was about to intervene and radically change the direction of his life. The first of his three Kiev concerts took place in the Contract Hall, the city's stock exchange. Kiev was then the centre for all grain transactions in the Ukraine, and the audience consisted mainly of farmers and landowners who had converged on the city from outlying areas to strike bargains, exchange contracts, and fix prices for next year's grain harvest. Liszt gave two more concerts, in the Great Hall of Kiev University, the first of them on February 2, 1847— a fateful day in the Liszt calendar.[27] Outwardly there was nothing to distinguish this particular concert from dozens of others he had given over the past few months. But sitting in the audience that night was Princess Carolyne von Sayn-Wittgenstein, a fabulously rich landowner with vast estates in the central Ukraine and more than thirty thousand serfs at her beck and call. Twenty-eight years old and separated from her husband, Prince Nicholas von Sayn-Wittgenstein, Carolyne now ran her holdings herself. She had travelled to Kiev from her home in Woronince, in the province of Podolia, for reasons of commerce, and attended Liszt's second concert only after hearing from her business contacts about the success of the first. After the concert she left an anonymous gift of 100 roubles for Liszt's charity subscription, and it was by seeking out his

26. Ibid., January 16, 1847.
27. The reader who is interested in chronological exactitude is likely to encounter increasing frustration with Liszt's itinerary from this point on. He is reminded that twelve days separated the old Julian calendar (still used in Russia at this time) from the new Gregorian calendar followed by Western Europe. Liszt sometimes forgets the distinction in his correspondence, with the result that discrepancies arise between his announced and actual whereabouts. The above-mentioned recital, for instance, took place on February 14, 1847 (New Style).

benefactress to thank her for her generous donation that Liszt first met Carolyne. The story of that meeting, of his sojourn in her country house at Woronince, and of their ultimate decision to unite their lives and settle in Weimar
is much too important to be dealt with as a mere footnote to a concert tour.
Their lifelong relationship, and its turbulent consequences in Weimar, will be
considered in depth in the second volume of this life of Liszt. Suffice it to say
that one immediate consequence of this chance encounter in Kiev was that Liszt
was finally prevailed upon to give up his career as a concert pianist, a career
that was slowly destroying him, and for this we must be grateful. That crucial
decision was probably taken sometime during February 1847, while Liszt was
a guest of the princess at Woronince. True, there were still firm engagements
to fulfil in the summer, but it was Liszt's intention to rejoin the princess at
Woronince in the autumn so that they could plan their future together.
Meanwhile, Liszt built a wall of silence around his visit to Woronince and his
relationship with the princess. He knew that his ten-day stay with her would
eventually be reported back to Paris, arouse curiosity, and prompt questions
from friends and family which he was not at the moment prepared to answer.

After leaving Woronince, Liszt gave recitals in Lemberg and Czernovtsy
during April and May. He then retraced his steps and returned to Jassy in order
to make preparations for his long-awaited trip to Constantinople. Turkey in
those days was a closed country, and the immigration formalities were severe.[28] Liszt had to proceed to Galatz, where he was placed in quarantine. He
then sailed down the Black Sea and entered the Bosporus Straits on June 8. Liszt
was not the first traveller to be overwhelmed by the panoramic view of
the Golden Horn as his ship approached the great harbour of Constantinople,
"the most splendid and astonishing marvel the eye might be permitted to behold."[29] As soon as he disembarked Liszt was taken to the royal palace at
Tchiraghan for an audience with the Sultan, Abdul-Medjid Khan. This poten-
tate had ruled Turkey since he was sixteen years old. The absolute master of
his millions of subjects, Abdul-Medjid was one of the last survivors of an exotic
line, although he had been given a modern education by his father, Sultan
Mahmoud II, and had immersed himself in Western culture.[30] After they

---

28. Liszt had taken the precaution of getting a Hungarian passport a few months earlier, signed by
Count Apponyi. (WA, Kasten 137, no. 4.)
29. LLB, vol. 8, p. 49. News of Liszt's long-awaited visit to Constantinople had already been published
in the Turkish newspaper *Takvimi Vekayi*, zilhicce 2, no. 309 (1262 [Islamic calendar]).
30. Abdul-Medjid (1823–1861) was said to have four hundred concubines in his harem, a modest
number amounting to self-denial when set beside that of his brother Abdul-Aziz, who promptly raised
the figure to nine hundred when he ascended to the throne in 1861. (ETE, pp. 287–312.) It should
be added here that Abdul-Medjid has always been regarded with favour by the Hungarians. After
the War of Independence against Austria, large numbers of Hungarian exiles (including Kossuth)
were granted asylum in Turkey, where they were protected by this sultan despite threats of reprisals
against him by both Austria and Russia. The sultan's prime minister, Mustafa Resit Pasa, was a

chatted in French for a few moments (a language Abdul-Medjid spoke fluently), Liszt noted with pleasure that "his highness was up-to-date about my bit of fame."[31] Liszt played twice at the Tchiraghan Palace, and Abdul-Medjid decorated him with the Order of Nichan-Iftikhar, encrusted in diamonds. He also gave him a precious casket studded with jewels. Liszt's other recitals were held in the Russian Embassy,[32] whose rooms offered a panoramic view of the Bosporus in one direction and the Sea of Marmara in the other. He was impressed by the fact that he could see both Europe and Asia at the same time, and he even deluded himself into thinking that he could pick out Mount Olympus on the distant horizon. For Liszt's Constantinople recitals Erard had sent over one of his best pianos from Paris. Liszt described it as "a magnificent instrument," and it was shuttled back and forth between the royal palace and the Russian Embassy for each recital. After his departure from Turkey, the piano was sold for 16,000 piastres to a young man, M. Baldagi, who wanted it as a present for his fiancée. "It is a quite romantic fate for this beautiful instrument," remarked Liszt.[33] By an amusing coincidence, Liszt found himself in Constantinople at the same time as another pianist, Listmann, who decided to capitalize on the situation by dropping the second syllable of his name. Liszt was displeased at this act of gamesmanship, the more so since his "double" received an expensive gift from the sultan intended for Liszt himself. Listmann apologized for his behaviour, but there is no record of his having returned the gift.[34]

Liszt's exit from Turkey took him back across the Black Sea to Galatz, where he was once more obliged to languish in quarantine in mid-July. He sailed aboard the cruiser *Peter the Great,* an esoteric experience we learn about from the columns of the *Odessa News,* which carried a report of his impending return

---

moving force behind Turkey's drive towards Europeanization, and Liszt's visit to Constantinople appears to have been arranged partly through Pasa's contacts with Lamartine. (ACLA, vol. 2, p. 388.) Abdul-Medjid's Kapellmeister, incidentally, was Giuseppe Donizetti, the brother of Gaetano and composer of Turkey's national anthem at that time, and Giuseppe was Liszt's constant companion during his stay in Constantinople. The sultan was an admirer of Italian opera, and it was therefore no accident that at his first recital in the Tchiraghan Palace, Liszt played three of his paraphrases in this genre—the "Andante" from *Lucia di Lammermoor* (Donizetti), the "Overture" from *Guillaume Tell* (Rossini), and the "Fantasy" on themes from *Norma* (Bellini)—to all of which the sultan listened "with growing interest, mingled with astonishment and admiration" (*Revue et Gazette Musicale,* July 11, 1847). The previous January, the wooden opera house in Constantinople had burned down, and during Liszt's visit the Turks had begun to raise a new one, built of stone, which was designed to have three balconies and hold between 1,200 and 1,400 persons.

31. ACLA, vol. 2, p. 388.

32. One of the Russian Embassy recitals, given on June 28, 1847, was for the benefit of the Association Commerciale-Artisane de Piété. The Weimar archives (WA, Kasten 27, no. 5) contain the association's formal letter of thanks. The scrolled diploma of the Order of Nichan-Iftikhar, presented by the sultan, is also kept at Weimar (WA, Überformate no. 168).

33. LLB, vol. 8, pp. 50–51.

34. LLB, vol. 2, p. 358.

to the Ukraine.[35] So bored was Liszt at having to endure yet another period of quarantine that he took with him a copy of "Daniel Stern's" newly published *Essai sur la liberté* (a volume for which he had searched for weeks), read it from cover to cover, and then wrote Marie a long letter in which he analysed her work in flattering detail.[36]

v

Liszt's *Glanzzeit* was now drawing to a close. The last concerts of his career took place in Odessa and Elisabetgrad, historic recitals which went virtually unrecorded. Liszt stayed for six weeks in Odessa and gave ten concerts in the Hall of the Stock Exchange, the largest auditorium in the city. Odessa was full of high-ranking military personnel gathered for the army manoeuvres, and Liszt's concerts were attended by brilliant audiences of officers in full uniform attended by their consorts. At Elisabetgrad Liszt saw Tsar Nicholas I pass eighty thousand of his troops in review;[37] Europe was about to explode, and Nicholas did not intend to be found wanting. It was in Elisabetgrad, in September 1847, that Liszt gave his last public recital for money and announced his intention of retiring from the concert platform for good. He was still only thirty-five years old. Thereafter he never again played in public for his own benefit. In retrospect we can see that this was one of the wisest decisions Liszt ever made. By stepping down when he was still relatively young, and at the height of his powers, he kept the legend of his playing untarnished. The hundreds of young pianists who now flooded the concert halls of Europe (Liszt's retirement was tantamount to declaring an open season on the piano) looked up to him and attempted to copy him in all things save one: his decision to retire early. In this, as in so much else, he proved himself to be their superior. The bad ones could not survive their lack of talent and came to ignominious ends. The good ones quickly became condemned to a life of endless routine and their dreams often turned into nightmares as the public's embrace became a stranglehold. Liszt had perceived this possibility as early as 1840, when he had exclaimed: "Always concerts! Always to be a valet of the public! What a trade!"[38]

---

35. July 16, 1847. Information about Liszt's little-publicized concerts in the Ukraine in the spring and late summer of 1847, which included visits to Zhitomir, Nemiriv, Berdichiv, and Kremianets, is contained in the pioneering article "Forgotten Pages of Musical Life in Kiev," by M. Kuzmin (Kiev, 1972), pp. 45–48.

36. ACLA, vol. 2, pp. 384–89. "Before I went into quarantine an indulgent friend sent me by steamboat a few letters and *L'Essai sur la liberté*. Yesterday I read the first four books all at once, and I offer you my hand, proud and happy by its grasp to have stirred in you at one time, perhaps, such valiant harmonies of thought and feeling." Liszt implies here that some of the ideas in Marie's *Liberté* essay came from him. If so, that might account for the fact that she ignored his repeated requests to send him a copy.

37. LBLCA, p. 21.

38. PBUS, p. 50.

Appendix

Sources

Index

Appendix

Catalogue of works which Liszt played in public,
1838–48, compiled by himself

The holograph of this catalogue, which is in the Weimar Archives (WA, ms. Z 15), is in the hand of August Conradi, with revisions and corrections by Liszt himself. Since Conradi was resident in Weimar for just a few months, in 1849, that helps to pinpoint the date of its completion. The document was written in French, and its original title runs: *"Programme général des morceaux exécutés par F. Liszt à ses concerts de 1838 à 1848."* Liszt was obviously relying on his memory when he compiled this inventory, since it contains some curious omissions (the "Waldstein" Sonata, for example, which he is known to have played). On the other hand, he did not invent such works as the transcriptions of the Berlioz *Carnaval romain* and Beethoven *Egmont* overtures, to say nothing of the operatic paraphrase on Mozart's *Die Zauberflöte.* The whereabouts of these pieces is unknown, but their presence in this catalogue confirms that at one time they existed. The grouping of the pieces by genre, into fifteen categories, is Liszt's own.

1. OVERTURES

Guillaume Tell (Rossini); *Oberon, Der Freischutz, Jubel* (Weber); *Egmont* (Beethoven); *Die Zauberflöte* (Mozart); *Carnaval romain* (Berlioz)

2. SYMPHONIES

Beethoven: Fifth, Sixth, Seventh; Berlioz: *Fantastic*

3. PIANO CONCERTOS

Beethoven: C Minor, E-flat major ("Emperor"); Hummel: A minor, B minor; Moscheles: E-flat major, G minor, E major; Mendelssohn: G minor, D minor; Chopin: E minor, F minor; Henselt: F minor; Weber: Concertstück; J. S. Bach: Concerto for three pianos; Beethoven: Choral Fantasy

4. CHAMBER MUSIC

Hummel: Septet in D minor; Beethoven: Quintet in E-flat Major; Spohr: Quintet in C minor; Prince Louis Ferdinand of Prussia: Quartet; Beethoven: Trios; Schubert: Trios; Mendelssohn: Trios; Hummel: Trios; Mayseder: Trios; Pixis: Trios; Beethoven: Sonatas for piano and violin, Sonatas for piano and cello

5. PIANO SONATAS

Beethoven: Op. 26, Op. 27, Op. 29, no. 2,* Op. 57, Op. 101, Op. 106, Op. 109, Op. 110, Op. 111; Weber: C major, A-flat major; E minor, D minor; Hummel: F-sharp minor; Czerny: A-flat major; Schumann: F-sharp minor; Schuberth: Sonata [Karl ?]; Hummel: Sonata for four hands; Moscheles: Sonata for four hands; Czerny: Sonata for four hands

6. LARGE-SCALE FANTASIES BY

Beethoven, Schumann (dedicated to Liszt), Schubert, Hummel, Czerny

7. FANTASIES BY LISZT ON MOTIFS FROM

Don Giovanni (Mozart), *Robert le diable* (Meyerbeer), *Les Huguenots* (Meyerbeer), *La Juive* (Halévy), *Norma* (Bellini), *La sonnambula, I puritani* (Bellini), *Lucia di Lammermoor* (Donizetti), *Lucrezia Borgia* (Donizetti), *Le nozze di Figaro* (Mozart); Fantasy on Swiss motifs, Fantasy on Spanish motifs, Divertimento on a cavatina by Pacini, Divertimento in the Hungarian style by Schubert, Paraphrase on "God Save the King," Paraphrase on the fourth act of *Dom Sébastien* (Donizetti) by Kullak

8. STUDIES BY

Chopin, Moscheles, Paganini, Kessler, Hiller, Döhler, Liszt

9. ORIGINAL VARIATIONS BY

Bach ("Goldberg"), Handel, Beethoven, Mendelssohn ("Variations sérieuses"), Czerny (Op. 14), Kroll ("Variations mignonnes")

---

*Here Liszt was mistaken. He probably meant the Sonata in D minor (Op. 31, no. 2), subtitled "The Tempest."

10. VARIATIONS BRILLANTES

Moscheles: On the *Alexander* March, On an Austrian melody; Czerny: On "God Save Franz the Kaiser"; Pixis: On a motif from *Il barbiere di Siviglia*; Chopin: "Là ci darem la mano"; Thalberg, Chopin, Czerny, Pixis, Herz, Liszt: *Hexaméron*

11. FUGUES

Bach: Organ fugues, Fugues from the "48," Chromatic fantasy; Scarlatti: "Cat's Fugue"; Mendelssohn: Fugues; Handel: Suites

12. MARCHES

Rákóczy March, Funeral March from Beethoven's "Eroica," Funeral March from Donizetti's *Dom Sébastien,* March to the Scaffold (Berlioz), Turkish March (Beethoven), March for the Sultan Abdul Medjid Khan (Donizetti), Hungarian March (Schubert), Three Characteristic Marches (Schubert), Circassian March (Glinka), Heroic March (Liszt), Heroic March (Vollweiler)

13. VARIOUS PIECES

Chopin: Waltzes, Polonaises, Mazurkas, Ballades, Nocturnes, Impromptus, Scherzos, Preludes; Mendelssohn: Scherzos; Weber: Polonaise, Momento capriccioso, *Invitation to the Dance*; Schumann: Carnaval; Kessler: Toccata; Nicolai: Trois Etudes mélodiques; Berlioz: *L'Idée fixe*; Liszt: *Harmonies poétiques et religieuses*, Three Petrarch Sonnets, *Feuille morte* (Elégie), *Gaudeamus igitur*, Valse mélancolique, Bravura waltzes, Caprice-Valse de Lucie et Parisina, Tarantelle from *La Muette de Portici*, Russian Galop by Bulhakow, Gypsy Polka by Conradi; Schachner: *Ombres et rayons*

14. SONGS

Schubert: fifty songs; Mendelssohn: six songs; Dessauer: three songs; Beethoven: "Adelaïde," Gellert Songs; Michael Wielhorsky: Melodies (transcribed by Henselt and Liszt); Weber: "Schlummerlied," "Leyer und Schwert"; Liszt: Songs, "Nonnenwerth," "La romanesca"; Schumann: "Liebeslied"; Meyerbeer: "Der Mönch"; Rossini: *Soirées musicales*; Donizetti: *Nuits d'été à Pausilippe*

15. NATIONAL MELODIES

Hungarian melodies, Nineteen Hungarian Rhapsodies; Döhler: Russian melodies; Henselt: Air bohémien; Liszt: Swiss melodies, Canzone veneziane, Canzone napolitane, Tarantella napolitana, Spanish melodies

Sources Consulted in the
Preparation of Volume I

AAM Apponyi, Count Albert. *Memoirs*. London, 1935.

AC Agoult, Marie d'. "The Unpublished Notebooks of Marie d'Agoult (1832–36)." Manuscript, Bibliothèque Nationale, NAF 14319.

ACLA Agoult, Marie d'. *Correspondance de Liszt et de la Comtesse d'Agoult*. Edited by Daniel Ollivier. 2 vols. Paris, 1933, 1934.

ACS Agoult, Colonel Count Charles d'. "Souvenirs." Unpublished holograph in the possession of Count Saint-Priest d'Urgel, Avignon.

Acta Mus. Acta Musicalia. Esterházy Archive, National Széchényi Library, Budapest.

AE Adelburg, August Ritter von. *Entgegnung auf die von Franz Liszt in seinem Werke "Des Bohémiens et leur musique en Hongrie" aufgestellte Behauptung: Dass es keine ungarische Nationalmusik . . . gibt.* Foreword by Alexander von Czeke. Pest, 1859.

AFFL Agoult, Marie d'. *Meine Freundschaft mit Franz Liszt*. Dresden, 1930.

AJF Agoult, Marie d'. "A Journal Fragment: Episode de Venise," unpublished manuscript, Heineman Collection, Library of Congress, Washington, D.C.

ALM Auvergne, Edmund d'. *Lola Montez: An Adventuress of the 'Forties*. London, 1909.

AM Agoult, Marie d' ("Daniel Stern"). *Mémoires, 1833–54*. Edited by Daniel Ollivier. Paris, 1927.

AMA Aragonnès, Claude. *Marie d'Agoult: Une Destinée romantique*. Paris, 1938.

AML Autexier, Philippe A. *Mozart and Liszt sub Rosa*. Poitiers, 1984.

APL *Abendblatt des Pester Lloyd*. Budapest.

AS Agoult, Marie d' ("Daniel Stern"). *Mes Souvenirs (1806–33)*. Paris, 1877.

ASSV Agoult, Marie d'. "The Second Scrapbook of Marie d'Agoult." Manuscript, Library of Versailles. A miscellaneous collection of newspaper cuttings, started by Adam Liszt and continued by Marie d'Agoult.

BA   Bayreuth Archive. Nationalarchiv der Richard Wagner Stiftung in Bayreuth.

BAEP   Bertha, Sándor. "Ch. V. Alkan: Etude Psycho-Musicale." *Bulletin Français de la Société Internationale de Musique,* February 15, 1909.

BALV   Bauer, Karoline. *Aus dem Leben einer Verstorbenen: Nachgelassene Memoiren von Karoline Bauer.* 4 vols. Berlin, 1880.

BBAG   Barbey-Boissier, C. *La Comtesse Agénor de Gasparin et sa famille: Correspondance et souvenirs 1813–94.* 2 vols. Paris, 1902.

BBM   Bache, Constance. *Brother Musicians: Reminiscences of Edward and Walter Bache.* London, 1901.

BBRC   Barzun, Jacques. *Berlioz and the Romantic Century.* 2 vols. New York, 1969 (3rd ed.)

BCLP   Blanc, Charles. Le Centenaire des concerts données par Franz Liszt à Pau; 1844–1944." *Bulletin de la Société des Sciences, Lettres et Arts de Pau.*

BDLL   Bory, Robert. "Diverses Lettres inédites de Liszt." *Schweizerisches Jahrbuch für Musikwissenschaft* (Aarau) 3 (1928).

BEM   Busoni, Ferruccio. *The Essence of Music.* London, 1957.

BK   *Ludwig van Beethovens Konversationshefte (Band 3, Hefte 23–37).* Herausgegeben im Auftrag der Deutschen Staatsbibliothek Berlin von Karl-Heinz Köhler und Dagmar Beck unter Mitwirkung von Günter Brosche. Leipzig, 1983.

BKMM   Beatty-Kingston, W. *Music and Manners: Personal Reminiscences and Sketches of Character.* 2 vols. London, 1887.

BL   Boutard, Abbé Charles. *Lamennais: Sa Vie et ses doctrines.* 3 vols. Paris, 1905–13.

BLB   Buchner, Alexander. *Franz Liszt in Bohemia.* Prague, 1962.

BLE   Bory, Robert. *Liszt et ses enfants Blandine, Cosima et Daniel.* Paris, 1936.

BLOD   Beale, Willert. *The Light of Other Days.* 2 vols. London, 1890.

BLP   Boissier, Mme Auguste. *Liszt Pédagogue: Leçons de piano données par Liszt à Mlle. Valérie Boissier en 1832.* Paris, 1927.

BLSC   Békefi, Ernö. *Liszt Ferenc: Származása és családja* [Liszt's Family and Its Origins]. Budapest, 1973.

BLU   Bezucha, Robert J. *The Lyon Uprising of 1834: Social and Political Conflict in the Early July Monarchy.* Cambridge, Mass., 1974.

BM   Berlioz, Hector. *Mémoires.* Paris, 1870. Trans. by David Cairns, London, 1969.

BMP   Boschot, Adolphe. *Musiciens, poètes.* Paris, 1937.

BNR	Brett-James, Antony, ed. *1812: Eye-witness Accounts of Napoleon's Defeat in Russia.* London, 1960.
BOM	Bull, Sara. *Ole Bull: A Memoir by Sara C. Bull.* London, 1886.
BQLE	Bory, Robert. "Quatre Lettres inédites de F. Liszt à Pierre Erard." *Mitteilungen der schweiz. musikforschenden Gesellschaft.* Zürich, January 1934.
BRRS	Bory, Robert. *Une Retraite romantique en Suisse: Liszt et la Comtesse d'Agoult.* Geneva, 1923; Lausanne, 1930.
BSE	Belgiojoso, Princess Cristina. *Souvenirs dans l'exil.* Milan, 1946.
BSM	Borowitz, Albert. "Salieri and the 'Murder' of Mozart." *Musical Quarterly* 59, no. 2 (April 1973).
BSO	Berlioz, Hector. *Les Soirées de l'orchestre.* Paris, 1852.
BSS	Baranyi, George. *Stephen Széchenyi and the Awakening of Hungarian Nationalism 1791–1841.* Princeton, 1968.
BULM	Bertha, Sándor. *Über Liszts Mutter.* Vasárnapi Ujság no. 22, Budapest, 1891.
BVL	Bory, Robert. *La Vie de Franz Liszt par l'image.* Geneva, 1936.
CAB	Cornelius, Peter. *Ausgewählte Briefe, nebst Tagebuchblättern und Gelegenheitsgedichten, herausgegeben von seinem Sohne Carl Maria Cornelius.* 2 vols. Leipzig, 1904, 1905.
CE	The Breitkopf and Härtel *Collected Edition* of Liszt's works, in thirty-four volumes. Leipzig, 1901–36.
CEL	Czerny, Carl. "Erinnerungen aus meinem Leben." Manuscript dated 1842. Edited and annotated by Walter Kolneder. Strassburg, 1968.
CFL	Corder, Frederick. *Ferencz Liszt.* London, 1925.
CFLW	Christern, Johann Wilhelm. *Franz Liszt nach seinem Leben und Wirken aus authentischen Berichten dargestellt von Christern.* [The Library of Congress copy, with annotations in Liszt's hand.] Hamburg and Leipzig, 1841.
CL	Chantavoine, Jean. *Liszt.* Paris, 1911.
CLBA	Csapó, Wilhelm von, ed. *Franz Liszts Briefe an Baron Anton Augusz, 1846–78.* Budapest, 1911.
CLFB	Csekey, István. *Liszt Ferenc Baranyában* [Franz Liszt in Baranya]. Pécs, 1956.
CLSH	Csekey, István. *Liszt Ferenc származása és hazafisága* [The Descent and National Identity of Franz Liszt]. Budapest, 1937.
CLV	Csekey, István. Franz Liszts Vater: Nach bisher unveröffentlichen Dokumenten dargestellt. *Die Musik,* 29, no. 9 (June 1937).
CMGM	Chorley, Henry, F. *Modern German Music.* 2 vols. London, 1854.
CMM	Chorley, Henry, F. *Music and Manners in France and Germany: A Series of Travelling Sketches on Art and Society.* 3 vols. London, 1841.

CPC   Cornelius, Carl Maria. *Peter Cornelius, der Wort- und Tondichter.* 2 vols. Regensburg, 1925.

CPG   Courcy, Geraldine de. *Paganini the Genoese.* 2 vols. Norman, Okla., 1957.

CPR   Chantavoine, Jean. *Pages romantiques.* Paris, 1912. Articles published over Liszt's signature in the *Revue et Gazette Musicale,* 1835–40.

CPV   Chiesa, Maria Tibaldi. *Paganini: La vita e l'opera.* Milan, 1940.

CVRL   Chiesa, Maria Tibaldi. *Vita romantica di Liszt.* Milan, 1937.

CSS   Carnot, Hippolyte. *Sur le Saint-Simonisme: Lecture faite a l'Académie des sciences morales et politiques.* Paris, 1887.

DDP   Doisy, Henri. *Les Débuts d'une grande paroisse: Sainte-Vincent de Paul.* Paris, 1942.

DFL   Drizen, N.V. "Franz Liszt v Moskve." Ezhegodnik imperatorskikh teatrov. Moscow, 1911, 1912.

DGG   Dörffel, Alfred. *Geschichte der Gewandhausconcerte zu Leipzig vom 25. November 1791 bis 25. November 1881.* Leipzig, 1884.

DHEd'A   Decourcelle, Maurice. *Histoire de la Société Academique des Enfants d'Apollon,* Paris 1881.

DJE   Devrient, Theresa. *Jugenderinnerungen.* Stuttgart, n.d. (3rd ed.).

DLFW   Deutsch-German, Alfred. *Franz Liszt und seine Familie in Wien.* Vienna, 1906.

DM   *Die Musik,* Liszt Number, 1905. "Aus Liszts erster Jugend. Ein Schreiben seines Vaters mit Briefen Czernys an ihn. Nach den Handschriften mitgeteilt von La Mara."

DMA   Dash, Countess. *Mémoires des autres.* 4 vols. Paris, 1898.

DML   Dunkel, Norbert. *Milyen Volt Liszt Ferenc?* [What Was Liszt Like?]. Budapest, 1936.

DPG   Day, Lillian. *Paganini of Genoa.* New York, 1929.

EDW   Eckhardt, Mária P. "Diary of a Wayfarer: The Wanderings of Franz Liszt and Marie d'Agoult in Switzerland, June–July 1835." *Journal of the American Liszt Society* (Louisville, Ky.), June 1982, pp. 10–17.

EGEL   *The George Eliot Letters.* Edited by Gordon S. Haight. 12 vols. New Haven, 1954.

ELP   Eckhardt, P. Mária. *Liszt és Párizs* [Liszt and Paris] (Ferenc Liszt Society Miniature Library no. 1). Budapest, 1982.

ENDL   Eckhardt, P. Mária: "New Documents on Liszt as Author." *New Hungarian Quarterly,* no. 95, Autumn 1984, pp. 181–94.

EOCR   Elkin, Robert. *The Old Concert Rooms of London.* London, 1955.

EPE   Erard, Pierre. *Le Piano d'Erard à l'Exposition de 1844.* Paris, 1844.

EPL   Eckhardt, P. Mária. *Párizsi Liszt-Dokumentum, 1849–böl* [A Liszt

Document in Paris, from 1849]. Budapest (Musicological Studies), 1979

ES   Escudier, Léon: *Mes Souvenirs: Les Virtuoses.* Paris, 1863, 1868.

ETE   Eversley, Lord. *The Turkish Empire from 1288 to 1914.* London, 1917.

FBLM   Frimmel, Theodor von. *Beethoven Studien II. Bausteine zu einer Lebensgeschichte des Meisters.* Munich and Leipzig, 1906.

FEL   Frankenburg, Adolf. "Erinnerungen an Franz Liszt." *Athenaeum* (Budapest), no. 16, 1873.

FFDS   Fleuriot de Langle: "Franz Liszt et Daniel Stern, ou les galériens de l'amour (documents inédits)," *Mercure de France,* February 1, 1929.

FJI   Fontaney, Antoine. *Journal intime (1831–36).* Introduction and notes by René Jasinski. Paris, 1925.

FM   Frankenburg, Aldolf. *Memoiren.* 2 vols. Budapest, 1861.

FMSG   Fay, Amy. *Music Study in Germany.* Chicago, 1881.

FR   *Fortnightly Review* (London) 40 (September 1886).

FSC   "Franz, Robert" (Olga Janina). *Souvenirs d'une cosaque.* Paris, 1874.

FSP   "Franz, Robert" (Olga Janina). *Souvenirs d'une pianiste.* Paris, 1874.

GAWZ   Genast, Eduard. *Aus Weimars klassischer und nachklassischer Zeit: Erinnerungen eines alten Schauspielers.* Edited by Robert Kohlrausch. Stuttgart, 1903.

GCR   Gros, Johannès. *Une Courtisane romantique: Marie Duplessis.* Paris, 1929.

GEFR   Gugitz, Gustav. *Die Ehetragödie Ferdinand Raimonds; nach dem unveröffentlichen Akten des Wiener Stadtgerichtes im Archiv der Stadt Wien,* Wiener Bibliophilen-Gesellschaft, Vienna, 1956.

GFLF   Gajdoš, Vševlad. *František Liszt a františkani (Františkansky Obzor)* [Ferenc Liszt and the Franciscans]. Bratislava, 1936.

GL   Göllerich, August. *Franz Liszt.* Berlin, 1908.

GLD   Grew, Eva Mary. "Liszt's Dante Sonata," *Chesterian,* vol. 21, January–March 1940, pp. 33–40.

GLEL   Gut, Serge. *Franz Liszt: Les Eléments du langage musical.* Paris, 1975.

GLK   Göllerich, August. *Franz Liszts Klavierunterricht von 1884–1886: Dargestellt an den Tagebuchaufzeichnungen von August Göllerich, von Wilhelm Jerger.* Regensburg, 1975.

GLMM   Gábry, György. "Liszt Ferenc emléktárgyai a Magyar Nemzeti Múzeumban" [Ferenc Liszt Relics in the Hungarian National Museum]. *Folia Historica* (Budapest) 5, 1977.

GMA   Gugenheim, Suzanne. *Madame d'Agoult et la pensée européenne de son époque.* Florence, 1937.

GP   Gárdonyi, Zoltán: "Paralipomena zu den ungarischen Rhapsodien von Franz Liszt," in *Franz Liszt: Beiträge von ungarischen Autoren, herausgegeben von Klára Hamburger.* Budapest, 1978.

GRT   Gregorovius, Ferdinand. *Römische Tagebücher (1852–74).* Stuttgart, 1892.

GVL   Giraud, Victor. *La Vie tragique de Lamennais.* Paris, 1933.

GWLF   Gajdoš, Vševlad. "War Franz Liszt Franziskaner?" *Studia Musicologica* 6 (1964): 299–310.

HBD   Herwegh, Marcel. *Au banquet des dieux.* Paris, 1931.

HC   Heineman Collection. Unpublished letters of Liszt. Library of Congress, Washington, D.C.

HCWL   Hueffer, Francis, trans. *Correspondence of Wagner and Liszt.* London, 1888.

HDF   Haraszti, Emile. "Deux Franciscains: Adam et Franz Liszt." *La Revue Musicale,* May 1937.

HFLA   Haraszti, Emile. "Franz Liszt: Author Despite Himself." *Musical Quarterly,* October 1947.

HGL   Haldane, Charlotte. *The Galley Slaves of Love: The Story of Marie d'Agoult and Franz Liszt.* London, 1957.

HHB   Hiller, Ferdinand. *Aus Ferdinand Hillers Briefwechsel, Beiträge zu einer Biographie Ferdinand Hillers von Reinhold Sietz.* 5 vols. Cologne, 1958–66.

HJL   Huneker, James. *Franz Liszt.* New York, 1911.

HK   Hiller, Ferdinand. *Künstlerleben.* Cologne, 1880.

HL   Haraszti, Emile. *Franz Liszt.* Paris, 1967.

HLB   Habets, A., ed. *Letters of Liszt and Borodin.* Edited and translated by Rosa Newmarch. London, 1895.

HLCE   Hárich, János. "Liszt Ferenc családja és az Esterházy hercegek" [Franz Liszt's Family and the Princes Esterhazy]. *Napkelet* (Budapest) 9, 1934.

HLL   Hallé, Sir Charles. *Life and Letters.* Edited by C. E. Hallé and Marie Hallé. London, 1896.

HLLM   Hevesy, André de. *Liszt, ou Le Roi Lear de la musique.* Paris, 1936.

HLOG   Hárich, János. "Liszt Ferenc ősei és gyermekévei" [Franz Liszt's Ancestors and His Childhood]. *Énekszó* (Budapest) 2, 1935.

HLP   Haraszti, Emile. "Liszt à Paris." *La Revue Musicale,* April and July, 1936.

HLSW   *The Letters of Franz Liszt to Marie zu Sayn-Wittgenstein.* Translated and edited by Howard E. Hugo. Cambridge, 1953.

HMB   Heine, Heinrich. *Musikalische Berichte aus Paris.* 1841. In *Sämtliche Werke,* vol. 9, edited by Fritz Strich. Munich, 1925.

HMBE	Hiller, Ferdinand. *Felix Mendelssohn-Bartholdy: Briefe und Erinnerungen von Ferdinand Hiller.* Cologne, 1875.
HMR	Hoffman, Richard. "Some Musical Recollections of Fifty Years." *Scribner's Magazine* 47 (New York) (March–April 1910).
HNTR	Hoffman, A, and Missir, N. *Sur la tournée de concerts de Ferenc Liszt en 1846–47 dans le Banat, la Transylvanie et les Pays Roumains.* Report of the second Liszt-Bartók musicological conference, Budapest, 1961.
HPD	Herwegh, Marcel. *Au printemps des dieux.* Paris, 1929.
HPL	Haraszti, Emile. "Le Problème Liszt" *Acta Musicologica,* December 1937.
HSD	Herwegh, Marcel. *Au soir des dieux.* Paris, 1933.
HSWMB	Heine, Heinrich. *Sämtliche Werke.* 10 vols. Munich, 1925. Contains *Musikalische Berichte aus Paris.*
IRL	Ille-Beeg, Marie. *Lina Ramann: Lebensbild einer bedeutenden Frau auf dem Gebiete der Musik.* Nuremberg, 1914.
JCR	Joubert, Solange. *Une Correspondance romantique: Madame d'Agoult, Liszt, Henri Lehmann.* Paris, 1947.
JFL	"Franz Liszt und die Gräfin d'Agoult in Nonnenwerth. Aus dem Nachlass Varnhagens von Ense." Edited by Emil Jacobs. *Die Musik,* October 1911. Part 1: pp. 34–45; Part 2: pp. 93–112.
KAS	Kapp, Julius, ed. "Autobiographisches Skizze (1881)," *Die Musik,* 1911.
KE	Kellermann, Berthold. *Erinnerungen, ein Künstlerleben.* Edited by Sebastian Hausmann and Hellmut Kellermann. Zürich, 1932.
KFL	Kapp, Julius. *Franz Liszt.* Berlin, 1909.
KHC	Király, Béla K. *Hungary in the Late 18th Century.* New York, 1969.
KJB	Kalbeck, Max. *Johannes Brahms.* 4 vols. Berlin, 1904–14.
KLB	Kapp, Julius. *Liszt-Brevier.* Leipzig, 1910.
KLG	Kling, Henri. "Franz Liszt pendant son séjour à Genève en 1835–36." *Guide Musicale de Bruxelles,* 1897.
KLV	Koch, Ludwig. *Franz Liszt: Ein bibliographischer Versuch.* Budapest, 1936.
LAFB	Liszt, Eduard Ritter von. *Franz Liszt: Abstammung, Familie, Begebenheiten.* Vienna and Leipzig, 1937.
LAG	La Mara (Marie Lipsius), ed. *Aus der Glanzzeit der Weimarer Altenburg.* Leipzig, 1906.
LBLB	La Mara, ed. *Briefwechsel zwischen Franz Liszt und Hans von Bülow.* Leipzig, 1898.
LBLCA	La Mara, ed. *Briefwechsel zwischen Franz Liszt und Carl Alexander, Grossherzog von Sachsen.* Leipzig, 1909.

LBW La Mara. "Beethoven's Weihekuss." *Allgemeine Musikzeitung,* No. 17, 1913.

LBZL La Mara, ed. *Briefe hervorragender Zeitgenossen an Franz Liszt.* 3 vols. Leipzig 1895–1904.

LCRT La Mara, ed. *Classisches und Romantisches aus der Tonwelt.* Leipzig, 1892. Franz Liszt aus seinem ersten Weltflug. Briefe seines Vaters an Carl Czerny.

LCS Litzmann, Berthold. *Clara Schumann: Ein Künstlerleben.* 3 vols. Leipzig, 1902–8.

LDML La Mara. *Durch Musik und Leben im Dienste des Ideals.* 2 vols. Leipzig 1917.

LEL Léon-Bérard, Marguérite. "Une Elève de Liszt." *La Revue des Deux Mondes,* April 15, 1960, pp. 682–94.

LGPZ Lenz, Wilhelm von. *Die grossen Pianovirtuosen unserer Zeit.* Berlin, 1872.

LHFL Lange, Fritz. "Im Heimatsdorfe Franz Liszts." *Der Merker* (Vienna), October 1911.

LLB La Mara, ed. *Franz Liszts Briefe.* 8 vols. Leipzig 1893–1905.
    1: *Von Paris bis Rom*
    2: *Von Rom bis ans Ende*
    3: *Briefe an eine Freundin*
    4, 5, 6, 7: *Briefe an die Fürstin Sayn-Wittgenstein*
    8: *Neue Folge zu Band I und II*

LLBM La Mara, ed. *Franz Liszts Briefe an seine Mutter.* Leipzig, 1918.

LLF La Mara. *Liszt und die Frauen.* Leipzig, 1911.

LLM Legány, Dezső. *Liszt Ferenc Magyarországon 1869–1873* [Ferenc Liszt and his country]. Budapest, 1976.

LMWP Loesser, Arthur. *Men, Women and Pianos: A Social History.* New York, 1954.

LMZK Legány, Dezső. *A magyar zene krónikája* [Chronicle of Hungarian music]. Budapest, 1962.

LSJ La Mara, ed. *An der Schwelle des Jenseits: Letzte Erinnerungen an die Fürstin Carolyne Sayn-Wittgenstein, die Freundin Liszts.* Leipzig, 1925.

LSS Legouvé, Ernest. *Soixante Ans de souvenirs.* 4 vols. Paris, 1887.

LT *Liszt tanulmányok,* by Zsuzsa Dömötör, Mária Kovács, and Ilona Mona. Budapest, 1980.

MAL Melegari, D. "Une Amie de Liszt, la Princesse de Sayn Wittgenstein." *La Revue de Paris,* September 1, 1897.

MAML Moscheles, Ignaz. *Aus Moscheles' Leben, nach Briefen und Tagebüchern herausgegeben von seiner Frau.* 2 vols. Leipzig, 1872–73.

MB Mendelssohn Bartholdy, Paul and Dr. Carl, eds. *Briefe aus den*

	Jahren 1830 bis 1847 von Felix Mendelssohn Bartholdy. 2 vols. Leipzig, 1863, 1864.
MBJ	*Briefe an und von Joseph Joachim.* Edited by Andreas Moser. 3 vols. Berlin, 1911–13.
MCPB	Malvezzi, Aldobrandino. *La Principessa Cristina di Belgiojoso.* 3 vols. Milan, 1936.
MCW	Moulin Eckardt, Richard Graf. *Cosima Wagner, ein Lebens- und Charakterbild.* 2 vols. Munich, 1929.
MD	*The Diaries of William Charles Macready (1833–51).* Edited by William Toynbee. 2 vols. London, 1912.
MFL	Milstein, Jacob. *F. Liszt.* 2 vols. Moscow, 1956.
MJ	Moser, Andreas. *Joseph Joachim: A Biography (1831–1899).* Translated by Lilla Durham. London, 1901. An expanded version of the German original, published in Berlin, 1898.
ML	Maurois, André. *Lélia: ou La Vie de George Sand.* Paris, 1953.
MLL	Main, Alexander. "Liszt's *Lyon*: Music and the Social Conscience." *Nineteenth Century Music,* spring 1981, pp. 228–43.
MLMR	Major, Ervin. "Liszt Ferenc Magyar Rapszódiái" [Ferenc Liszt's Hungarian Rhapsodies]. *Muzsika* (Budapest) 1 (1929): 47–54.
MMR	*Monthly Musical Record* (London). Cited by issue.
MPC	Marmontel, Antoine. *Les Pianistes célèbres.* Paris, 1878.
MQLN	*Musical Quarterly* (New York), Special Liszt Number, vol. 22, no. 3, 1936.
MRS	Maréchal, Henri. *Rome: Souvenirs d'un musicien.* Paris, 1904.
ND	Neumann, Baron Philipp von. *The Diary, 1819–50.* Translated and edited from the original manuscript by E. Beresford Chancellor. London, 1928.
NFL	Neumann, W. *Franz Liszt.* Cassel, 1855.
NHQ	*New Hungarian Quarterly,* (Budapest), Liszt-Bartók Issue, 1962.
NL	Nohl, Ludwig. *Franz Liszt.* Leipzig, 1882.
NLB	Nohl, Walter. "Der elfjährige Liszt und Beethoven." *Neue Musik-Zeitung* (Stuttgart), no. 14, 1927.
NLE	*New Liszt Edition: Complete Works.* Edited by Imre Sulyok and Imre Mezö. Budapest, 1970.
NLRW	Newman, Ernest. *The Life of Richard Wagner.* 4 vols. London, 1933–47.
NML	Newman, Ernest. *The Man Liszt.* London, 1934.
NPR	Niecks, Frederick: "Personal Recollections: Ch. V. Alkan." *Monthly Musical Record,* January, 1918.
NZfM	*Neue Zeitschrift für Musik,* 1834–44. Edited by Robert Schumann. Cited by issue.
OAAL	Ollivier, Daniel, ed. *Autour de Mme d'Agoult et de Liszt (Alfred de*

Vigny, Emile Ollivier, Princess de Belgiojoso): Lettres publiées avec introduction et notes. Paris, 1941.

OCLF   Ollivier, Daniel, ed. *Correspondance de Liszt et de sa fille Madame Emile Ollivier, 1842–1862.* Paris, 1936.

OFL   d'Ortigue, Joseph. "Franz Liszt: Etude biographique" *Revue et Gazette Musicale,* June 14, 1835.

OJ   Ollivier, Emile. *Journal, 1846–1869.* 2 vols. Text selected and edited by Theodor Zeldin and Anne Troisier de Diaz. Paris, 1961.

PBUS   Prahács, Margit, ed. *Franz Liszt: Briefe aus ungarischen Sammlungen 1835–86.* Kassel, 1966.

PCC   Pictet, Adolphe. *Une Course à Chamonix: Conte fantastique.* Paris, 1838.

PCM   Pardoe, Julia. *The City of the Magyar, or Hungary and Her Institutions in 1839–40.* London, 1840.

PCMHA   Pierre, Constant. *Le Conservatoire national de musique et de déclamation: Documents historiques et administratifs recueillis ou reconstitués par Constant Pierre.* Paris, 1900.

PD   "The Diaries of John Orlando Parry (1840–41)." Manuscript (m.s. 17717/8), National Library of Wales, Aberystwyth. For the published text, see *Liszt Society Journal* (London) 6 (1981) and 7 (1982).

PMPE   Pincherle, Marc. *Musiciens peints par eux-mêmes: Lettres de compositeurs écrites en français (1771–1910).* Paris, 1939.

PMW   *The Musical World of Robert Schumann: A Selection from Schumann's Own Writings.* Edited and translated by Henry Pleasants. London, 1965.

RA   Royal Archives, Windsor Castle, England.
(a) Queen Victoria's Journal
(b) Correspondence between Queen Victoria and her relations in Germany

RB   "La Comtesse d'Agoult: Lettres à Ferdinand Hiller (1838–57)," edited by Jean Chantavoine. *Revue Bleue* (Paris), November 8 and 15, 1913.

RFL   Rellstab, Ludwig. *Franz Liszt: Beurtheilungen-Berichte-Lebensskizze.* Berlin, 1842.

RGS   Ramann, Lina, ed. *Franz Liszts Gesammelte Schriften.* 6 vols. Leipzig 1880–83.
      1: *Friedrich Chopin*
      2: *Essays und Reisebriefe eines Baccalaurens der Tonkunst*
      3: *Dramaturgische Blätter*
        (1) *Essays,* (2) *Richard Wagner*

4: *Aus den Annalen des Fortschritts*

5: *Streifzüge: Kritische, polemische und zeithistorische Essays*

6: *Die Zigeuner und ihre Musik in Ungarn*

RL Ramann, Lina. *Lisztiana: Erinnerungen an Franz Liszt in Tage-buchblättern, Briefen und Dokumenten aus den Jahren 1873–1886/7.* Herausgegeben von Arthur Seidl. Textrevision von Friedrich Schnapp. Mainz, 1983.

RLKM Ramann, Lina. *Franz Liszt als Künstler und Mensch.* 3 vols. Leipzig, 1880–94.

RLL Reis, Pedro Batalha. *Liszt na sua Passagem por Lisboa em 1845.* Lisbon, 1945.

RLS Raabe, Peter. *Franz Liszt: Leben und Schaffen.* 2 vols. Stuttgart, 1931; rev. 1968.

RM *La Revue Musicale,* Special Liszt Numbers, May–June 1928.

RML Reeve, Henry. *Memoirs of the Life and Correspondence of Henry Reeve.* By John Knox Laughton. 2 vols. London, 1898.

RMV Ruiz de Lihory, José. *La musica en Valencia.* Valencia, 1903.

RWA Richard Wagner Archive, Bayreuth, Germany.

RWL Raabe, Peter. *Wege zu Liszt.* Regensburg, 1943.

SA Smith, Ronald. *Alkan. Vol. 1: The Enigma.* London, 1976.

SAW Saphir, M. G. *Saphiriana: Anekdoten, Witze und Charakterzüge aus dem Leben M.G. Saphir's.* Brünn, 1874.

SB Schober, Franz Ritter von. *Briefe über F. Liszt's Aufenthalt in Ungarn.* Berlin, 1843.

S-BC Sainte-Beuve. *Correspondance générale: Recueillie, classée et annotée par Jean Bonnerot.* 8 vols. Paris, 1935–38.

SBLB Schindler, Felix Anton. *Biographie von Ludwig van Beethoven.* 2 vols. Münster, 1860.

SC Sárosi, Bálint. *Cigányzene.* Budapest, 1971. Translated as *Gypsy Music* by Fred Macnicol. Budapest, 1978.

SCC Sydow, B. E., ed. *Correspondance de Frédéric Chopin.* 3 vols. Paris, 1953–60.

SD Shelley, Lady Frances. *The Diary of Frances, Lady Shelley (1787–1873).* 2 vols., edited by Richard Edgcumbe. London, 1912.

SEW Schilling, Gustav. "Liszt." *Encyclopädie der gesammten musikalischen Wissenschaften, oder Universal-Lexicon der Tonkunst,* vol. 4. Stuttgart, 1837.

SFL(1) Schilling, Gustav. *Franz Liszt: Sein Leben und sein Wirken aus nächster Beschauung.* Stuttgart, 1844.

SFL(2) Schrader, Bruno. *Franz Liszt.* Berlin, 1917.

SJI Sand, George. *Journal Intime.* Published posthumously by Aurore Sand, Paris, 1926.

SL   Sitwell, Sacheverell. *Liszt*. London, 1934; rev. 1967.

SLAB   Suttoni, Charles. "Franz Liszt's Published Correspondence An Annotated Bibliography." *Fontes Artis Musicae* (Kassel) 26, no. 3 (1979).

SLE   Schorn, Karl. *Lebenserinnerungen: Ein Beitrag zur Geschichte des Rheinlands im neunzehnten Jahrhundert*. 2 vols. Bonn, 1898.

SLFH   Sylvain, Rev. Charles. *Life of the Reverend Father Hermann*. New York, 1925.

SLJ   Smart, Sir George. *Leaves from the Journals of Sir George Smart*. London, 1907. By H. Bertram Cox and C.L.E. Cox

SLL   Sallès, Antoine. *Liszt à Lyon: Le Centenaire de Liszt*. Paris, 1911.

SLML   Stevenson, Robert. "Liszt at Madrid and Lisbon, 1844–45." *Musical Quarterly* (New York), vol. 65, no. 4 (October 1979).

SLV   Sand, George. *Lettres d'un voyageur*. Paris, 1869.

SLWB   *König Ludwig II und Richard Wagner Briefwechsel*. Edited by Otto Strobel. 5 vols.. Karlsruhe, 1936 (vols. 1–4); 1939 (vol. 5).

SLWT   Sayn-Wittgenstein, Carolyne von. "Last Will and Testament." Unpublished manuscript, Library of Congress, Washington, D.C.

SML   Searle, Humphrey. *The Music of Liszt*. London, 1954; rev. 1966.

SN   "Stern, Daniel" (Marie d'Agoult). *Nélida*. 2 vol. Brussels, 1846.

SNW   Schorn, Adelheid von. *Das Nachklassische Weimar*. 2 vol. Weimar, 1911.

SPP   Salaman, Charles: "Pianists of the Past." *Blackwood's Magazine* (London) 170 (1901).

SPR   Stearns, Peter N. *Priest and Revolutionary: Lamennais and the Dilemma of French Catholicism*. New York, 1967.

SPRL   Strelezki, Anton. *Personal Recollections of Chats with Liszt*. London, 1893.

SSEM   Stasov, Vladimir. *Selected Essays on Music*. Translated by Florence Jonas. London, 1968.

SSPS   Saint-Saëns, Camille. *Portraits et Souvenirs*. Paris, 1900.

SSR   Simoni, Dario. *Un soggiorno di Francesco Liszt a San Rossore*. Pisa, 1936.

SVKL   Schnapp, Friedrich. "Verschollene Kompositionen Franz Liszts." In *Von Deutscher Tonkunst: Festschrift für Peter Raabe*. Leipzig, 1942.

SWS   Speyer, Edward. *Wilhelm Speyer der Liederkomponist*. Munich, 1925.

TBC   Tiersot, Julien, ed. *Hector Berlioz: Correspondance (1819–55)*. 3 vols. Paris, 1904–30.

TE   Teleki, Sándor. *Emlékeim* [Memoirs]. 2 vols. Budapest, 1879.

TL   Trifonoff, P.: "François Liszt." *Nouvelle Revue Internationale* (Paris), 1884.

TLMF	Tiersot, Julien. *Lettres de musiciens écrites en français du XVᵉ au XXᵉ siecle.* 2 vols. Paris, 1924.
TM	Thierry, A. *Lola Montès: Favorite royale.* Paris, 1936.
TRW	*Lettres françaises de Richard Wagner.* Edited by Julien Tiersot. Paris, 1935.
TSCA	Toole Stott, R. *Circus and Allied Arts: A World Bibliography, 1500–1957.* Derby, 1958.
UB	"Unbekannte Briefe von Wagner, Liszt, Berlioz, Robert und Clara Schumann, und H. Heine." Edited by Gerhard Tischler. In *Rheinische Musik- und Theater-Zeitung,* No. 11 (1910), pp. 455–65.
VAMA	Vier, Jacques. *Marie d'Agoult—son mari—ses amis: Documents inédits.* Paris, 1950.
VCA	Vier, Jacques. *La Comtesse d'Agoult et son temps, avec des documents inédits.* 6 vol. Paris, 1955–63.
VFL	Vier, Jacques. *Franz Liszt: L'Artiste, le clerc: Documents inédits.* Paris, 1951.
VLC	Valkó, Arisztid. "A Liszt család a levéltári iratok tükrében" [Archive Documents in the National Széchényi Library Concerning the Liszt family]. *Magyar Zene* (Budapest), 1961.
VT	Varnhagen von Ense, Karl August. *Tagebücher.* 2 vols. Berlin, 1863.
VET	Verstovsky, Alexis. *Ezhegodnik imperatorskikh teatrov* [Annals of the Imperial Theatres]. Moscow, 1912, 1913.
WA	Weimar Archives. Liszt collection now held by the Nationale Forschungs- und Gedenkstätten der klassischen deutschen Literatur in Weimar. Das Goethe-Schiller-Archiv, Weimar.
WAF	Wamser, Heinrich. "Abstammung und Familie Franz Liszts." *Burgenländische Heimatsblätter,* 1936.
WEW	Weissheimer, Wendelin. *Erlebnisse mit Wagner, Liszt und vielen anderen Zeitgenossen.* Stuttgart, 1898.
WFL	Wagner, Cosima. *Franz Liszt: Ein Gedenkblatt von seiner Tochter.* Munich, 1911 (2nd ed.).
WFLR	Wohl, Janka. *François Liszt: Recollections of a Compatriot.* Translated by B. Peyton Ward. London, 1887.
WFWB	Walch-Schumann, Käthe, ed. *Friedrich Wieck: Briefe aus den Jahren 1830–1838.* Cologne, 1968.
WL	Walker, Alan, ed. *Franz Liszt: The Man and His Music.* London, 1970.
WLA	Winklhofer, Sharon. "Liszt, Marie d'Agoult, and the 'Dante' Sonata," *Nineteenth Century Music,* July 1977, pp. 15–32.
WLCC	Walter, Teréz. *Liszt Ferenc árvizi hangversenyei Bécsben 1838–39* [Liszt's Charity Concerts in Vienna, 1838–39, after the Flood in

Hungary]. Translated and annotated from the German diary of
Theresa Walter by Béla Coulta. Budapest, 1941.

WLLM   Waters, Edward N., ed. *The Letters of Franz Liszt to Olga von
        Meyendorff 1871–1886.* In the Mildred Bliss collection at Dumbarton
        Oaks. Translated by William R. Tyler. Dumbarton Oaks, 1979.

WLW   Weilguny, Hedwig. *Das Liszthaus in Weimar.* Weimar, 1973.

WLWP   Wallace, William. *Liszt, Wagner and the Princess.* London, 1927.

WML   Wagner, Richard. *Mein Leben.* Munich, 1911.

WMM   Wyndham, Horace. *The Magnificent Montez.* London, 1935.

WRP   Whitehouse, H. Remsen. *A Revolutionary Princess: Christina Belgi-
        ojoso-Trivulzio, Her Life and Times, 1808–1871.* New York, 1906.

WT   Wagner, Cosima. *Die Tagebücher.* 2 vols. Edited and with a com-
        mentary by Martin Gregor-Dellin and Dietrich Mack. Munich,
        1976, 1977. Translated (as *Cosima Wagner's Diaries*) by Geoffrey
        Skelton. London and New York, 1978 and 1980.

WTS   Winterberger, A. *Technische Studien für Pianoforte von Franz Liszt,
        unter Redaktion von Alexander Winterberger.* Leipzig, 1887.

WW   Wallace, William. *Wagner.* London, 1925.

ZAC   "Zorelli, Sylvia" (Olga Janina). *Les Amours d'une cosaque par un
        ami de l'Abbé "X."* Paris, 1875.

ZLEF   Zichy, Count Géza. *Aus meinem Leben: Erinnerungen und Frag-
        mente.* 3 vols. Stuttgart, 1911–20.

ZRPC   "Zorelli, Sylvia" (Olga Janina). *Le Roman du pianiste et de la
        cosaque.* Paris, 1875.

Index

Page numbers in italic refer to main entries.